SIXTH EDITION

Effective English

FOR BUSINESS COMMUNICATION

ROBERT R. AURNER, Ph.D.
Vice President
Management Consultant Division,
Scott, Incorporated

Formerly: Professor of
Business Administration in the
University of Wisconsin

PAUL S. BURTNESS, Ph.D.
Professor of English
Northern Illinois University

Published by

SOUTH-WESTERN PUBLISHING COMPANY

Cincinnati, OH   Chicago, IL   Dallas, TX   Burlingame, CA   New Rochelle, NY

E17

 # PREFACE

Verbal intelligence is the target of this book. Oral sounds and written marks are today, as in past centuries, the chief means of man's understanding his own behavior and that of his fellowmen. Through pencils, pens, typewriters, printing presses, dictating equipment, broadcasting, telecasting, and other devices, we use powerful and persuasive symbols of verbal intelligence in sophisticated ways. We exchange information. We question and reply. We act and interact. We learn and share. And we continue to develop what, in this new Sixth Edition of *Effective English for Business Communication,* we call *the verbal intelligence of man.*

The new Sixth Edition is based upon four vital principles of verbal intelligence proved through years of accumulated experience:

1 — The degree of success you will achieve as a participant in this exciting world will depend substantially upon your command of spoken and written English.
2 — The most direct way to strengthen your English command is to develop an understanding of the underlying resources of English. There is no other route to true mastery.
3 — Mastery of English resources includes increasing your sensitivity to the psychology of communication: Improving your skill and ability in recognizing and choosing the most effective procedure.
4 — Effectiveness depends ultimately upon the appropriateness of message content and form and upon the suitability of its language.

Your career depends upon disciplined preparation. Our national leaders know that the future of our country hinges upon your basic preparation for the vital responsibilities that lie ahead. They point out that the success of American society will depend upon your intelligence, initiative, and understanding. Furthermore, no one of us can escape the fact that the prosperity, welfare, and security of the United States rest upon the soundness of the American economy.

Leading universities, as well as the government, report that in the 1970's more and more young people are going on to college. If you decide to enter college, you will find that *your ability to use and to interpret English skillfully will largely determine your academic success. Extensive research proves that no other subject predicts success in college so reliably as does English mastery.*

When you take your place as a participant in the challenging economic world, you will discover that your mastery of English is equally important for success there. If you do not plan to attend college, this course, as one of your last chances to increase your mastery of English, is overwhelmingly essential. If you seize this opportunity to discover the importance of effective English to your personal, social, and business success, your entire career will benefit as a result. Your potential contribution and achievement as a participant in American society and as a citizen of the United States will greatly increase.

A perspective on English, your most basic tool. At the outset, recognize that effective English is indispensable at every waking hour. When you can communicate skillfully, ideas and knowledge gain enormous power. To be effective, messages must of course convey data and judgments accurately. But much more than accuracy is needed. To be truly effective, messages must also be persuasive. For instance, a supervisor informing his staff about a complex problem confronting them must not only convey the information clearly but must also arouse their concern and secure their intelligent cooperation.

Communication calls for problem solving. Each important message poses a challenge, a problem to be solved. Such problems require thought and skill for their imaginative solution. These abilities are equally vital to your effectiveness as a person and to the success of the enterprise which will employ your services in the future. L. C. Keyes, in a recent issue of the *Harvard Business Review,* dramatically emphasizes this point: "Eliminate written communication from the basic business functions for twenty-four hours, and the entire industrial commercial operation would freeze into immobility."

Organizing with the tools of language. Without the tools of language, both written and oral, cooperation and planning would be impossible. Without cooperation and planning, the progress of American industry and commerce would be likewise impossible. In a larger sense, without language, our social, political, military, and scientific enterprise would dissolve into confusion.

Knowing, then, that English mastery is vital to your future success, you can profit from each assignment as a means of increasing your language command. By doing so, you will increase your potential as a participant in the American economy. Once you understand that your mastery of English will greatly affect your paycheck and your chances for advancement, you will seize every opportunity for practice in developing verbal intelligence.

Realistic and modern: This is our approach. The new Sixth Edition of *Effective English for Business Communication* includes three major divisions. Each division develops a special subject phase.

Division I, The Resources of English, presents the principles of communication. Here you will have an opportunity to master the differences between spoken and written English, the basic patterns of English sentences, the forms and uses of various parts of speech, and the technique for achieving unity, coherence, and power.

Division II, Effective Business Messages, presents creative information concerning the development of a personal writing style. Here you will have an opportunity to master such topics as controlling tone, planning and styling specific kinds of messages, and assessing the effectiveness of various approaches to the creation of such messages.

Division III, The Reference Guide, presents in convenient form a summary of key information. Here you will be able to find the answers to the most common questions of detail that arise. Division III also includes a section on the *Sentence X-Ray,* an optional, graphic approach for better understanding of English resources.

Effective English for Business Communication, Sixth Edition, aims to stimulate your interest in language and to develop your sensitivity to words and phrasing. Each page offers you knowledge concerning the resources of the sentence. The book as a whole gives you insights necessary for shaping messages intelligently and for adapting them to special purposes and particular audiences. It also gives you the knowledge of English fundamentals and the practice that will enable you to continue increasing your language skill long after you graduate.

In your study you will swiftly find that effective messages do not just "happen." They are the result of careful planning, organizing, phrasing, revising, and polishing, all with a definite purpose and specific audience in mind. As you gain experience in preparing and analyzing messages, you will gradually acquire a sense of what makes one particular word or construction preferable to another in a given context. You will develop a feeling for its effectiveness in achieving a special purpose. You will learn to judge which words and expressions are likely to produce precisely the result you seek.

Understanding the motives of people. The new Sixth Edition also involves you in larger questions of psychology and problem-solving. Ultimately, effective English means communication that enables you to get along successfully with others. You will discover the need for taking account of the motives, opinions, attitudes, desires, and feelings of others. You will find, for example, that expressing a personal interest in people leads them to listen with greater interest to what you have to say. You will come to see that only when you win a sympathetic hearing can you really communicate.

Summary. In using this Sixth Edition, you will be making steady progress toward the attainment of five major goals:

1 — Developing accuracy and sensitivity in the use of words
2 — Learning to plan and organize important kinds of messages
3 — Becoming familiar with business procedures and principles
4 — Increasing your grasp of business problems and strengthening your ability to analyze such problems, assess them, and solve them
5 — Deepening your understanding of people—their interests, their preferences, their potentialities, their motives

By improving your ability to express yourself effectively and to evaluate what others have expressed, you increase your personal competence. And *competence* forms the basis for confidence and success.

Preparing for your future. The challenge of the 1970's is enormous and stimulating. Your authors are convinced that your experiences with this book will help you immensely in preparing to meet this challenge. They believe that these experiences will equip you with an understanding and mastery of language that will contribute immeasurably to your personal competence and lifelong success.

Acknowledgments. Grateful acknowledgment is expressed to those persons and companies who have extended many helpful courtesies and who have granted generous permission to use certain materials and illustrations. Wherever such materials have been included, specific credits appear. Warm appreciation is also extended to many associates and friends who have contributed so significantly to making this Sixth Edition sound and practical. First, our thanks go to our many colleagues in education who have helped strengthen this edition by offering valuable suggestions based upon their classroom experience. Second, our thanks go to associates in executive management who have offered many key insights and stimulating ideas based upon their business experience. The combination of these two sources—imaginative classroom teaching and effective, innovative business management —gives this book the intelligent priorities and the sense of reality that readers have found so valuable in earlier editions.

Robert R. Aurner
Paul S. Burtness

 # CONTENTS

DIVISION III. REFERENCE GUIDE

Contents

clear whom we meant by *they*. Our listeners might wonder whether *all* refers to all the books "they" own or to all those that are related to the class in question. Our listeners might wonder what class we meant —history, shorthand, marketing, typing, English, or some other class. In conversation, such questions can easily be raised and instantly settled. In writing, on the other hand, we must phrase our message so carefully that the questions never arise.

The written language differs, then, in many important ways from the spoken language. It is helpful to regard written English as a special, standardized dialect of English. This written "dialect" requires particular care concerning word form, phrasing, and organization. It also requires us to give attention to neatness, mechanics, punctuation, and spelling.

The need for especially careful phrasing in the written language. In writing we deal with words, sentences, and paragraphs appearing on paper. They must make clear our information and ideas. They must imply our feelings and our attitudes. They must express our personality and character. Only if we choose our words thoughtfully, can we communicate effectively our whole message.

The need for care in choosing words can be seen clearly in the fact that the same combination of letters may have quite different meanings and uses in different situations. Consider the following sentences:

1—The air was melodious.
2—The air was fragrant.
3—The air was escaping from the tire.
4—The air brake was defective.
5—They will air their winter clothes.
6—They will air their views.
7—He spoke with an air of authority.

Here the same combination of letters, *air,* has different meanings in each of the seven sentences. This possibility should remind us that words are sometimes slippery and hard to manage. That is one reason why care and thoughtfulness are essential in writing.

Making a favorable impression through writing. Our job in writing effectively is complicated by the need to do more than just make our ideas clear. In business writing, especially, we must also make a favorable impression on our reader. We should keep in mind that the words we use will influence the reactions of a reader. Thus, we must be alert and choose our words guardedly.

To judge whether our words will make our meaning clear and will impress our reader favorably, we should try to adopt the reader's viewpoint. It is not easy to do this. We must keep in mind the problems the reader will face when he interprets our message. We must estimate his probable reactions.

ADVANTAGES OF WRITTEN ENGLISH

Planning: the secret of effective organization. We lack the advantages of the spoken language when we write, but *we gain other important advantages.* In conversation we have little time to think out what we are going to say or how we should say it. If we pondered for a minute or two each time we responded to a question, our friends would wonder what was wrong.

In writing, on the other hand, we can almost always take time to order our thoughts and consider how best to express them. We can organize our material. We can decide how to develop our message— how many details to include and what examples to give. We can bring our discussion to an effective and courteous close. We can leave the reader with a clear understanding of our message and a favorable attitude toward it.

Revision: the key to improvement. Writing has further advantages. After we have planned our message and phrased it thoughtfully, we can check it over and attempt to improve what we have written. No one can do his best on a first try. Many professional writers rewrite important messages repeatedly to make their phrasing and organization effective.

An example of how a great writer shapes and revises his material is provided by the closing paragraphs of Lincoln's First Inaugural Address. Remember that a number of Southern states had already seceded by March 4, 1861, when Lincoln delivered his address. He was appealing to the South, desperately and earnestly, not to secede— not to try to destroy the Union. Here is the conclusion as Lincoln *first* wrote it:

> In *your* hands, my dissatisfied fellow countrymen, and not in *mine,* is the momentous issue of civil war. The government will not assail *you,* unless you *first* assail *it.* You can have no conflict, without being yourselves the aggressors. *You* have no oath registered in Heaven to destroy the government, while *I* shall have the most solemn one to "preserve, protect, and defend" it.

You can forbear the *assault* upon it; I can *not* shrink from the *defense* of it. With *you,* and not with *me,* is the solemn question of "Shall it be peace, or a sword?"

Lincoln rewrote this conclusion. In doing so, he made use of two suggestions—(1) The following paragraph proposed as a conclusion by William H. Seward, Lincoln's Secretary of State:

> I close. We are not, we must not be, aliens or enemies but fellow countrymen and brethren. Although passion has strained our bonds of affection too hardly, they must not, I am sure they will not, be broken. The mystic chords, which, proceeding from so many battle fields and so many patriot graves, pass through all the hearts and all the hearths in this broad continent of ours, will yet again harmonize in their ancient music when breathed upon by the guardian angel of the nation.

(2) A sentence Lincoln himself had jotted down on the back of a letter, adapting two sentences from Seward's proposal: "Americans, all, we are not enemies, but friends. We have sacred ties of affection which, though strained by passion, let us hope can never be broken."

Here is the conclusion as President Lincoln actually revised and delivered it:

> In *your* hands, my dissatisfied fellow countrymen, and not in *mine,* is the momentous issue of civil war. The government will not assail *you.* You can have no conflict, without being yourselves the aggressor. *You* have no oath registered in Heaven to destroy the government, while *I* shall have the most solemn one to "preserve, protect, and defend" it.
>
> I am loath to close. We are not enemies, but friends. We must not be enemies. Though passion may have strained, it must not break our bonds of affection. The mystic chords of memory, stretching from every battlefield, and patriot grave, to every living heart and hearthstone, all over this broad land, will yet swell the chorus of the Union, when again touched, as surely they will be, by the better angels of our nature.

The revised ending places great emphasis upon Lincoln's plea for understanding and reconciliation. Note that this essential theme was lacking in the original version.

Another excellent example of effective rewriting is offered by the Declaration of Independence. Thomas Jefferson and his collaborators worked carefully over Jefferson's rough draft. They added a word here, took out a sentence there, rephrased this expression, and changed the tone of that paragraph. They painstakingly revised the Declaration, strengthening the document greatly before the Second Continental Congress adopted it.

Not only messages of state—like Lincoln's First Inaugural Address and the Declaration—but every other important message deserves careful revision. Successful revision involves effort. It involves trial and error, patience and imagination. Through revision, we can almost always improve our rough drafts. Through revision, too, we can learn a great deal about how to make our English effective.

Proofreading for accuracy. We have time to plan a written message, to phrase it thoughtfully, and to revise it. In addition, we ordinarily have a chance to prepare a neat copy of our message and to check what we have prepared before submitting it. Our appearance inevitably makes an impression on those we meet. The appearance of a written message makes a similar impression. Neatness and accuracy are essential. A misspelling in a business message can make the same undesirable impression as a ragged margin or a soiled sheet of paper. Note the undesirable effect produced by the many careless errors in the following sentence:

Illiterate — Its to bad we didn't recieve that order of your's in time.

Either the writer was ignorant of important facts concerning written English, or he did not bother to check over and correct the sentence. The sentence should have read:

Acceptable — It's too bad we didn't receive that order of yours in time.

or

Acceptable — We regret that we did not receive your order in time.

Carefulness about neatness, spelling, apostrophes, punctuation, and capitalization makes a very favorable impression on the reader. For that reason we must pay special attention to preparing a neat and accurate copy of any message for which we share responsibility.

The process of catching and correcting careless errors is called proofreading. In proofreading, we must concentrate intently on each word, figure, and punctuation mark in the message we are checking. Such effort will be rewarded by the knowledge that we have submitted a message that represents us at our best.

NEVADA HARDWARE SUPPLY, INC.

SANDS BOULEVARD • (AREA CODE 702) 221-5304 • LAS VEGAS, NEVADA 89109

May 31, 19--

Mr. Everett L. Abrams
Jeffries & Abrams, Inc.
4687 Sunrise Way Dr.
St. Louis, MO. 63125

Dear Mr. Abrams

We appreciate your oder and shall give it our prompt attention.

We are temporarily out of B9871 Antenna Rotators; but they are on rush odre, and the manufacturer assurs us they will be de-livered in 3 days. We are holding, shipment of Order #1267 awaiting the arrival of these orators. If they are note delivered as promised, we shall ship the rest of your order without further delay.

The L9135 Antennas have been with drawn by the manufacturer because of technical difficulties and have been superseded by Model 39610 L 9140, an improved modle. May we ship this new model instead of L 9135?

Sincerely yours
R. L. McNaughton
Sales Manager

NEVADA HARDWARE SUPPLY, INC.

SANDS BOULEVARD • (AREA CODE 702) 221-5304 • LAS VEGAS, NEVADA 89109

May 31, 19--

Mr. Everett L. Abrams
Jeffries and Abrams, Incorporated
4687 Sunrise Way Drive
St. Louis, MO 63125

Dear Mr. Abrams

We appreciate your order and shall give it our prompt attention.

We are temporarily out of B9871 Antenna Rotators; but they are on rush order, and the manufacturer assures us they will be delivered within three days. We are holding shipment of Order #1267 awaiting the arrival of these rotators. If they are not delivered as promised, we shall ship the rest of your order without further delay.

The L9135 Antenna has been withdrawn by the manufacturer because of technical difficulties and has been superseded by Model L9140, an improved model. May we ship this new model instead of L9135?

Sincerely yours
R. L. McNaughton
Sales Manager

J1b

• APPLYING EFFECTIVE ENGLISH

Oral Applications

• **1.** Pronounce the following sentences in various ways, stressing different words, so as to give the sentences different meanings. Discuss the differences between these meanings of the spoken sentences and the meaning the sentences apparently have in their written form:

1 — Their Phoenix agency has not billed us for this month's shipment.
2 — His written report was carefully prepared.
3 — Some of the electric typewriters had not been adjusted.
4 — That appliance store will take a partial inventory.
5 — The new records clerk in the billing office began work last week.

• **2.** In the sentences of Oral Application 1, above, what words could *not* properly be emphasized? What explanation can you offer for the fact that certain words in some sentences cannot, meaningfully, be stressed?

• **3.** Discuss the advantages that a writer has over a speaker, and that a written message has over a spoken one.

• **4.** Discuss the ambiguity in the phrasing of each of the following sentences. Suggest a way of rephrasing each sentence to remove this ambiguity.

1 — Bill asked to leave at eight o'clock.
2 — When the payment arrived, the letter was sent.
3 — The Buckleys have a Chrysler and a Mustang; the boys were given permission to use it for their trip.
4 — Since Cheryl has come, the girls have decided not to go hiking.
5 — Sharon, Elaine, and Mary, who had been there before, were planning a visit to Dallas.

• **5.** Discuss the differences between the first and final versions of the conclusion to Lincoln's First Inaugural Address (pages 18 and 19). What effects do you think Lincoln was trying to achieve in making these changes? In particular, contrast the concluding sentences in the two versions. What impression was Lincoln trying to make in his conclusion? What details of phrasing can you cite to support your view?

Written Applications

• 1. The following sentences contain many obvious errors. Such errors in our writing may slip by, unless we proofread our messages and assignments carefully. Proofread the following sentences and correct all errors. Use a dictionary if you are in doubt about the spelling or meaning of a word. Write each sentence in correct form.

1 — These shipment must of arived.
2 — There anser has not came.
3 — That modle was to expencive.
4 — We except you're kind invitaton to diner.
5 — Preparring and writting these planes has taken much time and car.
6 — The windows was place their for light an ventilasion.
7 — Us boys finaly caughth site of the Statute of Liberty.
8 — The boxs our comming to the libary.
9 — The stenagrapher's are planing a meting of there organization for the neer future.
10 — The not was writen on cleen papper but know one proofred it.
11 — We could tell that they must of been halfing a grate time.
12 — The bord of director's, in going over the proposel, desided against changing the companies polisy.
13 — Writ you're letter to the klub president at onse so that he can be looking four someon to tacke your plase.
14 — He is writting the secretery.
15 — Massages stiled in that weigh loose there affectiveness.

• 2. Many spelling errors can be corrected by paying close attention to correspondences between spelling and pronunciation. From Written Application 1, list all such misspellings. After the misspelled word, provide the correct spelling. For example, note the correspondence in spelling and pronunciation between the following sets of words: *bit/bite/bight; can/cane; met/meat/meet/mete; not/note; rod/road/rode; shot/shoot; cut/cute.*

• 3. In addition to the examples of correspondence in spelling and pronunciation provided in Written Application 2, list at least five words which demonstrate (1) the use of silent *e*, (2) the doubling of a vowel, (3) the use of two vowels (for example, *ie* or *ea*), or (4) the use of doubled consonants (for example, *plan/planned*).

• 4. Write a paragraph explaining why proofreading is especially important in business.

SECTION 4

Approaches to Language Study

(1) Rhetoric deals with the effectiveness of messages.
(2) Grammar deals with language as a signaling system.

The differences between rhetoric and grammar. One purpose of this book is to encourage you to think about the English language. You should consider (1) how it can be used most efficiently in modern business and (2) how it works. These two topics represent two different but equally important approaches to a mastery of English. The first—the study of how messages can be made effective—is called *rhetoric.* The second—the study of how the English language operates as a signaling system to communicate our meaning—is called *grammar.*

THE EFFECTIVENESS OF MESSAGES: RHETORIC

The effective use of English in business. The question of how we can best use English for the purposes of modern business is an important subdivision of rhetoric. Business rhetoric must take into account such different uses of language as planning sales campaigns, giving instructions, and preparing reports and evaluations. It also concerns the writing of business messages and the composing of advertisements.

Many rules of business rhetoric relate closely to the general principles that apply in other areas of communication. For example, the principle that a writer should unify his material applies in all types of writing.

Business writing, however, involves many special problems. Business rhetoric must deal with these. For instance, the relationship between writer and reader in the business world involves special considerations. When a person writes as a representative of a company, he has a special responsibility. He is projecting an image not only of himself, but also of his employer. This image may greatly affect the attitude of the public toward the company. It may affect profits and the long-term success of the company.

The importance of anticipating the reaction of our readers. How a thing is said may often be just as important as what is said. Effective business writing requires a writer to be skillful at judging how people will react to various ways of presenting a fact or an idea. This concern for people's reactions, which is a form of courtesy and thoughtfulness, is essential in all business writing.

Assisting readers and getting them to want to do business with us are key aims of business rhetoric. All expert writers, of course, pay some attention to the probable reaction of their audiences. In business communications, however, the reader's reaction is of central importance. Courtesy—a friendly, winning, respectful attitude—is not merely advisable. It is the key to effective business communication. In studying business rhetoric, accordingly, we must develop skill in using language to convey the right impression. We must become aware of these special challenges of business communication.

Rhetoric, then, is concerned with what a writer can do to make a particular message successful. It is concerned with many different aspects of writing. It is concerned with how different subjects may be organized effectively and with the effect that various phrasings will have on an audience. Rhetoric deals with persuasion—with how to win the attention of an audience and how to hold their interest. It deals with the use of details for the purpose of presenting a precise account of a topic. It deals with the use of examples for the purpose of making a difficult subject clear. In short, whatever may contribute to the effectiveness of any piece of business writing belongs to the study of business rhetoric.

THE SIGNALLING SYSTEM: GRAMMAR

Studying the English sentence and its components. As a different approach to language, we may study the grammar of English. Grammar concerns (1) the forms of individual words in their various uses and (2) the ways in which words are combined into phrases and clauses. While rhetoric covers a variety of topics—from word choice to organization—grammar focuses on the patterns of the English sentence and its parts. Grammar may strike you at first as an extremely limited subject—only the patterns and parts of the English sentence! The English sentence, however, poses many interesting problems. From a different point of view, English grammar may be defined as the signaling system of the English language. Every meaning in speech and writing is communicated by some definite grammatical signal.

Grammatical meaning through word order. Word order is an essential signal in English grammar. Let us consider the following list of words:

1. repaired	6. the
2. the	7. supervisor
3. staff	8. the
4. has	9. of
5. typewriter	10. cardholder

In such a disorganized list, the words have no meaning beyond their meaning as items. Note what happens when we rearrange them:

1—The staff supervisor has repaired the cardholder of the typewriter.

The new and additional meaning which these words acquire in grammatical constructions is called *grammatical meaning*. The principles controlling the combination of words into such constructions is what we mean by the term *English grammar*.

The principle illustrated by Sentence 1, above, is that words must appear in a definite sequence if they are to have grammatical meaning. Another way of expressing this principle is that *word order* is an important signal of English grammar. In fact, word order is the most important signal we have in English for establishing grammatical relationships.

Note the change in the meaning of the sentence if we make one simple change in word order:

2—Has the staff supervisor repaired the cardholder of the typewriter?

The shift of *has* from the fourth to the first position has changed the sentence from a statement to a question. Thus, word order often determines the grammatical meaning of sentences—determines, for example, whether a sentence is a statement or a question.

Note the alterations in the meaning of the sentence when we make the following changes:

3—Has the staff repaired the cardholder of the supervisor's typewriter?

Grammatical meaning through function words. Another basic signal of English grammar—the use of function words—can be illustrated by the same sentence. Look again at the three preceding examples. In each the word *typewriter* is brought into the sentence by means of a special kind of word, the word *of*. Such a word acts as a "hook" to attach the word *typewriter* to the word *cardholder*. The phrase *of the typewriter* shows what kind of carriage we are talking about. The word *of* establishes this grammatical relationship. Words that serve special grammatical functions (such as the "hooking" function performed by *of*) are called *function words*. Thus, one word can be made a modifier of another word by means of a function word. This kind of function word is called a *preposition*.

Grammatical meaning through word form. The most important signals of English grammar are word order and function words. There are two other grammatical devices: (1) changes in the forms of words (inflectional changes) and (2) punctuation (oral or written segment markers). Punctuation indicates where one construction, or part of a construction, ends and the next begins.

The same sentence can be used to illustrate the grammatical significance of word form:

4—The staff supervisors have repaired the cardholder of the typewriter.

Note the addition of the *-s* (called the *plural suffix*) to the word *supervisor*. This suffix illustrates one of the most common types of change in form. We can make *cardholder* and *typewriter* plural in the same way: *cardholders, typewriters*. The grammatical distinction here involves the difference between one object and more than one object. This grammatical meaning is signalled by means of the *-s* (in some words the suffix will be *-es*) added to the singular form of the word. Any word that adds *-(e)s* to form a plural is a noun. This simple test will enable you to identify most nouns in English.

Note also the change from *has to have* which occurs when we change *supervisor* to *supervisors*. This correspondence of forms is called *grammatical agreement*.

An example of another kind of change in form occurs in the following sentence. Note that a change in word order is also involved:

5—The staff supervisor has repaired the typewriter's cardholder.

Here *-'s* (called the *possessive suffix*) is added to *typewriter*. (In Sentence 3 we had another example of the possessive case.) The grammatical meaning signalled by *-'s* can also be signalled by the prepositional phrase *of the typewriter*. Thus, we can say either *the boy's book*, or *the book of the boy*. Any word that adds *-'s* to form the possessive case is a noun. Like the -*(e)s* plural suffix, the possessive suffix -*'s* is a simple way of identifying most nouns in English.

Our last example of the grammatical significance of word-form also involves a change in word order:

6—Have the staff supervisor repair the cardholder of the typewriter.

The following signals make this construction a command: (1) *has* appears as *have* and *repaired* as *repair*, and (2) *have* stands first in the sentence.

The fact that word order determines meaning suggests that English grammar is based on certain basic patterns or formulas. Patterns of this kind provide the framework for all English sentences.

Grammatical meaning through punctuation. One additional signal of English grammar is punctuation—oral or written. The following sentences illustrate the grammatical significance of punctuation. Note how changes in punctuation affect the meaning of the sentences, each of which is composed of exactly the same words in exactly the same order:

7—The staff said the supervisor has repaired the cardholder of the typewriter.
(Orally, the pitch of the speaker's voice falls at the end of the sentence. The falling pitch and following pause correspond to a period.)

8—The staff said the supervisor has repaired the cardholder of the typewriter?
(Orally, the pitch of the speaker's voice rises at the end of the sentence. The rising pitch and following pause in this echo question correspond to a question mark.)

9—"The staff," said the supervisor, "has repaired the cardholder of the typewriter."

The *grammatical* meaning of these sentences depends upon their punctuation. End punctuation signals whether the sentence is a statement or a question. Internal punctuation sets off special segments.

Thus, all four kinds of grammatical signals in English can be illustrated by this one group of words. These signals are (1) word order, (2) function words, (3) word forms, and (4) segment markers (punctuation). These signals establish the grammatical relations in English sentences. We shall study them in greater detail in the following unit.

• APPLYING EFFECTIVE ENGLISH

Oral Applications

• **1.** Explain the distinction between rhetoric and grammar. Give examples.

• **2.** List some of the rhetorical factors involved in planning and writing a message. Discuss the importance of each of the factors you mention.

• **3.** What are the four basic kinds of grammatical signals in English? Give examples to illustrate how each of these kinds of signals operates.

• **4.** Discuss the following questions:

1 — What grammatical signals enable us to know whether Ken caused or received the injury mentioned in the following sentence?
Alan accidentally hit Ken with a pitched ball.

2 — What grammatical signals enable us to tell who performed the actions mentioned in the following sentences?
The notice was written by Mr. Kilmer.
Fred Case helped me proofread the report.

3 — What grammatical signals enable us to tell the time of the actions mentioned in the following sentences?
a — Those tallies were made by Jean Simpson.
b — The clerks will file the correspondence.
c — Most of the salesmen have submitted their reports.
d — Each student completed his assignment.
e — The accounting staff had left the office.

4 — What grammatical signals enable us to distinguish between the pairs of expressions shown below? What are the differences in meaning?
a — The moving van . . . (type of van)/The moving van . . . (van in motion)
b — The show boat . . ./The boat show . . .
c — The manager was there./Was the manager there?
d — The secretary has sent the announcement./The secretary had been sent the announcement.
e — He hits well against left-handed pitchers./He hit well against left-handed pitchers.

Written Applications

• **1.** Write a paragraph explaining the special importance of tone in business messages. Give examples. For instance, what reaction would you expect from a sarcastic directive?

• **2.** Discuss the tone of the following messages. Rephrase them in order to make their tone more appropriate for business messages. Try to make the requests as persuasive as you can.

1 — Your note of September 6 was illegible. We couldn't figure out your order for engine parts.

2 — Of course there are no appointments that would be open two days after we receive your request! Write again and this time ask for an appointment a decent period in advance.

3 — In the past your inquiries have distracted us from our work. Don't pester us with phone calls. Don't worry! When we finish repairing your TV set, we'll notify you! We won't steal it.

4 — Customers who are forever changing their minds are a great nuisance to us. You people cost us time and money! If you *must* exchange your purchase, the least you can do is return it personally.

5 — How in the world can you expect us to have parts in stock for a radio nine years old? We won't be able to supply those parts for at least a month. After all, they have to be shipped all the way from New York.

• **3.** Rewrite the following sentences, expressing the same idea but using different grammatical devices. Use other and additional words if necessary. For example, you may indicate the performer of an action by making him the object of the preposition *by*, as well as by making him the subject of the verb.

1 — Mr. Elliott sent everyone on the office staff a box of candy.

2 — Miss Jenkins prepared, typed, and proofread that memorandum.

3 — The inventory was taken by two of our merchandise clerks.

4 — That recording was given to each contestant by the sponsor.

5 — Andy Stein was elected president by the senior class, yesterday.

UNIT 2

MASTERING THE BASIC SENTENCE PATTERNS OF ENGLISH

All English sentences use one of four basic patterns. We can see these patterns clearly in minimum sentences. Minimum sentences omit nonessential elements so that only the framework remains.

The four basic patterns fall into two types. The first type (Patterns 1-3) uses normal word order. In normal word order the subject regularly precedes the verb. In Sections 1 and 2 you will discover that Patterns 1-3 are built on three different kinds of verbs. These kinds are: (1) transitive verbs, (2) intransitive verbs, and (3) linking verbs. The various constructions that follow such verbs provide the basis for classifying Patterns 1, 2, and 3.

The second type (Pattern 4) uses special formulas to signal that the logical subject will follow the verb. Section 2 shows how reversed word order can provide variety of sentence structure, informal tone, and emphasis.

Section 3 indicates that we analyze words and classify them as parts of speech in order to understand how English sentences work.

UNIT 2

Section 1

Sentence Patterns 1 and 2: Pattern 1 is based upon transitive verbs; Pattern 2, upon intransitive verbs.

Section 2

Sentence Patterns 3 and 4: Pattern 3 is based upon linking verbs; Pattern 4, upon special formulas for postponing the logical subject of the verb.

Section 3

The Importance of the Parts of Speech: The key positions in English sentence patterns can be occupied only by certain parts of speech.

SECTION 1

Sentence Patterns 1 and 2

Pattern 1 is based upon transitive verbs; Pattern 2, upon intransitive verbs.

All English sentences use one of four basic patterns. At this point we are interested in the essential framework of the sentence. Thus, we shall deal with short, simple sentences—minimum sentences. Such examples illustrate the patterns clearly. Any of them can be expanded by various kinds of modifiers. Any of them can be altered to form a question or command. Later, we'll take up the various ways in which minimum sentences may be altered and expanded. Right now let's consider them in their simplest forms.

PATTERN 1

With general-type transitive verb.[1] Pattern 1 sentences involve a subject, a transitive verb (a verb whose action "carries across" and affects a noun or a noun substitute, the *direct object*), and a direct object:

Subject +	Transitive Verb +	Direct Object
(noun)	*(verb)*	*(noun)*
The boy	earns	money.
Rusty Staub	hit	the ball.
The secretary	brought	the report.

Note these parts: (1) a substantive (a noun or any word used as a noun) preceding the verb, (2) a transitive verb, and (3) a substantive following the verb. The two substantives refer to *different* things: *boy* and *money, Rusty Staub* and *ball, secretary* and *report.* (The only exception occurs when a pronoun ending in *-self* or *-selves* is the direct object. For example: He criticized himself.)

---

[1] See "Guide to the Sentence X-Ray," pages 638-639, for additional help.

Pattern 1 sentences have two subclasses. These subclasses use special kinds of transitive verbs—sending-type and altering-type transitive verbs. There are comparatively few of these special verbs in the language. Therefore, we'll be able to recognize them easily.

Pattern 1 with sending-type transitive verb.[2] Such sentences contain a subject, a sending-type transitive verb, an indirect object, and a direct object.

Subject + (noun)	Sending-type Transitive Verb + (verb)	Indirect Object + (noun)	Direct Object (noun)
The girl	sent	the store	a message.
That clerk	brought	the manager	the report.
Miss Hadley	paid	the grocer	the money.
The supervisor	gave	the secretary	instructions.

A sending-type transitive verb indicates that something (the direct object) has been given by someone (the subject) to someone else (the indirect object). Three substantives (nouns or noun substitutes) occur. The subject occurs before the verb. The indirect object and the direct object occur after the verb—the indirect object first, the direct object second.

Thus, the indirect object relationship is established by word order. The same relationship can be indicated by a prepositional phrase [3]; here, emphasis is placed on the recipient:

The girl sent a message *to the store.*
That clerk brought the report *to the manager.*
Miss Hadley paid the money *to the grocer.*
The supervisor gave instructions *to the secretary.*

The preposition *to* indicates the relationship of *store, manager, grocer,* and *secretary* to the rest of the sentence. Each of these nouns is used as the object of the preposition *to.*

Pattern 1 with altering-type transitive verb.[4] Such sentences contain a subject, an altering-type transitive verb, a direct object, and an objective complement (either a noun or an adjective).

---

[2] See "Guide to the Sentence X-Ray," page 640.
[3] See "Guide to the Sentence X-Ray," pages 640-641.
[4] See "Guide to the Sentence X-Ray," pages 641-642.

Subject (noun)	+	Altering-type Transitive Verb (verb)	+	Direct Object (noun)	+	Objective Complement (noun)
The manager		made		John		his assistant.
Mr. Collins		found { *forming or altering an opinion*		her suggestion		the best solution.
The company (noun)		considered (verb)		the project (noun)		a success. (adjective)
The job		made		the boy		responsible.
The executive		found		the typist		reliable.
The janitor		painted		the office		green.

An altering-type transitive verb can express such meanings as these: (1) making a change in assignment or appearance, or (2) forming or changing an evaluation. The change may involve election or appointment to a new position. It may involve a reversal in someone's opinion or judgment. It may involve an alteration in appearance. In such sentences the subject occurs before the verb, and two substantives (or a substantive and an adjective) follow the verb—the first substantive being a direct object, the second the objective complement.

After altering-type transitive verbs, the word *as* is sometimes used to introduce the objective complement. For example: "The student senate elected James Fenton as their representative." When *as* occurs, the objective complement occasionally precedes the direct object: "The student senate elected as their representative James Fenton." In such sentences, *as* serves as a function word. It emphasizes the fact that *their representative* is an objective complement.

SUMMARY: Pattern 1 sentences involve this basic pattern:

Subject	+	Transitive Verb	+	Direct Object
The executive		dictated		a memorandum.

This pattern has two important variations:

Subject	+	Sending-type Transitive Verb	+	Indirect Object	+	Direct Object
The company		sent		its consumers		catalogues.

Subject	+	Altering-type Transitive Verb	+	Direct Object	+	Objective Complement
The president		appointed		Miss Evans		his secretary.
The decorators		painted		Helen's office		green.

PATTERN 2

Pattern 2 sentences contain a subject and an intransitive verb.[5] They may also contain an adverbial modifier, as illustrated below.

Subject (noun)	Intransitive Verb (verb)	Adverbial Modifier (adverb or noun-adverb)
The clerk	hurried	away.
The principal	left	immediately.
An eclipse	occurred	[last night].
The salesman	arrived	[this morning].
The team	returned	[Sunday].
The stenographer	came	[home].
The problem	existed	[last year].

An intransitive verb is a verb that does not take an object. (The *in-* of *intransitive* means *not.*) Some verbs never take an object. Such verbs are always intransitive. Examples are *occur, happen, exist, die, sit, lie* (meaning *recline*), *rise,* and *come.* On the other hand, many verbs sometimes take an object and sometimes do not. When a verb is used with an object, it is said to be *transitive.* When the same verb is used without an object, it is said to be *intransitive.* For example:

> *Transitive use:*   The choir sang Handel's Messiah.
>
> *Intransitive use:*   The choir sang [this afternoon].

In deciding whether a verb is transitive or intransitive, examine it in a particular sentence. If it has no object in that sentence, it is used intransitively. You may then go on to consider whether it ever occurs with an object. If it does not, it belongs with the group of verbs including *occur* and *exist* that are always intransitive (for one cannot "occur something" or "exist something").

Distinguishing between a direct object and an adverbial noun. There is only one problem that you are likely to face in recognizing sentences of Pattern 2. This problem is that a noun-adverb (a noun used as an adverb, usually telling *when* or *where* something happened) is often used to modify an intransitive verb. A noun in this position may seem to be a direct object. (Compare the sentences above in which the noun-adverbs are bracketed.)

To distinguish a direct object from a noun-adverb, see whether the noun after the verb answers the question "What?" or "Whom?"

---

[5] See "Guide to the Sentence X-Ray," page 643.

If it does, the noun is a direct object. On the other hand, if the noun answers the question "When?" or "Where?" it is an adverb. For example:

Morris sailed Tuesday.

Tuesday does not sensibly answer the question "Sailed what?" Hence, *Tuesday* cannot be a direct object (unless it happens to be the name of a boat). Note that *Tuesday* does answer the question "Sailed when?" This fact confirms our conclusion that it is used as an adverb. For contrast, let's consider the following sentence:

Kevin hit the ball.

In this sentence, *ball* answers the question "Hit what?" Hence, *ball* is a direct object, and we see at once that the sentence is an example of Pattern I: S + TrV + DO.

● *APPLYING EFFECTIVE ENGLISH*

Oral Applications

● **1.** In class discussion, make up sentences to fill out the following patterns. Each sentence involves a transitive verb.

1 – The _____ mailed the _____.
2 – All _____ completed the _____.
3 – Many _____ refused the _____.
4 – Some _____ will write a (or *an*) _____.
5 – That _____ has approved my _____.

● **2.** In class discussion, make up sentences to fill out the following patterns. Each sentence involves a sending-type transitive verb.

1 – My _____ gave her _____ that _____.
2 – This _____ told the _____ a (or *an*) _____.
3 – Her _____ sold the _____ the _____.
4 – His _____ taught all the _____ this _____.
5 – Our _____ sent that _____ many _____.

● **3.** In class discussion, revise the preceding five sentences, substituting prepositional phrases with *to* for each of the indirect objects.

● **4.** In class discussion, make up sentences to fill out the patterns at the top of page 38. Each sentence involves an altering-type transitive verb.

1 — The _____ elected _____ their _____.
2 — _____ painted the _____ _____.
3 — All the _____ considered _____ their _____.
4 — Her _____ called _____ a (or *an*) _____.
5 — This _____ thought the _____ a (or *an*) _____.

● **5.** In class discussion, make up sentences to fill out the following patterns. Each sentence involves an intransitive verb.

1 — A (or *An*) _____ occurred last _____.
2 — My _____ walked across the _____.
3 — That _____ will arrive next _____.
4 — Our _____ looked up from his _____.
5 — Many _____ came toward the _____.

Written Applications

● **1.** Using a different verb in each sentence, make up three different sentences illustrating the following pattern:

Subject + Transitive Verb + Direct Object.

● **2.** Using a different verb in each sentence, make up three different sentences illustrating the following pattern:

Subject + Sending-type Transitive Verb + Indirect Object + Direct Object.

● **3.** Revise the sentences in Written Application 2 above, expressing the indirect object as the object of the preposition *to* (or *for*).

● **4.** Using a different verb in each sentence, make up three different sentences illustrating the following pattern:

Subject + Altering-type Transitive Verb + Direct Object + Objective Complement.

● **5.** Using a different verb in each sentence, make up three different sentences illustrating the following pattern:

Subject + Intransitive Verb + Adverbial Modifier.

● **6.** Copy the sentences at the top of page 39 and supply three verbs for each blank. Indicate the pattern each sentence illustrates.

1 — Mr. Massey _____ George about the report.
2 — Miss Alcott _____ the clerk an urgent message.
3 — That tailor _____ the garment.
4 — The class _____ Maria their spokesman.
5 — Those delegates _____ through the building.
6 — The student finally _____ his lesson.
7 — The athletes _____ onto the field.
8 — The president _____ that new plans were being prepared.
9 — Our friend _____ Monday.
10 — The designer _____ the new office very bright.
11 — Laura _____ that book to the library.
12 — Each mechanic _____ his work carefully.
13 — Mother _____ the store a check.
14 — Warren _____ early.
15 — Dean Cass _____ the report yesterday.
16 — Dr. Morgan _____ the driver for the shipment.
17 — Eleanor _____ an excellent dinner.
18 — Martin _____ the story briefly.
19 — Her teacher _____ the class an interesting assignment.
20 — The team _____ home happily.

• 7. Proofread and correct each of the following sentences. Using examples from these sentences, show how correspondences between spelling and pronunciation can be used to correct the spelling errors. For example, point out that the silent *e* in *ate, rate, mate,* gives *a* the sound of its own name. The absence of *e* in *at* indicates that *at* rhymes with *mat* and *sat*. Using examples from these sentences, show that the rule "*i* before *e* except after *c* or when sounded as *a* in *neighbor* and *weigh*," while not universally true, can nevertheless be helpful. Refer to an up-to-date dictionary whenever you are in doubt about spelling, syllabication, or other details concerning the forms of words you plan to use.

1 — I believe the employees ratting on the test should be excepted as prove of his competense.
2 — There writting becam smother when they tryed to writte naturally.
3 — These man confered fur ours in the executives dinning room.
4 — All the secreterys from those too agencies new they're job compleatly.
5 — Know amount of practice cane help unles the students consentrats on detales and receives assistence from there teacher.

SECTION 2

Sentence Patterns 3 and 4

Pattern 3 uses linking verbs; Pattern 4, special formulas for postponing the logical subject of the verb.

PATTERN 3

Pattern 3 sentences contain a subject, a linking verb, and a subjective complement. The following sentences illustrate Pattern 3:

Subject *(noun)*	Linking Verb *(verb)*	Subjective Complement (either *predicate noun* or *predicate adjective*)
The youngster	is	a student.
The girls	are	receptionists.
The teacher	was	the referee.
The messengers	were	trustworthy.
Ed	seemed	certain.
The investments	appeared	sound.

After linking verbs, a predicate noun or a predicate adjective regularly occurs. The most common linking verbs are forms of the verb *TO BE (am, are, is; was, were; been; being).* Other linking verbs are *to seem* and *to appear.*

How to distinguish between a direct object and a predicate noun. A linking verb is a special kind of intransitive verb that *never* takes an object. Instead a linking verb is always followed by a subjective complement. A subjective complement is simply a predicate noun or a predicate adjective. A predicate noun always refers to the *same* person or thing as does the subject. A direct object, however, refers to a person or thing *other* than the subject.

Pattern 3:

Subject	Linking Verb	Pred. Noun
The secretary	is	an experienced stenographer.
Mr. Langford	was	the editor.

Pattern 1:

Subject	*Tr. Verb*	*Direct Object*
The patrolman	complimented	the driver.
She	finished	the report.
The students	completed	the assignment.

Note that both the predicate noun and the direct object answer the questions "What?" or "Whom?" "The secretary is—what?" A stenographer. "The patrolman complimented—what [or whom]?" The driver.

The possibility of altered word order in Patterns 1-3. In all three of the sentence patterns previously presented, the subject precedes the verb. This word order pattern is very general in English statements. To produce a special effect, a writer may occasionally reverse the usual order of subject and verb: "In trooped the reporters," or "Out marched the directors," or "Then came the climax." These sentences are merely a rearrangement of Pattern 2:

Subject +	*Intr. Verb* +	*Adverb*
The reporters	trooped	in.
The directors	marched	out.
The climax	came	then.
The girls	drove	over.

A reversal in word order can also occur in some sentences of Pattern 3:

Pred. Adj.	*Linking Verb*	*Subject*
Urgent	was	the tone of his voice.

In normal word order, this becomes:

Subject	*Linking Verb*	*Pred. Adj.*
The tone of his voice	was	urgent.

Reversals in Pattern 1 sentences are possible but rare:

Direct Object	*Subject*	*Tr. Verb*
That sales message	Leslie	had composed.

In normal word order this sentence would read as follows:

Subject	*Tr. Verb*	*Direct Object*
Leslie	had composed	that sales message.

Sec. 2 • Sentence Patterns 3 and 4

Patterns 1-3: the bases for various kinds of expansion. These three patterns can become the foundations for much longer clauses and sentences. In considering the basic pattern of any sentence, begin by reducing the sentence to its minimum form. For Pattern 1, the minimum form will be one of these three possibilities:

$$S + TrV + DO$$
$$S + TrV \text{ (sending-type)} + IO + DO$$
$$S + TrV \text{ (altering-type)} + DO + OC$$

For Pattern 2, the minimum form will be:

$$S + Intr. \ V$$

For Pattern 3, the minimum form will be:

$S + LV + SC$ (either *predicate noun* or *predicate adjective*) [1]

These patterns provide the skeleton for all sentences except those of Pattern 4, which we will discuss next. They also provide the skeleton for all English clauses. Most English clauses (both independent and dependent) are expansions or modifications of these three basic patterns. Learn these patterns thoroughly. Keep in mind that word order is the grammatical sign underlying each of the patterns.

PATTERN 4

Pattern 4 sentences involve special formulas ("There is . . . , There are . . . , It is . . . .") for postponing the logical subject of the sentence. Such sentences occur frequently in both speech and writing.

Pattern 4 with *there* (called an "expletive"): [2]

There is an explanation.

Note that this sentence is an informal way of saying "An explanation exists." We would not be using English if we said "An explanation is." Thus, *there* serves as a function word to fill out a convenient formula.

This formula involves a special use of the word *there* as an expletive or "filler" word. An expletive has no meaning itself but

---

[1] For assistance with minimum sentence Patterns 1-3, see "Guide to the Sentence X-Ray," pages 638-644.
[2] See "Guide to the Sentence X-Ray," pages 644-645.

fills out a grammatical formula. Let's examine the difference between *there* used as an expletive in Pattern 4 sentences, and *there* as an adverb of place.

There was a detective there.

The first *there* is an expletive, enabling us to postpone the subject, *detective*. The second *there* is an adverb of place. Note that *there* as an expletive is never strongly stressed (accented). If we say *"There* was a detective," stressing *there,* the word is being used as an adverb of place. The strong stress indicates this fact. Note that normal word order is possible when *there* is an adverb of place: A detective was there. (Pattern 2.)

The expletive *there* occupies the position normally occupied by the subject of the sentence. However, *there* never determines the form of the verb. The subject follows the verb and determines the form of the verb (for example, *is* or *are, was* or *were*). The expletive, then, may be regarded as a pointer to indicate that the subject is not in its normal position:

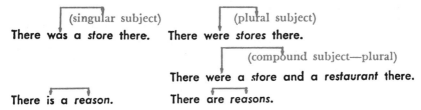

The lines with arrowheads symbolize the tie in form between the subject and verb. This tie (or correspondence) in form is called *subject-verb agreement.*

Pattern 4 with *it* (called an "expletive): [3]

It is easy to write.
It is a fact that he left.

Here the logical subjects are the infinitive *to write* and the dependent clause *that he left.* In this pattern, the expletive *it* serves as a substitute for the logical subject. The *it* also determines the form of the verb. Pattern 4 enables a writer:

1 — to vary the structure of his sentences
2 — to increase the informality of his writing
3 — to give added emphasis to the postponed subject.

---

[3] See "Guide to the Sentence X-Ray," pages 645-646.

Pattern 4 sentences with *it* can be rephrased with the logical subject in the subject position:

> To write is easy. *(Pattern 3, infinitive as subject.)*
> That he left is a fact. *(Pattern 3, dependent clause as subject.)*

The definition of a sentence. We have been analyzing the four basic patterns of English sentences, but we have not yet defined the word *sentence*. The examples we have considered have made us familiar with the patterns underlying English sentences. Now let's consider a useful definition of a sentence: *A sentence is a grammatical construction that is both complete and independent.*

A sentence is grammatically complete when it contains a subject and finite verb (a verb agreeing in form with its subject). A sentence is independent when it is not made subordinate to any other construction.

In Section 3 we shall consider the relationship between the various word-classes (or parts of speech) and the basic sentence patterns. Of these parts of speech, two are of outstanding importance in English grammar—the noun and the verb. Note that all four sentence patterns require at least one verb and at least one noun (or noun substitute). In Unit 3 we shall deal with nouns and verbs in detail, as well as with other parts of speech.

● *APPLYING EFFECTIVE ENGLISH*

Oral Applications

● **1.** In class discussion, point out every subject, direct object, indirect object, predicate noun, predicate adjective, adverbial noun, and objective complement that occurs in each of the following sentences. After identifying which of these structures occur in each sentence, classify the sentence as Pattern 1, 2, or 3.

1 — The drivers bought their license plates.
2 — Each applicant completed the test.
3 — The teacher taught her students the basic concepts of economics.
4 — Many companies send their customers samples.
5 — She baked her brother a cake.
6 — The teacher taught the basic concepts of economics to her students.
7 — Many companies sent samples to their customers.

8 — She baked a cake for her brother.

9 — The company made Mr. Bergen their new agent.

10 — Our coach considered David Watkins the best tackle on the team.

• **2.** In class discussion, identify the expletives and logical subjects in the following Pattern 4 sentences.

1 — It is necessary to reclassify these accounts.

2 — There are many opportunities available.

3 — There is a fine restaurant in Algonquin.

4 — There are a marina and a parking lot in their plans.

5 — It is certain that more students will apply.

• **3.** In class discussion, revise the sentences given in Oral Application 2, placing the logical subjects in their normal position and eliminating the expletives.

• **4.** In class discussion, classify each of the following sentences as Pattern 1, 2, 3, 4 with *there,* or 4 with *it.* Justify each decision.

1 — Many businessmen are expert readers.

2 — Mr. Lenox retired last August.

3 — There were four applicants at the luncheon.

4 — Miss Jackson made the test more difficult.

5 — The company sent its customers special announcements.

6 — It is true that accuracy is essential in business messages.

7 — There are a faculty member and an administrative officer on that committee.

8 — Each contestant seemed nervous.

9 — The Fourth of July falls on a Tuesday this year.

10 — The return address must include the ZIP Code.

Written Applications

• **1.** Write the following sentences, filling in the blanks with appropriate words. Each sentence involves a linking verb followed by a predicate noun.

1 — Each _____ became a (or *an*) _____.

2 — All _____ were their _____.

3 — The _____ seemed his _____.

4 — This _____ appeared to be a _____.

5 — Our _____ will be a _____.

6 — That _____ had been my _____.

7 — A (or *An*) _____ should be a _____.

• **2.** Write the following sentences, filling in the blanks with appropriate words. Each sentence involves a linking verb and should be followed by an adjective (for example, *tall, happy, rich, handsome*). An adjective in this position is called a predicate adjective.

1 — Their _____ was _____.
2 — The _____ is _____.
3 — That _____ will be _____.
4 — Our _____ became _____.
5 — A (or *An*) _____ has become _____.
6 — My _____ seems _____.
7 — The _____ may seem _____.
8 — Each _____ appears to be _____.
9 — Many _____ have been _____.

• **3.** Write the following sentences, filling in the blanks with appropriate words:

1 — There is a (or *an*) _____ scheduled for tomorrow.
2 — There are many _____ in the storeroom.
3 — It is _____ that these letters must be completed.
4 — There are a (or *an*) _____ and a (or *an*) _____ in our office.
5 — It would be _____ to submit that suggestion now.

• **4.** Revise the sentences you wrote in Written Application 3, eliminating the *It is* and *There is/are* formulas.

• **5.** Write the following Pattern 4 sentences, supplying the appropriate verb form. Be prepared to justify your choices.

1 — There is/are a calculator and a slide rule on my desk.
2 — There has/have been many advances in the design of office equipment.
3 — There is/are two typewriters that need repair.
4 — There was/were a pencil and two pens in the drawer.
5 — There has/have been a big improvement in her shorthand.

• **6.** Revise each of the following sentences, placing the logical subject in the subject position.

1 — It is necessary to proofread that sales brochure.
2 — There have been five applicants in the office this morning.
3 — There were two well-qualified stenographers on his staff.
4 — It is satisfying to prepare a neat and effective message.
5 — It is true that a reliable report must be accurate.

SECTION 3

The Importance of the Parts of Speech

Only certain parts of speech can occupy the key positions in English sentence patterns.

The relation between sentence patterns and the parts of speech. We have seen that English sentences are composed of words occurring in regular sequences. The order in which words occur communicates important grammatical meanings. The following unstructured list has no grammatical meaning: *A locked the man door.* On the other hand, three of the words, as items, have obvious meanings: *locked, man,* and *door.* When we rearrange the words according to an English pattern, at once a new meaning emerges:

A man locked the door.

The additional meaning that words acquire when they occur in a pattern is called *grammatical meaning*.

The word order illustrated by the sentence "A man locked the door" can be the basis of millions of different sentences. Each time we make a change, however, we must substitute an appropriate part of speech. For example:

S	+	TrV	+	DO
A man		locked		the door.
A statesman		praised		the governor.
A boy		painted		the picture.
A girl		baked		the pie.
A teacher		graded		the test.
An executive		mailed		the contract.
An employee		loaded		the truck.
A secretary		examined		the report.

The *grammatical* meaning of all of these sentences is identical:

(1) A person (indicated by the noun in the subject position) performed an action.

(2) The performer has not been named in the context (indicated by use of the indefinite *a* or *an*).

(3) The action was performed prior to the time the statement was made (indicated by the fact that the verbs all have an *-ed* suffix).

(4) The action affected some other person or thing (indicated by the noun in the direct object position).

To preserve this grammatical meaning, we must:

(1) keep the original word order;

(2) retain *a* or *an* and *the* (otherwise we alter the definiteness or indefiniteness of the reference);

(3) use a noun (or noun substitute) for both the subject and direct object;

(4) use a transitive verb between the subject and direct object.

Points 3 and 4 concern us here. They demonstrate the importance of the parts of speech in English grammar. They indicate the need to examine and describe these parts of speech. Such an examination will enable us to determine what classes of words can occupy what positions in an English sentence.

The definition and treatment of the parts of speech. In Unit 1 we saw that word order and function words are two basic kinds of grammatical signals. Now we know that word order enables us to understand which term is the subject, direct object, or some other structure. *The key positions convey these grammatical meanings.*

We can use this fact to set up our first general class of words. Words that can occupy these key positions in sentence patterns form the group called "pattern words." For example, *secretary* and *customer* have grammatical meanings in Sentence 1 different from those in Sentence 2:

1—The secretary wrote the customer a note.
2—The customer wrote the secretary a note.

Secretary is the subject in the first sentence, the indirect object in the second. *Customer* is the indirect object in the first sentence, the subject in the second. Position alone—word order—determines this difference in grammatical meaning.

Thus, nouns (such as *secretary* and *customer*) are examples of pattern words. Other types of pattern words include pronouns, verbs, descriptive adjectives, and most adverbs.

In addition to pattern words, we must recognize a second general class of words. Words belonging to this second class are, in themselves, grammatical signals. While they do not occupy key sentence positions, they do perform various special grammatical functions. For this reason they are called "function words." The following are the main types of function words:

1 — *Determiners* (articles, limiting adjectives, possessive nouns and pronouns, relative adjectives) (a) point out the person or object in question, or (b) indicate that the person or object has not occurred previously in the discussion, or (c) indicate the number of persons or objects involved: *a, an, the, this, these, that, those, some, all, seven,* etc.

2 — *Prepositions* establish a relationship involving the substantive (noun or noun substitute) which follows: *in, on, over, under, behind, to, from, by,* etc.

3 — *Coordinating conjunctions* link words, phrases, and clauses of equal rank: *and, but, or* and sometimes *for.*

4 — *Conjunctive adverbs* link independent clauses: *however, nevertheless, therefore, consequently, hence,* etc.

5 — *Subordinating conjunctions* link dependent clauses to independent clauses: *because, when, since, if, although,* etc.

6 — *Relative pronouns* link dependent clauses to words: *who, whom, which, that,* etc.

7 — *Auxiliary (helping) verbs* help form the passive voice, the perfect tenses, questions, and so on: *is* sent, *has* left, *will* study, etc.

8 — *Interrogative function words* signal that certain kinds of questions follow: *who, whom, which, what, when, why, where, how,* etc.

There are about 150 common function words in English. In contrast, there are tens of thousands of "pattern" words. Though the number of different function words is small, they gain tremendous importance from the fact that many of them are used repeatedly in every paragraph. Consider the number of *the's, in's,* and *of's,* for example, in this paragraph. The word *the* is used seven times. The word *of* is used six times. The word *in* is used five times. There is a reason why such function words occur so frequently. Almost every sentence involves relationships that are signalled by means of them. Thus, function words gain even greater importance from the fact that they communicate essential grammatical meanings. Many of these meanings cannot be communicated in any other way.

In Unit 3 we'll study pattern words. In Unit 4 we'll take up function words.

• *APPLYING EFFECTIVE ENGLISH*

Oral Applications

• **1.** Rearrange the following groups of words as Pattern I sentences.

    1 — that finished boy book the
    2 — the sent application girl her
    3 — assignment that made the teacher
    4 — the secretary report criticized this
    5 — discharged each committee the president board of the
    6 — attention that his needs street
    7 — his revised student paper each
    8 — Ellen Carl to the message sent
    9 — enjoyed those many courses golfers
    10 — many architect buildings the planned

• **2.** Rearrange each of the sentences you composed for Oral Application 1. Use exactly the same words, but change the grammatical meaning of the sentence by placing some of the words in different positions.

• **3.** In class discussion, classify the words in Oral Application 1 as pattern words or function words. Justify your classifications.

• **4.** What effect does position have on the *grammatical* meaning of a noun (or noun substitute). Use as examples the sentences you prepared for Oral Applications 1 and 2.

• **5.** Discuss the positions which the function words in Oral Applications 1 and 2 can occupy. Experiment with your sentences to determine all of the possibilities.

Written Applications

• **1.** By placing the nouns in different positions, construct two different sentences using the following group of words:

cooperation her for the customer the thanked receptionist

• **2.** By placing the nouns in different positions, construct three different sentences using the following group of words:

helping for the thanked clerk her typist friend the

• **3.** By placing the nouns in different positions, construct at least three different sentences using the following group of words:

called Greene Mr. manager competent a comptroller the

 **UNIT 3**

MASTERING THE FORMS AND USES OF THE PARTS OF SPEECH: PATTERN WORDS

Pattern words (the five types listed on the next page) differ in use from function words. Pattern words fill the key position in sentences. These <u>positions</u> establish the relations among the various pattern words. In contrast, function words are themselves grammatical signals which set up additional relationships among pattern words.

Two types of pattern words occur in every statement: (1) Nouns (or noun substitutes, including personal pronouns) serve as subjects. (2) Verbs serve as the essential term in predicates. Nouns and personal pronouns can also serve as objects and complements. Certain verb forms (participles and infinitives) can serve as descriptive adjectives. Certain verb forms (gerunds and infinitives) can serve as nouns.

Two other types of pattern words occur as optional elements in sentences—as modifiers: descriptive adjectives and adverbs. Their position ordinarily indicates what term they modify.

Adverbs often serve as verb modifiers. As such they can occupy numerous positions. For example, in the following sentence the adverb <u>then</u> can occupy any one of these five positions: (1) The efficient secretary (2) had (3) begun (4) her afternoon's work (5).

UNIT 3

Section 1

Nouns: Most nouns can be identified by the fact that they can have four distinct forms in writing. For example: <u>girl/girls/girl's/girls'</u>.

Section 2

Personal Pronouns: Personal pronouns have different forms for use as subjects and as objects. They also have special possessive forms for use as substantives. For example: <u>we/us/our/ours</u>.

Section 3

Verbs: Verbs can be identified by the fact that they have sets of forms similar to one of these:
 I: lift/lifts/lifted/lifted/lifting
 II: ride/rides/rode/ridden/riding
III: go/goes/went/gone/going

Section 4

Descriptive Adjectives: Descriptive adjectives modify substantives. They usually have sets of forms corresponding to <u>tall/taller/tallest</u> or to <u>adept/more adept/most adept</u>. They often have special adjectival endings, such as <u>-ful</u>, <u>-al</u>, <u>-ive</u>, and <u>-ous</u>.

Section 5

Adverbs: Adverbs can modify adjectives, adverbs, and verbs, indicating, for example, the time, place, or manner of an action. Many adverbs end in -ly; others resemble prepositions: <u>in, out, up, across, through, by, under,</u> etc. Many adverbs, like descriptive adjectives, have comparative and superlative forms.

Introduction

The importance of position in classifying parts of speech. Unit 2 pointed out that the position a word can occupy in English sentence patterns is one of the tests used for classifying parts of speech. In classifying a word as a particular part of speech, work with the word in a particular context. For example, consider the word *man* in the following sentences:

Subject Position	Verb Position	Object Complement Position
1 — The man	entered	the lifeboat.
2 — The sailors	man	the lifeboat.

The word *man* is spelled identically in both sentences, but it functions in entirely different ways. As a result, the forms *man* can have in Sentence 1 are different from those it can have in Sentence 2.

The importance of word form in classifying parts of speech. In the first sentence *man* is the subject of the verb *entered*. *Man* occupies the normal subject position. In this position, the word can have either the singular form *man* or the plural form *men*. That is, it can distinguish between one man and more than one man. Any word capable of making such a distinction is a noun or a personal pronoun.[1]

In the second sentence *man* is a transitive verb and has as its subject *sailors*. Here *man* occupies the normal verb position. In this position, the word can occur either in its singular form *mans* ("The sailor mans the lifeboat.") or in its plural form *man* (The sailors man the lifeboat."). The distinction between the singular and plural forms of *man* in Sentence 2 is not related to the distinction between one or more than one man. Instead, it is a distinction involving a correspondence in form between the verb and its singular or plural subject. This correspondence is called agreement. Thus, in the present

---

[1] The only exceptions to this extremely useful generalization are the determiners *this/these* and *that/those*, which can also be used as substantives.

tense, verbs with subjects like sailor (or *he/she/it* or any singular noun) have the suffix *-(e)s*.

Accordingly, both position and form indicate that in Sentence 2 *man* is a verb. Another test for identifying a verb is to see whether it has a special form for indicating past action. If it has, it is a verb. Thus, in reference to past action, Sentence 2 could be written: "The sailors manned the lifeboat." Here the word has the special past tense form *manned*. This form signifies that the action occurred prior to the time when the statement was made. Any word whose forms can express a distinction between present and past time is a verb.

Suppose someone asked what part of speech *man* is, and made no reference to any particular sentence. We would have to answer that it is either a noun or a verb. We could point out that when *men* can be substituted for *man* in a sentence, *man* is being used as a noun. On the other hand, when *mans* or *manned* can be substituted, *man* is being used as a verb. Thus, both form and function (position) can be used in classifying the parts of speech.

A dictionary lists all possible parts of speech to which a word might be assigned. We shall not attempt to do this. Instead, we shall classify words in terms of the forms they can have in certain sentence positions. Thus, in the sentence "They list the contributors each month," *list* occupies the second key position. In this position, it can have the form *listed*. Hence we classify *list* in this sentence as a verb. In the sentence "The list was posted," *list* occupies the first key position and can have the form *lists* designating more than one list. Hence we classify *list* in this sentence as a noun.

Occasionally a word found in a position normally occupied by a noun may not have all the formal characteristics of a noun. Such a word is called a *substantive* or *noun substitute*. Take, for example, the sentence, "The strong can look out for themselves, but the weak cannot." The words *strong* and *weak* occupy noun positions, though they do not have singular or plural forms. In *this* sentence these words are substantives. Ordinarily they serve as adjectives: "The strong wind . . .," "The weak tea. . . ."

The plan to be followed in treating pattern words. In the discussion of pattern words, we'll cover the following points, as appropriate, for each part of speech:

1 — The conventional definition of the part of speech.
2 — One or more simple test-frames for identifying the part of speech.

3 — The formal characteristics of the part of speech; that is, the possible changes in form resulting from the addition of suffixes or from alterations in the spelling of the word—for example, *write/writes/wrote/written/writing.*

4 — The main subclasses or varieties of the part of speech.

5 — The grammatical constructions in which the part of speech normally appears.

• *APPLYING EFFECTIVE ENGLISH*

Oral Applications

• **1.** The following words can be used both as nouns and as verbs. Make up sentences to illustrate these different uses of the words. Discuss the various changes in form which are possible for each word in its different uses.

change   copy   hand   swing   fish   wall   help   dance   dish

• **2.** Explain why a word like *wish* cannot, out of context, properly be classified only as a noun. What other part of speech can it be? On what basis can we decide what part of speech *wish* is in a sentence? Give examples to illustrate and clarify your answer.

• **3.** In the following sentences indicate whether the italicized words are nouns or verbs. Discuss how word order and, sometimes, word form have enabled you to identify the part of speech.

1 — The *fence needs repairs.*
2 — They *fenced* in their *garden.*
3 — Don *repairs* old lawn mowers.
4 — There is an urgent *need* for improvement.
5 — He *gardens* every afternoon.
6 — Ken *repaired* that *light.*
7 — The *hammer* had been mislaid.
8 — Eric *hammered* the spike persistently.
9 — Joan's *hands* were unusually strong.
10 — Mrs. Essex *handed* the *bill* to her husband.

Written Application

Make a list of five words, such as those in Oral Application 1, that can be used as either nouns or verbs. Try to find examples that were not used in the Oral Application. Compose sentences which illustrate the use of each word, first as a noun, then as a verb.

SECTION 1

Nouns

We can identify most nouns by the fact that they can have four distinct forms in writing. For example: girl/girls/girl's/girls'.

Conventional definition. A noun is the "name" of a person (*girl, man, lady, Guy, Betty, Alan Lerner, Maria Callas*), place (*city, ocean, the Green Mountains, Chattanooga, Isthmus of Panama, Lake Erie*), thing (*book, car, chalkboard, U.S.S. John F. Kennedy, United Nations Building*), event (*hike, race, earthquake, election, promotion, Olympics*), or concept (*justice, hope, goodness, evolution*). Certain kinds of nouns based on verbs designate actions ("His *running*," "Her *writing*," "Their *swimming*," "The dog's *barking*"); verbal nouns ending in the suffix *-ing* are called *gerunds*.

Test-frame for identifying nouns. Any noun can fit the blank in one or the other of the following sentences.[1]

1 — The _____ was good.
2 — The _____ -(e)s were good.

These test-frames provide a fast and easy way to determine whether a particular word is a noun (or can be used as a noun; the four forms characteristic of nouns will provide a further check). For example, the following words fit the blank in Test-frame 1: *airplane, test, book, pencil, boy, fishing, picture, lady, cloud, man, house, girl, corporation.* The following words fit the blank in Test-frame 2: *airplanes, tests, books, pencils, boys, pictures, ladies, clouds, men, houses, girls, corporations.* (Note that *men* fits the second frame, although it forms its plural by means of changing its spelling rather than by adding the suffix *-(e)s.* Similarly, such words as *women, teeth, mice,* and *feet* fit the second frame.)

---

[1] The word *the* in the test-frames is omitted before people's names and some other proper nouns. Any descriptive adjective may be substituted for *good*; for example, *large, acceptable, colorful.*

Formal characteristics of nouns. Most nouns in English have four distinct forms in writing.

1 — Singular form, general case. (The term *general case* refers to the forms nouns have in all their uses except as possessives.) For example, *tool, typist, ticket, friend.*

2 — Plural form, general case. For example, *tools, typists, tickets, friends.*

3 — Singular form, possessive case. For example, *tool's, typist's, ticket's, friend's.*

4 — Plural form, possessive case. For example, *tools', typists', tickets', friends'.*

Formation of the plurals of nouns (general case). The great majority of nouns in English form their plural by adding the suffix *-s* or *-es* to their singular. If the singular form of the noun ends in *e* (for example, *name*) or in any sound other than a hissing sound like *s* or *z*, add the suffix *-s* to form the plural.

If the singular form of the noun ends in a hissing sound (spelled *s, ss, z, ch, sh,* or *x*—for example, *kiss/kisses, box/boxes, church/churches*) and if the noun does not end in silent *e*, add the suffix *-es* to form the plural.

Nouns adding -s to form their plural		*Nouns adding -es to form their plural*	
pen	pens	watch	watches
typewriter	typewriters	hatch	hatches
desk	desks	wish	wishes
shoe	shoes	class	classes
ring	rings	slash	slashes
finger	fingers	twitch	twitches
head	heads	itch	itches
lock	locks	flash	flashes
tree	trees	fuzz	fuzzes
toe	toes	blush	blushes
book	books	catch	catches
record	records	gas	gases
judge	judges	pass	passes
fence	fences	church	churches
radio	radios [2]	potato	potatoes [2]

[2] Nouns ending in *o* preceded by a vowel symbol (a, e, i, o, u) generally form their plural by the addition of *s*; nouns ending in *o* preceded by a consonant generally form their plural by the addition of *-es*. When in doubt, consult a dictionary.

A few nouns which form their plural by the addition of the -s or -es suffix also change from *f* in the singular to *v* in the plural:

Nouns adding -s and changing an f sound to v in the plural		*Nouns adding -es and changing a final f sound to v in the plural*	
knife	knives	thief	thieves
wife	wives	calf	calves
life	lives	half	halves

Nouns ending in *y* preceded by a consonant, form their plural by the addition of the suffix -es after the *y* has been changed to *i*. Nouns ending in *y* preceded by a vowel character form their plural simply by the addition of the suffix -s.

Nouns ending in y preceded by a consonant and adding -es after changing y to i		*Nouns ending in y preceded by a vowel character and merely adding -s*	
baby	babies	valley	valleys
lady	ladies	Sunday	Sundays
country	countries	volley	volleys
beauty	beauties	trolley	trolleys
candy	candies	key	keys
currency	currencies	day	days
pantry	pantries	holiday	holidays

A few nouns form their plural by a change in spelling, without the addition of the -s or -es suffix.

Nouns changing their spelling to form the plural

man	men
woman	women
salesman	salesmen
tooth	teeth
goose	geese
foot	feet
mouse	mice
louse	lice

In addition a small number of nouns in English follow none of the patterns thus far discussed. For example, one noun adds the suffix -ren (*child-children*). A few nouns use exactly the same form for the singular and plural: *sheep, swine, moose, deer,* etc. Some nouns which have been borrowed from foreign languages retain their foreign plural forms. Other borrowed nouns have acquired an English plural instead of or in addition to their foreign plural. For example: *alumnus/alumni* (referring to male graduates), *alumna/alumnae* (referring to women graduates), *index/indexes* or *indices, antenna/antennae* (in connection with biology) or *antennas* (in connection with radio and television), and so on.

Whenever you are in doubt about the proper plural form of any noun, consult an up-to-date dictionary. If the noun has an irregular plural, the dictionary will give it.

Forming the possessive case of nouns. When you use the expression "the man's car" or "the manager's desk," the first noun (*man's, manager's*) is a "possessive" modifier of the second noun. In written language the possessive noun must be given an apostrophe and a suffix *-s*. This form is called the possessive case.

Only nouns (and pronouns) have special possessive forms. And again only nouns (and pronouns) have different forms to refer to one thing (singular) and to more than one thing (plural).

The possessive case normally refers to possession. Sometimes, however, it expresses other relationships. Note the difference in the following examples.

Possessive case used to indicate ownership

The boy's wagon (= the wagon of the boy)
The school's station wagon (= the station wagon of the school)
The man's ticket (= the ticket of the man)
The child's shoes (= the shoes of the child)

Possessive case used to indicate relationships other than ownership

The boy's mother (= the mother of the boy)
The school's principal (= the principal of the school)
The man's baldness (= the baldness of the man)
The child's happiness (= the happiness of the child)

The parenthetical phrases given with the preceding examples illustrate that the meaning of the possessive case can be expressed by a prepositional phrase introduced by *of* or occasionally by *for*. For example: "A sale of *children's snowsuits*" means "A sale of *snowsuits for children.*" Thus, these two grammatical devices—the suffix *-'s* (a change in word form) and the *of*-prepositional phrase (use of a functional word)—can express essentially the same meaning. The writer, then, may choose whether to express this relationship by means of an inflectional ending or a prepositional phrase.

All nouns form their singular possessive in the same way; they add *-'s* to their singular form. For example: *student/student's, lady/lady's, judge/judge's, car/car's, John/John's.*

The plural possessive is formed in either of two ways. (1) For all nouns adding *-s* or *-es* to form their plural, add an apostrophe after the *-s* to form their plural possessive. Nouns that change a final *y* to *i* before *-es* is added and nouns that change an *f* to *v* before *-(e)s* is added, belong in this group.

For example:

Singular Possessive

the **boy's books** (= the books of the boy)
the **girl's gloves** (= the gloves of the girl)
the **student's car** (= the car of the student)
the **teacher's pens** (= the pens of the teacher)
the **baby's rattles** (= the rattles of the baby)
the **country's manpower** (= the manpower of the country)
the **lady's appearance** (= the appearance of the lady)
the **dean's report** (= the report of the dean)

Plural possessive

the **boys' books** (= the books of the boys)
the **girls' gloves** (= the gloves of the girls)
the **students' car** (= the car of the students)
the **teachers' pens** (= the pens of the teachers)
the **babies' rattles** (= the rattles of the babies)
the **countries' manpower** (= the manpower of the countries)
the **ladies' appearance** (= the appearance of the ladies)
the **deans' report** (= the report of the deans)

For this large class of nouns (all those adding *-(e)s* to form their plural) it is easy to tell whether to add the apostrophe before or after the *-s* suffix. Mentally rephrase the construction, substituting an *of*-phrase for the possessive case, as in the parenthetical expressions in the preceding examples. If the object of the preposition *of* would be singular, add *-'s*. If it would be plural, add *-(e)s'*.

(2) For all nouns that form their plural in any other way than by adding a suffix *-(e)s*, add *'s* to the plural to form the plural possessive.

For example:

Singular possessive

the man's clothes (= the clothes of the man)
the child's toys (= the toys of the child)
the sheep's tail (= the tail of the sheep)
the woman's hats (= the hats of the woman)
the goose's honking (= the honking of the goose)
the alunma's record (= the record of the alumna)

Plural possessive

the men's clothes (= the clothes of the men [or "for men"])
the children's toys (= the toys of the children)
the sheep's leader (= the leader of the sheep)
the women's hats (= the hats of the women [or "for women"])
the geese's honking (= the honking of the geese)
the alumnae's record (= the record of the alumnae)

In summary, a word is a noun if it follows any of the preceding patterns for forming plurals or possessives. Any such word can occupy the blank position in the test-frame "The _____ is/are good." Special problems concerning the possessive are taken up in Unit 5, pages 178-181.

Subclasses or types of nouns. Nouns may be subdivided in many different ways. We shall consider two important kinds of distinctions: (1) those among common, proper, and collective nouns, and (2) those between concrete and abstract nouns.

Common, proper, and collective nouns. A common noun is one that names an object as the member of a class. All of the objects making up a class have essential characteristics in *common*. That is why such nouns are called *common nouns*.

Common nouns may designate (1) a substance, (2) a class of things, or (3) the members of a class of things. Examples are: *sugar, coal, soldier, table, city, architect, bug, snail, tree, lamp, airport, car.*

In contrast, a proper noun is the special name of one person, place, thing, or event; for example, *Miss Joan Sutherland; Houston, Texas; Frank Lloyd Wright; Candlestick Park; Arbor Day; Lincoln High School; Borden, Inc.; the Empire State Building.* Thus, a proper noun is the special name associated with a particular thing, whatever it may be. A common noun is a name that applies to a *class* of things or to *members* of a class of things. This distinction will become much clearer when you compare the following lists. The individual names (proper nouns) on the right correspond to the class names (common nouns) on the left.

Common nouns	Proper nouns
city	Denver
state	New York
ocean	Atlantic
airport	O'Hare Airport
automobile	Pontiac
corporation	Ford Motor Company
hotel	The Palmer House
person	Richard M. Nixon
explorer	Christopher Columbus
conductor	Leonard Bernstein

Each proper noun names a member of the class designated by the corresponding common noun. This distinction is essential in writing, for all proper nouns are capitalized, while common nouns are not. (For guides to the capitalization of proper nouns, see pages 198-202.)

A collective noun is a special kind of common noun that names, by its singular form, a group or collection of individuals; for example, *band, troop, army, orchestra, jury, family.* A collective noun can be used to refer to a unit as a whole or to the individuals comprising the unit. If a collective noun refers to a unit as a whole, it takes a *singular* verb, and *singular* pronouns are used in referring to it. If a collective noun refers to the individuals comprising the unit, it takes a *plural* verb, and *plural* pronouns are used in referring to it.

For example, if the collective noun *family* refers to the group as a unit, it is considered a singular noun:

The family *is going* on a trip to Sequoia National Park and *is taking its* new station wagon.

Note that the verbs *is going* and *is taking* and the pronoun *its* are singular; hence, in this sentence the writer is regarding the family as a unit.

In contrast, if the collective noun *family* refers to the individuals comprising the group, plural verbs and pronouns are used in connection with it:

The family *are discussing their* destinations, for *they* have different preferences.

Note that the verb phrase *are discussing* and the pronouns *their* and *they* are plural. The most important point to remember about a collective noun is to be consistent in regarding it as singular or plural.

The distinction between concrete and abstract nouns. A concrete noun designates some object(s) or event(s). In contrast, an abstract noun designates a quality considered apart from (*abstracted from*) an actual object or event.

For example, the following nouns name persons, things, or occurrences rather than qualities: *paper, desk, pencil, test, typewriter, promotion, employment, inspection, visit.* Concrete nouns name things that can be perceived and events that can be observed.

In contrast, the following nouns name qualities rather than things or events: *happiness, ability, persistence, loyalty, love, urgency.* The following test sentence can give help in recognizing abstract nouns:

_____ **is a quality characteristic of them.**

Abstract nouns can fill the blank in this sentence; concrete nouns cannot. Some nouns have both concrete and abstract meanings. For example, *charity* can refer to generosity (abstract meaning) or to an organization which performs charitable work (concrete meaning).

Many abstract nouns are formed by adding special suffixes to descriptive adjectives. Since such adjectives name *qualities,* nouns based upon descriptive adjectives also name qualities. For example, the abstract noun *sweetness* is formed by adding the suffix *-ness* to the descriptive adjective *sweet.* In the lists below the descriptive adjective appears to the left, the abstract noun based upon it to the right.

Descriptive Adjective	*Corresponding Abstract Noun*
happy	happiness
secure	security
wise	wisdom
loyal	loyalty
continuous	continuity
rough	roughness
confident	confidence
heavy	heaviness
free	freedom
true	truth
sweet	sweetness

The advantages of concrete nouns. The distinction between concrete and abstract nouns is an important consideration in one's style of writing. A style that emphasizes concrete nouns and active verbs has vigor. Apt examples and illustrations reinforce this effect. On the other hand, a style that remains at the level of vague generalizations will be boring and ineffective. Compare the following sentences:

1 — Precision of diction and variety of sentence construction and sentence length should not be overlooked as qualities of importance to be strived for in connection with effectiveness in writing.

2—An effective writer chooses words with precision and varies sentence length and type.

Note that the two sentences say approximately the same thing. The first is difficult and general. It calls up no picture. It is roundabout. In contrast, the second sentence is brief, concrete, and straightforward. It asks the reader to imagine a writer at work, deciding how best to express his ideas. In business, only writing that captures the reader's attention can be expected to win profits. Such writing harnesses the power of concrete nouns.

The constructions in which nouns occur. Nouns are used in many different structures (or constructions) in the English language. The most common and most important of these structures have already been discussed in some detail in Section 2 of Unit 2, "Mastering the Basic Sentence Patterns of English." Hence, many of the structures summarized here will already be familiar to you.

The various structures in which nouns appear involve all four kinds of grammatical signals. These signals are word order, word form, function words, and oral or written punctuation. In the following discussion, fourteen noun structures will be considered.[3]

Each of these structures involves a definite grammatical meaning. For example, "Glenn praised Adele" does not mean the same thing as "Adele praised Glenn." The words are the same, but their grammatical meanings—their relationships—are different. In the first *Glenn* is the subject and *Adele* the direct object. In the second these relationships are reversed. Equally important contrasts in meaning are involved in each of the following constructions.

---

[3] These fourteen constructions represent all the important uses of nouns in English, except for certain absolute constructions and certain subclasses (e.g., noun as direct object of a present participle, of a gerund, of an infinitive, and so on). All of these structures, of course, could occur in compound form.

Noun as subject.[4] A single noun which precedes the verb and, in some situations, is tied to the verb by agreement of form is the subject.

A careful *writer* revises his first drafts.[5]

Noun as direct object.[6] A single noun which follows a transitive verb, refers to something different from the subject, and answers the question "The subject did *what?*"[7] is a direct object.

The carpenter built the *house.*

Noun as indirect object.[6] If two nouns follow a "sending type" transitive verb, one denoting the receiver and the other what was received, the first (the receiver) is an indirect object. You can also convey the same meaning by using the function word *to* followed by the noun denoting the receiver. Use this second method as a simple test for identifying an indirect object. Example: "I told *Allen* the story." Now apply the test: "I told the story to *Allen.*" In *this* sentence *Allen* is the object of a preposition; accordingly we know that in the previous sentence *Allen* is the indirect object.

Noun as objective complement.[6] If an "altering-type" transitive verb is followed by two nouns, one indicating what was affected or altered and the other indicating the result of the alteration, the one indicating the result of the alteration is an objective complement.

The president appointed Rosanne his personal *representative.*

Noun as object of a preposition.[6] A single noun "linked" to some other element in a sentence by means of a preposition (for example, *in, on, to, from, by, of, under*), and usually immediately following the preposition, is the object of that preposition.[8]

The principal of the *school* brought his *report* to the *meeting.*

Noun as appositive.[6] If two nouns occur together and the second could substitute for the first, the second is called an appositive: "Washington, the *father* of his country, chaired the Constitutional Convention." If the appositive is needed to identify or limit the meaning of its head, it is a *restrictive* appositive and is not set off by

---

[4] See "Guide to the Sentence X-Ray," page 646.

[5] Note that if the subject were *writers* (third person plural), the form of the verb in the present tense would be *revise.* This correspondence in form between a finite verb and its subject is called subject-verb agreement.

[6] See "Guide to the Sentence X-Ray," page 647.

[7] For *did* substitute the appropriate verb; for example, "built *what?*"

[8] For a discussion of prepositions, see pages 134-136.

commas. If the appositive merely provides additional information about its head, it is a *nonrestrictive* appositive and is set off by commas in writing and by pauses in speech.

Mr. Perry, our *teacher*, is fascinated by Shaw's play *Pygmalion*.

Note that *teacher* is a nonrestrictive appositive. It merely gives added information about Mr. Perry. Hence, *teacher* is set off by commas. *Pygmalion,* on the other hand, is a restrictive appositive. It identifies which of George Bernard Shaw's plays fascinates Mr. Perry. As a restrictive appositive, it is not set off by commas.

We got Julius, our *dog*, from the pound.

Noun as noun-adjunct (or *adjectival noun*).[9] A noun used to modify a following *noun* is called a noun-adjunct. For example, *ball player, file clerk, station wagon, truck driver, steam engine, stone wall.* Note that a noun-adjunct cannot be separated from its head by an adjective or by any other modifier. Sometimes such expressions have become compounds: *showboat, bookstore, wallpaper, flowerpot, football, bathhouse.*

The *house* builder consulted the landowner about the *tax* rate.

The *airplane* pilot followed that route for ten years.

Noun used in direct address.[9] A noun or title addressed directly to a reader or listener is called a noun in direct address. It is set off from the rest of the sentence by commas in writing and pauses in speech.

We need your help, *Shirley*, on this job.

Kevin, send for a replacement.

In the second example we can tell that *Kevin* is a noun in direct address since it is a name set off from the rest of the sentence. In addition, if *Kevin* were the subject of the verb *send*, the verb would end in the third-person singular, present tense suffix *-(e)s*: "Kevin sends for a replacement."

Noun as possessive modifier (determiner).[9] A noun in the possessive case indicates the "possessor." Its head indicates what is possessed.

---

[9] See "Guide to the Sentence X-Ray," page 647.

For example, "The teacher's dictionary. . . ." This construction also applies to relationships similar to possession: "The chairman's patience. . . ."

The *company's* agent delivered the *woman's* package.

Russell's note gave *Irene's* new address.

The possessive form of a noun as substantive.[10] Sometimes the possessive form of a noun does not modify a following noun. In this event, the possessive form may stand for a phrase implied by the context.

Doug took his golf clubs, and Art took *Father's.*

In this example *Father's* is a short way of saying *Father's golf clubs.* The term *golf clubs* is understood from the context.

Noun as predicate noun (subjective complement).[10] A single noun occurring to the right of the verb and referring to the same person or thing as the subject is a predicate noun. This construction occurs in three situations:

(1) It is most frequent after linking verbs, which require a predicate noun (or adjective) to complete the predicate. Examples of linking verbs are the various forms of *to be, to seem, to appear,* and *to become.*

Drew became the *leader.*

In the sentence above, *leader* is a predicate noun occurring after the linking verb *became.* Note that a predicate noun (or adjective) is required to *complete* the assertion being made about the subject of the sentence. For this reason, predicate nouns are also given the name *subjective complements.* Note also that the words *Drew* and *leader* both refer to the same person.

(2) Predicate nouns sometimes appear after verbs other than linking verbs:

Barry returned from his vacation, a happy and enthusiastic *man.*

This construction is similar to an appositive. However, an appositive follows its head directly, without being separated from it.

Laura came back again, a determined and persistent *girl.*

---

[10] See "Guide to the Sentence X-Ray," page 648.

(3) Predicate nouns also occur after the passive voice forms of "altering-type" transitive verbs.[11]

The man was considered a *hero*.

The noun *hero,* occurring in the predicate, refers to the same person as the subject *man.*

Brad was appointed the president's *representative*.

Noun as adverb.[12] When a noun designates such meanings as time or place and is not one of the structures already listed, it is a noun adverb (or *adverbial noun*). Note the difference between these two sentences:

1—Mike went home.
2—Mike painted his home.

In Sentence 1, *home* follows the intransitive verb *went* and designates a place. Hence it is a noun adverb. In Sentence 2, *home* is the direct object of the transitive verb *painted.* Here is another example:

Fridays, the construction workers from Decatur return *home*.

Noun as retained direct object.[13] "Retained" constructions require a word of explanation. Two important points about them must be kept in mind: First, they occur *only* after verbs in passive voice.[14] Second, they occur only after the passive voice forms of "sending-type" transitive verbs.[15] Let us compare two sentences involving a "sending-type" transitive verb and expressing essentially the same idea. The first uses active voice, the second passive voice. This comparison will show that the direct object in active voice can be "retained" in passive voice.

1 — "Sending-type" transitive verb in active voice followed by an indirect object and a direct object:

Keith sent Mr. Randolph a *telegram*.

2 — "Sending-type" transitive verb in passive voice followed by a "retained direct object":

Mr. Randolph was sent a *telegram* [by Keith].

---

11 See "Guide to the Sentence X-Ray," page 642.
12 See "Guide to the Sentence X-Ray," page 648.
13 See "Guide to the Sentence X-Ray," page 648.
14 For an explanation of passive voice and the grammatical signals involved in passive voice, see pages 123-126.
15 For a discussion of "sending-type" and "altering-type" transitive verbs, see pages 34-35.

In Sentence 1, *telegram* is a direct object. It occupies the characteristic position of a direct object and it tells what was sent. In Sentence 2, *telegram* is a "retained direct object." It is retained as a direct object even though the verb has been converted to passive voice. Here is another example:

The supervisor was told the *story* by Carl.

Note that the verb *was told* is in passive voice. The subject *(supervisor)* is not doing the telling—is not performing the action—but is "receiving" it. *Story* occupies the position of a direct object and indicates *what* the supervisor was told. Hence, it is a "retained direct object."

The same sentence, in active voice, would read: "Carl told the supervisor the story." After the transitive verb *told,* in active voice, *story* is an ordinary *(not* a retained) direct object.

Noun as retained indirect object.[16] "Retained" indirect objects occur only after "sending-type" transitive verbs in passive voice. Let us compare two sentences involving a "sending-type" transitive verb and expressing essentially the same idea. The first uses active voice, the second passive voice.

1 — "Sending-type" transitive verb in active voice followed by an indirect object and a direct object:

   Miss Benson offered *Susan* good advice.

2 — "Sending-type" transitive verb in passive voice followed by an indirect object.

   Good advice was offered *Susan* [by Miss Benson].

Note that the verb *was offered* is in passive voice. The subject *(advice)* is not doing the offering—is not performing the action—but is "receiving" it. *Susan* occupies the position of an indirect object and indicates *to whom* the advice was given. The same meaning could be expressed with *Susan* as object of the preposition *to.* Thus: "Good advice was offered to Susan." This possibility confirms that *Susan* is an *indirect object.* Hence, in Sentence 2 Susan is a retained indirect object. Here is another example:

The report was given the *supervisor* by his assistant.

Note that *supervisor* occurs after a passive verb and indicates *to whom* the report was given. Thus, it is a retained indirect object.

---

16 See "Guide to the Sentence X-Ray," page 648.

In summary, a word which follows any of these patterns for forming plurals or possessives is a noun: [1]

General case singular	General case plural	Possessive case singular	Possessive case plural
boy	boys	boy's	boys'
lady	ladies	lady's	ladies'
woman	women	woman's	women's
deer	deer	deer's	deer's
child	children	child's	children's

Any word which has such forms can occupy the blank position in the test-frame.[2]

The _____ is/are good.

---

[1] A very small number of words which are nouns on the basis of their ability to fit the blank in the test-frame may not have all four forms. For example, *chaos*.

[2] Any descriptive adjective (for example, *swift, urgent, beautiful*) may be substituted for *good* in the test-frame.

● *APPLYING EFFECTIVE ENGLISH*

Oral Applications

● 1. Give the conventional definition of a noun.

● 2. Using the test-frame for identifying nouns, decide which of the following words can be nouns:

repeated	skating	wonderful	beside	mirror
an	paper	off	love	blush

● 3. Which of the following nouns form their plural by the addition of *-es*? Which by the addition of *-s*? Explain the principles determining the form of the suffix that is appropriate.

couch   basket   train   slice   fox   book   patch   whistle   judge

● 4. Which of the following nouns ending in *y* change the *y* to *i* before *-es* is added to form the plural? Explain the principle which determines which form of the suffix is appropriate.

Monday	candy	county	sympathy	entry	valley
baby	trolley	key	currency	money	fly

● **5.** Rephrase the following expressions, substituting an *of*-phrase for each possessive form. Be certain that you do not alter the grammatical number of the nouns.

the teams' spirit
the lady's reply
the committee's work

the men's decision
the manager's answer
the children's toys

Written Applications

● **1.** Give the four forms possible for each of the following nouns, listing them under these headings: (1) general case, singular; (2) general case, plural; (3) possessive case, singular; (4) possessive case, plural.

president   commission   person   woman   secretary   car   child

● **2.** Arrange the following common nouns in a column. Opposite each, write two corresponding proper nouns.

airport   country   building   park   school   lake   president   state

● **3.** Arrange the following proper nouns in a column. Opposite each, write one or more corresponding common nouns.

Sweden   Utah   Pope Paul   Sinclair Lewis   U.S.S. Long Beach   Miss Marian Anderson   Dallas   Twentieth Century Limited   Ford   *Macbeth*   United Nations   *New York Times*   *Newsweek*

● **4.** Set up three columns headed: Common Nouns, Proper Nouns, and Abstract Nouns; classify each of the following nouns under one of these headings.

ticket
message
goodness
suitcase

whiteness
London
Mr. Truman
devotion

Hamlet
honesty
chalkboard
consistency

● **5.** Write out each of the following sentences and label the function of each noun as subject, indirect object, etc.

1 — The secretary mailed each customer a notice of the coming sale.
2 — The young man, a hard worker, completed his assignment this afternoon.
3 — The committee named Carol Bates their chairman.
4 — The school board praised the principal's report.

5 — The athletes were given awards for their achievements.
6 — The school gave the athletes awards for their achievements.
7 — Awards were given the athletes for their achievements.
8 — Mr. Graham, Mr. Monroe's assistant, prepared the summary.
9 — The analysis was submitted to the bureau chief.
10 — Miss Gordon was named the consultant of the budget committee.

• **6.** Revise the following expressions, substituting the appropriate possessive form for each prepositional phrase. Do not alter the grammatical number of the nouns.

1 — the stamina of the athletes
2 — the colors of the drapes
3 — the sound of the trumpet
4 — the texture of the material
5 — the surface of the tables
6 — the excitement of the youngsters
7 — the actions of the officials
8 — the complaints of the critic
9 — the return of the supervisors
10 — the content of the books
11 — the praise of the dean
12 — the skill of the corporation president
13 — the wisdom of the rabbi
14 — the energy of the team members
15 — the strength of the fabric
16 — the enthusiasm of Edward Kennedy
17 — the persistence of the demonstrators
18 — the alertness of the competitor
19 — the conviction of the speaker
20 — the reluctance of the investors

• **7.** Revise the following expressions, substituting an appropriate prepositional phrase for each possessive case form.

1 — the lawyer's insistence
2 — the coach's encouragement
3 — her mother's expectations
4 — Richard's answer
5 — the vice-president's suggestion
6 — the underwriter's ideas
7 — the collaborators' revision
8 — the committee's proposals
9 — the mayors' plans
10 — the councilmen's motion

SECTION 2

Personal Pronouns

Personal pronouns can be identified by the fact that they have different forms for use as subjects and as objects and that they have special possessive forms for use as substantives. For example: we/us/our/ours.

Conventional definition. A pronoun is a word that can stand for (take the place of) a noun. For example, *he* and *him* can replace *Neal, Jim, Don; his* can replace *Neal's, Jim's, Don's. She* and *her* can replace *Sherry, Gina, Jennifer; her* can replace *Sherry's, Gina's, Jennifer's. It* can replace *organization, car, tree; its* can replace *organization's, car's tree's. They* and *them* can replace *boys, girls, things; their* can replace *boys', girls', things'*.

These examples illustrate third-person personal pronouns. Third-person personal pronouns can replace nouns referring to persons or things we are talking about.

We can also use personal pronouns to refer to ourselves (*I, me, my; we, us, our*). These are called first-person personal pronouns. Finally, we can use personal pronouns to refer to the persons we are addressing (speaking to) (*you, your*). These are called second-person personal pronouns.

Test-frames for identifying and for classifying the forms of personal pronouns. Personal pronouns are easy to identify. There are, altogether, only thirty-two different forms, and many of them are closely related. Personal pronouns can be classified as subjective (or nominative), objective (or accusative), and two separate possessive case forms. Four test-frames are useful in making this classification. Nouns can occupy some of the blanks, but can be distinguished from personal pronouns on the basis of form.

In Section 1 we found that nouns have four forms: *stenographer/ stenographer's/stenographers/stenographers'*. In contrast, personal pronouns have the characteristics shown on page 74.

1 — Subjective case: _____ am/is/are good.

(Appropriate forms: I/we/you/he/she/it/they)

2 — Objective case: The ball struck _____.

(Appropriate forms: me/us/you/him/her/it/them)

3 — Possessive case as determiner: Jan says _____ car is good.

(Appropriate forms: my/our/your/his/her/its/their)

4 — Possessive case as substantive: The car is _____.

(Appropriate forms: mine/ours/yours/his/hers/theirs)

Only personal pronouns have two distinct forms for use as subject or object in a sentence pattern.[1] In addition, only personal pronouns have two distinct possessive forms like *my/mine* and *their/theirs*.

Subclasses of personal pronouns. Personal pronouns can be classified with reference to case, as above—subjective, objective, and possessive. Case is determined by the use of the personal pronoun in a sentence.

Personal pronouns can also be classified with reference to "person": First-person personal pronouns refer to the speaker—*I, me, my, mine; we, us, our, ours.* Second-person personal pronouns refer to the person addressed—*you, your, yours.* Third-person personal pronouns refer to the person or thing being discussed—*he, him, his; she, her, hers; it, its; they, them, their, theirs.*

Finally, third-person personal pronouns include masculine, feminine, and neuter forms. These forms refer to males, females, and inanimate objects. Neuter pronouns, in addition, are used to refer to lower animals, to plants, and sometimes to pets and infants. Feminine pronouns are sometimes used to refer to ships and countries. The table on page 75 gives all the forms of personal pronouns.

The effective use of personal pronouns. Personal pronouns enable us to refer to nouns without repeating the nouns themselves. They also enable us to refer to the reader or listener and to the speaker or writer without using names. As a result, personal pronouns help us tie sentences together neatly, clearly, and economically. (See pages 227-228, 259-260.)

---

[1] The only exceptions are the interrogative function words *who/whom/whose* and *whoever/whomever.* These words are also used as relative pronouns to introduce dependent clauses.

FORMS OF PERSONAL PRONOUNS

Case	Number	
	Singular	*Plural*

First-Person Personal Pronouns

Subjective (or nominative)	I	we
Objective (or accusative)	me	us
Possessive (Form I: determiner [1])	my	our
Possessive (Form II: substantive [2])	mine	ours
Intensive [3] and Reflexive [4]	myself	ourselves

Second-Person Personal Pronouns [5]

Subjective (or nominative)	you	you
Objective (or accusative)	you	you
Possessive (Form I: determiner [1])	your	your
Possessive (Form II: substantive [2])	yours	yours
Intensive [3] and Reflexive [4]	yourself	yourselves

Third-Person Personal Pronouns

	Masculine	*Feminine*	*Neuter*	
Subjective (or nominative)	he	she	it	they
Objective (or accusative)	him	her	it	them
Possessive (Form I: determiner [1])	his	her	its	their
Possessive (Form II: substantive [2])	his	hers	its	theirs
Intensive [3] and Reflexive [4]	himself	herself	itself	themselves

---

[1] The possessive as determiner is a limiting adjective occurring before its head; for example, "*Her* best friend. . . ." (For a discussion of determiners, see page 114.)

[2] The possessive as substantive substitutes for a noun. For example: "Dolores brought her book, and I brought *mine* [= *my book*]."

[3] The intensive is used for purposes of emphasis: "Miss Nelson herself made the arrangements"; "Mr. Langley revised the message himself."

[4] The reflexive is used to indicate that the person or thing designated by the subject of a verb is also designated by the object of the same verb: "The football player criticized himself"; "The student disciplined himself."

[5] It is interesting to observe that the singular forms of the second-person personal pronouns are identical to the plural forms. The old singular forms (*thou, thee, thy/thine*) have died out in Modern English, except when they are used with reference to God in prayer.

A writer must use special care with personal pronouns. He must make certain that there is no possible question about their reference. First- and second-person pronouns, of course, refer to the writer (or speaker) and to the reader (or listener). They involve few problems.

Third-person pronouns, on the other hand, refer to persons or things being talked about. Most discussions refer to many persons and things. Hence, the writer must make certain that the reference of each third-person pronoun is clear. If the reader is not sure what noun a third-person pronoun refers to, effective communication stops. Confusion results. If the antecedent (the noun to which the pronoun refers) is not clear, the sentence may have to be revised so that the noun can be repeated. The following sentences illustrate the confusion resulting from careless use of pronouns:

Unclear pronoun reference

a) Bob turned in the report and grammar assignment and received a high grade on it. (Was the high grade given to the grammar assignment or to the report?)

b) The committee studied the organization plan and the report system at Tugwell Tool and Die Company, and it was satisfactory. (Was the committee, the organization plan, the report system, or the company satisfactory?)

Revised for clear pronoun reference

a) Bob turned in the report and the grammar assignment and received a high grade on the report (or on them or on both).

b) The committee studied the organization plan and the report system at Tugwell Tool and Die Company, and found the organization plan satisfactory.

Pronouns with collective nouns as antecedents will be singular if the writer wishes to emphasize the group as a unit. Such pronouns will be plural if the writer wishes to emphasize the individual members comprising the group. The important point here is that the writer should be consistent. If he uses a singular verb with the collective noun, to be consistent he should use singular pronouns in referring to that noun. If he uses a plural verb with a collective noun, to be consistent he should use plural pronouns in referring to that noun. Here are two examples:

1—The class *are* going on a picnic and will bring *their* lunches.
2—The commission *is* preparing *its* report.

In the first of these sentences, the collective noun *class* is regarded as plural; as a result, both the verb *are going* and the personal pronoun *their* are plural. In the second, the collective noun *commission* is regarded as singular; as a result, both the verb *is preparing* and the personal pronoun *its* are singular.

Consistency is important when pronouns are used with other kinds of nouns, as well as with collective nouns. A pronoun must be consistent in number with its antecedent. If it is not, the reader will be baffled. For example:

Inconsistent pronoun number

The reports will be ready next week, and it will be comprehensive. (Has the writer made a mistake in writing *reports* as a plural and *it* as a singular? Or does *it* refer to something other than *reports*? No one can tell from this sentence.)

Revised for clear pronoun reference

The reports will be ready next week, and they will be comprehensive.

The writer must check to make sure that the reader cannot misunderstand the reference of each pronoun. He must also ensure that the form of each pronoun is consistent with that of its antecedent. When used thoughtfully, pronouns help form compact sentences that are clear and unified.

The constructions in which personal pronouns occur. Personal pronouns, in their appropriate forms, can occur in many of the constructions in which nouns occur. The following examples illustrate the principal functions of personal pronouns. Note that some of the constructions possible for nouns (see pages 64-70) do not ordinarily occur with pronouns.

Subject of a verb:

I (we/you/he/she/it/they) finished the job.

Direct object:

The teacher greeted me (us/you/him/her/it/them).

Indirect object:

The secretary sent me (us/you/him/her/it/them) a message.

Object of a preposition:

Abby took the book from me (us/you/him/her/it/them) to her (me/us/you/him/it/them).

Direct address (second person only—abrupt and urgent):
You! Get out of the way of the truck!

Possessive as determiner (occurring before the noun it modifies):
My (our/your/his/her/its/their) car is parked in the street.

Possessive as substantive (used as a subject, direct object, indirect object, etc.):
Mine (ours/yours/his/hers/theirs) is at home.
The students found mine (ours/yours/his/hers/theirs) where I had left it.
The mechanics repaired Mr. Emerson's car and gave mine a checkup.
The book was mine (ours/yours/his/hers/theirs).

Subjective complement:
It was I (we/you/he/she/it/they) who gave the book report.[2]

Retained direct object (that is, a direct object retained in a passive construction):
Mr. Freeman was assigned them (us) as his special assistants.

Retained indirect object (that is, an indirect object retained in a passive construction):
The story was told me (us/you/him/her/it/them) by a witness.

• *APPLYING EFFECTIVE ENGLISH*

Oral Applications

• **1.** Explain the differences in form between personal pronouns and nouns.

• **2.** Explain what the following terms mean and give examples to illustrate your explanations: (1) first-person personal pronouns, (2) second-person personal pronouns, (3) third-person personal pronouns, plural number.

• **3.** Point out the ways in which the third-person singular personal pronouns entail special considerations not involved in the first- and second-person personal pronouns, nor in the third-person plural personal pronouns.

---

[2] In business writing, this construction does not occur often. When it does occur, and especially if the construction is repeated for emphasis ("It was he who did this; it was he who did that; it was he . . ."), the subjective case is regularly used. In casual conversation, however, educated speakers sometimes use the objective case for the subjective complement: "It was me."

Discuss the meaning of the term *gender*. Be prepared to give examples to illustrate what determines whether masculine, feminine, or neuter pronouns are appropriate.

• **4.** In class discussion identify and analyze each personal pronoun in the following sentences and tell why the particular form is used:

1 — She brought sandwiches for him and his friends.
2 — Between you and me, there is a good chance that we will get next Friday off.
3 — Send them a notice that I expect to arrive in their fine city sometime next week.
4 — Our house is clean, but it needs painting badly.
5 — Martha brought her favorite records, and we brought ours.

• **5.** Give the forms of the personal pronouns (1) that are used in referring to the person we are addressing, (2) that are used when the person speaking refers to himself, and (3) that are used in referring to the person or thing we are speaking about. What designation is given to each of these three classes of personal pronouns?

Written Applications

• **1.** Copy the following sentences and draw an arrow from each personal pronoun to its antecedent (the noun to which it refers). If the pronoun refers to the speaker or the listener, an antecedent will usually not occur; if no antecedent occurs, draw an arrow pointing straight up from the personal pronoun. This arrow indicates reference to a person (the speaker or writer; the listener or reader) rather than to an antecedent.

1 — Barbara and Robin brought their puppets to school and showed them to the class.
2 — I gave Stanley my knife and asked him to return it later.
3 — The orchestra are coming and are bringing their instruments, which they will store in the gymnasium.
4 — Miss Nelson gave her assignment to the class and let them use the rest of the hour to work on it.
5 — Did you tell Mr. Morris that his daughter planned to go straight to her piano lesson and that he should not wait for her?

• **2.** Write a short sentence to illustrate one use of each of the following forms of personal pronouns:

1 — First-person singular, possessive case (the form occurring before a noun).
2 — Second-person singular (and plural), possessive case (the form occurring as a substantive).
3 — First-person plural, objective case.
4 — Third-person plural, subjective case.
5 — Third-person singular, feminine gender, objective case.
6 — First-person singular, objective case.
7 — Second-person plural (and singular), objective case.
8 — Third-person plural, possessive case (the form occurring before a noun).
9 — Third-person singular neuter gender, possessive case (the form occurring before a noun).
10 — First-person plural, subjective case.

• **3.** Write each of the following sentences and label each personal pronoun to indicate its person, number, and case.

1 — We gave Ned his prize.
2 — You should have heard from her.
3 — They complimented him for his good work.
4 — We students considered her our best athlete.
5 — She told them her story yesterday.
6 — The assignment was given them.
7 — Their letter indicated their enthusiasm.
8 — Her work pleased them.
9 — He was praised by their supervisor.
10 — Your committee should revise its procedures.

• **4.** Revise the following sentences to remove the vague reference of pronouns or to correct inconsistencies between the form of a pronoun and its antecedent.

1 — The council holds a special meeting to review their annual report.
2 — Each boy brought their own pen and paper.
3 — Hal Riley and Ward Lane drove his car to the game; but he had trouble starting it.
4 — Take your radio and typewriter with you on vacation, if you wish, but don't forget to bring it back.
5 — The group investigated morale and performance, and it was outstanding.

SECTION 3

Verbs

Identify verbs (excluding auxiliaries) by the fact that they have sets of forms similar to one of these:
I: lift/lifts/lifted/lifted/lifting
II: ride/rides/rode/ridden/riding
III: go/goes/went/gone/going

Definition. A verb is a word indicating action (*run, jump, see*) or state of being (*is, are, seem, appear*). Verbal *nouns* (sometimes called gerunds: *running, seeing, being*) also convey actions and states of being, but they fit into sentences as nouns. To identify and understand *verbs*, therefore, we must consider word order and form.

Test-frame for identifying main verbs. The base form of verbs (but not of auxiliaries, which are function words, see pages 118-130) can fit the blank in the following sentence:

He/it will _____ (it).

This test-frame provides a simple way to determine whether a particular word is a verb. The word *it* (given in parentheses) will occur with transitive verbs (verbs followed by objects) and with linking verbs (verbs followed by subjective complements). The word *it* will not occur with intransitive verbs (verbs which are not followed by objects or subjective complements). For example, the following words fit this frame and, hence, can be classified as verbs: *go, believe, hear, buy, elect, leave, occur, sink, rise, raise, swim.*

Formal characteristics of verbs. In this unit "verb" will regularly refer to a word and not a phrase. We will discuss verb *phrases* when we take up auxiliary function words [1] in the next unit.

---

[1] Auxiliary function words are "signal words" used to help *main verbs* express special grammatical meanings, such as passive voice and present perfect tense. For example, in the following verb phrases, the "helping verbs" (or *auxiliary function words*) are italicized: "The message *was* written by the director"; "The first baseman *has* completed two double plays"; The reports *have been* checked for accuracy." In a verb phrase, the main verb *always* occurs last.

A verb may have a maximum of five different forms. Many verbs have fewer than five distinct forms, because some forms overlap and are used in more than one way. All verb constructions in English are based on these five forms. Three of the five are often used in combination with various auxiliary function words.

In the following lists, we recognize three types of verbs on the basis of the kind of signal each verb uses to show past tense. It is important to remember that almost all full verbs (in contrast to some auxiliaries) can indicate both present and past tense. Present tense expresses customary action: "She walks." Past tense expresses action that occurred before the statement is made: "She walked."

Type 1

Regular verbs add -d or -ed to their unchanged base to form the past tense.[2] Most verbs belong to this class.

TYPE 1: EXAMPLES OF REGULAR VERBS

Base form [3]	Present tense 3d person singular	Past tense	Past participle	Present participle (and gerund)
walk	walks	walked	walked	walking
paint	paints	painted	painted	painting
try	tries [4]	tried [4]	tried [4]	trying
wade	wades	waded	waded	wading
mow	mows	mowed	mowed	mowing
look	looks	looked	looked	looking
lift	lifts	lifted	lifted	lifting
lay	lays	laid [5]	laid [5]	laying
play	plays	played	played	playing
sew	sews	sewed	sewed	sewing
report	reports	reported	reported	reporting
add	adds	added	added	adding

---

[2] If the base has only one syllable and ends in a single consonant preceded by a single vowel, however, the final consonant is doubled before -ed is added; for example, tan/tanned, pet/petted, trim/trimmed, mop/mopped, cup/cupped. If the base has more than one syllable, the preceding rule applies only when the accent falls on the last syllable of the base; for example, refer/referred, confer/conferred.

[3] The base form of a verb is used (1) as the present tense (except for the third person singular, which ends in -(e)s); (2) as the infinitive, which is preceded by to, except when the infinitive occurs with will/would, shall/should, may/might, can/could, and must; (3) as the imperative—the form of the verb used in commands; and (4) as the base to which most suffixes are added.

[4] Verbs ending in y preceded by a consonant, change the y to i before -es or -ed is added.

[5] A few verbs ending in ay change the y to i before adding -d; for example, say/said.

Type 2

Irregular verbs (1) add *-d, -ed,* or *-t* to an altered base to form the past tense, or (2) change their base without adding *-d, -ed,* or *-t* to form the past tense, or (3) occasionally have no signal for past tense.

TYPE 2: EXAMPLES OF IRREGULAR VERBS

Base form	Present tense 3d person singular	Past tense	Past participle	Present participle (and gerund)
1. buy	buys	bought	bought	buying
catch	catches	caught	caught	catching
bring	brings	brought	brought	bringing
sell	sells	sold	sold	selling
teach	teaches	taught	taught	teaching
sweep	sweeps	swept	swept	sweeping
creep	creeps	crept	crept	creeping
sleep	sleeps	slept	slept	sleeping
2. hold	holds	held	held	holding
write	writes	wrote	written	writing
ride	rides	rode	ridden	riding
hide	hides	hid	hidden	hiding
fly	flies [6]	flew	flown	flying
lie (recline)	lies	lay	lain	lying
rise	rises	rose	risen	rising
sit	sits	sat	sat	sitting
get	gets	got	got/gotten	getting
read	reads	read [7]	read [7]	reading
lead	leads	led	led	leading
speed	speeds	sped/speeded [8]	sped/speeded [8]	speeding
3. burst	bursts	burst	burst	bursting
set	sets	set	set	setting
cost	costs	cost	cost	costing
broadcast	broadcasts	broadcast	broadcast	broadcasting
hurt	hurts	hurt	hurt	hurting
cast	casts	cast	cast	casting

---

[6] When the verb ends in *y* preceded by a consonant, the *y* is changed to *i* before *-es* is added. We have already noticed that this same principle applies to the plurals of nouns ending in *y*; for example, baby/babies, lady/ladies.

[7] Note the difference in pronunciation between the present tense and base forms, on the one hand, and the past tense and past participle on the other.

[8] Sometimes a verb has more than one set of acceptable forms, as a result of historical changes. When in doubt, check a dictionary to determine the acceptable principal parts of any verb.

Type 3

Three verbs have unique past-tense forms: (1) *to go*—"Kathy *went* to the conference"; (2) *to do*—"Mr. Miller *did* the work"; (3) "I *was* there but the others *were* not."

TYPE 3: THE THREE VERBS WITH SPECIAL PAST TENSE FORMS

Base form	Present tense 3d person singular	Past tense	Past participle	Present participle (and gerund)
go	goes	went	gone	going
do	does	did	done	doing
be (Present tense: *am/are/is*) [9]	is	was/were [9]	been	being

Key points to note concerning verbs.

1 — The three main types draw attention to the signal used to form the past tense. Note there are three important sub-groups under Type 2.

2 — The present tense third-person singular usually has the suffix *-(e)s*. (The only exception is the very small number of subjunctive forms [10] found in such sentences as, "He asked that Leo leave at once." Here *leave* is third-person singular. After a verb of ordering, commanding, or suggesting, subjunctive forms without the *-(e)s* occur. Almost the only other traces of subjunctive forms in modern English are in such exclamations as "Long live the king!" in which *live* lacks the suffix *-(e)s*. Contrast this construction with "The king lives long," in which the normal *indicative* third-person singular present tense ending *-(e)s* occurs.

3 — For Type 1 verbs and a few Type 2 verbs, the past tense and past participle are always identical in form.

4 — The present participle and gerund are identical in form but differ in use. They always end in the suffix *-ing*. Present participles are used as adjectives and as parts of verb phrases: "The *barking* dog," "The girls are *hiking*," "The teacher is *lecturing*." Gerunds are verbal nouns: "*Hiking* is fun," "Leo enjoys *hiking*," "These shoes are for *hiking*."

---

[9] *To be*, one of the most frequently used verbs in English, is the only verb which (1) has a base form different from its present tense forms, (2) has three different forms for the present tense, and (3) has two different forms for the past tense.

[10] Three categories (or moods) of verbs are recognized: (1) indicative, used in all statements and questions; (2) imperative, used in commands; and (3) subjunctive, used in object clauses after verbs expressing a desire. The verb *to be* uses special subjunctive forms in assumptions which are contrary to fact; for example, "If I *were* you. . . ."

5 — Three verb forms never occur with auxiliary function words: (1) the present tense, (2) the present tense third-person singular, and (3) the past tense. These three forms always occur alone as the verb in a clause, never with a helping verb. They are called *finite verbs* because they are sometimes limited in form by their subject. For example, we say "I see" but "Frank sees." This correspondence or "tie" between the form of the verb and the subject of the verb is characteristic of finite verbs only; it is called subject-verb agreement. For a further discussion of agreement, see pages 85-88.

6 — Four verb forms are called *nonfinite* verb forms because they are never "tied" to a subject: the infinitive, present participle, past participle, and gerund. The gerund never occurs in verb phrases. The other three nonfinite verb forms may occur in verb phrases, as well as outside of verb phrases. Nonfinite verb forms are discussed on pages 88-90.

7 — The term *principal parts of a verb* is often given to three forms: the infinitive, the past tense, and the past participle. These are the principal (or main) parts of a verb because on the basis of these forms, with appropriate inflectional endings and auxiliary verbs, we can form every construction in which the verb may appear. When five principal parts are given, as in the lists of verbs on pages 82-84, only auxiliary verbs ("helping verbs") are needed to form all of the possible verb constructions.

8 — Difficulties with the principal parts of verbs occur primarily with verbs belonging to Type 2. Whenever you are in doubt about the principal parts of a verb, look in a recent dictionary. The use of a wrong principal part (for example, "The girls have *went* [for *gone*]," "He has *wrote* [for *written*]," "Kenneth *swang* [for *swung*] the bat," and "The teacher *ringed* [for *rang*] the bell") suggests that the writer has not been careful. The principal parts of the intransitive verb *lie/lies/lay/lain/lying* (meaning "recline"), which are particularly tricky, should be carefully distinguished from those of the transitive verb *lay/lays/laid/laid/laying* (meaning "put something down"): "Annie is lying down"; "They were laying the linoleum floor."

Agreement of subject and verb.[11] *Finite* verb forms are those that change form to correspond with the number and person of the subject. In the present and present perfect tenses (and, for the verb *to be* only, in the past tense) adjustments of form tie the subject to

---

[11] In a verb phrase, the first auxiliary and only the first auxiliary is finite. In other words, the first auxiliary is the only verb form in the phrase which is "tied" to its subject. All subsequent auxiliaries and the "idea" verb, which always stands last in a verb phrase, are one of the following nonfinite forms: (1) infinitive, (2) present participle, or (3) past participle. Verb phrases will be discussed later; see pages 118-130.

its verb. This limitation in form—called agreement of subject and verb—occurs in the present tense and present perfect tense of all verbs. It occurs in the past tense of only one verb, the verb *to be*.

Agreement in number. In connection with nouns and pronouns, number refers to the distinction between singular (one object) and plural (more than one object). In connection with verbs, number refers to an entirely different concept. A verb is singular if its subject is singular. A verb is plural if its subject is plural. For example, "The boy drives to school"; "The boys drive to school." The difference between *drives* and *drive* is the difference between a singular and plural third-person verb, present tense.

Agreement in person. The term *person,* in connection with verbs, refers to the three possible categories of subjects. A first-person verb has as its subject the person speaking. Hence, the subject of a first-person verb will always be either *I* or *we.* A second-person verb has as its subject the person addressed. Hence, the subject of a second-person verb will always be *you.* A third-person verb has as its subject the person or thing spoken about. Hence, the subject of a third-person verb can be any noun in the language or any third-person pronoun (for example, *he/she/it/they*). Agreement in person, then, involves the correspondence in form which concerns changes in person.

Agreement of subject and verb in person and number is an important factor in writing. The verb *to be* illustrates these distinctions more fully than any other verb in English:

PRESENT TENSE

Person	Singular	Plural
First:	I am	we are
Second:	you are	you are
Third:	he/she/it is	they are

PAST TENSE [12]

First:	I was	we were
Second:	you were	you were
Third:	he/she/it was	they were

---

[12] Because the only verb in Modern English that has more than one form in the past tense is the verb *to be*, agreement of subject and verb in the past tense is possible only for this verb. We have already seen that, in the present tense, all finite verbs are "tied" to their subjects.

Special problems involving subject-verb agreement. The basic principle that a verb agrees in person and number with its subject covers the vast majority of sentences. Occasionally, however, the number of the subject may involve special considerations. Thus, subjects that are compound or collective require special attention.

1 — *Compound subjects govern plural verbs.* For example, "Marcia and Julia are good students and expect to receive high grades." Writers must be particularly alert when a compound subject occurs after the verb, in Pattern 4 sentences: "There were a teacher and a student from our school at the conference."

Note that when a compound subject is joined by *or* or *nor,* the part of the compound subject next to the verb determines the form of the verb. For example, "Either Roy and Paul or their father is going to pick up the groceries"; "Mr. Gregory or his daughters are delivering the programs."

2 — *Compound subjects which govern plural verbs are formed only by the coordinating conjunction* and. Such expressions as *in addition to, together with, along with, as well as,* and *including* do not form compound subjects; hence, "Roby, as well as Barbara, is attending the conference," and "Miss Forbes, in addition to Miss Layton and Mr. Walters, leaves for Seattle tomorrow." Nouns occurring in prepositional phrases do not influence the form of the verb: "A factory with many employees is a busy place." In this sentence, the subject of the verb is *factory*; it governs the singular verb *is. Employees* is the object of the preposition *with*; it does not influence the form of the verb. Note that if we make *factory* a plural noun, the form of the verb must change: "Factories with many employees are busy places."

3 — *A few subjects which are compound in form refer to a unit of some kind and govern singular verbs.* For example, "The secretary and treasurer [if one person holds both titles] is already here"; "The halfback and team captain [when these titles refer to the same person] is now entering the game." Similarly, a few subjects, though plural in form, refer to a unit of some kind and thus govern a singular verb: "Twenty dollars is a good price for that bicycle"; "Five cents is the sales tax on a purchase amounting to one dollar."

4 — *Compound subjects modified by determiners like* each *and* every *govern singular verbs.* "Each boy and girl is expected to visit the post office"; "Every manager and assistant manager was present at the meeting."

5 — *Collective nouns* (see pages 62-63) *govern singular verbs if the writer wishes to emphasize the group as a unit:* "The class is finishing its unit on punctuation." Collective nouns govern plural verbs if the writer wishes to emphasize the individual members of the group: "The class are finishing their papers." Note that pronouns having such collective nouns as antecedents may be singular or plural. The choice should be consistent for both verb and pronoun.

Classes of main verbs. The basic patterns of the English sentence depend upon three different types of verbs: (1) transitive verbs, occurring with objects; (2) linking verbs, occurring with predicate nouns and predicate adjectives; and (3) intransitive verbs, occurring without objects.

The constructions in which nonfinite verb forms appear. The following table summarizes the essential facts about the four types of nonfinite verb forms and their uses. Nonfinite verb forms are also called *verbals.*

Name of the Nonfinite Verb Form	*Characteristics*	*Principal Functions*
I. Infinitive [13]	(1) base form, without suffix (2) preceded by *to,* except when used with these auxiliary function words: *may/might, will/would, shall/ should, can/could, must.*	(1) as part of certain verb phrases: "Kathy will *go.*" "Lynn ought *to try.*" (2) as a subject: "*To study* takes concentration." (3) as an adjective: "The place *to go* is California." (4) as a predicate noun: "To swim is *to exercise.*" (5) as a direct object: "Gay likes *to write.*" (6) as an adverb expressing purpose: "Chester went *to get* the paper."

---
[13] See "Guide to the Sentence X-Ray," page 649.

Name of the Nonfinite Verb Form	Characteristics	Principal Functions
II. Gerund [14]	(1) base form + -ing (Sometimes the final consonant must be doubled before the -ing is added; for example, *swimming, patting, mopping.* Sometimes a silent *e* must be dropped before -ing is added; for example, *flaming, preceding, biting, hoping, fluting.*)	(1) as a subject: "*Hiking* is good exercise." (2) as a direct object: "Susie studies *dancing*." (3) as object of a preposition: "In *driving*, be careful." (4) as a noun adjunct (that is, as a noun used adjectivally): "The *dining* car was ready." [15] "Pam threw coins into the *wishing* well."
III. Present participle	(1) base form + -ing (Sometimes the final consonant must be doubled before the -ing is added; for example, *hopping, sledding, canning, planning.* Sometimes a silent *e* must be dropped before -ing is added: for example, *taming, sliding, planing, curving.* Note that the present participle is identical *in form* to the gerund. They differ in use only.)	(1) as an adjective, in various positions: "The *running* boy fell." "*Running,* the boy fell." "The boy, *running,* fell." "The boy fell, *running.*" (2) as part of certain verb phrases: [16] "Betty is *studying*." "The problem is *being* studied." "Ed will be *returning*." "Our car was *being* repaired."

[14] See "Guide to the Sentence X-Ray," page 649.

[15] Note that *dining* does not describe what the car was doing. If it did, *dining* would be classified as a present participle, like *barking* in the phrase "The barking dog." What *dining* indicates is the type of railroad car under discussion. Compare "The moving van . . ." with stress on the first syllable of *moving,* with "The moving van . . ." with stress on *van. Moving* in the first example is a gerund used as a noun adjunct. In the second it is a present participle used as a descriptive adjective. Note that gerunds do not occur in verb phrases.

[16] This form of verb-phrase is called *progressive aspect.* For a discussion of progressive aspect, see pages 125-126.

Name of the Nonfinite Verb Form	Characteristics	Principal Functions
IV. Past participle	Type I: Regular verbs: base form + -d or -ed. Type II: Irregular verbs: (1) suffix -d, -t, or -ed added to altered base forms; (2) no suffix -d, -t, or -ed; altered base form; occasionally the suffix -n or -en, for example, ridden, written; (3) identical with the base form; for example, set, cost. Type III: Three special forms: been, gone, and done.	(1) as an adjective in various positions: "The *written* request . . . ." "The *painted* fence . . . ." "The reply, *written* yesterday, was not sent." "The fence, *painted* white, looked new." "*Written* out, the plan seemed sensible." "*Painted*, the fence looked new." (2) as part of certain verb phrases: "Dorothy has *written* her message." "The message has *been written*." "Tim will have *painted* the fence." "The fence will have *been painted*."

Tips for recognizing nonfinite verb forms.

1 — The infinitive is the form of the verb that can be used with *to* for example, *to go, to be, to see, to catch, to study, to think.*

2 — The present participle and the gerund always end in the suffix *-ing.* They can be distinguished from each other because the gerund is used as a noun, while the present participle is used either as a descriptive adjective or as part of a verb phrase. For example, "Proofreading [gerund] takes practice"; "The prancing [present participle] horse . . ."; "Greg is swimming [present participle]."

3 — The past participle is the nonfinite verb form that can follow the auxiliary function word *have;* for example, *seen* (thus, *have seen*), *written, talked, ridden, sung, gone, been, believed, hoped, praised.*

This section has dealt with the forms and uses of *individual* verbs. Many of the grammatical meanings associated with verbs in English require the use of auxiliary function words. The patterns of English verb phrases are discussed in Unit 4, pages 118-130, in connection with auxiliaries.

In summary, any word which has a special form to signal past time is a verb. The kinds of changes in form characteristic of verbs are illustrated by the following examples:

Base form	Present tense 3d person singular	Past tense	Past participle	Present participle (and gerund)
Type I. finish	finishes	finished	finished	finishing
raise	raises	raised	raised	raising
Type II. (1) feel	feels	felt	felt	feeling
think	thinks	thought	thought	thinking
(2) ring	rings	rang	rung	ringing
(3) set	sets	set	set	setting
Type III. be (am/are)	is	was/were	been	being
do	does	did	done	doing
go	goes	went	gone	going

The following test-frame, in addition to the preceding characteristics of form, may be used to identify verbs. All main verbs will have one form (specifically, the infinitive) which can fill the blank in the following sentence: "He/it will _____ (it)."

• APPLYING EFFECTIVE ENGLISH

Oral Applications

• 1. Give the five forms—base form, third-person singular present tense, past tense, past participle, and present participle (and gerund)— of those words which can be *verbs* in the following list.

for, each, typewriter, chalkboard, walk, hear, find, under, see, mend, sell, cost, seem, catch, actor, ride, down, urge, top

On the basis of this test, which words in the preceding list cannot be verbs?

• 2. Give the conventional definition of a verb and apply it to the preceding list of words to check the classifications you made in Oral Application 1.

● **3.** The differing signals that various kinds of verbs use to indicate past time show something about how verbs work. On pages 82-84 we saw that verbs can be divided into three large classes (regular verbs, irregular verbs, and verbs with unique past tense forms). Assign each of the following verbs to one of these classes and explain the basis of your assignment:

> swing, print, sweep, trim, go, fight, smile, lay, raise, hurt, lie (recline), lie (prevaricate), lead, train, be, prejudice, rise, sit, set

● **4.** Give the five forms for each of the verbs listed in Oral Application 3.

● **5.** There are only four types of suffixes that occur on verb forms in English: (1) -(e)s, (2) -ing, (3) -(e)d (sometimes t), and (4) -(e)n. Two of these suffixes can occur on all verbs; two of them occur only on certain verbs. Study the forms of verbs classified on pages 82-84 and 88-90. Be prepared to discuss the uses of each of these suffixes and to give three different verbs illustrating each of these suffixes.

● **6.** What are the names and uses of the following italicized nonfinite verb forms?

> The *sealed* letter   Joe was *hurrying*   The *shouting* cheerleader
> To *open,* press here   Finley must *pay*   The *selling* price of
> A. T. and T.

● **7.** In verb phrases, the first auxiliary is always finite. Each other auxiliary, as well as the main verb, must be one of three possible forms: (1) infinitive, (2) past participle, or (3) present participle. Classify the *nonfinite* verbs in the following verb phrases:

> 1 — Marian has been promoted.
> 2 — Kelley will be leaving tomorrow.
> 3 — Mr. Tate had written the recommendation.
> 4 — The message is being prepared by the sales director.
> 5 — Miss Quinn should go to the next meeting.

● **8.** Finite verbs are either (1) verbs occurring alone in a clause or (2) auxiliaries occurring as the first term in a verb phrase. Whenever possible, in business messages a finite verb must agree in person and number with its subject. For each finite verb in Oral Application 7, state its person and number. Take the subject of the verb into consideration in your answer.

Written Applications

• **1.** Present participles can be used (1) in verb phrases ("The boy is *fishing*") and (2) as adjectives ("The *floating* log . . ."). Write three sentences illustrating the use of present participles in verb phrases and three illustrating the use of present participles as adjectives. Underline each present participle in your sentences.

• **2.** Past participles can be used (1) in verb phrases ("The message was *written*") and (2) as adjectives ("The *broiled* lobster . . ."). Write three sentences illustrating the use of past participles in verb phrases and three illustrating the use of past participles as adjectives.

• **3.** Gerunds can be used in most of the ways nouns are used. Write three sentences to illustrate how the gerund *swimming* may be used (1) as a subject, (2) as a direct object, and (3) as the object of a preposition. Do the same thing for the gerunds *writing* and *revising*.

• **4.** When they occur as subjects, as direct objects, as adjectives, and as adverbs expressing purpose, infinitives are preceded by *to*. Write three sentences to illustrate how the infinitive *to dance* may be used (1) as a subject, (2) as a direct object, and (3) as an adverb expressing purpose. Do the same thing for the infinitives *to proofread* and *to study*.

• **5.** Taken together, present participles, past participles, gerunds, and infinitives are called nonfinite verb forms. Nonfinite forms of transitive verbs may be followed by objects. Nonfinite forms of linking verbs may be followed by predicate nouns or adjectives. Copy the following sentences and draw a single line under the direct object of a *nonfinite* verb. Draw two lines under the indirect object of a *nonfinite* verb. Draw three lines under a predicate noun or adjective following a *nonfinite* verb.

    1 — Repairing automobiles was Larry's hobby.
    2 — Audrey studied hard to learn English grammar.
    3 — Roger was praised for giving his brother assistance.
    4 — Mr. Maxwell, by being enthusiastic, made others enthusiastic.
    5 — Finishing his homework early, Ted decided to play a game of golf.

• **6.** Label each nonfinite verb in Written Application 5 as (1) an infinitive, (2) a present participle, (3) a past participle, or (4) a gerund.

SECTION 4

Descriptive Adjectives

Descriptive adjectives modify substantives. They usually have sets of forms corresponding to tall/taller/tallest *or to* adept/more adept/most adept *and often have special adjectival endings, such as -ful, -al, -ive, and -ous.*

Definition. A descriptive adjective is usually defined as a word which modifies a noun or pronoun, naming some quality or characteristic of the substantive which it modifies. This definition does not exclude noun-adjuncts (nouns immediately preceding and modifying other nouns) like *stone* in "The stone wall." Noun-adjuncts,[1] however, can easily be distinguished from adjectives: in different contexts, *stone* can also have the other three forms characteristic of nouns (stones/stone's/stones'). As with other kinds of words, the characteristic forms of adjectives, as well as the positions they normally occupy, are helpful guides in recognizing and understanding adjectives.

Test-frames for identifying descriptive adjectives. Descriptive adjectives (and some noun-adjuncts, which have the set of forms characteristic of nouns) can occupy the blanks in the following sentences: [2]

1—The man's ＿＿＿＿＿＿ idea succeeded.
2—The idea seemed ＿＿＿＿＿＿.

For example, the following words can fit either of these blanks: *colorful, best, expensive, admirable, friendly, boyish, wonderful, chaotic, satisfactory, exciting, mysterious, final.*

Formal characteristics of adjectives. Two characteristics of form can help us recognize and understand adjectives. First, many descriptive adjectives have a series of three distinct forms, as illustrated on page 95.

---

[1] For a discussion of noun-adjuncts, see page 66.
[2] Any noun may be substituted for *idea* in the test-frames.

Positive degree	Comparative degree	Superlative degree
short	shorter	shortest
long	longer	longest
thin	thinner	thinnest
thick	thicker	thickest
fancy	fancier	fanciest
sweet	sweeter	sweetest
calm	calmer	calmest

Many other descriptive adjectives use function words to fill out a similar series.

Positive degree	Comparative degree	Superlative degree
alert	more alert	most alert
industrious	more industrious	most industrious
capable	more capable	most capable
serious	more serious	most serious
observant	more observant	most observant
careful	more careful	most careful
attentive	more attentive	most attentive

Second, many descriptive adjectives end in special, adjective-forming suffixes. In the preceding list of adjectives, for example, the following adjective-forming suffixes occur: *-ous, -able, -ant, -ful,* and *-ive.* Such suffixes indicate that the word in question is an adjective. More examples of adjective-forming suffixes will be given later under a separate heading (see page 97).

Thus, adjective-forming suffixes, as well as comparative and superlative forms, can help us recognize and understand adjectives. Keep in mind, however, that many descriptive adjectives do not have adjective-forming suffixes (for example, *large, small,* and *young*). Keep in mind, also, that many descriptive adjectives do not have comparative and superlative degrees (for example, participial adjectives like *swimming* and *written*).

The comparison of adjectives. The base form—called the *positive degree*—of descriptive adjectives is used to assign various qualities to substantives (nouns and noun substitutes). For example: "The difficult puzzle," "A gay party," "Those energetic students," "Each helpful assignment," "This heavy snowfall." Note that the descriptive adjectives *difficult, gay, energetic,* and *helpful* can fit the blank in the test-frame on page 94.

Persons, objects, and concepts can possess varying degrees of any quality. It is often necessary or useful to make comparisons involving such differences in degree. For this purpose, descriptive adjectives have special grammatical signals: (1) the suffixes *-er* and *-est* and (2) the function words *more* and *most*. Examples are given on page 95 in the lists headed "Positive degree," "Comparative degree," and "Superlative degree."

When *two* items are involved in the comparison, the comparative form of the adjective is used. For most one-syllable and many two-syllable adjectives, the comparative involves the suffix *-er*. Thus, *gayer, heavier, stronger*. For other adjectives the comparative involves the function word *more*. Thus, *more apt, more helpful, more difficult, more congenial*. Three types of formula are commonly employed in sentences comparing two items:

Formula I: Thing one is _____-er than thing two.
Example: Ernie is taller than Kirby.

Formula II: Thing one is _____-er than any other thing.
Example: Ernie is taller than any other boy in the class.

Formula III: Of the two things, thing one is the _____-er.
Example: Of the two boys, Ernie is the taller.

When more than two items are involved in the comparison, the superlative form of the adjective is used. For most one-syllable and many two-syllable adjectives, the superlative involves the suffix *-est*. Thus, *gayest, heaviest, strongest, wealthiest*. For other adjectives the superlative involves the function word *most*. Thus, *most apt, most helpful, most intricate, most congenial, most beautiful*. Two types of formula are commonly employed in sentences comparing more than two items:

Formula I: Thing one is the _____-est thing [in the world, city, room, etc.]
Example: Ernie is the tallest boy on the team.

Formula II: Thing one is the _____-est of all the things [in the world, city].
Example: Ernie is the tallest of all the boys at the camp.

A few adjectives use an entirely different word for their comparative and superlative. See the examples on page 97.

Positive	Comparative	Superlative
well (in good health)	better	best
good	better	best
bad	worse	worst
little	less/lesser	least

Some adjectives, like *round, square,* and *perfect,* theoretically have only positive forms. A thing is either round or not round, perfect or not perfect. However, when these attributes are thought of as approximations to an ideal, the use of comparative and superlative degrees becomes understandable.

Adjective-forming suffixes. A large number of adjectives are formed by the addition of adjective-forming suffixes to other parts of speech. You have already met a number of these in the discussion of adjectives compared by the use of *more* and *most.*

Adjective-forming suffixes enable us to recognize many words as adjectives. In the following examples the symbol "<" means "is derived from."

-ive. conducive (<conduct), elusive (<elude), inventive (<invent)

-ful. wonderful (<wonder), dutiful (<duty), beautiful (<beauty)

-able. considerable (<consider), understandable (<understand)

-ible. digestible (<digest), edible, divisible (<divide), legible

-ly. friendly (<friend), gentlemanly (<gentleman) (This suffix occurs much more frequently on adverbs.)

-al. royal, detrimental (<detriment), continual (<continue), visual, usual (<use), special (<species)

-ous. continuous (<continue), viscous, contiguous, sinuous, vicious.

-ic. hygienic (<hygiene), scientific, specific (<species), geographic (<geography)

-ical. practical (<practice), whimsical (<whimsy), physical, comical, biological (<biology)

-ish. childish (<child), girlish (<girl), womanish (<woman), fiendish (<fiend)

-y. hasty (<haste), speedy (<speed), homey (<home)

Positions in which descriptive adjectives occur. A descriptive adjective can occupy the following positions in English sentence patterns:

(1) *Attributive position* (immediately preceding its head) [3]

The clever advertisement attracted many enthusiastic customers.

(2) *Appositive position* (immediately following its head)

The secretary, eager and competent, reported for work.

(3) *Predicate adjective* (required after a linking verb) [3]

The automobile was expensive and powerful.[4]

(4) *Predicate adjective* (optional after an intransitive verb) [5]

The scouts returned from their hike, sleepy but still eager.

(5) *Introductory position* [5]

Confident and attractive, the young lady represented the company well.

• *APPLYING EFFECTIVE ENGLISH*

Oral Applications

• **1.** Give the definition of an adjective.

• **2.** What are the principal characteristics of form and use which assist in identifying and understanding adjectives?

• **3.** Using both the definition and the test frame for descriptive adjectives, pick out the descriptive adjectives from the following list of words.

> impression, tough, each, accident, wishful, accidental, suddenly, gentle, friendly, competence, geographic, competent, ingenious

• **4.** Many adjectives have special endings (like *-ful* on *wonderful*) which indicate at once that they are adjectives. Give three adjectives that illustrate each of the following adjective-forming suffixes: -ic, -ous, -ful, -al. How are the comparative and superlative degrees of these adjectives formed?

---

[3] See "Guide to the Sentence X-Ray," pages 649-650.

[4] A predicate adjective following a linking verb is often called a *subjective complement,* since an adjective (or noun) is required in this position to *complete* what is being said about the subject.

[5] See "Guide to the Sentence X-Ray," page 650.

• **5.** Descriptive adjectives and determiners (or limiting adjectives) both modify substantives, but they occupy different positions and behave in different ways. For example, most descriptive adjectives have comparative and superlative forms (*taller* and *tallest,* or *more beautiful* and *most beautiful).* Determiners like *that, the, an,* and *each* do not. Determiners occurring in the same construction with descriptive adjectives precede the descriptive adjectives: "Many considerate employers" (not "Considerate many employers"). Thus, descriptive adjectives can fit the blank in the following test-frame, while determiners cannot:

This very ＿＿＿＿＿＿ action will be taken.

Using these tests, distinguish between the descriptive adjectives and determiners (discussed in detail in Unit 4) in the following list:

final, interesting, each, intelligent, few, expensive, kind, sudden, special, an, conclusive, tentative, seven, moderate

Written Applications

• **1.** Write five sentences illustrating the use of the comparative form of different adjectives. Choose three adjectives that use the inflectional signal *-er* and two that use the function word *more.*

• **2.** Write five sentences illustrating the use of the superlative form of the same adjectives you used in Written Application 1.

• **3.** The use or omission of descriptive adjectives before substantives is an important feature of style. Descriptive adjectives enrich a sentence and appeal to the reader's imagination.

On the other hand, too many descriptive adjectives make writing ineffectively ornate. Experimentation, practice, and wide reading are the best ways to develop judgment in the use of descriptive adjectives. Advertisements offer some brilliant examples of clever, attention-getting descriptive adjectives. From advertisements in *Life, Look, Newsweek,* or some other magazine of national distribution, make a list of twenty phrases that utilize vivid descriptive adjectives.

• **4.** For the purpose of experimenting with the stylistic effect of descriptive adjectives, write two versions of a short paragraph explaining why you admire a certain late model automobile. In the first version, make a special effort to use numerous descriptive adjectives to spotlight the features of the car that appeal to you. In the second version, omit *all* descriptive adjectives.

SECTION 5

Adverbs

Adverbs can modify adjectives, adverbs, and verbs, indicating, for example, the time, place, manner, or extent of an action. Many adverbs end in -ly. Others resemble prepositions: in, out, up, across, through, by, under, etc. Many adverbs have comparative and superlative forms.

Conventional definition. An adverb is a word which can modify a verb, an adjective, or another adverb. We shall find, however, that adverbs can also modify other parts of speech. The following questions suggest four of the most common and important kinds of meaning adverbs communicate: "Where?" "When?" "How?" "How much?" [1] For example: "Arnett went *upstairs*." ("Where did Arnett go?"); "Sherrie went *later*." ("*When* did Sherrie go?"); "Peter typed the letter *skillfully*." ("*How* did Peter type the letter?"); "Josephine hesitated *slightly*." ("*How much* did Josephine hesitate?")

Test-frame for identifying adverbs. Adverbs, as verb modifiers, can occupy one or both of the blanks in the following sentences: [2]

1—Dora went _____.
2—Maureen praised the student _____.

---

[1] Note that a small group of words including *very, quite,* and *too* (when it means "to an excessive degree") cannot occupy the blanks in the test-frames for adverbs; like many other adverbs, however, they can modify descriptive adjectives and adverbs (for example, "A very good plan"; "He left quite promptly"). This special subclass of adverbs of degree can be called *intensifiers*.

The words *more* and *most* when used to form the comparative and superlative degrees of adverbs (*more aptly/most aptly*) and of descriptive adjectives (*more conspicuous/most conspicuous*) are classified as function words. In these uses the words *more* and *most* correspond to the suffixes *-er* and *-est*.

Finally, "linking adverbs" (or "conjunctive adverbs") such as *therefore, thus, consequently,* and *however,* though they can occupy the blanks in the test-frame for adverbs, are classified as function words, because they establish relationships between clauses.

[2] Some noun-adverbs can also fit these blanks. Since adverbial nouns, in other contexts, can occur in any of the four forms characteristic of nouns (for example, *home/homes/home's/homes'*), they can easily be distinguished from adverbs.

Note that the adverb *not* requires the auxiliary *do/did*: "Mr. Conte did *not* leave."

For example, the following words fit one or both of these blanks:

Adverbs of place or direction: *in, out, up, down, across, through, under, by, back, here, there, past, upstairs.*

Adverbs of time or frequency: *now, soon, then, immediately, before, afterwards, thereafter, presently, once, late, eventually, always, often, seldom, never,* etc.

Adverbs of manner: *happily, slowly, swiftly, enthusiastically, wearily, hastily, earnestly, contentedly, unhesitatingly, determinedly.* Since most descriptive adjectives can be made into adverbs of manner by the addition of the suffix *-ly,* this class of adverbs is extremely large.[3]

Adverbs of degree: *somewhat, excessively, badly, however* ("However expensive . . ."), *slightly, much, extremely, more* ("Nancy ran more than Hazel."), *most* ("Of all the girls, Denise studied most.").

Other types of adverbs: *probably, not, indeed, perhaps, conceivably, certainly,* etc.

Formal characteristics of adverbs. Many adverbs are formed by the addition of the suffix *-ly* to a descriptive adjective. Note, for example, many of the adverbs cited in the previous lists. Others are studiously (<*studious* + *ly*), willingly (<*willing* + *ly*), resentfully (<*resentful* + *ly*), harmoniously (<*harmonious* + *ly*), tenderly (<*tender* + *ly*), steadily (<*steady* + *ly*).

Many adverbs, on the other hand, do not end in *-ly.* For example, those adverbs which are identical in form to prepositions do not end in *-ly.* Thus, *in, out, up, by, across, through, under, near, past,* etc. On the distinction between adverbs and prepositions, see pages 104-106.

Occasionally adverbs may have two acceptable forms—one with *-ly* and one without. For example, *slow* and *slowly, loud* and *loudly.* The form without *-ly* will be identical to the corresponding adjective. Adjectives, however, occupy different sentence positions. Pairs of adverbs with and without the *-ly* suffix usually are not interchangeable.

---

[3] Remember that an *-ly* suffix does not guarantee that the word is an adverb. For example, *friendly, gentlemanly, maidenly, fatherly,* and *manly* are adjectives formed by the addition of the *-ly* suffix to a noun. Occasionally a word ending in *-ly* can be either an adjective ("Mrs. Jenkins' *kindly* attitude") or an adverb ("Miss DeBord *kindly* invited the entire class"). The *-ly* suffix does, however, signal the difference between a great many descriptive adjectives and the corresponding adverbs. For example: *calm/ calmly, swift/swiftly, intelligent/intelligently.*

"Drive slowly" and "Drive slow" are both correct. In some sentences, however, only the -ly form is possible. For example: "Slowly the train picked up speed." In business writing the -ly forms are preferable.

The comparison of adverbs. Like descriptive adjectives, many adverbs can occur in comparisons involving the comparative or superlative degree. In such comparisons adverbs use either (1) special forms for the comparative degree (the -er suffix) and superlative degree (the -est suffix) or (2) the comparative function word *more* and the superlative function word *most*. Most adverbs of manner (ones answering the question "How?" or "In what manner?") can occur in these constructions.

One-syllable and some two-syllable adverbs add the suffixes -er and -est. Other adverbs, including most of the large number of adverbs ending in -ly, use the function words *more* and *most*.

Patterns of comparison of adverbs using the suffixes -er and -est:	*Patterns of comparison of adverbs using the function words more and most:*
Sam ran fast.	Sam answered courteously.
Sam ran faster.	Sam answered more courteously.
Sam ran faster than his brother.	Sam answered more courteously than his brother.
Sam ran faster than any of the other boys.	Sam answered more courteously than any of the other boys.
Sam ran fastest.	Sam answered most courteously.
Sam ran fastest of all the boys.	Sam answered most courteously of all the boys.
Of all the boys, Sam ran fastest.	Of all the boys, Sam answered most courteously.

The preceding sentences illustrate the formulas involved when the comparative and superlative degrees of adverbs are used. Note that the comparison may be implied by the context ("Ron was quicker"). On the other hand, the contrast may be made explicit ("Ron was quicker than his father").

The constructions in which adverbs occur. As we have seen, an adverb can indicate, among other meanings, the time, place, manner, or extent of an action. We know from our test-frames that virtually all adverbs can modify verbs. Frequently more than one adverb is used to modify the same verb. For example:

Becky *hastily* climbed *up there again.*
Nick went *back there often.*

Note that while we can say "Nick often went back there," we do not say "Nick there went back often" or "Nick back went there often." Thus, adverbs are not always interchangeable in the positions they occupy. In addition, many adverbs, especially adverbs indicating manner or frequency, can occupy various positions in sentences:

1—*Happily* Nora awaited the beginning of the dress rehearsal.
2—Nora *happily* awaited the beginning of the dress rehearsal.
3—Nora awaited, *happily,* the beginning of the dress rehearsal.
4—Nora awaited the beginning of the dress rehearsal *happily.*

We have noted that adverbs are used to modify many parts of speech in addition to verbs. For example, adverbs are often used to modify adjectives: "*Encouragingly* and *unhesitatingly* optimistic, Ben left"; "Confident *then,* Victoria returned"; "*Always* persistent, Ethel resumed"; "The *amazingly* proficient secretary completed the report."

Adverbs are also used to modify other adverbs: "The shoppers departed, *sometimes* impatiently"; "*Still* upstairs, Rose picked up the telephone"; "*However* reluctantly, Irma paid the bill." [4]

Some adverbs can modify nouns: "This phone *here* is out of order"; [5] "Lonnie told that policeman *there*"; "Dewey gave the wrench to the man *below*"; "The entertainment *afterwards* was as good as the dinner."

Finally, adverbs often modify phrases and clauses: "*Finally* out of last place, the Cherry Grove High School baseball team redoubled their efforts"; "Fortunately, Mr. Holyoke found the records."

In summary, when adverbs modify verbs, they can occupy various positions. When adverbs modify adjectives, adverbs, or nouns, however, they stand adjacent to the word they modify. The following examples demonstrate these points:

Adverbs modifying verbs: optional positions offering possibilities for variety of style

Spencer skirted the opposing tacklers *swiftly.*
Spencer skirted, *swiftly,* the opposing tacklers.
Spencer *swiftly* skirted the opposing tacklers.
Swiftly, Spencer skirted the opposing tacklers.

---

[4] Note that *however* in this example is an adverb of degree, not a function word used to link clauses. It is important to keep in mind that the same word may have more than one use.

[5] *Here* and *there* regularly follow the nouns they modify: "This item here," "That man there." Note that such expressions as "this here item" and "that there man" suggest that the speaker is uneducated.

Adverbs modifying nonfinite verbs: optional positions

Finally completing his annual report, the controller . . .
Completing, *finally*, his annual report, the controller . . .
Completing his annual report *finally*, the controller . . .

In *finally* completing his annual report, the controller . . .
In completing, *finally*, his annual report, the controller . . .
In completing his annual report *finally*, the controller . . .

Greatly encouraged by their fans' support, the players . . .
Encouraged *greatly* by their fans' support, the players . . .
Encouraged by their fans' support *greatly*, the players . . .

Adverbs modifying adjectives: adjacent position

The *wonderfully* ingenious pattern . . .
Their defense, *rigorously* attentive, amazed . . .
Jack's *understandably* boyish approach . . .
The company's *astonishingly* economical arrangements . . .
The scissors, *extremely* sharp, were . . .
Ready *then*, the vice president welcomed . . .

Adverbs modifying other adverbs: adjacent position

Always willingly, the youngsters helped Frank do the chores.
Across *first*, Keith looked back . . .
The submarine passed *directly* under.
Soon thereafter, the invoice arrived.
Perhaps unwittingly, Mr. Claxon repeated the word.
Immediately above, James placed his new sign.

Adverbs modifying nouns: adjacent position

The girl *above* tied the rope to a tree.
Maria found a way *through*.
The teacher has noticed an improvement in his attitude *now*.
That lad *there* has been especially cooperative.
Clyde's apology *afterward*—unexpected as it was—pleased his parents.

The distinction between adverbs and prepositions. We have repeatedly noted that the same word can often be used in more than one way. For example, the word *that* is used in four different ways in the following sentence:

> *"That* (determiner) repairman *that* (relative function word) was here last night reported *that* (subordinating conjunction) he had not said *that* (substantive).

Similarly, some words that occur as adverbs can also occur as prepositions. As prepositions, these words are always accompanied by a substantive, their object. The function of the preposition is to "hook" the substantive to some other part of the sentence. (See Unit 4, pages 134-136.)

As adverbs, these words do not serve to "hook" a substantive to some other part of the sentence. Instead, they occur as modifiers in their own right. Adverbs may contribute their meaning directly to the sentence in which they occur. Or they may combine with a verb to form a unit with a special meaning. The distinction between abverbs and prepositions can be seen in the following examples:

Preposition + object	*Adverb*
He walked *on the grass.*	He walked *on.*
Beth hurried *across the street.*	Beth hurried *across.*
The salesmen passed *by the booth.*	The salesmen passed *by.*

Note that the preposition introduces a subunit—a prepositional phrase—composed of itself and its object. The prepositional phrase as a whole serves to modify some other element in the sentence. For further information about prepositional phrases, see pages 134-136.

In the following examples, the adverb forms a special unit with the verb. The meaning of the unit is somewhat different from the meaning the verb and adverb have separately. This tendency for verbs and adverbs to combine and form special units is an important characteristic of Modern English.

Verb and adverb forming a special unit

Rita looked after the child. ("Looked after" = tended)
Miss Crawford tried out the typewriter. ("Tried out" = tested)
The brothers fitted out the boat. ("Fitted out" = equipped)
Look out! ("Look out" = be alert)
The clerks carried out the orders. ("Carried out" = obeyed)

Confusion may result if the same word can be used either as an adverb or as a preposition. For example, the sentence "Ellen rolled up the mat" may have either of two meanings. These two meanings are made distinct in speech by contrasting patterns of stresses and pauses. In the written language, however, the appropriate meaning must be inferred from the context. The example can mean: (1) "Ellen rolled the mat up" (that is, made a roll of it). (2) "Ellen, lying down, rolled over and over from one end of the mat toward the other."

With the first meaning, the sentence can be expressed either "Ellen rolled up the mat" or "Ellen rolled the mat up." The fact that *up* can occupy both positions demonstrates that it is an adverb. Note that the adverb *up* forms a kind of unit with the verb *rolled* when the two stand adjacent.

With the second meaning, *up* must precede *mat*, and these two words form a prepositional phrase.

The following sentences illustrate the same kind of ambiguity:

"The driver of the car turned on the spot." ("turned the car on the spot" or "turned on the spotlight.")

"The neighbors talked over the fence." ("talked across the fence" or "discussed the fence.")

The value of adverbs for exact and vivid phrasing. Only one sentence pattern requires an adverb as an indispensable part. This pattern is one in which an abverb of place occurs with a form of *to be*:

Dave was *there*. Bruce is *outside*. I am *upstairs*. Father is *here*.

With the exception of this one sentence pattern, adverbs, like descriptive adjectives, are optional stylistic features. In this sense, adverbs are not basic elements in sentence patterns. Like descriptive adjectives, adverbs can be used to capture attention and to add significant details. Compare the impression these sentences make:

Mr. Cohen answered.
Mr. Cohen answered *honestly*, *confidently*, and *convincingly*.
Miss Elt typewrites.
Miss Elt typewrites *accurately* and *speedily*.

The first sentence of each pair is so bare that its effect is likely to be negative. The second sentence, on the other hand, conveys the writer's enthusiasm and respect, and appeals to the reader to react in the same way.

Excessive use of modifiers, however, weakens the force of writing. For example, if a long succession of adverbs occurred in the second sentence, the effect would be grotesque: "Mr. Cohen answered honestly, confidently, convincingly, forthrightly, intelligently, moderately, earnestly. . . ." Such a style suggests a broken record. It is monotonous and boring. The writer faces the problem, then, of deciding what modifiers in what arrangement will best convey his message.

• APPLYING EFFECTIVE ENGLISH

Oral Applications

• **1.** Give the conventional definition of an adverb. Explain what characteristics of form can help in recognizing adverbs.

• **2.** Adverbs are used, for example, to indicate place (answering the question "Where?"), time (answering the question "When?"), manner (answering the question "How?"), and degree (answering the question "How much?"). Using both definition and the test-frames, identify the adverbs in the following sentences and classify them as adverbs of place, time, manner, degree, etc.

1 — Then Mr. Bailey came in late.
2 — Eventually Linda turned her paper back in.
3 — Soon the young man turned and walked by again.
4 — Mrs. Thomas notified the members quickly, frankly, and efficiently.
5 — Mr. Hughes worked there briefly and then was unexpectedly promoted.
6 — Steadily diversifying its line of products, the Todd Corporation has expanded its plant tremendously.

• **3.** State what term is modified by each adverb in the sentences of Oral Application 2.

• **4.** Some adverbs are identical to prepositions in appearance, differing from them only in use. Prepositions are accompanied by "objects"—substantives which are connected to the rest of the sentence by means of the preposition. In the following sentences distinguish between the prepositions and those adverbs which are identical to prepositions in form. Explain the basis of your classifications. In addition, identify any other adverbs in the sentences.

1 — Rex decided to walk around the block for some exercise.
2 — Rex decided to walk around for some exercise.
3 — Up went the lineman to repair the connection.
4 — Up the pole went the lineman to repair the connection.
5 — Chatting enthusiastically, the clerks walked by the open door.
6 — Chatting enthusiastically, the clerks walked by.
7 — At that point, Mr. Rosenthal quietly went out.
8 — At that point, Mr. Rosenthal quietly went out the door.
9 — The final report was due in by May 23.
10 — The final report was due in the vice president's office by May 23.

• **5.** The positions of most pattern words in an English sentence are relatively fixed. As verb modifiers, however, adverbs can occupy more than one position. The writer must decide which position for the adverb gives the sentence the rhythm and emphasis he desires. What positions can the adverbs occupy in the following sentences and what change in emphasis results from each change in position.

1 — Finally the company's consultant returned from his vacation.
2 — Mr. Mundy completely revised our production schedule.
3 — The shipment of machine parts, fortunately, did arrive in time.
4 — The senior class postponed their trip reluctantly.
5 — New typewriter ribbons were promptly installed.

Written Applications

• **1.** Compose five sentences illustrating the various positions that adverbs can occupy as verb modifiers.

• **2.** Make a list of ten adverbs ending in -*ly* and ten adverbs not ending in -*ly*. (A few adjectives end in -*ly*. To be sure that you understand that the -*ly* suffix does not guarantee that a word is an adverb, add a list of at least four adjectives which end in -*ly*.)

• **3.** Like adjectives, carefully chosen adverbs can add liveliness to sentences. The paragraph below is written without adverbs. Write the paragraph, suggesting at least two possible adverbs to fill each blank. Do not suggest the same adverb more than once in the paragraph.

_____ confident that sales could be _____ increased, Mr. Kerr _____ reviewed the previous year's sales policies. He _____ concluded that an increased volume of sales could _____ be achieved if products were more _____ advertised and more _____ available. _____ writing up his conclusions, Mr. Kerr argued _____ that a small additional expenditure for daily newspaper advertisements and some local radio and television advertisements would _____ result in _____ increased sales. Furthermore, he _____ asserted that _____ selected dealers located _____ near new housing developments would _____ reach an _____ important group of potential buyers. The president _____ read the report and decided _____ to try Mr. Kerr's plan _____.

● **4.** Write five sentences involving adverbs which resemble prepositions. Then write five sentences using the corresponding preposition. Remember that the prepositions will be used with nouns as objects; the adverbs will not.

● *REVIEW*

● **1.** Label the structure of each noun in the following sentences. For example, label the appropriate terms *subject, direct object, adverbial noun.*

1 — The manager sent each employee his bonus check.
2 — The interviewers were representatives of the government.
3 — Yesterday the customer received the company's answer.
4 — The class made Harlan their delegate.
5 — The typists were remarkably efficient and accurate.
6 — The committee made its report extremely interesting.
7 — The secretary told her superior the whole story.
8 — It had been a mistake to include all those details.
9 — There were three possible approaches to the problem.
10 — The editor made the cover colorful.

● **2.** Classify each verb in the sentences of Review Item 1 as (a) transitive; (b) transitive, sending-type; (c) transitive, altering-type; (d) intransitive; or (e) linking.

● **3.** Classify each sentence in Review Item 1 as a Pattern 1, 2, 3, or 4 sentence.

● **4.** Write the four forms of each of the following nouns:

child, committee, lady, building, manager, salesman, secretary, valley, man, school, country, mouse

● **5.** Write the five forms for each of the following verbs; classify the verbs as (1) regular, (2) irregular, or (3) verbs with unique past tense forms. Refer to the dictionary if in doubt about any form.

look, see, patch, fly, speak, find, lead, lie (recline), lay (place), shoot, teach, lie (prevaricate), swing, rise, raise

● **6.** Give the various forms for each of the following personal pronouns and classify each form as to person, number, case, and (where appropriate) gender.

I, he, they, you, we, it, she

• **7.** Use each of the following forms in a sentence and be prepared to explain the difference in use between the forms at left and those at the right.

mine		yours			my		your
	ours					our	
theirs		hers			their		her

• **8.** Write the comparative and superlative forms for each of the following adjectives which can have such forms. Circle all adjective-forming suffixes and give the word on which the adjective is based. Use two comparative and two superlative forms in sentences.

> friendly, accidental, beautiful, long, quick, applicable, easy, foolish, smart, digestible, good, biological

• **9.** Some adverbs can be compared, while some cannot. Some use the suffix *-ly*, while others do not. Adverbs indicate place, time, manner, and extent, answering the questions "Where?" "When?" "How?" and "How much?" For each of the following adverbs, give the comparative and superlative forms wherever possible. If the adverb ends in *-ly*, give the adjective upon which it is based. Classify each adverb as an adverb of place, time, manner, or degree.

> slowly, accidentally, there, fast, easily, continuously, too, well, extremely, then, fortunately, basically

• **10.** The following paragraph contains numerous errors involving faulty knowledge of the forms and uses of pattern words. Rewrite the paragraph, correcting all errors. Be prepared to explain your corrections.

> The employment manager at this companies business offices were having trouble finding qualified office workers. There was a surplus of unskilled applicants' and a shortage of competent typists and stenographers. Consequently, a special committee who were to find and hire the necessary personnel was appointed. They were to begin work just as soon as the committee could find them, for a backlog of assignments had piled up at many of the offices. The committee thought its' first step should be to prepare a careful worded newspaper advertisements. Next they decide to interview interest students in there final semester of high school. This committee succeeded in finding the additional skilled office personnel in less than three weeks.

 **UNIT 4**

MASTERING THE FORMS AND USES OF THE PARTS OF SPEECH: FUNCTION WORDS

Function words are an important part of the grammatical system of English. While thousands of pattern words occur in business messages, there are probably fewer than two hundred function words. These function words recur time and again in almost every English sentence. For example, consider the number of the's, a's, and an's in any paragraph.

Sometimes function words express grammatical meanings that can also be expressed by other grammatical signals. For example, "Al gave a corsage to Jan" is equivalent to saying "Al gave Jan a corsage." In the first sentence the function word to signals the recipient; in the second, word order signals this meaning.

Many of the grammatical meanings signalled by function words cannot be signalled in any other way. Thus, in verb phrases in English many grammatical meanings require auxiliaries. For example: (1) the future and perfect tenses, (2) passive voice, and (3) progressive aspect.

In this unit you will become acquainted with the most important types of function words. In addition you will learn the most important grammatical meanings they signal.

UNIT 4

Section 1

Determiners: Determiners (or "limiting adjectives") identify or limit the substantives they precede. For example: "A/the/that/this/each/every/one student."

Section 2

Auxiliaries: In conjunction with particular forms of main verbs, auxiliaries signal such special grammatical meanings as passive voice ("The note was written.") and future tense ("He will go.").

Section 3

Prepositions: Prepositions serve as "hooks" to connect substantives to various other sentence elements, thus making the substantives modifiers. For example: "The executive walked to/in/into/from/by/beyond/across his office."

Section 4

Connectors: (1) Coordinating conjunctions link elements of equal rank. (2) Movable clause connectors link main clauses. (3) Subordinating conjunctions and (4) relative pronouns link dependent clauses to main clauses.

Section 5

Sentence Varieties: Sentences can be classified (1) as simple, compound, complex, or compound-complex and (2) as statements, questions, or commands.

 ## Introduction

Unit 3 dealt with pattern words, the first of the two main categories of parts of speech. Pattern words included nouns, personal pronouns, verbs (except auxiliaries), descriptive adjectives, and adverbs. The second main category of parts of speech consists of function words of all kinds. Function words are an important feature of the grammatical system of English. There are only about 150 different function words in common use.[1]

Function words sometimes communicate grammatical meanings which can also be indicated by other kinds of grammatical signals. For example, we can say either "The boy's duties" or "The duties of the boy." In the second expression the preposition *of* indicates the same grammatical meaning as does "*-'s*" in the first expression. Another example will help make this point clear. To signal past tense meaning, we add the suffix *-ed* to the verb *paint*—"He painted." To signal future tense meaning, we cannot use a suffix. Instead we use the function word *will*—"He will paint." For this reason the function word *will* is called a "future auxiliary."

In Unit 4 we shall consider four principal types of function words:

(1) determiners (used with substantives),
(2) auxiliaries (used with verbs),
(3) prepositions (used to make modifiers of substantives),
(4) connectors (used to link words, phrases, dependent clauses, main clauses, and sentences).

In addition, we'll take into account the two main ways of classifying English sentences. We'll examine the characteristics which distinguish simple, compound, complex, and compound-complex sentences. Then we'll consider the characteristics which distinguish statements, questions, and commands.

---

[1] In studying the language contained in about fifty hours of recorded telephone conversations, Professor C. C. Fries found only 154 different function words. Some of these words, however, were repeated so frequently that function words comprised about one third of all the words in the conversations.

SECTION 1

Determiners

Determiners (or "limiting adjectives") identity or limit the substantives they precede. For example: A / the / that/this/each/every/one *student.*

Function words that identify or limit a following noun or noun substitute are called *determiners.* Determiners fit one or both of the following test-frames:

1—_____ good, helpful idea. . . .
2—_____ good, helpful ideas. . . .

For example, the determiners, *a, an, one, every, each, this,* and *that* fit only Test-frame 1. The determiners *these, those, many, all, both, some, two, few,* and other determiners fit only Test-frame 2. Many determiners can be used with either the singular or the plural test-frame; for example, *my, our, your, his, her, its, their, John's, Jane's, Jones's, any, some,* and *the.* Sometimes pairs of determiners occur together; for example, *such a, many a* (singular); *both the, both these, all the, all those, all his,* and *all their* (plural).

Determiners regularly precede descriptive adjectives when both modify a noun. Take, for example, the following phrase:

All ambitious, young, and imaginative businessmen

The descriptive adjectives *ambitious, young,* and *imaginative* can occur in any order between the determiner *all* and the noun *businessmen.* The determiner *all,* however, occupies a fixed position. It cannot be shifted about as the descriptive adjectives can. Notice also that the descriptive adjectives can be compared: *ambitious/more ambitious/most ambitious; young/younger/youngest; imaginative/more imaginative/most imaginative.* In contrast, most determiners cannot be compared.

In the singular, some nouns require a determiner, while others do not. For instance, we must use a determiner in the sentence "The boy left." Without the determiner, the sentence is unnatural ("Boy left"): It violates a basic pattern that native English speakers invariably, and unconsciously, follow. Singular nouns that require a determiner refer to one of many objects belonging to the same class. Therefore, they may be called *countable nouns.* Some nouns, however, do not require a determiner; for example, *butter, sugar, hay, coal, mud, dirt, gravel, pepper, salt.* Note that these nouns name materials that interest us as a mass or aggregate, rather than as individuals belonging to a class. Such nouns may be called *mass nouns.* Thus we say, "Butter is nutritious," "Coal is a fuel," "Gravel is used in concrete." If, however, we are referring to a particular, identifiable quantity of butter, coal, or gravel, we say *"The* butter is in the refrigerator," *"The* coal has been delivered," *"The* gravel was expensive."

Determiners are not required with plural nouns. In this respect, plural nouns are like mass nouns. Thus we say "Girls love pretty clothes" when we are making a general statement. But we say "The girls are coming to the dance" when we have specific girls in mind.

Note that determiners can be recognized by the fixed position they occupy. The whole class of determiners can be broken down into various subclasses. Thus, the possessive forms of nouns (*boy's, boys', man's, men's, Foster's, Sue's,* for example) would make up one subclass. The possessive forms of personal pronouns (*my, our, your, his, her, its, their*) would be another. A third subclass would be made up of determiners like *some* and *those.* Such words can be used both as nouns, and as determiners: "Some left early" and "Some students left early"; "Those are new" and "Those typewriters are new." Other subclasses could also be set up. Such function words are classified together as determiners because they all occupy the same relative positions when they serve as noun modifiers. In addition, they have characteristics different from those of descriptive adjectives and noun adjuncts, which also serve as noun modifiers.

• *APPLYING EFFECTIVE ENGLISH*

Oral Applications

• 1. Explain the difference between determiners (limiting adjectives) and descriptive adjectives. Cite examples.

• 2. Most singular common nouns occur only with a determiner. However, a few can occur without one. Explain the difference in meaning between singular nouns that require determiners and those that do not. Cite examples to illustrate your explanation.

● **3.** Discuss the use or omission of determiners before plural nouns. Cite examples.

● **4.** Function words are used to establish special relationships—to communicate special grammatical meanings. Try substituting different determiners in the illustrative sentence below. In this way, explore the possible variations in meaning that depend upon determiners. Use the following determiners, making the nouns and verbs singular or plural as appropriate: *the, a, each, all, both, many, some, most, few, that, these, his, Gordon's.*

_____ youngsters enjoy _____ rides.

Written Applications

● **1.** List five determiners for each blank in the following sentences. Whenever it is possible to do so, make one of the five determiners the possessive case of a proper noun and one the possessive case of a personal pronoun.

1 — _____ typewriter needs _____ repairs.
2 — _____ clerk in _____ office received _____ award.
3 — _____ students completed _____ unusual assignment.
4 — _____ form should be submitted to _____ officials next week.
5 — In _____ store, the shoppers found _____ excellent bargains

● **2.** Determiners signal the occurrence of noun-headed phrases. Copy the following paragraph and draw rectangles around all noun-headed phrases that are introduced by determiners, as has been done in these directions. Note that these expressions introduced by determiners operate as subunits within sentences.

> The expression *mastering English* is ambiguous. There are at least three different meanings which this expression can have. (1) It can be used to mean the ability a child acquires, through imitation and practice, to manage the basic structures and the working vocabulary of his native language. For example, by the time he enters kindergarten he utilizes such structures as subjects, objects, indirect objects, predicate nouns, modifiers, and various kinds of verbs. A child has no awareness of these structures, of course, and could not identify them or explain the principles which enable him to communicate by means of the spoken language. (2) *Mastering English* can be used, also, to mean the knowledge of English grammar which a person acquires as a

student. Gradually he becomes aware that words can be classified into parts of speech and that each part of speech has special peculiarities of form and function. Later he becomes aware that word order, word form, function words, and oral or written punctuation establish various relationships among individual words and that these relationships communicate grammatical meanings. For example, any native speaker knows at once what the relationship is between *manager* and *president* in the following sentence:

> The president praised the manager.

The first noun in this sentence is the subject—the speaker; the second noun is the direct object—the "receiver" of the action. A knowledge of English grammar—of the signalling system of the English language—then, is a second important meaning of the term *mastering English*. (3) *Mastering English* is used, finally, to mean a highly sophisticated control over the language, a full awareness of the strategies of communication.

• **3.** Using the paragraph you copied in Written Application 2, circle all nouns that are *not* marked by determiners but that *are* marked by various characteristic noun forms, such as plural suffixes.

• **4.** Certain determiners can stand without an accompanying noun. Occurring in this way, they are regarded as substantives—noun substitutes.

    A. Rephrase the following sentences so as to convert the determiners into substantives. For example: "That answer is correct" would be converted to "That is correct."

        1 — Each inspector is well qualified.
        2 -- Many reports include statistics.
        3 — Few games will be played at night.
        4 — Those commas are unnecessary.
        5 — Two tires were badly worn.

    B. Rephrase the following sentences so as to convert the substantives into determiners. For example: "All will be increased" could be converted to "All salaries will be increased."

        1 — These do not fit.
        2 — All have given assistance.
        3 — Many participated.
        4 — Each is inspected periodically.
        5 — Six were late.

 **SECTION 2**

Auxiliaries

Used with particular forms of main verbs, auxiliaries signal such special grammatical meanings as passive voice ("The note was written.") and future tense ("He will go.").

Auxiliaries are function words that contribute grammatical meaning in verb phrases. In studying verb phrases, we must keep three general principles clearly in mind:

(1) In a verb phrase all verbs except the last one are auxiliaries. The last verb is the "idea" verb or main verb. As pointed out in Unit 3, it is the main verb that controls the structure of the sentence. The main verb determines what other constructions may occur in the sentence: (a) direct objects, indirect objects, or objective complements, or (b) subjective complements, or (c) a clause which is complete without objects or complements. We call the three types of verbs that control these structures (a) transitive verbs, (b) linking verbs, and (c) intransitive verbs.

(2) Each auxiliary verb has a distinct function. For example, some auxiliaries indicate that a verb is in the future tense: "Edward *will* learn." Other auxiliaries, occurring with the past participle of the main verb, signal that a verb phrase is passive voice: "The sales letter *was* typed by the secretary." Still other auxiliaries, occurring with a present participle, signal that a verb phrase is progressive aspect: "They *are* planning a conference."

(3) The first and only the first auxiliary in any verb phrase is finite. The main verb *in a verb phrase* and any auxiliaries *except the first* are always nonfinite verb forms. As nonfinite verb forms occurring in a verb phrase, they will be infinitives, present participles, or past participles. If the main verb occurs alone, without auxiliaries, it will be finite. (For an explanation of finite and nonfinite verb forms, see pages 85-91.)

The fact that only the first auxiliary in a verb phrase is finite means that in present tense, third-person singular, the first auxiliary will end in the suffix *-(e)s*. The only exceptions are the ten single-form auxiliaries: *will/would, may/might, can/could, shall/should, must,* and *ought*; or a form of *to be*. This fact also means that in present perfect tense, *has* will be the auxiliary used for third-person singular. *Have* will be used elsewhere. Finally, it means that in the past tense, *was* will be the auxiliary used for first- and third-person singular. *Were* will be used elsewhere. These changes in form illustrate the principle of agreement between a finite auxiliary and its subject. (On subject-verb agreement, see pages 85-88.)

Thus, a verb phrase involves an elaborate system of auxiliaries used to indicate many kinds of grammatical meanings. Any verb phrase illustrates the fundamental importance of function words. We shall now consider the main grammatical meanings signalled by auxiliaries. These meanings involve tense, voice, and aspect.

AUXILIARIES RELATED TO TENSE

The discussion of verbs in Section 3 of Unit 3 (pages 81-91) noted that present tense and past tense are generally signalled by word form, without the use of auxiliaries. Even in present and past tenses, however, auxiliaries are used for special purposes; for example, to give emphasis ("He *does* study," "He *did* apply"), to provide for a negative verb phrase ("He does not study," "He did not apply"), and to indicate a question ("Does he study?" "Did he apply?").[1]

For all tenses other than present and past, English requires the use of special tense auxiliaries. Thus, *shall* and *will* are auxiliaries which establish future tense. *Has* and *have* are auxiliaries which establish present perfect tense. *Had* is an auxiliary which establishes past perfect tense. *Shall have* and *will have* are combinations of auxiliaries that establish future perfect tense.

Note that each auxiliary occurs in a fixed sequence and form. The form of the main verb and each auxiliary helps complete the formula. The complete verb phrase conveys the intended grammatical meaning.

Future tense. To convey the idea of future action, English often uses the auxiliary *will* and, in rather formal usage, *shall*.[2] *Will* and, in

---

[1] The auxiliary *to do* will be examined on page 129.

[2] *Shall* is regularly used in only two situations in present-day spoken English: (1) When another person is being asked to participate in making a decision—"Shall we go out to dinner tonight?" and (2) when a regulation is being stated in formal language—"Each member shall pay his dues on the first Monday of each month." In writing, especially in writing with a somewhat formal tone, *shall* is used with first person subjects (*I* and *we*). Do not make the mistake of carelessly substituting *shall* for *will*.

speech, its contracted form *'ll* are probably the most common ways of forming future tense. In a verb phrase, the verb form following *will* (and following any of the other nine one-form auxiliaries—*would, shall/should, can/could, may/might, must,* and *ought*) is invariably an infinitive. Note that in such verb phrases *to* (the so-called "sign of the infinitive") does not occur, except after *ought*. For example:

I shall go (rather formal)   we shall go (rather formal)
I will go (informal)   we will go (informal)
you will go   you will go
he will go   they will go

It is also true that the present tense form of the verb can often be used with appropriate adverbial expressions to indicate future time:

Martin leaves for Dallas tomorrow.
Eleanor enters college next September.

Use of the future auxiliary *will* would emphasize the future significance of these statements:

Martin will leave for Dallas tomorrow.
Eleanor will enter college next September.

In addition, we all use many other formulas to express future tense:

I am to fly to Portland.
I am going to fly to Portland.
I am about to fly to Portland.

The perfect tenses. The simple tenses (present, past, and future) ignore the question of whether an action has been completed. In contrast, the perfect tenses focus attention on this question. The term *perfect,* in grammar, means *completed.* For example, present perfect tense indicates completion of an action (or some phase of an action) at the time the statement is made:

Jerome has cut down three trees.	At the time the statement is made, this action has been completed.
I have studied United States history for two years.	Two years of such study have been completed. Perhaps the speaker is continuing his studies. The sentence is indefinite about this possibility.

He has come into the room.	At the time the statement is made, the action has been completed.
They have left.	At the time the statement is made, the action has been completed.

In addition to present perfect tense, English has auxiliaries to signal other perfect tenses. Past perfect tense designates an action completed at some specified time before the statement is made. Future perfect tense designates an action expected to be completed before some specified future time. For example:

Present perfect: *We have written the report.* (Action completed by the time the statement is made.)

Past perfect: *We had written the report before the request came.* (One action completed before some other action.)

Future perfect: *We will (formal, shall) have written the report before they arrive.* (One action to be completed before some other action occurs.)

The formula-like characteristics of the English verb are apparent from the fact that each perfect tense uses a special auxiliary:

Present perfect: *has* (third person, singular) /*have*
HAS/HAVE + PAST PARTICIPLE OF MAIN VERB [3]
He *has* written/they *have* written ■ He *has* seen/they *have* seen

Past perfect: *had*
HAD + PAST PARTICIPLE OF MAIN VERB [3]
He *had* written/they *had* written ■ He *had* seen/they *had* seen

Future perfect: *will have (shall have)*
WILL + HAVE + PAST PARTICIPLE OF MAIN VERB [3]
He *will have* written/they *will have* written
He *will have* seen/they *will have* seen

Thus, some form of the auxiliary verb *to have* is the signal for the perfect tenses. The present tense forms *has* and *have* are used as auxiliaries in present perfect tense. The past tense form *had* is used as an auxiliary in past perfect tense. The infinitive *have* is used after the future auxiliary *will* (or *shall*) in future perfect tense. In the perfect tenses the main verb, always the last term in a verb phrase, is regularly a past participle.

---

[3] Note that the past participle of any verb can be used in these formulas without changing the *grammatical* meaning of the verb phrase.

In summary, here is the conjugation of an English verb in all the forms thus far considered:

PRESENT TENSE

I write	we write
you write	you write
he writes (Note the inflectional ending *-s*.) [4]	they write

PAST TENSE

I wrote	we wrote
you wrote	you wrote
he wrote	they wrote

FUTURE TENSE

I will write (formal: I shall write)	we will write (formal: we shall write)
you will write	you will write
he will write	they will write

PRESENT PERFECT TENSE

I have written	we have written
you have written	you have written
he has written (Note *has* replacing *have*.) [4]	they have written

PAST PERFECT TENSE

I had written	we had written
you had written	you had written
he had written	they had written

FUTURE PERFECT TENSE

I will have written (formal: I shall have written)	we will have written (formal: we shall have written)
you will have written	you will have written
he will have written	they will have written

---

[4] Inflectional *-s* (in present tense) and the auxiliary *has* (in present perfect tense) are the only signals involving formal agreement of subject and verb in English, except for the various forms of the verb *to be*.

AUXILIARIES RELATED TO PASSIVE VOICE [5]

The distinction between active and passive voice. *Voice* is a technical term. In grammar, *voice* refers to the relation between a verb and its subject. If the subject performs the action expressed by the verb, the verb is said to be in the active voice. For example:

The boy hit the ball.
The executive read the summary.
The man received his check.

Here the verbs indicate the actions of *hitting, reading,* and *receiving.* In each sentence the subject (*boy, executive, man*) is performing the indicated action.

If the subject "receives" the action expressed by the verb, the verb is said to be in the passive voice. In other words, if the subject is acted upon rather than acting, the voice of the verb is passive. Here are examples:

The ball was hit by the boy.
The summary was read by the executive.
The check was received by the man.

Here the subjects (*ball, summary, check*) are being acted upon; they are "receiving" the actions of *hitting, reading, receiving.* The persons performing these actions are indicated by the prepositional phrases *by the boy, by the executive, by the man.* If these prepositional phrases are omitted, the performer of the action remains unmentioned:

The ball was hit.
The summary was read.
The check was received.

This impersonal construction sometimes has advantages. Such an advantage is obvious if the writer wishes to omit reference to the performer of the action. Except in special situations of this kind, however, active constructions are preferable. They are more direct and more forceful. Usually they are more effective.

The "formula" for passive voice. [6] We have already seen that future tense and the perfect tenses use special function words in

---

[5] See "Guide to the Sentence X-Ray," pages 639-640.
[6] For example, see the chart on page 126.

special patterns. Passive voice uses the following formula: Some form of the verb *to be* (*am, are, is, was, were, been, being,* depending upon person, number, tense, and aspect) + the past participle of the main verb.[7] For example:

Kirk was sent: *was* (form of *to be*) + sent (past participle of *send*)
The package has been delivered: *been* (form of *to be*) + delivered (past participle of *deliver*)
The boat will be built: *be* (form of *to be*) + built (past participle of *build*)
Songs are sung: *are* (form of *to be*) + *sung* (past participle of *sing*)
The records are filed: *are* (form of *to be*) + filed (past participle of *file*)

The last example reveals a double meaning that sometimes occurs in this construction. *Filed* is a past participle. As a past participle it may function as a part of the verb phrase to form passive voice. It may also function as a predicate adjective (subjective complement) modifying *records*. If an agent (performer of the action) is expressed or implied in such a construction, the passive voice of the verb is involved. For example:

The records are filed by Jenny each day.

This passive-voice construction is roughly equivalent to the following active-voice construction:

Jenny files the records each day.

If, however, the past participle *filed* merely describes the situation, the past participle is serving as a predicate adjective:

The records are filed and safe.

This construction is similar to the following one:

The records are complete.

Active voice occurs whenever the formula for passive voice is missing. The contrasting signals of active and passive voice show what relationship is intended between the verb and its subject. Keeping in mind the formula for passive voice, you will find it easy to determine the voice of a verb.

---

[7] In very informal speech, some form of the verb *to get* is sometimes substituted for the corresponding form of the verb *to be* in the formula for passive voice. Thus: "Cheyenne got shot last night." This substitute does not occur in business writing.

Two basic grammatical signals of English are exemplified by passive voice. The first involves function words—the forms of *to be* used as passive auxiliaries. The second involves word form—the past participle of the main verb, which is necessary to complete the passive construction.

AUXILIARIES RELATED TO PROGRESSIVE ASPECT

Progressive aspect: action in progress. Progressive aspect emphasizes that a certain action *is* (*was, will be, has been, had been,* or *will have been*) in progress. In other words, the construction indicates that the action expressed by the verb phrase is going on over a span of time.

Progressive aspect is signalled by some form of the verb *to be* plus a present participle (that is, an *-ing* verb form) as part of the verb phrase. See page 126 for examples.

When a writer wants to establish certain time relationships between two actions, he may use the progressive aspect for one or both verbs. Note the somewhat different time relationships between the clauses in each of the following examples:

1—When the message came, Orville wrote a reply. (Both verbs in simple aspect.)

2—When the message cáme, Orville was writing a reply. (Second verb in progressive aspect.)

3—When the message was coming, Orville was writing a reply. (Both verbs in progressive aspect.)

Sentence 1 reports a sequence of actions. The verbs in both the dependent and the independent clauses occur in simple aspect. The use of simple aspect indicates that the actions occurred consecutively, one after the other. Sentence 2 states that the action of the main clause was in progress at the time the action of the dependent clause occurred. Sentence 3 states that the action of the main clause and of the dependent clause were in progress simultaneously.

There is another related use of progressive aspect. This use draws attention to the fact that the activity in question is in progress at the time indicated by the tense. For example: What is Joe doing right now? The answer to this question would also use progressive aspect: He is studying English grammar.

ACTIVE VOICE

	Simple Aspect (No emphasis that action is in progress. No *-ing* verb form.)	*Progressive Aspect* (Emphasis that action is in progress. Form of *to be* [progressive auxiliary] + *-ing* form of main verb.)
Present tense	Si washes cars.	Si is washing cars.
Past tense	Si washed cars.	Si was washing cars.
Future tense	Si will wash cars.	Si will be washing cars.
Present perfect tense	Si has washed cars.	Si has been washing cars.
Past perfect tense	Si had washed cars.	Si had been washing cars.
Future perfect tense	Si will have washed cars.	Si will have been washing cars.

PASSIVE VOICE

	Simple Aspect (No emphasis that action is in progress. No *-ing* verb form.)	*Progressive Aspect* (Emphasis that action is in progress. Form of *to be* [progressive auxiliary] + *being* [passive auxiliary] + past participle of main verb.)
Present tense	Cars are washed by Si.	Cars are being washed by Si.
Past tense	Cars were washed by Si.	Cars were being washed by Si.
Future tense	Cars will be washed by Si.	
Present perfect tense	Cars have been washed by Si.	
Past perfect tense	Cars had been washed by Si.	
Future perfect tense	Cars will have been washed by Si.	

> THE FUTURE TENSE AND THE PERFECT TENSES OF VERB PHRASES IN PASSIVE VOICE, PROGRESSIVE ASPECT, SELDOM OCCUR.

OTHER KINDS OF AUXILIARY VERBS

Ten single-form auxiliaries. Ten important auxiliaries in English—*may/might, can/could, shall/should, will/would, must, ought*—

form a special class. They are treated as a group because they share the following characteristics:

1 — They have no principal parts.
2 — They take no inflectional endings.
3 — They regularly precede the infinitive form (with or without the function word *to*) of the next verb in the verb phrase.
4 — They never occur as main verbs.

The single-form auxiliaries refer to ability, possibility, permission, obligation, and intention. Each idea looks toward the future for realization and thus involves some degree of future meaning.

The list below and on page 128 summarizes the most frequent meanings of each of the single-form auxiliaries and provides examples to illustrate each of these meanings.

	Frequent Meanings	*Examples*
1—May	(1) possibility	Lee may pass the test.
	(2) permission	Nan may attend the dance.
2—Might	(1) less definite possibility than *may*	Jill might win this race.
	(2) possibility, in connection with clauses stating contrary-to-fact assumptions (for example, "If I were you/ Were I you")	If I were you, I might go.
3—Can	(1) ability	Lou can pass the test.
	(2) colloquially, permission	You can leave now.[8]
4—Could	(1) ability, though with some reservation	Maurice could fix it.
	(2) ability, in connection with clauses indicating contrary-to-fact assumptions	If Beth were here, she could help us.
	(3) ability, in indirect discourse	Lou said that she could do it. Compare: Lou said, "I can do it."

---

[8] Since there is a widespread prejudice against the use of *can* to indicate permission, it is unwise to use the word in this meaning in business writing. Use *may* instead.

	Frequent Meanings	*Examples*
5—Should	(1) obligation	Ben should pay for the ticket.
	(2) intention, with first person subjects, after clauses stating contrary-to-fact assumptions	If I were you, I should reply courteously.
6—Would	(1) intention or expectation, in connection with clauses stating contrary-to-fact assumptions	If I were you, I would reply courteously. If Harry were here, he would solve the problem.
	(2) intention, in indirect discourse	Sam said that he would go. Compare: Sam said, "I'll go/I shall go/I will go."
7—Must	strong obligation	Gustav must attend.
8—Ought	somewhat less binding obligation than *must*	Gustav ought to attend.
9—Will	*Will* and *shall* are used as future auxiliaries (see pages 119-120). In addition, *shall* is used in documents and regulations to indicate a formal requirement. For example, "Every student shall participate in at least two team sports."	
10—Shall		

Two additional auxiliaries indicating obligation. We have already seen that the verb *to have,* in its various forms, is the auxiliary used for the perfect tenses. There it is followed by a past participle. The verb *to have* is also used as an auxiliary, in a different pattern, to indicate obligation. In this pattern the auxiliary is followed by an infinitive. For example:

Lloyd has to pay the bill.
We have to finish our assignments.
Mr. Burke will have to return the equipment.
You have to admit that they were right.
I had to leave early.
Miss Lewis will have to reply at once.
The equipment has to be returned for repairs.
Mr. Garcia and Mr. Adams have to analyze the problem.
She has to proofread that report.
You have to answer that letter.
They have to obtain two estimates.

Thus, this formula involves an appropriate form of *to have* plus the infinitive form of the following verb. In the spoken language, *got* is sometimes added to this formula for further emphasis:

Dirk has got to pay for the record.
Margie and I have got to finish our assignments.
They have got to return the equipment.
Gretchen has got to be more accurate.

When *got* occurs, the *has* and *have* auxiliaries frequently occur as contractions, especially if the subject is a personal pronoun:

He's got to revise his last paragraph.
We've got to find volunteers for that project.
They've got to reconsider that assignment.
You've got to proofread more carefully.

An auxiliary for use with *not*. The auxiliary *do, does/did* is used whenever *not* modifies a verb in the present or past tense.[9] Thus, we say "Grace didn't finish," "The boys don't want to go," "The principal doesn't believe the rumor." Note that these negative constructions would not be possible without the *do, does/did* auxiliary. Without this auxiliary the previous examples would read: "Grace finished not," "The boys want not to go," "The principal believes not the rumor." Such sentences are not acceptable in Modern English. Their impossibility makes clear the importance of *do, does/did* as a negative auxiliary.

Verb phrases as formulas. In summary, keep in mind that the last verb in any phrase is the main verb, the *key* verb. It is the key verb for two reasons. First, the final verb in a verb phrase determines the constructions that can occur in the rest of the clause. Second, while the preceding verb forms in the phrase are auxiliaries, the last verb in the phrase states the *idea* the writer had in mind. For example:

An announcement has been sent.

Has makes the verb phrase present perfect tense. Occurring with the past participle of the main verb, *been* makes the verb phrase passive. *Sent*, on the other hand, reveals what idea the writer had in

---

[9] The only exception is the verb *to be*. For example, "He isn't here," "I am not ready," "They weren't at the meeting." The verb *to have* occurs both with and without the negative auxiliary *do, does/did*: "Joseph hasn't any excuse" or "Joseph does not have an excuse"; "They haven't any explanation" or "They do not have an explanation."

mind. The writer did not mean *refused, sold, offered,* or *promised,* but *sent.* Any of these verbs, as well as thousands of others, can fit the same formula. The auxiliaries, however, must remain the same if the grammatical meaning of the construction is to be the same. When other main verbs occur in this formula, they must be past participles of transitive verbs. Thus:

> An announcement has been sent.
> . . . has been refused.
> . . . has been sold.
> . . . has been offered.
> . . . has been promised.

Here is another demonstration of the way word form and function words work together to convey meaning in English.

• *APPLYING EFFECTIVE ENGLISH*

Oral Applications

• **1.** The various verb phrases in English are formulas. They communicate such grammatical meanings as voice, tense, and aspect. Each auxiliary communicates some part of the grammatical meaning of the whole phrase. The sequence and form of each auxiliary, as well as of the main verb, are fixed. In class discussion identify each verb phrase in the following sentences. Give its (1) person, (2) number (person and number will be determined by the subject of the verb), (3) tense, (4) voice, and (5) aspect.

> 1 — The new calculator was delivered by the firm's sales manager.
> 2 — We were sending them a replacement.
> 3 — The fluorescent light has been installed.
> 4 — The notice is being written by Mr. Fox.
> 5 — Miss Warner will have finished dinner by the time the plane lands.
> 6 — You had mailed the statement before the error was found.
> 7 — A corsage will be given Connie by Steve.
> 8 — Mr. Hamilton and Gary had been assigned new responsibilities.
> 9 — Steve will give Connie a corsage.
> 10 — You will be promoted next year.

• **2.** In class discussion, identify the main verb in each verb phrase in the sentences at the top of page 131. Indicate whether it is finite or nonfinite. The nonfinite forms are the infinitive, past participle, or present participle. They can occupy any position in an English verb phrase except the first. Finite verbs occur as the *first* auxiliary in a verb phrase *or* as individual verbs without auxiliaries.

    1 — The analysis was submitted by Miss Tarr.
    2 — Dr. Fenn had signed the application.
    3 — The fixture has been cleaned by the janitor.
    4 — Harold will be driving with us.

• **3.** In class discussion, identify each passive auxiliary in the verb phrases in Oral Application 1 and indicate its form. (For a list of the possible forms of the individual verbs comprising verb phrases, see Oral Application 2.)

• **4.** In class discussion, identify each progressive auxiliary in the verb phrases in Oral Application 1 and indicate its form. (For a list of the possible forms of the individual verbs comprising verb phrases, see Oral Application 2.)

• **5.** In class discussion, identify each tense auxiliary in the verb phrases in Oral Application 1 and indicate its form. (For a list of the possible forms of the individual verbs comprising verb phrases, see Oral Application 2.)

• **6.** Give the ten single-form auxilaries that make up a special group in English. What are the principal characteristics of this group of auxiliaries? What justification is there for grouping them together in a special class?

• **7.** Give the formula for past perfect tense. Compose ten verb phrases to illustrate this formula.

• **8.** Give the formula for passive voice. Compose ten verb phrases to illustrate this formula.

• **9.** Give the formula for progressive aspect. Compose ten verb phrases to illustrate this formula.

• **10.** Review Section 3 of Unit 3, which deals with individual verbs and their forms. Explain the difference between a finite and nonfinite verb, citing examples to clarify your explanation. What position does a finite verb occupy in a verb phrase? What position does the main (or *idea*) verb occupy in a verb phrase? Give examples.

Written Applications

• 1. Give the verbs or verb phrases which communicate the grammatical meanings specified below. For example, the answer to Number 1 is "We have been selling."

Main Verb	Person	Number	Tense	Voice	Aspect
1 — sell	1	plural	present perfect	active	progressive
2 — lie (recline)	3	singular	past	active	simple
3 — lie (prevaricate)	3	plural	past perfect	active	simple
4 — lay	3	singular	past	passive	progressive
5 — sing	2	singular	future	active	progressive
6 — write	3	singular	present perfect	passive	simple
7 — go	1	plural	present	active	progressive
8 — swing	3	singular	past	passive	simple
9 — rise	2	plural	past perfect	active	simple
10 — raise	3	plural	present perfect	passive	simple
11 — paint	3	plural	present	passive	progressive

• 2. The main verb in a verb phrase determines whether objects and subjective complements may or may not occur in a sentence. The effect is the same as if that verb occurred alone, as a finite verb. For example, in the following examples *Randy* is the indirect object and *invitation* is the direct object. The sending-type transitive verb *give* and word order determine these relationships. Whether the sending-type transitive verb occurs alone or as part of a verb phrase makes no difference:

    1 — Sam gives Randy an invitation.
    2 — Sam gave Randy an invitation.
    3 — Sam will give Randy an invitation.
    4 — Sam has given Randy an invitation.
    5 — Sam will be giving Randy an invitation.

Make up five sentences with verb forms corresponding to those in the five examples above. Use *offer* as your verb, *explanation* as direct object, *supervisor* as indirect object, and *Jess* as subject. Use whatever auxiliaries and other function words are needed.

• 3. Copy the verb phrases given at the top of page 133, and fill in the blanks. Some of the blanks can be filled only by the appropriate form of one or two verbs. Others can be filled by the appropriate form of hundreds of different verbs. Wherever possible, supply five different verbs in their appropriate form to fill each blank. Some adverbs can fill these blanks; however, do not give adverbs in this exercise.

1 — The mimeographed statements have _____ completed.

2 — The plane _____ landing as I reached the airport yesterday.

3 — Each change will _____ approved by the board.

4 — The alternatives are _____ considered.

5 — All members will have _____ the plan by tomorrow.

6 — The store will _____ the sewing machine.

7 — While Esther was sealing the envelopes, I _____ addressing them.

8 — The monthly statements should _____ mailed by May 5.

9 — Mr. and Mrs. Worth will _____ left before we reach Augusta.

10 — Miss Payne has already _____ the report.

• 4. Write a brief explanation of the principle that determines whether the blanks in Written Application 3 can be filled only by one or two verbs or by a great many different verbs. Cite examples from Written Application 3 to illustrate your points.

• 5. Write out the general formulas for the following verb constructions:

1 — past perfect tense
2 — passive voice
3 — progressive aspect
4 — future tense
5 — present perfect tense

• 6. Review the classification of verbs on pages 81-85; this classification was set up on the basis of the inflectional signal for past tense meaning. The groups were as follows: Type I. Past tense signalled by the addition of -ed or -d to the unchanged base of the verb; Type II. Past tense signalled by a change in the base form of the verb, with or without the addition of an -ed, -d, or -t suffix; Type III. Past tense signalled by the substitution of a different base or by an irregular form in the past tense. (Remember that only three verbs belong in Type III.) Classify each of the main verbs given in Written Application 1 under one of these three categories.

• 7. Copy the following sentences. Draw a circle around each finite verb and a square around each main verb.

1 — The clerk has been cooperating fully.
2 — Lester is being asked to join.
3 — Miss Conner speaks to our club tomorrow.
4 — Fran was collecting the suggestions.

SECTION 3

Prepositions

Prepositions are "hooks" that connect substantives to other sentence elements, thus making the substantives modifiers. For example: The executive walked to/in/into/from/by/beyond/across *his office.*

The function of prepositions. *Prepositions* serve as "hooks" for making modifiers of substantives (nouns and noun substitutes). A preposition is always accompanied by its object,[1] a substantive which it "hooks" to some other part of a sentence. The object of a preposition usually follows the preposition. The preposition is frequently used to indicate a relationship involving position and time. For example, *in the bottle, in the afternoon; between the houses, between the games; on the shelf, on the next day; by the store, by morning.* Prepositions "hook" their objects to such other sentence elements as the following:

(1) to other substantives: "The liquid *in the bottle,*" "The space *between the houses,*" "The cat *under the stairs,*" "The box *on the shelf,*" "The mailbox *by the store.*" (Note that a prepositional phrase used as an adjective regularly follows its head.)

(2) to verbs: "They ran *into the yard,*" "He stood *on the platform,*" "She answered *in anger,*" "They called *to the owner,*" "*From the train* the scouts waved goodbye." (Note that a prepositional phrase used as a modifier of a verb can sometimes occupy positions both preceding and following the verb.)

(3) to adjectives: "Enthusiastic *about their chances,* the team left for the game"; "The delivery man, weary *at the end of the day,* set down his last bundle." (Note that a prepositional phrase used as a modifier of an adjective regularly follows the adjective.)

---

[1] Many words can function both as prepositions (with objects) and as adverbs (without objects). For example, in "Lester went out the door," *out* is classified as a preposition because it is used as a function word to link the noun *door* to the rest of the sentence. In "Lester went out," *out* is classified as an adverb because it occurs, not as a "hook" to relate a substantive to other parts of the sentence, but solely to complete the meaning of the sentence. As a preposition, *out* is a function word. As an adverb, *out* is a pattern word. For a fuller discussion of this distinction, see pages 104-106.

(4) to adverbs: "Here *in the city,* everything seems exciting"; "Then *at noon,* the telephone rang." (Note that a prepositional phrase used as a modifier of an adverb regularly follows the adverb.)

Prepositions have come to indicate many relationships other than those involving time and place. For example: "He was *in the room*"/ "He was *in luck*"; "The squad was *under the tree*"/"The squad was *under attack*"; "They walked *on the sidewalk*"/"They acted *on his advice.*" These derived (or metaphorical) meanings for prepositions are extremely frequent.[2]

Prepositional phrases themselves are sometimes modified by adverbs. For example: "Immediately *after the show,* the tent was taken down"; "The runner paced himself entirely *according to his coach's advice.*"

Most prepositions are short, simple words. Some English prepositions, however, were originally phrases; for example, *into, onto, across, beside, between.* Some English prepositions are even today made up of more than one word. They are called *phrasal prepositions*; for example, *in spite of, because of, on account of, instead of, by means of, in front of, in case of, in lieu of.*

The positioning of prepositions. While a preposition usually precedes its object, it does not always do so: "What did you ask about?" "Which tools were the boys sent for?" "Who (more formally, *whom*) did they talk about?" Such questions occur primarily in speech, rather than in writing. Note that these questions can be rephrased so that the prepositions precede their object: "About what did you ask?" "For which tools were the boys sent?" "About whom (immediately after the preposition, only the objective form *whom* occurs) did they talk?" The sentences in which the preposition precedes its object are not necessarily more correct; however, they are more formal.

The word *preposition* comes from the Latin word *praepositio,* meaning "something placed before." As a result, some grammarians used to insist that a sentence should never end with a preposition. The name, however, is merely a convenient label derived from the pattern in which the preposition usually occurs. Such a name cannot reasonably be used for settling points of grammar. An editor once revised one of Sir Winston Churchill's sentences because it ended in

---

[2] The great thirteen-volume historical dictionary of the English language, *The Oxford English Dictionary,* lists, for example, some thirty-nine meanings of the preposition *in.*

a preposition. The great British statesman and writer made fun of the editor by commenting: "This is a sort of impertinence up with which I will not put." His point is unmistakable. Such a sentence is much more natural when it *does* end with a preposition: "This is a sort of impertinence which I will not put up with." Effective writers let naturalness, clarity, and emphasis determine the placement of all words, including prepositions.

Prepositions used to introduce clauses. Occasionally prepositions "'hook" whole clauses to some other part of a sentence. For example: "The question of who has paid his dues can easily be answered." Here *who has paid his dues* is brought ("hooked") into the sentence by means of the preposition *of*. The entire clause (called a *noun clause* because it is used as a noun) is the object of the preposition *of*. Note that *who*, as the subject of the verb *has paid*, is in the subjective case. It is the entire clause, not *who* alone, that is used as a direct object. Another example is provided by the following sentence: "They gave a bonus to whoever had finished his assignment." [3]

• *APPLYING EFFECTIVE ENGLISH*

Oral Applications

• **1.** Identify the prepositions and adverbs in the following sentences and explain the distinction between them.

1 — Mr. Raleigh went out later to the store.
2 — When the mail was given to her, Miss Porter immediately took it to the manager.
3 — The young man applying for the job went into the outer office.
4 — Later that day the steps up were being recarpeted by workmen.
5 — The shipment from Cleveland did not go out until the afternoon.
6 — The meeting of the executives was put off because of Mr. Sawyer's absence.
7 — The report of each division on last year's expenses is due in Miss Carlyle's office soon.

• **2.** Confusion sometimes results if a word may be interpreted either as an adverb or as a preposition. For example, "Higgins looked over the sink" may have two different meanings: (1) He examined the sink. (2) He looked across the sink. When the sentence has

---

[3] See "Guide to the Sentence X-Ray," pages 654-655.

the first meaning, the following rephrasing is possible: "Higgins looked the sink over." The possibility of this rearrangement indicates that *over* is an adverb. With the second meaning, the position of *over* before *sink* is fixed. This fact indicates that in this construction *over* is a preposition. (Sometimes, however, the position of the abverb *is* fixed. For example, in the sentence "The babysitter looked after [that is, tended] the children," the position of the adverb *after* is fixed.)

Discuss the possible confusion in the following sentences. Indicate for each meaning whether the word in question is a preposition or an adverb. Explain the special meaning of each verb-adverb combination. For example, "looked over" means "examined." The verb-adverb combination tends to be pronounced as a unit. Similarly, the preposition-object combination tends to be pronounced as a unit. Use these differences in pronunciation as clues in detecting double meanings in the following sentences.

1 — Mr. Reagan looked over the newspaper.
2 — Miss Hardy looked up the building.
3 — The wind blew over the park benches.
4 — The adults talked over the noisy television program.
5 — The dormitory attendant turned in the messy room.
6 — Horace called off the boat.
7 — The nurse looked after the patient.
8 — Miss Weaverly turned up the steps of the ancient temple.
9 — The carpenter turned out the door very promptly.
10 — The janitor looked into the dirty window.

• 3. The objective case is used when personal pronouns occur as objects of prepositions. On the other hand, if an entire clause is used as the object of a preposition, the function of the personal pronoun *within the clause* determines its form. Indicate the correct forms for the personal pronouns in the following sentences. Explain why the forms you choose are appropriate.

1 — Between you and I/me, the phrasing of that message should be revised.
2 — The question of who/whom prepared the report has not been considered.
3 — Please send a copy of your speech to we/us students.
4 — The president will give an award to whoever/whomever can solve this problem.
5 — Because of Marty and I/me, the plan will be reconsidered.

• **4.** Prepositional phrases can be used to modify almost any term in a sentence. Discuss the function of each of the following prepositional phrases. Note the position of each prepositional phrase and discuss whether it can occupy a different position in its sentence.

1 — The youngster was afraid of the dark.
2 — The bill for books was sent last month.
3 — Mr. Plimpton went to the bank.
4 — Jim's urgent request, delayed for hours, finally reached us.
5 — Planning his campaign in a careful way, Mr. Maloney consulted many experts.
6 — Clara was encouraged by the response to Tuesday's advertisement.

Written Applications

• **1.** Copy the following sentence seven times, each time providing a prepositional phrase to modify a different underlined word. Do not use more than one prepositional phrase in any sentence in this exercise.

The representative who attended the meeting and spoke there will send our agents copies.

• **2.** Like determiners, prepositions set up subunits in sentences and indicate to a listener or reader that this group of words is bound together by a common function. Copy the following paragraph and, to get a clearer understanding of how prepositions signal the occurrence of subunits within sentences, enclose all of the prepositional phrases in the following sentences in boxes, as has been done in these instructions:

Prepositions in the English language perform a function of great importance. They serve the purpose of establishing relationships between their objects, on the one hand, and various other elements in the sentence, on the other. Many relationships, of course, are established by word order, and others by word form. But a great many meanings and relationships are communicated primarily by means of these grammatical "hooks," which are given the name of *prepositions*. The number of prepositional phrases which you have put into boxes in this one paragraph should give you some idea of the frequency of occurrence and of the importance of this type of construction in English grammar.

Unit 4 • Mastering the Forms and Uses of the Parts of Speech: Function Words.

138

SECTION 4

Connectors

(1) Coordinating conjunctions link elements of equal rank. (2) Linking adverbs join main clauses. (3) Subordinating conjunctions and (4) relative pronouns link dependent clauses to main clauses.

Four main types of function words serve as connectors: [1]

(1) Coordinating conjunctions connect two or more elements of equal rank. Thus they form pairs or series of items with the same grammatical structure.
(2) Movable clause connectors (or "linking adverbs") connect sentences or independent clauses in a compound sentence.[2]
(3) Subordinating conjunctions connect dependent clauses to different parts of a sentence. Dependent clauses introduced by subordinating conjunctions may serve various functions. For example, they may serve as modifiers, as subjects, as appositives, as direct objects, and as predicate nouns.
(4) Relative pronouns connect adjective clauses to substantives and introduce noun clauses.

Such connectors can indicate exactly the relationship between the elements being joined.

COORDINATING CONJUNCTIONS[3]

The following function words are coordinating conjunctions: *and, but, or, nor,* and *for.* Sometimes *either* is paired with *or, neither* with *nor,* and *both* with *and.* These combinations of conjunctions are called "correlative conjunctions."

---

[1] Prepositions, too, are connectors. They have the special function of making substantives modify other sentence elements. For that reason prepositions have been discussed separately, in Section 3.

[2] For a discussion of sentence varieties, including compound sentences, see pages 146-148.

[3] See "Guide to the Sentence X-Ray," pages 651-652.

Examples of words joined by coordinating conjunctions:

Larry *and* Bruce are leaving. (compound subject)

The boys *or* May is responsible.　　　　(Note that the number of
May *or* the boys are responsible.　　　　the subject term coming
Neither Ron nor the students have left.　after *or* or *nor* determines
Either Edmund or the referees are wrong.　the form of the verb.)

Examples of phrases joined by coordinating conjunctions:

The car went down the street *and* around the corner.
The secretary had drafted the report *but* had not typed it.
To prepare good advertising copy *or* to draft an effective letter,
　one must use imagination.
The lawyer *either* had not seen the evidence or had forgotten about it.

Examples of coordinate (equal ranking) clauses joined by coordinating conjunctions:

The director dictated the reply, *and* his secretary typed it at once.
The equipment had been wrapped carefully, *but* it was damaged by
　careless handling.
The clerk took two hours on that job, *for* he didn't finish it until noon.
Either the inquiry never reached Mr. Finch, or he failed to answer it.
The evening paper carried no account of Mr. Branden's departure,
　nor did the news summary on television mention it. (Note that
　after *nor*, the finite verb precedes its subject.)

Linking adverbs (or movable clause connectors). The following are common linking adverbs: *therefore, consequently, thus, hence, accordingly, nevertheless, nonetheless, however, yet, furthermore.* Linking adverbs may occupy two main positions. First, they may stand at the beginning of an independent clause. In this position they are generally preceded by a semicolon or by a period. Second, they may stand within a sentence or clause. Within a sentence they are often set off by commas.

Examples of compound sentences in which the second clause is introduced by a linking adverb. Note that the clause connector could be moved to a position within its clause:

The book makes the main ideas clear; *however,* it does not provide
　enough details.
The monthly report will be late; *nevertheless,* these changes must be
　made.

Two additional clerks will be required; *therefore,* advertise for them in the morning newspapers.

The meeting began on time; *furthermore,* all members of the committee were present.

The policy was changed last year; *however,* no one was happy about the change.

Examples of linking adverbs which occur within sentences or clauses. Note in these sentences that the linking adverb could be moved to the first position in its clause:

Buddy left early. He was, *therefore,* unable to participate in the discussion.

Mr. Burhan's secretary is out to lunch. If she returns in time, *however,* I shall notify you.

The vice president was pleased with that color of paint. It was used, *accordingly,* in his office and in his conference room.

Our sales have improved considerably this quarter. The advertising campaign we began in March will be extended, *consequently,* into the next quarter.

That notice concerning the great importance of neatness in correspondence will be revised; the main idea, *however,* will not be altered.

Each study submitted by our firm is proofread many times; we have, *therefore,* an enviable record for accuracy.

SUBORDINATING CONJUNCTIONS

Subordinating conjunctions signal that dependent clauses follow. Subordinating conjunctions introduce dependent clauses which are used in a variety of ways. For example, such clauses serve (1) as adverbial modifiers, (2) as adjectival modifiers, (3) as subjects, (4) as direct objects, (5) as appositives, and (6) as predicate nouns. Here are examples of various dependent clauses serving various functions. Each clause is introduced by a subordinating conjunction.

Adverb clauses introduced by subordinating conjunctions [4]

When the mail arrived, it was taken directly to the comptroller.

The policy of granting a two-week vacation after one year of service has improved morale *because it provides an incentive for new employees.*

---

[4] See "Guide to the Sentence X-Ray," page 653.

If the new equipment is installed by Friday, the training program will begin next week.

While the secretary was away on vacation, few estimates were sent from Mr. Sutton's office.

The annual financial statement cannot be prepared *until all departments have submitted their reports.*

Adjective clauses introduced by subordinating conjunctions [5]

The plant *where this suggestion originated* is located in Albany.

The salesman came at a time *when everyone in the office was busy.*

The reason [*why*] [6] *Miss McGowan returned* was to type the statement.

At the moment [*when*] *Troy entered*, Mr. Herndon was beginning to speak.

The stadium *where the big game had been held* was now empty.

Noun clauses used as subjects, introduced by subordinating conjunctions [5]

That the plan would succeed was a foregone conclusion.

Whether the president can convince the board is anyone's guess.

That construction expenses will rise next year seems obvious.

When Ernest will come can be inferred from his reply.

Noun clauses used as appositives,[7] introduced by subordinating conjunctions [5]

The idea *that profit-sharing will encourage employees to work harder* appealed to the president.

The objection *that better packaging would be more expensive* had been anticipated by the committee.

The statement that *effective English had increased the efficiency of our office* came from the board chairman.

Noun clauses used as direct objects, introduced by subordinating conjunctions

The designer said [*that*] *color would improve the interior.*

Why the public responded so enthusiastically, no one really knows.

---

[5] See "Guide to the Sentence X-Ray," page 653.

[6] Note that in some situations the writer may omit the subordinating conjunction because position and context show the appropriate relationship. Brackets have been used to draw attention to this possibility.

[7] The distinction between appositive clauses and adjective clauses is sometimes tricky, since both kinds of clauses can be introduced by *that*. An adjective clause, however, can be recognized from the fact that *which* (a relative pronoun) can be substituted for *that* in an adjective clause. Such a substitution is not possible in an appositive clause.

Noun clauses used as predicate nouns, introduced by subordinating conjunctions

Our agent's comment was *that the new clients were pleased with our service.*
The best suggestion is *that we should increase our sales staff.*

RELATIVE PRONOUNS

Relative pronouns introduce both adjective and noun clauses. The relative pronouns *that, which,* and *what* (= *that which*), have only one form. The relative pronoun *who* (used when a definite antecedent occurs) and the relative pronoun *whoever* (used when no definite antecedent occurs) have distinct case forms. In this respect they resemble personal pronouns:

	Relative pronoun (definite)	*Relative pronoun (indefinite)*
Nominative (subjective) case	who	whoever
Objective (accusative) case	whom	whomever
Possessive case	whose	. . . . . .

In spoken English the objective forms occur infrequently. In conversation, *who* and *whoever* are widely used for the objective as well as the nominative case. In business writing, however, the distinction between *who* and *whom* is generally retained. As the subject of a clause, *who* (or *whoever*) is used. As a direct object or as the object of a preposition, *whom* (or *whomever*) is used.

Examples of adjective clauses [8] introduced by relative pronouns [9]

1—The car *that Eugene bought* had been driven only 14,500 miles.
2—The president's secretary unfortunately mailed a reply *which she had failed to proofread.*
3—The man *who paid for the tickets* is my uncle.

---

[8] Dependent adjective clauses are divided into two classes: (1) Restrictive adjective clauses cannot be expressed in a separate sentence without falsifying the meaning of the original sentence: "Anyone *who steals* is dishonest." Restrictive clauses, as necessary parts of the sentence, are not set off by commas. (2) Nonrestrictive adjective clauses are merely descriptive and can be expressed in a separate sentence. They are set off by commas: "Evanston, *which is a suburb of Chicago,* is the site of Northwestern University." The information in the nonrestrictive clause could equally well be expressed in a separate sentence: "Evanston is the site of Northwestern University. Evanston is a suburb of Chicago." For further discussion of the distinction between restrictive and nonrestrictive clauses, see pages 164-166.

[9] See "Guide to the Sentence X-Ray," pages 654-655.

4—The office manager, *whom I introduced you to,* is in line for promotion.

5—The office manager, *to whom I introduced you,* is in line for promotion.

6—The personnel director, *whose office you just visited,* is out of town.

7—The company promoted Mr. Tracy, *whom they made their agent in Mexico.*

8—Anyone *whose output is consistently greater than average* deserves a bonus.

Examples of noun clauses introduced by relative pronouns. [10]

9—*Whoever cleared the table* misplaced the ledger.

10—The contest director revealed *who had won the prize.*

11—The supervisor informed them of *what their responsibilities are* and of *whom they should ask questions.*

12—*What Mr. Barker said* pleased them.

13—The major greeted *whomever he recognized.*

14—I knew *who had submitted that suggestion.*

15—The winner would be *whoever turned in the most coupons.*

16—Miss Pleska understood *what you said.*

• *APPLYING EFFECTIVE ENGLISH*

Oral Applications

• **1.** In the following sentences, identify the coordinating conjunctions and the equal-ranking elements which they connect:

1 — Daniel or Max checked and corrected the computations.

2 — When Sandy came and before Jolene left, we agreed to alter our plan and leave either Friday or Saturday.

3 — The bill has arrived, but the merchandise has not yet been delivered.

4 — Not Mr. Butler but Mr. Jackson made the reservation.

5 — Mr. Planer considered Stewart his friend and advisor.

• **2.** In the following sentences, identify the dependent clauses and the function words which introduce them.

1 — When Dee examined the records, she found that they were accurate.

2 — Mr. Harmon said that he would attend the conference if his schedule permitted.

---

[10] See "Guide to Sentence X-Ray," pages 654-655.

3 — Although Peter had seen the samples, he had not inspected them closely.

4 — The secretary who filed the papers will know where they are.

5 — The bank teller checked the account which had been referred to him.

• **3.** State the function of each dependent clause in Oral Application 2. Indicate whether it is (1) an adjective clause and, if so, what it modifies; (2) an adverbial clause and, if so, what it modifies; (3) a noun clause and, if so, whether it serves as a subject, direct object, or appositive.

• **4.** Identify the linking adverbs in the following sentences. Suggest other positions which they could occupy in these sentences. Note that a semicolon is used to join the independent clauses.

1 — The texts of the advertisements are ready; moreover, the illustrations will be available tomorrow.

2 — The football team did not win all their games; however, they did have a good season.

3 — The waiting room will be enlarged soon; we are, therefore, looking for an imaginative decorator to supervise the job.

4 — Mr. Drake will address the sales conference; hence, most of our staff will be attending.

5 — A new shipment of rugs is scheduled to arrive Monday; the coffee tables, however, will not arrive until next week.

Written Applications

• **1.** Write two sentences illustrating the use of each of the following subordinating conjunctions:

if, whether, that, when, while, because

• **2.** Write two sentences illustrating the use of each of the following relative pronouns:

who, that, which, whose, whom

• **3.** Write two sentences illustrating the use of each of the following linking adverbs; if you combine two independent clauses in the same sentence, remember to use a semicolon between them.

however, thus, nevertheless, therefore, consequently

SECTION 5

Sentence Varieties

Sentences can be classified with reference to (1) clause-types and (2) purpose.

SENTENCE CLASSIFICATIONS BASED ON VARIOUS COMBINATIONS OF CLAUSES

The distinction between main and dependent clauses. In the preceding section we saw that a clause may be made dependent by a function word or, sometimes, by position alone. A dependent clause that is introduced by a subordinating conjunction cannot stand by itself as a sentence. For example, "Because the newspaper advertisement had not been carefully prepared" is a dependent clause. It is made dependent by the subordinating conjunction *because.* If this conjunction were omitted, the clause would become a main clause. Thus, "The newspaper advertisement had not been carefully prepared."

A dependent clause that is introduced by a relative pronoun cannot stand by itself, except as a question. For example: The man who repaired the car is my best friend. If we separate the adjective clause from the rest of this sentence, we have: "Who repaired the car." This construction makes no sense as a statement. However, it is a perfectly good question: "Who repaired the car?" Thus, the significance of the clause would be basically altered if it stood by itself.

A dependent clause that is made dependent by position alone can stand by itself as a sentence. Of course, the meaning of the clause would change if it stood as a separate sentence. For example: "Mr. Harrison said the statements were very effective." Here the dependent clause can stand by itself as a separate sentence: "The statements were very effective." Its grammatical meaning is different when it stands alone. Then it is no longer the direct object of the transitive verb *said.* The dependent clause can also be introduced by the subordinating conjunction *that.* When introduced by a subordinating conjunction, the clause cannot stand by itself as a sentence. Thus, "That the statements were very effective" can only be a dependent clause.

The simple sentence. A simple sentence has only one clause. Such a sentence may be long and elaborate, for it may contain any number of single-word and phrasal modifiers. Here are simple sentences which vary greatly in length:

The visitors left.

The friendly visitors from the city left.

The friendly, enthusiastic, and observant visitors from the great city of Los Angeles finally left after a long visit with their relatives in the mountainous region near Gatlinburg, Tennessee, on the edge of Great Smoky Mountains National Park.

These sentences are classified as simple sentences, since each contains only one clause. The differences in length are a result of the additional words and phrases used as modifiers in the second and third sentences. Note that such differences in length are an important technique for introducing variety into sentences.

The compound sentence. A compound sentence is a sentence made up of two or more main clauses but no dependent clauses. Great differences in length can occur in compound sentences, just as in simple sentences. For example:

The accident damaged the cars, but no one was hurt.

The sudden accident severely damaged both the cars, but no one in either of the cars was badly hurt.

The sudden, surprising, and altogether unnecessary accident severely damaged both the cars, but fortunately no one in either of the cars was hurt, except for superficial wounds and bruises on the arms and right shoulder of the driver of the north-bound vehicle.

The complex sentence. A complex sentence is a sentence made up of one main clause and one or more dependent clauses. The dependent clause may be a modifier. It may also be a noun clause used as a subject, direct object, appositive, or predicate noun. The following are examples of complex sentences:

The principal believed [that] Fritz had left.

Mrs. Weinburg said [that] more business courses would be offered in the future.

When she returns, send Pam to me.

Whoever suggests a good slogan will receive a prize.

The secretary who typed that page is thoroughly reliable.

That an outline might help him write better was a helpful suggestion.

The length of a complex sentence depends partly upon the number of dependent clauses it contains. It also depends upon the number of single-word and phrasal modifiers in both the main clause and the dependent clause or clauses.

The compound-complex sentence. The compound-complex sentence is a sentence made up of two or more main clauses and one or more dependent clauses. For example:

> Mr. Lyman said [that] he would go, but he never found time.
> The teacher whom we had seen was Mr. Parsons; he did not, however, teach at our school.
> When the mail came, it was given at once to the secretary, but she did not examine it.
> Unless the typewriters are repaired, our work will be delayed; however, no competent repairmen are available now.
> The report that more shipping clerks are needed reached this office yesterday, but there has not yet been time to advertise for them.

The significance of sentence classification based on clausal type. One of the most important features of effective style in writing is variety. We have seen that variety involves both sentence length and sentence type. An awareness of the four types of sentences—simple, compound, complex, and compound-complex—can help you write better. Such an awareness can enable you to avoid overuse of any single sentence type. Paragraphs composed of one short simple sentence after another are choppy and hard to follow. Paragraphs composed of a series of long compound sentences tend to be ponderous and strung out. Of course, no writer sets out to write first a simple sentence, then a complex one, then a compound one, and so on. The type of sentence which is appropriate in a given situation will generally be determined by what is being said. Nevertheless, it is useful to guard against excessive and perhaps unconscious use of one type of sentence. Seek variety in sentence type, as well as in sentence length.

THE SIGNIFICANCE OF SENTENCE CLASSIFICATION BASED ON FUNCTION: STATEMENTS, QUESTIONS, AND COMMANDS

Sentences may have one of three possible functions. They may (1) make statements, (2) pose questions, and (3) embody commands. These distinctions in function are clearly indicated by grammatical signals in the language. Every native speaker will have unconsciously mastered these grammatical signals when he begins school. He may never have thought, however, about the mechanisms which enable him to communicate these different grammatical meanings. Knowing how English works can increase our command of the language. For this reason, in the following pages we shall look into the grammatical signals which distinguish statements, questions, and commands.

Statements in English. In Unit 2 we discovered that English statements conform to one of four patterns:

Pattern 1. Subject + Transitive Verb + Direct Object
Pattern 2. Subject + Intransitive Verb
Pattern 3. Subject + Linking Verb + Subjective Complement
Pattern 4. There/It + Linking Verb + Subject

Except in Pattern 4, the normal word order involves a subject preceding its verb. In Pattern 4 the expletives *there* and *it* signal that the logical subject of the sentence follows the linking verb.

These minimum sentence patterns may be expanded and elaborated in many ways. The subject (as well as a direct object, indirect object, objective complement, subjective complement, etc.) may be compound. It may be preceded by one or more single-word modifiers. It may be followed by one or more phrasal modifiers. Furthermore, one sentence may be joined to another sentence; the result is a compound sentence. A dependent clause also may be added to the sentence. These, briefly, are the structural resources upon which we draw when we speak or write English. Questions and commands are special functions of language. They are used much less often than are statements.

Questions in English.[1] Questions occur primarily in speech or in writing intended to represent speech. In writing, rhetorical questions (questions to which no response is expected from the listener or reader) are sometimes used to focus attention on a particular point. Questions are always indicated by special signals, in speech as well as in writing. A question mark in writing ordinarily reinforces other signals. Note that we instantly recognize questions during a conversation. Yet no question mark can occur in speech. It is true that an "echo" question uses a slight rise in the pitch of the speaker's voice at

---

[1] Questions may embody any of the four basic sentence patterns of English. For example: Pattern 1—"Who paid the bill?" Pattern 2—"Who left?" Pattern 3—"Who is responsible?" Pattern 4—"When is there hope for a change?"

the end of the sentence to indicate that the sentence is a question. This rise in pitch is a kind of oral question mark. In the written language an echo question can be recognized only by the presence of a question mark:

The packages have been shipped.
The packages have been shipped?

In speech, as well as in writing, there could be no doubt that the first sentence is a statement and that the second is a question. The falling pitch at the end of the first signals a statement. The rising pitch at the end of the second signals an echo question. In writing, only the question mark differentiates the statement from the echo question.

Except for echo questions, all questions in English use special question-signals in addition to the question mark. We shall now examine these special signals.

Reversed word-order as a question signal.[2] Yes-no questions are regularly formed by placing the first auxiliary in the verb phrase before the subject.[3] Transposition as a question signal is illustrated by the contrasting sentences given below. The left column presents the statement. The right column presents the corresponding question:

Statement	*Yes-No Question*
1—Buck left.	Did Buck leave?
2—Jill will go.	Will Jill go?
3—Larry has finished.	Has Larry finished?
4—Mr. Anders can do that.	Can Mr. Anders do that?
5—Mrs. Nix writes well.	Does Mrs. Nix write well?
6—Their experiment had succeeded.	Had their experiment succeeded?
7—Dr. Scott will have left by then.	Will Dr. Scott have left by then?
8—The boys help.	Do the boys help?
9—Nell is trying.	Is Nell trying?
10—The assembly will be held in the auditorium.	Will the assembly be held in the auditorium?
11—The students have paid.	Have the students paid?

[2] See "Guide to the Sentence X-Ray," pages 655-656.

[3] For the verb *to be* in the present and past tenses, the verb itself (rather than an auxiliary) is transposed. Thus, "Am I wrong?" "Were you there?" "Are they sure?" "Were the folders in the file?" The verb *to have* can also be transposed to form a question: "Have you their reply?" Compare, "Do you have their reply?"

Note that the auxiliaries *do, does,* and *did* in Questions 1, 5, and 8 do not occur in the corresponding statements. Many statements do not contain an auxiliary verb. In such a situation, the "question auxiliary" *do, does* (present tense) /*did* (past tense) must be used to convert the statement to a question. (But see footnote 3, page 150.)

Interrogatory function words as question signals.[4] Questions that call for an answer other than *yes* or *no* require the use of interrogatory function words. Examples of interrogatory function words are *when, where, how, how much, which, who, whom,* and *what.* In addition to these interrogatory function words, the first auxiliary is sometimes transposed before the subject. In such sentences reversed word order reinforces the effect of function words. Words that serve as interrogatory function words can serve, *in other patterns,* as subordinating conjunctions or relative pronouns. No confusion is caused by this double use. As interrogatories these function words introduce independent constructions. As subordinating conjunctions or relative pronouns, they introduce dependent constructions.

The following examples illustrate the contrast between statements and corresponding questions requiring more than a yes-no answer.

Statement Form	*Question Form*
1—Mr. Adkins left.	Who left?
2—Mr. Adkins left to attend a meeting.	Why did Mr. Adkins leave?
3—Mr. Adkins left at 10:30 a.m.	When did Mr. Adkins leave?
4—Mr. Adkins left in a taxi cab in haste.	How did Mr. Adkins leave?
5—Mr. Adkins went downtown.	Where did Mr. Adkins go?
6—Mr. Adkins left two hours ago.	How long ago did Mr. Adkins leave?
7—Mr. Adkins was going to see Mr. Brewer.	Whom was Mr. Adkins going to see?
8—Mr. Adkins was responsible to Mr. Brewer.	To whom was Mr. Adkins responsible?
9—Mr. Adkins was going to attend the morning meeting.	Which meeting was Mr. Adkins going to attend?
10—Mr. Adkins was the principal speaker.	What was Mr. Adkins' role at the meeting?

---

[4] See "Guide to the Sentence X-Ray," pages 656-657.

Note that the first auxiliary verb is placed before the subject with most of these interrogatory function words. The only exceptions are those (like *who* and *which*) that serve simultaneously as interrogatory function word and as subject ("Who paid?" "Which was found?") or as subject-modifier ("What team won?").

Commands in English.[5] Commands occur primarily in speech and in writing intended to represent speech. They also occur frequently in connection with instructions and directions. In commands, the verb has one and only one form, always identical with the infinitive. The verb form used in commands is called the *imperative mood* of the verb.[6] A noun in direct address (or, in speech, an exclamatory expression) sometimes occurs with the imperative verb. Such an element is generally set off from the imperative verb by a comma (corresponding to a pause and shift in pitch, in speech).

The differences between a statement and command can be seen by comparing the examples given below. The following signals are involved in distinguishing statements from commands: (1) oral or written punctuation, (2) the form of the verb, (3) the presence or absence of a grammatical subject, which governs the person and number of the verb.

Statement	*Command*
1—Boys leave the room.	Boys, leave the room.
2—You set the table yesterday.	You, set the table. (Discourteous tone.)
3—You are ready for the new task.	Be ready for the new task.
4—You move out of the way.	You! Move out of the way! (Urgent tone.)
5—Students help.	Students, help!
6—Jan is here on time.	Jan, be here on time.

When a noun (or pronoun) in direct address, or an exclamatory expression, occurs in a command, it can always be omitted. Any command may be given an exclamatory tone—indicated in writing by use of an exclamation point instead of a period.

---

[5] See "Guide to the Sentence X-Ray," pages 657-658.

[6] The other moods are *indicative*, used in almost all statements and questions; and subjunctive, used in certain dependent clauses after verbs of asking and commanding ("I request that he *be* promoted," where the indicative form would be "is promoted") and in a few special expressions ("If I *were* you. . . .," where the indicative form would be "was").

• APPLYING EFFECTIVE ENGLISH

Oral Applications

• **1.** Classify the following sentences as simple, compound, complex, or compound-complex.

1 — When Chuck left, he promised to return.

2 — In the fall, Mr. Cortina and Mr. Fortas decided to visit the Atlanta plant in order to survey operations there at first hand.

3 — Miss Oliver brought sandwiches to the picnic, and Miss Albers brought dessert.

4 — John Wycliffe, who lived in the fourteenth century, helped make the first English translation of the Bible.

5 — In preparing his speech, Mr. Brown included many helpful examples.

6 — While the facilities are being enlarged, manufacturing continues; moreover, we have almost equalled last year's levels of production.

7 — Wyatt went to night school because he was trying to improve his chances for a promotion.

8 — The United States is shipping great quantities of agricultural produce to Japan.

9 — The impression that next year's models will not be changed much seems to have stimulated sales.

10 — Linoleum and vinyl are attractive and durable floor-coverings.

• **2.** Suggest function words (appropriate kinds of connectors) to fill the blanks in the following sentences. Discuss which kinds of connectors (A. coordinating conjunctions, B. subordinating conjunctions, C. relative pronouns, and D. movable clause connectors) can occupy each blank. Some of the blanks can be occupied by more than one kind of connector; others can be occupied by only one kind. Determine for each blank whether more than one kind of connector is possible.

1 — The game had, _____, proved extremely interesting.

2 — _____ the train was late, our schedule was upset.

3 — The agent _____ sold us the ticket made several suggestions.

4 — Each customer was offered two tickets; _____, some tickets remained at the end of the day.

5 — The annual company golf tournament was postponed _____ it rained.

• **3.** Identify the signals which introduce the dependent clauses in the sentences of Oral Application 1.

• **4.** The statement "Meg paid the bill" is the basis for the following questions—"Did Meg pay the bill?" "What did Meg pay?" "Who paid the bill?" Experiment with the questions that can be based on these statements:

    1 — You listened to the speech very thoughtfully.
    2 — Marshall left.
    3 — Jerome completed his assignment.
    4 — Miss Lee has written a book.
    5 — Donald is a sincere, hard-working lad.

• **5.** Change the statements of Oral Application 4 into commands. For example, the statement "Meg paid the bill" becomes, as a command, "Pay the bill," or "Pay the bill, Meg."

• **6.** Change the following commands into statements. Make up names as subjects for the verbs in your statements and use verbs in various tenses, adding whatever function words may be necessary.

    1 — Report tomorrow.
    2 — Return the envelope.
    3 — Be patient.
    4 — When you pay the bill, ask for a receipt.
    5 — Mail those cards at the post office.
    6 — Have dinner with us.
    7 — Name a substitute for Miss Osborne.
    8 — Study the proposals carefully.
    9 — Turn on all the lights in the room.
    10 — Be attentive.

• **7.** Change the commands of Oral Application 6 into various kinds of questions. Make up names as subjects for the verbs in your questions and use verbs in various tenses, adding whatever function words may be necessary.

• **8.** Change the following questions into statements that answer the questions. Invent any additional information needed for the answers. Give complete sentences as answers.

    1 — How much did this eraser cost?
    2 — Where did Mr. Perkins leave the folder?
    3 — Is this flight usually on time?
    4 — Who received the bonus last year?
    5 — Has that inquiry ever been answered?

Written Applications

● **1.** Convert the following statements into (a) questions and (b) commands. Whenever possible, base more than one question on each statement. Try to convert each statement into a yes-no question. Also try to form questions concerning *who, what, where, when, why, how,* or *how much.* Make whatever changes may be necessary to convert the statements into various kinds of questions and into commands. For example:

Mr. Hartley left early.

As a command, the sentence would read: "Leave early" or "Leave early, Mr. Hartley." The following kinds of questions could be made from this statement:

Yes-no question:	Did Mr. Hartley leave early? Has Mr. Hartley left early?
Who question:	Who left early?
When question:	When did Mr. Hartley leave?
Why question:	Why did Mr. Hartley leave early?
How questions:	How did Mr. Hartley leave? How early did Mr. Hartley leave?

Here are sentences for you to work with:

1 — Mr. Houston attended the delegates' symposium.
2 — When the concert ended, the audience remained for the lecture.
3 — Miss Rodgers arrived in the afternoon.
4 — The brothers went to the store to buy an evening paper.
5 — The cook found the recipe in an old manuscript.
6 — We found the fourth question especially difficult.
7 — Mrs. Bacall had visited her cousin in Montreal.
8 — In 1927 Charles Lindbergh made the first trans-Atlantic solo flight.
9 — A knowledge of the grammatical constructions of English can help a writer avoid monotony in his sentences.
10 — *Webster's New International Dictionary,* Third Edition, was published in 1961.

● **2.** Revise the sentences of Oral Application 1. Retain the same ideas but change complex sentences into compound sentences or into two or more simple sentences. Similarly, change compound sentences into complex sentences, and so on. Experiment with the various kinds of sentences that can be used to express the same basic ideas.

• **3.** Make the following pairs of simple sentences into other kinds of sentences by combining them in various ways. Use coordinating conjunctions, subordinating conjunctions, relative pronouns, and movable clause connectors whenever necessary.

1 — Warren answered the telephone. No one else made a move to do so.
2 — The equipment was delivered in the morning. The office was ready for business that afternoon.
3 — Mr. Gross will be chairman of the spring meeting. He has been chairman often in past years.
4 — Miss Hatchin filed the correspondence. Miss Lang typed the annual report.
5 — The background of the advertisement will be dark blue. The lettering will be white.
6 — The seminar begins at 7:00 p.m. The seminar is held yearly.
7 — Mr. Stevens appointed Emmett as his assistant. Emmett has had three years' experience in accounting work.
8 — The error was caught. It was too late to correct it.
9 — That problem will require legal advice. Mr. Leake is consulting the corporation counsel.
10 — The address of the Turner Canning Company has been changed recently. Their shipment is being delayed until we learn the firm's new address.

• **4.** Combine, whenever possible, the following pairs of simple sentences into a single complex sentence. Use subordinating conjunctions (such as *when, because, if, while, until, since, where*) before either the first or the second clause, making this clause dependent. Or use a relative pronoun to make an adjective clause out of one of the sentences.

1 — Mr. LaMaster will make the inspection. Mr. LaMaster is an engineer.
2 — Gretchen is checking the word in the dictionary. The dictionary is kept in the outer office.
3 — The summary should be completed by tomorrow. The summary concerns the rise in costs over the past year.
4 — The revised version is an improvement. The revision includes many more details and examples.
5 — The messenger delivered the telegram. The telegram had been sent by Mr. Clayton.
6 — The bowling team is scheduled to play at 8:00 p.m. The team is made up of members of the personnel department.

7 — All applicants for the position must pass a written test. The position will require knowledge of legal procedures.

8 — The machinery was crated yesterday. The machinery will be sent to Louisville.

9 — The manager prepared a statement for the company newspaper. The statement explained the proposed changes in company policy.

10 — The supervisor included the details of the study in his annual report. Miss Wilson assisted the supervisor last week.

• **5.** Combine the pairs of simple sentences in Written Application 3 in such a way as to make one compound sentence. Use appropriate movable clause connectors (such as *therefore, however, nevertheless, thus, accordingly, hence*). Experiment by placing some of these movable clause connectors before the second clause and some within it. Remember that a semicolon is used to join the independent clauses of a compound sentence when a coordinating conjunction is not used.

• *REVIEW*

• **1.** Explain how word order, function words, word form, and oral or written punctuation are involved in communicating the grammatical meanings of the following sentences. Take into account such matters as how we know (1) who performs the action, (2) when the action occurred, (3) whether one or more than one person or thing is involved, (4) whether a completed action is involved, (5) whether the action is in progress, (6) which words and phrases are modifiers, and so on.

1 — Mr. Browne mailed Mr. Sands a description of our program.

2 — The rearrangement of the office has been approved by Miss Wallace.

3 — The mechanic will quickly repair Avery's desk.

4 — Miss Swanson's resourceful and industrious secretary is revising the program.

5 — Mr. Mazzella, safety supervisor of the company, prepared the safety code.

• **2.** Each of the sentences below and at the top of page 158 contains one error. Correct these errors.

1 — A supervisor of experienced workers have few problems.

2 — Our car needs it's engine checked.

3 — Elmer's friends brought there dog with them.

4 — Mr. Corwell did not hear the mens' answers.

5 — Whom do you think will win?

6 — Each contestant brought their own equipment.

7 — Gordon should of returned the pliers at once.

8 — Miss Collins has went home.

9 — The reports concerning our project is favorable.

10 — Our experience with restaurants don't support that claim.

• **3.** First convert each of the following sentences into a yes-no question. Then point out the signals used to produce this question.

1 — The dean brought the report with him.

2 — The questions were excellent.

3 — Many swimmers thought the water was too cold.

4 — The instructor has my manual.

5 — Each applicant should type his answers.

6 — That room has been cold all morning.

7 — Illustrations add interest to an article.

8 — The Carters decided to repaint their house.

9 — I have enough change to buy the newspaper.

10 — The car didn't start easily this morning.

• **4.** First convert each of the following sentences into a question of the *who/where/why/when/what/which/how* variety. Then point out the signals used to produce each question.

1 — Mr. and Mrs. Eckstrom sail for England tomorrow.

2 — Laura revised her paper last night.

3 — The furnace has already been repaired.

4 — My car needs a washing badly.

5 — Those books are overdue at the library.

6 — A white vase would look attractive there.

7 — The switch in your room doesn't work properly

8 — The Linds receive broadcasts directly from Italy on their radio.

9 — Our English class has been cancelled.

10 — The back window was broken by the ballplayers.

• **5.** Convert the following pairs of simple sentences into single, compound, or complex sentences. Get as much variety into your sentences as you can. Use whatever additional words may be necessary, and rearrange the sentences however you wish.

1 — Lon's taxi arrived late. He missed his airplane connection.

2 — The paper is excellent. Warren's letter looks impressive.

3 — That message is not clear. The times given are contradictory.

4 — Mr. Kloss's car is old. He plans to drive it to San Diego.

5 — The weather may moderate. The wind is shifting to the south.

UNIT 5

DEVELOPING SKILL IN THE USE OF PUNCTUATION, CAPITALIZATION, AND NUMBERS

A page of writing without punctuation or capital letters would puzzle you completely. You wouldn't be able to tell where one sentence ended and the next began. You would have to analyze the entire passage word by word to understand the message. The main purpose of punctuation, then, is to enable the writer to present his ideas in units that will be clear and effective.

Sentences are indicated by an initial capital letter and by a period, question mark, or exclamation point at the end. Subunits are indicated by commas, colons, semicolons, dashes, parentheses, and brackets.

The proper use of apostrophes to indicate possessives and contractions shows the interrelationships among terms. The proper sequence for adjacent punctuation marks shows the writer's attention to detail and pride in careful work. The expression of numbers in consistent and appropriate form simplifies understanding and comparison of such detail.

In this unit you will learn the principles of punctuation, capitalization, and number expression.

These will help you present your ideas clearly, correctly, and effectively.

UNIT 5

Section 1

The Period: The period concludes each separate statement or command.

Section 2

The Comma: The comma sets off certain subunits within the sentence.

Section 3

The Semicolon, Colon, Question Mark, and Exclamation Point: The semicolon can join independent clauses. The colon points to what follows. The question mark ends each question. The exclamation point substitutes for a period to show emotion.

Section 4

The Apostrophe: The apostrophe, with the suffix s̲, can make a noun into a special kind of modifier.

Section 5

Quotation Marks; the Dash, Parentheses, and Brackets; Omission Marks; the Hyphen: Quotation marks enclose quoted material. The dash, parentheses, and brackets set off incidental comments. Omission marks indicate incomplete quotations. The hyphen makes one unit of two or more words.

Section 6

Rules of Order Among Punctuation Marks: Punctuation marks occurring together follow a fixed sequence.

Section 7

Capitalization: Capitals signal the beginning of a new sentence and the occurrence of proper nouns.

Section 8

Expression of Numbers: General rules govern the use of figures or words.

SECTION 1

The Period

The period ends each separate statement or command.

The purposes of punctuation. Written punctuation serves two purposes:

1 — Written punctuation draws the reader's attention to the various units and subunits in writing. For example, punctuation identifies sentences as units and identifies the independent clauses of a compound sentence as subunits. Written punctuation of this kind corresponds to various features of oral punctuation. These features include the pauses, the variations in pitch, and the stresses which every native English speaker employs unconsciously whenever he speaks.

2 — Written punctuation also serves an entirely different purpose. It satisfies various special formulas and conventions of writing which enable us to make our messages uniform and neat. Written punctuation of this kind does *not* correspond to oral punctuation. For example, the use of periods after abbreviations is exclusively a convention of *written* English.

Both types of punctuation are important in business writing, for businessmen are intelligent and demanding readers. To be well-received, a business message must be thoughtfully written, and the final copy must be prepared with serious concentration.

The period: The major stop sign in writing. The period is the basic stop sign controlling the traffic of ideas in writing. It enables us to draw attention to the unifying idea set forth in a single sentence. It enables us to present ideas in emphatic and easy-to-understand spans.

The period in writing corresponds to the following features of the spoken language:

1 — A rapid fading away of one's voice at the end of a statement

2 — An accompanying distinctive fall in the pitch of one's voice

3 — A pause before a new sentence is begun.

When we talk, we are ordinarily quite unaware that we are punctuating our speech in elaborate ways. All of us learned to do this as children, through years of unconscious imitation. Awareness of the features of oral punctuation can increase mastery of the corresponding features of written punctuation.

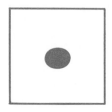

1 — Most sentences end with a period, which is the mark indicating *full stop* at the end of a statement. On every page of writing are many examples, for all declarative sentences end with a period.

The new plant is in Maine.

2 — The period is used at the end of an imperative sentence.

Meet me at the drugstore.
Mail the enclosed card by next week.

3 — The period is used after initials and after most abbreviations.

Mrs. C. T. Irwin; Closson's, Inc.; Ph.D.; a.m.; f.o.b.; oz.; C.O.D.

Abbreviations composed of several capitalized initial letters are often written solid without periods: TWA (Trans World Airlines); FDIC (Federal Deposit Insurance Corporation); FEPC (Fair Employment Practices Committee); NASA (National Aeronautics and Space Administration).

4 — The period is used between dollars and cents expressed in figures; for example, $9.63. Note, however, that a period and ciphers are not required when an amount in even dollars is expressed in figures.

The bill totals $33.92.
He donated $800 to the college.

• *APPLYING EFFECTIVE ENGLISH*

Oral Application

Read aloud in class the unpunctuated paragraph at the top of page 163. First read it in a monotone. Then read it normally, inserting oral punctuation to signal the end of each sentence in spoken English. In class discussion try to identify, as precisely as possible, the characteristics of the "oral period." This is a signal of the spoken language that corresponds to the period in writing and makes clear where each sentence ends.

Frank walked down the country road finding an interesting path to the right he turned onto it that afternoon he walked seven miles never before had he found the crisp autumn air so invigorating nor felt so close to the beauty of nature

Written Applications

● **1.** Rewrite the following sentences, inserting periods wherever they are needed.

1 — The price of the imported vase was $38 62 f o b Los Angeles

2 — Mr Clyde Ingle received an M A degree at the spring commencement exercises

3 — Policy No 3876295 was issued to Mrs Barbara Noonan

4 — Willoughby, Ltd, of Ontario, is a large and distinguished firm

5 — The Hickory Falls Dental Clinic will close tomorrow at 1:15 p m

6 — The shipment was forwarded to Mrs Mann, who lives at 413 Ash St, Washington, D C

7 — The statement sent to Col C B Osborne listed three purchases at $5 50 each

8 — Dr William S Terrill has office hours from 1:30 to 3:00 p m, Monday through Friday

9 — Burton-Phillips, Inc, sent the diamonds by air to the R T Angston Co

10 — J M Reisner, Ph D, is the author of many textbooks and articles

● **2.** Rewrite the following paragraphs, inserting periods wherever they are needed.

Dr Eld J Judson, the well-known authority on U S history, has accepted our invitation to address the International Relations Club at its spring meeting He will be introduced by Prof Thomas Elwood, Ph D, who was a colleague of Dr Judson in the State Department

Please send an announcement to all members that Dr Judson will lecture on the subject "The Place of Commerce in the Modern World" The program will be held Wednesday, May 17, at 12:45 p m A group of three panelists will be selected at our next regular meeting, Wednesday, March 13, at 12:30 p m They will follow Dr Judson on the program and will discuss the ideas that he presents in his lecture

SECTION 2

The Comma

The comma sets off certain subunits within sentences.

When speaking with someone, you are communicating information from your mind to his. To communicate effectively, you must control the flow of information in such a way that the listener can follow you. You do this by the use of changes in stress and pitch and by the use of pauses. Similarly, you use punctuation to control the flow of information in writing. Punctuation separates one sentence from another. Punctuation also sets off various segments within the sentence, making clear the relationships among certain parts of the sentence. The comma is especially important for this purpose.

The comma. The comma marks off various kinds of subunits within the sentence. The comma corresponds to a minor pause (with slightly rising, slightly falling, or unchanged pitch) in speech. *Many pauses in speech, however, go completely unmarked in writing.* Be on guard against inserting commas automatically wherever pauses occur in speech. The following guides will enable you to use the comma effectively and confidently.

1 — Use the comma to point off a subordinate clause preceding its principal clause. Such clauses are introduced by subordinating conjunctions like *if, unless, since, because, when, after, although, while, as.*

When the rough draft has been revised, the secretary will prepare final copies.

If errors occur, the reports will have to be retyped.

2 — Use the comma to set off a nonrestrictive clause. A nonrestrictive clause gives information that could be given equally well in a separate sentence. Nonrestrictive clauses are sometimes called *descriptive clauses.*

For example:

1) Our high school principal, *who formerly was our teacher of English,* is extremely popular.

2) This corporation, *which has a good record of earnings,* is recommended as an investment.

The meaning of these sentences is preserved even when the nonrestrictive clauses have been converted into separate sentences. The sentences then read:

1) Our high school principal is extremely popular.
He was formerly our teacher of English.

2) This corporation is recommended as an investment.
This corporation has a good record of earnings.

A restrictive clause is one that restricts the meaning of the term it modifies. It cannot be dropped or expressed in a separate sentence without clouding or falsifying the meaning of the original sentence. Restrictive clauses are sometimes called *identifying clauses.*

3) Anyone *who has committed a crime* should be brought to trial.

4) All corporations *that are making large earnings* are able to pay satisfactory dividends.

To drop the relative clauses or to make them separate sentences would destroy the intended meaning:

3) Anyone should be brought to trial. He has committed a crime.

4) All corporations are able to pay satisfactory dividends. All corporations are making large earnings.

Restrictive clauses are not set off by commas. In oral punctuation, a pause immediately precedes a nonrestrictive clause; this pause corresponds to the comma in written punctuation. Before a restrictive clause no such pause occurs. A pause may occur *after* either a nonrestrictive or a restrictive clause.

3 — Use the comma to set off a nonrestrictive appositive but not a restrictive appositive. An appositive is a second noun (or noun clause) set beside another noun and giving additional information about it. Examples: Elizabeth II, Queen of England: Dr. Rhoten A. Smith, president of Northern Illinois University.

The rules for appositives are similar to those for relative clauses. Nonrestrictive appositives (those not necessary to identify the term they accompany) are set off by commas in writing and by pauses in speech. Restrictive appositives (those necessary to identify the term they accompany) are *not* set off by commas or pauses.

1) Albany, the capital of New York State, is the second oldest permanent settlement in the thirteen colonies.

2) Please consult the book *The Close Reading of Factual Prose* as soon as possible.

The appositive in Sentence 1 is properly set off by commas because the appositive is not required to make clear the meaning of the sentence. We can identify the Albany in question without the appositive "the capital of New York State." A nonrestrictive appositive, like a nonrestrictive clause, can be satisfactorily expressed in a separate sentence. Such a change will not cloud or falsify the meaning of the original sentence.

1) Albany is the second oldest permanent settlement in the thirteen colonies. It is the capital of New York State.

The appositive in Sentence 2, above, is not set off by commas because it is required to convey the essential meaning of the sentence. Without this appositive the reader cannot know what book is meant.

4 — Use the comma to separate coordinate clauses joined by one of the coordinating conjunctions: *and, but, for, or, nor.*

This company is strong financially, *and* its sales policy will assure its continued success.

A large reserve fund had been accumulated, *but* the directors were reluctant to use it.

This rule concerns coordinate *clauses* joined by conjunctions. It does not refer to a clause containing two verbs, even though in speech a pause might separate the verbs. *Remember that many pauses in speech are not indicated by any mark of punctuation in writing.*

Undesirable: The CPA audited the books, and submitted an extremely helpful report.

Better: The CPA audited the books and submitted an extremely helpful report.

5 — Use the comma to set off an introductory phrase containing a verb form. In general no comma is used after an introductory phrase which does not contain a verb form. Exceptions occur if the phrase is parenthetical (for example, *on the contrary, in the second place, on the other hand,* and *for example*) or if it is unusually long.

Right: *After making the survey,* the committee will meet again.
Right: *To complete the job,* they increased the work force.

Right: *After much debate* the motion was defeated.
Right: *As chairman of the committee* he addressed the convention.

Right: *For example,* consider the modern compact automobile.
Right: *In view of the large sum of money necessary,* there is some doubt about whether the current tax rate is adequate.

6 — Use the comma to set off a word or word group that interrupts the basic sentence pattern. In the spoken language these interruptions are preceded and followed by pauses.

There is some doubt, *in view of the large sum of money necessary,* about whether the current tax rate is adequate.
The members of the executive conference, *their calendar for the day completed,* adjourned until the following week.

Such interruptions are frequently parenthetical or transitional. Examples of words often used parenthetically are *however, moreover, therefore, consequently, finally, besides, perhaps, accordingly, also.*

They have agreed, *however,* to make the necessary changes.
It was certain, *moreover,* that his request would be refused.
It should be added, *finally,* that the expenses were unavoidable.

Examples of phrases often used parenthetically are *in fact, of course, in short, in brief, without doubt, if possible.*

There is no reason, *as a matter of fact,* why the improvements should not be made.
Our company, *of course,* will submit bids on the new highway project.
All our members hope that you will, *if possible,* attend the meetings of the Willow Park Press Club.

Examples of clauses often used parenthetically are *I think, I believe, I repeat, he says, as you know.*

There is, *as you know,* a reason for stopping this practice.
To believe that rumor is, *we think,* both foolish and irresponsible.

7 — Use the comma to point off words or word groups used in a series consisting of at least three units.

Series of words: Among the more important commodities are iron, steel, cotton, wool, silk, and leather.

Series of phrases: Herbert returned without his flashlight, without his fishing gear, and without his enthusiasm.

Series of clauses: The committee finished the assignment, the chairman reported the committee's views, and the faculty began its deliberations.

8 — Use the comma between successive adjectives when the word *and* can be inserted between the adjectives. Such adjectives are said to be coordinate, since they are of equal rank. Orally, they receive equal stress and are separated by a slight pause. Either adjective may occur first.

a self-reliant, healthy boy (a self-reliant and healthy boy)
a healthy, self-reliant boy (a healthy and self-reliant boy)
an honest, reliable man (an honest and reliable man)
a reliable, honest man (a reliable and honest man)

No comma is used when the modifiers are not coordinate. For example, no comma is used when the second modifier forms a kind of unit with the noun. Orally, such modifiers do *not* bear equal stress, are not separated by a pause, and occur in a fixed sequence. For example, we do not say "a swimming stylish suit."

a stylish swimming suit   laughing blue eyes
long-rooted blue grass   an intelligent young woman

9 — Use the comma to set off words used in direct address.

Mr. Chairman, the Finance Committee is ready to report.
We are glad to know, Dr. Knight, that our service has been helpful.

Notice the difference between the following sentences:

1) Don set the margins.
2) Don, set the margins.

Only the comma enables us to distinguish between *Don* as a subject (Sentence 1) and as a noun in direct address (Sentence 2). In speech a pause corresponding to the comma in Sentence 2 would provide the necessary signal.

10 — Use the comma to set off sentence elements that might otherwise be wrongly joined in reading.

Misleading:	Ever since the annual report has been published.
Clear:	Ever since, the annual report has been published.
Misleading:	In the inventory books in sets were not counted individually.
Clear:	In the inventory, books in sets were not counted individually.
Misleading:	They left early for the business conference was to begin promptly at 8:15 a.m.
Clear:	They left early, for the business conference was to begin promptly at 8:15 a.m.

11 — Use the comma to indicate the omission of words that are understood by the reader.

The high-fidelity amplifier had been quoted at $190; the loudspeakers, at $110 each.

The personnel committee dealt with various grievances; the finance committee, with the preparation of next year's budget.

Do not use commas where they are not necessary. In general, do not put a comma where no pause is made in reading. Remember also that many pauses are possible in spoken English that do not correspond to a comma in writing. For example, in speech, many people might pause after the subject *man* in the sentence "The young man walked gaily home." In speech the subject is often separated from the verb by a slight pause. No comma, however, should be used to mark the many optional pauses of this kind that may occur in any sentence.

• *APPLYING EFFECTIVE ENGLISH*

Oral Applications

• **1.** Proofread the following sentences. Explain all errors and indicate your corrections.

1 — If Clyde goes to Miami he will fly from John F. Kennedy Airport New York New York.

2 — The manager of the sales department was pleased when he heard that his secretary Miss Priscilla Sabatelli had won the typing contest.

3 — After Peter reported the accident the authorities inaugurated a safety campaign.

4 — Notebooks of this kind are widely used by stenographers, who take dictation with a ball-point pen.

5 — I disagree that Mr. Dale the chief clerk should be criticized for his action which was based on the best information available.

6 — The salesman, who has the best record, will receive the bonus.

7 — The lincoln expressway to be completed this spring will relieve traffic congestion in the west part of the city.

8 — After introducing the speaker the toastmaster took out pencil and paper, and took down the entire speech in shorthand.

9 — The man the woman and all three children were badly shaken up in the accident.

10 — Although the wreck was a serious one the damage to the automobile was surprisingly small.

11 — The bearer of this introduction Mr. Mark Johnson formerly worked for our company.

12 — The package, which is on the counter is for Miss Doty; the package, which is under the counter is for Harold Spears.

13 — To increase the demand for the product we have planned an extensive advertising program.

14 — The chairman Mr. Bell appointed Dr. Walker, Miss Barnett and Mrs. Thomas to the nominating committee.

15 — Mr. Hoagland who is always on time was early again this morning.

• **2.** Read the following sentences aloud, with the pitches indicated by the arrows. Discuss the correspondence between the oral and written punctuation. Experiment with placing the "oral period" earlier in each sentence. Note that either a rising or falling pitch can correspond to the commas punctuating items in a series.

1 — On the hike, the boy scouts took beans ↗, potatoes ↗, frankfurters ↗, candy bars ↗, and rice [↘ extra low fall in pitch].

2 — The clerk counted out the five-dollar bills: "One ↘, two ↘, three ↘, four ↘, five ↘, six [↘ extra low fall in pitch].

Written Applications

• **1.** Rewrite the following sentences, inserting commas at the proper points.

1 — After making her decision Miss Marie Roberts left the store and her father returned to his office.

2 — Miss Highfield who prepared the manuscript in duplicate wrote the memorandum about the need for more stenographers.

3 — I shall send you a copy of the announcement Miss Ramsey within a week.

4 — The Donald Marshalls are as a matter of fact leaving for a trip to New York and New England.

5 — That action eventually resulted in a reduction in wages a lowering of efficiency and the resignation of ten clerks.

6 — There was consequently a shortage of properly trained office help.

7 — A president was elected two committee chairmen were appointed and dues were collected from the members present.

8 — There is I believe no easy solution to this problem.

9 — The members of the debating team their evidence well in mind presented a strong affirmative argument.

10 — It may be said in conclusion that this recommendation is fully justified by all the facts.

11 — The directors wanted to declare a dividend but the earnings of the company did not warrant such a move.

12 — The house that has green shutters was constructed by E. B. Jenkins who is one of the most reliable contractors in the city.

13 — Mr. Dean Lampros an employee of the company was present.

14 — His brother Joe I understand will be attending college this fall.

15 — Ever since the clerk has had to be more careful in filling orders.

16 — The Glenview Country Club which is located west of Glenview Colorado has scheduled a tournament for August 7 8 9, and the club professional will send applications to all those who are interested in competing.

17 — Mr. Emil Renfrew vice president for public relations will visit Kankakee Illinois during April June August and October.

18 — The sidewalk in front of the building needs to be repaired.

● **2.** The following example has all the necessary punctuation except commas. Rewrite it, supplying the necessary commas.

Under the law the Attorney General is authorized to advise only departmental heads the seventy-one district attorneys and other individuals specified in the statutes. For that reason the Attorney General cannot advise you officially.

The Railroad Commission has jurisdiction over the administration of the common-carrier law as you know; I suggest therefore that you communicate with the Railroad Commission which has detailed information and which is in a position to obtain any additional information you may need. If you give the facts in detail the Commission will be able to make a preliminary investigation of the situation. The Commission will I am sure cooperate in every possible way.

SECTION 3

The Semicolon, Colon, Question Mark, and Exclamation Point

The semicolon can join independent clauses. The colon points to what follows. The question mark ends each question. The exclamation point substitutes for a period to show emotion.

The semicolon. The semicolon substitutes for a period whenever the writer wishes to emphasize the close connection between two independent clauses. He can indicate this close connection by including the clauses, without use of a coordinating conjunction, in the same sentence.

1 — Use the semicolon between the members of a compound sentence when no conjunction is used.

The desks arrived last week; the chairs have not yet been delivered.

The book concerns leadership in business; its advice is both dependable and practical.

2 — Use the semicolon between the clauses of a compound sentence that are joined by such phrases as *in fact* and *on the other hand* or by certain transitional words. Examples of such transitional words (called *linking adverbs*) are *also, consequently, accordingly, hence, however, moreover, nevertheless,* and *therefore.*

The builders are making excellent progress; in fact, they have almost completed the job.

He arrived early; consequently, he was able to assist in planning the whole program.

Mrs. Campbell declined; hence, the committee resumed its research.

The comma after the introductory phrase or linking adverb, though optional, is generally used in business writing.

3 — Use the semicolon before certain expressions when they introduce an independent clause or an enumeration of several items. The expressions are as follows: *that is, namely, e.g.* (from Latin *exempli gratia,* which means "for example"), *i.e.* (from Latin *id est,* which means "that is"), *to wit, viz.* (from Latin *videlicet,* which means "namely"), and *for example.*

Kerner and Company is a shipping firm; that is, it transports various kinds of cargo.

All the participants had interesting suggestions; e.g., the salesmen thought we should experiment with television advertising.

Four men were appointed to the program committee; namely, L. K. Kerley, S. W. Bagby, A. M. Foster, and J. D. Dean.

Mr. Brandenburg has solved some interesting problems; for example, he arranged our current vacation schedule.

4 — If a semicolon increases the clarity of the sentence, use it to separate the clauses of a compound sentence when one or both members are punctuated with commas. In effect, then, a semicolon is substituted for the comma which normally precedes a coordinating conjunction joining the clauses.

If he is nominated, he will run; but since there are three other popular candidates, he does not really expect the convention to nominate him.

The contracts, which Mr. Adams prepared, will be finished today; and the report, which he reviewed, will be ready tomorrow.

It is easy to read about how to write good business messages; but it is not so easy to write a truly effective application, acknowledgment, collection notice, or sales promotion piece.

5 — Use the semicolon between the members of a series, if the members contain commas.

The designer states that the craft will land vertically; that, furthermore, it will fly faster than sound; and, finally, that it will fly higher than previous piloted craft.

The enterprising businessman visualizes an opportunity; he secures the necessary materials, organizing them effectively; and he creates a going business.

The staff included an assistant manager; a research assistant, eager but inexperienced; and six clerks, five of whom were recent high school graduates.

The colon. The colon indicates that what follows will be an explanation, an expansion, or a clarifying restatement of what precedes:

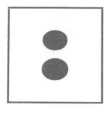

1 — Use the colon between two independent clauses having no connecting word between them, the first clause pointing forward to the second.

> Progress lies in one direction: extensive basic research will inevitably lead to important advances in technology.

An understanding of the connection between oral and written punctuation will help a student: it will enable him to punctuate his written sentences more accurately and more confidently.

2 — Use the colon after forward-looking expressions—expressions that introduce items of information.

> Please ship the following athletic equipment at once: one pitcher's glove, two baseballs, and one catcher's mask.
> These are the members of the board of directors: Mr. Kemper, Mrs. Norton, and Mrs. Morgan.
> The camp will enforce these three regulations: (1) swimming will be permitted only when lifeguards are present, (2) no nonswimmers will be allowed on the pier, and (3) no swimmers will be permitted under the raft.
> Note these special features: feather touch, velvet carriage, instant margins, and one-half space key.

3 — Use the colon before a quotation that is long or one formally introduced by such words as *thus, the following, as follows.*

> The Secretary of Defense made the following statement: "The United States will continue to build up its fleet of atomic-powered submarines."
> The lawyer stated his interpretation as follows: "Under the contract you are obligated to return the equipment as soon as you are finished with it."

Before a direct quotation that is short, however, or one that is informally introduced, a comma is customary.

> Mr. Ober said, "It's late; let's go home."
> At that time the chairman announced, "The committee has decided that all reports must be submitted, in duplicate, by Monday, June 15."

If the quotation does not interrupt the sentence pattern, no punctuation is used.

At that time the chairman announced that "all reports must be submitted, in duplicate, by Friday, May 23."
The efficiency expert stated that he had "completed the preliminary check of the company's operating procedures."

4 — Use the colon to separate hours and minutes expressed in figures: 11:30 a.m., 7:49 p.m. Where all figures refer to time, as on a timetable, the period is often used instead of the colon.

The question mark. The question mark reinforces the use of interrogatory function words and inverted word order in signaling questions.

1 — Use the question mark after a direct question.

How many pages of manuscript has she typed?
He asked, "Where is the conference to be held?"
Did many people respond to the questionnaire?

The question mark should not be used after an indirect question, that is, after a question that the writer is not reporting word for word.

The program chairman asked Mr. Murphy whether he would address the spring meeting.
The new customer asked whether the company had a plan for installment buying.
Jack asked whether the mail had come.

The question mark is not necessary after a courtesy question. That is, after a sentence disguised as a question out of courtesy but actually embodying a request or command, one may omit the question mark.

Will you please send me a credit memorandum at once.
Will you please ship me the order not later than July 20.

2 — Use the question mark after the individual members of a series, if each member might be expanded into a complete question. In such situations the question mark corresponds to a comma or a semicolon and should be followed by a small letter.

How do you like botany? history? typing?
What is the population of Texas? of New York? of California?

In business messages, many writers avoid the use of multiple question marks (???) for emphasis.

The exclamation point. The exclamation point is used after a word, a phrase, or a sentence to indicate strong emotion or sharp emphasis.

Note that overuse of the exclamation point weakens its effectiveness. In business messages (except, perhaps, humorously), most writers do not use multiple exclamation points (!!!) for emphasis.

What an astonishing answer!
Don't give up!
No! That's not true!

• APPLYING EFFECTIVE ENGLISH

Oral Applications

• **1.** Discuss all errors in punctuation in the following inquiry. Be prepared to explain your corrections.

I am writing to learn what scholarships are available at Northeastern University? The field in which I plan to major is business administration, the scholarships in that area; therefore, are of greatest interest to me.

What is the deadline for submitting applications for admission. What is the deadline for submitting applications for scholarships. Would it be possible for me to consult with some member of the Department of Business Administration. If so, what procedure should I follow in arranging such a consultation?

In high school I have taken the following courses in business; typing; shorthand; consumer economics; and business English. I am interested in determining whether this background will qualify me for some business electives during my freshman year?

If possible, I would like to live in a dormitory, please send me; therefore, the necessary application form. Would you please send me; also, the current undergraduate catalog?

• **2.** Act out the following situations. One student should take the role of supervisor; another, the role of typist:

1 — The supervisor explains to the typist, with examples, the distinction in use between a comma and a semicolon.
2 — The supervisor explains to the typist, with examples, the distinction between a semicolon and a colon.

Written Applications

● **1.** Rewrite the following sentences, inserting colons and semicolons where necessary.

1 — The books were shipped promptly as a result they were received in time for the fall term.

2 — The discussion brought out these points about the reproductions of the paintings fine quality, excellent appearance, reasonable price, and immediate availability.

3 — The plane leaves Chicago at 10 30 a.m. it arrives in Miami at 1 15 p.m.

4 — The principal said that the graduates of his school are well trained that they have had no difficulty, in recent years, in obtaining desirable positions and that they easily fulfill all of the requirements of the positions they hold.

5 — His check was not filled out properly consequently, the bank would not honor it.

6 — A great deal of research, you understand, has gone into the preparation of our proposal data and materials have been collected from business, educational, and governmental sources.

● **2.** Rewrite the following sentences, adding needed marks of punctuation.

1 — Although the weather is favorable the plane will not take off this morning in fact it may not make the trip at all

2 — Your application must be postmarked no later than 2 00 a m Friday October 16

3 — What I can hardly believe it

4 — The difficult we do at once The impossible takes a little longer

5 — Do you believe that the center of population is in Illinois in Missouri in Ohio in Indiana

6 — Will you please send me your new spring summer and fall catalogs

7 — Mrs McCoy asked whether the children had seen the parade

8 — When will it be possible for Thelma to finish this work

9 — The Internal Revenue Service wishes this matter to be taken care of promptly in fact it has asked us to submit our records before the end of the week.

10 — The history book cost $4 55 the typewriting and shorthand books $4 each

SECTION 4

The Apostrophe

The apostrophe, with the suffix -s, can make a noun into a special kind of modifier.

The apostrophe. A surprising number of messages improperly use or improperly omit apostrophes. Many messages containing such mistakes reach enormous audiences. These errors cause observant readers to react with amusement or with contempt. A contemptuous or amused reaction to business writing is likely to be highly unprofitable. Accordingly, whenever you add a suffix -s to a noun, consider first whether an apostrophe is necessary. If it is necessary, be sure to place the apostrophe correctly.

THE APOSTROPHE WITH THE SUFFIX S SHOWS POSSESSION

One important way to show your ability in writing English is to use the apostrophe correctly in forming the possessive case of nouns. The principles governing the use of the apostrophe are simple. Once you have mastered them, only careful proofreading will be needed to insure that your writing (as well as the texts of messages for which you must prepare perfect copies) is free of errors in the use of the apostrophe.

Three kinds of errors are common: (1) omitting an apostrophe when it is needed, (2) inserting an apostrophe in the wrong place, and (3) using an apostrophe when none should be used.

The "possessive" form is used to show possession (Kermit's football, Mr. Adler's house), but also to show many other relationships. For example, it is used to show origin or source (the fire's warmth, the lamp's glow, America's businessmen), kind or type (a man's hat, a children's book). It is also used to show authorship (Shakespeare's *Macbeth*, Hemingway's *A Farewell to Arms*), and other connections (Barbara's red hair, Mr. Godfrey's freckles, Rembrandt's "The Night Watch," Grandmother's cooking skill, etc.).

Singular possessive forms. The possessive case of a singular noun is formed by adding the apostrophe and *s* ('s) to the noun. The same relationship can be indicated by a prepositional phrase introduced by *of* (or, occasionally, by *for*).

> The attorney's office is on the second floor. (office of the attorney)
> A month's notice is required. (notice of a month)

The possessive of a few singular nouns ending in *s* may drop the final *s* to avoid an awkward succession of *s* or *z* sounds. Thus, if a singular word ending in *s* (or *s* sound—like *conscience*) contains more than one syllable, one may use the apostrophe alone (') to form the possessive. If a singular word ending in *s* contains one syllable only, use the apostrophe and *s* ('s).

> They approved Mr. *Corliss'* suggestions. (Two syllables)
> Many courtesies are extended for *politeness'* sake. (Three syllables)
> The *class's* performance was excellent. (One syllable)
> He examined *Ross's* statement. (One syllable)

Words like *someone, one,* and *anyone* add the apostrophe and *s* to form the possessive. Note, however, that the possessive forms of the personal pronouns never involve the use of an apostrophe: my/mine, our/ours, you/yours, his/his, her/hers, its, their/theirs.

> Someone's accounting text was left on the desk. Is it yours?
> Is anyone's report ready? Rosanne has not finished hers.

Plural possessive forms. The small group of nouns which form their plurals without an *s* suffix (e.g., *child/children*) form the plural possessive by adding the apostrophe and *s* to the plural form of the noun (*children's*).

> The salesmen's duties included keeping accurate records. (duties of the salesmen)
> That store sells women's and children's clothing. (clothing for women and for children)

The plural possessive of nouns whose plurals involve an *s* suffix (for example, *boy/boys*) is formed by adding an apostrophe after the suffix *s* (*boys'*). Most nouns in English follow this pattern.

> The boys' baseball equipment is kept in the club house. (baseball equipment of the boys)
> The ladies' answers were promptly submitted. (answers of the ladies)

Put the apostrophe in the right place. A singular possessor and plural possessor are distinguished *by the part of the word that comes before the apostrophe.* Note that the phrase form of the possessive provides an instant check of whether the possessor is singular or plural:

Apostrophe Form		*Phrase Form*
the firm's patent rights	=	the patent rights of the firm
the firms' patent rights	=	the patent rights of the firms
the trainman's wages	=	the wages of the trainman
the trainmen's wages	=	the wages of the trainmen
Mr. Haymond's office	=	the office of Mr. Haymond
Mr. Haymonds' office	=	the office of Mr. Haymonds

RULES FOR FORMING SPECIAL KINDS OF POSSESSIVES

1 – To show joint ownership, add the possessive sign to the last word only.

West and Fox's stores (the stores owned by West and Fox) are on Northern Boulevard.

2 – To show separate ownership, add the possessive sign to the name of each owner.

West's and Fox's stores (stores owned separately by West and Fox) are on Northern Boulevard.

3 – In compound expressions add the sign of possession to the last word only.

The editor in chief's responsibility is great.
His mother-in-law's home was in Algonquin, Illinois.
The Senator from Iowa's observations were most helpful.

4 – In such expressions as *our friend Mr. Packard* and *your cousin Leroy* (noun plus restrictive appositive), the sign of possession is added to the last word.

That is our friend Mr. Packard's magazine.
Your cousin Leroy's performance was superb.

If the appositive is nonrestrictive, it is preferable to substitute the phrase form with *of.*

For example:

The display of Vaughn, the florist, was unusually ·attractive.
The profits of Day, the jeweler, showed an increase last year.

5 — Nouns and pronouns used to modify a gerund (a verb form ending in *ing* and used as a noun) have the possessive form. Thus, just as we say "Joe's car is . . ." and "His car is . . . ," we say "Joe's proofreading is . . ." and "His proofreading is. . . ."

Robert's typing needs improvement.
What is your reaction to Mr. Payne's resigning from the club?
You can count on the printer's delivering the books next week.
Sheldon improved his swimming by daily practice.

6 — Nouns naming concepts or inanimate objects are often used in the possessive when the resulting expression is not awkward. Here are common examples: *a stone's throw, the war's end, the ship's fuel supply, the car's axle, a dollar's worth, Chicago's new harbor,* etc. Nouns showing various time spans are often used in the possessive:

SINGULAR	PLURAL
a day's work	five days' work
a week's journey	two weeks' journey
a year's trial	three years' trial

Avoid the possessive form of nouns naming inanimate objects, however, when the resulting expression seems clumsy. For example:

AVOID	BETTER
The door's hinge	The hinge of the door
The porch's roof	The roof of the porch
The typewriter's keyboard	The keyboard of the typewriter

7 — Follow the official or customary form for titles and place names, many of which omit the apostrophe.

Central Executive Secretaries Association
National Sales Executives Club
Western States Merchants Association
Eastern Newspaper Editors Association
Veterans Administration
Teachers College, Columbia University
Harpers Ferry, Virginia
The Explorers Club

THE APOSTROPHE SHOWS THE OMISSION OF LETTERS IN A CONTRACTION

Be careful to place the apostrophe properly in a contraction. The apostrophe stands for and replaces the missing letter or letters. Contractions are used for two main reasons. First, they are used in messages and memorandums to people whom the writer knows in a friendly, informal way. Second, they are used in sales presentations and advertisements to give a personal tone. In formal reports, policy statements, regulations, directives, and similar kinds of business writing, contractions are generally considered inappropriate. The following contractions occur frequently in informal writing:

I'm	I am	*she's*	she is	*haven't*	have not
I'll	I will	*she'll*	she will	*hadn't*	had not
I've	I have	*it's*	it is	*couldn't*	could not
we're	we are	*they're*	they are	*wouldn't*	would not
we'll	we will	*they've*	they have	*can't*	cannot
we've	we have	*they'll*	they will	*shan't*	shall not
you're	you are	*isn't*	is not	*shouldn't*	should not
you'll	you will	*aren't*	are not	*doesn't*	does not
you've	you have	*wasn't*	was not	*don't*	do not
he's	he is	*weren't*	were not	*didn't*	did not
he'll	he will	*hasn't*	has not	*won't*	will not

Take special care to distinguish between the contraction *it's,* which means "it is," and the possessive form *its.* Because *its* is a personal pronoun, no apostrophe is used to form its possessive.

The contraction *won't,* meaning "will not," originated in the Middle English expression *wol not.* The auxiliary verb *wol* has otherwise vanished from the English language.

Words like *o'clock* involve the same principle of contraction as that illustrated in the list of contractions above. The apostrophe indicates that *ten o'clock* is a contraction of *ten of the clock.*

THE APOSTROPHE IS CUSTOMARILY USED TO FORM THE PLURAL OF ABBREVIATIONS, LETTERS, FIGURES, AND CITED WORDS

The company hired two Ph.D.'s to organize the program.
Carelessly written *l's, i's,* and *t's* often cause confusion.
The 5's, 10's, and 20's had already been totalled.
Too many *and's, but's,* and *for's* make sentences unnecessarily long.
His *if's* and *maybe's* make me doubt that he will adopt the plan.

• *APPLYING EFFECTIVE ENGLISH*

Oral Application

In class discussion, revise these sentences. Whenever a phrase indicating possession is used, substitute the possessive form of the noun.

1 — The achievement records of the students were on file.
2 — The leaders of the country had formulated careful plans.
3 — The coats of the teachers were in the office of the principal.
4 — The report of the Department of the Treasury was optimistic.
5 — The orders of the president were carried out exactly.
6 — The secretary of the committee was reappointed by the chairman.
7 — The student council of the school held a meeting each week.
8 — The recommendations of the commission will not be made public.
9 — Terry was delighted by the decision of the teacher.
10 — The representatives of the counties are considering joint action.

Written Applications

• 1. In the following sentences, insert apostrophes wherever necessary.

1 — Carelessly formed *ms* and *ns* sometimes cause misreadings.
2 — The library stays open until nine oclock every night.
3 — Its time to leave, isnt it?
4 — Mr. Kings conversation contained too many *Is* and *mes*.
5 — The mens club planned the clean-up campaign.
6 — Six M.S.s and two Ph.D.s were conferred at the commencement.
7 — In six months time the new highway will be in use.
8 — Didnt you transcribe Mr. Eysters dictation yesterday?
9 — The presidents secretary was entitled to a three weeks vacation, wasnt she?
10 — The three boys little sister sang their fathers latest songs.
11 — The 2s, 3s, and 4s are the issues that were specified.
12 — The doctor prescribed a years rest for the exhausted man.
13 — Wouldnt Jeans sister tell her teacher the actress name?
14 — Didn't Kevin receive the message his fathers secretary delivered?
15 — That firms policies have been violated on several occasions.

• 2. Rewrite the following sentences. Whenever the possessive case is used, substitute a prepositional phrase introduced by *of* (or *for*).

1 — The executive's office was richly carpeted.
2 — The sale of boys' suits reduced the store's inventory.
3 — The stockholders' money financed the company's expansion.
4 — High speeds are hard on a car's tires and on a driver's nerves.
5 — The audience applauded the actor's skillful performance.

SECTION 5

Quotation Marks; the Dash, Parentheses, and Brackets; Omission Marks; the Hyphen

Quotation marks enclose quoted material. The dash, parentheses, and brackets set off incidental comments. Omission marks indicate incomplete quotations. The hyphen makes one unit of two or more words.

Quotation marks. Quotation marks show the reader that the

enclosed material was originally written or spoken somewhere else. Usually someone other than the present writer wrote the passage. When quoting, the writer should make clear whose words are being quoted. Only in this way can the reader judge for himself whether the quoted information or opinions are likely to be reliable.

1 — Use quotation marks to enclose every direct quotation. A direct quotation consists of the exact words of the original. An indirect quotation expresses the thought of the original in different words and does not require quotation marks.

Right: Mr. Bruce said, "America has, since 1941, achieved the status of a world leader."

Right: Mr. Bruce said that America has become a world leader.

Right: Mr. Bruce said that "America has, since 1941, achieved the status of a world leader."

Wrong: Mr. Bruce said that "America has become a world leader."

This is an important convention. To omit quotation marks around material written by others would often imply that the material is one's own writing. Such a practice, whether deliberate or not, is called plagiarism. It is regarded as a form of dishonesty. Even if footnotes indicate one's source, quotation marks *must* enclose all material not phrased by the writer himself.

When the quotation is interrupted by words inserted by the speaker or the writer, both parts of the quotation are enclosed.

"Let us hope," said the Speaker of the House of Representatives, "that the vote is favorable."

In a continuous quotation of several complete sentences, quotation marks are used only at the beginning and at the end of the quotation.

General Collins commented as follows: "America is one of the two most powerful countries in the world. America carries heavy responsibilities. To meet the crisis ahead, the nation needs educated and devoted leaders."

If a quotation has several paragraphs, use quotation marks at the beginning of each paragraph and after the last paragraph. Sometimes, as a substitute for quotation marks, a long quotation is written in shorter lines (lines indented more than the main text).

Single quotation marks (' ') enclose a quotation within a quotation.

"Then," the speaker went on, "the manager said, 'Excellent, I approve the report,' and shook hands with the committee chairman."

2 — Use quotation marks to enclose the titles of subdivisions of published works (parts, chapters, sections, etc.) and the titles of magazine articles, reports, lectures, and the like.

In contrast, titles of books, booklets, essays, newspapers, magazines, plays, and other separately published works should be italicized. In typewriting, each word to be italicized is underlined.

Mr. Boyd's latest lecture, "New Methods in Data Processing," will be given next week.
I have read Mr. Abbott's article "See the World with the U. S. Navy," but have not read any of his other articles.
"Playing Tennis" is an interesting chapter in The Book of Sports.

3 — Use quotation marks or underlining to set off expressions cited for discussion, expressions regarded as inappropriate in your message, and expressions given as definitions.

His action was an example of "steam roller" methods.
An outworn expression is called a "stock phrase" or "cliche."
At this point the word "furthermore" may be used.
Because of is an example of a compound preposition.
The abbreviation e.g. means "for example."

Beware of using quotation marks too often for unusual words. In general, if a word or expression is inappropriate, find a substitute.

The dash. Make the dash of sufficient length to avoid confusion with the hyphen. The typewritten dash is made by striking the hyphen twice.

1 — Use the dash to show a sudden break in thought.

> He could learn in an hour—yet why should we
> try to convince him?

2 — Use the dash to separate the name of an author from an extract from his writings.

> "Determination is a key to success."—Blenheim.
> "Love truth, but pardon error."—Voltaire.

3 — Use the dash before an appositive to give special emphasis to the appositive. If the appositive is separated from its head, the dash sometimes increases the clarity of a sentence.

> Our history teacher asked us to study a particularly interesting report—
> the Berger Commission Report.
> One of the candidates for the scholarships—a boy named Steve
> Coulson—was interviewed by the committee.

4 — Use the dash to set off and emphasize important words or important points expressed parenthetically.

> Courtesy—for success in business, no trait is more essential.
> Those who opposed him—and there was vigorous opposition from
> many—still admired him for his courage.

Caution: Use the dash sparingly. To use it excessively suggests that one is ignorant of how to use other punctuation marks.

Parentheses. Parentheses enclose supplementary material which the writer wishes to include for the reader's convenience or for accuracy or clarity.

1 — Use parentheses when an amount expressed in words is followed by an expression of the same amount in figures.

> We agree to pay the sum of one hundred
> dollars ($100).
> The assessment will be fifty-five (55) dollars.

2 — Use parentheses to enclose numbers or letters in enumerations that are run into the text.

The investigator divided his report into four parts: (1) background of the problem, (2) evidence, (3) findings, and (4) recommendations.
Mr. Brinker advanced three objections to the plan: (a) excessive cost, (b) lack of public interest, and (c) unrealistic planning.

3 — Use parentheses to set off parenthetical, explanatory, or supplementary material.

The pictures of this event (see Illustrations 9-12) convey the President's elation.
In further announcements (watch for them in your local newspaper) details concerning dates and times will be given.
The revision (see page 127) corrected the errors.

Brackets. Brackets are used to enclose remarks a writer wishes to insert within material that he is quoting.

1 — Use brackets within quotations to enclose explanations, comments, or criticisms which you are inserting in the quoted material.

Austin makes the following statement: "Three counties [Winchester, Lake, and Wilson] opposed the amendment, but it became law."
Miss Tarr concluded: "These words [to, two, too] must be checked for spelling everytime they occur."

2 — Use brackets around the Latin word *sic* (meaning "thus") to indicate that an incorrect form within a quotation reproduces the original text exactly. Responsibility for the construction is thus referred to the author who is being quoted.

The announcement contained the following statement: "The principle [sic] will be chairman of the meeting."
Mr. Ringwald writes: "Under no circumstances will this company compromise it's [sic] high standards of service to the community."

3 — Use brackets to enclose a parenthetical expression within material already in parentheses.

He confirms your opinion (see, for example, *Business Leadership* [Third Edition] page 1).

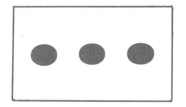

Omission marks, or ellipses. Ellipses signify the omission of words, sentences, or longer passages in quoted material. Three periods or dots (. . .) signify an omission. Four periods (. . . .) are used when the omitted portion ends at a period.

"The document, now in a rough draft, was submitted to the committee . . . for approval."

The report stated: "Each man had the responsibility for making suggestions. . . ."

In using ellipses, be certain that your omissions do not misrepresent, distort, or obscure the author's intended meaning.

The hyphen. The hyphen makes a unit of two or more words or parts of words.

1 — Use the hyphen to indicate the division of a word at the end of a line. Rules for the division of words at a line ending are given on page 666.

2 — Use the hyphen to join the parts of certain compound words. There is considerable variation in the form used to write compound words, especially compound nouns. Some are written as two separate words; some, as two words joined by a hyphen; and some, solid as one word. Any form recognized in the current edition of a good dictionary (like *Merriam-Webster's Collegiate Dictionary, Webster's New World Dictionary, American College Dictionary,* or Thorndike-Barnhart's *High School Dictionary*) is acceptable.

Like other rules in language, rules for hyphening compound words depend upon usage, which is always subject to change. The following statements summarize current practice.

a — A hyphen is frequently used with the prefixes *ex, self,* and *vice.* It is also used to join a prefix to a proper noun or adjective. It is not used with *co, de, pre, pro,* or *re,* except to prevent misinterpretation or mispronunciation.

ex-president	co-op (for co-operative)
self-made	recover (to regain)
vice-commander	re-cover (to cover again)
un-American	co-worker
pro-French	coauthor

b — A hyphen is usually used between two or more words serving as a single adjective *before* a noun. (In speech, stress is placed on the first element of such a compound. The compound is pronounced as a unit.)

a forty-hour week	some ready-to-wear suits
their eight-room house	those high-stepping majorettes
the hit-and-run driver	two man-eating tigers
each first-class ticket	all low-cost housing
her Book-of-the-Month Club notice	Mel's happy-go-lucky attitude

When such modifiers occur as predicate adjectives, they are usually not hyphened. In speech, such modifiers occurring as predicate adjectives are not marked by stress on their first element.

She is a well-known singer.
The singer is well known.
His up-to-the-minute review was interesting.
His review was up to the minute.
This wash-and-wear shirt is well made.
This shirt is for wash and wear, according to the label.

When an adverb ending in *ly* is used with an adjective or a participle, the phrase is usually not hyphened.

a widely praised action	the highly effective argument
an understandably difficult decision	an amazingly accurate prediction

c — A hyphen is used in compound numbers from twenty-one to ninety-nine when they are written as words.

twenty-three employees	ninety-six students
thirty-two of the applicants	forty-nine of his daily reports

d — A hyphen is used between the numerator and the denominator of a fraction written in words when it is used as a limiting adjective. When the fraction is used as a noun, the hyphen is omitted. (In addition, if the numerator or denominator contains a hyphen, the hyphen between them is omitted.)

a one-third share	three sixteenths of an inch
one third of the amount	a three-sixteenths allowance
a three-fourths majority	twenty-six hundredths
three fourths of the members	twenty-two sixty-fourths

e — A series of hyphened compounds with a common element usually retains the hyphen even though the common element occurs only once.

one-, two-, and three-year contracts
six-, seven-, and eight-room houses
short- and long-term policies

• *APPLYING EFFECTIVE ENGLISH*

Oral Applications

• **1.** Pronounce each of the following sentences aloud, as naturally as possible. Through class discussion try to identify the features of "oral punctuation" which distinguish the contrasted sentences; then explain the differences in meaning.

A. (1) There was a blackbird sitting on the telephone wire.
   (2) There was a black bird sitting on the telephone wire.
B. (1) Mr. Higgins said that.
   (2) Mr. Higgins said that?
   (3) Mr. Higgins said that!
   (4) Mr. Higgins said that—. [Here the speaker stops short.]
C. (1) The greenhouse was damaged by the hailstones.
   (2) The green house was damaged by the hailstones.
D. (1) "The principal," said the teacher, "is well liked."
   (2) The principal said the teacher is well liked.

• **2.** Act out the following situations. One student should take the role of the employer; another, the role of a new clerk-typist:

1 — The employer explains why words must be spelled accurately in all company correspondence.
2 — The employer explains how the new clerk-typist can learn to proofread accurately by concentrating and pointing at each word as he checks it.

Written Applications

• **1.** Rewrite these sentences, inserting the necessary punctuation marks.

1 — The title of Chapter IV is Writing That Wins Sales
2 — The point of this report though I do not believe I can accept it as correct is that the company cannot remain solvent
3 — The vice president of the firm was a self made man

4 — Only two salesmen were given this high honor Bill Duffy and Jim Hawley

5 — His salary as an accountant is twelve thousand dollars $12,000

6 — The teacher said I want this assignment to be handed in Monday without fail

7 — Cawler headed his column Up to the Minute News

8 — It will be difficult the secretary said for me to complete the review in so short a time.

9 — The correct balance is $19.76 $23.76—$4

10 — Truth is the highest thing that man may keep Geoffrey Chaucer

11 — The following accounting records are required 1 the voucher register 2 the check register 3 the general journal and 4 the general ledger

12 — The speech was entertaining and well organized

13 — It was a well organized entertaining speech

14 — The increase in our sales see Charts 1 to 3 is undoubtedly a result of the spring promotional campaign.

15 — Depreciation amortization and accumulation all of these are explained in the section on bookkeeping.

- 2. In the following sentences, insert the necessary punctuation.

1 — The corporations slogan is Quality First.

2 — The remnants of material came in three five ten and eleven yard lengths

3 — The plant manager said I will assign Mr. Mason to take care of this problem

4 — When the furniture becomes worn it will be recovered by an expert upholsterer

5 — The police recovered the mans car the thief however was not captured until two weeks later.

6 — This widely used product is an invention of the exforeman

7 — The personnel manager the speaker concluded said Go ahead with the plans to hire two more secretaries I agree that additional help is necessary

8 — The article Plan for Tomorrow appeared in the August issue of Economic Pointers

9 — The trend of sales see the charts on pages 10 and 11 is slowly improving.

10 — Miss Eversole made the following announcement in her English class If anyone in the class wishes to do additional work outside of class for extra credit he should discuss the matter with me I shall assign the work for him to do The student may have two weeks in which to complete the assignment

SECTION 6

Rules of Order Among Punctuation Marks

Punctuation marks occurring together follow a fixed sequence.

Rules of order in punctuation. Two or more punctuation marks often occur at the same point in a sentence. In such a situation the punctuation marks should be arranged according to the following rules of order:

1 — A period following an abbreviation is used before any other mark of sentence punctuation. When the abbreviation occurs at the end of a declarative sentence, a single period follows. Do not use two periods in a row.

> Did he arrive before 10 a.m.?
> Do you expect him to send it C.O.D.?
> E. D. Mountz, Ph.D., whom you met last week, is the
>   new research director of the Ribicoff Laird Corp.
> Miss Roth arrived at 7:45 p.m.
> The dean has an M.A.; he is working toward a Ph.D.

2 — Quotation marks are used with other marks of punctuation as follows:

a — At the end of a quotation, a comma or a period is always placed inside the quotation mark. At the end of a quotation, a semicolon or a colon is always placed outside the quotation mark.

> "I saw him," she said, "as he entered the door."
> Mr. Elliott has not yet read the article "Education and
>   Business"; he has, however, read "Business Cycles."
> I have this to say about her "intuition": it is fictitious.

> "The Clark Report," according to the *Tribune*, "omits
>   certain facts"; however, the paper makes this con-
>   cession: "Improvements should result from the study."

b — A question mark, an exclamation point, or a dash occurs inside the quotation mark if it punctuates the quotation.

> Mr. Todd inquired, "Where are you going?"
> Miss Ellis said, "Well done!"
> Leif remarked, "Our plan—if you can call it a plan—"
>   when he was interrupted.
> The letter ended with this question: "Will *you* help?"

An initial quotation ending with its own mark of punctuation is not set off by a comma or period.

> "I'm late!" Mrs. Barr explained as she hurried down
>   the street.
> "I am so busy that—" is all I heard Miss Chilton say
>   as she rushed past my desk.
> "Can you be there?" Major Shelton asked.
> "Watch out!" exclaimed the workman.

c — A question mark, an exclamation point, or a dash occurs outside the quotation mark if it punctuates the entire sentence.

> Why was Barry Ingram "fired"?
> Did the supervisor really say, "This is good work"?
> How enthusiastically that crowd received Stephen
>   Douglas, "The Little Giant"!
> Why did Eunice say, "I shall type the memorandum"?
> "A good book is the precious life-blood of a master-
>   spirit, embalmed and treasured up on purpose to a
>   life beyond life."—John Milton.

d — Punctuation for a quotation within a quotation follows the preceding rules. When the quotation within a quotation occurs at the end of a sentence, the single quotation mark precedes the double quotation marks.

> Miss Brown said, "I read the article 'Small Business Management.' "
> Did Mr. Nesbitt say, "I read the article 'Small Business Management' "?
> Laura said, "Did you read the article 'Small Business Management'?"
> Marvin said, "I read the article 'What Lies Ahead for Small Business
>   Management?' "

3 — Parentheses are used with other marks of punctuation as follows:

a. If the punctuation mark applies to the whole sentence and not specifically to the material in parentheses, the punctuation mark follows the second parenthesis.

Pride (generally unrecognized by the proud man himself), can be a motive for extraordinary effort.

The chemical analysis of those cleansers has been completed and is included in the report (as in Formula 2).

b. If the punctuation mark applies specifically to the material in parentheses, the punctuation mark precedes the second parenthesis.

This article ("Successful Business Practices") was written five years ago.

When I heard his voice (he whispered, "Who is there?"), I was greatly startled.

Mr. Mott phrased the original question ("When were you last employed?"); Mr. Singer suggested the revision.

4 — A parenthetical expression set off by dashes sometimes requires a question mark or an exclamation point. In such a situation, the punctuation mark is placed before the second dash.

Ron Baker—is he the treasurer or the secretary?—has made an appointment with you for ten o'clock.

Spacing after punctuation marks. Within a sentence, space once after each mark of punctuation, with the following exceptions:

1 — Within a sentence, space *twice* after a colon:

He said: "A competent secretary is essential."

2 — Within a sentence, *do not space* after:

a. A period within an abbreviation, or a colon within a time designation.

Dr. Young, Ph.D., and Dr. Floyd, LL.D., left at 12:30 p.m.
to attend a meeting.

b. A period used as a decimal—

A difference of 1.638 resulted.

c. A dash—

Then we went to--but you are not interested in that.

d. A hyphen—

```
The well-known editor will be the first speaker.
```

e. An initial quotation mark—

```
The plant manager asked, "Have you finished your work?"
```

f. An apostrophe within a word—

```
Mr. Castleman didn't arrive on time.
```

g. A beginning parenthesis—

```
(See page 5 of the price list.)
```

h. A beginning bracket—

```
The contractor's letter stated:   "The estimate was submitted
     in May [19--]."
```

3 — At the end of a sentence, space *twice* after a punctuation mark.

```
There you are!  What are you doing?  Please type this page
     next.  How soon will it be finished?
```

● *APPLYING EFFECTIVE ENGLISH*

Oral Applications

● 1. Be prepared to justify, in class discussion, all punctuation you use in the sentences of Written Applications 1 and 2.

● 2. In class discussion indicate what punctuation mark would be appropriate at each point numbered in the following passage. Justify each decision you make.

> The twenty-fifth anniversary report concluded (1) (2) When Mr. Jordan asked (3) twenty-five years ago (4) (5) How can this firm best prosper (6) (7) his answer to his own question was as follows (8) (9) By giving full value and prompt service to all our customers (10) (11) That has been the secret of Jordan Manufacturing Company's extraordinary growth (12) and that will be the key to its future success (13) (14)

● 3. A committee of three has been formed to improve the following form letter intended to invite customers to the company's annual spring showing of women's clothing. The firm's president wants the letter to be friendlier and less stuffy. He has suggested using shorter sentences and simpler, more natural words.

One student may take the role of committee chairman, while two others serve as committee members. Through discussion of suggestions with the committee members, the committee chairman should attempt to develop a revised letter that will satisfy the president. Make the customer seem more important whenever possible. Here is the text of the original letter which the president found unsatisfactory:

Nathan R. Walworth and Co. is pleased to issue this announcement concerning its annual vernal exhibition of fashionable ladies' dresses and coats—stunning garments designed by some of the world's fashion leaders from Paris and New York, and many of them originals never before shown to the public— ranging in price from $18 to $325. This showing, which will be limited to 1,507 of our best customers who have charge accounts with us, will be held in the twelfth floor showroom of our Oak Ridge store at the intersection of Kennedy Boulevard and Highway 57 (the showroom is in the northwest corner of the main building), at three o'clock on the afternoon of March 13, 19--.

Nathan R. Walworth and Co. takes pleasure in including your name on its select invitation list, and it wishes to extend to you the special privilege of bringing with you to this gala event a guest of your choosing.

You will regret it sorely if you pass up the opportunity offered by Nathan R. Walworth and Co. in this letter, or if you fail to take advantage of our invitation to you to be accompanied by a guest.

Sincerely,

Nathan R. Walworth
President

Written Applications

● **1.** Rewrite these sentences, inserting the necessary punctuation.

1 — Did the principal really say This program has been very carefully planned

2 — We shall leave Mrs. Kidwell said as soon as everyone is ready

3 — Sue said I have finished reading the article English for Everyone

4 — Isnt there a clearer way to phrase this idea the editor asked

5 — Michael Murphy Ph D will succeed Dr Abrams as head of the English department

6 — Mr Fisher is he the president of the group

7 — Sandra who had voted against the proposal exclaimed Wonderful when she heard it had been defeated

8 — Mr. Edwards answered Thats a great plan

9 — Let me tell you what I was all Mrs. Hill had a chance to say before she was interrupted

10 — Help she shrieked the moment she saw the burglar at the safe

- **2. Rewrite these sentences, inserting the necessary punctuation.**

1 — Although Dr Hackers flight was scheduled to depart at 2 30 p m he did not arrive at the airport until 3 30 p m

2 — The difference amounted to but its not important remarked the clerk

3 — What is the name of the senior class president the senior class secretary the valedictorian

4 — The head of the department Dr John M. Greer became chairman of the board at Smith Brothers Inc

5 — Lonzo Kidwell M D of the Ferguson Clinic subscribes to Business Week Time and The New Republic

6 — The physician asked Have you read Dr Hicks latest article Healthy People are Happy People

7 — I havent read the article The Secretarys Responsibilities however I am reading the one entitled Using Time Wisely

8 — The interviewer had not yet come in therefore the applicants for the job had to wait

9 — What is the capital of France of Japan of Argentina

10 — The graphs see pages 15 to 21 reveal the growth of our foreign business during the last three decades

11 — The boy answered I have written a theme entitled Do You Want a Summer Job

12 — Berry Bros Inc sent out over two thousand invitations to their grand opening

13 — How long have you been a stenographer the employment manager asked

14 — Good heavens I seem to have misplaced the report

15 — Mr. Austings speech Private Enterprise and Democracy concerned the importance of the profit motive his speech Business and Government dealt with regulations intended to prevent monopolistic practices

16 — The two paper salesmen spoke as if they were old friends but in fact they had never met until the sales conference

17 — Mr. Fawcett started with the company she said as an office boy now he is the president

18 — To sell the salesman must believe in his product

19 — A past characteristic of business writing has been its deadly monotony its pompous unnaturalness its ponderous formality and its stifling dullness

20 — My old friend who is from my hometown is leaving for St Paul Minnesota on the 8 45 flight

SECTION 7

Capitalization

Capitals signal the occurrence of proper nouns, as well as the beginning of a new sentence.

Capitalization of proper nouns. The general rule is that any proper noun must be capitalized. There are, however, many irregularities involved in the conventions governing capitalization in Modern English. In deciding what words to capitalize, you will find the following guides helpful.

1 — Capitalize the name of a person exactly as he himself capitalizes it.

Marianne MacMurray	Patrick O'Brian
Herbert von Karajan	Robert McDowell
Fred C. Van DeRyt	Rey de la Torre
Ray McL. van Metre	Giuseppe di Stefano

2 — Capitalize a word when it is used as a part of a specific name, even though the word is otherwise used as an adjective or as a common noun.

Little Rock	Executive House
Green Mountains	Connecticut Avenue
Eastern Michigan University	Glacier National Park
Sunbeam Baking Company	Missouri River
Ocean View Restaurant	Lake Geneva

Do not capitalize a geographic term such as *ocean, river, harbor,* or *valley* that is not used as part of the name. This rule holds even though the term precedes the name. Do not capitalize a geographic term that is used in the plural, unless it is an integral part of a proper name.

the valley of the Colorado	the Arctic and Antarctic oceans
the river Nile	the Colorado and Rio Grande rivers
the Allegheny Mountains	Warm Springs, Georgia

3 — Capitalize names of regions and localities. Do not capitalize nouns or adjectives indicating direction.

Capitalize:	*Do Not Capitalize:*
North Carolina	eastern Pennsylvania
the South (also, a Southerner)	the southern part of Florida
the Far East	hiking west through the park
Upper Peninsula	southern California
Latin America	northern Idaho
the West (also, a Westerner)	an east wind

4 — Capitalize the names of specific buildings, locations, ships, trains, etc.

Building:	the Wrigley Building	*Room:*	the Rainbow Room
Library:	the Omaha Public Library	*Train:*	the Broadway Limited
Hall:	Carnegie Hall	*Ship:*	U.S.S. Nautilus

5 — Capitalize the names of specific groups and organizations.

Churches:	the Second Presbyterian Church
Associations:	the National Geographic Society
Clubs:	the Rotary Club, the Columbian Yacht Club
Organizations:	the North Atlantic Treaty Organization
Departments:	the Department of Health, Education, and Welfare
Firms:	the Hammond Organ Company
Corporations:	the Standard Products Corporation
Institutions:	the Smithsonian Institute, the Reading Institute
Schools:	North High School, Lincoln Elementary School
Magazines:	the *Atlantic,* the *Reader's Digest,* the *Scientific American*
Newspapers:	the New York *Times,* the Chicago *Daily News*

6 — Capitalize the names of days of the week and months of the year. Do not capitalize names of the seasons.

The report will be distributed on Monday, May 30.
The fall and winter catalog will be ready late in the summer.

7 — Capitalize words based on proper nouns unless these words have developed specialized meanings.

Capitalize:		*Do Not Capitalize:*	
American	French	boycott	italicize
English	Georgian	chinaware	pasteurize
Italian	Danish	mercerize	turkey (dinner)

8 — Capitalize the names of divisions of knowledge only as titles of specific courses. Do not capitalize such names when they are used to denote studies in general or common divisions of knowledge.

Merle is taking World History, Typing II, and Chemistry I.
The required subjects are history, mathematics, and English.

9 — Capitalize principal words (including the first word) in headings and in the names of books and articles.

See Chapter IV, "The History of English Pronunciation in the Modern Period," of Professor Wyld's book *A History of Modern Colloquial English*.
The Close Reading of Factual Prose teaches the student to read analytically and critically.

10 — Capitalize business, professional, military, and honorary titles when they accompany a proper name. (Some established writers prefer to capitalize such titles only in the following situations. First, when the title *precedes* the proper name. Or, second, when the title indicates a world-recognized position. Since there is divided usage among reputable authorities on this point, either practice is acceptable as long as it is followed consistently.)

Dr. Ellis P. Jann, Professor of English, and Dr. Rufus J. Talbott, Associate Professor of English, have collaborated on many books.
Mr. John Drake, Honorary Chairman of the Board, Universal Motors Corporation, addressed the annual meeting of stockholders.
Edward Levi, Chancellor of the University of Chicago, is a former dean of the University of Chicago Law School.
General George C. Marshall was Chief of Staff of the United States Army during World War II.
The Honorable Thomas Waters, Director-General of Harrod's, Ltd., arrived in the United States to consult with business leaders here.

11 — Capitalize the titles of high government officials when the titles are being used instead of proper names.

The President of the United States will hold a press conference later this week.
The President will hold a press conference later this week.
When the Senator returned, he was informed of the invitation.
The Secretary of State made an official visit to the Far East.
As the Prime Minister finished his speech, the entire assembly cheered.

12 — In addition, capitalize the following words:

a. The first word of every sentence.

b. The first word and all titles and nouns in the salutation of a letter.

My dear Sir: Dear Mrs. Beatty:
My dear Mr. Ashby: My dear Glenn:

c. The first word in the complimentary close of a letter.

Yours sincerely,   Sincerely yours,
Yours very sincerely,   Very sincerely yours,

d. Sometimes, the first word of a complete sentence or passage following a colon. The use of a capital emphasizes the independent status of the following passage.

The latest quarterly evaluation contained one extremely important observation: The bonus plan has been effective in raising morale.

Here, the statement following the colon, since it begins with a capital letter, is emphasized. In the following sentence the statements after the colon are treated as an ordinary continuation of the sentence.

He gave two reasons for his decision: the club members are willing to do the work, and the materials are now available.

e. The first word of a quotation that is introduced formally.

The dispatch concluded as follows: "Later this month, representatives of foreign business firms will meet with State Department officials."
Mr. Holland said, "Standards must be kept high in our schools."
President Ankers commented, "Our records demonstrate that competent use of English is indispensable for success."

Sometimes, however, the first word of the quoted material was not capitalized in the original text. This situation often arises if the quotation is brought into the sentence without use of a comma or colon. In this event, do not capitalize the first word of the quotation.

President Ankers commented that "competent use of English is indispensable for success."

f. The pronoun *I* and the interjection *O*.

g. Any noun or pronoun used to refer to the Deity.

The missionary spoke of God and His mercy.

h. When followed by a number, a noun or an abbreviation designating the formal parts of a written work.

Volume I	Vol. I	Chapter 5
Book II	Article II	Section 9
Unit III	Act V, Scene I	Canto XX
Part 4	Paragraph XV	But: page 1

If you are in doubt whether to capitalize a word, you can generally find the answer by referring to an up-to-date dictionary. When you are proofreading, keep proper capitalization in mind. Careless or foolish errors in capitalization stand out and will be noticed by any attentive reader.

• *APPLYING EFFECTIVE ENGLISH*

Oral Applications

• **1.** Nothing in spoken English corresponds to the use of capitals in the written language. In class discussion identify as many other features of the written language as you can that have *no* corresponding feature in the spoken language. Does the absence of such features cause ambiguity or confusion in the spoken language? What advantages do these features offer in the written language?

• **2.** In class discussion identify as many features of the written language as you can that *do* have corresponding features in the spoken language and indicate as precisely as possible what these corresponding features are.

• **3.** An inexperienced typist has just joined an office staff. She did not succeed in mastering the principles of capitalization during her formal schooling. The supervisor believes the typist has ability and takes time to explain the distinction between common nouns and proper nouns. She uses numerous examples involving streets, parks, schools, churches, and companies, among others. One student may take the role of the supervisor; another student, the role of the typist.

Written Applications

● **1.** Supply all necessary capitals and punctuation in the following sentences. Correct all errors.

1 — the board of education of the edgebrook school district holds its regular meetings at the forest park university club

2 — traveling through the rocky mountains and visiting rocky mountain national park yosemite national park and other national parks in the west is an enjoyable way to spend a vacation

3 — speed and accuracy in typing and in transcribing said our instructor Mrs. Martha Thomas are essential to the success of a stenographer

4 — when his dictating improves Mr Ronald Blair our new assistant sales manager will begin to dictate his executive messages.

5 — the prestige of the firm was increased by the favorable publicity given to the presidents speech the future of american business

6 — The marvel products company was located near the maumee river because of the excellent facilities for shipping available there.

7 — the office manager of the mayfield printing company made the following announcement accuracy is of utmost importance in proofreading in the future we must make a determined effort to eliminate all mistakes

8 — Its difficult to lecture when an audience is rude or inattentive

9 — the delegation from france visited farms in kansas in iowa and in illinois

10 — the student council of cincinnatis taft day school discussed the best methods for encouraging students to exercise initiative

● **2.** Punctuate, capitalize, and correct the following sentences.

1 — his Office is in the bankers trust building

2 — he lives on the South side of english square

3 — when r s watts became a member of the bankers club; He was made responsible for the Entertainment for the year

4 — the new york times, advertises Our Spring Sale of Novelties in its' may 3 issue

5 — chapter vii, of our textbook, applied economics begins on Page 273

6 — the oak lawn pottery company specializes in Chinaware

7 — the airliner follows a Northern route then, turns sharply East, and flies a Northeastern route, landing at the westend airport

8 — the Honorable Bond Nelson gave the address

9 — please address Inquiries to 2733 mason drive boise idaho

10 — Charles F Conners m d has his office in the doctors building

SECTION 8

Expression of Numbers

General rules govern the use of figures or words.

How to handle numbers. Should a number be written in words or in figures? This can be a puzzling question. The problem does not arise in the writing of business forms such as invoices, sales tickets, or purchase orders. In such records figures are used almost entirely. In letters, memorandums, and business reports in paragraph form, however, sometimes words and sometimes figures are appropriate. In messages of this kind a careful writer expresses numbers in accordance with the following guides. These guides serve the convenience of the reader.

GENERAL RULES FOR EXPRESSING NUMBERS

1 — Use words for a number at the beginning of a sentence. If the number requires too many words, reverse the sentence so that the number falls elsewhere.

> Nineteen dozen pairs of slippers were shipped yesterday.
> Ten thousand dollars is our goal for United Appeal.
> The cost of the new electronic equipment was $2,750.

2 — Use figures for numbers greater than 100, except for isolated round numbers. (See Rule 3.)

> The public relations office reported that 933 persons attended the first meeting, 1,588 attended the second, and 1,931 attended the dinner meeting.
> The Better Business Bureau made 103 investigations in May and 114 investigations in June.
> More than fifty-five pages appear in the report.

3 — Write round numbers (numbers in even units, such as tens, hundreds, or thousands) in words. However, when such numbers are

used in the same context with other numbers that cannot be expressed conveniently in words, use figures.

Mrs. Barnard paid him ten days ago.
Mr. Brooks offered units ranging in price from $23 to $75,000.
In the first month over three thousand carloads were shipped.

Large round numbers may be written in words or figures or both (for example, $20 million). When figures are used elsewhere in the same context, however, use figures.

4 — If several numbers are used in similar constructions within a sentence, ordinarily write all the numbers in figures. If the numbers are small or round numbers, use words if figures do not occur in the same material. If the first word is a number, it may be written out even though the other numbers are written in figures. On the other hand, it may be possible to improve the sentence by revising it so that the first word is not a number.

The order called for 115 English books, 125 arithmetic books, and 68 geography books.
Paul bought three suits, eight shirts, and two belts.
Forty-one men, 53 women, and 79 children live in Oak Dale.
In Oak Dale live 41 men, 53 women, and 79 children.

5 — Sometimes a small number is used in the same sentence with a large number but with a different application. In such a situation it is advisable to use words for the smaller number, figures for the larger.

The three investors received a net profit of $317,623.

Similarly, when two numbers occur as parts of the same construction in a sentence, use words for the smaller number.

Miss Burke had 73 four-cent stamps and 15 seven-cent stamps.
Paul Manning bought three 50-cent pads of paper.

When two adjacent numbers occur as parts of different constructions in a sentence, separate the numbers by a comma for purposes of clarity.

In 1962, 127 discount stores were established in the state.
By 1975, 15,000 students will be enrolled here.

RULES FOR EXPRESSING NUMBERS USED IN SPECIAL WAYS

Addresses

1 — Express house numbers in figures, except for house number *One*.

Mary lives at One Ocean View Drive; Toni, at 462 Oak Lane; and Dianne at 9 Fairmont Avenue.

2 — Spell out the number naming a street if the number is ten or below; for larger numbers, use figures. When a street has a number as its name, separate a house number from the street number by a hyphen. Use a space before and after the hyphen. The letters *d, st,* or *th* may be added to the number that represents a street name.

Mr. Bogard moved from 753 Fifth Street to 1247 - 49th Street.
Dr. Eaton's office address is 1336 - 231st Street.

Dates

1 — After the name of a month, use figures to express the day.

Your inquiries of February 27 and March 2 were answered on March 4.

2 — When the day of the month stands alone or when it precedes the month, it may be written in figures with *d, st,* or *th* added. In this situation the date may also be written in words.

Mr. Huff sent a check for $275 on the 17th of August.
In my request of the 9th I asked for an itemized bill.
In my request of the ninth I asked for an itemized bill.

Amounts of money

1 — Except in legal documents, sums of money (whether in dollars or foreign denominations) should be typed in figures.

The invoice totaled $926.71.

2 — Write even sums of money without the decimal and ciphers.

The customer promptly sent a check for $297.

3 — When stating sums in cents, use figures without the decimal and spell out *cents*.

Miss Justice bought a rain hat for 97 cents.

4 — In legal documents spell out sums of money, and write figures in parentheses. If the figure in parentheses precedes the word *dollars,* omit the dollar sign.

I agree to pay the sum of Nine Hundred Thirty-Two Dollars ($932).
I agree to pay the sum of Nine Hundred Thirty-Two (932) Dollars.

Fractions and decimals

Simple fractions that stand alone are usually written in words. (For the use of hyphens in written fractions, see page 189.) Mixed numbers and decimals are written in figures. When a decimal fraction is not preceded by a whole number, a cipher is used before the decimal point unless the decimal fraction itself begins with a cipher.

Mr. Lee, ordered one-half dozen bottles of permanent red ink.
The length of the boards is 6½ feet.
The length of the boards is 6.5 feet.
The calculator operator swiftly found the quotient—0.578.
The answer to the math problem was .03.

Quantities and measurements

Quantities and measurements should usually be written in figures, as in the following examples:

1 — Age, especially when it is specific:

Ruth is 18½ years old.

Approximate age, however, is often written in words: "Ruth is almost nineteen years old." Within the same context, do not write some ages in words and others in figures. Be consistent.

2 — Dimensions:

The paper is of standard size, 8½ by 11 inches.

(Spell *by* in full, except in technical writing, where *x* is used for *by*.)

3 — Distance:

The distance from my home to my office is 8 miles.
It is 2,795 miles by road from Seattle to Baltimore.

(When the distance is a fraction of a mile, use words; for example, "Monterey Airport is one-half mile away.")

4 — Measures:

Mr. North raises 162 bushels on every 3 acres.
The dictionary states that 1 meter equals 39.37 inches.

5 — Percentages:

Mr. Nelson computed interest on the debt at 5 percent.

6 — Temperature:

A temperature of 100° Centigrade equals 212° Fahrenheit.

7 — Time:

The committee chairman arrived at 10:45 a.m.

(But spell the hour in full when *o'clock* is used in stating time; for example, "The office opens at eight o'clock.")

8 — Weights:

It takes 14 pounds to make 1 stone.

Pages and divisions of a book

Page numbers are written in figures. Often capitalized Roman numerals are used for major divisions of books and Arabic numerals for minor divisions. In writing about a particular book, follow the usage of that book.

The explanation is given in Unit XII, Part 3, Figure 9, page 425.
Chapter X deals with changes in English spelling.

Numbers used in official titles or designations

Follow the official or customary form for numbers used in titles or designations.

The 12th Infantry will soon go on field maneuvers.
Emerson Kingsley, of the Fifth Congressional District, was elected to the Eighty-Eighth Congress.
The First Methodist Church now has 1,358 members.

• *APPLYING EFFECTIVE ENGLISH*

Oral Applications

• **1.** In class discussion, consider the question of why it is important in business messages to follow the accepted conventions for expressing numbers.

● **2.** Point out and explain the errors in Written Applications 2 and 3 other than those related to expression of numbers.

Written Applications

● **1.** Most of the following sentences contain one or more errors in the expression of numbers. Correct all errors.

1 — The desk sold for the advertised price of $135.00.
2 — We must order ½ dozen erasers for the new classroom.
3 — I paid six hundred eighty-nine dollars for my new furniture.
4 — When we returned from our one hundred and twenty mile trip, there were four gallons of gasoline in the tank.
5 — Our purchase amounted to $.98.
6 — Mr. Mann's inquiry of June 10 was answered on June 15th.
7 — Our office hours are from 9 o'clock in the morning until 5 o'clock in the afternoon.
8 — The drive-in theatre is ten miles from town.
9 — Standard stationery is eight and a half by eleven inches in size.
10 — The salesman began making calls at 9:30 o'clock.
11 — Our church is located at 4117 10th Street.
12 — 12 of the items on the order were to be shipped immediately; the other 24 were to be shipped by the end of the week.
13 — There were 3,000 1-dollar items included in the special sale.
14 — There were 12 695 votes for the bond issue and one thousand ninety against it.
15 — The invoice was mailed January 13th.
16 — The note bears interest at the rate of five and one-half per cent.
17 — The two invoices totaled $367 and .98 cents.
18 — At noon the temperature was ninety-four degrees.
19 — Miss Kelly had 2 10-dollar bills in her purse.
20 — My broker paid one hundred sixty-seven dollars for the stock.

● **2.** Most of the following sentences contain one or more inappropriate expressions of numbers, as well as other mistakes. Correct all errors.

1 — The 87th Congress was adjourned promptly.
2 — The package weighed five and one-quarter pounds.
3 — The style manuals were advertised for $.64.
4 — The plastics plant is fourteen miles north of the city.
5 — The temperature in the freezer should be twenty-seven degrees.
6 — In 1889 136 new laws were passed in hiram county.
7 — Jan lives at 8508 62nd Street Carol lives at 2 West 8th Street

8 — The bank charged four and one-half per cent interest on the six hundred and fifty dollar loan.

9 — A service charge of 25 cents is made each month.

10 — The room measures ten by twelve feet.

11 — He had three appointments in the afternoon one at 1.15 another at 2.30 and the last at 4.10.

12 — The chart is given on Page twenty of Volume ii.

13 — 34 offices were built when the company enlarged it's quarters.

14 — The summary was 4 pages long.

15 — June Gale will be 18 years old, next February, her sister will be sixteen years old.

16 — The June bill was $16.74 the July bill, $18.00.

17 — 35 men, 31 women, and 17 children attended the family reunion.

18 — A payment of four hundred ($400) dollars is due at this time.

19 — Standard scores were compiled for only six of the eleven bookkeeping tests for only two of the fifteen grammar tests and for only three of the 20 typewriting tests.

20 — In your specifications of the 16, did an error appear in the quotation on seventy-four engines?

● **3.** Most of the following sentences and paragraphs contain one or more errors or inappropriate expression of numbers. Express all numbers in appropriate form. Correct all other errors.

1 — This babys blanket, selling at $4.00 dollars, is 100% wool, measures 40x40 inches, weighs a pound and one-half.

2 — The class chose two students to write an inquiry to a local department store. Each of the students wrote a 2-page draft in which 10 questions were asked. The inquiries were mailed on October eleventh; they were answered by the general managr of the department store on October twentieth.

3 — The inventory included a total of one thousand two hundred fifty-one items of merchandise. The most expensive item retailed at $29.95; the least expensive, at $0.75. The average price was ten dollars and fifteen cents.

4 — When the president of the company retired, he began to draw a monthly income from his twenty-three thousand five hundred dollar annuity within 4 weeks after his retirement.

5 — The clerk helped in taking the inventory of 2 departments in the department store. In the first department the inventory showed a total of 1,265 articles on hand, in the second department the inventory showed a total of four thousand articles on hand, thus the 2 departments had a total of five thousand two hundred sixty-five articles.

● *REVIEW*

● **1.** The following example of business writing has been correctly divided into paragraphs; the individual sentences have been numbered for your convenience. All punctuation and capitalization, however, have been omitted. Supply all necessary punctuation and capitalization. Correct any errors you may find. In your version do not number the individual sentences.

(1) it is with regret that i must decline your request of march 25th for leaves of absence for cadets prewitt and ogden from friday april fourth until sunday april sixth.

(2) at sterling arms military academy saturday is a school day monday is our weekly holiday (3) however I would permit the cadets to leave the academy saturday afternoon about 3 30 oclock after their duties have been completed and to return sunday afternoon in time for parade at 4 oclock (4) i might add too that this arrangement would be dependent upon certain additional considerations they must have their parents approval and must be free from any disciplinary duties

(5) will such an arrangement be satisfactory to you

● **2.** Correct the capitalization in the following sentences.

1 — the boys played at south crest golf course.
2 — the fredericks plan to hike in the rocky mountains.
3 — each spring the water level rises in walden pond.
4 — frank belongs to boy scout troop 212.
5 — miss bell expects the american telephone and telegraph company to increase its dividend this fall.
6 — an answer has come from professor elsman.
7 — did the remco corporation refund your payment?

● **3.** Correct the punctuation in the following sentences.

1 — Anyone, who plays golf, needs to practice diligently.
2 — The report was duplicated yesterday copies were mailed today.
3 — The word, which I misspelled, is *accommodation.*
4 — After checking Dean Conner carefully made a second reservation for August 3 at the Birchwood Motel Augusta Oklahoma.
5 — Miss Jennifer Wrenn applied for the position this spring and the Fletcher Construction Company answered her letter of application in a prompt courteous and personal reply.
6 — When the term ends Professor Buckley will be visiting Vienna.
7 — With the prices going up investors may delay their purchases.

Sec. 8 • Expression of Numbers

211

• **2.** Correct all errors in punctuation, capitalization, and grammar in the following sentences.

1 — The press club of rolling meadows high school will hold its regular weekly meetings at the springfield youth club.

2 — We will go said the scout master unless the weather turns colder.

3 — If the class wins the prize, the money can be used for it's labor day picnic.

4 — If this were saturday we would start our two week canoe trip down the rock river.

5 — The 3 first prize winners were Bill Ed and Joe.

6 — Miss Rodgers studied chapter III the importance of alertness in proofreading.

7 — Of the 3 dresses Josephine likes the pink one better.

8 — The scouts' said there camp accommodations had been superb.

9 — Many capable men have to many responsibilitys.

10 — After scheduling the meeting Dr Thornberry announce to the class that he had arranged for two scientist to serve as consultants.

11 — The counselor said do not take it for granted that Mr. Vickers is one of those people who is easily persuaded.

12 — The reference was to Page 53 in volume III of the encyclopedia americana.

13 — The managers' work was increased because of his assistant resignation, furthermore, their were many reports that had to be completed before September thirtieth.

14 — The teacher ordered 23 copys of Dr Walkers latest book integrated secretarial projects for class use but she had to begin meeting her classes before it arrived.

15 — The new professor dr edwin e green has 2 classes in Business Law 3 classes in Economics and 1 class in Accounting, all of them meet in room 216 reavis hall.

16 — Their were as a matter of fact 4 decided factors one scholastic rating two character 3 participation in extra-curricular activities 4 leadership

17 — jim caswell the valedictorian of this years senior class is a young man who I sincerely believe will succeed in whatever he does

18 — the veterans day program will be given in roy j bell memorial auditorium at 7.45 oclock.

19 — The message was addressed to professor Grace A. Hyde who teaches Shorthand and Typing in the saxman school of business.

20 — The students use to be prejudice against the course many of them however now realize that they are acquiring much practical information, and mastering essential skills that will help them in there business careers

UNIT 6

DEVELOPING SKILL IN WRITING SENTENCES

Sentences are the basic building blocks of writing. Strong, clear sentences will enable him to communicate his ideas with accuracy and force. They will represent you to the best advantage. They will help one make a favorable impression on the readers. In this unit you will learn to make your sentences more effective.

In Sections 1 and 2 you will learn to identify and correct frequent errors in sentence structure. Once you understand such errors, you will be able to eliminate them from your writing.

In Section 3 you will learn to emphasize major points. By following the suggestions given in this section, you will increase your power as a writer.

Practice is the key to improving your writing! The section-end exercises will give you a good start.

UNIT 6

Section 1

Sentence Unity: Each sentence should present one central idea.

Section 2

Sentence Coherence: The parts of a sentence should be clearly and logically connected.

Section 3

Sentence Power: Key points must attract the reader's attention.

 **SECTION 1**

Sentence Unity

Each sentence should present one central idea.

The basic aim in writing is to communicate effectively. Effective communication involves two key factors. First, you must make your meaning unmistakably clear. Second, you must express your ideas in such a way that your reader's response will be favorable.

The conventions of modern written English have resulted from the experience of countless authors and editors over hundreds of years. One such convention is our system of marking off each separate sentence. This practice enables a reader to grasp a writer's message rapidly and easily. Imagine how difficult it would be to read a paragraph if you had to figure out where each sentence ended.

Your success in writing depends largely upon your mastery of the conventions of written English. It depends particularly upon your ability to write unified sentences. Sentence *unity* means that everything in a sentence must help convey one central point. To write unified sentences, follow these two basic principles:

1 — Include in a single sentence only closely related points that you can show are parts of one unifying idea.
2 — Punctuate as sentences only those units that are conventionally regarded as sentences—units that contain a subject and a predicate, and that are grammatically *independent*.

Failure to follow these principles may confuse or irritate your reader. Needless to say, a confused or irritated reader will *not* be favorably impressed by your message.

An expert writer uses sentences to make his thoughts clear to the reader. In addition, he uses sentences in such a way as to hold the reader's interest. An important trick for this purpose is sentence variety. A paragraph made up of sentences of *varying lengths* and of *varying types* [1] helps keep a reader's attention. On the other hand, a paragraph of sentences all very much alike soon grows boring.

---

[1] For a discussion of the various types of sentences, see Unit 4, Section 5, pages 146-148.

Four weaknesses common in sentences. The remainder of this section deals with four serious and common errors. All of them may confuse the reader. All suggest that the writer is incompetent.

1 — The sentence fragment
2 — The run-on sentence
3 — The comma fault
4 — Awkward and ambiguous phrasing

1 — The sentence fragment. A common mistake in writing is the practice of punctuating phrases or dependent clauses as sentences. This practice is explained, in part, by the fact that sentence fragments occur frequently in conversation. The following exchange illustrates the fragmentary character of many sentences that occur in conversation.

Guy: "Neil around?"
Carl: "He left yesterday for Boston."
Guy: "Boston?"
Carl: "Yes, to take his brother to the clinic."
Guy: "For treatment?"
Carl: "No. Just for an examination, as far as I know."
Guy: "Why go way up there just for an examination?"
Carl: "Because a good friend of theirs is interning there."

In written English only the second line would be considered a sentence. The language in the entire passage is, however, perfectly acceptable in conversation. Our practice of using incomplete sentences in conversation often traps us into *writing* such sentences. While sentence fragments are acceptable in conversation, they are seldom used in business writing. Learn to recognize them in your own writing and to correct them.

Sentence fragments are of two kinds:

(1) Dependent clauses punctuated as though they were sentences.

Objectionable

a) Albert left quickly. Because he was afraid he would be questioned.
b) He had been there. When the door was being locked by the janitor.
c) He did not get the job. Although much of his data sheet was impressive.

The clauses introduced by the subordinating conjunctions *because, when,* and *although* are dependent clauses. They are made dependent *by* the subordinating conjunctions. In conversation they might be added to a completed sentence as a kind of afterthought. In expository writing dependent clauses are almost never punctuated as separate sentences. Many corrections of this error are possible.

Acceptable

a) Albert left quickly because he was afraid he would be questioned.

a) Albert left quickly; he was afraid he would be questioned.

a) Because he was afraid he would be questioned, Albert left quickly.

b) He had been there when the door was being locked by the janitor.

b) He had been there. At that time the door was being locked by the janitor.

c) He did not get the job, although much of his data sheet was impressive.

c) He did not get the job. Much of his data sheet, however, was impressive.

c) He did not get the job; still his data sheet was impressive.

(2) Various kinds of phrases punctuated as though they were sentences.

Objectionable

a) The revision having been suggested by Mr. Carr. It was made.

b) The firm hired a new clerk. More help being desperately needed.

c) Mr. Brent accepted their congratulations. It seeming clear now that he had won the election.

This type of sentence fragment lacks an appropriate verb form. The participial forms *having been suggested, being,* and *seeming* cannot serve as the predicate of a sentence. Such an error can be corrected in either of two ways.

(1) A finite verb can be substituted for the participial form and the phrase thus changed into a clause.

(2) The nominative absolute (noun plus its modifying participial phrase) can be joined, with a comma, to an adjacent sentence.

Acceptable

a) The revision had been suggested by Mr. Carr. It was made.

a) Since the revision had been suggested by Mr. Carr, it was made.

a) The revision, having been suggested by Mr. Carr, was made.

b) The firm hired a new clerk; more help was desperately needed.

b) The firm hired a new clerk, for more help was desperately needed.

b) The firm hired a new clerk, more help being desperately needed.

c) Mr. Brent accepted their congratulations, since it seemed clear now that he had won the election.

c) Mr. Brent accepted their congratulations, it seeming clear now that he had won the election.

2—The run-on sentence. Sometimes a writer has trouble keeping up with his thoughts. This difficulty may lead him to run separate sentences together without a conjunction or punctuation. Such an error makes writing difficult to understand, since separate thoughts are not kept apart. Business executives regard such carelessness as impolite. A writer can hardly make a worse impression.

The following examples illustrate the run-on sentence.

Objectionable

a) The meeting had started before Mr. Newman arrived almost all hope of agreement had been abandoned.

b) The shipment was found to be in error when it was re-examined the letter was also found to be wrong.

c) Statements were sent last week the complaints were still coming in.

In each example, complete sentences are run together without a conjunction and without punctuation. Furthermore, do the modifiers (*before Mr. Newman arrived, when it was re-examined,* and *last week*) belong with the preceding or with the following independent clause?

Acceptable

a) The meeting had started. Before Mr. Newman arrived, almost all hope of agreement had been abandoned.

a) The meeting had started before Mr. Newman arrived. Almost all hope of agreement had been abandoned.

b) The shipment was found to be in error when it was re-examined. The letter was also found to be wrong.

b) The shipment was found to be in error. When it was re-examined, the letter was also found to be wrong.

c) The transcript was sent last week. The complaints were still coming in.

c) The transcript was sent. Last week the complaints were still coming in.

As you write, proofread, and revise, remember that run-on sentences will confuse a reader. They suggest that the writer is inept.

3—The comma fault. We have seen that the run-on sentence merges two independent clauses without a conjunction or punctuation. The comma fault joins two independent clauses by *only* a comma. Except for special effects, experienced writers avoid this practice.

Run-on sentence: The money had been sent the documents had been filled out and signed.

Comma fault: The money had been sent, the documents had been filled out and signed.

One may link independent clauses in a compound sentence in any of the following ways:

a. By a comma plus one of the coordinating conjunctions (*and, for, but, or*):

> The money had been sent, and the documents had been filled out and signed.
>
> The money had been sent, for the documents had been filled out and signed.

b. By a semicolon:

> The money had been sent; the documents had been filled out and signed.

c. By a semicolon plus a linking adverb (for example, *however, nevertheless, therefore, hence, still, consequently, thus*):

> The money had been sent; the documents, therefore, had been filled out and signed.
>
> The money had been sent; consequently, the documents had been filled out and signed.

One may always punctuate independent clauses as separate sentences. Here are other examples of comma faults and run-on sentences:

Objectionable

a) The president left for the airport before 6 a.m., he didn't reach the airport until 12:30 p.m.

b) The advertising campaign has been very expensive, it has, however, brought about widespread interest in the product.

c) When the message came, it was answered immediately, nevertheless, the misunderstanding persisted for some time.

d) The new typewriter ribbons were thoroughly satisfactory they were purchased at the local office supply company.

Acceptable

a) The president left for the airport before 6 a.m. He didn't arrive there until 12:30 p.m.

b) The advertising campaign has been very expensive. It has, however, brought about a wide interest in the product.

c) When the message came, it was answered immediately. Nevertheless, the misunderstanding persisted for some time.

d) The new typewriter ribbons were thoroughly satisfactory. They were purchased at the local office supply company.

4—Awkwardness and confusion resulting from improper omission of words. In business messages, some writers omit words to give the impression of conciseness. The resulting sentences are awkward.

Objectionable

a) Yours of January 10 received with thanks. Shipment sent day order arrived. Appreciate order and are ready to serve further at any time.

b) Ship sails October 13.

Such phrasing can often be misleading. For example, in the second example, above, is *ship* a noun or verb? No one can tell from this message. Seek conciseness through phrasing your ideas accurately and through sticking to the point. Avoid glaring omissions.

Acceptable

a) Thank you for your letter of January 10. The shipment was sent the same day your order arrived. We appreciate your business and are ready to serve you further at any time.

b) The ship sails on October 13. [Or, depending on the meaning:]

b) Please ship the sails on October 13.

Careful revision and painstaking proofreading are necessary for effective business writing. Only by these means can one avoid sentence errors. Guard especially against the sentence fragment, the run-on sentence, the comma fault, and awkward omissions.

● APPLYING EFFECTIVE ENGLISH

Oral Applications

● **1.** In class discussion: (a) consider the effect the following message would make upon an educated reader; (b) identify the errors which produce this effect; (c) suggest two alternative corrections for each error.

I am writing in response to your advertisement in the *Chicago Reporter* of June 10, for an experienced typist. Because I feel that I meet the requirements which were in the advertisement.

The advertisement stated that applicants should be able to type at least 60 words a minute, be able to turn out clean copy, be good at spelling, and be familiar with the conventions of written English I meet all of these qualifications. In school I studied typing for two years. Typing being one of the subjects which was required of business majors. I am able to type well over 60 words a minute, I have had experience on many different kinds of typewriters, including electric typewriters.

In my high school English courses I always made high grades my teachers complimented me on the care I used in preparing my written assignments. This fact making me certain that I can easily meet your high standards.

I have had two years of experience as a typist, this experience was with three different firms the reason I have changed jobs so often is that I was interested in learning to adjust to new situations. Getting to know people being one of my greatest pleasures. Now, however, I am looking for a permanent position, I shall be happy to come in for an interview at your convenience. Hope to hear from you soon.

• **2.** The manager of the customer relations section of a manufacturing company is serving as chairman of a committee of four employees. This committee is responsible for handling correspondence with customers who pose inquiries about the company's products. The manager, with the help of the other committee members, is trying to develop a brief announcement to be sent out to customers during the next month. The contents of the announcement have been sketched out in rough outline form by the design engineer. The committee's assignment is to develop an effective paragraph seeking to interest the reader in visiting his dealer so that he can examine the new product. One student may take the part of the manager; four others, the roles of the committee members. Each committee member, as well as the manager, may prepare a draft of the announcement. The committee can choose the most promising of these drafts as the basis for its consideration. Through discussion the committee should try to improve the draft, incorporating promising suggestions from the four other drafts.

1 — An AM-FM transistor radio only 3″ x 1″ x ¾″
2 — No antenna required
3 — AM reception up to 75 miles; FM reception up to 30 miles
4 — Long-lasting battery operation—up to four months on a single battery
5 — Handsome, rugged plastic case available in buff, gray, or black
6 — Guaranteed for 18 months, provided warantee card is returned
7 — Tone quality comparable to that of table model radios
8 — Price—$17.75

Written Applications

● 1. Rewrite each of the following items and correct all errors. The following kinds of mistakes are emphasized in this application: (a) sentence fragments, (b) run-on sentences, (c) comma faults, and (d) awkward phrasing.

1 — Our company maintains a research division. The home office being in Dallas.

2 — The repairs were made yesterday fortunately the defect was found before it caused an accident.

3 — It may be that some of the tables were damaged in shipping, if this is the case, should like you to make adjustment.

4 — Report cash receipts at the end of each day's business, prepare a summary of sales to be presented to the board every Tuesday evening.

5 — If you are uncertain about the stock number, consult our new catalog. This being the surest way of receiving your exact order.

6 — Each day we meet pressing problems. Which require immediate solution.

7 — Here are two copies of our reports these summarize the results for the year.

8 — This is the usual procedure. Although there is no reason why we cannot modify it.

9 — Feel sure you'll be interested in this opportunity. The price quoted being the lowest offer of the year.

10 — Your letter of April 6 received. Glad to learn shipment suited. Was sure it would. Wish to state you can depend on us at all times. Credit terms satisfactory. Hope for further business.

11 — We have not yet heard from you regarding your order, please contact our representative before Thursday, September 21.

12 — Pleased to state, in reply your inquiry February 17, that economy is at highest peak in three years, hope business activity and high wages continue.

● 2. Revise the message in Oral Application 1 according to the plan given below:

(a) Prepare a revised draft. Correct all the mistakes that were mentioned in class discussion as well as any other mistakes you find. Make the revised draft as effective as possible.

(b) Copy your revised work in final form from your corrected draft.

(c) Proofread the finished copy carefully.

SECTION 2

Sentence Coherence

The parts of an effective sentence will be clearly and logically connected.

In sentence structure, *coherence* means the careful arrangement of sentence elements, so that their relationships are clear. To write unified, coherent sentences, think through each sentence individually. Experiment with various phrasings to find the one that most precisely expresses your intended meaning.

Cultivate a critical attitude toward your own writing. Learn to revise sentences that you suspect might not convey your meaning clearly to the reader. Thus you will develop the ability to analyze your writing *from the reader's point of view.* You will also gain skill in expressing your ideas effectively.

This section deals with six errors that destroy sentence coherence:

1 — Misplaced modifiers
2 — Ineffective placement of special modifiers
3 — Misrelated modifiers: dangling constructions
4 — Indefinite and unclear reference of pronouns
5 — Lack of parallelism
6 — Inconsistent point of view

1—Misplaced modifiers. A modifier should stand as close as possible to its head (the term it modifies). This idea is a basic principle of coherence. If the connection between a modifier and its head is not clear, the sentence will be confusing and may be silly.

Objectionable

a) He bought a car for his daughter with a sleek chassis and wire-spoked wheels.
b) Mr. Nelson examined this product with a careful eye.
c) Lou sent a letter to the man with a check enclosed.
d) The old man entered carrying a book with a broad smile.
e) Miss Finley completed filing the invoices in the afternoon shipment.
f) Mr. Hays answered the telephone call from the conference room.

Sentences like these are ambiguous and sometimes laughable. To catch such slips, able writers proofread all their messages. Sometimes sentences with misplaced modifiers can be satisfactorily corrected by minor changes in word order. Sometimes thorough-going revision is necessary.

Acceptable

a) The car he bought for his daughter had a sleek chassis and wire-spoked wheels.
b) With a careful eye Mr. Nelson examined the product.
c) Lou sent the letter, with a check enclosed, to the man.
d) With a broad smile the old man entered, carrying a book.
e) Miss Finley completed filing the invoices which arrived in the afternoon shipment.
f) From the conference room, Mr. Hayes answered the telephone call.

2—Ineffective placement of special modifiers, such as "only," "alone," and "at least." In conversation we ordinarily pay little attention to where we place these modifiers. The pauses and emphasis we use as we speak clarify our meaning. Take, for example, the following sentence.

The new students only paid three dollars for their tickets.

If a pause occurs after *only* when the sentence is spoken, the speaker means *the new students* were the ones charged three dollars; others were charged more or less. If no pause occurs after *only*, the speaker means that three dollars was not a high price to pay for the tickets. In writing this sentence, an author cannot rely on pauses or lack of them. If he wants to single out *the new students,* he must alter the word order of the sentence as follows: "Only the new students paid three dollars for their tickets." But if he wants to show that the price was not high, he might place *only* immediately before the phrase *three dollars.* Thus: "The new students paid only three dollars for their tickets." Note the following contrasts in meaning:

Only Mr. Dye inquired today about the company's account.
Mr. Dye only inquired today about the company's account.
Mr. Dye inquired only today about the company's account.
Mr. Dye inquired today only about the company's account.
Mr. Dye inquired today about only the company's account.
Mr. Dye inquired today about the company's only account.
Mr. Dye inquired today about the company's account only.

These examples show the importance of placement if such expressions are to be used with precision in writing.

Pauses can sometimes be used in writing, as well as in speaking, to alter meaning. Such pauses are usually indicated by commas. Hence, punctuation is sometimes an important factor in the accurate use of terms like *only* and *at least*. In the following sentence the comma indicates a desired pause that makes the meaning approximately that of the first sentence in the list on page 224.

Mr. Dye, only, inquired today about the company's account.

3—**Misrelated modifiers: dangling constructions.** Verbals used as modifiers in constructions at the beginning of sentences often cause trouble for writers. The following *verbal* constructions are involved:

1 — **Present participles:** *Studying* composition, Esther learned much.
2 — **Past Participles:** *Written* carefully, the notice was very brief.
3 — **Gerunds:** In *studying*, one should concentrate.
4 — **Infinitives:** *To improve*, one should study.

For an explanation of verbals, see pages 88-90.

One other kind of dangling construction sometimes causes difficulty—the elliptical clause. An *elliptical clause* is one in which some element is omitted. For example:

When practicing, a writer learns.

Note that the elliptical clause may be expanded: "When a writer is practicing. . . ." In this example the elliptical clause contains a present participle, "practicing." Elliptical clauses may also contain past participles. For example:

When studied thoughtfully, Latin increases a student's vocabulary.

Here the elliptical clause may be expanded: "When Latin is studied thoughtfully. . . ."

The problem of dangling constructions, then, concerns these four varieties of introductory modifiers: participles (both present and past), gerunds, infinitives, and elliptical clauses.

The principle governing the effective use of these introductory constructions is simple. The action expressed by such a construction must be done *by* or *to* the subject of the following clause. (The subject can be identified as the term that determines whether a singular or plural verb occurs in the clause.) Some examples of how this principle operates are given on page 226.

Acceptable

a) Walking along 35th Street on a scorchingly hot day, the visitors to New York City wonderingly observed the Empire State Building. (Present participial phrase)

b) Typing a letter, an efficient secretary will be careful about spelling. (Present participial phrase)

c) To type a good letter, a secretary must be careful about spelling. (Infinitive phrase)

d) In typing a letter, a secretary should be careful about spelling. (Gerund phrase, object of a preposition)

e) When typing a letter, a secretary should be careful about spelling. (Elliptical clause)

f) When typed by an efficient secretary, a letter should contain no misspellings. (Elliptical clause)

g) Typed by an efficient secretary, a letter should contain no misspellings. (Past participial phrase)

Sentences in which this principle is ignored seem silly:

a) Walking along 35th Street on a scorchingly hot day, the Empire State Building was wonderingly observed by visitors to New York City. (Dangling present participial phrase)

b) Typing a letter, spelling will be watched by an efficient secretary. (Dangling present participial phrase)

c) To type a good letter, spelling must be watched carefully by a secretary. (Dangling infinitive phrase)

d) In typing a letter, spelling should be watched by a secretary. (Dangling gerund phrase)

e) When typing a letter, spelling should be watched by a secretary. (Dangling elliptical clause)

f) When typed by an efficient secretary, misspellings should not occur in a letter. (Dangling elliptical clause)

g) Typed by an efficient secretary, misspellings should not occur in a letter. (Dangling past participial phrase)

Sentences like these sound foolish because of their dangling elements. Consider the reader's initial reaction in reading the first objectionable sentence. The sentence seems to be saying, "The Empire State Building is walking along 35th Street"! The second objectionable sentence seems to be stating that "Spelling is typing a letter." A reader can sometimes puzzle out what the writer is trying to say in such awkward sentences. The reader cannot help smiling, however, at the writer's ineptness.

4—Indefinite and unclear reference of pronouns. Pronouns enable us to avoid undesirable repetition of nouns and to knit our sentences neatly together. Pronouns work efficiently only when their reference is clear. Note the confusion in the following sentences.

Ambiguous

a) When our accountant talked with Mr. Turner, he felt sure the audit report would be completed by noon.

b) The typewriter was found in the typewriter compartment of an old desk; it was badly in need of repair.

Here the pronouns do not refer clearly to one of the preceding nouns. *He* could refer to *accountant* or to *Mr. Turner. It* could refer to *typewriter, typewriter compartment,* or *desk.* In using pronouns, therefore, make sure that each pronoun refers accurately to its antecedent.

Acceptable

a) Our accountant felt sure, when he talked with Mr. Turner, that the audit report would be completed by noon.

a) Mr. Turner felt sure, when our accountant talked with him, that the audit report would be completed by noon.

b) The typewriter, which was badly in need of repair, was found in the typewriter compartment of an old desk.

b) The typewriter which was found in the typewriter compartment of an old desk was badly in need of repair.

Confusion of the same kind may result if a writer uses relative pronouns carelessly.

Ambiguous

a) The teacher of the boy, who made an outstanding record on his tests, was asked to come in for a conference.

b) The report in the consumers' magazine that received a national journalism prize discussed a new synthetic fiber.

Acceptable

a) The boy's teacher, who made an outstanding record on his tests, was asked to come in for a conference.

a) The teacher who coached the boy that made an outstanding record on his tests was asked to come in for a conference.

b) The consumers' magazine that received a national journalism prize contained the report discussing a new synthetic fiber.

b) The consumers' magazine contained the report that received a national journalism prize. This report discussed a new synthetic fiber.

Use pronouns to refer only to antecedents *not* in the possessive case.

Objectionable

a) Mr. Vaughn's suggestion was not considered, because he arrived late for the conference.

b) The president's day was a full one; he was extremely busy throughout his tour.

c) One of the salesman's suitcases was lost because he had been careless while checking out of the hotel.

Acceptable

a) Because Mr. Vaughn arrived late for the conference, his suggestion was not considered.

b) The day was a full one for the president; he was extremely busy throughout his tour.

c) Because the salesman had been careless while checking out of the hotel, one of his suitcases was lost.

c) The salesman lost one of his suitcases because he was careless while checking out of the hotel.

Use relative pronouns to refer to a specific word, rather than to the general idea or meaning of a preceding construction.

Questionable

a) They will arrive early for the meeting, which will give them time to review their material.

b) The shipment had not been properly crated, which explained the damage to the fragile parts of the apparatus.

Acceptable

a) Their early arrival for the meeting will give them time to review their material.

a) Since they will arrive early for the meeting, they will have time to review their material.

b) The shipment had not been properly crated. As a result, the fragile parts of the apparatus were damaged.

b) The fragile parts of the apparatus were damaged because the shipment had not been properly crated.

5—**Lack of parallelism.** In sentence structure, the principle of parallelism is often a source of emphasis. This principle is that a similarity of construction indicates a similarity in function.

Ignoring such similarities leads to ineffective phrasing. For example:

Objectionable

a) They went to enjoy the fresh air and so that they could learn about life in the out-of-doors.

b) In composing a message and when it is typed, the writer should consider the effect the message will have.

Acceptable

a) They went to enjoy the fresh air and to learn about life in the out-of-doors. (Note that *to enjoy* and *to learn* have the same relation to the rest of the sentence. Both express the purpose of the trip.)

b) In composing a message as well as in typing it, the writer should consider the effect the message will have.

A special problem involving parallelism arises whenever correlative conjunctions occur. Correlative conjunctions are pairs of conjunctions such as *not only . . . but also, either . . . or, both . . . and, neither . . . nor.* The principle here is that the same grammatical construction should follow both parts of the correlative conjunction.

Objectionable

a) That employee not only studies shorthand, but also accounting.

b) He neither responded to my letter nor to my visit.

c) He either lost the telegram or his sister did.

d) I was either confused about the date or the time.

Acceptable

a) That employee studies not only shorthand, but also accounting.

b) He responded neither to my letter nor to my visit.

c) Either he or his sister lost the telegram.

d) I was confused about either the date or the time.

Finally, the principle of parallelism applies when a writer is making comparisons. The phrasing of a comparison should draw attention clearly to the elements that are being compared.

Objectionable

a) A letter that is typewritten has a neater appearance than handwriting.

b) The gas economy of the compact car is greater than any other model.

a) A letter that is typewritten has a neater appearance than one that is handwritten. (*One* stands for "A letter.")
b) The gas economy of the compact car is greater than that of any other model. (*That* stands for "The gas economy.")

When using such comparisons, phrase them so as to make clear the elements being compared. The reader may be able to tell what you mean even if your phrasing of the comparison is inexact. Your purpose in preparing business messages, however, involves more than barely conveying your meaning. It involves conveying that meaning accurately and neatly. It involves making a favorable impression upon your reader. Inexact phrasing will not only obscure your meaning but irritate your reader.

6—Inconsistent point of view. Maintain a consistent point of view in deciding whether to use:

1 — first-, second-, or third-person pronouns (I/we; you; he/she/it; they; and so on);
2 — a particular noun as a singular or plural (for example, whether to say, "a student of writing," or "students of writing");
3 — active or passive voice.

This guide does not mean that you must necessarily use the same forms throughout a message. Rather, it means that careless and thoughtless inconsistency will be confusing to a reader.

Inconsistent	*Consistent, Direct, Clear*
A student learning to write needs a great deal of practice. All of the writing done by them should be revised and proofread carefully. Composition cannot be learned by students merely through their reading about it. Nor can you learn to write effectively unless various different ways of phrasing the same idea are considered. As students we learn most by doing. By *doing,* I mean by actual writing, by industrious and imaginative revising. Of course, careful proofreading is also meant.	A student learning to write needs a great deal of practice. He should carefully revise and proofread everything he writes. He cannot learn to write effectively merely by reading about composition. Nor can he learn to write effectively unless he experiments with various ways of phrasing his ideas. For a student learns most by *doing.* In connection with composition, *doing* means (1) writing, (2) revising for clarity and accuracy, and (3) careful proofreading.

• APPLYING EFFECTIVE ENGLISH

Oral Application

The paragraph below contains (a) misplaced modifiers, (b) dangling constructions, (c) improperly used pronouns, (d) errors in parallelism, and (e) confusing shifts in point of view. Locate each error and be prepared, in class discussion, to explain the error and to suggest a correction for it. The sentences are numbered for convenience in discussion.

(1) In revising a piece of writing, a good point for the student to keep in mind is that grammatical errors may confuse or annoy the reader. (2) The reader not only considers basic meaning but also tone, accuracy, and neatness. (3) You may be able to see this better if you put yourself in the reader's place and try to imagine, at least, their response. (4) Students realize that a neat, accurately phrased, and grammatically correct message makes a better impression than carelessness about these factors. (5) Another factor in a message which influences the reader greatly is spelling. (6) Only the student must make a habit of looking up words about the spelling of which he is in doubt in a dictionary. (7) Looking words up in a dictionary, errors are avoided by conscientious writers. (8) Students who wish to learn to write effectively and so that they can make a favorable impression must form the "dictionary habit."

Written Applications

• **1.** Each of the following sentences illustrates at least one of the errors discussed in this section. Revise and rewrite each sentence, correcting whatever errors it contains.

1 — A student can build their vocabulary through careful reading. We must learn, however, the meanings of new words by looking them up in the dictionary.

2 — In order to prepare a polished message, time is required by a writer, especially one who has not written many messages.

3 — Revision is not only required but also proofreading. Errors caused by carelessness are just as objectionable as ignorance.

4 — Mr. Delaney sent his representative to the afternoon meeting; he was to report to the president as soon as the conference was over.

5 — The boys mowed the lawn to get exercise and so that they could make some spending money. Spending a great deal on their car, however, little was left for other purposes.

 # SECTION 3

Sentence Power

Key points should capture the reader's attention.

Sections 1 and 2 have been largely concerned with grammatical mistakes. In contrast, this section is concerned with various ways by which you can increase the emphasis of your sentences. *Emphasis* means forcefulness. *Emphasis* captures and holds the reader's attention.

In speaking, each of us emphasizes important points in a **variety of ways:**

1 — By stressing certain words and phrases as we say them
2 — By using gestures and facial expressions
3 — By using accurate, forceful diction (word choice)
4 — By repetition
5 — By drawing attention to certain ideas through stating that these ideas are important
6 — By organizing and presenting sentences so that important ideas are given prominence

Some of these devices are available to a writer and some are not. Like a speaker, a writer may choose words effectively, may state that certain ideas are important, and may organize his material carefully. All of these procedures will enable him to get special attention for his key points.

Other devices for securing emphasis in writing are capital letters, underlining, quotation marks, italics, and contrasting colors of ink. Unless these mechanical devices are used sparingly, however, they soon become monotonous and hence ineffective.

Emphasis through clear phrasing and precise diction. When you write, one of the most important factors in determining your success is phrasing. Phrasing has to do with the words you choose and the way you arrange them. A good vocabulary used to phrase ideas precisely, emphatically, and appealingly is an asset in shaping messages which will win the approval of your reader.

The contrast between the following two sentences is revealing:

Vague and Imprecise Phrasing

The writing had a part which said anyone who told them something that could be used, about how to improve the way they ran the firm, would get something extra for what they had done in the way of making good suggestions.

Definite and Emphatic Phrasing

The contract's final clause stated that employees suggesting practicable methods for increasing the firm's efficiency would receive a bonus in recognition of their initiative and imagination.

The second version is superior because it conveys the message more fully and more accurately, though it uses fewer words. A comparison of the words used in the two versions will reveal the advantage of using specific and exact phrasing.

Vague and Imprecise	*Definite and Emphatic*
writing	contract's
part	final clause
anyone	suggesting
told	employees
them (no antecedent)	(*management* is understood from the context)
something that could be used	practicable methods
the way they ran the firm	firm's efficiency
get	receive
something extra	bonus

Finally, the terms *initiative* and *imagination* draw attention clearly to the qualities which this company was trying to encourage. The first version omits reference to these qualities!

Emphasis through variety in sentence length and sentence structure. Monotony is the greatest enemy of emphasis. Repeated look-alike sentences lull a reader to sleep. Sameness in sentence length or type kills interest. Emphasis becomes impossible.

To combat monotony, consciously shape your material. Phrase your ideas vigorously. Vary the types of sentences you use. Vary the length of your sentences. Such variety will keep the reader alert and enable you to emphasize key ideas by contrast.

One of the most useful methods of getting attention for important ideas is the short, forceful sentence. Of course, a short sentence will not produce emphasis when surrounded by other short sentences. When buried in this way, the key sentence is wasted. The reader will have no reason to give it special attention. But occurring after a series of long sentences, the short sentence jolts the reader. It hammers your point home.

Emphasis through careful placement. You have probably noticed that the opening scene of a movie is usually striking. The director sets out to capture the attention of the audience instantly. If he fails at the outset, it becomes increasingly difficult to gain their attention.

Similarly, the opening part of a letter, a paragraph, or a sentence is particularly important for catching the reader's interest. Only the concluding part is more important in making an impression. Since the opening and closing parts of any unit receive greatest attention, it makes sense to present key points in these positions. Place routine details and minor points in less eye-catching positions.

Note how short sentences and variety of sentence arrangement are used to emphasize different points in the following messages.

a) Under the terms of the new contract arranged last week and due to go into effect in five weeks, you will receive a large increase in salary as a reward for your excellent work.
(Routine opening, emphatic close.)

b) A new contract was arranged last week. Under it you will receive, beginning in five weeks, a large increase in salary. This increase is a reward for your excellent work.
(Routine opening, very emphatic close.)

c) A new contract was arranged last week in which certain salary increases were granted in recognition of excellent work. Among other employees, you were granted an increase according to this contract. The contract will not become effective until five weeks from now.
(Minor points and details emphasized.)

d) For your excellent work, you have been granted a large increase in salary under the terms of the new contract which was arranged last week; the new contract goes into effect in five weeks.
(Emphatic opening, routine close.)

e) Your salary for next year has been greatly increased. The increase, which was arranged in a new contract last week, goes into effect very soon—in five weeks. The increase recognizes your excellent work.
(Emphatic opening and close.)

f) Under the terms of last week's new contract, a large increase in salary will be granted to you in recognition of your excellent work last year. The increase will go into effect in five weeks.
(Routine opening and close.)

Any one of these versions of the message might be acceptable for certain purposes. Each message makes a somewhat different impression on the reader. The same information in approximately the same words is given in each message. Different points are, however, emphasized in each. This difference in emphasis, together with minor changes in the phrasing, affects the tone of each message. Notice that message *e*, in particular, has been arranged to please the recipient. Complimentary observations are given prominence through both sentence position and sentence brevity. On the other hand, notice that message *c* has a distinctly negative, almost grudging tone.

The decision about what should be emphasized in any message depends entirely upon the writer's intentions. To write effectively, you must first decide what it is you wish to accomplish. You must then plan your message—work out your strategy—in a way calculated to accomplish that purpose.

Active voice for punch. We have examined the use of key sentence positions to gain attention for important points. A related technique is the conscious use of active or passive voice for purposes of emphasis. Many writers have a tendency to use passive voice; active voice is, however, almost always more appropriate and more forceful. Use active voice, *unless you have a specific reason for not doing so.*

Passive voice—indirect and wordy

a) It was stated in the telegram that the detachment had been sent on a dangerous mission by the colonel.
b) That weaknesses in the company's accounting procedures had been found by the inspector was reported by the committee.

Active voice—direct and brief

a) The telegram stated that the colonel had sent the detachment on a dangerous mission.
b) The committee reported that the inspector had found weaknesses in the company's accounting procedures.

Active voice is direct and forceful. Still, passive voice can be used effectively for specific purposes. Under certain circumstances the writer of the preceding examples might prefer passive voice in the dependent clauses. For example, he might want to emphasize the detachment of soldiers (first sentence) or the company's accounting procedures (second sentence). Note that in passive voice, these terms are used as subjects. Attention is focused on them.

Passive voice is also useful when the writer wishes to avoid mentioning his informant, or when the writer wishes to avoid mentioning the person responsible for a certain action. It is useful, too, when the writer does not know the source of his information or the person responsible for an action. Because confusion often results when the agent or informant is omitted, careful writers use the passive voice with caution.

Agent or informant emphasized: active voice

a) My brother repaired the window last night.
b) Senator Lyons reported that the Senate will pass the bill later this week.

Agent or informant mentioned: passive voice with prepositional phrase

a) The window was repaired by my brother last night.
b) It was reported by Senator Lyons that the Senate will pass the bill later this week.

Agent or informant not mentioned—unknown or concealed?

a) The window was repaired last night.
b) It was reliably reported that the Senate will pass the bill later this week.

As you experiment with various ways of phrasing your ideas, make a point of exploring the use of both active and passive voice. Use voice as a tool for the purpose of controlling point of view and emphasis. As you read, note the use professional writers make of these resources.

Emphasis through parallelism and climactic arrangement. In Section 2 we considered parallelism as a feature of grammar. Here we shall consider it from the point of view of rhetoric (effective presentation). A writer wishing to present an idea with great force may arrange his points in a series of similar (parallel) constructions. Lincoln uses this device frequently in the Gettysburg Address, for example, in this sentence:

But in a larger sense we cannot dedicate—we cannot consecrate—we cannot hallow this ground.

Let's examine the use of parallelism in the following example:

In a national crisis the true patriot is prepared to sacrifice luxuries, to sacrifice leisure, to sacrifice financial advantage, to sacrifice happiness, and, if need be, to sacrifice life itself.

Here a number of factors help make the sentence forceful:

1 — the series of infinitive phrases
2 — the repetition of the word *sacrifice*
3 — the climactic arrangement of the words *luxuries, leisure, advantage, happiness,* and *life*

In a series of parallel constructions, the terms become more effective if they are arranged in order of increasing importance. Because it works toward a climax, such a pattern is called *climactic arrangement.* A failure to arrange terms climactically is called *anticlimax.* Note the effect of interchanging the words *leisure* and *life* in the preceding example. Once the term *life* has been used in the list, it becomes ridiculous to add the other terms.

As we have seen, climax is a device for emphasis often used in a series of parallel constructions. Another such device is the repetition of key words and phrases. The powerful concluding sentence of the Gettysburg Address provides an excellent example of emphatic repetition, together with parallelism and climax:

It is rather for us to be here dedicated to the great task remaining before us—that from these honored dead we take increased devotion to that cause for which they gave the last full measure of devotion; that we here highly resolve that these dead shall not have died in vain; that this nation, under God, shall have a new birth of freedom; and that government of the people, by the people, for the people, shall not perish from the earth.

Parallelism involving balance and contrast. Parallelism may involve other forms than the kind of climactic series of similar constructions that we have just considered. For example, a writer may phrase two clauses so that the structure of one balances the other. This arrangement can gain increased attention for each of the balanced elements, and thus can provide emphasis for points that deserve special treatment. Emphasis results, however, only when a writer does not use such sentences repeatedly. As we have noted often, variety is indispensable for interest and emphasis. Note the use of balance for emphasis in the following sentences.

It was the secretary who prepared the faulty letters; it was the executive who signed them.

Before it is sent, you can proofread your letter; before it is sent, you can correct your mistakes.

Balanced construction can be used to especially good advantage to emphasize a contrast between two statements.

> As usual, Mr. Babin arrived on time. As usual, Mr. Hale arrived late.
> Last year's price was reasonable. This year's price is not.
> The wise student is primarily concerned about what he is learning, not about his grades. The foolish student is primarily concerned about his grades, not about what he is learning.

Emphasis through postponing key ideas. A writer can achieve a measure of suspense by placing his main point toward the end of a sentence. The reader's interest is then maintained to the very end, the most emphatic part of the sentence. This delay reinforces the emphasis which results from placing an important point near the end of the sentence. Both of the following sentences are acceptable.

> *Key idea revealed at once:*

> You will receive a bonus when your sales increase markedly, when you have been with the firm for at least one year, or when you suggest ideas for increased efficiency which are adopted by the firm.

> *Key idea postponed:*

> When your sales increase markedly, when you have been with the firm for at least one year, or when you suggest ideas for increased efficiency which are adopted by the firm, you will receive a bonus.

Emphasizing essential relationships between ideas. The relationships between ideas are often as important as the ideas themselves. If relationships are not made definite, confusion may result. Thus:

> Since taxes were raised, sales declined.

Here the writer may mean: (1) Because taxes were raised, sales declined. (2) After taxes were raised, sales declined. The reader has no way of knowing which meaning was intended. Even more serious is the possibility that the reader may not notice the confusion. He may simply accept a meaning, and it may very well *not* be the one intended by the writer.

When you are writing, try to imagine what difficulties the reader may encounter in interpreting your words. He has no way of knowing what you *really* mean, except through the words you put on paper. Make sure those words convey your meaning unmistakably.

It is helpful to realize the great variety of relationships that can exist between two simple ideas. This awareness will remind us of the importance of indicating relationships precisely. The following sentences illustrate some of the many possible relationships between two simple ideas. These ideas are (1) Tom makes high grades, and (2) Tom will be elected to the honor society. (Note in the following examples that the same relationship—such as cause and effect—can often be expressed in many different ways.)

Tom makes high grades: he will be elected to the honor society.
   (Cause and effect. Note the use of the colon.)
Tom will be elected to the honor society; he makes high grades.
   (Conclusion and explanation.)
Tom will be elected to the honor society, for he makes high grades.
Tom will be elected to the honor society because he makes high grades.
Tom will be elected to the honor society if he makes high grades.
Tom will be elected to the honor society as long as he makes high grades.
Tom will be elected to the honor society while he makes high grades.
Tom makes high grades; so he will be elected to the honor society.
Tom makes high grades, so that he will be elected to the honor society.
   (Note the ambiguity here. The conjunction "so that" may signify either *purpose* or *result*.)
Tom makes high grades; hence, he will be elected to the honor society.
Tom makes high grades; therefore he will be elected to the honor society.
Because Tom makes high grades, he will be elected to the honor society.
   (Note that the order of the clauses can be reversed in many of the other sentences, as well as in this one.)

Thus we see that many different relationships can exist between two simple ideas. The nature of the relationship between clauses is an essential part of their significance, and sometimes is central to a writer's purpose.

To appreciate the value of actually stating such relationships, let's examine the following passage. It is composed entirely of short, simple sentences. Words expressing relationships have been omitted. Here is the passage:

Leo went to the track every afternoon. He ran for hours and hours. The all-city meet was to be held in less than two weeks. He wanted desperately to win at least one event. A letter would then be presented to him at the annual athletic banquet.

Such a series of simple sentences seems childish. Compare the much different impression this passage makes when relationships are thoughtfully expressed.

> Because he wanted desperately to win at least one event in the all-city meet, which was to be held in less than two weeks, Leo went to the track every afternoon. He ran for hours and hours. If he succeeded, he would earn his letter, to be presented at the annual athletic banquet.

Omit sentence padding. Inexperienced writers sometimes pad their sentences with unnecessary words. Perhaps they do so, at times, to make a letter or assignment appear longer that it otherwise would be. Perhaps they are writing down whatever comes into their heads, without stopping to think. Note the following examples.

Objectionable

Because they were late, the result was that they were fined.

Here the writer apparently does not realize that "the result was" expresses the same idea as "because." Repetition of this kind is unemphatic and distracting. Its effect is undesirable, self-defeating. In contrast, planned and skillful repetition of key words and phrases can produce striking emphasis.

Objectionable

> A necessity arising because of the existence of a depressing condition of uncleanliness in the quarters in which the staff regularly carried on their activities, the improvement of these quarters was undertaken during that time of year when workers are being given rest from their regular employment.

Wordiness of this kind is called *gobbledegook*. Such writing is ridiculous and confusing. The rules for avoiding gobbledegook are simple. (1) Write only when you have something to say. (2) Express your ideas simply, concisely, and straightforwardly.

Here are sample revisions of the two awkward and objectionable sentences given above:

Acceptable

> Because they were late, they were fined.
> They were late; as a result they were fined.
> The office was redecorated during the summer, because it had become dingy.

• *APPLYING EFFECTIVE ENGLISH*

Oral Applications

• **1.** From the *Reader's Digest* or some other magazine choose an article which interests you. Select for class discussion passages which illustrate some of the following techniques of effective composition:

1 — Variety of sentence structure
2 — Emphasis obtained by careful placement
3 — Parallelism involving climactic arrangement
4 — Parallelism involving balance and contrast
5 — Sentence structure postponing the key idea
6 — Emphatic repetition of key words and phrases
7 — Clearly indicated relationships between ideas

In class discussion try to decide what effect the author was trying to achieve in using these particular devices. Concern yourself not only with *what* the author has said but also with *how* and *why* he has said it.

• **2.** A committee of five has the responsibility of revising the J. R. Loras Company's announcement of its approaching expansion. One student may take the role of committee chairman; four others, the roles of committee members. (More than one committee may be formed in any class.) Here is the announcement the committee must try to make more effective:

> It is not without a substantial degree of genuine pleasure that it is announced at this time, by the J. R. Loras Company, that a new division will be opened at our Sulter Valley plant which will employ over three hundred and twenty-seven additional employees, and it will manufacture our newly designed stereo high-fidelity automobile tape player.

Written Applications

• **1.** Rewrite the following sentences in balanced form. Make whatever changes seem desirable in order to produce a sentence as effective as possible. Many different effective sentences can be obtained through imaginative revision of these awkward sentences.

1 — Tony's height is six feet, but Lloyd is only five feet, six inches tall.
2 — The package was mailed by us yesterday; however, we did not mail the letter until this morning.
3 — An experienced writer carefully revises and proofreads anything that he writes for others to read. What is written by an inex-

perienced writer is often submitted unrevised and even without being proofread.

4 — The head office was located, in accordance with the decision of the board, in New Orleans. They decided, however, that they would establish the research laboratories in Birmingham.

5 — Reading and study make a man well-informed. A man is made mature and steady by experience.

• **2.** Rewrite the following sentences in such a way as to make them more emphatic.

1 — By the time we arrived, he had left already, however.

2 — The largest sales campaign in the history of the company will begin early next month, we were informed today.

3 — The expert affirmed that the reorganization could be carried out without great expense, in his opinion.

4 — Mr. Lucas has had a great deal of executive experience; he was vice-president of Diefenbach Manufacturing Company for eleven years, for example.

5 — Five employees will be eligible for promotion this year, according to the personnel department.

• **3.** Revise the following sentences, placing the dependent clause in a less emphatic position.

1 — Yesterday the board ordered a revision of the firm's advertising policies, because sales have been low during the last six months.

2 — The company has appealed to the high schools to give greater emphasis to writing, because many recent graduates are unable to write even an acceptable application for a job.

3 — His suggestion was rejected when it became known that there was insufficient evidence to support it.

4 — The engine can be made more cheaply and rapidly, if we are willing to sacrifice its dependability.

5 — Mr. Drummond also bought a briefcase when he observed that all of the other executives carried them.

• **4.** Revise the following sentences, omitting unnecessary words. Make similar elements parallel whenever possible.

1 — When they looked into the costs of such improvements, it was at that time that they decided not to go ahead.

2 — Because Miss Muller can express herself fluently and pleasantly, consequently she was chosen as receptionist.

3 — The reason a second shipment was ordered is because many items from the first shipment had already been sold out.

4 — Mr. Miller had three special reasons for going to night school. The first reason was that he wanted to improve his ability to write reports. A possible increase in salary in recognition of his efforts to improve was his second reason. Also, he had a genuine interest in the problems of management psychology.

• *REVIEW*

• **1.** Revise the following sentences to improve their unity, coherence, and emphasis. Combine sentences if such an arrangement offers an improvement.

1 — A student may fail who doesn't study. Such students cannot reasonably expect to benefit from going to school.

2 — Decorated with colored frosting and whipped cream, you will be very much pleased with the birthday cake that has been ordered.

3 — He passed the first test with a high grade; however, the second test was passed by him with one of the lowest grades in the class.

4 — That man should go far in the business world: his character is excellent, his personality is pleasing, and an ability to mix easily with other people is another of his traits. Also, he has a good reputation.

5 — Elroy borrowed from the library many books on American history. He was preparing for a scholarship test. He is very much interested in the subject. He wants to major in American history in college.

• **2.** Revise the following sentences. Insert necessary punctuation and correct all errors. Attempt to make the sentences more emphatic whenever possible.

1 — He dont want to come because these kind of meetings ain't interesting to him.

2 — Mr. Martin use to visit us real often.

3 — Nothing you, and I speak on the basis of my own experience, can say will change his mind he is not willing to consider others suggestions.

4 — One of his employees, in the near future, are being sent to a special school, he is one of those executives who likes to give his employees a chance to improve yourself.

5 — Each and every person in all the companies departments are given their own choice of vacation time.

6 — Its much to hot to cut the grass today, at least lets wait until this evening.

• **3.** Copy the following promotional message. Supply proper capitalization and proper punctuation. Correct all errors you find.

dr jacob l barnes has written us suggesting that you might be interested in subscribing to business month a magazine devoted to professional analysis of business trends throughout the country and indeed throughout the world

let me point out at once that business month does not solicit subscribers on a random or mass basis individuals are invited to become subscribers only upon recommendation by one of our present subscribers it is in fact a mark of distinction to be invited to subscribe to business month it is an even greater mark of distinction of course to be a subscriber among the intelligent business leaders who subscribe to business month are the directors of many of our countries largest and most important corporations

were sure youll feel right at home among these distinguished subscribers to our fine publication a publication which dr thomas c nelson vice president of the supreme electronics equipment company pittsburgh pennsylvania has called the key to treasures of vital up to date business information

not everyone of course realizes the value of such a key but we feel confident that you should be numbered among the select group that appreciates up to the minute accurate and confidential business reporting

on the first monday of each month business month reviews all of the important news in the world of business during the preceding 30 days surveys government activities and pending legislation which may affect business and provides informed predictions of business trends no one interested in american business no one contemplating investments no one having managerial responsibilities can afford to neglect a single issue of business month

the enclosed folder explains the publishing policy's of business month the order blank which you will find on the last page of the folder offers you 3 options all with a money back guarantee 1 a years subscription at $15.00 2 a two year subscription at $285.0 3 a trial subscription for 6 issues at $6.00

whichever offer you accept i am confident that you will find you're subscription to business month a tremendous asset

UNIT 7

DEVELOPING SKILL IN WRITING PARAGRAPHS

From your study of Unit 6 you have learned important principles of writing. You know what makes sentences correct and forceful. Such sentences are the basis of good writing. However, good writing requires more than effective individual sentences. These sentences must be combined into logical paragraphs and well-organized messages. While Unit 8 will deal with complete messages, Unit 7 will show you how to build effective paragraphs.

In the first section you will learn the fundamental idea behind paragraphing. You will learn to appreciate the value of topic sentences to the writer as well as to the reader. You will also learn various techniques for developing paragraphs logically.

In the second section you will examine key methods of increasing the unity, coherence, and emphasis of paragraphs.

The more practice you have in thoughtful writing, the sooner you will master the principles of organization and emphasis.

UNIT 7

Section 1

Paragraph Structure and Development: An effective paragraph must develop a definite topic.

Section 2

Paragraph Unity, Organization, Coherence, and Power: To be forceful, paragraphs must be carefully planned—organized, knit together, and phrased—to fulfill some specific functions.

SECTION 1

Paragraph Structure and Development

An effective paragraph develops a unified topic.

A *paragraph* is a span of writing which develops a unit of thought. The unit is larger than a single sentence but more limited than the unifying idea of a whole message. (This definition holds except when a single sentence functions as a paragraph or a message contains only one paragraph.)

For the convenience of the reader, individual sentences are set off by means of periods (or other full-stop punctuation marks), spacing, and capital letters. For the same reason, paragraphs are set off by indenting the first line, by spacing, or by both devices.

The purpose of paragraphing. Paragraphs, like sentences, are important tools which the writer uses in communicating his ideas. Paragraphs are not merely arbitrary units of copy. They should draw the reader's attention to definite divisions in the writer's thought. Thus, by beginning a new paragraph, you give the reader a signal that you are turning to a new phase of your presentation. As a result, he can follow your thoughts much more readily than he otherwise could. Without the help of paragraphing, a reader would be forced to analyze a message sentence by sentence to identify its topics. To understand the message thoroughly, he would have to study it to determine the relationships among its sentences.

Besides marking off divisions in thought, paragraphs present material in units that encourage the reader to continue reading. A long message not divided into paragraphs is extremely forbidding, as well as difficult to understand. On the other hand, a message containing only very short paragraphs is dull. The principle of variety in length is as important for paragraphs as for sentences.

The length of paragraphs varies somewhat with the *audience* and the *subject*. Young readers or those with limited education will respond more readily to short paragraphs (and sentences). Mature readers, however, are not likely to respond favorably to artificially simple writing.

The paragraph as a unit of thought. As we have noted, paragraphs serve the purpose of marking off divisions in the writer's thought. Thus, a paragraph will represent one phase of the writer's outline for his memo, letter, or report. There are two tests to insure that a paragraph will be efficient. First, be certain that each paragraph contains a definite, unifying idea (its topic). Second, see that all irrelevant material—anything unrelated to the point being developed—is excluded from the paragraph.

If you include information not clearly related to the topic of a paragraph, the reader may lose his bearings. He may not be able to tell what the real point of the paragraph is. Of course, information that is irrelevant in one paragraph may be essential in some other paragraph. For this reason every message requires planning. Prepare at least a general outline of key ideas, and follow your plan as you write. Thus you will be assured of arranging your ideas in a purposeful sequence. You will find that this practice also assists in keeping each paragraph tightly centered around a definite idea.

The topic sentence as a key to the paragraph. Writers often state the basic idea of a paragraph in a single sentence. Such a sentence is called a *topic sentence.* It often, but not always, comes at the beginning of a paragraph. A topic sentence is extremely helpful to the writer, as well as to the reader. For the reader it provides a guidepost which reveals the thought of the paragraph. For the writer it provides a reminder of the main point he should be developing in the paragraph.

Types of paragraph development. All the sentences in a paragraph should bear a definite relationship to the topic of the paragraph. The nature of that relationship, however, can vary considerably. Six types of relationships commonly used for developing paragraphs are presented and illustrated below and on the following pages:

(1) The paragraph may narrate an incident or describe a process. Narration and process description are types of *time arrangement.*

Narration

For weeks the boy scouts planned their three-day hike. They studied various maps and eventually decided what route to take and where to camp each night. They agreed on what equipment and food to bring. At last, on the morning of May 19, twelve scouts and their leader drove 150 miles north to Elm Hill Forest Preserve. There they parked the station wagon and set out along the Willibee River Trail.

Description of a process

To operate the record player, first turn on the power switch. Give the amplifier adequate time to wārm up. Place a record on the turntable. Set the selector switch at the speed appropriate for the record you intend to play. Lift the tone arm and move it slowly away from the turntable a distance of about two inches. This action engages the turntable motor. When you hear a click, gently place the needle on the lead-in grooves of the record. After the record has been played, the turntable will stop automatically.

(2) The paragraph may describe some physical object, such as the layout of a building, a campus, or an office. When the shape of an object determines the sentence sequence, the paragraph involves a *space arrangement*.

Description according to space arrangement

The new high school building is laid out in the form of a large U, with its base running from southwest to northeast. The left-hand wing contains the auditorium, home economics room, and shops. The base contains the school offices, the science classrooms and laboratories, and the rooms with various kinds of office equipment. The right-hand wing contains all the classrooms which do not require special equipment or machinery. If more space is needed in the future, a new wing will be built across the open end of the U.

(3) The paragraph may present an analysis. One kind of analysis divides a subject into its logical parts. Another kind of analysis arranges related objects or ideas into classes. The first type of development by analysis is called *partition*. The second is called *classification*.

Partition

The university has five schools: (1) a liberal arts college, (2) a graduate school, (3) a medical school, (4) a law school, and (5) a school of business administration. The liberal arts college, the graduate school, and the school of business administration have expanded very rapidly since 1945. On the other hand, the medical school and the law school, although they were established long before the school of business administration, have not grown in size since World War II.

Classification

The phonograph records in his collection include three principal types: (a) solo performances by singers and instrumentalists, (b) operas and oratorios, and (c) instrumental works, such as symphonies, concertos, and tone poems. His new high-fidelity stereo system reproduces the first type of recording with somewhat greater brilliance than his former record player did. But the most striking improvement in reproduction concerns the second two types—recordings of large ensembles.

(4) The paragraph may present a comparison, pointing out either similar or contrasting features of the objects or ideas being compared. This type of presentation is called *development by comparison.* The following paragraph illustrates paragraph development involving definition and examples, as well as comparison. The purpose of this comparison of the two types of analysis is to clarify the meaning of the word *analysis.*

Comparison

The word *analysis* comes from two Greek roots, *ana-* (throughout) and *lysis* (a loosening). Thus, in origin the word means a loosening of the parts throughout any whole or unit. In other words, analysis is the process of identifying the components of any whole. Analysis applied to a single object is called *partition.* Thus, if an essay is divided into its introduction, main body, and conclusion, the analytical process may be referred to as partitioning. On the other hand, the whole may be a group of objects that are considered as making up some kind of unit. Analysis applied to a group of objects to make clear the various categories or classes comprising the group is called *classification.* Thus, if students are divided into groups on the basis of I.Q., the analytical process is called classification.

(5) The paragraph may present an argument. If the argument establishes some generalization on the basis of specific details, the paragraph is being developed inductively. In other words, it is being developed according to the principles of *inductive reasoning.* If the argument applies some general principle to a particular situation, the paragraph is being developed deductively. In other words, it is being developed according to the principles of *deductive reasoning.*

Development by inductive reasoning

The number of small cars imported into the United States has been increasing at an impressive rate during recent years. Many different small cars manufactured in various European countries are frequently seen on our streets and highways. Furthermore, various United States

manufacturers are now producing compact models, and other manufacturers have announced plans to do so. This evidence indicates that
public taste is coming to favor smaller cars. It may foreshadow a
decline in popularity for the tremendously powerful, sleek limousines
of the last decade.

Development by deductive reasoning

Our state should adopt any measure which will help us cut the
accident rate on our highways. The number of people killed in automobile accidents over the last two decades has steadily increased.
Unless something is done to correct this situation, the increase in the
accident rate will continue as more and more cars operate on our roads.
Many states have adopted a strictly enforced maximum speed limit of
60 or 65 miles an hour. Such limits have significantly reduced the
number of fatal accidents on their highways. Therefore, it seems
obvious that our state should enact such a law and then enforce it.
Otherwise we can hardly claim to be serious about wanting to make
our roads safer.

(6) The paragraph may present *details* or *examples*. The details
or examples may be used in order to increase clarity, accuracy, or
emphasis.

Development by examples and details

Many high school graduates cannot write effectively. Their difficulty
results largely from a lack of concentration when they write. They
have never learned to proofread with scrupulous care. They have
never formed the dictionary habit. Sentence fragments, comma faults,
awkward and imprecise phrasing are common in their reports, term
papers, and examinations. Such errors occur even in their letters of
application! Misspellings are frequent. Even misspellings of such common words as *believe, receive, written,* and *writing* occur. Words that
sound alike, such as *to-too-two, there-they're-their,* and *affect-effect*
are often confused. A letter containing such mistakes makes the writer
seem nearly illiterate.

These types of paragraph development are not the only possible
ones, but they are among the most important. You will discover that
most paragraphs involve a combination of various types of development. For example, note the combination of factors involved in the
paragraph presenting a development by comparison. The principle in
organizing the paragraph, however, is the distinction between partitioning and classifying, the two main forms of logical analysis.

• APPLYING EFFECTIVE ENGLISH

Oral Application

• Study the following paragraphs carefully. In class discussion,
  (1) decide what the unifying idea of each paragraph is,
  (2) identify the topic sentence wherever possible,
  (3) determine the technique used to develop each paragraph,
  (4) consider how these paragraphs could be condensed or expanded. In your opinion, would omitting or adding anything improve any of them? Be specific in justifying your answer.

(a)

The United States is attempting to strengthen the free world in many ways. In the first place, it is giving economic aid to many underdeveloped countries—to some countries still not committed in the struggle between democracy and totalitarianism, as well as to those already on the side of democracy. It is giving valuable assistance to some countries in the form of technical aid and advice in the areas of agriculture, education, and industry. It encourages foreign students to visit the United States, to observe our way of life, and to study in American colleges and universities. It is also giving military assistance wherever its allies require such assistance.

(b)

Anyone who has studied seriously in school and who is interested in working hard toward a definite goal can enjoy a successful career in American business. Executives are always looking for such applicants to fill important jobs—jobs promising a bright future. You in this class—most of you—are taking your studies seriously and are doing your best to learn as much as possible while you are in school. You wish to succeed. You have ambition. You have, therefore, the prospect of an exciting business career opening before you when you finish your education.

(c)

A trip to historic locations can make history seem much more real than it does when one merely reads about it in books. Last summer we visited Independence Hall, in Philadelphia. We saw the rooms where the delegates to the Second Continental Congress met; we saw the Liberty Bell; we saw the very room and furniture used by the great men who wrote, debated, and signed the Declaration of Independence. As we stood in the room where the text of the Declaration was debated, the Founding Fathers and the exciting events of the American Revolution seemed more real to us than ever before.

(d)

The accounting department office, according to present plans, will be laid out in the form of a capital L, the upright stroke of which is about three times the length of the horizontal one. The private office of the comptroller and the office of his secretary will occupy the horizontal stroke; a continuous picture window will stretch the entire length of this wall. From these offices the view north over the lake will be beautiful. The main part of the office, occupying the vertical stroke of the L, will have three rows of 25 desks each, with broad aisles between the rows and with ample room between the desks.

Written Applications

● **1.** Choose any whole-page magazine advertisement, and, using its slogan or selling point as a unifying idea, write a paragraph developing that idea. Use one of the methods of paragraph development discussed in this section. Attach the advertisement to your paragraph.

● **2.** Write a paragraph developing the following topic: "Student government in high school is effective preparation for citizenship in a democracy." Be prepared to point out and explain the method (or methods) you have used in developing this topic.

The following points, which you may wish to expand, modify, or rearrange, may be helpful to you as you write this paragraph:

1 — The student body nominates candidates.
2 — The candidates campaign for election.
3 — Members of the student senate (or whatever this organization may be called at your school) represent the student body, derive their authority from the student body and must act in accordance with a constitution.
4 — Parliamentary procedures are followed at meetings of the senate.
5 — The rights of minorities are protected.
6 — Decisions are reached by majority vote of senate members, and those holding other views accept such decisions.
7 — Difficult problems may be referred to the student body for its decision.

• **3.** Write a paragraph developing each of the following topic sentences according to the method suggested. Be prepared to explain at least one other method that might be used to develop each paragraph.

> 1 — Team sports teach young people the value of cooperation. (Develop by using examples and details. Use personal experiences, if possible.)
>
> 2 — Careful reading can help one improve his writing. (Develop by narrating an experience of your own.)
>
> 3 — Voting privileges in national elections should be extended to all citizens when they reach the age of eighteen. (Develop by arguing from a general principle.)

• **4.** Write a paragraph developing the topic sentence, "Effective English is indispensable in modern business." Be prepared to explain to the class the method or methods you have used in developing this topic sentence.

The following points, which you may wish to expand, modify, or rearrange, may be helpful to you as you write this paragraph:

> 1 — A letter containing mistakes in grammar makes a bad impression on the person who receives the letter. It may lose customers for the firm.
>
> 2 — Careless mistakes in writing can lead to confusion and misunderstandings. Costly errors in shipments and arrangements may result. Such blunders may lose business for the firm.
>
> 3 — If the recipient of a letter has to puzzle out or guess at what the writer was trying to say, a great deal of time and goodwill may be lost.

• **5.** Write a paragraph developing the following topic: "Summer employment (or after-school employment) provides valuable practical education for a business career." Be prepared to point out and explain the method (or methods) you have used in developing this topic.

SECTION 2

Paragraph Unity, Organization, Coherence, and Power

To be forceful, paragraphs must be carefully planned—organized, knit together, and phrased—to fulfill specific functions.

The principle of unity. The principle of unity in writing applies on three levels:

1 — Individual sentences must be unified, the component words functioning together to present a clear point.
2 — Individual paragraphs must be unified, the component sentences functioning together to present a larger unit of thought.
3 — The message as a whole must be unified, the component paragraphs functioning to present the writer's thesis—his overall meaning.

The unifying idea of a paragraph, of course, will be broader than the unifying ideas of the sentences making up the paragraph. Likewise, the unifying idea of the message will be broader than the unifying ideas of the paragraphs making up the message.

All the sentences in a paragraph should help present, explain, or illustrate the idea being developed in that paragraph.

In contrast to a report, theme, or essay, a letter sometimes deals with several comparatively unrelated points. For instance, one paragraph in a letter may be devoted to placing an order for certain pieces of equipment. Other paragraphs may request replacement of parts damaged during a recent shipment. Still another paragraph may request an operating manual for a certain machine. Even such a letter does have a kind of unity. Everything in it relates to matters of mutual concern to the two firms.

The importance of organization. In developing a topic, a writer seeks to exclude irrelevant material. In addition, he takes pains to present ideas systematically, in logical order. The significance of this principle is most obvious in narration. In telling a story, a writer ordinarily begins with the earliest events in his account. He then devotes successive sentences and paragraphs to successive incidents. Other types of development often require more thought than does simple narration. The writer must decide what sequence of topics will best develop his main point.

For instance, suppose you were writing a letter to sell a customer a 20-volume set of *The Space-Age Encyclopedia*. You might begin by listing various sales points. You might eventually decide to use only a few of the points that occurred to you as possibilities.

1 — Economical cost of the set, when its value is fully realized
2 — Reliability and authority of the set
3 — Usefulness of the set for all citizens who wish to be accurately informed. Science, government, history, and literature are among the fields covered
4 — Rich appearance of the set, making it a desirable adornment for the living room of a distinguished home
5 — Availability of convenient credit terms
6 — Special advantages of the set for students: large print, readability, attractive illustrations (many of them in color)
7 — Bonus offer of a bookcase for the set
8 — Comparison with other encyclopedias, showing the superiority of this set
9 — Prestige value of owning this particular encyclopedia
10 — Quotations from authorities praising the set

You must determine which of these points to include. A sales message that is too long will not be effective. Similarly, a sales message cluttered with ideas—even convincing ideas—will merely distract the reader. Points omitted in the first message may, of course, be used in a follow-up.

After determining what to include, you must decide how much attention to devote to each sales point. You must also consider how the message may be most convincingly organized and presented. So far you have merely selected certain items from a disorganized list. Encountering ideas in this random order, beginning with the cost (say $350), few readers would read beyond the first sentence! The organization of these ideas into an effective message poses a challenging problem of psychology, of persuasion.

The following sales message illustrates one way in which a writer might organize and present some of the sales points listed above. Each successful message must take into account the special interests of the particular sales audience being addressed.

> For a limited time only, the beautifully illustrated new edition of *The Space-Age Encyclopedia*—World's Ultimate Authority—is being offered for just $6.00 a month. Never before has *this* encyclopedia been available at so low a cost—only pennies a day!
>
> This is an exciting opportunity to provide the finest set of reference books in all the world for your children! As Professor Hewitt, Dean of Grandview College, has recently pointed out:
>
>> The key to success is knowledge, and *The Space-Age Encyclopedia* is an open door to knowledge.
>
> Think what it will mean to your children in school, to your whole family, and to you personally! This impressive set of richly bound volumes will be available for immediate reference in *your own* living room or study!
>
> *The Space-Age Encyclopedia* will place at your finger tips a treasury of vital information. Each article has been prepared by leading experts. How necessary such reliable information is to *the thinking person* in today's demanding world!
>
> Act now! Simply fill out the enclosed, self-addressed postcard, and you will receive *The Space-Age Encyclopedia*, plus a custom bookcase for your set . . . at *no additional charge!*
>
> Send the postcard for your set and free bookcase *today!*

Note that some of the original ten sales points have been omitted in the message. The writer has tried to say just enough and to make exactly the right points to achieve his purpose.

The concept of function in planning the paragraphs of a message. Study the organization of *The Space-Age Encyclopedia* message. Note that different parts of the message have distinct functions. Each has a definite job to do. For example, the message begins by asserting that this offer is the chance of a lifetime! If the first paragraph is successful, the recipient will read further.

The second and third paragraphs appeal to the reader's pride in ownership. The fourth paragraph has the function of complimenting the prospective buyer. It suggests that he is a thinking person. Accordingly, he will appreciate the value of having this resource available at home.

The fifth and sixth paragraphs make it easy for the recipient of the letter to order his set. The fifth paragraph provides a final incentive to convince anyone who is still doubtful—the free book-case! The short sentence comprising the sixth paragraph urges immediate action. The sentence reminds the reader, indirectly, that this wonderful offer is being made "for a limited time only."

Coherence: tying ideas together. Thus far we have considered two important rhetorical principles. The first is unity—sticking to a unifying idea; the second is organization—presenting ideas in a logical sequence in which each paragraph has a definite function.

Now we shall consider a third principle—coherence, tying together the various ideas and topics in a message. We have seen that the logical connection between sentences in a paragraph must be communicated to the reader. In a similar way the relationships between paragraphs and groups of paragraphs must be made clear. Elements which set up this essential linkage are called *transitional* elements. Words, phrases, sentences, and whole paragraphs may be used to provide smooth transitions from one part of a message to another.

A reader can work out the relationships among paragraphs in a carefully organized message even if the transitions are missing. However, a writer can greatly assist the reader by providing a clear transition whenever he takes up a new phase of his subject. The transition announces that something new is coming. At the beginning of a message, a similar type of sentence or paragraph is often used. Such an introductory sentence may indicate the main points and plan of the entire message. In this way the writer provides a kind of outline to guide the reader through the message.

Examples of transitional words and phrases are *for example, on the other hand, furthermore, therefore,* and *finally.* These signals can make clear the relationships among paragraphs, as well as among sentences. Various limiting adjectives used with a key noun from the previous sentence or paragraph may function as transitional elements. For example, *these* adjectives, *this* noun, *that* sentence, *those* paragraphs. This device provides emphasis through repetition and shows the connection between ideas in adjacent sentences or paragraphs. Pronouns, also, can serve this connecting function.

An important type of transitional device is a sentence or paragraph stating that a change in topic is coming. Sometimes such a sentence or paragraph will also briefly summarize preceding material. For instance, consider the material after the heading "Coherence: tying ideas together," above. The first sentences restate the two rhetorical principles just discussed—unity and organization. The new paragraph begins the next topic to be considered—coherence. The first paragraph, then, provides a transition from the previous subjects to the discussion of coherence.

Headings may be used to draw attention to the separate parts of a discussion, as in this book. These headings keep the various sections separate from one another. At the same time, they provide a capsule version of the material to be presented.

Sometimes, instead of headings, a writer will use numbers to set off different topics. Headings and numbered lists are supplementary devices. They are used in connection with other transitional devices that occur in the text itself.

Now, let's look more closely at some of the devices commonly used to gain coherence. (Note that this paragraph provides a transition from the general introductory remarks concerning coherence.)

(1) **Coherence through repetition of key words or phrases.** Writers frequently repeat important words in various sentences or paragraphs. Such repetition draws attention to the fact that these sentences or paragraphs deal with aspects of the same idea. Thus, the repetition not only serves as a link, but it also emphasizes the idea.

For example, coherence is provided by the repeated words in the following paragraph:

> The standard model of this typewriter is equipped with *three extra keys. These extra keys* may be *adapted for* use in typing *special kinds of material. Such material* as market summaries can be conveniently typed on a typewriter with a specially *adapted keyboard.*

(2) **Coherence through the use of pronouns and limiting adjectives.** Pronouns can provide the same linking effect as the repetition of key words and phrases. However, pronouns can be repeated, without danger of monotony, much more freely than nouns. Limiting adjectives also help provide variety. In the example under (1) above, for instance, repeating the entire phrase *three extra keys* would have been awkward. At the beginning of the second sentence, the phrase was varied to *these extra keys.* Thus, pronouns and limiting adjectives are useful in establishing smooth connections between sentences and between paragraphs. The following are the most common and useful: *he, she, it, they* (plus the objective and possessive case forms *him, his;*

her, hers; it, its; them, their, theirs); who (whom, whose), which; that, those; this; these; such, another, other, one.

Note how the pronouns and their antecedents in the following passage serve to tie the sentences together. The pronouns are italicized; their antecedents are given in capital letters.

> MR. ALMAN criticized THE COMPANY'S EMPLOYMENT PRACTICES. *He* felt that *they* were out of date. *He* felt *they* should include APTITUDE TESTING and other PSYCHOLOGICAL TECHNIQUES *which* have been worked out in recent years. *His* CRITICISMS were contained in a report submitted to the president. *They* were expressed in frank but objective language.

Without pronouns the sentences would read as though they were separate and unrelated units. They would not sound like parts of a coherent paragraph. Furthermore the sentences would seem wordy and clumsy if the words in capitals were substituted each time for their corresponding pronouns. Try substituting them and see for yourself!

(3) Coherence through the use of special linking words and phrases. Special linking words and phrases make clear and definite the relationships between two or more ideas. When a relationship is made definite, the reader cannot overlook it. Thus, a writer can increase both clarity and emphasis by careful use of transitional words and phrases. (See pages 139-144 and 238-240.)

The list on the facing page includes the most common linking words and phrases. It comprises coordinating conjunctions, subordinating conjunctions, correlative conjunctions, linking adverbs, and various kinds of phrases. Examples of these transitional devices can be found in practically any paragraph. Try to find at least ten different linking words or phrases in the present section (Section 2 of Unit 7). For each example you find, decide exactly what relationship the transitional element indicates.

Emphasis in paragraphs. Thus far we have considered the importance of *unity, organization,* and *coherence.* We have also noted the interrelationships among these concepts. One further characteristic of an effective paragraph is *emphasis.* Emphasis means presenting key ideas forcefully. For emphasis, variety is essential. If all sentences in a paragraph are emphatic individually, the paragraph as a whole will be monotonous. The contrast between the phrasing and positioning of routine points and of important points helps keep the reader's attention. This contrast makes emphasis possible.

COMMON LINKING WORDS AND PHRASES THAT SHOW RELATIONSHIPS BETWEEN TWO OR MORE IDEAS [1]

Indicating *Result*

so that
with the result that
thus
consequently
hence
accordingly
for this reason
as a result
therefore
so

Indicating *Purpose*

in order to
so that
for the purpose of
with this in mind
with this in view
to + infinitive

Indicating *Examples*

for example
for instance
to illustrate

Indicating *Emphasis*

indeed
truly
of course
certainly
surely
in fact
really
in truth
above all

Indicating *Addition*

and
in addition
furthermore
moreover
besides
then
too
also
another
equally important
not so obvious
first, second (etc.)
again
further
lastly
finally
not only . . . but also
both . . . and
as well as

Indicating *Exclusion*

neither . . . nor
all except
all but
not that
but not

Indicating *Condition*

if
whether

Indicating *Alternatives*

or
either . . . or
whether . . . or

Indicating *Similarity*

similarly
likewise
in like fashion

Indicating *Contrast*

on the contrary
on the other hand
by way of contrast
contrastingly
notwithstanding
but
however
nevertheless
in spite of
in contrast
still
yet

Indicating *Details*

specifically
especially
in particular
to list
to enumerate
in detail
namely
including

Indicating *Concession*

although
at any rate
at least
still
though
even though

---

[1] Some of these terms can indicate more than one relationship.

The following techniques are useful for giving emphasis to an important idea: [2]

(1) **Give the idea a prominent position.** Spotlight essential material by placing it in such attention-getting positions as the beginning and the end of a paragraph. The most emphatic positions are at the beginning of the first paragraph and the end of the final paragraph of a message. The opening and closing sentences of paragraphs within a message are important for another reason. They must provide a smooth transition from the preceding paragraph to the following one.

(2) **Devote more space and more attention to the idea.** Focus the reader's interest on your key idea. Then provide enough repetition, elaboration, and detail to insure the reader's mastery of your point. (Note that this technique contrasts with No. 5 below.)

(3) **Repeat the idea in a variety of forms.** Present the idea from a number of points of view, or in contrasting phrasings.

(4) **Repeat key words.** Do not hesitate to use important words more than once. This device can serve to emphasize central points and also to knit sentences (and paragraphs) closely together.

(5) **Compress the important idea into a short paragraph.** The effectiveness of this technique depends upon a change of pace. If most paragraphs in a message are short, a slightly shorter one will not produce much emphasis. In contrast, an important idea expressed in a paragraph strikingly briefer than adjacent paragraphs will stand out. Like a short sentence contrasting sharply in length with longer sentences, a brief paragraph jolts the reader. It is the writer's "right jab."

(6) **Express the idea as a slogan or pithy saying.** The best illustrations of effective slogans are to be found in advertising and politics. Sometimes a writer is able to hit on an extremely catchy phrasing for an idea. The reader may not be able to get the idea out of his head.

(7) **State that the idea is important.** This is a forthright approach, and sometimes a highly effective one. A careful writer uses statements of this kind sparingly, however, or he defeats his own purpose. Suggesting that almost everything is important erases distinctions in importance.

---

[2] Compare these techniques for controlling emphasis at the paragraph level with those which apply to sentences. See Unit 6, Section 3, pages 232-240. Note the similarity of many of these points.

(8) For special effects, use mechanical methods for emphasis. Some of these devices are spacing, headings, enumerations, underlining, capitalization, and ink of contrasting color. The first three of these (spacing, headings, and enumeration) must be used with special attention to parallelism. Corresponding parts may be most effectively presented if they are developed in a similar way. The last three (underlining, capitalization, colored ink) should be used sparingly. If not used sparingly, they become monotonous and weaken the reader's interest.

Planning the whole composition. Like the paragraph, the whole composition must be clearly organized if it is to be effective. The various means of developing paragraphs are also used for developing the whole composition. Similarly, the characteristics of an effective paragraph are essential to a clear and forceful message. In Unit 8 you will have an opportunity to take up these principles as they apply to complete messages.

• *APPLYING EFFECTIVE ENGLISH*

Oral Applications

• **1.** In class discussion, expand the following list of advantages that could be claimed for the new compact Panther automobile. One way of expanding the list would be to include more details.

    1 — extraordinary maneuverability
    2 — rugged new 4-cylinder engine
    3 — complete dependability
    4 — outstanding comfort
    5 — remarkable economy of operation
    6 — impressive durability
    7 — appealing advanced design
    8 — luxurious interior
    9 — aluminum engine block and parts
   10 — low original investment
   11 — service available everywhere
   12 — sports car pick-up and handling qualities
   13 — five models available
   14 — many colors and color combinations available

• **2.** Consider the general topics under which it would be possible to outline all the sales points you consider advantageous. Classify each sales point under the appropriate topic. You might, for example, classify them under the following topics: (1) economy appeal, (2) esthetic appeal, (3) novelty appeal, (4) quality appeal, and (5) driving appeal.

• **3.** In the paragraph below, the principle of unity is violated. The writer has included sentences that do not relate closely to the unifying idea of the paragraph but introduce new and different aspects of a broader topic. Furthermore, as it stands the paragraph is rather long.

By means of class discussion, try to reach agreement concerning what idea the writer seems to have in mind as the unifying topic of the paragraph. Then decide which sentences do not properly develop this topic and hence do not belong in this paragraph. Give reasons for your conclusions. Finally, suggest a rearrangement by which two effective, unified paragraphs can be made from this defective one. Discuss what sort of transition should be provided between the two paragraphs you propose. Explain how improving the unity of this paragraph also leads to improved organization and increased emphasis.

The development of the modern automobile tire promises to revolutionize the tire industry. One of the main advantages of this tire is that it remains almost perfectly in its original shape even at top highway speeds. In contrast, conventional tires tend to become deformed at speeds above 60 or 65 miles an hour. Such distortion causes disturbing noises, leads to undesirable roughness in the ride, and increases tire wear as a result of thumping and friction. Synthetic rubbers were successfully developed during World War II as a substitute for natural rubber. For a period of half a decade during the 1940's the United States did not have access to the resources of natural rubber in Southeast Asia. One of the construction features of the latest tires is an improvement whereby the layers of cord comprising the body of the tire are applied in diagonal strata. Each successive layer wraps around the tire at a ninety-degree angle to the preceding one. This criss-cross design enables the modern tire to maintain its shape even under severe conditions. The fact that the tire remains in shape also leads to a reduction of friction between tire and pavement. The experimentation with synthetic rubbers, mentioned previously, also led to improvements in the manufacture and processing of natural rubber. As a result, the modern tire is much more durable and heat-resistant than tires manufactured just a decade ago. Accordingly, the modern tire reduces friction, maintains a nearly perfectly round shape at all speeds, and increases the amount of rubber actually in contact with the pavement. Thus, research leading to improved materials has brought about significant advances in driving safety, as well as comfort.

Written Applications

• **1.** Using (a) the economy appeal, (b) the driving appeal, or (c) the quality appeal, outline and write a paragraph to be used in a sales message for the Panther automobile described in Oral Application 1. First, decide which of the three appeals you wish to use; then, select for use in the paragraph those advantages or features that you classified under this appeal in Oral Application 2. Try to observe the principles of unity, coherence, and emphasis as you develop the paragraph.

• **2.** The following paragraph from a letter of application for a position is supposed to deal with two topics: the applicant's education and his business experience. Revise the material so that it is properly unified and effectively organized. Use more than one paragraph, if necessary.

> Throughout my high school career I maintained a better than C average. Incidentally, I attended Nelson High School, Harrison, Florida, graduating in June, 19—. Then I went to work for the Town House Shipping Company in Harrison. While attending high school I took many courses in commerce and typing. At the Town House Shipping Company I worked as a file clerk, but I did some typing in the office too. That reminds me that when I worked as a receptionist in Dr. Karnes' dental office, I also did some typing. I typed his bills and professional correspondence. In addition to typing, I studied shorthand, bookkeeping, and business English in high school. I was elected secretary and then, in my senior year, president of the business club at Nelson High School. In my business subjects I had almost a B average. During my two years as receptionist at Dr. Karnes' office, I frequently had an opportunity to take dictation. This experience enabled me to increase my speed considerably.

• **3.** Using (a) the quality appeal, (b) the esthetic appeal, or (c) the economy appeal, write an effective sales paragraph for the Soundking High Fidelity AM-FM Table Radio. Select from the list given at the top of the next page the sales features to include in the paragraph.

1 — Finishes: light oak, mahogany, maple, and fruitwood
2 — Cost: $97.50
3 — Operates on A.C. current or on battery power
4 — Wood cabinet for quality appearance and for outstanding sound quality
5 — Eight-inch high-fidelity speaker
6 — Nine transistors
7 — Excellent reception even in fringe areas
8 — Handsome styling: modern, early American, or provincial
9 — Built-in antenna, including di-pole antenna for FM
10 — Push-button tuning

• REVIEW

The following sentences contain various errors in punctuation, spelling, and grammar. (a) Be prepared to explain what is wrong in each sentence. (b) Rewrite the sentences, correcting each error.

1 — Although Kenneth claims that he rides the bus to school every day. Really, he takes his fathers car whenever he is late, which is about twice a week!

2 — The office staff is expected to attend these meetings, but they are not very conscientious about doing so.

3 — The manager of the companies two plants in Lexington are planning to attend. Provided, of course, that he does receive an invitation.

4 — Seeing that I now have the necessary information, I shall be able to quickly, accurately, and completely fill out that form.

5 — Revised three times, he was sure that the letter was now equally as effective, as he could make it.

6 — The difficulty with Mr. Lunn proposal was that no one could understand it, however now that he has rewritten and simplified the plan, he hopes it will be reconsidered.

7 — The advertising in the newspaper has been effective the advertising on the radio has been more effective. The television advertising having been most effective of all.

8 — Investigating the complaints from neighbors, the dogs were found by the policemen running loose.

9 — The man brought his new car, that owned the garage and paint shop.

10 — Even in the eighteenth century the widest known rivers in the Country, early trappers used the Mississippi and Ohio rivers for transporting furs long before other settlers came west.

 **UNIT 8**

DEVELOPING COMPETENCE IN WRITING THE COMPLETE MESSAGE

The fact that you are reading these lines suggests that you want to develop competence in writing a complete message. In order to develop such competence, you must understand clearly what your main thought is.

Your main thought is the basic subject of your discourse, the central idea that you intend to communicate. It is your corethought. The corethought is the commander. It marshals all the ideas into a well-planned unit. It takes control.

To put ideas into the right relation to one another, you must first identify your message corethought. Once the identity has been established, your ideas fall into order. Your complete message takes shape.

In Section 1 you will review the characteristics of an effective message: unity, coherence, and power. You will learn some of the specific steps for planning the message. You will also learn how to shape your material around the corethought.

In Section 2 you will become acquainted with methods for developing effective first and last sentences. You will also learn how to write such sentences yourself.

UNIT 8

Section 1

How to Plan the Complete Message: A good plan guides you in framing an intelligent message that is unified, coherent, and powerful.

Section 2

How to Write Forceful First and Last Sentences: Make your first sentence the headline, and let your last sentence leave a favorable impression.

 **SECTION 1**

How to Plan the Complete Message

A good plan guides you in framing an intelligent message that is unified, coherent, and powerful.

A well-planned message generates a favorable attitude toward the sender. It draws on your reason or your emotions. Perhaps it builds up within you a desire to act as the sender wishes you to act. To achieve these outcomes, three vital elements of effective writing have been applied:

1 — Words have been chosen and put together expertly into smooth-flowing sentences.
2 — The sentences have been linked together into smooth-flowing paragraphs.
3 — The paragraphed ideas have been welded together into a complete message of clearness and force.

You will observe this kind of skill each time an expertly framed statement makes a complicated problem seem crystal-clear. In the hands of the expert, the words of a complete message are the precise equivalent of pure power. In this and the following section you will be given an opportunity to examine and practice this power.

Study the characteristics of an effective message. Leaf through some of the feature articles of the newsmagazine, *U.S. News and World Report.* Note the exceptional skill with which the articles have been developed into effective messages. At the opening of each article, note the careful placement of the unifying corethought. Distinguishing every effective message are certain basic characteristics. Let us examine each one.

(1) The characteristic of unity. Your message must have a *unifying* idea that binds the whole statement together. This unifying idea, sometimes called the thesis, is the essential, central, key idea. It is the basic reason for creating and writing the communication. Example: "The central purpose of this book is to train you to become an

effective communicator." In this example you see a typical unifying statement that sets forth its subject, establishes its precise purpose, and supplies the key idea.

(2) The characteristic of organization. Your message should have a logical beginning, middle, and conclusion. The paragraphs of your statement should move systematically from point to point. You should be able to explain why you have included certain points in the opening section, others in the middle section, still others in the conclusion. Your clearly thought-out plan is the one sure path to effective organization.

(3) The characteristic of coherence. Make crystal clear to your reader the logical progression of your ideas. Through the transitions you provide between the parts of your message, help your reader to follow your plan. Let him see that all parts of your message contribute to the corethought or thesis.

(4) The characteristic of emphasis. Make your key ideas forceful. Let them be prominent. You may lose your reader's attention if you present your entire message at the same dead level. You must work for the emphasis that comes from variety. To spotlight important points, use deliberate contrast and variety (a) in your phrasing, (b) in your sentence length, (c) in your sentence structure, and (d) in your paragraphing.

How to plan and prepare the complete message. To assure its effectiveness, your complete message must be planned with intelligent care. You actually have a good running start toward this end. Why? Because you now apply, at the higher level of the *complete* message, the same principles you use in developing paragraphs. At this point you will find it most helpful to review these principles and procedures of paragraph development; see pages 247-251.

Develop your plan for the complete message by asking and answering the following question-guides:

1 — What is my *purpose* in writing (the corethought)?
2 — What facts and ideas do I wish to express? (These are the materials from which you will determine the method you will use in developing each paragraph.)
3 — In what exact order should I express these facts and ideas? (Your decision on order will provide the basic outline structure of the complete message and the unity and emphasis it must have.)

4 — How shall I link them together into a coherent whole that will support the corethought? (Select transitions that logically tie the sentences together into unified paragraphs and that logically tie the paragraphs together into the complete unified message.)

The illustrative case of the high-school yearbook. Let us examine the situation that might easily be taken out of the authentic records of your school. You are the chairman of the high-school yearbook sales committee. Your responsibility is to prepare a sales message designed to encourage each student to buy a copy of this publication. Applying the four-part procedure outlined above, you create the following set of guides:

1 — Your purpose: To get every student to buy a copy of the yearbook.
2 — The facts and ideas you will want to express: Suggest the outstanding features of the yearbook. List the reasons each student should buy a copy.
3 — The order in which you will want to arrange your material: Select with care a limited number of facts and ideas. Determine the order in which you wish to present them.
4 — Create a paragraph-by-paragraph sequence of effective topic sentences. Weld your message into a coherent and progressive whole that supports your basic purpose: "Buy a copy of the yearbook."

Now let us begin by listing selected sales points for the yearbook, entitled *The Golden Record*.

1 — A vivid, valuable permanent record of fond memories of your classmates and of the stirring events in which you all participated
2 — Classmates: pictures of all the graduating seniors (and of certain other undergraduates), with career records
3 — Class prophecy: future of the seniors as seen through the eyes of the editors and through comments of fellow students
4 — Athletic events and activities: the "Little Conference" football championship; the football king; cheerleader platoon; baseball, tennis, golf, hockey, swim meets
5 — Important organizations: choir groups, a cappella; Music Club, sponsoring musicals and operettas held in the high school auditorium; Latin Club; Dramatic Club, sponsoring two annual stage plays; social clubs
6 — Student trips to various cities to inspect activities related to school courses: display marts, business market exchanges, music programs, special programs

7 — Major special events for the year: fall homecoming, junior hop, senior prom, class queen selection

8 — Pictures of the superintendent, the principal, and teachers

9 — Pictures of class officers, editorial staff of the annual, chief officers of all school organizations, leaders of the outstanding campus activities through the year, together with a "memory record" of editorial comment for each, and a summary of the senior class achievement

10 — Pictures of winners of scholarships and major awards

11 — Your permanent "vintage" library record of high school life, bound in tough vinyl covering between boards with titles handsomely stamped in 14-karat gold

Under these eleven headings you have now listed a considerable number of sales points available for possible use. You may ultimately decide that your message will be more effective if you use only a few of the points. Hence, you must determine which of these points to include. A sales message too long will not be effective, nor will one "cluttered" with ideas, even though they may be good ideas. Obviously you will want to apply the limit-rule. Select, with great care, the points you feel to be most valuable in your first message. Some of the points you have omitted in the first message may, of course, be used in your follow-up.

Here is the commander-sentence that you might use as the main topic or central theme of your message:

The school yearbook that everyone wants—the book filled with pictures of people and events that will set up fond memories for years to come—will be off the press on May 5.

How will you expand this central theme? The following message illustrates one way in which you might present some of the feature points we have listed under the eleven sales points on pages 271 and above. You will note that some of the points in the original list have been omitted. You want to say just enough and select just the right items to assure the success of your message.

The school yearbook that everyone wants—the book filled with pictures of people and events that will set up fond memories for years to come—will be off the press on May 5.

As a student at Westport High, you have been in the very center of many of these events. You've seen the teams win the Little Conference football championship, and the trophies for baseball, tennis, and hockey.

You've been on the trips to the stock exchange and other interesting places. You've attended the music festival in the auditorium, the two senior class plays, and perhaps the senior prom. All these big events of the year are imperishably recorded for you in THE GOLDEN RECORD for 19—. This is the yearbook that will keep your memories vivid all your life long.

Then, of course, there's the class prophecy that predicts what is going to happen to all the seniors. Possibly the teachers helped to prepare some of these intriguing predictions. The faculty pictures are all there to bring your classroom experiences alive again, no matter how many years go by!

THE GOLDEN RECORD will be bound in tough vinyl-covered hard boards with titles handsomely stamped in 14-karat gold. It will form your lasting record of fond memories of your classmates and of the events you helped to make exciting!

To reserve your copy of THE GOLDEN RECORD, you must come to Room 212, English Hall, no later than February 1 to fill out a subscription form. Room 212 will be open every week day from 9 a.m. to 4:30 p.m. Your subscription now will assure you that your copy of THE GOLDEN RECORD will be waiting for you on May 5!

Note how this theme is swiftly expanded through the use of sharply concrete details, particulars, and examples. From opening to closing sentence, the fond-memory theme continues. It runs like a thread to unify the message and to give it psychological, persuasive force.

"One Hundred Years of Business History." Can you identify the corethought of the following message?

Would you like to see one hundred years of business history in a three-foot chart?

On this chart you may study the ups and downs of a century of business activity. You may observe the ebb and flow of important economic factors. You may view the play of wages, prices, real-estate values, and the stock market. This play is clearly shown.

We shall be glad to send you one of these charts as our small contribution toward business progress. If you would like to have one, please return the attached card; and we shall see that you get one at once. No charge, of course.

The corethought is announced like a trumpet call in the first sentence. You cannot mistake it. You cannot misunderstand it. The corethought defines itself in just fifteen words. "Would you," it inquires, "like to see one hundred years of business history in a three-foot chart?" The subject is (1) an offer (2) of a chart (3) three feet long (4) showing what has happened to business (5) in a hundred years.

Now you have identified the corethought and have decided exactly what it is. You can now see the essential ideas. All of them are simple. They have been put into the proper order to make sense and to bring about the result the writer wishes. The subject is first announced. Then the rest of the message tells (1) what may be done with this chart, (2) what advantages may come from its use, (3) the reason for its distribution, (4) how it may be had.

Sports, Incorporated, answers an inquiry. Let us try still another test. The situation is this: Sports, Incorporated, manufacturer of precision sports equipment, wishes to send a message to prospective customers (ages fifteen to eighteen years). These messages are to answer inquiries about Sports, Incorporated, .22-caliber sports and target rifles.

How should Sports, Incorporated, handle this situation? What should be the corethought of the message? How should this corethought be expanded in order to stimulate an intelligent interest?

First, of course, the company should decide exactly what the subject should be. The one who plans the message should study the inquiries. He must determine what particular .22-caliber sports and target rifle would best suit the needs of those who have inquired. He can then assemble the material into a list of unassorted but valuable ideas in the following manner:

> Features of the Precision Sportmaster: accurate target rifle; durable; built of wear-resisting materials to stand hard usage; larger barrel, heavier-gauge steel; husky, man-sized stock; new peep sights; eight sighting combinations; Lyman No. 422 Expert scope sight optional at additional charge; genuine walnut stock of selected wood; special tempered-steel barrel; precision workmanship; prices now low; for further information see your dealer; handle the unit; try it, test it, sight it.

Notice the sharp, concrete detail in these features. Now (1) he studies them. (2) He assorts the ideas into related groups. (3) He organizes each group into suitable paragraphs. (4) He puts the paragraphs into the right order to make sense. (5) He prepares his final draft.

Presented on page 275 is the message he prepares.

INCORPORATED

412 DUNCAN AVENUE

CHATTANOOGA, TN 37404

TELEPHONE: 615-432-6656

Manufacturers of Precision Sports Equipment

January 23, 19--

Mr. John M. Berry
1250 Harrison Boulevard
Ogden, UT 84404

Dear Mr. Berry

Thank you for asking about the Sportsmaster .22-caliber automatic repeating sports and target rifle. Enclosed is a folder that describes the features of the new Sportsmaster Precision 500.

You will enjoy the Precision 500 for its accurate target shooting. It replaces the Model 400 bolt-action and was built for hard service. The Precision 500 has all the advantages of the 400 and, in addition, has many new features.

Examine the man-sized stock with wide semibeavertail fore-end, and the larger, heavier barrel. Notice, too, the new Precision 500 adjustable sights giving ten sighting combinations.

Read about the Lyman No. 422 Expert scope sight, which you may buy with the Sportsmaster Precision 500 if you wish. This polished scope sight, although moderately priced, is of high grade, in keeping with the superior quality of the 500.

Why not ask your favorite sporting-goods or hardware dealer to show you the Sportsmaster Precision 500. Handle this beautifully balanced unit. Bring it to your shoulder. Compare it with others at or near the price. Notice the fine workmanship and materials--the high-grade polished steel, the high-gloss seasoned walnut stock.

You'll be wise to buy your Sportsmaster Precision 500 now while the price is low. If your local Sports, Incorporated, dealer does not have it, he will be glad to get it for you.

Sincerely yours

D. K. Floyd

D. K. Floyd
Sales Manager

mal

AN EFFECTIVE COMPLETE MESSAGE

You are told, in the first thirty words, precisely what you are going to read about. The corethought shines like a headlight. It is the new Sportsmaster Precision 500, .22-caliber automatic repeating sports and target rifle. The next five paragraphs describe the Model 500.

In two sentences the opening paragraph expresses courteous thanks for the inquiry and directs attention to the enclosed Sportsmaster folder. Thus, the subject has been announced. Then the facts are listed in effective order. They explain (1) the uses for the Precision 500, (2) the needs it will fill, (3) the convenient features, (4) the way in which to test it, and (5) the favorable price. The facts have been put into intelligent order and have been brought together into related groups. You now see how the body of a message is developed.

(1) Identify your subject, (2) select what is important, and (3) drop the rest. Perhaps you remember in *Aesop's Fables* the story of the monkey that tried to take a handful of sweetmeats from a jar with a small neck. But he was greedy. He seized such a large fistful that he could not draw his hand out of the jar. Some who write are like the monkey. In their haste to cover the subject, they seize too big a fistful. Failing to identify the corethought, they are liable to talk about things that do not matter. They are also liable to ramble along about trivial side issues and to smother, in a cloud of minor details, the significant facts and the important arguments.

Follow two simple rules:

1 — Choose the chief point you want to make.
2 — Stick to it.

Discipline your facts: multiply your success. Every day in some offices, communicators who fail to discipline their facts, who fail to organize their assembled materials are wasting precious company resources. Their business messages that should make friends and win new business miss the targets and simply go to waste.

The reason? Because the persons who wrote those messages were untrained in one terribly costly way. In twelve simple words: *They did not know (1) what to say or (2) how to say it.*

But *you will* now know what to say and how to say it. All you have to do is to apply the straightforward and tested principles set forth in this section, and to practice the art of unity, coherence, and power.

● *APPLYING EFFECTIVE ENGLISH*

Oral Applications

● **1.** Discuss the following concepts as they apply to the preparation of a complete business message: (1) unity, (2) organization, (3) coherence, and (4) emphasis.

● **2.** By means of class discussion, plan the texts of six different posters to be used for the purpose of drawing attention to *The Golden Record* (see pages 271-273). Limit the text for each poster to a dozen words or so. Select the corethought for each poster from the sales points listed on pages 271-272.

● **3.** In class discussion, develop a list of eight or more sales points for the Whirlaway Vacuum Cleaner. After you have these sales points on the chalkboard, organize them into various categories (for example, economy, convenience, performance). Consider which of these points might best be included in a sales message. Consider the order which would make these points most effective. Be prepared to give reasons in support of your suggestions. Take notes on the discussion, so that you can use these ideas in connection with Written Application 3.

● **4.** In class discussion, develop a list of ten or more sales points for the Fantasia Color Television set—portable, and battery operated. Organize this random list into appropriate sales categories. Take notes on the discussion, so that you can use these ideas in connection with Written Application 4.

Written Applications

● **1.** On pages 272-273 the sales message for *The Golden Record* contains 284 words. Using your own phrasing and selecting the points that appeal to you as most persuasive, prepare a 75-word sales message for *The Golden Record* for distribution by postcard.

● **2.** Make up a list of ten possible sales points for the Handywrite Electric Typewriter. Use three or four of your most persuasive sales points in a 150-word sales message.

● **3.** Using several of the most appealing sales points which were developed through class discussion of Oral Application 3, prepare a 150-word sales message for the Whirlaway Vacuum Cleaner.

● **4.** Incorporating what you regard as the best sales points worked out in class discussion concerning the portable, battery-operated Fantasia Color Television set, prepare a 175-word sales message. Be prepared to explain *why* you chose the particular sales points you used.

SECTION 2

How to Write Forceful First and Last Sentences

Make your first sentence the headline, and let your last sentence leave a favorable impression.

The headline spot in a message is its opening sentence. That is the position of strength. Play to it. Make use of it. Pivot an important key thought at the opening.

With equal force, let your last sentence leave a favorable impression. By lighting up your prominent ideas so that they stand forth, you make your reader's task lighter.

THE POWERFUL LEAD-OFF POSITION

In a news story the headline instantly tells you what the story is about. The expert newsmen who choose the words for these news headlines strive to make each one dynamic, strong, and brief.

Your message, too, through its first sentence, has the advantage of a powerful lead-off position. Your reader's eye sees your first sentence first. That powerful first impression counts heavily. You may be opening a stack of mail in a business office. Or you may be opening a very personal message. In either case the first sentence keys the message—or *should* do so. So choose your headline words with the greatest care because double importance rides on what comes first— the lead-off position.

Memorize the four duties of the first sentence. Let your first sentence do four vital things:

1 — Show courtesy and, if appropriate, express action in favor of the reader.
2 — Indicate the subject of the present message.
3 — Refer briefly to the subject of the preceding message, if such reference is desirable for clearness.
4 — *In a subordinated position,* refer to the date of the preceding message. The communicator may then check the filed copy for needed reference and review.

You are on the staff of the Madison National Bank. A customer sends in a deposit totaling $325.25 and asks for an acknowledgment. What will be the corethought of your reply to him? Clearly, the corethought is the remittance of $325.25 and what has been done with it. Simple as this situation appears, it requires care if it is to be handled well. You have established the corethought, and you must now meet and master the problem of the first sentence. What should the first sentence do? Look back at the four duties. You find the first sentence should be courteous. It should announce the subject. It should refer briefly to the subject of the preceding message. It should refer in an incidental way to the date of that message. To do these four things, the following first sentence is created:

> Thank you for the deposit of $325.25 enclosed in your note of August 20.

Tell your reader what he wants to know. Let us picture your reader. He is likely to be even busier than you. He has his pile of mail to go through. The bigger it is, the less attention he will pay to each message. He will read rapidly. Perhaps he will only glance. His eye will sweep down the page, searching for the answer to the insistent question, "What's this all about?" The first sentence is your opportunity to headline the news, to flash the answer.

Ask yourself, "What does he want to know first?" And, again, "*Exactly* what does he want to know first?" This question is the starting point of a clear plan. When you have answered your own question, you have your corethought. When you once have your corethought, you can bring your ideas into good order.

Give your first sentence a flying start. Action in favor of the reader makes a favorable impression. It is perhaps the most effective style of opening. Suppose you want a two weeks' vacation with pay during the Christmas season. You ask your employer, in a written memorandum, whether you may have the vacation. What more pleasing first sentence could you read than the one in the following note:

> It is a pleasure to grant your request of December 10 for two weeks' vacation with pay. Your record has been of such faithful character that you have earned the privilege. Your vacation runs from December 16 to December 30, inclusive.

Action first implies alertness, energy, and decision. Most of us like to have our requests treated with alertness, energy, and decision.

In the following examples, action gets the message off to a flying start:

1—You have 24-hour delivery on your order of June 7 at these quantity quotations:
2—Promptly after your telephone call this morning, we instructed our New York distributors to release the shipment specified in your request of April 11.

Streamline the message. Many readily accept the most modern systems in every part of their work except in communications. There they remain stalled. They bumble along with first-sentence "horse-and-buggy" wordiness of bygone days. Contrast these examples:

The Old Way (58 words)	*The New Way* (16 words)
We desire herewith to acknowledge the receipt of your inquiry of January 25, in which you ask whether you are fully protected under our policy No. 2-40378, and we wish to inform you that an examination of our records shows that your policy is in force and that you are protected according to the terms and stipulations therein.	Your policy No. 2-40378 is in force, and you are definitely protected according to its terms. SAVED: 42 words

To use fifty-eight words to say something that could be said far better in sixteen is intolerably wasteful. Yet many "clop-clop" around in "surreys with too much fringe on top" in their first and last sentences. Compare these examples:

Intolerable Wordiness	*Crisp Information*
We beg to acknowledge receipt of your kind favor of the 30th inst. and wish to state that we appreciate the interest you have shown in the present situation. In the matter of your inquiry relative to your illustrations, we beg to advise that they have had our attention and are enclosed herewith.	Here are the illustrations you requested on July 30. We were glad to have a chance to see examples of your work. We shall now be better guided in placing our future orders.

In the left column the wordy example smothers the reader. That in the right column gives, in the first eight words, the headline facts.

MAKE YOUR CLOSING SENTENCES FORCEFUL

Leave your reader with a favorable impression. The beginning and end of anything, because they are prominent, are places of emphasis. Any person, for instance, who values his appearance should look to his hat and his shoes. Why? Because hat and shoes are prominent at head and foot. The eye of a rapid reader is a skipping eye. It leaps from paragraph to paragraph. Anything that stands out, that serves as an eye stopper, will get more attention than the rest. The eye best "takes in" the start and the finish of the message.

The last sentence should do three important things: (1) It should round out the message plan. (2) It should bring to a sharp point the action desired. (3) It should leave an echo of courtesy.

Notably *weak* as closing expressions are forms like *thanking, assuring, hoping, trusting, believing,* or the like. Such expressions hinge all their weight on a participle. Never use them to express important ideas. Give closing ideas top strength. You get top strength by doing the following things: (1) Make a definite statement. (2) Train attention on the action desired. (3) Leave a sound of courtesy.

Undesirable	*Improved*
Assuring you in advance of our appreciation for your kind attention, and hoping that we may have the opportunity to return the same, we are	Thank you for the care with which you have handled this transaction. We hope to return the courtesy soon.
Thanking you for your order, and assuring you of our careful attention, we remain	Your order is greatly appreciated, and we are confident it will reach you in excellent shape.
Regretting our inability to comply with your demand, and assuring you of our best regards	It's our regret that we are unable to fill your exact requirements. May we serve in other ways?
Believing that you will find this number suitable to your requirements, we beg leave to remain	This article will, we feel, suit your needs. We're basing our judgment on the profits of our other dealers.
Trusting you will give this request your prompt attention, we are	We'll appreciate it if you will act promptly upon this request.
Hoping this will be satisfactory, and thanking you for past favors,	Believe me, we do appreciate your business.
Looking forward to filling your order, we are	May we look forward to filling your next order promptly?

Thank people for services rendered—but NEVER "in advance." As a matter of courtesy and good manners, you will thank people for their services. But express the thanks *after* the service has been performed, not in advance. "Thank you in advance" is no longer an admissible expression in the modern communicator's equipment.

Its use is basically unwise, even if it were not an exhausted phrase. Why? Because anyone who "thanks in advance" leaves the impression (whether true or not) that he *expects* his wish to be granted. He leaves the further impression that he wants to save himself the trouble of expressing his appreciation later at the proper time. Yet no one wants to be taken for granted. Hold the good thought that your request *will* be granted. But let your thanks be conveyed later *after* the event, and at the proper time.

• *APPLYING EFFECTIVE ENGLISH*

Oral Applications

• **1.** Discuss the reader appeal of the following sentences. Suggest ways by which these sentences could be made more effective by being made more courteous.

 1 — What justification can you have for complaining about the design of the desk lamp you bought from us, since you examined the item before making the purchase?

 2 — Why didn't you give the second part of our shipment time to reach you before you started complaining about not receiving it?

 3 — What makes you think that we can afford to send our illustrated catalog to every person who happens to want one?

 4 — Our total order was for only 700 brochures; so we cannot afford to send them to strangers.

 5 — How can we reasonably be expected to send you the tennis racket you ordered when you didn't even indicate the grip size or weight of the racket you wanted?

• **2.** In this unit you have found how wordiness obscures meaning, confuses the reader, and creates a bad impression. Through class discussion try to determine the writer's meaning in the wordy sentences at the top of page 283. See whether you can convey the same essential meaning in sentences of about a dozen words. Compare your concise versions with the original ones to insure that no important point has been omitted.

1 — About this extremely important principle of written communications in the world of modern business there cannot very well be any questions: in the preparation of messages which must have a high degree of effectiveness, the keeping of extraneous information and minor points to a minimum or, better, the excluding of them entirely and the focusing of attention on those considerations which are felt by the writer to be of greatest significance will without any reasonable doubt greatly increase the degree of clearness possessed by the message.

2 — The improvement that can be achieved with reference to the effectiveness of any message by the employment of material by which the writer's idea is brought into clear focus so that the general meaning is made specific and an abstract meaning is made concrete cannot be stressed too strongly.

● 3. Examine critically the following conclusions for business messages. Suggest and discuss various ways for improving these sentences.

1 — Expressing our appreciation in advance for your assistance in providing us with the necessary data, we remain

2 — Confident that you will not object to our request for additional information concerning the scope of your planned expansion so that we can submit an accurate bid, we are

3 — With sincere apologies for our failure to be able to comply with your request for our fall catalog and knowing that you will understand, George Newall and Company begs leave to remain

4 — Emphasizing that it will be impossible for our representatives to inspect the siding on your house or to make a bid on installing aluminum siding until after July 4, the volume of our business being too great, we are

Written Applications

● 1. Revise the following old-fashioned opening sentences, making them more courteous and efficient. Use more than one sentence when such an arrangement would improve the opening.

1 — This will acknowledge receipt of yours of the 17th in which you make inquiry as to whether or not an additional copy of the operating instructions for the Model 127C Ice Crusher is available, and give you notice that, barring unforeseen events, a copy will be sent in the near future, before the end of the month.

2 — We beg leave to advise you that your order of April 3, in which you indicate a willingness to accept the *Webster's New Collegiate*

Dictionary either with or without thumb-indexing, will be filled soon with a thumb-indexed volume, for we recently sold out our supply of those without thumb-indexing.

3 — Enclosed herewith as per your instructions included with yours of September 24, are fifteen copies of our most recent bulletin, "Arranging Attractive Window Displays," which it is our pleasure to send you gratis in hopes that you will find the bulletin helpful in training those who are employed in this work for you.

• **2.** As the person in charge of customer relations for the H. J. Bennett Company, prepare a 150-word notice drawing the attention of your staff to the importance of a business message's closing sentence. Emphasize the qualities which you wish your staff to incorporate in such sentences.

• *REVIEW*

Proofread the following sentences and correct all errors:

1 — Upon entering the lobby, a decorative fountain is seen by the visitor.
2 — The handling qualities of a sports car are better than a family limousine.
3 — Anyone, who expects to master a difficult subject, must study diligently.
4 — The students in Miss Cable's afternoon class in shorthand is planning to visit the Coe Corporation next week.
5 — The companies vice president for planning has recommended that the committees principle efforts be devoted to market analysis.
6 — The firm has replaced its' fleet of cars.
7 — The supervisor in charge of the plant's parking facilities don't believe that reserved spaces will solve the problem.
8 — As a result of it's increased sales, the Wilcox Company consequently plans to expand it's facilities for research and development.
9 — The fact that the plan was not adopted did not effect Mr. Darby's enthusiasm.
10 — The Bentons have taken there collie to a veterinarian for treatment.

UNIT 9

MESSAGE POWER: THE FAMOUS C-QUALITIES

Message power in particular, and effective expression in general, are based on certain vital qualities. These qualities you will recognize in all good writing.

It happens that each of these vital qualities has a name that begins with the letter C. For convenience, therefore, we call them the C-Qualities.

In the first section you will learn why it is that thinking first of your reader rather than of yourself generates courtesy. You will also learn why courtesy takes you a long step toward writing success.

In the second section you will study the way the experts determine exactly what and how much to put in a message to make it complete.

In the third and fourth sections you will discover how clearness and correctness pack your meaning with power and make it easy to grasp.

In the fifth section you will see how, in your expression, you can chisel away needless words and streamline every phrase. You will also discover how to flash colorful pictures through the powerful qualities of sharp conciseness and vivid concreteness.

UNIT 9

Section 1

Courtesy: The You Attitude: Generate courtesy power by thinking of your reader first.

Section 2

Completeness: Careful planning tells you what and how much to put in your message.

Section 3

Clearness: Clearness power packs your meaning, gets your message through, makes it easy to grasp.

Section 4

Correctness: Add force, focus your reader's attention, and train it on the message, through correctness.

Section 5

Conciseness and Concreteness: Cancel needless words, and flash sharp word pictures.

SECTION 1

Courtesy: The You Attitude

Generate courtesy power by thinking of your reader first.

When a person becomes a great success, you will usually find an inquiring reporter asking "What's the key to your success?"

One of the wisest of business advisors gives the all-inclusive answer: "I do not know of a more certain key to success than courtesy. It will carry you further in this world and cost you less than any other single quality you could possess. If I could talk in twenty languages, I would preach courtesy in all of them."

Everyday courtesy is simply a part of good manners. But you can also take the straight dollars-and-cents point of view. Then you find that showing courtesy is not only the right thing but it is also the profitable thing. Indeed, some business firms value their public good-will—the way the public feels toward them—at millions of dollars.

COURTESY, FRIENDSHIP, AND GOODWILL GO HAND IN HAND

"Goodwill," states a famous court decision, "is the decision of the customer to return to the place where he has been well served." When your customer makes this pleasant decision, he does so because he likes the way you have treated him. He senses that your expressions of courtesy mirror an attitude in your mind, generated by how you feel. For example, he finds your written messages to be effective because they mirror courtesy. You have made them effective by the language and tone in what you say, the manner you display toward him, and the generous attitude you maintain.

The courtesy test. Ask yourself these four key questions: (1) Will your message win goodwill? (2) Have you used positive, pleasant-toned words? (3) Have you expressed appreciation somewhere in your message? (4) Would *you* enjoy reading what you have said? Hopefully you should be able to answer yes to each of these four tests.

Yet the first thing everyone has to learn about courtesy is its *elusive* character. You can say the courtesy words all day long. You can write them by the yard. But unless you *mean* what you say, the words won't work. Courtesy is more than the mechanical repetition of the words *thank you* and *please*. Important as they are, you must not only write these expressions but you must also feel them toward your reader. The important point is this: You must *mean* sincerely what you say.

"The broadness of our hospitality . . . the diameter of our circle of friends . . . and the depth of our courtesy." Not long ago these words caught the eye of customers of a highly successful firm, recording gratitude for its success in its current annual report. "We're proud that our swift growth has contributed to the safety of your savings and that we now rank third in size among the great associations of the United States. But it is not by size alone that we wish to be measured. It is not by our billions in assets that we want you to measure us. Instead, we want you to measure us by the broadness of our hospitality . . . by the diameter of our circle of friends . . . and by the depth of our courtesy." The management of this organization had drawn forth the secret jewel of the treasurehouse: the pervasive quality of courtesy.

Cooling the world's friction points. A famous cartoonist on the staff of the Chicago *Tribune,* the late John T. McCutcheon, created a cartoon, later published on the front page of the *Tribune,* showing a giant figure holding an equally huge oil can from which he aimed a stream of oil on the axis-poles of the revolving world. "Courtesy," ran the caption of the cartoon, "is the lubricant that cools the world's friction points." The cartoon became internationally famous.

COURTESY-POWER IS A BUSINESS BUILDER

Introducing a book on the impact of goodwill, the following message discusses courtesy-power:

> Developing the value of friendship in holding business, Mr. Ames shows how goodwill may be acquired and how friendship may be built by the written word. He emphasizes the value the appearance of daily communications plays in building a good public attitude. In brief, Mr. Ames shows the business world how to leave an ever-widening trail of goodwill.

Three top employees of a famous mail-order house were asked this question: What are the responsibilities of our correspondents?

The first answered, "We have the responsibility, first of all, of satisfying the customer. A good correspondent should be able to put himself in the customer's place. The message he writes should be the kind of message he would like to receive—friendly, courteous, and sympathetic."

The second said, "To exhibit a thorough knowledge of the company's policies, the catalog, and the inquiry we are answering is our prime responsibility. But an even greater one is to convey to the customer the facts in an honest, concise, tactful way that will insure goodwill and friendliness."

Concluded the third, "Our messages represent this company. They must show friendliness. On our messages depend the customer's goodwill and future business."

You will discover amazing advantages in applying the power of courtesy in everything that you write. Blue ribbon businesses across the country have used courtesy-power to win notable successes. Consider, for example, the following instructions set forth in each of hundreds of district offices of the Metropolitan Life Insurance Company:

"Every patron of the Company must receive courteous attention, unstinted service, and helpful counsel. Our policyholders own the Company. Their goodwill must be cherished and sustained by the exertion of every reasonable effort to comply with their wishes."

"Thank you, call again," is the standard imprint on the face or the back of countless millions of cash-register receipts that find their way into the hands of buyers every business day.

"Sling" or "swing"? The Hilton Hotels Corporation paints a "courtesy picture" so vivid that you will remember it for a long time. "A doorman," says a Hilton message, "can SLING the door in such a way as to make the incoming guest expect to find a rusty pen stuck in a potato when he gets to the desk, or he can so SWING the door as to make him feel that this is His Hotel."

Spending millions for the word *please*. In the telegraph and telephone offices of America and the rest of the free world, the word *please* costs many millions of dollars a year just to be transmitted many thousands of times a month over the air, the wires, or the cables.

Obviously the firms that spend millions to transmit cordial words have come to the conclusion that courtesy is an investment just like other investments, and that it will pay dividends just as other good investments pay dividends. It matters little whether people spend a million or a billion dollars on courtesy and on courtesy words. Returns from this well-spent money are goodwill, friendship, and respect— three of the world's most valuable assets. Suppose we let Ralph Waldo Emerson, famous essayist and one of America's wisest men, sum it up. "Life is not so short," wrote Emerson, "but there is always time for courtesy."

THE YOU ATTITUDE GENERATES COURTESY

Did you ever try to see through another person's eyes? Did you ever try to get into another person's shoes? At first thought perhaps these may seem to you like odd ideas. But are they, after all? When you do these things, you are practicing the art of assuming the other person's point of view, of seeing things as he sees them. When you have learned how to do that, you will then have discovered another priceless secret called the YOU attitude. The YOU attitude is the art of getting outside of yourself. You release yourself from attention concentrated exclusively on your own personal affairs.

"A smile is the one thing the people of every country understand." In the days before world cruises had become common, and when native people were less accustomed to world-ranging tourists, a veteran world traveller once said, "A smile is the one thing the people of every country understand. *So I have smiled myself around the globe, and I have made friends in every country—without the help of an interpreter."* He unleashed the kind of leverage that works everywhere. The secret was unbelievably simple. But it was also unbelievably powerful. This world traveller discovered that a smile given to shopkeepers, hotel clerks, rail conductors, airline attendants, porters, and waiters worked magic. The language barrier? There wasn't any! *Anyone of any country and any age can understand a smile!*

Now what was there so magical about that smile? The answer is simple: it set up a common bond, a platform of understanding, an assurance of courtesy and mutual consideration.

"That fellow is an ace in getting along with other people," you may hear someone say. "He knows how to 'OTHER' himself." Do you know how to 'OTHER' yourself? This art may take you some time to learn. But you can learn it if you set out with determination to do so. One of the surest time-tested ways to "other" yourself and thus to be considerate of others is to smile, no matter how rough the going. And the smile we are talking about here is the considerate and thoughtful smile in your feelings and words, not merely the superficial smile on the face.

> Good nature begets smiles,
> Smiles beget friends,
> And friends are better
> than a fortune.

You may remember that in an earlier paragraph we asked the question, "Did you ever try to get into another person's shoes?" Difficult though this art may sometimes be, you will find it one well worth mastering, even as did the American Indians centuries ago. In the spirit of consideration and tolerance and thoughtfulness of others, a member of the famous Sioux Indian Tribe sent forth this prayer:

> Great Spirit, help me never to judge another until I have walked two weeks in his moccasins.

Getting along with others is an art you can master. The normal tendency of everyone is to live "off in his own little world." He is inclined to give small consideration to the world of anyone else. His natural pattern is to be self-centered. If he allows himself to become too self-centered, he becomes egotistical beyond hope. In such case he should never become a business communicator. On the other hand, if he recognizes his tendency to be self-centered, and if he is willing to take steps to correct the tendency, he can become a skilled communicator on his way to a responsible position in life. The first step is to climb out of the self-centered world and to visit the many worlds of others. How do you do this? You *other* yourself into their worlds. You may meet them across a desk, or you may meet them across a thousand miles. As you meet them for the first time, you try to think first of *their* ambitions, hopes, and aims, or of *their* work, interests, and hobbies. As a part of your preparation to make your words on paper carry friendly warmth, you deliberately interest yourself *first* in what the other fellow is doing and thinking.

Practice visualizing your reader: SEE him in your mind. When you talk about your reader, you please him because you are discussing what is to him the most interesting thing in the world—himself. Make his hopes, his preferences, his interests, his wishes as nearly as possible your own. Take his viewpoint. Look through his eyes. Back up your message with the burning power of his attention by talking about *him* in *his* terms. Say to yourself, "If I were over there where my reader is, instead of where I am, what would I like to have myself say?"

Will it be YOU or WE? If any of the expressions below were addressed to you, which would be more effective, do you think, in commanding your attention and interest?

"You"	"We"
Have you wondered	We are firmly of the belief
You will find	We think that
You may be interested in	We are going to tell you
Your experience may have shown	It is our opinion
Have you noticed in your work	We wish to announce

To any given person the most interesting thing in the world is of course himself. Hence every writer faces something of a struggle to bridge the gap between himself and someone else. He naturally thinks of his own world: *our* factory, *our* policy, *our* files, *our* company. Only with a considerable effort can he get over the barrier into *your* company, *your* policy, *your* wants, *your* interests.

Get twice the force. If you think ahead and take the right YOU-stance, you can double the power of everything you write. Follow these two power-guides:

1 — Make what you say have some value to your reader.
2 — Put your reader in the center of what you say.

You can't fake. Merely sprinkling *you's* over a page does not of itself assure a *you* attitude. The choice of the pronoun *you* instead of *we* is the first step, a mechanical help, but it does not in itself make

"TO SELL JOHN SMITH WHAT JOHN SMITH BUYS, YOU MUST SEE JOHN SMITH THROUGH JOHN SMITH'S EYES."

Dear Bill:

You don't know how much I appreciated your inquiry of July 7. If you'd made it just a couple of months earlier, it would have been easy to run over and have a direct look at the situation. Now, however, you catch me in the midst of a busy consulting schedule that will, I think, last a long time. So, much as your thought pleases me, it wouldn't be feasible to switch plans at this time.

You'll find the latchstring out over here whenever you can spend a couple of days with us. Can you come soon?

Sincerely,

Paul

SAMPLE THE YOU-APPROACH

One professional man writes another, and the YOU-feeling is as comfortable as your bedroom slippers!

the attitude. It simply helps to make you think first of your reader's interests and desires. You can in fact adopt the *you* attitude without once using the pronoun itself.

Suppose, for example, that you ran on to the following old-fashioned we-centered sentence:

Inferior: Acknowledging recent order Number 7711, we wish to state that it has been duly filled and sent in accordance with our usual policy.

You wish to convert it into a you-centered form without once using the pronoun *you*. You can do it:

Effective: Sincere thanks for order No. 7711. It has been promptly filled and sent within the customary 24-hour time limit.

Clearly you are dealing with not just one multiplied pronoun but something much bigger and deeper: the spirit back of what you write. To have that spirit, you must live it, you must believe in it, and you must feel it. It must come from the heart. It has to be real.

Touch the reader's interest-spark. If you stand behind the reader, look over his shoulder, and see through his eyes, you'll never fall into the trap of talking "at" him. Instead you'll touch the spark of his interests and make everything *sound* interesting. When you get over on his side of the fence and begin to prove to him that his interests are yours, all kinds of promising things begin to happen.

"If you can show your reader you have something for him," writes a skilled manager, "and do not want to get something from him, if you can show that you are offering something for his personal good, you at once break down the barriers between. Suddenly you are walking with him. Instead of trying to sell him, *you are helping him to buy*. And what a tremendous difference in sales results that little difference in attitude makes!"

"You may well ask how we tie this point of view to our production," he concludes. "You may want to know how we put the *you* attitude into our products. I'm glad to give you the answer. Every piece of material, every brass rod, every strip of iron or other metal, every piece of steel wire, goes through tests to see that it measures to the standard we can confidently talk about in our messages. The word *you* may be important—but it isn't final. It's the spirit within."

The case of the loser that turned into the winner. A sheet metal contractor who knew a lot more about the sheet-metal business than he did about the qualifications of a good communicator, tried his hand at preparing a message to prospective customers. This is how it went:

THE LOSER

We wish to announce that we are in the sheet-metal business, using Dreadnaught Satin Finish sheets and specializing in cottage and residence work, such as gutters, downspouts, roofing, etc.

We can give immediate service with the best material and mechanics and will be glad to furnish you with an estimate.

We do not care how large or how small the job may be, for we can assure you that it will be handled satisfactorily.

Please let us hear from you.

The effort was a dismal failure. The sheet-metal contractor gave up and turned the task over to an experienced communicator (1) who knew how to analyze the requirements, (2) who knew how to plan the appeals, (3) who knew how to talk the reader's language, and (4) who knew how to write. Why did his version bring in a satisfactory number of inquiries that were turned into profitable contracts?

THE WINNER

Did you know that rust eats away about as much sheet metal every year as is produced in the same period? Will it prey on your new building, or will you select lasting material?

Dreadnaught Satin Finish galvanized sheet metal, which
we use, is highly durable. Actual tests in service,
covering many years, have proved the lasting qualities of
this rust-resisting material, resistant because it is pure
and dense.

Dreadnaught Satin Finish galvanized sheets have been
used in important buildings in which durability is needed.
The Lincoln Memorial Building, Washington, D.C., the
Empire State Building, and the Ford Hospital are structures
in which this material proves its lasting qualities.

From us, you'll get immediate service with the best of
material and mechanics. Whether your building is large or
small, plan to get an estimate from us. Dreadnaught Satin
Finish is excellent for roofing, gutters, downspouts, and
other metal work.

Just dial 624-1234, or write us a line, today.

Why did the first version lose, the other win? Note the striking
points of difference in the two versions: the emphasis on *we* in the
first, the emphasis on *you* in the second. The first wrapped itself
around the contractor's interests and failed to touch the reader. It
produced nothing but ineffective generalities. Even the closing
clincher (the element that seeks to get favorable action) was vague
and inconclusive in its words, ". . . let us hear from you." The reader
might quite well react by asking: How? When? Where? What's
your telephone number? Why bother? Or he might merely drop the
item into the wastebasket. This was an outcome which apparently
must have been common.

Test the Winner

1. Is the writer of this message writing directly to you?
2. Is his thinking logical and orderly?
3. Does he have you and your interests in mind?
4. Does he make it plain why he wrote?
5. Does he accept responsibility?
6. Do you trust him?
7. Would you like to meet him?

Now how does the second version open? A startling statement
about the colossal waste of rust, striking directly at the reader's instinct
for economy and dollar-protection, grips his attention. Then, representing a second appeal to thrift, follows a challenging question. Each
sentence is studded with concrete detail. Famous buildings are cited

by name in proof of severe practical tests of the product. The over-all effect of the message? Vivid and convincing. Action? Specific, easy, and inviting.

"Think across." In considerable measure every written message is something like a voice in the dark. We seek clues to the writer. We need help to visualize the kind of person he may be. Do we like him? Is he, we ask, thoughtful, trustworthy, dependable?

The "we and our company" approach blocks the clues and the help we seek. It smothers the individual behind the message and bars our efforts to define his personality. With no hint about the writer, we are forced to depend on what other thin clues we may be able to detect.

But when the message is expressed with courtesy, warmed with consideration, illuminated with a desire to be helpful, we may form an impression that glows. So to make your words "pull," appreciate your reader's feelings, put yourself in his shoes, visualize his personality, and, if you can, see through his eyes.

> "To sell John Smith
> What John Smith buys
> You must see John Smith
> Through John Smith's eyes."

Try this test. You now conclude this section with the following test-challenge:

Can You Pass This Test?

1 — Do you "think across" to your reader in terms of YOU? Can you break out of the "WE-US prison?" ☐

2 — Do you successfully apply the communicator's Golden Rule: "How would I like this to sound if I were going to get this message?" ☐

3 — Do you talk your reader's language? ☐

4 — Do you show appreciation of his problem? ☐

5 — Do you see John Smith through John Smith's eyes? ☐

If you can meet this test as you study the coming sections, you will have the treasured gift that others continue to seek.

• *APPLYING EFFECTIVE ENGLISH*

Oral Applications

• 1. In class discussion examine ways in which courtesy and good manners can be built into a business message.

• 2. What effect would the following sentences have on you as a customer? Revise the sentences so that they will be appealing rather than sarcastic. In your revisions try to adopt the point of view of the reader and encourage him to want to do business with the company you represent. Be appropriately polite.

1 — We received your order but can't read your writing. As a matter of fact, we are just guessing at your address. Send us your order again and make it legible if you expect us to be able to serve you.

2 — Your letter of August 27 assumes that we are in the business of providing complimentary dictionaries to anyone who happens to ask for them. If you send in an order for at least ten copies, it is our policy to supply a desk copy free.

3 — You did not even take the trouble to give the catalog number of the lamp you ordered. We cannot very well ship a lamp to you until we know which model and finish you want. After all, our floor lamps come in a wide variety of models and finishes.

4 — The guidebook you requested is not free, though you seem to think it is. Follow the directions contained in our advertisement, send us a check or money order for fifty cents, and the guidebook will be sent to you. Your carelessness just makes more trouble for yourself, as well as for us.

5 — If you don't bother to specify whether you want steel or aluminum shafts, how in the world are we going to know which? Why don't you resubmit your order and make it complete this time.

• 3. A friendly clerk who takes a genuine interest in his customer increases his chances (a) of making a good sale and (b) of influencing the customer to return in the future. In the same way courteous messages build and encourage additional business. Try to find various ways by which the following "we-centered" sentences from sales messages can be rephrased to emphasize the customer's point of view.

1 — I am convinced that after 20,000 miles an automobile needs a safety inspection.

2 — There can be little question, we believe, that use of our high quality antenna will improve the reception of any radio.

3 — There is, in my opinion, no doubt that intelligent newspaper advertising will increase sales.

4 — It has been our experience that professional cleaning restores carpets to their original colors.

5 — This letter will explain our position that White-Maid Cupboards will make any kitchen a brighter more efficient room.

• 4. Discuss the following message with reference to each question in the seven-point test (page 295). Be prepared to indicate evidence in the message to support your judgments.

Thank you for your recent request. It reached us after Miss Parr had left on a business trip to London, England. As soon as Miss Parr returns, she will answer your inquiry personally.

In the meantime, it is a pleasure to send you the eight additional copies of "Safety Measures" that you requested.

Written Applications

• 1. Revise the following announcement. Alter the "we-centered" attitude of the message.

I am beginning delivery of Linwood Dairy Products in your neighborhood. Deliveries will begin next August 24, since I won't finish my vacation until August 22.

I plan to stop by sometime in the next few weeks to see if I will be delivering milk to you in the future.

I shall carry homogenized milk, skim milk, cream, butter, yogurt, and other dairy products, as well as fresh eggs.

• 2. Revise the following "we-centered" announcement. Adopt the "you-attitude."

We plan to establish a new bookstore in Oak Grove. We plan to carry all current best-sellers, standard reference books, and classics. We plan also to stock many paperback books.

We shall be open for business March 4. Our hours will be 9 a.m. to 6 p.m.

We shall be happy to see you, and we hope our bookstore will be convenient for our customers.

SECTION 2

Completeness

Careful planning tells you what and how much to put in your message.

Build an effective plan. You will recall (if you have taken a course in geometry) that a straight line is the shortest distance between two points. Hence, if you want to get from point A—your mind—to point B—your reader's mind—*plan* your facts in a straight line. Then *transmit* your facts in a straight line. Alexandre Dumas (the son) may have been thinking about this topic when he asked, "How can you tell what road to take unless you know where you are going?"

Let us suppose, for example, that one of your important customers asks you for a quotation on a Xerox 3600-IV copier-duplicator. Or perhaps another requests information about a Friden desk-type electronic computer, or an Olivetti Airliner Portable, or a Magnavox Theatre Stereo with stereo FM. You will need to supply the customer with the complete information, explanation, or quotation he wants. It won't do to give him only part of it. He will want *all* of it— *complete*. Under an effective plan you can give it to him. To do so, know all your facts and marshal them in intelligent order.

Your responsibility as a communicator is two-fold. On the one hand, you must be an intelligent receiver of information. You must know how to read and interpret incoming facts and ideas. On the other hand, you must know how to plan and shape your outgoing message so that it will be complete and easily understood.

Not long ago the operator of a variety store sent the following airmail message to a container manufacturer:

> I am interested in learning the prices and in seeing some samples of your *Super-Strength* bags, Line 203, advertised recently in *The Retailer*. Since I am not yet certain what sizes I may need, please let me have size-samples of the line.
>
> It will be most helpful if you can promptly give me a price quotation for each size in lots of 1,000, 5,000 and 10,000. And please quote me your quantity discount on the larger orders.

Two weeks later came the following (incomplete) reply:

Your message addressed to our Rochester branch has been forwarded to this office since your city is in our territory. Already on the way to you are several samples of our bags which we believe may prove suitable for your operation. These *Super-Strength* units are produced in distinctive colors. Patrons will carry your store identity home with them because each unit can be imprinted with your store name.

If you will let us know the quantity you are planning to use, we can then quote you as you request.

Why was the reply incomplete? What central fact was missing? Answer: The manufacturer gave no price information. The customer was, of course, inconvinced because he was in a hurry to make a decision and place an order.

"What I wanted to know," he said, "was the price of the bags in various sizes and in specified quantities. Why didn't this company quote me a price?" The customer was right. This case is a clear example of an incomplete message. The test question, "What does he want to know?" was not properly answered. Hence, two *extra* messages had to be exchanged.

The specific purpose of planning is to *guide* your writing. Your thoughts will then be easy for your reader to grasp. You can learn to write straight only after you learn to think straight. In a business situation you will put a certain part of your thinking on paper. Of course you'll try to avoid being a clumsy communicator. But if you are (and there are many), you'll make your reader pull and haul in his unsuccessful efforts to follow your thought. If you have been too clumsy, he won't pull and haul very long. He'll simply file the whole thing in the wastebasket.

If, on the other hand, you are a carefully trained communicator, you find that good writing is simply straight thinking put on paper. You make the situation supremely easy for your reader. No longer does he have to tug and pull and haul. You have put your words together in such skillful form that his mind easily grasps the message. Your thought, framed according to an effective plan, comes smoothly off the page.

Be guided by the experts. Plan your message according to the steps at the top of page 301.

1 — Gather together your basic material. Get all the *figures, facts, illustrations, and examples* you will need to make a *planned and complete* reply.

2 — Review your material. Organize it into thought units, seeing that each is clear in its relation to the others. Decide what *facts* are needed, what elements should come first, and how the rest of the facts should be arranged.

3 — Last, *double-check your fact-material: see that it is complete* and that its arrangement is right.

Use great care to give all the information asked for, to the extent that you have it. For instance, if you are answering a request for some specific thing, you may jot down notes on the points you want to make in your reply. You then arrange your notes in the order of their importance. You make sure you will cover all the necessary points. But you do not start to write until your facts are as complete as you can make them.

"Say enough, but say *just* enough." That is the slogan of the experts. The neat trick, of course, is to know precisely when just enough has been said.

For example, an extremely *short* message asking someone to do a favor for you may be so short that it fails. It fails because it does not get enough ideas into the mind of the reader. In short, it does not bring him to the point where he is ready to grant the favor requested.

It helps to ask yourself questions like the following:

1 — If I include this material, will my message be easier to understand?

2 — If I include this material, will my message be as factually complete as I can make it?

3 — If I include this material, will my message be more valuable to my reader?

4 — If I include this material, will my message, because of its completeness, get quicker results?

The cost of business messages that are dictated and typewritten has risen to spectacular heights. As a result, the cost-pressure is heavy

to keep written messages as brief as possible. As far as actual physical preparation goes, the shorter the message, the less its cost.

There could hardly be a more serious error, however, than the error of admiring briefness just for the sake of briefness. The expensive fact is this: Suppose a message is so short that it is not complete. It may then cost ten or twenty times as much to correct the mistake as it would have cost to write an original message two or three times as long. Thus we come to an inevitable conclusion proved in countless thousands of practical situations: No message is too long if an examination proves that every word is needed.

The risks of incompleteness. Would you like to do a lot of unnecessary writing? Be incomplete. Would you like to multiply your troubles and misunderstandings and costs? Be incomplete. Would you like to complicate the operation of your business and cut the heart out of your profit? Be incomplete.

The irony of all this is that one complete message, well planned and intelligently drafted, will do everything that otherwise may require three. Hundreds of perfectly futile messages are exchanged week in and week out because the first efforts were prepared with only a slipshod grasp of the subject. When the first message failed, a long string of others became necessary to cure the original fault.

Let's consider a concrete example in sequence. You send in a question. Your question is perfectly clear because it has been transmitted in a well-framed message to your reader.

> Can you spare me one copy of your *Illustrated Index* and let me know the approximate date on which the *Index Supplement* will be issued?

Unfortunately your reader scans your message too hurriedly. Or it may be that he handles the reply too hurriedly. Or he may be afflicted with a touch of familiar forgetfulness. He answers only half your question.

> We're happy to send along one copy of our *Illustrated Index* as you have requested. It will, we're sure, prove useful.

You now have to write a second request asking for the other half of the answer. To avoid hurting anyone's feelings by implying careless forgetfulness or oversight, you'll make every effort to be tactful. But at the same time you want to keep the record straight.

> Thank you for so promptly sending along the copy of your *Illustrated Index*, requested in my first note in which, by the way, I also inquired as to the approximate date on which the *Index Supplement* will be issued. Can you let me have a line with this information?

Tactfully reminded of his prior oversight, your reader now has to reply with his second effort.

> You have my apologies for overlooking the second part of your original inquiry. I hasten to tell you that the *Index Supplement* will be issued about the first week in August. We shall see that your name is on our list to receive a copy.

You will note that your reader substantially offsets his oversight and reclaims goodwill by taking initiative in your favor: "We shall see that your name is on our list to receive a copy." In taking this action, he shows excellent judgment. But the fact remains: Through replying too hurriedly the first time, he answered only half your question and his reply was only *half complete*. That fact adds up to two additional messages, both of which were quite needless. In a sizable business office those two additional but needless messages may have cost a minimum of $2.75 each. With costs per dictated message now crossing the $3.00 mark, the actual total money waste may have been in the region of five or six dollars!

How Trans World Airlines Assures Completeness

On the inside flap of the business reply envelope, used by TWA to generate inquiries for its travel publications, appear the following reminders:

"Did you fill in your name and complete address?"

"Did you check the guides you want?"

"Did you detach the form and enclose your remittance?"

"Then moisten this gummed flap, seal, fold, and mail. No postage necessary."

What is the greatest single threat to completeness? Perhaps the greatest single threat to completeness is *lack of a sensible plan*. As you have seen in the study of Unit 6, a good basic plan is your best guide in framing a complete message. Recently a professional expert made a survey of two thousand business messages that had been exchanged over a period of a month. His survey revealed that only one out of six had an intelligent plan. The other five rambled on more or less pointlessly. They were characterized by a type of planlessness that puts a penalty on everyone. They literally multiplied further needless exchanges. At perhaps $2.75 or more each, you need only consult your imagination to estimate what such basic faults of incompleteness may do in multiplying costs.

"Neglect," "carelessness," and "oversight." As long as human nature is as human nature is, we shall have incompleteness because of human oversight. Probably no one knows better than the executives of mail-order houses and the managers of mail-order divisions of department stores *how often customers forget*. Customers forget to mention the size, or the dimensions, or the color. Customers also forget to mention the catalog number, or the serial number, or the number of yards, or some other similar important detail necessary to the filling of an order. Forgetting essential facts like these is so commonplace that it has become an accepted business problem. The truth is that *stores can predict* how many mail orders out of every hundred will be so incomplete as to require further correspondence. As long as people are people, they will continue to forget the most obvious things.

To the following you will be able to supply many additional concrete examples:

This writer forgot:	*This writer remembered:*
Please send me one "Arctic" Zipper Jacket, silver finish, Catalog No. Z23477.	*Please send me one "Arctic" Zipper Jacket, size 38, color silver, Catalog No. Z23477.*
Please send me one of your beige cashmere sweaters, size 14.	Please send me one cashmere sweater, color beige, size 14, *Catalog No. X14491.*

With some further research into human nature, you will find that size, color, and catalog number are not the only items that people forget. Actions may also be incomplete.

Here, for example, is a message that opens with the following words:

"Enclosed are several samples. . . ."

What error do you suppose has been committed this time? You guessed it. The sample enclosures have been left out. Now you have to write for them just as if you were making your original inquiry. So the costly exchange of messages has now been multiplied by a factor of two.

Let us take another example. An important inquiry is neglected for a week. Or an agreement calling for a signature is overlooked because it gets lost in a shuffle of papers on a desk top. The delay itself may cost everyone something. But the specific cost is the cost of the reminder telegram, the reminder telephone call, or the written reminder message. All of the conspicuous waste would have been avoided, had the inquiry been promptly answered, had the agreement been signed at once.

Summary: the chief guides to completeness. One effective way to cut business costs is to check each outgoing message for completeness. In summary, the chief guides to completeness are delightfully easy to remember. They are: (1) to know what and how much to put in and (2) to know what to leave out.

● *APPLYING EFFECTIVE ENGLISH*

Oral Applications

● **1.** Suggest three situations in which an error or omission of essential information would make an additional message necessary. For example: (a) A customer forgets to specify whether he wants a dictionary with or without thumb indexing. (b) A mail-order firm sends a blue sweater instead of the black one ordered by the customer.

● **2.** What steps will insure that your message will include all essential data? Explain the purpose of each step. Give examples to clarify your explanations.

● **3.** Examine the orders at the top of page 306 with reference to their completeness. Point out defects.

1 — Please send me one pair of men's black oxfords, Catalog No. N.A.16237. I require a C width.

2 — Please send me several pairs of your best print dacron, ankle-length, men's socks, in an argyle pattern. I am happy to know that they are available in five color combinations: brown-yellow, black-white, brown-tan, red-black, and blue-green.

3 — Your recent advertisement in the *Washington Post* indicated that you have picture frames available in both white and natural oak finish and that the eighteen by twenty inch size costs $7.75, while the twelve by fifteen inch size costs $5.25. Please send me three as soon as possible.

4 — Please send me one pair of ladies' long pigskin gloves, size $7\frac{1}{2}$, Catalog No. H739. I understand that these gloves carry a one-year guarantee, that they are available in either black or brown, and that they will be repaired free of charge if any seams should open during the guarantee period.

5 — Please send me your finest cotton drapery material, Catalog No. K93216, which, according to the catalog description, is available in five color-fast pastel tones.

• 4. Discuss whether the following messages are complete. If they are not, indicate specifically what essential information is lacking.

1 — Please send me a set of four 7.00-16 Firestone tires, blackwall, at your special sale price. I understand that both standard and belted tires are on sale.

2 — Please reserve space for me and my family. We shall arrive the afternoon of December 3 and remain in San Francisco until the afternoon of December 10.

3 — Send me three striped ties, Catalog No. 13052, in the following color combinations: blue-grey and green-black.

4 — Please send me one Janzen ladies' swimsuit, pink, No. 1312.

5 — Please send me two $4.25 balcony tickets to the matinee performance of "Man of La Mancha," which I understand will be playing in Chicago for three weeks beginning March 21.

• 5. Why is completeness so important in business messages? What delays and additional expenses would be caused by the orders given in Oral Application 4?

• 6. Evaluate the message at the top of the next page in terms of completeness. Point out how disorganization, irrelevant material, or forgetfulness spoil this message.

Your letter concerning the opening date of the Madison County Toll Road is much appreciated.

You may be surprised to learn we receive some 225 similar inquiries every day. This is convincing proof, isn't it, that the Madison Toll Road will be satisfying a real public need.

It is a pleasure to be of service to you. If there is any way we can be of further help, just let us know.

• **7.** Are the following replies complete? Explain in detail what additional information should have been included.

> 1 — No more copies of our brochure, "Painting as a Pastime," are available right now. We regret, inasmuch as you have taken the trouble to write requesting a copy, that we cannot now send you a copy of this brochure. It's unfortunate that we didn't order a larger first printing, but, frankly, we had no idea how popular the booklet would be. Sorry we can't oblige you!
>
> 2 — We do not have seven table-tennis nets in stock at this time. Since we have no more than three nets available, we shall not be able to fill your order. May we inquire how soon you will be needing these nets?

Written Applications

• **1.** For each situation you have suggested in connection with Oral Application 1, write one of the messages which the firm must prepare as a result of its own or the customer's error.

Even if it is a foolish error on the customer's part, be tactful and courteous. Do not give the customer any reason for dissatisfaction or resentment. Catch his interest and offset his disappointment at learning that the shipment will be unavoidably delayed.

• **2.** Rewrite the defective orders given in Oral Application 3. Supply any missing information.

• **3.** Angus Combs orders ten yards of green vinyl plastic upholstery material to match a sample he intends to include with the order. The shade of green is important, since it must match that of other pieces of furniture. Mr. Combs, however, forgets to enclose the sample.

> 1 — Write Mr. Comb's original order for the material
> 2 — Write the store's answer to Mr. Combs

• **4.** Rewrite the replies given in Oral Application 7. Supply the additional information which would create a favorable impression.

SECTION 3

Clearness

Clearness power packs your meaning, gets your message through, makes it easy to grasp.

When business enterprises were small and run for the most part by individuals or partnerships, communication was relatively simple. In those days the proprietor called his assistant and issued instructions. Or the manager told Neil, Mike, and Ed, his three helpers, what to do. Or one partner personally discussed with the other plans for the next month. If what one person said to the others left any uncertainty, the latter could promptly ask, "What do you mean by that?" They could instantly clear up the point.

Then, following the American pattern, firms began to grow. Employees in many businesses began to number hundreds and then thousands. No longer was there time enough for the manager to talk daily with everyone on his payroll. No longer was there time enough to tell each one individually what to do. Instructions had to be put into writing. At that point businessmen had to meet the challenge of clearness in communication.

Multiplying personal power. Clarity—the quality of clearness—is a prime business essential. It gives you personal power in two vitally important ways.

1 – Your effective use of language helps you to make an excellent impression on those with whom you deal. A firm control of language is your mark of distinction.

2 – Clarity in speaking and writing is a strategic instrument in persuading other people to think or act as you wish them to do.

An instrument of personal power, clearness is the quality of transmitting thought lucidly—that is, without hinderance, clumsiness, or ambiguity. The chief requirement for clearness is a precision of statement combined with (a) simplicity of word choice and (b) orderliness of structure. For example, when you say, "I will sign that report," you leave no doubt as to the action you are about to take. You indicate by your assertion that you, yourself, will take a certain specific action. You indicate what that action will be: to sign. You indicate exactly what you are about to sign: a report. Furthermore, you indicate precisely which report you are about to sign: *that* one. There is nothing ambiguous about your assertion, "I will sign that report."

On the other hand, ambiguousness in meaning is a common fault. It arises from the use of language that admits of more than one interpretation. For example, suppose someone writes:

The manager said the supervisor has hired four more typists.

Here you have a statement that has the quality of being double, questionable, mistakable, indistinct, indefinite. It is capable of being understood, or misunderstood, as the case may be, in either of two possible senses:

The manager said that the supervisor has hired four more typists.

"The manager," said the supervisor, "has hired four more typists."

The ambiguousness is removed through the use of the changes shown.

When you are in a situation that calls for you to communicate something to someone, can you, with certainty, say what you mean? Can you say it so that you can be understood?

What is far more important, can you say it so *clearly* that you can*not* be misunderstood? Can you so skillfully transmit from your mind to another mind what you have to say that he'll grasp it all in a flash? Do you believe that you, yourself, at this moment, can express your thoughts in a form that is crystal-clear and spike-sharp?

Speaking of the art of writing, the famous Lord Chesterfield put it this way: Every paragraph should be so clear and unambiguous that the dullest fellow in the world will not be able to misstate it, nor be obliged to read it twice in order to understand it.

How can you make your writing and speaking spike-sharp and crystal-clear? Once again, as you have seen in prior pages, a good plan is the very foundation of clearness. If your mental "grooves" are clear and well cut, your thought will flow with ease. Your thought processes will travel swiftly down the clear straightaway of a good plan, just as a powerful car rolls easily down a smooth expressway.

You can go much faster when you *know* where you are going, on the basis of a clear route. You don't have to waste valuable time puzzling out a route as you go. You aren't tempted to wander off into wrong turnings. You don't get mixed up in dead ends. You seldom have to go back and hunt up the place where you made a wrong turn. You seldom have to retrace any part of your thought-journey. Why? Because you stay on the planned route of a "thought-highway." You have prepared your mind so that it knows what it wants to say and how to say it . . . *clearly.*

Can you answer this test question? Here is the test question to ask yourself: WHAT, PRECISELY AM I TRYING TO SAY?

When you can give the right answer, start to write. But don't touch the paper until you *can* give the right answer. Otherwise, you will grope in a mental fog. You will try unsuccessfully to transmit your idea without knowing where you are headed. Practically every poor sentence that has ever been written has been the direct result of mental fog. Obviously, if you are trying to write something in a mental fog, you can expect to set up in the mind of your reader only a confusing haze.

Contrast the two paragraphs below. Note how, by carving away twenty surplus words, the *impact and clarity* of the idea have been many times multiplied.

Wordy, Cloudy (34 Words)	*Concise, Clear* (14 Words)
We believe that by giving these independents an opportunity whereby they can have the same functions and weapons of attack as have been developed by the cooperatives, they too will succeed in the trade.	The independents will succeed if they are given the same weapons as the cooperatives.

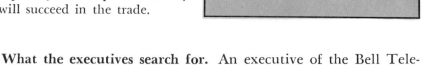

What the executives search for. An executive of the Bell Telephone Company considers as many as two hundred applications for jobs each week. "The characteristic we look for, and the quality we demand," he says with emphasis, "is clearness." But he goes further: "We can hire any number of people who can write something that can be understood. But the people *we* are after are those *who can write something that cannot be misunderstood!*"

The vice president in charge of legal matters for the Goodyear Tire and Rubber Company applies this interesting clearness-test: "I never," he says, "send out a contract or communication I have written until I allow some one or two other persons in the organization to read it. If that person questions the thought at any place, I rewrite that sentence, for I know a slight vagueness to any one right here will quite likely become a serious misunderstanding to a stranger, and misunderstandings cost both time and money."

A Curious Contrast in Clearness

Can you unravel the following cloud of negative verbiage?

"The multiple communication effort does not enhance the complete or efficient flow of work, but rather tends to confuse it and extend unnecessarily all of our individual involvements."

Here is a clarified positive translation:

"Please send all mail to the same person."

—*Teachers Insurance and Annuity Association of America*

The mountaineer didn't understand. Do you? An insurance man once wrote the following message to a mountaineer in the eastern part of our country. As you read it, put yourself in the mountaineer's place:

> Surrender of the policy is permissible only within the days attendant the grace period in compliance with citation relevant options accruing to the policy. We are stopped from acquiescing to a surrender prior to the policy's anniversary date. We are confident that an investigation relevant to the incorporation of this feature will substantiate that the policy is not at variance with policies of other companies.

Discussing this cloudy haze of words, one commentator remarks: "I suppose most of us in business are a little better equipped to understand the English language than that man of the hills. But tell me truthfully—did you understand the meaning of those sentences? . . .

CLEARNESS MAGNIFIES YOUR MEANING, MAKES IT EASY TO GRASP.

Writing skill becomes visible every time a well-planned sentence makes an idea crystal clear.

I think the insurance man should have been ashamed when he read the mountaineer's simple answer:"

> Dear Mister: I am sorry, but I do not understand what you have written. If you will explain what you mean, I will try to do as you ask.

Light up your reader's path: use pointer-words and focus-phrases. Fighter pilots riding the cockpits of America's hottest jet planes speak of "zeroing-in" on their targets—hitting them on the absolute bullseye, the accuracy-pinpoint.

To zero in on the subject, ask yourself these two useful questions:

1 — What do I wish to make known?
2 — What do I want to say about it?

Try to pinpoint the exact nature of the subject you are handling. Select "pointer-words" and "focus-phrases" like these examples:

> Here is our progress to date . . .
> Let us summarize these points . . .
> Here is the target we're aiming at . . .
> The ten guide rules are these . . .
> Look for these three objectives . . .
> The final result was this . . .

When you use expressions like these, pointing the direction and focussing the thought, you help your reader to pick out your important ideas. You focus your reader's attention and highlight your important points. The more sharply you focus and pinpoint your thoughts through similar pointer-words and focus-phrases, the more certain you will be of transmitting your thought forcefully.

Generate new power through clarity. Of course, you don't want your reader to have to grope through a dark maze of confusion. Try, therefore, to train the searchlight of a well-made plan and the flood-light of well-thought-out clearness on every line that you write. Make your reader's way an easy one. Light up his path. Always remember that the simpler your language, the clearer your words, the greater will be the power-impact of what you say.

• *APPLYING EFFECTIVE ENGLISH*

Oral Applications

• **1.** Discuss the possible ambiguity in the following sentences and suggest ways of making the sentences clear.

> 1 — Marsha and Michelle, who had never taken a course in typing, had to prepare the memorandum together.
> 2 — Each student, under the guidance of Miss Allen, our speech teacher, who competed in the contest, won approval from the judges.
> 3 — The desk from the vice president's office which had just been refinished looked like new.
> 4 — Mr. Hixon suggested to Mr. Norden that he drive his car.
> 5 — Passing O'Hare Airport, the Hancock Building could be seen in the distance.
> 6 — Carefully corrected by the manager, the messenger delivered the final report to the vice president.

• **2.** Make an effort to determine the meaning of the technical jargon in the message from the insurance man to the mountaineer (page 311). After the class has reached agreement about its meaning, simplify the message so that the mountaineer will be able to understand it easily.

• **3.** Careful organization is one extremely important way of making a message clear. Evaluate the following announcement. Make an outline organizing this information in logical units.

> Title of play: Twelfth Night
> Play opens Wednesday
> Box Tickets cost $5.00 each

Orchestra tickets $4.00 each
Balcony tickets $3.50 each
Time of performance 8 p.m.
The beginning date of the performances is April 7
Closing date Friday, May 16
Sir Toby Belch will be played by Mr. Douglas Allen
The role of Olivia will be played by Miss Karen Schweitzer

• 4. Compare and evaluate the following two messages in terms of these questions:

1 — Does the message make you want to get to know the writer?
2 — Is the purpose of the message unmistakably clear and does every part of the message contribute in some demonstrable way to this purpose?
3 — Is it well organized, logical, and persuasive?
4 — Does the writer convey the impression that he is a thoughtful, sincere, and responsible person—that he is worthy of your trust?
5 — Does the writer understand your point of view and interests and take them into account?
6 — Is this message written directly to you?

I

How does your wallet represent you? What kind of impression does it make on your colleagues and clientele?

Take a second right now. Is your wallet a bit tattered? Are the edges frayed? Does it look a little the worse for wear? Chances are it does.

If so, you have the chance of a lifetime—the chance to get a Count Hilton genuine calfskin, modern-design wallet at an unbelievably low price. These wallets are designed to provide maximum convenience. They are slim as can be. Yet they hold more than you can imagine. They prove your good taste every time people see them.

Just sign the enclosed card and drop it in the mail. No need to send even a penny now. You'll have your Count Hilton wallet in a matter of days. Then you'll really be proud to have your wallet represent you!

II

We want to sell you our finest set of bookends—Atlas bookends. These bookends are made of real stainless steel.

Our artists—some of the cleverest men in the business—have produced a design that we think is superb. Incidentally, these bookends are polished to a high degree.

Knowing that most bookends are too light and insubstantial to do the job, we inserted extra weights in Atlas bookends. They can be relied on to hold up many books.

The enclosed picture of a set of Atlas bookends isn't really too good. The bottoms of these bookends have green felt cemented to them, so that Atlas bookends can be used even on the surface of a finely finished table. If the picture we are enclosing were in color, you would be able to appreciate our product.

Send us a postcard ordering a set of Atlas bookends. We would even be willing, if after examining them you decide you don't want them, to refund your money. Our address is as follows:

Crown Metals Manufacturing Company
4900 East Sill Boulevard
Miami, Florida 33167

Written Applications

• **1.** Write a clear description of two of the following objects. Using no more than 50-100 words for each object, be as precise as possible.

1 — a desk	5 — a door
2 — a lamp	6 — a ring
3 — a flashlight	7 — a pen
4 — a table	8 — a chair

Include information, for example, about the appearance, size, material(s), style, design, make, color, parts, and condition of whatever you are describing. Your description should be accurate and detailed, so that the object could be identified even if there were other similar objects in the same room.

• **2.** Write short paragraphs indicating the meaning of each of the following terms. Use examples to help make your explanations clear.

1 — Competence	3 — Cooperativeness
2 — Accuracy	4 — Courtesy

• **3.** Prepare a carefully organized, clear announcement incorporating the information in Oral Application 3.

• **4.** Write a new version of Sales Message II in Oral Application 4. Organize the letter carefully, bringing together points that are closely related. Adopt the "you-attitude." Use a tone that will win goodwill. Eliminate the negative elements that spoil the original version.

SECTION 4

Correctness

Add force, focus your reader's attention, and train it on the message, through correctness.

When, sometime in the future, you prepare a business message that may cost your company more than three dollars [1] to put in the mail, you will hope that your reader will give it the close attention you think it deserves.

Will he, in fact, do so? You must remember that perhaps two dozen other writers may have sent him messages the same morning. With limited time for each message, what can you realistically expect from your reader?

This is what will probably happen: First, he will form a quick first impression. If your message is well prepared with handsome margins and balanced layout, his eye will first seek your opening sentence. This is the natural point for his attention. Next, he will search for your core idea. This will be the answer to his question, "What's this about?" Swiftly he scans your paragraphs for the gist of your message. Finally, he may pencil a note or two in the margin, draw his conclusions, make his decision, and formulate his reply. Now how much time has he given you? One minute? Two minutes? Three minutes? Whatever the amount of time that he has been willing to devote to your message, that message has been made more effective, more productive, if you have been *accurate*.

Don't make your reader "trip over" errors. In business messages, mistakes can be both irritating and embarrassing. They are costly to look for and costly to correct. *Just one* omitted (or wrongly inserted) apostrophe can sharply lower your status and reputation. If you should doubt this unpleasant conclusion, run a brief personal test of your own and discover the facts.

Can you at this moment confidently handle such words as *affect/ effect, accessary/accessory, capitol/capital, calendar/calender?* Can you

---

[1] Systematic cost surveys by The Dartnell Corporation reveal that the cost of a personally dictated business letter has now crossed the three-dollar mark.

accurately distinguish, in usage, the words *counsel/council/consul?*
And should it be *principal* or *principle* in the context of the passage
before you?

Obviously, in these and in dozens of similar instances, you don't
want your reader to trip over an error. As we have seen, he may have
only a minute or two to devote to what you have to say. If he doesn't
have to hurdle any errors, he is likely to get your points with force
and clearness. With every error you plant in his way, with every
additional mistake he has to hurdle, you disrupt his attention and
destroy the impact of your message.

Errors block thought flow. Suppose, for a moment, we use a
purposely distorted example to see what happens to thought-flow
when errors block the way. Try wading through the following lines:
"The free pension system is, in theorey, a nobel idea. But in passed
years it ran into an un happy expereince. So keen analists promtly
startted to formlate the principals of a selfsupporting programm to
replac it. It was beleived that such a plan should be contributary from
both employe and emploier. It was sugested that the pension re-serves
should be sistematicaly accummulated, should have no cashsurrender
value, and should be keppt intac untill retirment too provide life-time
suportt."

If you are like the average reader, you may have found that each
of the glaring errors in the foregoing lines annoyed you, got in your
way, and derailed your thought. Anyone who voluntarily or involun-
tarily indulges in the expensive habit of poor spelling, haphazard
punctuation, defective grammar, surely risks clogging the channels of
thought-flow. The reason is simple. The errors simply distract the
eye through which the thought is picked up. Sprinkling the message
with errors is, therefore, the surest way to derail the reader's train
of thought.

**Can this be true? "English mistakes more costly than engineering
mistakes?" YES.** An executive of the Westinghouse Electric Corporation recently made a startling statement. He was discussing his work
after a transfer from the engineering group to the communications
and corporate-report group.

"Mistakes in English," he asserted, *"cost the company more than
mistakes in engineering."*

He explained further. He pointed out that if messages and
specifications from sales offices or from within the East Pittsburgh

Works were (1) incorrect, (2) incomplete, or (3) ambiguous, the result might well be serious. Why? Because, if wrong designs and shipments were avoided, it would only be through corrective—perhaps prolonged and costly—message exchanges.

When he was in the engineering division, he accepted the tradition that it was engineers who made the mistakes. But, he said, when he was transferred, he found that those who handle communications can make mistakes too. "And," he added, "unless these [mistakes] are watched and avoided, they offer a constant threat of unnecessary operating expense and intolerable rising costs."

One of the greatest single business savings that can be made is that of increasing written accuracy. One communications supervisor keeps before his eyes the following statement: To economize the reader's attention, and to focus it on the message, be correct.

A sheet of plate glass. In one respect a written message is like a sheet of plate glass. It should be clean and polished. It should permit the light of the thought to pass through with crisp clearness. The language, like plate glass, should be flawless. It should be accurate enough, and therefore clear enough, to let the reader grasp the thought easily and smoothly, just as you would see a clear picture through flawless glass.

Tiny errors may grow into towering trouble. A small mistake in an office may become a giant mistake a thousand miles away. The error may be in figures or words: the wrong addition or subtraction of a unit or cipher, the omission of a vital phrase, the blunder of a misleading statement. Many can write a message that can be understood. Few can write a message that cannot be misunderstood. Hence, strive for a clear plan and guard against misunderstanding.

Consider, for example, the difficulties that might beset a utility company operating electric lines and transportation if:

(1) A customer was quoted the wrong size of motor, and after purchase the motor proved too small to drive the machinery; or

(2) A farmer were to find that the contract price for the extension of an electric line to his farm turned out to be three times as much as he was quoted; or

(3) An extra cipher were, in error, added to the amount involved in the settlement of a thousand-dollar claim; or

(4) An engineer's instructions from the freight dispatcher's office told him to take the siding at 2:10 P.M. instead of 2:01 P.M. and he

BRADFORD HEATING CO.

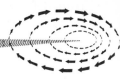

385 WEST SHIELDS AVENUE, BELLEVUE, WASHINGTON 98004 (206) 264-7769

June 19, 19--

Omit; colon only here

Weak opening, hackneyed

Omit -th, -st, -nd, -rd after the number when name of month appears

Spelling

Repetition

Bad form to omit needed words

Stock phrase

Capital

Stock phrase

Repetition

Overemphasizes the negatives

Repetition

Negative

Typing Error

Stock word

Repetition

Weak, trite close; participial conclusion; no longer considered good business usage

Entirely vague; shows no desire to be helpful; disinterested

Spell surname for identification of signature

Stock word; should never be used in this manner

Spelling

Negative and unpleasant

Wordy; omit

Negative

Repetition

Stock phrase

Negative

Word omitted

Spelling

Negative

Stilted

Stock word

Repetition

Violates parallel construction

Impossible division

Ineffective complimentary close

Avoid abbreviation here

Noticeable erasure and "strike over"

Stock phrase

Typing error

Necessary?

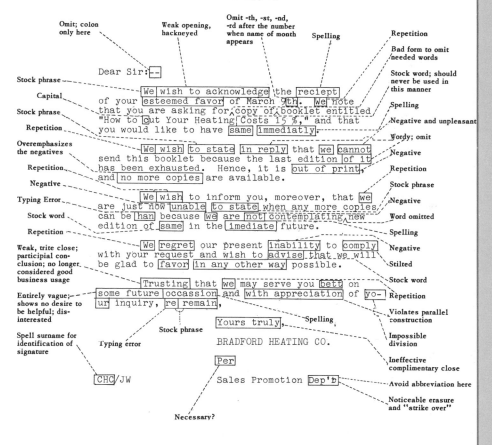

Dear Sir:--

We wish to acknowledge the reciept of your esteemed favor of March 9th. We note that you are asking for copy of booklet entitled "How to Cut Your Heating Costs 15 %," and that you would like to have same immediatly.

We wish to state in reply that we cannot send this booklet because the last edition of it has been exhausted. Hence, it is out of print, and no more copies are available.

We wish to inform you, moreover, that we are just now unable to state when any more copies can be han because we are not contemplating new edition of same in the imediate future.

We regret our present inability to comply with your request and wish to advise that we will be glad to favor in any other way possible.

Trusting that we may serve you bett on some future occassion and with appreciation of yo-ur inquiry, re remain,

Yours truly,

BRADFORD HEATING CO.

Per

CHC/JW   Sales Promotion Dep't

SOME MESSAGES <u>ARE</u> ACTUALLY THIS BAD

continued for nine minutes on the right-of-way when he should have been on the siding. In this instance the dispatcher might prevent an expensive pile-up of freight cars, and probably would; but the high risk still remains.

Anyone can realize what such cases might cost a company. Nor are such errors impossible. Exactly such errors *have* occurred.

Your checklist for correctness. Here is a convenient checklist to guide you in conveying *correct* information in accurate form:

1 — When, in preparation for writing, you make a list of facts, figures, and details, check your finished list against the original sources.
2 — In writing the message, check all names, addresses, and amounts against the original sources.
3 — When you have completed the message in rough draft, *proofread it* closely and carefully—first, for clearness; second, for accuracy of facts, figures, spelling, punctuation, and like details.
4 — As a final special precaution—and before you start the final draft—check *any* doubtful fact or figure against the original source; *any* doubtful spelling against the dictionary; and any doubtful point of punctuation against your punctuation guide.
5 — When you *do* make a mistake, *correct it at once.*

Show good manners. Correctness is one form of good manners. Good manners are expected of you. To the best of your ability, try to make everything you write from this point on correct in grammar, spelling, punctuation, and all other writing details. Clear away the error-blocks that clog the normal flow of thought. Haul away the hurdles that derail the thought-train.

Take the important steps listed above and you will achieve two major goals.

1 — You display your basic good manners.
2 — You show thoughtfulness and consideration.

Your reader will appreciate both. Of that you may be sure.

Summary. Prior pages of this section illustrate how gross errors may amuse or irritate your reader. If they amuse him, he is laughing at you. Your message loses its dignity. It draws an ironic smile and perhaps the comment, "He should know better than that." If, on the other hand, you irritate him, you have created (not solved) a communication problem.

Your reader may, of course, forgive you for your bad grammar, your faulty punctuation, your careless spelling. But you do not want him to take time to forgive you. You want him to invest his time in your message.

One ironic truth you must face: He himself may make many mistakes. But that fact will not prevent his noticing yours!

• *APPLYING EFFECTIVE ENGLISH*

Oral Applications

• 1. Mr. C. F. Schweitzer, an experienced plumber, sent the following inquiry to a distributor of the products of the Brooks Manufacturing Company:

> In the *Plumber's News,* I have seen advertisements for Brooks Manufacturing Company's No-Splash Faucets. Are these faucets available in different sizes? If so, what is the unit price for each size? Are replacement parts available?

Evaluate the following answers, which were prepared by the distributor's public relations department.

1 — We appreciate your inquiry concerning Brooks No-Splash Faucets. These faucets provide dependable service for years and seldom require replacement of parts. They are available in beautiful long-lasting chromium finish. You will also be interested in the matching towel racks. The faucets and towel-racks do, indeed, make an impressive set. We hope you will write us if we can be of further help.

2 — Thank you very much for your inquiry. No-Splash Faucets are available in a seven-inch size for the bathroom, a ten-inch size for the kitchen, and a ten-inch size, unpolished, for the basement. The kitchen and basement faucets swing through a 160 degree arc. The prices are as follows:

bathroom (7"): $7.65
kitchen (10"): $9.25
basement (10"): $5.65

These faucets and replacement parts for them are in stock and available for immediate delivery. You may be interested to know that No-Splash Faucets were used in the Michigan Towers Building—Milwaukee's most modern apartment development. Your faucets will be shipped the same day we receive your order.

3 — Thank you for your inquiry. The faucets come in a kitchen variety (10 inch-$9.25), and unpolished basement variety (10 inch-$5.65). They are available for immediate delivery.

4 — Thank you for your inquiry concerning No-Splash Faucets. We are happy to inform you that No-Splash Faucets come in three sizes, costing $5.65, $7.65, and $9.25.

• **2.** Compare the following statements in terms of their completeness and the impression made by each. Cite evidence to support your conclusions.

1 — With reference to your order for two Sure-Spot Flashlights, Catalog No. 25739, we are sorry to report that temporarily the model is out of stock. We received a notice yesterday from the manufacturers indicating when more of these flashlights will be available. Since we don't have this model on hand, of course we won't be able to fill your order. We look forward to the opportunity of serving you again.

2 — In answer to your request for our spring sale catalog and for information concerning our credit plan, we regret to have to report that this catalog will not be off the presses until March 9. We are placing your name on our mailing list and shall send you a copy of our spring sale catalog just as soon as it is available.

3 — We are sorry that you were put to the trouble of writing a second time in order to learn the opening date of our annual spring house furnishings show, the hours of the show, and the times when the modern kitchen demonstration will be held.

The pressure of answering inquiries from interested people and of filling orders for tickets led to our unfortunate oversight. Haste makes waste! We apologize and assure you that such a mistake will not recur.

This year the show promises to be one of the most exciting shows ever. The show opens August 28 and runs for four weeks. Hours are from 9:00 a.m. to 8:30 p.m. daily. Tickets will be available at the door. We hope you enjoy the show and urge you to make a special point of attending the demonstration of the largest home intercommunication system, of new heating techniques, and, especially, of the world's most modern kitchen. If we may be of further service in any way, please let us know.

• **3.** Examine the message below and at the top of the next page for correctness:

We are pleased to supply the itemization requested in your letter of July 3.

The three ballpoint pens cost $2.50 each. The eight automatic pencils cost $1.25 each. The six reams of paper cost $3.95 each. The four bottles of ink cost 39¢ each. The total cost, therefore, is $42.76.

A 20% discount is granted to schools, Thus your discount is $8.55. The total cost to you is $34.21.

Eager to give satisfaction, any assistance desired will be extended by us to you with promptness and pleasure.

Written Applications

• **1.** Rewrite each message given in Oral Application 2. Make certain that you provide complete and accurate information.

• **2.** Rewrite the message in Oral Application 3.

• **3.** Prepare replies to the following inquiries. Provide the information necessary for a complete and correct answer. Organize your message carefully, and use a courteous tone that emphasizes your appreciation for the inquiry.

1 — I am interested in attending the annual spring play at Washburn High School. Since I live almost 135 miles away, I must make special arrangements in order to attend. Would you please let me know the dates of the performances? The name of the play you are producing? The time of the performances? And the names of the principal actors? What is the cost of tickets? Will tickets be available at the door? Thank you for your assistance.

2 — I have just moved to Edmonton, and am interested in learning what days and hours the public library is open. Since I work during the day, I am particularly interested in learning whether the library is open Saturdays and Sundays, and, if so, during what hours. Will I be able to withdraw books at once or will I be forced to wait until a regular library card is processed? How long will that take?

Thank you for your help.

3 — I am considering a visit to Ash Mountain Lodge next July. How long in advance shall I make reservations? Do you have cooking facilities in any of your rooms? What are your weekly rates? What recreational facilities are available? Is transportation available from the airport to the lodge? I shall appreciate any help you can give me.

SECTION 5

Conciseness and Concreteness

Cancel needless words, and flash sharp word pictures.

Would you like to win *twice* the comprehension of your message in *half* the time? You can if you economize your use of words. Behind this call for word economy is powerful "cost-cutting" pressure. The very characteristics of modern industrial organization—machine tools, assembly lines, standardization, swift transportation—demand word economy.

Let us turn to a dictionary definition. Referring to style in writing or speaking, *conciseness* means to express much in few words, to be condensed, brief, and compact. The term *concise* (the opposite of *diffuse*) implies cutting away extra material.

Again referring to style in writing or speaking, *concreteness* is a quality relating to actual things or events, objects or actions that are real, specific, and particular. (The term *concrete* is the opposite of *abstract* and *general*.)

You will become familiar, in this section, with some of the characteristics of conciseness and concreteness. These are the joint qualities that multiply the central force of writing and speaking.

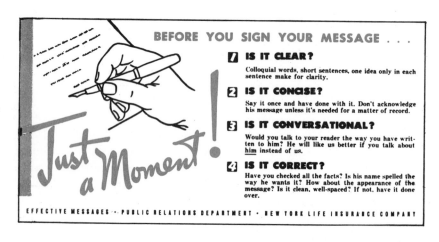

BEFORE YOU SIGN YOUR MESSAGE . . .

1 IS IT CLEAR?
Colloquial words, short sentences, one idea only in each sentence make for clarity.

2 IS IT CONCISE?
Say it once and have done with it. Don't acknowledge his message unless it's needed for a matter of record.

3 IS IT CONVERSATIONAL?
Would you talk to your reader the way you have written to him? He will like us better if you talk about him instead of us.

4 IS IT CORRECT?
Have you checked all the facts? Is his name spelled the way he wants it? How about the appearance of the message? Is it clean, well-spaced? If not, have it done over.

EFFECTIVE MESSAGES · PUBLIC RELATIONS DEPARTMENT · NEW YORK LIFE INSURANCE COMPANY

CONCISENESS IS WORD SAVING

"Words are about the most expensive thing we have, and we ought to treat them with more care."

So believes J. N. Hook, Executive Secretary of the National Council of Teachers of English. He continues:

"About half of all the taxes you pay every year are spent on words.

"When you buy a new $3,000 car, you are getting about $1,500 worth of words.

"About half the astronomical billions of dollars Uncle Sam pays annually for national defense buy nothing but words.

"You also pay for all the words, written or spoken, in board meetings, order forms, telegrams, telephone calls, newspaper, radio, and television advertisements, sales conferences—you name it, you're paying for it.

"About those taxes and the words they pay for: Most of the people in Washington, and most of the state and local government people as well, are communicators. They make not something that is tangible—they make words." [1]

You may say, "Well, the words I produce aren't worth much—at least not yet—because I'm not earning much of anything these days while I'm in school." True enough. But as you start climbing the ladder of experience on your first job, your words will become increasingly expensive as your salary increases.

Saving words cuts costs. If all those government employees previously spoken of were able, at national, state, and local levels, to save just ten words out of every one hundred they use, we might easily be able to reduce over-all government expenditures by ten percent, or by tens of millions of dollars a year!

Without leaving gaps or holes in what you write, without smothering your thought in useless wordage, your aim is to give forth your ideas in as few words as you can. Learn to use economy and concision in words, and you will pack more power in everything you say.

Suppose you want to send a greeting to a good friend. Instantly you face a decision. How long do you want to make it? Should it be five lines long? Ten? Twenty? Thirty? Forty? Nobody can give you a precise "figure" answer because the answer does not lie there.

Then how will you decide? Probably the best solution is to be found in the old story made famous by President Lincoln. Although

---

[1] As quoted in the *Bulletin* of the American Bus...ess Communication Association, Volume XXV, Number 1.

it has been told thousands of times, it will give you the exact answer. "How long should a man's legs be?" someone asked President Lincoln. "Just long enough to reach to the ground," he replied.

Your greeting to your friend should be just long enough to carry out its mission, just long enough to do its job—*and no longer.* By this test thousands of writing efforts are too long. A few, trying for brevity, fall into an opposite pit, sacrifice completeness (see Section 2 of this unit), and get only unpleasant curtness. A good effort falls in between. It strikes a happy medium. Completeness assures that the greeting will be given in full; conciseness that it will be carved down to the minimum.

President Lincoln knew "what to put in and what to leave out." Turn to page 396 of this book. There you will find the original draft of the immortally famous Gettysburg Address, thought by many competent judges to be the greatest utterance ever made by any President of the United States in the history of our country.

The concise simplicity of this brief piece of writing has come to be the standard of the world. This is not to say that all of the words are simple. Not all of them are. Yet rare indeed is any document into which is packed so much meaning in the measured conciseness of two hundred seventy-one words, rounded by the President's genius into an ultimate conception famed throughout the world. With immortal power the Gettysburg Address stands as a superb example of the kind of writing most fitted for its purpose.

Learn to condense. To seize attention and economize time and dollars, train yourself to pack the maximum of thought into the minimum of words. Cut through the nonessentials the way this writer does it in talking about rugged Stillson wrenches:

—and all they did was bend the handle.
Four brawny boys in our wrench foundry once put a pipe on the end of an 18-inch Stillson and swung on it—to see what would happen. The wrench handle bent, as tough steel should. The heavyweight committee got tired and fell off. But the Stillson never budged a tooth.

A real Stillson always bends before it breaks. It took four big men to bend this one. Any mechanic who risks his neck on high scaffolding knows what that means.

But most men look for the Stillson trademark (on the top jaw) just to make sure of getting a husky tool that will turn anything and will probably last until their grandchildren need it more than they do.

"This is the age of condensation in news and its related field of advertising," writes Kenneth Collins in his book *The Road to Good Advertising*. "Many newspapermen used to be paid for the amount of space they filled in the paper. Today they are rewarded for their ability to boil down news and ideas to their very essence. The great editorial writers and the successful advertising writers have this talent. It is what makes their copy so readable, their message so vivid. They *cut directly to the core*."

With attention to compactness you can cut down the length of your writing from one third to one fourth without sacrificing courtesy or completeness. Study the two examples illustrated in parallel on page 328. Note in the 82-word example these four features:

1 — How startling the contrast in compactness
2 — How outmoded words have been cut out
3 — How the sentences have been made brief and simple
4 — How untactful phrases have been avoided

Here is another example showing how to deflate surplus wordage. You may find it hard to believe that the two sentences say the same thing, but they do.

Wordy	*Concise*
(42 Words)	(7 Words)
Assuming that you are in search of valuable information that may increase your earning capacity by a more complete knowledge of any subject in which you may be interested, we desire to state most emphatically that your wages increase with your intelligence.	You earn more as you learn more.

Try out your writing on somebody else. Once there was a sales executive who won remarkable results with direct mail. His messages were sent to people of low to medium income. Each message brought a gratifying response. He was asked, "How do you do it?" His answer was simple. He never, he said, sent any written material to a large group without first trying it out on his friend, the bus driver.

"I have often boarded a bus to ride to the end of the line with a driver in order to read him what I have written. I found those men get into the habit of thinking clearly and dealing in short, direct

The Bumbling Original
(244 Words)

We have your kind favor of the 7th inst., and wish to state that we have very carefully gone over its contents.

In reply to your statement that you received a consignment of nine NX-211 Whirlwind Motors without the latest style valves, wish to state that this is in no sense a shortage. You state that you cannot understand why same were not packed with the engines in the original shipment and that something must have gone wrong in our shipping department. Beg to advise that the latest style valves do not come as standard equipment. You probably did not know that these are special and not covered in the original price of the motors are quoted to you in our letter of April 19th.

In other words, you ought to specify more carefully on your orders that you want the latest style valves on your orders, in any case where you want us to supply you with this extra equipment. If you will use a little extra care in this direction, we shall always do as you request. Of course you must remember that we will have to add an extra charge of $19.00 each for every job. In addition, if you want these for the jobs you just ordered, you will have to send us another order.

Trusting our explanation as outlined above is entirely satisfactory, and awaiting your further favors which will always receive the best of service and attention, we remain

As Revised and Condensed
(82 Words)

Apparently our catalog was not available at the time you ordered the nine NX-211 Whirlwind Motors mentioned in your letter of May 7.

On page 26 of the enclosed catalog will be found the latest style cam-and-roller valves, specified as extra equipment ($19 each, net). These valves could not, of course, be included at the unusually low price you obtained.

May we send you the valves? Simply telegraph us collect, and we will rush nine sets by prepaid express, billing them net.

This blank space represents the net saving in time, words, mental effort, human energy—and dollars—all as the result of SMART CONDENSING.

TO ECONOMIZE DOLLARS, CUT OUT USELESS WORDS!

statements. They taught me the fine art of cutting out extra words. Often, too, I have read these messages to the janitor who cleans out the office at night. He has given me splendid help, unknowingly, in the line of simplifying my thoughts. That is why the writing I send out now is mighty crisp and to the point. Some think I am too plain. The facts, however, are that my words bring me the business." [2]

Strike a happy medium. As you revise your writing, you will be constantly surprised at the relatively large number of words you can "red-pencil" without harm to the meaning. But good as strict word economy is, it should be applied with some caution. If you run it into the ground, you may damage goodwill that may have taken much effort to build. Only a small step separates brevity from curtness. If there is any question, the cancelled words should be reinstated.

The great military commander, Napoleon, was once asked what rule he followed in preparing his army orders. His famous reply:

"BEGRUDGE," he said, "EVERY WORD YOU PUT IN AN ORDER; BUT NEVER SACRIFICE CLEARNESS FOR BREVITY."

Generalizations such as "Short messages are better than long ones," "Short statements will always be read first," are unsound. To follow them uncritically may damage both your writing and the manner in which you have written. Follow this simple and trustworthy guide:

1 — First assure clearness, completeness, correctness, and courtesy.
2 — Then apply the red pencil vigorously on any word that does not contribute to those four paramount qualities.

CONCRETENESS FLASHES WORD PICTURES

You make words, phrases, and sentences easier to grasp when you infuse into them the forceful quality of concreteness. You make them easy to grasp because their ideas become vivid, specific, sharp. Abstractness and generality are the opposite of concreteness. Abstractness is generalized, perhaps fuzzy, in its outlines. Concreteness is sharp and vivid in its definition.

MAGNETIZE YOUR LETTERS WITH CONCRETENESS

---

[2] Bulletin of the Direct Mail Advertising Association.

For example, you speak of:

a point	as	"sharp as a needle"
a light	like a	"flaming skyrocket"
darkness	of an	"ink-black sky"
an edge	as	"razor-keen"

What you have done is to create vivid comparisons because they refer to concrete objects that are familiar to all of us. Here are some more contrasts:

General and Abstract	*Vivid and Concrete*
This hi-fi set will give you good service and pleasure.	Apex stereo high-fidelity, with static-free FM, offers you an amplifier 33% more powerful than comparable sets and delivers rich bass and sparkling treble tones over two 7-inch oval coaxial speakers.
This camera will serve your photographic needs well.	You'll find in the Graflex just the right lens speeds, film index, flash synchronization, and cross-coupled meter.
Get a quick shave	Enjoy a 75-second shave
It is a wide concrete road.	The new 6-lane concrete turnpike, 200 feet wide, stretches away like a long, wide ribbon.
This soap gives generous lather.	Multiplies itself in lather 250 times.
These tires stop the car within a short distance.	Four Champion steel-belted, radial heavy-duty tires stop this 2-ton car, from 60 miles an hour, in 235 feet.
The airplane comes down fast.	Like a great hawk the Vulcan-Fighter, its four cyclone jets whining, swoops down in a screaming dive.
This military jet is fast.	The USAF B-70 Valkyrie holds the world's air-breathing-engine trophy at 10,000 mph over a closed course.

Use concreteness to multipy descriptive power and vivid word choice. You develop descriptive power through the skillful use of nouns, verbs, and abjectives that picture facts, situations, events, and actions in colorful terms appealing to the senses of seeing, hearing, feeling, touching, and tasting. Words that stimulate these senses convert generalities into colorful vividness.

For additional material on concreteness, review the discussion of nouns, verbs, and adjectives (Sections 1, 3, and 4 of Unit 3), and refer to the discussion of effective vocabulary and vivid word choice.

SUMMARIZING THE SIX C's

Through the tested and now-famous six C's, effective communication has become forceful, courteous, human, and cost-saving. Taken together, the six C's make up a guide-series important to apply and easy to remember. Each one has over the years proved itself to be essential. Memorize the six C's. Make (1) Courtesy, (2) Completeness, (3) Clearness, (4) Correctness, (5) Conciseness, and (6) Concreteness your targets in the challenging situations that lie ahead.

Courtesy and the YOU-attitude—your consideration of your reader—are essential in order that your writing may win a favorable reception and your reader may be truly helped; *completeness,* in order to assure that you have determined what and how much to put in your writing to make it carry out its task; *clearness,* in order to power pack your meaning and make it easy to grasp; *correctness,* in order to focus your reader's attention and to train it on your message; *conciseness,* in order to chisel away needless and costly words; and *concreteness,* in order to flash vivid pictures to make every fact interesting, definite, and informative.

When you have mastered these six guides, you will be well on your way to becoming an effective writer. In the genuine sense of the word, you will be *well versed in the fundamentals* that will make you a trained communicator.

• *APPLYING EFFECTIVE ENGLISH*

Oral Applications

- 1. Explain each of the six C-qualities.

- 2. How can a message be concise and complete at the same time? How can the apparent conflict between these two principles be explained? For example, consider the examples of concise writing in this section. Do they also meet the test of completeness? Explain.

- **3.** Examine the following example in terms of the C-qualities.

Your letter of the 9th received and in reply must state that these awnings would have to be made up and it would be necessary for us to have, at this particular time of the year about ten days to do the job, if this amount of time would not inconvenience you to much. We can turn them out in about half that time if absolutely necessary and when the hot weather comes, it generally slows us up to, but we can work faster now, since the volume of our business is smaller during this slack time of the year for us.

We are sending you under separate cover two folders containing awning samples and patterns. In figuring the size these awnings should be, the height of the window as well as the width is necessary to be known to us. We need these measurements so that we can cut the awnings to the right size. Otherwise your awnings won't fit properly when you go to install them.

- **4.** Many writers find it useful to secure the advice of others in revising their messages. Note the practice of the sales executive cited on page 327.

Ask a classmate to suggest ways of improving the message you write in connection with Written Application 2. Then discuss the possible advantages of getting someone else's reaction to your message before sending it.

- **5.** Suggest a more vivid and concrete version for each of the following flat, unimaginative statements. Provide the names and details necessary to make the statements interesting and forceful. For examples, see page 330.

1 — Renee's report was nice.
2 — Jeffry moved down the incline on his sled.
3 — Michelle fell down.
4 — Randy is a good student.
5 — These tires go through snow.
6 — This stereo record is excellent.
7 — Attention should be obtained by a message.
8 — A Sure-Line ball-point pen writes well.
9 — This T.V. set gives reception in fringe areas.
10 — With this gasoline you can start easily.
11 — An accident occurred.
12 — This is a good carpet.

Written Applications

• **1.** Assume you are manager of the public relations department of Paulson Office Equipment, Inc. Write a 150-200 word explanation making clear to your staff why conciseness is necessary for effectiveness. Cite evidence from the contrasting letters on pages 326-328 to illustrate your points.

• **2.** Rewrite the example given in Oral Application 3. Incorporate the six C-qualities.

• **3.** Revise the following sentences, making them concise. Do not, however, sacrifice any of the other C-qualities.

1 — One of these days in the future in your business it is not unlikely in your case that additional machine tools will be needed, and when this situation arises and is realized by you, it will be with great pleasure that prompt service will be offered to you by us at that time and any other time, always.

2 — It is possible, Mr. Kinnee, that we—you and I—have personally met each other at some time or other in the past, but if so, at the present time, that occasion does not seem to come to mind now and I just can't recall it.

3 — Mr. Lidbeck pointed out last week and said that, in view of the success that was experienced as a result of the advertising campaign carried on by us for six weeks before July last spring, it would seem to him that it would not, everything considered, be inadvisable to consider a similar campaign for possible adoption by our company.

4 — The plan is that this organization, which has, after all, no other purpose than that of conducting various business operations such as securing the necessary materials, manufacturing automobile radios, and merchandising them, is to produce as soon as possible an AM-FM instrument for installation in automobiles at a much lower cost than any now available without sacrificing quality.

5 — We beg to be allowed the honor of communicating to you the important information that a research division is to be maintained at the home office by us with the idea, perfectly normal and usual in any business enterprise, that valuable help can be obtained from such an organization as this and problems can be avoided, perhaps, too, by means of its studies and recommendations.

6 — If this corporation had unlimited funds, great financial resources, and all of the money anyone could want, we should proceed ahead on this plan and idea and carry it out to the fullest possible extent in every detail.

• *REVIEW*

Correct all errors in the following sentences:

1 — Mrs. Ford, as well as her husband, were sincerely apolagetic.
2 — Miss Sutton may of answerd his inquirys.
3 — Tacked firmly in place, the installer's felt that the carpet would not slip.
4 — A package of paper clips are laying on the desk.
5 — Lets revise our plan completly.
6 — Mrs. Schrubbe has went home to.
7 — Them students, just between you and I, will no what the teams chance of winning is.
8 — That secretary is a young lady whom, I believe, has excellant prospects with our company.
9 — The employees have there own restaurant.
10 — Mr. Warren Ford is dinning at the Hinsdale university club this evening.
11 — Naturally we only can send you in this sales message a few of our suggestions for your Christmas shoping.
12 — One of our representatives are assigned to the district accross the river.
13 — All staff members must attend the conference this afternoon plans will be layed for our next sales campaign.
14 — If Katharine takes her umbrella, Judy wont bother to take her's.
15 — We not only will review our proceedures but our policys.
16 — The board is bringing their own copy's of the financial statement.
17 — Miss Pat Fontecchio, as well as Laura Allen and Linda Hammer, are on vacation this week.
18 — These mistakes of your's has been occuring to often.
19 — Waiting in the outer office, an unusual incident was witnessed by Mr. Richard Bourke our representative.
20 — Each student and teacher in the High School are excited about the contest.

UNIT 10

MESSAGE POWER THROUGH EFFECTIVE STYLING

What your reader is going to <u>think</u> about you and your message will depend in part on what your reader first <u>sees</u> on the page. The opening impression you make will be the launch pad from which your message will take off.

Be sure at all costs to provide an attractive <u>visual</u> invitation as a basic requirement. Only when you are sure that your message will make an excellent first impression can you safely send it.

You will learn in the first two sections how a business message should be attractively placed on a sheet. You will also review the seven parts of a business letter and learn how to arrange and space them to invite easy reading.

You will learn in the third and fourth sections more fully about the nature of the seven parts and how they help to launch the message.

Finally, in the fifth section you will learn how to guarantee that your message will get to where you want it to go in an attractive form that will make the impression you desire.

UNIT 10

Section 1

Make an Excellent First Impression: Place your message attractively on the sheet.

Section 2

How to Gain Effective Styling: The seven parts of a business letter, properly spaced and arranged, invite easy reading, assure excellent form.

Section 3

The Introductory Parts: The heading, the introductory address, and the salutation instantly launch your message.

Section 4

The Body and the Concluding Parts: The concluding steps present the message swiftly over your signature.

Section 5

Putting the Message in the Mail: Careful envelope addresses, handsome letter folds, and well-prepared postal cards all help speed your message.

SECTION 1

Make an Excellent First Impression

Place your message attractively on the sheet.

As we shall soon see in later units, truly effective communication in business requires creativity and a sensitive *awareness* of your reader. For example, when your reader picks up a page on which you have sent him a message, what is the first thing he will see? Visual form is the first to strike his eye. Handsome arrangement reinforces visual impact. Make it command respect. See that it looks "right" on the page.

If we were to put it the other way around and use the warning approach, we could say it differently. "No matter how careful your word choice, no matter how thoughtful your plan, no matter how vivid your ideas, you can, by a few ill-chosen typing strokes or a few slovenly lines of your pen, instantly ruin visual form."

Whether you like it or not, people trademark you every day. Although you may never be aware of it, every day they see you, people are putting a trademark on you. An experienced executive puts it this way: "People look at you. They judge you. They trademark you. Then they put you in what they think is your right pigeonhole. What they are saying is, 'That is where we think you belong.' Just by *looking at you,* they do all these things."

Regrettable though it may seem, people continuously form quick first impressions through instantaneous snap judgments. You may argue vigorously that making snap judgments is superficial. You may say that it is sometimes grossly unfair. You are quite right. Many snap judgments *are* superficial and grossly unfair. But your arguments will be of no avail. People will go right ahead making snap judgments. You may be sure they will make snap judgments about *you.* And they will keep right on making them, whether these judgments are right or wrong.

You are at a public lecture. The speaker walks up the steps of the platform, approaches the rostrum, prepares to address the group.

He has not yet uttered a word. Yet you have already started to size him up. You are in the process of making a snap judgment. Perhaps you like him at first glance. When you draw these quick conclusions of a person, an object, a situation, you are indulging in a recognized human habit. It is an unavoidable human habit that you and all others will follow. Prepare for it. Expect it. You will be subjected to it as long as you live.

You and your messages *both* get trademarked. Just as you get trademarked, so does all the work you produce, and all the messages that you write.

You can give them handsome and powerful impact, if you will do these things: (1) Make your message attract the eye. (2) Give it handsome display. (3) Place it carefully on the sheet.

WHAT KIND OF MESSAGE WILL GO ON THAT SHEET?

Will it be handsome? Will it be courteous? Will it build goodwill? Will you be proud of it?

Nine o'clock in the morning. Suppose you are a visitor in a sky-scraper office. The time is nine in the morning. An executive is at work. He elects to open his mail.

Before him lies a stack of incoming messages. He picks up a slender paper knife, slits an envelope flap, draws forth the sheet, unfolds it with a snap, gives it a quick and appreciative appraisal. A "picture" strikes his eye!

"Handsome," is his thought. "Quality . . . importance . . . better give this item special attention." The slender paper knife slits into the next envelope.

"Well! What a contrast! Can't this outfit hire a stenographer who can spell? Look at those strikeovers . . . this is certainly a piece of slovenliness . . . Maybe this company is slipping . . . I wonder? . . . Reminds me, I'd better have a look at our stuff . . . I hope we're not letting anything like this out of *our* office!"

And the paper knife slits on, with the critical "subconscious" of the executive doing its snap-judgment work for or against, as the case may be.

Marshall Field & Company

111 NORTH STATE STREET · CHICAGO · ILLINOIS 60690 · TELEPHONE STATE 1-1000

May 23, 19--

Mrs. Kathryn Lambert
1124 Highland Avenue
Des Moines, IA 50315

Dear Mrs. Lambert:

If there's one place in the world where every member of
your family can have a completely rounded and highly enjoyable vacation--it's <u>Chicago</u>!

There's everything here! Bathing, beaches, boat regattas,
zoos and museums, Ravinia's symphony concerts, restaurants
of all nationalities, gala dining and dancing--a whole
world of entertainment in one great city. And this year
the celebration of Chicago's Charter Jubilee will make
your visit brimful of excitement.

Marshall Field & Company is anxious to help you get the
most out of every minute of your time in Chicago, whether
it is a full-length vacation, a gay weekend, or just a
day between trains. Think of our store as your own personal tour headquarters.

You'll find our Personal Service Bureau ready to give you
detailed hotel information, to make your hotel reservations, to assist in solving your transportation problems,
and to help plan your sightseeing and entertainment.

We hope you will come in with the enclosed card and let
us help you as soon as you arrive in Chicago. If there
is anything we can do for you now, let us hear from you
by mail.

Sincerely yours,

MARSHALL FIELD & COMPANY

R. J. Cameron

Credit Manager

RJCameron:jc

LIFE

TIME & LIFE BUILDING
ROCKEFELLER CENTER
NEW YORK, 10020

November 21, 19--

Dr. Lester N. McDevitt
Doctors Building
140 Glendale Boulevard
Ocean View, DE 19970

Dear Dr. McDevitt

Thank you for the interest you have expressed
in the special article published in the November 11 issue. The questions you have raised
in your letter of November 17 are so important,
in our opinion, that we have made plans to deal
with them at length in a subsequent issue.

Accept our appreciation for your thoughtfulness
in writing and for giving us the valuable benefit of your research.

Sincerely yours

W. L. Wills

For the Editors

WLWills:rr

HARRINGTON-KIELY, INC.	**ODELL AND PERRY ATTORNEYS AT LAW**	**FP&W** Ferguson, Plevyak, & Wood Management Consultants

(letterhead details)

HARRINGTON-KIELY, INC.
399 North Michigan Avenue   Chicago, IL 60601   Telephone 312-477-700

Customer Service Department

March 15, 19--

Mr. Darrell Buckley
Meridian Products Corp.
2200 Grand Avenue
Des Moines, IA 50306

Dear Mr. Buckley

SUBJECT: Letter Cost

Sincerely yours

John A. Ohms, Manager
esp
Enclosure

ODELL AND PERRY   ATTORNEYS AT LAW
750 PETROLEUM BUILDING   TULSA OK 74103   (918)291-4000

March 15, 19--
AIRMAIL-SPECIAL DELIVERY

Mrs. Alice Mozelle McGowan
6402 Classen Boulevard, N.
Oklahoma City, OK 73116

Dear Mrs. McGowan:

SUBJECT: Contract #OL-417-28-400

Very truly yours,
ODELL AND PERRY

Richard S. Perry

sa

FP&W   Ferguson, Plevyak, & Wood   Management Consultants
821 Second Avenue   Seattle, WA 98104   Telephone (206)641-5000

March 15, 19--
CERTIFIED MAIL

Northwest Pacific Van Lines
222 Morrison, S.W.
Portland, OR 97204

Attention Mr. O. J. Burnside

Gentlemen   File: DL-47-395

Sincerely yours

Paul P. Plevyak
Vice President

rn

cc Mr. James S. Curtis
   Mrs. Janice McCall

SHORT   *AVERAGE*   *LONG*

Attractive placement of letters of varying length

Try the "Twenty-Five" Test. From the files of a business office pull at random twenty-five messages. Lay them out before you. Doubtless you will find several of low rank. Others will seize your favorable attention. Of these, sort out the several that rank highest in your judgment. Now compare them. You will find that certain features make winners stand out:

1 – The design of the letterhead
2 – The feel of the paper
3 – The accuracy and appearance of the typing
4 – The balanced placement on the letterhead

Visualizing. Refer to the Marshall Field & Company message and the *Life* magazine message on page 339. Note how crispness of form brings respect, builds prestige. Form is the first thing you see. It flashes a picture. Get into the habit of following high standards of excellent form. Then you can always turn out handsome work. You will have learned to "visualize."

Note that the longer message has narrower side margins and begins higher on the letterhead than does the shorter letter. Even though, for efficiency of message production, modern business no longer calls for exactly balanced margins and "picture-framing," messages are still placed on letterheads in such a way as to achieve attractive balance. Furthermore, "estimating" the placement of the date, margin width, and message length has become the practice. To aid in the accuracy of estimation, many office manuals specify, 2-, 1½-,

Jeffrey Sellwood, President

C̄R̄A

CENTURY RESEARCH ASSOCIATES, INC. ◢━━━━━━━━━━━

562 State Street

Chicago, Illinois 60610

(312) 751-4829

INDUSTRIAL BUILDERS, INC.

(216) 721-4723

715 SUPERIOR AVENUE
CLEVELAND, OHIO 44114

western
electronics, inc.

(213) 331-3310

1154 Westwood Boulevard
Los Angeles, California 90024

THE MODERN TREND IN LETTERHEAD DESIGN

and 1-inch margins for short, average, and long messages because shorter distances are easier to estimate than longer ones such as 48-, 60-, and 72-space lines.

Choosing stationery. Even the paper upon which you write leaves its impression. White, unruled, rag-content bond of firm texture and surface, of standard size 8½ by 11 inches, is most popular. For short notes the half sheet of 8½ by 5½ inches is used. Note, however, that it cannot always be filed well with larger sheets.

Tinted paper with matching envelopes is used to an increasing extent, especially in sales work.

Second-sheet stationery should match the first in quality, weight, and size. Carbon copies for office files are written on inexpensive paper, thin but firm in texture to assure a clear carbon impression.

Letterhead designs. Handsome letterheads can be created by the use of simple lines and angles and blocks of type. An attractive letterhead adds "pull" to the message and stature to the firm. But some business organizations in twentieth-century competition still use horse and buggy styles.

In a space depth of not more than two to two and a half inches, an effective letterhead gives (1) the name of the enterprise, (2) mail address, (3) sometimes the nature of the business, (4) the telephone number, and when appropriate (5) the address of the main office, and

(6) the location of branch offices. These classes of information may be reproduced on the letterhead in printed, lithographed, or engraved form.

Elaborate colors, illustrative devices, and impressive trademarks sometimes appear in the designs. In general, however, experts provide arrangements that direct attention to the character of the company without drawing attention away from the message.

• *APPLYING EFFECTIVE ENGLISH*

Oral Applications

• **1.** What impression concerning a corporation is conveyed by careless and inept styling of correspondence?

• **2.** What are some important outcomes that result from attractive placement of material? Discuss the importance of each of these outcomes.

• **3.** What information should be given on a letterhead?

Written Applications

• **1.** Design attractive letterheads for the following firms. Use 8½ by 11 inch stationery and print the words in the style and size you think most effective.

    1 — Cartriseal Division
        Rex Chainbelt, Incorporated
        634 Glenn Avenue
        Wheeling, Illinois 60090
    2 — Minnesota Rubber Company
        3630 South Wooddale Avenue
        Minneapolis, Minnesota 55416
    3 — Precise Machine Company, Inc.
        7131 Barry Avenue
        Rosemont, Illinois 60018

• **2.** As an office supervisor of the Todd K. Zimmerman Insurance Company, 504 Lexington Street, Kingsford, Michigan 49801, write to the members of your staff a 150-word explanation of the importance of style in business messages.

• **3.** Design a letterhead for the insurance company mentioned in Written Application 2.

SECTION 2

How to Gain Effective Styling

*The seven parts of a business letter, properly spaced
and arranged, invite easy reading, assure excellent form.*

Your dictionary defines a layout as the act or process of planning;
the arrangement of something planned. For example, when you achieve
an attractive arrangement of the several parts of a finished message,
you have a good layout. A good layout achieves three desirable aims:

1 — It makes your message attractive.
2 — It directs attention to the message as a whole, to its important
parts, and from part to part.
3 — Your message is easy to read because your layout presents it so
clearly.

It is wise to consider the following questions in planning your
first layout:

1 — How can you make it most attractive?
2 — How can you design it to get the greatest attention?
3 — How can you build it so that your reader can most easily understand what you have to say?

THE SEVEN LETTER PARTS AND THEIR ARRANGEMENT

The standard structure of the modern business message usually
has the following parts:

1 — Heading
2 — Address
3 — Salutation
4 — Body
5 — Complimentary Close
6 — Signature
7 — Signature Identification and Stenographic Reference

1—Heading. The *heading* is a device for indicating where the message comes from and when it was written.

When the message is written on plain paper without a letterhead, the heading includes the exact address of the writer and the date. The first line of the heading begins at the center of the sheet. For a message of medium length, the first line is typed about fourteen lines from the top. If the message is short, the first line of the heading is typed from four to six lines lower on the sheet.

On letterhead paper the writer's address is printed in the letterhead itself. Hence, there is no need to repeat it in the heading, which will then consist only of the dateline. On letterhead paper the dateline "floats"; that is, its vertical placement varies from Line 20 (for short letters) to Line 12 (for long letters). The dateline is often (1) begun at the horizontal center of the sheet, (2) placed so that it will end at the right margin, or (3) begun at the left margin in block style.

2—Address. The *address* contains the name of the person (if used) to whom the message is to be sent and his official title (if he has one), the name of the business, the street address, the city name, the state name, and the ZIP Code. The lines of the address are typed even with the left margin. Three blank line spaces separate the dateline and the address.

3—Salutation. The *salutation* is the complimentary greeting with which a message begins. (Examples: Dear Mr. Burke: or, Gentlemen: or, My dear Burke:) The salutation is typed even with the left margin and two line spaces below the last line of the address. Double spacing is used between the salutation and the first line in the body.

4—Body. The *body* is the material between the salutation at the beginning and the complimentary close at the end. The body begins two line spaces below the salutation. Your aim is to lay the dark type symmetrically on the white paper in such a way as to gain crisp contrast and emphasis. The body of a single-spaced message requires double spacing between paragraphs. Every line of a paragraph may be written flush with the left margin, or the first line alone may be indented several spaces, depending on the writer's preference.

5—Complimentary close. The *complimentary close* is typed two line spaces below the last line of the body. It is usually begun at the center of the sheet, but it may be started to the left of the center to prevent the longest of the closing lines from extending beyond the right margin.

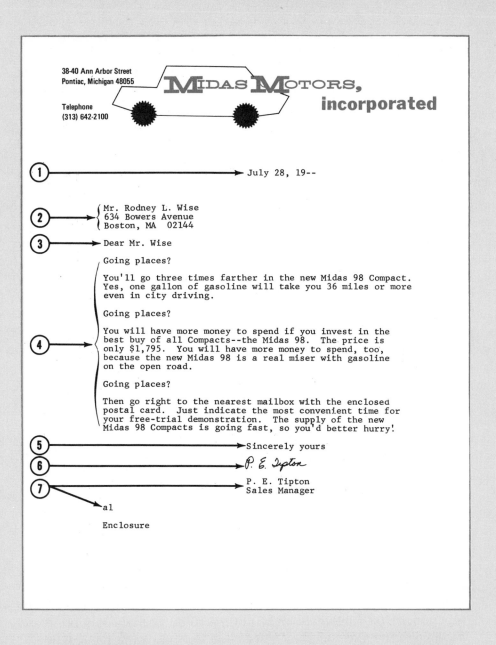

1　July 28, 19--

2　Mr. Rodney L. Wise
634 Bowers Avenue
Boston, MA 02144

3　Dear Mr. Wise

Going places?

You'll go three times farther in the new Midas 98 Compact.
Yes, one gallon of gasoline will take you 36 miles or more
even in city driving.

Going places?

4　You will have more money to spend if you invest in the
best buy of all Compacts--the Midas 98. The price is
only $1,795. You will have more money to spend, too,
because the new Midas 98 is a real miser with gasoline
on the open road.

Going places?

Then go right to the nearest mailbox with the enclosed
postal card. Just indicate the most convenient time for
your free-trial demonstration. The supply of the new
Midas 98 Compacts is going fast, so you'd better hurry!

5　Sincerely yours

6　*P. E. Tipton*

7　P. E. Tipton
Sales Manager

al

Enclosure

A WELL-ARRANGED MESSAGE SHOWING CORRECT LAYOUT

*The numbers at the left of the letter correspond to the seven standard letter parts
explained on pages 344 and 346; (1) heading, (2) address, (3) salutation, (4) body,
(5) complimentary close, (6) signature, and (7) signature identification and
stenographic reference.*

Sec. 2 • How to Gain Effective Styling

6—Signature. The signature may consist only of the name of the writer with his name typed, directly below his written signature, on the fourth line below the complimentary close. This typed signature is begun even with the beginning of the complimentary close. Sometimes in business communication the signature consists of (a) the firm name, typewritten in solid capitals on one line, (b) the written signature of the person accepting responsibility, and (c) the typed official position of the person who is writing. In this case the company name is typed on the second line space below the complimentary close. It is begun even with the beginning of the complimentary close. The signer's name is typed on the fourth line below the company name. It is begun even with the beginning of the company name. The official title is usually typed on the line immediately below the typed name. If, however, the official title is short, it may be typed on the same line preceded by a comma.

7—Signature identification and stenographic reference. *The signature identification* and *stenographic reference* are devices to indicate who has dictated the message and who has transcribed it. These items should be typed flush with the left margin and two spaces below the dictator's official title. If the signature does not carry a typewritten name of the dictator or an official title, the signature identification and stenographic reference are typed flush with the left margin on the fourth line below the company name. If the message is short and if it has neither a typed company name nor a typed official title, the identification and reference lines should be typed flush with the left margin six to eight line spaces below the complimentary close.

PUNCTUATION AND MESSAGE STYLES

Punctuation styles. *Open punctuation* permits the omission of punctuation at the *ends* of opening and closing lines, unless a line ends in an abbreviation. An abbreviation must always be followed by a period. *Mixed punctuation* requires a colon after the salutation and a comma after the complimentary close but omits the punctuation at the ends of the lines of the heading and the address. Modern usage approves either of these forms of punctuation. Even with open punctuation, it remains necessary to separate with a comma the name of the city from the name of the state, and the day of the month from the year.

```
February 8, 19--              February 8, 19--

Miss Carolina Perez           Miss Carolina Perez
850 Park Avenue               850 Park Avenue
New York, New York  10021     New York, New York  10021

Dear Miss Perez:              Dear Miss Perez

Sincerely yours,              Sincerely yours

William H. LaMaster           William H. LaMaster
Executive Director            Executive Director
```

Letter styles. Messages may be arranged in the block or the modified block style.

Block style. In the block style each line begins at the left margin. This style is thought by some to give less symmetry than do the other styles, but it enjoys some favor because it saves time for the typist. The amount of time saved may become important when the number of units handled becomes large.

Modified block style. The modified block style contains variations from the complete block style. On both letterhead and plain paper the dateline is ordinarily begun at the horizontal center of the sheet or typed to end at the right margin. When letterhead paper is not used, the heading is ordinarily typed to end at the right margin. The paragraphs may be typed in the block style, each line flush with the left margin, or the first line of each paragraph may be indented five to ten spaces. The closing lines are blocked (a) beginning at the center or (b) beginning at a point so that the longest line will not extend beyond the right margin. Because it presents a well-balanced appearance and is relatively easy to type, the modified block style enjoys the widest use of all the styles. It is illustrated on page 349.

Single spacing. Business prefers single spacing for the paragraphs of the body. We assume here the use of a typewriter or of similar spacing in handwritten drafts. Single spacing brings economy and better display. Many more words can be put on a page typed with single spacing. Hence less stationery may be needed. This saving may mean a considerable sum in a year. The eye is accustomed to reading the printed book and magazine. Hence, it finds single spacing familiar. Appearance is improved too when single spacing is used. Paragraphs

Block Style—Open Punctuation

Sabatelli, Guffey, & Holyoke management consultants

August 1, 19--

Mr. James K. Fawley, President
Southern National Corporation
2761 Benton Boulevard
Kansas City, MO 64128

Dear Mr. Fawley

SUBJECT: Effective Communication

You may be sure that we appreciate your most interesting comment on the introductory booklet of the series we have presented to the business executives of America under the sponsorship of our Communications Division.

Comments like yours are encouraging. They make us more certain that we are giving a valuable service to American business, a service all the more appreciated because it has an immediate and practical application to problems that beset every company from coast to coast.

Executives are just coming to the full realization that business messages are one of America's most powerful communication channels. Most universal of all, available to every man, they are the one medium that everyone can command. Instruments of great individual power, business messages win the headlines in the history of our American business.

Sincerely yours

SABATELLI, GUFFEY, & HOLYOKE

Donald Blair

Director
Communications Division

DBlair:jlb

2913 fountain ave. st. louis, missouri 63113

BLOCK STYLE—OPEN PUNCTUATION

Block Style—Mixed Punctuation

Sabatelli, Guffey, & Holyoke management consultants

August 1, 19--

Southern National Corporation
2761 Benton Boulevard
Kansas City, MO 64128

Attention Mr. Fawley

Gentlemen:

You may be sure that we appreciate your most interesting comment on the introductory booklet of the series we have presented to the business executives of America under the sponsorship of our Communications Division.

Comments like yours are encouraging. They make us more certain that we are giving a valuable service to American business, a service all the more appreciated because it has an immediate and practical application to problems that beset every company from coast to coast.

Executives are just coming to the full realization that business messages are one of America's most powerful communication channels. Most universal of all, available to every man, they are the one medium that everyone can command. Instruments of great individual power, business messages win the headlines in the history of our American business.

Sincerely yours,

SABATELLI, GUFFEY, & HOLYOKE

Donald Blair

Donald Blair, Director
Communications Division

jlb

2913 fountain ave. st. louis, missouri 63113

BLOCK STYLE—MIXED PUNCTUATION

August 1, 19--

Mr. James K. Fawley, President
Southern National Corporation
2761 Benton Boulevard
Kansas City, MO 64128

Dear Mr. Fawley:

    Subject: Effective Communication

    You may be sure that we appreciate your most inter-
esting comment on the introductory booklet of the series
we have presented to the business executives of America
under the sponsorship of our Communications Division.

    Comments like yours are encouraging. They make us
more certain that we are giving a valuable service to
American business, a service all the more appreciated
because it has an immediate and practical application to
problems that beset every company from coast to coast.

    Executives are just coming to the full realization
that business messages are one of America's most powerful
communication channels. Most universal of all, available
to every man, they are the one medium that everyone can
command. Instruments of great individual power, business
messages win the headlines in the history of our American
business.

                        Sincerely yours,

                        SABATELLI, GUFFEY, & HOLYOKE

                        Donald Blair

                        Donald Blair, Director
                        Communications Division

jlb

2913 fountain ave. st. louis, missouri 63113

Sabatelli, Guffey, & Holyoke management consultants

August 1, 19--

Mr. James K. Fawley, President
Southern National Corporation
2761 Benton Boulevard
Kansas City, MO 64128

Dear Mr. Fawley

        Effective Communication

You may be sure that we appreciate your most interesting
comment on the introductory booklet of the series we have
presented to the business executives of America under the
sponsorship of our Communications Division.

Comments like yours are encouraging. They make us more
certain that we are giving a valuable service to American
business, a service all the more appreciated because it
has an immediate and practical application to problems
that beset every company from coast to coast.

Executives are just coming to the full realization that
business messages are one of America's most powerful
communication channels. Most universal of all, available
to every man, they are the one medium that everyone can
command. Instruments of great individual power, business
messages win the headlines in the history of our American
business.

                        Sincerely yours

                        SABATELLI, GUFFEY, & HOLYOKE

                        Donald Blair

                        Director
                        Communications Division

DBlair:jlb

2913 fountain ave. st. louis, missouri 63113

MODIFIED BLOCK STYLE WITH INDENTED
PARAGRAPHS—MIXED PUNCTUATION

MODIFIED BLOCK STYLE WITH BLOCKED
PARAGRAPHS—OPEN PUNCTUATION

have greater visual unity when typed in single-spaced blocks with double spacing between them. Through use of the principle of visual contrast, their darker mass is better displayed against the light background of the letterhead. The same principle may be used in penwritten messages.

Simplified styles. Rules in regard to form are not fixed. They undergo constant change. For example, open punctuation, which is now generally accepted as a correct form, was a daring innovation a few years ago.

An interesting example of the movement toward further simplification is the *AMS simplified* style supported by the Administrative Management Society. An illustration of the *AMS simplified* form is presented on page 351. This form follows the block style. It differs from the usual block style in the following details:

1 — The salutation is omitted.
2 — The subject heading is typed in capital letters at least three spaces below the address.
3 — Questions, listings, or like items in the body of the letter are indented five spaces from the left margin except when they are preceded by a number or a letter.
4 — The period after a number or letter used in an outline form may be omitted.
5 — The complimentary close is omitted.
6 — The name of the dictator is typed either in all capital letters or in capital and lower case letters at the left margin at least three blank spaces below the end of the message.
7 — In the case of messages covering more than one sheet, the page number is placed on the lower left margin about one inch from the bottom of each sheet.
8 — This style is filed with the left margin up in order to bring the essential filing information in line at the top for easy reference.

Shown in the illustration on page 351 is a second simplified style. This form is a less radical shift from the usual form than is the AMS simplified arrangement. It drops the "Dear" in the salutation, making "Dear Mr. Rolfe" simply "Mr. Rolfe." It also drops the complimentary close. In all other respects, it follows a standard modified block style.

The official style. The official style, which is illustrated on page 352, is used in: (1) Situations of an official character; (2) formal

Formerly NOMA

ADMINISTRATIVE MANAGEMENT SOCIETY
Cincinnati Chapter

August 12, 19--

Mr. Jacob L. Karnes
3001 Lexington Road
Louisville, KY 40206

AMS SIMPLIFIED STYLE

This message is typed in the timesaving simplified style recommended by the Administrative Management Society. To type a message in the AMS style, follow these steps:

1. Use block format with blocked paragraphs.

2. Omit the salutation and complimentary close.

3. Include a subject heading and type it in ALL CAPS a triple space below the address; triple-space from the subject line to the first line of the body.

4. Type enumerated items at the left margin; indent unnumbered listed items five spaces.

5. Type the writer's name and title in ALL CAPS at least four line spaces below the body.

6. Type the reference initials (typist's only) a double space below the writer's name.

Communicators in your company will like the AMS simplified style not only for the "eye appeal" it offers but also because it reduces communication costs.

B. Edward Neimand
B. EDWARD NEIMAND - CHAIRMAN

jlb

BUSINESS RESEARCH SERVICE

(214) 899-5313
1412 COMMERCE STREET
DALLAS, TEXAS 75222

January 27, 19--

Mr. Harry Rolfe
Rolfe and Associates
1203 Chicago Street
Green Bay, WI 54301

Mr. Rolfe

Many thanks for your most interesting query of August 1, asking about visualizing.

Visualizing is the process of seeing in your mind's eye how a message should look when typed in its final form. If you develop an eye for symmetry, proportion, and balance, if you learn how a picture should look in its frame on the wall, you can give a message great advantages.

No matter how long or short a message, it should assume the proportions of the sheet upon which it is typed. The result is an attractive and attention-getting message.

Most business firms standardize upon an approved form that all typists are asked to follow. The larger the organization, the surer you may be that a standard form has been determined.

Accept my best wishes, Mr. Rolfe, for all your business activities in the coming year.

Larry F. Wright
Larry F. Wright

vfa

PERSONAL STYLE

198 Terrace Drive
Omaha, Nebraska 68134
January 4, 19--

Dear Alex,

May I say how much I appreciated the time you devoted to giving me many helpful suggestions and data for the article that I was asked to prepare for the April issue of Reader's Digest.

The final draft of the manuscript was mailed to the editor several days ago and has been accepted with only a few minor changes. As soon as proofs of the article are sent to me, I shall drop one in the mail for you so that you can check the final accuracy of the data you provided.

Cordially,

Jerry

Dr. Alexander G. Lambert
321 Easton Circle
Lincoln, Nebraska 68520

OFFICIAL STYLE

HUROK CONCERTS INC.

S. HUROK, PRESIDENT

730 FIFTH AVENUE, NEW YORK 19, N.Y.   TELEPHONE: CIRCLE 5-0500   CABLE: HURAT, N.Y.

January 17, 19--

Dear Dr. Ogilvy:

On Monday evening, January 30, NBC will present FESTIVAL OF MUSIC, an event unprecedented in musical history and unique in television. For one hour and a half, the world's great concert and opera stars will perform on television the world's greatest music.

Appearing on this program, which I am personally producing, are Alexander Slobodyanik, Byron Janis, Edith Peinemann, Maureen Forrester, Lili Kraus, Lorin Hollander, and Claudio Arrau, among others.

To those who direct music in schools, we suggest that FESTIVAL OF MUSIC be assigned to the students as required out-of-school viewing, since it offers in a single evening a galaxy of opera stars and world-famous instrumentalists whom it would be impossible to muster in a live performance in any other medium.

This letter serves merely to alert you to the program, since we know that every devotee of great music will want to set aside Monday evening, January 30, 8-9:30 p.m. (EST) for FESTIVAL OF MUSIC.

Sincerely,

S. Hurok

Dr. James A. Ogilvy
1307 St. Catherine Street
Monterey, California 93940

messages to persons of prominence; (3) nonbusiness messages to individuals not personally known.

This type differs from the ordinary business communication only in the position of the inside address, which is placed flush with the left margin from two to five spaces below the final signature line. The reference initials, when used, are placed on the second line below the final line of the inside address.

The personal style. The personal style, which is illustrated on page 352, is used for informal messages to personal friends and acquaintances. The address may, if desired, be omitted in this purely personal type.

● *APPLYING EFFECTIVE ENGLISH*

Oral Applications

● 1. What are the seven parts of a modern business letter?

● 2. Identify the features that make the illustration on page 345 so attractive. Take into account all the factors you believe contribute to the visual impression made by the message. Discuss the effect of changes in these factors.

● 3. What is the meaning of the following terms?
1 — Open punctuation
2 — Mixed punctuation

● 4. State the features of the following message styles:
1 — Block style
2 — Modified block style
3 — Official style
4 — Personal style

Written Applications

● 1. Type the following material (a) in modified block style with blocked paragraphs, (b) in modified block style with indented paragraphs, and (c) in block style. Use mixed punctuation in the modified block styles. Use open punctuation in the block style. Use your own initials in the stenographic reference and current date.

Mr. Dan Flaminio 1644 Park Street Lansing Michigan 48917
Dear Mr. Flaminio The report which you mentioned in your

inquiry of June 9 has been filed, and the proceedings will be published in full within the next four weeks. [New paragraph.] If you will kindly let us know how many copies you wish, we shall see that they are sent to you just as soon as they are issued. Very sincerely yours Harwood Products, Inc., Jerome Walsh (penwritten signature) District Supervisor

• **2.** Write personally to a friend, discussing some of the points covered in the present section of this book. For example, explain and illustrate the two styles of punctuating the salutation and complimentary close. Pattern your material after the example on page 352.

• **3.** Type the message given below. Use the current date, open punctuation, and modified block style with indented paragraphs. Address the message to Mr. Stanley J. Pyzik, Director of Public Relations, Cohen Printing Company, 634 Lunt Avenue, Lincolnwood, Illinois 60645.

The sentences are given as separate paragraphs. As you prepare the material, combine in single paragraphs sentences that deal with closely related points. Careful paragraphing increases the clarity of messages by focusing attention on unified phases of the discussion.

Insert necessary commas. All other marks of punctuation are given.

You are writing as a communications consultant with Trendright Market Research, Incorporated, 323 Royal Drive, Seattle, Washington 98122. Design an appropriate letterhead.

> In your inquiry of September 23 in which you enclosed twenty sample messages of the Cohen Printing Company you raised the following question "How can we increase the effectiveness of our communication?"
>
> The suggestions offered in this comment you understand concern only the question of tone.
>
> Detailed problems concerning grammar and organization can be handled much more effectively in a personal conference which we can arrange if you choose in the near future.
>
> Let's consider briefly the tone of the examples you forwarded for criticism.
>
> Notice how seldom "courtesy-expressing" words and phrases occur.
>
> Such expressions as *please thank you kindly* and *appreciate* very seldom appear.
>
> Your August 13 message to the Nelson Painting Supplies Company illustrates the point.

Take for example the following sentence: "You failed to specify what colors should be used on the labels you ordered; accordingly you will have to resubmit that order."

Here you are criticizing and blaming your customer for a mistake.

Wouldn't it be more effective to exclude any hint of complaint!

Consider for example the positive effect of this substitute version:

We are ready to start printing the labels you ordered last week but wish to check with you first concerning the colors you prefer.

The blue-green and yellow-orange combinations which you have used at various times in the past are of course available.

But many other color combinations are also possible.

Our color experts will be happy to confer with you if you would like advice from them.

If we may be of service in any other way, please let us know.

The main contrast Mr. Pyzik between your version and this one, can be summed up as the difference between the "we-attitude" and the "you-attitude."

In the suggested version the writer anticipates the customer's point of view and is as helpful and considerate as possible.

Nowhere is the customer criticized.

Nowhere is the customer made to feel foolish or embarrassed.

Instead the message offers constructive suggestions which lead the customer to supply the necessary additional information.

The customer rather than the writer is treated as the focus of concern.

The strategy of making the customer's interests the target of such messages is what we mean by the "you-attitude."

Company after company has found that the "you-attitude" increases sales.

In this sense every letter incorporating the "you-attitude" pays dividends. You'll be amazed at the results if you give it a try for just a few weeks.

Your writing can capitalize on the "you-attitude" in many other ways.

If you are interested in exploring such possibilities for increasing the effectiveness of your correspondence we shall be happy to meet with you at your convenience.

SECTION 3

The Introductory Parts

The heading, the introductory address, and the saluta-tion instantly launch your message.

Business messages, in most modern practice, contain the following introductory parts:

1 — The heading
2 — The introductory address
3 — The salutation

In addition, modern messages may also include:

1 — An attention line
2 — A subject line
3 — A reference line

The heading. To show where the message comes from and when it was written is the purpose of the heading. It contains the return address and the date. In printed letterheads the name of the company, the return address, and often the telephone number appear. The date, as part of the typed material, is varied in vertical position according to the length of the message.

Of course there are many cases in which printed letterheads are not used. For example, most individuals and some small, individually operated businesses do not use printed letterheads. Hence it is necessary for them to type an appropriate heading on business and personal-business communications. In typing such headings, observe the following guides:

1 — For the return address for a company, the preferred order is: company name on the first line; room and building (if they are included) on the second line, otherwise street and number or box on that line; city and state followed by the ZIP Code on the next line. The date follows from 12 to 20 spaces below, depending upon the length of the message.

2 — For the return address for an individual the preferred order is: street and number on the first line; city and state followed by the ZIP Code on the next line. The date follows on the last line.

3 — The lines of a company return address should be centered on the sheet of paper.

4 — The lines of a personal return address are blocked at the left and positioned either at the left margin (in the block style) or begun at the horizontal center (in the modified block styles).

Typing the dateline. Type the date in full: February 8, 19 - -. Upon the accuracy of the date may rest a legal decision. Figures alone, like 2/8/71, 2-8-71, 2:8:71, invite misunderstanding. Avoid their use except in office memorandums. Avoid also the needless additions *st, d, nd, rd,* and *th* after the day of the month.

Armed forces dateline. The armed forces favor typing the date thus: 17 October 19 - -, with the number of the day in Arabic numerals first, the name of the month second, and the figures for the year third. This procedure has come into approved civilian use.

Special arrangements of the dateline. With certain kinds of letterheads unusual arrangements of datelines are sometimes pleasing, but they are time consuming to type. Although few offices adopt them, it is well to know about them.

```
August 18,          August            August    Eighteenth
   19--               18              Nineteen Seventy-one
                      19--


  August            Eighteenth         Eighteenth    August
Eighteenth           August           Nineteen Seventy-one
  19--                19--
```

The introductory (or message) address. The introductory address states (1) the name of the person or the business to which the message is to be sent, (2) the street address, (3) the city and the state with ZIP Code. In the block and modified block styles each line of the address is typed at the left margin. Three lines are normally used. When a title or a descriptive phrase is used with the name of the person or the business, four or more lines may be necessary to avoid the use of an unattractive long line.

```
Mr. R. B. Muncey, Vice President     Mr. John Harris
R. A. Neale Company                  Sales Manager
2142 Jefferson Street                Baker Electric Company
Harrisburg, Pennsylvania  17110      1941 Bishop Lane
                                     Louisville, Kentucky  40218
```

The introductory address is typed four single spaces below the date. Double spacing is used between the last line of the address and the salutation.

In messages to persons of prominence and to others for whom a formal style may be desired, the introductory address is often typed below the signature in the manner illustrated on page 352. This style is also frequently used when the message is addressed to a friend. The complete address may be desired so that it will show on the carbon copy and thus be available for filing purposes. But the message seems a bit more personal if the address is given at the bottom rather than in its usual beginning position.

If window envelopes are used (envelopes with small transparent "windows" through which an address may show), the address must be placed so that it will show in full through the window when the message is folded and inserted.

Numbers in the address. 1—Express house numbers in figures except for house number *One.*

    Baird lives at One Locust Drive; Ayer, at 6308
    Melbourne Drive; and Littell, at 9 Lansing Street

2—Spell out street names that are numbers ten and below. When a street name is expressed in figures, separate the house number from the street number by a hyphen preceded and followed by a space. The letters *d, st,* or *th* may be added to the number that represents a street name.

    He moved from 148 Sixth Street to 340 - 65 Street.
    Our office is located at 105 - 55th Avenue.

Choosing the correct title. Use the correct title before the name of the person addressed, both in the introductory address and in the envelope address. Do not address a message to an individual without using Mr. or whatever *other* personal title is correct. The correct general titles for the first line of the address are:

Individual: *Mr., Miss, Mrs.*

Firm: *Messrs.* (the abbreviated form of the French *Messieurs*) is used in addressing men, or men and women; *Mmes.* (the abbreviated form of the French *Mesdames*) is used in addressing women. Modern usage tends to omit these two titles and to use the name of the firm instead.

Corporation: *Name of the Corporation.* To determine whether to use or to omit the word *The* before a company name, and to settle any other possible points of doubt, follow the exact styles used on the letterhead of the company to which the message is addressed.

Punctuating titles. The period must be used with the following titles because they are abbreviated forms:

Mr.   for a man
Messrs. for two or more men
Mrs.   for a married woman

The period is not used with the following titles, which are not abbreviated forms:

Miss [1]   for an unmarried woman
Misses   for two or more unmarried women
Mesdames for two or more married women

Professional titles, etc. Certain titles, in addition to those already mentioned, are often called for. They are:

Dr. is the title of one who holds a doctor's degree, whether of philosophy, law, literature, theology, medicine, or education. As a title, it is abbreviated.

Professor (Prof.) is the proper title of one holding a professorship in a college or a university. It should be written in full, although abbreviation is common.

The Reverend (Rev.) is a title properly carried by a minister, a priest, or a rector. The following guides are important:

1 — *The,* as an article preceding the title Reverend or the title *Honorable,* is conservative and preferable usage, although the growing practice in America (as distinguished from that in England) is to use the title *Reverend* or *Honorable* alone.

Preferable:

```
The Reverend Dr. D. A. Burhans
The Reverend Mr. Hales
The Reverend W. E. Hull
The Honorable Dwight Whitt
The Honorable Mr. Whitt
```

In the case of direct *oral* address *The* is dropped.

---

[1] It is proper to assume that women are to be addressed as *Miss* unless they themselves indicate that they are married. (See page 372.) A few organizations have experimented with "Ms." as a "universal" form covering both *Miss* and *Mrs.,* but the practice has not been generally adopted.

2 — Although abbreviation is common, it is better usage to write such titles in full.

3 — When preceded by *The,* such titles should *not* be abbreviated.

4 — Correct usage does not approve the use of *Reverend* or *Honorable* with the last name alone. Avoid: The Reverend Burhans; The Honorable Whitt.

5 — When *the* is not the only word used before Reverend or Honorable, it should not be capitalized.

```
        We sent this suggestion to the Reverend William Prewitt
and to the Honorable Clifford Nuxoll.
```

The Honorable (Hon.) is a title given to an individual who holds, or has held, a prominent governmental position. It is used with the names of cabinet officers, ambassadors, members of both houses of Congress, governors, mayors, and judges. Courtesy often extends it to others. As in the case of *Professor* and *Reverend,* it is better to write *Honorable* in full, although abbreviation is common. When preceded by *The,* the title *Honorable* should not be abbreviated. Do not use *Honorable* with the last name alone. Always avoid: The Honorable Whitt.

Titles for special groups. For certain public officials, educators, and church dignitaries, other special titles and salutations are reserved. For these titles and the matching salutations, see the Reference Guide, pages 668-671.

Using double titles. Common sense dictates when it is correct or incorrect to use a double title.

The multiplication of titles and degrees with a given name is not objectionable *if each one represents a different kind of status or achievement from the other.* Hence, double titles are justifiable when the second title adds new information or distinction and does not merely duplicate that which appears in the first title.

Compare these examples:

Right	*Wrong*
Dr. Roy Meredith, Director	Dr. Roy Meredith, M.D.
Mr. Leroy Vogel, Manager	Mr. Leroy Vogel, Esq.[2]
The Reverend M. J. Alsip	Dr. M. J. Alsip, D.D.
The Honorable S. L. Kuley, President	
Mrs. C. T. Lieb, Superintendent	

---

[2] *Esquire* is rarely used in the United States. It is never combined with *Mr., Dr.,* or *Honorable.*

Typing the official title. The official title in an address should be placed at the beginning of the second line and followed by a comma and a space. This title indicates the official position in relation to the company named in the second line. If the second line is long, however, the official title may be typed on the first line, with the personal name, to equalize line lengths.

```
Mr. William Sabatelli          Mr. D. A. Eckman, Manager
Director, Hall Associates      Barnett Lumber Company
403 Whitfield Mill Road        1004 Louisville Avenue
Jackson, Mississippi  39203    Memphis, Tennessee  38107
```

How to use proper names. It is a colossal error to misspell the name of the person addressed or take undue liberty with that name in the way of abbreviation or the omission of an initial. Men with the names of *Robert* and *Albert* may detest seeing them slashed to Robt. and Alb. Men with the initials R. R. and A. C. may have a deep personal distaste for initials cut to R. and A. Nothing is more individual than our names as we spell them and present them to others. Do not alter names. In a message address and elsewhere, write a name exactly as it is written by the bearer. This rule applies likewise to the word Company, which should be shortened to Co. only when the business itself does so in its own letterhead.

Misspelling a proper name is serious indeed; but even worse is mispronouncing it. In a sales presentation it is a cardinal sin to mispronounce the name of the man you are addressing. Such mispronunciation is almost certain to offend. In using the name of another, pronounce it exactly as it is pronounced by the bearer himself.

The attention line. Two acceptable ways may be used to reach by written message an individual in a business concern. One is to address him personally at the address of the business. The other is to address the concern and to follow that address with an attention line, which directs the item to his notice. The attention line is typed on the second line below the last line of the address, and begun even with the left margin between the address and the salutation.[3]

```
Carr and Lee, Inc.
General Contractors
75 Bedford Street
Portland, Maine  04101

Attention Mr. Carr

Gentlemen
```

---

[3] *Mr. Carr, Please* is sometimes used as a variant of *Attention Mr. Carr.*

On the envelope type the attention line in the lower left corner or immediately below the name of the company in the address itself. (See page 381 for illustrations.)

A message carrying an attention line will be opened at once. If the person specified is absent, and a prompt answer is required, the item will be referred without delay to another member of the staff. A message bearing a personal address may await the attention of the addressee and, as a result, may lie for some time unanswered on his desk. In large companies, however, all communications, irrespective of the character of the addresses, are opened, except those marked *Personal*.

The subject line. The subject is sometimes emphasized with a subject line, thus: *Subject: Convention Program*. If the printed letterhead does not indicate the place for the subject line, the subject (if one is used) may be typed a double space below the salutation (a) at the left margin, (b) at the paragraph point, or (c) centered. In the block style, of course, the subject line is begun at the left margin. The word *Subject* may be typed in all capitals or with only the first letter capitalized, or if the position of the subject line makes its nature clear, the subject heading may be omitted.

```
Brewer Metal Works, Inc.
4289 Newport Highway, North
Spokane, Washington  99218

Gentlemen:

SUBJECT:  Convention Program
```

```
Brewer Metal Works, Inc.
4289 Newport Highway, North
Spokane, Washington  99218

Gentlemen:

        Subject:  Convention Program
```

```
Brewer Metal Works, Inc.
4289 Newport Highway, North
Spokane, Washington  99218

Gentlemen:

            Convention Program
```

Attention and subject lines used together. If the same message should call for the use of both subject and attention lines, follow this procedure: (a) Type the attention line on the second line below the last line of the address; (b) type the salutation on the second line below the attention line; (c) center the subject line over the body a double space below the salutation.

```
Brewer Metal Works, Inc.
4289 Newport Highway, North
Spokane, Washington  99218

Attention Sales Manager

Gentlemen:

                Subject:  Convention Program
```

The reference line. Occasionally a communicator will place, somewhere at the top of his message, the following request: "In your reply please refer to File 101." Your reply will then carry the following reference line, typed at the same point as the subject line:

```
                Reference:  Your File 101
```

The salutation. The salutation is a form of courtesy to the reader, an interpretation of good manners exemplified in business usage.

When you meet another, perhaps you say, "How do you do?" Just so you may write: Dear Sir (or) Gentlemen. For the business message these are two common salutations. *Dear Sir* is always singular. *Gentlemen* as a term is always plural. Do not use *Dear Sirs*.

Type the salutation on the second line below the address and at the left margin. If there is an attention line, type the salutation on the second line below it. Double-space between the salutation and the first line in the body.

Approved salutations. Certain salutations are approved by authorities and by widespread usage of well-known companies. In the order of increasing formality, these salutations are:

FOR MEN	FOR WOMEN
Dear Russell	Dear Josephine
My dear Russell	My dear Josephine
Dear Wilson	
My dear Wilson	
Dear Mr. Wilson	Dear Mrs. Wilson
My dear Mr. Wilson	My dear Mrs. Wilson
Dear Sir	Dear Madam
My dear Sir	My dear Madam
Sir	Madam

In the plural the approved salutations are as follows:

FOR MEN OR BOTH MEN AND WOMEN	FOR WOMEN
Gentlemen	Mesdames
Dear Sir and Madam	Ladies
Ladies and Gentlemen	

The salutation *Gentlemen* is standard for addressing a company, a committee, a numbered post-office box, a collective organization made up entirely of men, *or of men and women*, and other group units of similar type. It is optional to use (1) *Dear Sir and Madam* in writing to a firm consisting of a man and a woman; and (2) *Ladies and Gentlemen* in writing to a club or social organization consisting of both men and women.

The salutation *Mesdames* is standard for addressing a company, a committee, or a collective group made up exclusively of women. *Ladies* is an alternate salutation that is gaining favor.

How well do you know your correspondent? You will want to know how to choose the correct salutation from these lists, whatever the situation may be. The key is this: How well do you know your correspondent?

Choose the salutation that reflects the degree of acquaintance you enjoy, that properly represents the relation existing between you and the person addressed, and that matches the tone of your message. For those whom you have never met, the formal *Sir* or *Madam* may be used, although in such instances the less formal *Dear Mr. Wilson* (or whatever the name may be) is fully approved.

For a personal acquaintance, use the informal salutations. Modern communication prefers personal directness.

How to capitalize a salutation. Capitalize the first word of a salutation. The word *dear* is not capitalized unless it is the first word. The words below are always capitalized.

Sir
Mr.
Every surname (*Wilson*, for example)
Every first name (*Walter*, for example)
Madam
Mrs.
Miss
All titles (*President, Professor, Superintendent, Director, Dr.,* and the like)

How to punctuate a salutation. The only correct punctuation for the *business* salutation is the colon (:). It should be placed at the end of the salutation line. Example: `Dear Mr. Wilson:` Do not use a comma as the punctuation after a *business* salutation. (The comma, in this usage, is acceptable in personal correspondence.)

In mixed punctuation the colon is used after the salutation. In open punctuation the colon is omitted after the salutation.

Salutations involving familiar titles. Certain familiar titles are used almost every day. Many of these find their places in salutations. The most important follow.

Dr.: You may abbreviate this title in the salutation, although many leading concerns write it in full.

`Dear Dr. Shirley`   `Dear Doctor Shirley`

Professor (Prof.): Although the abbreviation is common in salutations, it is better to write this title in full.

`Dear Professor Turner`

The Reverend (Rev.): Although the abbreviation is common in salutations, it is better to write this title in full.

`My dear Reverend Powell`   `Dear Reverend Father`

Salutations to special groups. Some business messages must go to persons not directly, and in some instances not even remotely, connected with business. To address these people correctly, you must be familiar with the special titles and salutations or you must know where to go to find them.

Two special groups of persons considered difficult to address are:

1 — governmental and other officials prominent in public life;
2 — church dignitaries.

The difficulty is that the suitable titles and salutations are unfamiliar because they are not often used. Furthermore, in messages to these special classes formal address must be observed. In the Reference Guide of this book is a list of special address forms and matching salutations for these special groups. This list has been carefully edited and will prove a helpful guide. The list is based upon the prevailing practice of the leading organizations of America.

Dropping salutations. The simplified style of the American Management Society drops the salutation (see the illustration on page 351) and puts a subject heading in its place.

A few firms have also experimented by dropping the salutation and substituting such forms as:

```
Mr. Wilson, Please
Greetings, Mr. Wilson
How Do You Do, Mr. Wilson
Thank You, Mrs. Robinson
```

A variation lifts the opening words of the first paragraph into the salutation position:

```
Here, Mr. Wilson,

is our idea of how you should proceed.
Lay your plans for the first month, [etc.]

So You May
Get Acquainted

I am going to send you for one month the
weekly United Forecasts of Business, [etc.]
```

Still another variant launches the message abruptly without lifting the introductory words:

```
Mr. Harold Wilson
1605 Brim Drive
Toledo, Ohio  43612

Here, Mr. Wilson, is our idea of how you should proceed in
the matter about which you wrote on June 16.  Lay your
plans, [etc.]
```

It is likely that the salutation will go on being used by business people for many years to come, simply because of long-time tradition and the weight of custom.

• APPLYING EFFECTIVE ENGLISH

Oral Applications

• 1. What are the introductory parts of a business message? Discuss the reasons why accuracy is a vital consideration in these parts.

• 2. Why is careful form especially important in the introductory parts of a message?

Written Applications

● **1.** Using the current date, adapt the following headings, addresses, and salutations to the modified block style with blocked paragraphs and open punctuation.

    1 — 2800 Lakeway Drive Bellingham Washington 98225
       Mrs. Steve Datko 68 Birch Street Youngstown Ohio 44507
       Dear Mrs. Datko

    2 — 223 North Hollywood Street Memphis Tennessee 38112
       Mr. William J. Haws 520 High Street Burlington New Jersey 08016
       Dear Mr. Haws

    3 — 148 Gould Lane Independence Missouri 64055
       Miss Lynne M. Haymond 356 King Street Alexandria Virginia
       22314
       Dear Miss Haymond

    4 — 9127 Parkview Drive, N.E. Atlanta Georgia 30329
       Dean Robert H. Kaylor College of Business Southeastern University 3544 Crestwood Street Jacksonville Florida 32208
       Dear Dean Kaylor

    5 — 4932 Kensington Drive Ann Arbor Michigan 48104
       Mr. Vincent Roger Lamont General Manager Monsford Manufacturing Company 1341 Betts Road Chattanooga Tennessee 37411
       Dear Mr. Lamont

● **2.** Using the current date, adapt the following headings, addresses, and salutations to the block style with mixed punctuation.

    1 — 149 Mockingbird Lane Auroraville Wisconsin 54920
       Mrs. Joan Woods 1410 Marne Drive Reno Nevada 89503
       Dear Mrs. Woods

    2 — 161 Harding Avenue Trenton New Jersey 08638
       Mr. Arthur Voigt 36 Cedar Street Milwaukee Wisconsin 53213
       Dear Art

    3 — 708 North Humboldt Avenue Minneapolis Minnesota 55411
       Mrs. George Voelker 47 Wayneroy Drive Austin Texas 78721
       Dear Mrs. Voelker

    4 — 832 Darcy Lane Yonkers New York 10709
       Mrs. Barbara Tuttle 521 DeKalb Street Staten Island New York
       10304
       Dear Barbara

    5 — 1661 Siskiyou Court, N.E. Portland Oregon 97230
       Dr. Willard M. Aldrich Administration Building Henderson School of Electronics Portland Oregon 97220
       Dear Doctor Aldrich

SECTION 4

The Body and the Concluding Parts

The concluding steps present the message swiftly over your signature.

BODY OF THE MESSAGE

The paragraphs in the body of the message are in block form or are indented according to the style you decide to use. In office work you will, of course, follow the style that has been formally adopted by the company.

Paragraphs in block form are used in messages written in block or AMS style and may be used in modified block style. Indented paragraphs may be used in messages written in modified block or official style. When the indented paragraph style is used, the first line of each paragraph is most commonly indented five or ten spaces.

Paragraphs are usually typed single-spaced with double spacing between paragraphs. In very short messages with indented first lines of paragraphs, however, the entire body of the message may be double-spaced.

Paragraphing in the body. As a rule, paragraphs in business messages are shorter than those in other forms of writing. The rapid pace of the modern office has made them so. The business paragraph is on its way to get something done. It aims straight at the bull's-eye of the target. The path of its thought should be arrow-straight.

Consider your reader's convenience. Make it easy for him to understand what you have written. Keep your first paragraph short. Two to five lines will be instantly easy to grasp and inviting to see.

It is much easier to read four paragraphs of six lines each than one solid paragraph of twenty-four lines. At the same time, you'll also find it easier to read four paragraphs of six lines each than twelve paragraphs of two lines each. It is just as objectionable to *over*-paragraph as to underparagraph. Strike a happy medium. Vary your paragraphs within a normal range of four to ten lines.

Abbreviations. You extend a thoughtful courtesy to your reader when you write his name, title, and address in full. Abbreviations, if used at all, should be used sparingly; and certain abbreviations should be avoided under all circumstances. Here are some examples for your close study:

Use	*Avoid*	*Use*	*Avoid*
New York	N. Y.	account	Acct., a/c
Cincinnati	Cinti.	amount	amt.
Los Angeles	L. A.	received	rec'd
Robert	Robt.	Secretary	Sec'y.
Professor	Prof.	Gentlemen	Gents

In interoffice memorandums, of course, in which there is company-wide familiarity with all terms used, shortened forms are not only quite admissible but usually customary. Even then it is wise to use a list of abbreviations like that in the United States Government Printing Office *Style Manual* as a source for standardizing all abbreviations.

Second sheets. You will find it possible to put most business messages on one sheet. Second sheets should be used only when necessary. Yet consider this warning: Never crowd page one merely to avoid the use of page two.

The side margins on a second sheet are the same as those on page 1. The heading is started one inch from the top and is followed by two blank lines, as illustrated below. See also the illustration at the top of page 370.

In size, color, weight, and quality the second sheet stationery should exactly match the first.

```
Consolidated Electric Company
Page 2
September 11, 19--


Will it be possible to wire the building for less than the
regular hourly labor charge?  As we are a nonprofit group,
```

[Message continues here]

Consolidated Electric Company   -2-   September 11, 19--

Will it be possible to wire the building for less than the regular hourly labor charge? As we are a nonprofit group,

[Message continues here]

~~~~~~

CONCLUDING PARTS

Complimentary close. The complimentary close is the fifth structural part. Like the salutation, its choice is controlled (1) by good taste, (2) by the practice of leading business organizations, and (3) by how well you know the reader.

Match the complimentary close to the salutation. Note the direct link between the salutation and the complimentary close. Let both match the tone and spirit of the message. Keep them in step. If the salutation is familiar because of a long-standing acquaintance, the complimentary close may be so. If the salutation is reserved because the message is directed to a person of high position, let the complimentary close be likewise. Let the two parts match at beginning and end. Keep them in step, grade by grade, from the most familiar and friendly at one extreme to the most severely formal at the other. Here is the approved list of closes in the order of increasing formality:

Close personal friendship with or without business Close confidential relations involving business	Faithfully yours, Yours faithfully, Faithfully,
Daily business contacts Close business friendship Informal business relations Personal friendship	Cordially yours, Yours cordially, Cordially,
Semiformal Ordinary business matters Business acquaintance Ordinary business friendship	Very sincerely yours, Yours very sincerely, Sincerely yours, Yours sincerely, Sincerely,

| Formal, but widely used | } Very truly yours,
Yours very truly, |

| Severely formal or for use in official
messages, reports, or communica-
tions to superior authority, or to
indicate special respect. | Respectfully yours,
Yours respectfully,
Respectfully submitted, |

Closes that pivot on the goodwill words *sincerely, cordially,* and *faithfully* are favored. Their choice is governed by the spirit of the message and by good taste.

Form of the complimentary close. The complimentary close is typed a double space below the last line of the body. It is (1) begun at the left margin in block style, (2) begun at the horizontal center of the sheet, or (3) placed so that the longest line ends at the right margin. Capitalize only the first word of the complimentary close. With mixed punctuation the complimentary close is followed by a comma; with open punctuation the comma is omitted after the complimentary close.

Signature. In its usual form the signature has two parts: (1) the dictator's signature (penwritten), and (2) the dictator's name, his title in the organization, or both his name and title (typed). Each part of the signature is begun even with the complimentary close.

Company name. The company name is sometimes used in the signature. When the company name is used, type it in solid capital letters on the second line below the complimentary close. If the company name is long, it must begin far enough to the left so that it will not extend noticeably into the right margin.

Penwritten signature. Every penwritten signature should be readable. *Make your signature legible,* if it is not already so, before your writing habits become set. Standardize your personal signature in a simple form and do not deviate from that form. This plan reduces the chance of questions arising when signatures of the same individual vary. In legal disputes signatures are scrutinized to the minutest detail. Use at all times the form of your name that you like best. Standardize on that form.

Dictator's name and title. As a courtesy, type the name of the dictator (not just the initials). The spelling of the dictator's name may thus be positively identified even if the handwriting is beyond the power of the eye to decipher.

(1) Type the dictator's name (aligned with the complimentary close) on the fourth line space below the company name or on the fourth line below the complimentary close when a company signature line is not used. (2) An optional arrangement is to type the dictator's official title on the fourth line below the complimentary close or the company name (if used) and to combine the full name of the dictator with the stenographic reference initials at the left margin.

If the name of the signer appears on the letterhead in such a line as *Office of T. R. Jefferson, Executive Vice President,* you need not type an identification. Here initials are sufficient.

If the dictator's name is typed below the complimentary close or the company name, the official title is placed on the line below the dictator's name. Only when both the name and title are short can you conveniently combine these two items on the same line.

(With company name)

Very truly yours,

MARSHALL-WELLS, INC.

Jm Anchor

J. M. Anchor
Vice President

(Without company name)

Sincerely yours,

A. M. Holland

A. M. Holland, Manager

Indicating the status of women. Married women should identify their status by one of the following methods:

Sincerely yours,

Julia K. Dykes

Julia K. Dykes
(Mrs. R. J. Dykes)

Sincerely yours,

Julia K. Dykes

(Mrs.) Julia K. Dykes

An unmarried woman should type the title (Miss) preceding her typewritten signature. The parentheses are optional.

Signature identification and stenographic reference. When there are more than one dictator and more than one stenographer in the office, it must be possible to know who has dictated a message and who has transcribed it. Initials or figures are used to indicate the stenographer.

If the name of the dictator is typed in the closing lines, the stenographic identification is typed after his initials, which appear at the left margin, thus: RRA:sst. Otherwise the name of the dictator is typed flush with the left margin, followed by the stenographer's initials. The preferred form is:

```
CharlesTAinsworth          or          CharlesTAinsworth:sst
```

Type the stenographic reference line even with the lowest line of the signature or on the second line space below that line, flush with the left margin. The first method keeps the base line of the letter *even* and hence greatly enhances the attractiveness of the message, thus:

~~~~~~

Very truly yours,

J. W. Craig

```
JWCraig:eb                          Executive Director
```

~~~~~~

Enclosures. Call attention, in the body of the message, to enclosures if any are included. Add a notation (usually the word *Enclosure,* or the abbreviation *Enc.* or *Encl.*) at the left margin, on the second line space below the stenographic reference.

```
DDL:ble                             DanielDLogan:ble

Enclosures 2 (or Encs. 2)     or    Enclosures:
                                        Estimate Report
                                        Catalog A
```

Use of a double space after the identification line causes the word *Enclosure* or the abbreviation *Enc.* to stand out for the attention of the mail clerk. When the messages have been signed by the dictator and are being prepared for the mail, the enclosure reference provides a check to guarantee the actual inclusion of the enclosure.

Separate-cover notations. When the body refers to items sent in a separate envelope or package, an appropriate notation should appear at the left margin below the last enclosure line or below the stenographic reference line if there is no enclosure line. The notation should indicate the method of transportation used in sending the separate-cover material and the number of envelopes or packages.

```
Separate Cover - Express
Separate Cover - Mail 2
```

Mailing instructions. When a special postal service is to be used (airmail, special delivery, or registered mail), a notation to that effect should be typed even with the left margin (a) midway between the dateline and the first line of the address or (b) below the reference, enclosure, or separate-cover notation line (whichever is last).

```
July 27, 19--                           ArnoldFOdin:blc

AIR MAIL                                Enclosures:
                                  or       Price List F
                                           Financial Report
Mr. Wade Wright, President                 Credit Report
Wright Manufacturing Corporation
7510 Lanett Avenue
Far Rockaway, New York  11691
                                        Separate Cover - Parcel Post

Dear Mr. Wright                         REGISTERED MAIL
```

Carbon copies. A carbon copy of each typewritten message is usually filed for reference. Additional copies are sometimes made for special purposes, such as conveying information to others interested in the matter involved. In such instances it is correct to sign the carbon copy. If the carbon copy is used under circumstances that make a personal tone desirable (e.g., an identical message to several committee members), place the signature on each as if it were an original.

If you wish to indicate on the original those to whom copies are being sent, you may write *Copy to* or *Copies to* (optionally *cc*) on the second line below the stenographic reference, enclosure, separate-cover notation, or mailing-instruction line (whichever is last), flush with the left margin, with the names of the copy recipients on the spaces immediately following, thus:

```
HOC:se                                  HOC:se

Copies to Dr. W. R. Crocker             cc Dr. M. A. Knight
          Mr. V. C. Field
```

If the information regarding carbon copies is not for the benefit of the addressee, this notation may be placed on the carbon copies only. In that case it may be placed at the top of the sheet.

When carbon copies are sent to several persons in an organization, the names may be arranged optionally in the following ways:

1 — Alphabetically
2 — According to rank (highest on down)
3 — According to the relative degree of interest in the particular subject

The alphabetical arrangement is the simplest and most foolproof of the three.

Postscripts. A postscript consists of one or more paragraphs added to the message after it has been typed in the usual form. It may be used for the following purposes:

1 — To cover a point thought of after the material has been typed
2 — To give special emphasis to some particular point

Logical construction of the body makes most postscripts unnecessary, except for those cases in which you wish to introduce deliberate special emphasis.

When you do wish to introduce deliberate special emphasis, a prominent postscript, used as part of a *planned* structure, draws attention to itself because of its position. For example, in sale work an important point is often *intentionally* featured as a PS. In one case a magazine publisher announces a special offer in a facsimile-handwritten postscript reading, "This special offer saves you $6.00 under the newsstand price." Any item set off by itself tends to attract attention. For this reason visual activity is almost always caught by a postscript or a footnote, which seems to *stimulate visual curiosity.* In a study of the subject, the late Henry G. Weaver, then head of the Customer Research Division, General Motors Corporation, found that footnotes (like postscripts) generally receive higher attention than an identical passage in the main text.

A postscript may be started on the second line below the stenographic reference initials and may be typed in the same form as any other paragraph of the body. If special guide lines are used, the postscript may be started on the second line below the last one. The postscript may also be preceded by the letters P. S., the abbreviation for *post script;* or, less often, by the letters N. B., the abbreviation for the Latin *nota bene,* meaning "note well."

• *APPLYING EFFECTIVE ENGLISH*

Oral Applications

• **1.** What are the regular concluding parts of a message? What is the function of each part?

- **2.** Why should the complimentary close be matched to the salutation? Explain how this can be done.

- **3.** What special notations sometimes occur among the concluding parts of a business message?

- **4.** Explain the two parts of the signature. Why is each part important?

- **5.** What are the reasons for adding "Enclosures" to the concluding parts of a business message? How does this reference help the stenographer or secretary? the person to whom the message is sent?

Written Applications

- **1.** Select five of the complimentary closes listed on pages 370 and 371. Write each of these complimentary closes with an appropriate matching signature. For each instance write a sentence or two describing the degree of acquaintance which makes this complimentary close appropriate.

- **2.** Arrange the following concluding parts in proper order as they should appear in a business message, and punctuate the material appropriately.

1 — Respectfully yours. Kathy Nedrow (Mrs. William Nedrow) (Use your own initials for stenographic reference.)
2 — Sincerely yours. Mr. Jim Kelley. Sales Manager. (Use your own initials for the stenographic reference.) Enclosures 3. Current (January) Price List. Current Fiscal Report. Latest Credit Reference. Separate Cover—Parcel Post. Registered Mail.
3 — Respectfully yours. (Mrs.) Linda O'Connell, Manager. (Use your own initials for the stenographic reference.) Enclosures 2. Copies to Mr. Gerald Clarke, Mr. Terry Tett, and Miss Mary Lynn Stein.
4 — Very truly yours. HALMGREN FURNITURE COMPANY. Randy D. King. Interior Decorator. (Use your own initials for stenographic reference.)
5 — Very truly yours. William Solly. Assistant Comptroller. (Use your own initials for stenographic reference.) Copy to Mr. Earl Markosen. Registered Mail. Enclosure.
6 — Very sincerely yours. Robert Leflar. Supervisor. Enclosures 3. (Use your own initials for the stenographic reference.)

SECTION 5

Putting the Message in the Mail

Careful envelope addresses, handsome letter folds, and well-prepared postal cards all help to speed your message.

To assure that your message will reach its proper destination in an attractive form that will make the impression you want it to make, what steps can you take?

One of your first steps is to learn how to address the cover in which your message will travel to precisely where you want it to go.

ADDRESSING THE ENVELOPE

Procedures for the correct addressing of envelopes (and postal cards) have undergone certain changes since the introduction of (1) the ZIP Code system and (2) the electronic mail sorter (called the Optical Character Reader).

The ZIP Code system of mail sorting was initiated by the Post Office Department on July 1, 1963. Originally designed for large volume mailers, its proved efficiency has resulted in a determination of the Post Office Department to have all mail, personal as well as business, sorted and dispatched to its destination by ZIP Code rather than by regular address.

ZIP (*Z*oning *I*mprovement *P*lan) divides the country into delivery units, each designated by a 5-digit number. The first digit represents one of ten geographic areas. The second digit represents a specific portion of a geographic area. The third digit represents one of the Section Center areas for sorting mail. The last two represent a within-the-city zone number for internally zoned cities or the delivery station for smaller ones.

But ZIP Coding was only *one* of the steps in a massive program designed to bring efficiency to future mail handling. The ZIP Code system foresaw the eventual use of an electronic mail sorter (the

Optical Character Reader) that could *read* not only the ZIP Code but also the other parts of the typewritten address.[1]

The first successful joining of ZIP and OCR took place on August 14, 1967. On that day the first Optical Character Reader completed its shakedown tests and began full-time operation in the Detroit Post Office. Since that time, Detroit has received an additional OCR, and others have been installed in Houston, Boston, Los Angeles, New York, Philadelphia, Chicago, San Francisco.

Addressing for the Optical Character Reader. New guides for addressing envelopes (and postal cards) have been shaped to suit the exact "reading habits" of the Optical Character Reader. OCR reads first from right to left to locate the beginning of the address lines. Then it reads from left to right, beginning with the bottom line.

New guides result in quite acceptably placed addresses, mailing notations, and addressee notations. Hence their universal adoption by business is likely to come swiftly. For that reason, you as a student and communications trainee should learn the new practices and procedures that are presented in the following pages. The discussion and the correlating illustrations emphasize the two commonest sizes of business envelopes (Number 6¾ and Number 10) and postal cards. (Recommended practices for special-size envelopes and parcels should be obtained from the Post Office Department when needed.)

General Guides. The six general guides that follow apply to all envelopes and postal cards, regardless of size.

> 1 — *Use standard typewriter faces—either pica or elite.* Addresses must be prepared in a type style that the Optical Character Reader can read accurately. Otherwise, the envelope will be rejected and will have to be sorted by hand. Script-like type faces and italics confuse the Reader.

Good: Houston, TX 77018   Poor: *Chicago, IL 60618*

Portland, OR 97219   *New York, NY 10012*

---

[1] A concise and systematic review of mail-handling progress can be found in the excellent summary by Dr. Jerry W. Robinson, Assistant Vice President and Senior Editor, South-Western Publishing Company, Cincinnati, Ohio 45227.

Dr. Robinson's article, "The Marriage of ZIP and OCR," appears in *Typewriting News* (Spring, 1969), pages 3-4.

The general guides, recommendations, and procedures outlined in Section 5 of this unit are parallel with those of Dr. Robinson's paper. These general guides and procedures have been officially approved by the United States Post Office Department (as of February 11, 1969).

2 — *All lines of the address should be* **blocked** *at the left.* (Indented lines confuse the line-finding logic of the OCR.)

```
Good:  Mr. John Harris       Avoid:  Mr. Richard L. Wendt
       122 Union Avenue              23 Lyons Street
       Columbus, OH  43223           Mobile, AL  36603
```

3 — *All addresses (even two-line ones for standardization) are preferably* **single-*spaced*.** This recommendation looks forward to the time when the OCR reads not only the city and state names and ZIP Code of the bottom line, but also the street address and other lines as directed, line by line from bottom to top.

```
Good:  Mr. Paul E. Tipton
       5610 Irving Street
       Camden, NJ  08109
```

4 — *The bottom line of the address must contain the city and state names and the ZIP Code—and in that order.* No longer is it permitted to place the ZIP Code on a separate line. The ZIP Code must appear on the same line as the city and state (spelled in full, abbreviated in the standard manner, *or* abbreviated according to the two-letter ZIP abbreviation.) The ZIP Code should be separated from the state name by two typewriter spaces. The two-letter state ZIP abbreviations should be used *only* when ZIP Codes are also used.

5 — *The next-to-last line of the address should be reserved for the street address or the Post Office box number, if either is known.* A building name or suite number, if used, should appear on the line above the street address. An apartment number *can* appear after the street address, provided it appears on the same line with the street address and is separated by a comma. Otherwise it should appear on the line above the street address.

```
Good:  Mr. John W. Roberts    Avoid:  Mr. Donald Blair
       241 Alva Drive, Apt. 9         1509 Leestown Road
       Tampa, FL  33614               Apartment 54
                                      Lexington, KY  40505
```

6 — *In addressing an envelope or card, the area immediately above the address (½ inch) and to the left of the address (⅝ inch) must be kept clear.* The *entire* space below and to the right of the address block should be kept clear. In brief, the address must be surrounded by white (clear) space, enabling the OCR to zero in on the address without obstruction or confusion.

Each of the specifications set forth in the foregoing paragraphs is of great importance in assuring the successful application of the new ZIP and OCR procedures.

MAILING PIECE	ADDRESS	
	Inches from Top	Inches from Left
Small Envelope	2	2½
Large Envelope	2½	4
Postal Card	2	2

Specific guides for addressing envelopes and postal cards. The table at the left will result in acceptable address placement for OCR sorting without requiring the typist to remember a wide assortment of needless figures representing "read zone" tolerances.

Return address. Type the return address, blocked and single-spaced, on the second line from the top edge of the envelope and three spaces from the left edge.

Addressee notation. Type addressee notations, such as *Hold for Arrival, Please Forward,* etc., a triple space below the return address and three spaces from the left edge of the envelope. The notations may be either underlined or typed in all capitals. Typing in solid capitals provides adequate attention-value in fewer typewriter strokes.

If an *attention line* line is used, type it immediately beneath the company name. For an example, see the illustration on page 381.

Mailing notations. Type mailing notations, such as AIRMAIL, SPECIAL DELIVERY, REGISTERED, CERTIFIED MAIL, and the like, below the stamp position and at least three line spaces above the envelope address. Type the notations in all capitals.

Abbreviations. The Optical Character Reader can read speedily and accurately state names spelled in full or abbreviated in the standard manner. The Post Office Department, however, is encouraging (particularly for large mailings) the use of the two-letter ZIP abbreviations (without periods and spaces) presented below.

STANDARD	ZIP	STANDARD	ZIP	STANDARD	ZIP	STANDARD	ZIP
Ala.	AL	Ill.	IL	Mont.	MT	P.R.	PR
Alaska	AK	Ind.	IN	N.C.	NC	R.I.	RI
Ariz.	AZ	Iowa	IA	N. Dak.	ND	S.C.	SC
Ark.	AR	Kans.	KS	Nebr.	NE	S. Dak.	SD
Calif.	CA	Ky.	KY	Nev.	NV	Tenn.	TN
Colo.	CO	La.	LA	N.H.	NH	Tex.	TX
Conn.	CT	Maine	ME	N.J.	NJ	Utah	UT
D.C.	DC	Mass.	MA	N. Mex.	NM	Va.	VA
Del.	DE	Md.	MD	N.Y.	NY	Vt.	VT
Fla.	FL	Mich.	MI	Ohio	OH	Wash.	WA
Ga.	GA	Minn.	MN	Okla.	OK	Wis.	WI
Hawaii	HI	Miss.	MS	Oreg.	OR	W. Va.	WV
Idaho	ID	Mo.	MO	Pa.	PA	Wyo.	WY

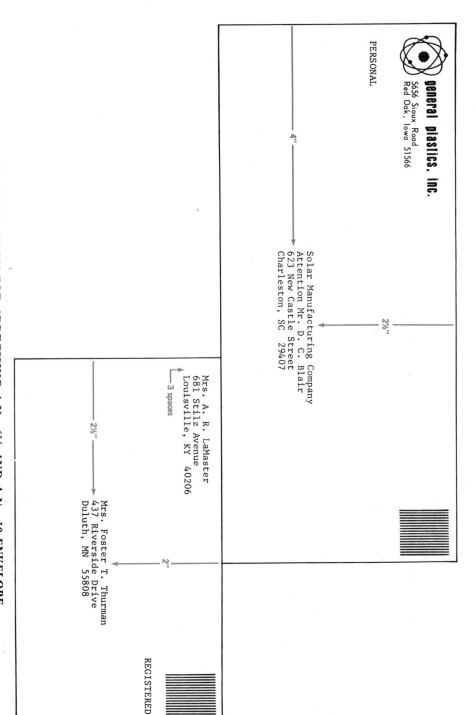

general plastics, inc.

5656 Sioux Road
Red Oak, Iowa 51566

PERSONAL

|← 4" →|

Solar Manufacturing Company
Attention Mr. D. C. Blair
623 New Castle Street
Charleston, SC   29407

|← 2½" →|

Mrs. A. R. LaMaster
681 Stilz Avenue
Louisville, KY   40206

|→ 3 spaces

|← 2½" →|

Mrs. Foster T. Thurman
437 Riverside Drive
Duluth, MN   55808

|← 2" →|

REGISTERED

APPROVED FORM FOR ADDRESSING A No. 6¾ AND A No. 10 ENVELOPE

Some mailings never arrive. Why? Literally millions of pieces of mail each year are (a) undeliverable, (b) delayed in delivery, or (c) returned to the sender. As much as ten percent of the staff of a main metropolitan post office spends full time correcting common errors. *And all of these common errors could easily have been avoided.*

Why do some mailings never arrive? Answer: Pure carelessness.

1 — Failure to give street and number in the envelope address
2 — Failure to put the complete return address in the upper left corner of the envelope
3 — Careless errors in typewriting or handwriting addresses
4 — Omission of North, South, East, or West (N., S., E., W.) street directions
5 — Failure to place the necessary postage on the envelope (millions of pieces of unstamped mail are received each year in one metropolitan main office alone)
6 — Failure to wrap parcel-post packages securely

All of such expensive waste could be easily avoided by one simple remedy: *careful attention to detail.*

FOLDING THE MESSAGE

How the message itself should be folded is controlled by the size of the envelope in which it will travel. The smaller envelope is generally used for sending a single page or one page with a small enclosure that is folded not more than twice, such as a circular or a card. The larger envelope is often used to carry more than one page or when accompanying enclosures might make a smaller envelope too bulky. The fold of the message should be even, neat, and attractive, should save time, and make unfolding easy. Here is your guide:

FOR THE SMALL ENVELOPE

(Size: Approximately $6\frac{1}{2}$ by $3\frac{5}{8}$ inches)

1 — Place the sheet face up on the desk.
2 — Fold the sheet up from the bottom to a point a half inch from top edge. With the edges even at the sides, crease the fold.
3 — Fold from right to left not quite a third of the width of the sheet.
4 — Fold from left to right, leaving a margin of about a half inch at the right.
5 — Hold the envelope in your left hand, face downward, flap open toward the right; take the folded sheet in your right hand, last crease at left, last fold up; insert it into the envelope.

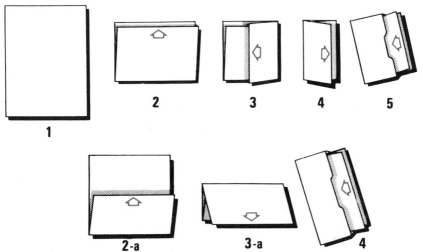

FOLDING THE SHEET FOR SMALL AND LARGE ENVELOPES

FOR THE LARGE ENVELOPE

(Size: Approximately 9½ by 4⅛ inches)

1 — Place the sheet face up on the desk.

2-a. Fold the bottom third of the sheet toward the top. With the edges even at the sides, crease the fold.

3-a. Fold the top downward, leaving a margin of about a half inch at the bottom. With the edges even at the sides, crease the fold.

4 — Hold the envelope in your left hand, face downward, flap open toward the right; take the folded sheet in your right hand, last crease at left, last fold up; insert it into the envelope.

These folding methods illustrated above assure the natural reading position, top edge up, as the sheet is opened.

Window envelopes. The window envelope—a special type—has a window of transparent material at or near the center of its face, permitting the address typed on the message itself to show through. The advantage of the window is that it eliminates the cost of addressing the envelope by letting the address on the inside sheet serve the purpose. The window envelope is popular for sending out checks, invoices, bills, and similar "form" items. For use with individually prepared messages its disadvantage is that it requires special spacing and folding. Such special spacing may mar the desired attractive placement of the message itself by forcing the layout arrangement out of balance.

Sec. 5 • Putting the Message in the Mail

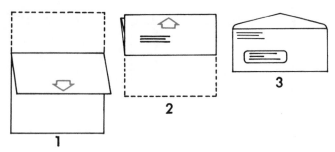

FOLDING THE SHEET FOR WINDOW ENVELOPES

Special folds for window envelopes. A sheet of stationery 8½ by 11 inches to be inserted in a window envelope measuring 9½ by 4⅛ inches, known as the No. 10 envelope, is folded as follows:

1 — With the sheet face down, top toward you, fold the upper third down.
2 — Fold the lower third up so the address is showing.
3 — Insert the sheet into the envelope with the last crease at the bottom.

The sheet should be folded and inserted in such a way that the contents of the envelope will not slide back and forth and make difficult the reading of the address through the window. The illustration above shows how a properly folded sheet is inserted.

To simplify the insertion of the message and to guarantee correct positioning of the address behind the transparent window, most forms and letterhead sheets are coordinated in size and arrangement to fit the window envelopes in which they are to be mailed.

POSTAL CARDS

Advantages. For routine or brief and impersonal correspondence, postal cards enjoy these advantages: (1) Their postal carrying charge is less than that of the first-class message; (2) they reduce all costs of stationery, envelopes, folding, sealing, and stamping; (3) they call for the simplest arrangement, making it easy to type the message and to speed its preparation.

Layout. A typewriter with elite type will get the message on the limited space of the card without sacrificing appearance. Elite type permits 20 percent more material in the same amount of space, or will allow 20 percent more space in the margin for the same amount of material.

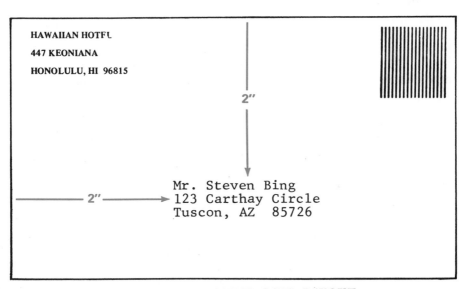

```
March 13, 19--


As requested in your note of March 11, we have
made a reservation for you at the Hawaiian Hotel
for the week of March 16.

We are very glad to be of assistance to you.  When
you arrive in Honolulu, we will do our best to
make your stay a pleasant one.


R. J. Gomes
Reservation Clerk
```

```
HAWAIIAN HOTEL

447 KEONIANA

HONOLULU, HI  96815


                            2"


                        Mr. Steven Bing
        2"              123 Carthay Circle
                        Tuscon, AZ  85726
```

A STANDARD POSTAL CARD LAYOUT

The message side of the card usually includes the date and name (either typed or written) of the sender. The return address is either typed or printed on the address side.

Penwritten signatures. Penwritten signatures add force to every message, but when space and time are limited typewritten signatures are acceptable.

● APPLYING EFFECTIVE ENGLISH

Oral Applications

● **1.** Explain the meaning of the abbreviations ZIP and OCR and the importance of these developments with reference to business correspondence.

● **2.** State the six main causes of mailing wastes. How can these expensive mistakes be avoided?

● **3.** Discuss the advantages of postal cards. For what uses are postal cards appropriate?

● **4.** Discuss the way envelopes and postal cards should be addressed for the Optical Character Reader.

● **5.** Demonstrate the proper way to fold a message for a small (6½" by 3⅝") envelope. Demonstrate the proper way to fold a message for a large (9½" by 8⅛") envelope.

Written Applications

● **1.** From typing paper, cut 4 rectangles 6½ by 3⅝ inches and 9½ by 4⅛ inches to represent the faces of large and small envelopes. Using your own return address, address a large and small envelope to each of the following persons.

1 — Mrs. Eleanor Armao 3245 Westwood Road Apartment 25 Brookfield Wisconsin 53005

2 — Personal Mr. David Bath Manager Solar Manufacturing Company 123 Brock Street Benton Harbor Michigan 49022.

3 — Keller Printing Company Attention Mr. William Cody 329 Chambers Street San Diego CA 92103 Special Delivery

4 — Miss Mary Frederick 116 West Manchester Drive Wheeling WV 26003

● REVIEW

Correct all errors in the following sentences:

1 — Mr. Brants departure will not effect Mrs. Petersons plans nor ours, unless Mrs. Brant goes along.

2 — Miss Judy Allen who don't never refuse a request for help agreed to chaperon the dance.

3 — Mr. Larry Schwartz, with his two daughters, plan to visit Saint Paul next month.

4 — Miss Longano is one of these ladies who always volunteers her help.

5 — Whom do you believe is responsible.

6 — Buttered and salted, you'll love our fresh cashews.

7 — Not all the delegates were present because of the bad weather.

8 — The report was delivered to me two accounts for checking were given to Mr. Laser my assistant.

9 — Thoroughly upset by the inclemeant weather, the hike was postponed by the troop leaders.

10 — Mr. Blaire Davidson who works at the Champion Electric Company will address the rotary club.

Class "Corporation" Project

Contemporary School Supplies, Inc., deals in all kinds of equipment and supplies for schools—students' desks and chairs, teachers' desks, storage cabinets, motion picture screens and projectors, opaque projectors, typewriters, adding and calculating machines, duplicating machines and supplies, chalkboards, lighting fixtures, synchronized clocks, venetian blinds, maps, globes, books, notebooks, paper and other writing supplies.

All members of the class will have responsibilities as "employees" of this corporation and are entitled to participate in discussion of various projects under the guidance of the "general manager" (your teacher). During the coming weeks, you will have an opportunity to write a number of messages and reports concerning the operations of Contemporary School Supplies, Inc. When you have completed such an assignment and it has been approved by the "general manager" of the company, file it in a special folder. Soon you will have a file illustrating many of the kinds of communication required in the day-to-day operation of any business.

As an employee, you have the responsibility for carrying out some of the following activities:

Present responsibilities

1 — Addressing envelopes to be used as "models"

2 — Typing a message to be used as a "model"

3 — Planning and drawing a letterhead

Future responsibilities

1 — Announcing special events

2 — Requesting information or assistance

3 — Ordering goods; arranging for services

4 — Writing collection messages
5 — Requesting adjustments
6 — Writing catalog descriptions
7 — Granting or refusing adjustments
8 — Writing sales messages
9 — Granting or refusing requests
10 — Acknowledging orders
11 — Making inquiries; replying to inquiries

Corporation project 10-A. As "office manager" of Contemporary School Supplies, Inc., design a new letterhead for company correspondence. Use the following address: 400 West Olive Avenue, Memphis, Tennessee 38106. The telephone number is (901) 392-5808. Since the company uses *modified block style with indented paragraphs* for all letters, the letterhead design should harmonize with this style.

Corporation project 10-B. As "secretary" to the office manager of Contemporary School Supplies, Inc., type the example illustrated on page 348 of your textbook in the new letterhead designed in Project 10-A. Use the *modified block style with indented paragraphs and mixed punctuation.* Since this example will be the model for all other outgoing messages you will write for the company, take unusual care in arranging it effectively on the letterhead stationery.

Corporation project 10-C. Address a No. 6¾ and a No. 10 envelope for each of the following addresses. When the envelopes have been approved by the "general manager," place them in your company file as "model" arrangements for future company assignments.

Airmail	*Airmail*
Mr. Elwood Hughes	Stone Business Machines
Hughes Industrial Supplies	Attention Mr. D. C. Allen
333 Dundee Drive	1220 South Orange Drive
Indianapolis, Indiana 46227	Los Angeles, CA 90019

UNIT 11

MESSAGE POWER THROUGH EFFECTIVE TONE

Choose your words with sensitivity. You can give your messages courtesy, sincerity, color, and strength. How? By sensitive word choice. You can erase grating discord and harsh irritability by deliberately employing tones that are pleasant, persuasive, and convincing. These are the tones that carry the impact of friendliness.

To tell you how these seeming miracles are performed is the aim of the following sections.

In Section 1 you will learn the nature of fact-writing and power-writing. You will also learn the difference between positive tone and negative tone. You will also discover the constructive end results of the positive.

Words are very much like people. They will work for you, or they may work against you. It all depends on how you treat them. Section 2 will tell you how to make them work for you and how to draw on their positive power.

Finally, you will learn in Section 3 how the experts choose their words. You will discover that the surest way to word power is to say things naturally.

UNIT 11

Section 1

Light Up Your Writing with the Right Tone: Let your written words generate pleasant overtones.

Section 2

Let Your Words Work FOR You: Your word power will predict your future success.

Section 3

Be Natural: Use the Words YOU Would Naturally Use: Let the experts guide you. They <u>talk</u> their messages <u>naturally</u> on to the paper. They avoid the pompous and the artificial.

SECTION 1

Light Up Your Writing with the Right Tone

Let your written words generate pleasant overtones.

Dozens of different tones. Someone may ask: "How many different kinds of tones are there?" In writing and speaking, there are dozens of different kinds of word tones. Naturally you would like to be able to write messages that are courteous, confident, straightforward, earnest, and sincere. Look back for a moment at that list. You have your choice of five different kinds of tone, and this is only the shortest kind of list. From this brief set of tones, you may choose to use several in combination with any or all of the others. Or you may choose to use just one. Whichever one you select, you know you will be on the positive side of the "tone line."

From your own experience you must, however, be aware that there are other kinds of tones. Some messages are filled with discord. They reflect the harsh, the unpleasant, the irritating, the corrosive. Let's try an experiment. Let's list some of the tones that we would *not* want anyone to use upon us: for example, tones that are sharp, stern, lofty, superior, overbearing, insistent, blunt, boastful, insolent, bragging, curt—just a few of the disagreeable tones that sometime you may meet. Of course you could change such unpleasant tones into ones that are pleasant, convincing, and persuasive. In fact you could gather enough expressions and tone shadings to create a regular color-chart.

Think of words as bridges between people. In these days the word *communication* is highly fashionable in business. What you seldom hear about communication is that unless you stimulate a welcome acceptance of your message, you simply don't communicate.

How do you establish warm contact with your reader? First, you forget yourself and think about your reader. You remember that there are just two of you: your reader and yourself. Second, you must care about what you are writing. So you set up a bridge of pleasant words. Over this bridge your thoughts flow with two objectives: (1) to win your reader's goodwill, his willingness to accept your message, and (2) to achieve the purpose for which your message is sent.

Stimulate welcome acceptance of your message. Let's suppose that two different corporations want to invite you to attend an annual meeting of shareholders. The first one does it this way:

Cold and Formal Tone

TAKE NOTICE that the Annual and a General Meeting of Shareholders of Logwood Corporation will be held in the Rosewood Room, Statesman Hotel, New York City, New York, on Wednesday, the 9th Day of April, 19— *[Continues]*

The second corporation does it this way:

Warm and Informal Tone

You are cordially invited to attend the Annual Meeting of Stockholders of Southern Airlines, Inc., which will be held in Wilmington, Delaware, on Tuesday, May 14, 19—, Eastern Daylight Time. We take pleasure in enclosing with this message a notice of the meeting, a proxy statement, and a form of proxy. If you find you cannot come, we'll appreciate it if you will execute and return the proxy in the enclosed envelope so that your shares may surely be represented.

The contrast in the two approaches is clear enough. A reasonable measure of care in preparing an annual message of invitation can completely change the *tone* of that invitation.

Let us now turn to a consideration of two major types of communication, each of which involves a certain kind of tone.

Power writing (to persuade) and fact writing (to inform). You will readily recognize two major types of communication:

1 – THE AIM: to arouse emotion and to move or impress with power
2 – THE AIM: to convey matter-of-fact information or knowledge

Although these two types of communication are often combined in varying degrees, let us for the moment take them up separately.

Power writing, to arouse emotion and to move or impress with power, is found in sales work and in other forms of promotional writing. The aim of this type is to stimulate lively interest and to move the reader to favorable action. The manner and the tone are persuasive, imaginative, alive, and powerful.

You will find power-writing examples illustrating all different levels of pressure. The greater the emotional content and the more gripping the appeal, the higher the pressure level tends to become. Yet, on the other hand, some of the "low-pressure" examples turn out to have the highest degree of persuasive force. Note the following one.

```
Dear Mr. Mason:       A friend in need,

--we all quote the old adage frequently, but here is a chance
to do something about it.  Your friend and ours, Fred Reese,
of the Reese Company, is confined to his home because of ill
health, and it is not likely that he will be back on the fir-
ing line for some time.

We who are his competitors (as well as his friends) need
business, but we do not want it at the expense of a fellow
worker in the field who is temporarily out of the race.
You who are his customers (as well as his friends) can help
by loyalty to his organization, which will carry on during
his absence.  They will give you the same careful attention
and service as in the past.

So let's all pitch in and do our little bit to keep Fred's
business going as usual--you can't tell--you may need a friend
yourself some day.
```

Notice in the first example on page 394 how the vivid, picture-making words build up a gripping appeal founded on a dynamic, emotional tone.

Fact writing, to convey matter-of-fact information, is found in business reports, direction books, summaries, statistical reports, abstracts, catalogs, fiscal reviews, quarterly reports, and the like. In documents of this kind, clearness, exactness, and accuracy are important. Attention and interest are less vital matters because they are already assured. Fact writing, dealing with matter-of-fact material, uses a calm, direct, and explanatory style illustrated in the second example on page 394.

The literature of knowledge and the literature of power. Thomas De Quincey, writer of gorgeous and glittering prose, in the following famous passage describes the difference between the literature of knowledge and the literature of power. The first he likens to a rudder through which to steer; the second to a sail through which to generate power.

> There is the literature of knowledge and there is the literature of power. The function of the first is to teach; the function of the second is to move. The first is a rudder; the second, an oar or a sail. The first speaks to the mere discursive understanding; the second speaks . . . to the higher understanding of reason. . . .

O. C. Deal Co.

financial analyst

132 Marion Avenue
Boston, MA 02185
617- 225- 0689

September 22, 19--

Miss Lynne M. Haymond
Lynne's Dress Shoppe
678 Greenview Drive
Portland, OR 97222

Dear Miss Haymond:

ENDANGERED!

In every city of the country, retail merchants today feel the tightening grip of severe competition. Welded link by link, the threat of cut prices is sinking into the flesh and blood of normal profits.

Panicky and fearful of the future of his business, many a dealer has tried to fight his way to success by wiping out his own profit with cut prices or, worse still, by reducing the quality of the articles he sells.

Both methods lead only to destruction.

Let's have a heart-to-heart talk about this serious situation. There is a way out for you, and we want to help you find it. First of all, let us make this point clear. We have organized our entire program for the single purpose of helping every client of ours to increase the efficiency of his store. If we accomplish that purpose, we, as advisors assure ourselves an expanding market for our services. Thus we all win!

Take heart! The small merchant is not going to have to go out of business. Provided both he and the manufacturer from whom he buys are prepared, through mutual cooperation and understanding, to establish their business methods on the solid rock of rapid turnover and small inventories, then a bright new future of better profits is already assured!

Our next letter will go into further details. Meanwhile don't lose your nerve. You have us with you through the current troubles. YOU ARE GOING TO WIN! With our organization we are going to help you win.

Sincerely yours,

O. C. Deal

O. C. Deal, President

byh

POWER WRITING: TO AROUSE EMOTION AND TO MOVE TO ACTION

DAVID G. PREWITT AND ASSOCIATES

INVESTMENT COMPANY
3343 SPRING VALLEY STREET
HOUSTON, TEXAS 77055
713-346-6636

January 3, 19--

Mr. Andrew Adams
27 Croell Avenue
Buffalo, NY 14227

Dear Mr. Adams

The Missouri-Iowa Railroad, controlled by the Missouri-Pacific Railroad through ownership of 51 percent of its capital stock, is primarily a freight carrier and, with the Mississippi River and Bonne Terre Railway (its wholly owned and leased subsidiary), is the only railroad in its territory serving the St. Joseph Lead Company, the St. Louis Smelting-Refining Company, and the Dresledge Consolidated Lead Company.

First-mortgage 5% Series A bonds totaling $3,500,000 constitute the only funded debt of the Missouri-Iowa Railroad Company. The bonds are secured by a first-mortgage lien on the Company's fixed property and a pledge of the lease and 29,992 shares of the outstanding 30,000 shares of the subsidiary's capital stock. These properties, with those of the subsidiary, have been valued at $6,361,756.

The net income of the company and its subsidiary has averaged $483,052 per annum for the six-year period ended December 31--approximately 2 3/4 times the maximum annual interest requirements of $175,000 on the Series A bonds. For the year ended December 31, the company reported a surplus of $528,881 applicable to interest, and the like.

These bonds are legal investment for life insurance companies in New York, Connecticut, and Pennsylvania.

We offer a limited amount of this issue at 87 and accrued interest--less a concession of 1 1/2 from this price.

Sincerely yours

D. G. Prewitt

President

DGPrewitt:jm

FACT WRITING: TO CONVEY INFORMATION

SOME TYPES OF WRITING TONE

The interesting tone. Express what you have to say *interestingly.* One of the easiest ways to accomplish this is to strive for *change of pace* in your sentences and paragraphs. Three simple guides will help you to achieve change of pace.

Vary sentence length. For business purposes most sentences are a bit briefer than other types. They average about seventeen words each. But to get variety, see that your sentences are not all of the same length. True, fifteen to twenty words is the *average* you should aim for. But some of your sentences may be as short as eight or ten words. Others may be as long as thirty or forty words. Follow the occasional long sentences with a short one of ten words, seven words, or even three or four words. The shorter sentence whips the reader's mind to new attention. In fact, the extremely short sentence placed between longer ones is called, by professional writers, a "sentence whip."

To see how monotonous it can become to have all sentences the same length, look back at pages 239-240. Then note how variety introduced in the same message lends new interest.

Vary sentence structure. Humdrum and choppy is the message made up entirely of simple sentences of average length. And hard to decipher is the message made up primarily of long, cumbersome compound and complex sentences in a continuous chain.

By using a *variety* of simple, compound, and complex sentences you can whip up interest, clarify your thoughts, and multiply emphases. Emphasize the most important points in the independent clauses. Subordinate less important ideas by placing them in dependent clauses. Tie your sentences together with transitional words and phrases carefully selected for smooth transition.

Choose active, colorful words. You have already learned that active verbs, concrete nouns, and picture-making adjectives have far greater impact than do passive verbs, abstract nouns, and general adjectives. You are rarely likely to make a message over-active and overly picturesque. Hence, sprinkle your writing with generous helpings of words that skillfully paint word pictures.

The sincere versus the sham. Much shoddy language, much worn-out phrasing, much false "pep," much cheap vocabulary, and much trite wordage may creep into a day's work. Hence, you should ever be on guard against such shams.

Through typewriters, printing presses, and high-speed duplicating and copying machines millions of pages of prose roll each year. Not all of this prose is good. Some is appallingly bad. Guide your own writing by the experience of others. Never approve shoddy language. Beware of a threadbare vocabulary. And only under suitable circumstances should you use slang.

Here and on page 397 is the famed Gettysburg Address written in two styles. First is presented the original text of immortal fame. Then follows a cheap, low-grade "popularization" expressed in words utterly trite. Note how the beauty of the original has been smothered in the "sham" version.

THE FAMOUS GETTYSBURG ADDRESS: POWERFUL SINCERITY

Four score and seven years ago our fathers brought forth on this continent a new nation, conceived in liberty, and dedicated to the proposition that all men are created equal.

Now we are engaged in a great civil war, testing whether that nation, or any nation so conceived and so dedicated, can long endure. We are met on a great battlefield of that war. We have come to dedicate a portion of that field, as a final resting place for those who here gave their lives that that nation might live. It is altogether fitting and proper that we should do this.

But, in a larger sense, we can not dedicate—we can not consecrate—we can not hallow—this ground. The brave men, living and dead, who struggled here have consecrated it, far above our poor power to add or detract. The world will little note, nor long remember, what we say here, but it can never forget what they did here. It is for us, the living, rather, to be dedicated here to the unfinished work which they who fought here have thus far so nobly advanced. It is rather for us to be here dedicated to the great task remaining before us—that from these honored dead we take increased devotion to that cause for which they gave the last full measure of devotion—that we here highly resolve that these dead shall not have died in vain—that this nation, under God, shall have a new birth of freedom—and that government of the people, by the people, for the people, shall not perish from the earth.

THE SHAM VERSION: WRITTEN IN LOW-GRADE TRITENESS

Back in 1776 our fathers founded a new nation based on the proposition that all men are born equal.

Now we are engaged in a great civil war, the aim being to save the Union. We are met on a great battlefield of that war to dedicate a portion of that field as a cemetery for those who here made the supreme sacrifice. This is a good idea.

Of course, the brave men, alive and dead, who fought it out here have consecrated it better than anything we can do. [Give the size of our army here.] It's not so much what we say. It's what they did that counts. It's up to us to carry on the unfinished work which they who fought here brought so far along. It is also up to us to dedicate ourselves to the real job ahead of us— namely, to be brave and true, to support the Constitution of the U. S., and to carry Old Glory to the heights, from the rock-ribbed coast of Maine to the sun-kissed shores of California.

The positive vs. the negative. Each type of expression carries its own tone: the positive, the neutral, or the negative. The positive tone is dependable, constructive, and cooperative. The negative tone is dangerous, destructive, and antagonistic. The neutral tone, on dead center, is usually factual, machinelike, often statistical, and without emotion.

The positive tone is of enormous value to the business communicator. Even in situations like advanced stages of collection, when forceful and insistent language may prove necessary, one can maintain the positive tone. If it can be done under these circumstances, it can be done under all others.

The Negative Tone May Result from Any One of These Attitudes:		*The Positive Tone May Result from One or More of These Attitudes:*	
defeat	uninterestedness	success	desire to serve
failure	slothfulness	triumph	initiative
displeasure	irritability	pleasure	level-headedness
discontent	insolence	satisfaction	diplomacy
refusal	bluntness	cooperation	tact
hesitance	curtness	willingness	courtesy
suspicion	slovenliness	trust	neatness
complaint	laziness	adjustment	ambition
fear	anger	assurance	calm
uncertainty	obstinacy	confidence	understanding
carelessness	egotism	accuracy	thoughtfulness
trickery	selfishness	honesty	generosity

SCORE CHART FOR BUSINESS COMMUNICATION
(Perfect Score: 100)

PLAN (25)	Direct Subject Opening 5 Sentence Sequence 5 Paragraph Sequence 5 Transitional Elements 5 Courteous Ending 5		Select a business message from a suitable source. Score your example according to the chart at the left. The number at the end of each line is the score to be awarded if the example is perfect in that item.
CONTENT (25)	Unity 5 Coherence 5 Proper Emphasis 5 Correct Data 5 Complete Data 5		For example, if sentence sequence is perfect, score 5 in the right-hand column opposite "Sentence Sequence." If the example is a little short of perfect, score it 4 or 3. If the sentence sequence is badly disorganized, score it 0.
TONE (25)	Courteous, YOU Viewpoint 5 Positive Approach 5 Sincere Attitude 5 Interesting Individuality 5 Effective Word Choice 5		If the writing style is interesting and holds your attention and is free from all trite, outworn expressions, score 5 opposite "Interesting Individuality." If the style is just above average and two or three worn-out expressions are used, score 3 for the item.
APPEAR-ANCE (25)	High-quality Stationery 5 Acceptable Style 5 Attractive, Informative Heading 5 Well-framed Margins 5 Sharp, Error-free Typing 5		Follow the same plan with other items. The highest possible total score is 100. An example scoring less than 70 is poor; above 80, good; above 90, excellent.

Put a smile in your writing with positive tone. In personal conversation you have the help of your personal gestures, physical presence, or smile. But your *written* words stand alone as a permanent record of what you said. Hence you try to mold your written words so that they carry pleasant overtones. These overtones take the place of the missing gestures and the facial expressions you would use if you were speaking face-to-face. Helpful in this respect is to visualize yourself (as you prepare your message) talking to your reader through a television screen.

Have you ever mailed a message—and then wished you hadn't? Remember this: Once your message is in the mail, you cannot easily get it back. It's too late, then, to correct an error in tone. Once it starts its flow into the receiving mind of your reader, you can't recall the stream of impressions for change or correction. If you write while you are excited or resentful or irritated and, in error, mail what you've written, you can't be with your reader to excuse yourself, or to erase your error, or to soften his scarred feelings. Make this your rule: *BEFORE you drop the message into the mailbox, be sure you've maintained the positive tone.*

If you are ever in the slightest doubt about the tone you have used, mail your message twenty-four hours later. You may be glad that you waited!

WHAT THE POSITIVE TONE CAN DO: SOME EXAMPLES

A bank strengthens its customer contact. A bank executive submitted to an expert a communication acknowledging the receipt of two checks. "Can this sample be improved?" he asked. "Yes," replied the expert. Let us see what happened. Watch the tone *shift* from (1) impersonal routine to (2) pleasant courtesy.

The Original Version: Wordy and Impersonal

We have your brief note of November 15, and we acknowledge the receipt of the two checks that were enclosed. We have credited these checks in the sum of $192.75 to your account.

Somewhat Improved

We acknowledge receipt, in your brief note of November 15, of two checks totaling $192.75, which we have credited to your account.

Still Better Versions

Thank you for the deposit of November 15, totaling $192.75. We have today credited it to your account.

or

We have promptly credited your deposit totaling $192.75, received today, to your account.

or

We are glad to credit to your account today the deposit of $192.75 received in your brief note of November 15.

In the original the tone is routine and impersonal, the expression wordy. In the improved version some of the wordiness is corrected, but the action is still hidden. In the still better versions the tone becomes positive through the expression of courtesy or action in the opening words. Simple though these tone shifts are, it takes practice to learn how to make them. Millions of people never learn.

A mail-order house keeps a customer happy. Not long ago a rural customer sent to a mail-order house an order for a heater that could not be shipped for three weeks.

Negative Disappointment *(As the Reply Was First Written)*	*Positive Satisfaction* *(As It Was Revised)*
We regret that we are unable to fill your order for three weeks.	Thank you for your order for a Thermador heater, which we shall be able to send you in about three weeks, in plenty of time to be installed before cold weather.

The reply at the left was a stark disappointment. It emphasized what the company could not do. As revised at the right, the answer was gratifying. It emphasized what the company *could* do. It showed that the company was thinking of the customer's interests.

How to lose business and alienate customers—or win them back. The patron of The Fifth Avenue National Bank, a man who had done business with the institution for years, asked for a loan. Somebody in the bank drafted a reply. It was just a routine reply. In fact, when you read it in just a moment, you may say to yourself, "Why . . . that isn't bad . . . seems to me it could be a lot worse. What's so wrong about that?" Here it is:

> Your recent request has been received. Before we would consider granting you a new loan, we would have to make a thorough investigation as to your credit. We would ask, then, that you fill out and return to us the enclosed financial statement, to replace the one now in our files dated two years ago.

That was the item that tripped the trigger. This was the item that lit the fuse! Our friend, the customer, came up to the desk of one of the officers with the reply clenched in his hand. Choked with anger, he was ready to close out for good his connections of many years. The institution was about to lose a steady patron, a profitable account. Goodwill of great value was about to be destroyed.

WILL YOUR MESSAGE REPEL WITH A FROWN OR
ATTRACT WITH A SMILE ?

What went wrong? All the facts were true. The practice of banks is to keep their financial statements up to date, and never to consider loans to persons about whom they have insufficient credit information. But because this routine reply had made an ordinary request in such an untactful and repellent tone, this good customer was so antagonized that he considered withdrawing his profitable account. Some skill in applied psychology and a positive tone would have saved the bank much embarrassment and would not have risked the imminent loss of one customer.

How could it have been done? Banks, like other organizations, are in business to serve the public, and to do so as efficiently as possible. They want to deal with their customers in such a way as to win friends and generate goodwill. Like other businesses, they want to keep their messages as brief as the situation will permit. Yet they want to cement friendship in the process. Let us see what they could have done:

```
        I was glad to learn from your request of May 10 that you
have another loan for us.  It is about two years since you
made out a financial statement, I believe, so I am enclos-
ing another blank.
        Just as soon as you fill it out for us, I'll see that
the loan goes at once before the loan committee.
```

Courteous, friendly, informal, simple? Yes—all of these things. But don't let the *apparent* simplicity fool you! This reply is most carefully expressed to do a job and to do it well through highly skilled "word judgment."

Why the second version won. In the new version the first three words choose the courteous tone for the send-off. The dictator who creates this version chooses to apply the rule, *courtesy first*. The next fifteen words, with exceptional tact, express appreciation to the customer for bringing his loan business to The Fifth Avenue National

Bank: "I was glad to learn . . . that you have another loan for us." That is, "YOU deserve the credit for bringing in some new business to *us,* and we want you to know that we appreciate it."

In an incidental way, the next twenty words refer to the two-year time lapse since the last financial statement and the customary routine of filling out the enclosed blank. But note: *this* time there is no implied doubt about the present status of the customer's credit standing ("Before we would consider granting you a new loan . . ."). This time there is no implied challenge, no discourteous implication that the customer may fail the test of investigation (". . . we would have to make a thorough investigation as to your credit."). This time there is no hint that the institution stands more or less like a juggernaut to block the customer's request and turn him away.

Finally, the last twenty-two words are filled with pleasant feeling-tone, the pleasant suggestion of action, and not just ordinary action, but quick, efficient action. The customer has reasonable justification for believing that the action will be favorable.

How to turn a failure into a success. A bond house sent out a follow-up message to those who had received a valuable illustrated booklet. The firm requested the return of the book after two weeks had passed without an order. The results from the follow-up were almost zero. Then, *without any other change whatever,* the second paragraph was put first and the first paragraph was put second. The results increased 40 percent. The two versions:

What Is Your Impression of This Original? (A Failure)	*Why, in This "Reversed" Version, Did Returns Jump 40%?*
If you have decided not to accept the invitation to ownership in this company, please return the book that we sent you twelve days ago in response to your request. Postage for the return is enclosed.	If you have decided to accept our invitation, you will still be in time to obtain one of the ownerships allotted to your state. But your application should be mailed promptly.
If you have decided to accept our invitation, you will still be in time to obtain one of the ownerships allotted to your state. But your application should be mailed promptly.	If you have decided not to accept the invitation to ownership in this company, please return the book that we sent you twelve days ago in response to your request. Postage for the return is enclosed.

The simple switch of these two paragraphs may at first seem like an incredibly small change to bring about such startlingly different results. The secret? The psychological impact of the opening tone.

• APPLYING EFFECTIVE ENGLISH

Oral Applications

• 1. Explain the difference between fact-writing and power-writing. How does this difference influence phrasing? Give specific examples.

• 2. Choose the words and expressions that develop a strong appeal in the first example on page 394. Discuss the effect of each item you cite.

• 3. Evaluate the tone of the following business replies. Cite words and expressions to illustrate your points.

> 1 — Your request for a complimentary calendar arrived too late. If you had written earlier, we would have been glad to send you one. In future, if we may offer a suggestion without giving offense, why don't you send in your request about the middle of October.
>
> 2 — No more red paint No. 1004 is being manufactured by our firm. You must have referred to an out-of-date color chart. We hope you check our current color chart before you order elsewhere.

• 4. Under your teacher's supervision obtain a business message from a suitable source. Analyze the message in terms of Score Chart for Business Communication given on page 398.

Written Applications

• 1. Rewrite the replies given in Oral Application 3. Make the tone of each reply positive. Adopt the "you-attitude." Eliminate unnecessary verbiage.

• 2. The following reply is written in a single monotonous, hard-to-follow sentence. In revising the reply, divide it into several varied sentences. Eliminate unnecessary words and elements. Make the sentence divisions highlight important points.

> The recent book *Tips on Successful Selling*, which you ordered in your letter of October 3, is temporarily out of stock, probably because of the tremendous demand—a demand incidentally which has been nationwide in scope—but should be available again in a matter of days, and the shipment of your order, accordingly, will be delayed a short time, although we regret the delay as much as you do, and the book should reach you, with luck, by next week-end; we value your business highly and apologize for the unavoidable delay, and assure you that we are doing everything in our power to give satisfactory service.

SECTION 2

Let Your Words Work FOR You

Your word power will predict your future success.

YOUR WORD POWER MAY PREDICT YOUR SUCCESS

"A wide and accurate vocabulary, a command of words, is closely linked with personal success." So states Johnson O'Connor, director of the Human Engineering Laboratories, in his *Atlantic Monthly* article, "Vocabulary and Success."

"An extensive knowledge of the exact meanings of English words accompanies outstanding success in this country more often than any other single characteristic which the Human Engineering Laboratories have been able to isolate and measure. The measured English vocabulary of an executive correlates with his salary," declares O'Connor. "This does not mean that every high-vocabulary person receives a large salary, but the relation between the two is close enough to show that a large vocabulary is one element, and seemingly an important one."

"Why do large vocabularies characterize executives and possibly outstanding men and women in other fields?" asks O'Connor in summarizing the connection between vocabulary and success. *"The final answer seems to be that words are the instruments by means of which men and women grasp the thoughts of others and with which they do much of their own thinking. They are the tools of thought."*

Words are like people in one dramatic way. They will work for you. Or they will work against you. It depends on how you treat them. You have your choice. What will your choice be?

Here is the crucial question: Can you make your words work for you? If you command them in the right way, they will serve you well. They will help you to win life success. Proof after proof overwhelmingly demonstrates that this is the plain truth.

Calling up the right word. Each of us has his own set of words. This set of words is like a bank deposit. Every time you deposit a new word, you increase your savings account. Then it bears more interest. Each of us must experiment with his own word supply and increase it, refine it, and improve it. Every new word is another deposit on personal success, a new shield against ignorance, and a tool for winning friendship and understanding.

Does the right word come when you call for it? Can you summon the one word you want when you need it most? Certainly there are plenty from which to choose. The English language offers you three million. A million of these are basic terms. The other two million are grammatical variants of these basic terms. Yet even with a good part of this treasure between the covers of the unabridged dictionary, most people privately admit that they are deficient in word power. At the very time they urgently need them, they find themselves hamstrung for lack of the right words.

Let vigorous vocabulary take command. The average business office desperately needs fresh words and clean, new phrases. Look for vivid word qualities and cultivate exactness in the use of words, and you will be in great demand the moment you are graduated. The statistics of employment prove this statement true. Hence, if you would like to be in demand when you leave school—study words!

"We've made the Sandman night manager in each of our hotels," runs a charming sales promotion message from a famous hotel chain. "At bedtime your nightlamp is turned on. Everything's ready for you to slide between the crisp, snowy-white sheets. A bit of chill in the air? Then tuck the fluffy, virgin wool blanket around you—it's featherweight, yet warm as toast. Snap off the light, and sink down into your soft pillow. Take a trip to our own special Land of Nod."

How easy, fresh, and natural is every word in this invitation. Yet every persuasive detail makes its pleasant mark in your mind, leaves you with the positive thought, "Let's go there sometime."

Stanley Walker, in his book *City Editor* discusses his old friend, Clark: "Clark . . . had a gift of knowing instantly the right word. His deft touches lifted stories out of the ordinary. He never hesitated; when he wrote a headline it was a *Sun* masterpiece. He handled the living language, and was not afraid to use a word or a phrase merely because it was unusual. His pencil slew a million clichés."

Other wise men have had much to say about the vast power of words and the way they may be used. "How forcible are right words," says the Book of Job in the Bible. "With words we govern men," wrote Disraeli, famous statesman and one-time Prime Minister of England. "The selection of the right word," wrote Alexander Hamilton, great American statesman of revolutionary days, "calls for the exercise of man's greatest faculty—that of judgment."

"TELEVISING" WORD PICTURES

Almost every group of words, whether spoken or written, "televises" some kind of picture in the receiving mind. When, for example, a story not only seizes your attention but, more than that, rivets your lasting interest to the very end, its author has made you see things as vividly as he sees them—and he has done this through his *words*.

Your mind "thinks in pictures," based on words. Your mind thinks in pictures. It reacts to anything in picture form. Picture magazines like *Life* and *Look* have risen to enormous circulation because the picture language they use can be grasped at almost any age level.

You can transmit ideas almost as if they were pictures, if you use words skillfully. In a sense you can be somewhat like your television set. Of course your TV uses both words *and* pictures. Yet in actual fact it does the same thing you are about to do with words alone: it transmits a message to a distant point. The faraway scanning camera, picks up, let us say, the action of the inauguration in Washington of a president of the United States; an exciting Rose Bowl game in Pasadena; or the firing of a giant missile in the Apollo program. The scanning TV camera, at its far-distant point, transmits the picture continuously, detail for detail, by electronics so that it paints an image on the picture-tube of your TV exactly like the picture in the scanning camera thousands of miles away.

You will find that that is precisely what you are going to do when you put the right words together to transmit a message in writing. From your "sending" mind you will transmit the detailed "picture" *in words* that, once it has finished its journey through the mails, will paint the same "picture" on the "receiving" mind of the reader who gets your message.

Choose words for picture power. Someone says, "Hey, there goes a streamliner." The statement makes no impression, creates no pictures. But imagine you are now back in the historical days when the great trains still ran. How different it turns out to be when sharp-cut concrete words go to work.

The Southern Pacific's de luxe *City of Los Angeles* flashes through the California countryside and slides majestically into the great Union Terminal at Los Angeles. The Santa Fe's crack streamliner, *The Super-Chief,* streaks around a long curve out of La Junta, Colorado, on its way past fabled Indian pueblos of New Mexico. The powerful diesel-electric, pulling with deep throated roar the long sleek stream-line of gleaming cars, winds between the shoulders of the mountain pass. *The California Zephyr* rolls majestically into the great Moffat Tunnel through the crest of the High Rockies and on toward the spectacular views of the Feather River Canyon in the High Sierra. Sentences like these, out of the historical past, *rivet* our attention and flash messages.

Of different atmosphere is the following rugged narrative of an engineering triumph in the Mosul Province of Iraq: "On this, the world's longest petroleum pipe line built as a single construction job, the U.S. and British building crews turned in one of the smoothest jobs of pipe laying ever seen. They had to build camps, dig water wells, run water lines, telephone and telegraph lines. Huge 18-wheel trucks carried the 12-in. pipe in 40-ft. lengths over some of the world's worst terrain. An automatic ditch-digging caterpillar tractor scraped out the 3-foot trench; compressor drills took care of the rock; Texan welders joined the firing lines of six or eight lengths; Sudanese painted and poured boiling asphalt over the section, wrapped it in brown paper, and lowered it into the trench. Two crews worked inland from the ports of Tripoli and Haifa, the third out from Kirkuk."

A descriptive passage with deft choice of words tells of an historical route along the Mississippi River, "crossing a hundred ravines where wild ferns flourish; over the Wisconsin River, and the Chippewa and the St. Croix; around the big bulge of Lake Pepin where the Mississippi widens to three miles. Willows and dogwood line the small creeks that hustle busily down from the hills. In the marshes, red-wing blackbirds teeter on the cattails."

Capturing the vivid spark, the throbbing energy, the dynamic movement, and the pictorial zest of words expertly put together, these examples illustrate how skillful word choice can transmit swift messages to receptive minds. The "picture phrases" literally glow.

Generating idea-power with verbs, nouns, and adjectives. In the order named, verbs, nouns, and adjectives—because they are idea words—are your strongest allies. Fortunately, you can call them to

Words are almost living things. There are weak words and strong words, pallid words and red-blooded words, words splendid as precious gems . . . words as scorching as fire, words incandescent with heat and light—words that seem to have dropped hissing upon the page that holds them. There are words as dreadful as murderers, words that boil and swirl with meaning as dark as the black broth of a witch's caldron.

For me words have colors, form, character . . . moods, humors, eccentricities . . . tints, tones, personalities.

Because people cannot see the color in words, the tints of words . . . Because they cannot hear the whispering of words, the rustling of the procession of letters . . . Because they cannot perceive . . . the frowning and fuming of words, the weeping, the raging and racketing and rioting of words . . . Because they are insensible to the phosphorescing of words, the fragrance of words . . . the tenderness and hardness of words . . .

Is that any reason why we should not try to make them hear, to make them see, to make them feel?

— Lafcadio Hearn

your service as you choose. Heading the list of power-makers are vivid verbs like *streak, flourish, hustle, teeter, scraped, painted, poured,* and *shoveled.*

Vivid verbs likewise lend rhythm. G. K. Chesterton, famed English author, writes in *Lepanto:*

Strong gongs groaning as the guns boom far,
Don John of Austria is going to the war. . . .[1]

In the heavy beat and accent are heard the throbbing alarm of general military uproar and frenzied excitement.

Choose the right verb, and you may not need an adverb. *Very,* used to intensify an adjective, often weakens instead of strengthens. For example, in the sentence, "The motor runs very smoothly," you gain no more word power over that in the sentence, "The motor runs smoothly." The quality of running smoothly is already indicated.

---

[1] You will enjoy the word vividness, as well as the fascinating rhythm, of (1) G. K. Chesterton's *Lepanto,* (2) John Masefield's *Cargoes,* (3) Vachel Lindsay's *The Congo,* (4) Bliss Carmen's *A Vagabond Song,* and (5) William Rose Benét's *Merchants from Cathay.*

The English language is rich in verbs. Note how, in the following picture-painters, color fuses into action.

alarm	clutch	glare	munch	sling
ally	dangle	glimmer	probe	slip
badger	dare	glitter	pry	snip
beguile	dash	gleam	rake	soothe
caper	dip	glow	ransack	surge
carve	drag	juggle	rivet	swoop
cheer	drive	loaf	rummage	tickle
chill	fidget	lock	skimp	track
chisel	flog	lug	slice	tremble
clang	floor	lunge	slide	wring

Whether for business or pleasure, writing is made forceful by verbs that flash pictures. Experts use the verb dynamo.

Call for the jolly Eskimo kid. *Uncap* a bottle of his gingery old drink. See the little bubbles *sparkle* to the top.

Perfectly proportioned, delicately balanced, the Gray Goose *cleaves* the air in his effortless flight.

Keep your curtains *a-flutter* with a Robbins and Myers fan.

To build an atmosphere of calm, a sense of peaceful beauty, writing in the quiet mood draws upon verbs. Study these sentences in the quiet tone of a Christmas Eve. "We cannot find the magic words that will make the spirit march forward off the page and into your Season's joy. We cannot word-mirror the leaping flames that warm the hearth and paint a rosy tint on the deepening twilight. We cannot make our plodding language foretell the dainty jingle of reindeer bells, nor the pearly twinkle of distant stars."

Your attention fastens on the movement in the expressions *march forward, word-mirror, leaping, paint, deepening, plodding, foretell, jingle, twinkle.*

The following couplets, taken from John Masefield's *Cargoes*, are, through sheer verb-and-word choice, a world apart in both tone and connotation: The first is a picture of romantic dignity, relaxed ease, and warmth. The second is a picture of an unromantic trade freighter, the struggle of windy sea-spray, and raw chill.

1 — Quinquireme of Nineveh from distant Ophir,
    Rowing home to haven in sunny Palestine . . .
2 — Dirty British coaster with a salt-caked smokestack,
    Butting through the Channel in the mad March days. . . .

Figures of speech are word painters. Good writing speeds its message and adds force through every element it can use. Concrete figures of speech, for example, drive ideas home because they fire the imagination. They make messages easier to read by creating lively pictures. Compare the following statements:

Inferior *The Generalized Abstract* *Statement*	*Strong* *The Vivid and Forceful* *Figure of Speech*
Many fine roads will be built.	The country will be ribboned with great new 4-lane interstate highways.
When you reduce it simply to the essential facts. . . .	When you boil it all down. . . .
We are approaching the fundamental factors involved here.	We are now getting down to the bedrock facts.
He succeeded in finding the exact location of the difficulty.	He put his finger squarely on the problem.
Words are pleasing or harmful.	Words are like flowers—or knives.

Use "TALK" words. Avoid big words when simpler ones are as good. The English language has a one-syllable word for many a three-syllable one. Sometimes the one-syllable word does a better job. Contrast the following example:

Pompous	*Simple*
Here is a common species of that feathered creature belonging to the general classification of gallinaceous biped, and noted for its egg-laying propensities.	Here is a hen with a fine record for laying eggs.

TALK YOUR MESSAGE
TO YOUR READER.
USE EASY "TALK"
WORDS – BUT
USE THEM
ACCURATELY.

Words like *scan, dig, snag, foil, split, go, slay, flay, pact, woe, wed, hop, bid, tilt,* and *bloc* are popular because they are simple, direct, and contain but one syllable.

BUILD YOUR OWN VOCABULARY—BEGIN TODAY

To build your vocabulary, cultivate the dictionary habit. There is no royal road to word command. If you want an adequate command of words, *you have to work for that command.*

How many different words do business communicators use? How large are their "writing" vocabularies? To find out, J. E. Silverthorn analyzed three hundred thousand words written by people across the country in a wide variety of businesses. Here are the results: (1) In all, approximately twelve thousand different words were used. (2) In the order named, the ten commonest words were *the, of, to, and, in, you, a, for, we,* and *your.*[2] (3) The fifty commonest words with their repetitions made up 45 percent of the words used. (4) The five hundred commonest words and their repetitions made up 70 percent of the writing. (5) The five thousand commonest words account for approximately 95 percent of the words used.

An adult with a small range of information can understand three thousand words when he reads; a skilled technician, ten thousand; a college graduate, twenty thousand.

A business vocabulary is composed of words used more commonly in business than elsewhere. The words so used are the common property of the English language. They may be used by others than businessmen, but they find their wider service in commerce.

Today the American dictionary contains more than a half-million terms. Excellent communication can be carried on with the use of only a fraction of this number. But the words that should be known and used should be accurately known and used.

Two hundred twenty out of one. Translating one general word into all its possible specific meanings yields startling results. Let us take the common verb *said.* This hard-working daily servant of the English language can be translated into not less than two hundred twenty specific substitutes. *Each one of these is descriptively more powerful than the original from which it sprang.*

---

[2] James Edwin Silverthorn, *The Basic Vocabulary of Written Business Communications,* Doctoral dissertation, Indiana University, June, 1955.

Here are a few of the two hundred twenty:

Specific Offshoots of the General Verb "Said"

announced	cried	exclaimed	grumbled	promised
argued	declared	explained	hinted	recommended
blurted	denied	exploded	insisted	responded
burst out	drawled	faltered	maintained	whispered
conceded	droned	growled	predicted	yelled

(plus one hundred ninety-five more)

Try this type of translation once a week, each week selecting a new business verb. This exercise will help you to greater word power.

Which of these two kinds will you write? "Two kinds of messages cross my desk," writes an executive at the top of a large enterprise. "One—paper, ink, and formality—goes the way of the wastepaper basket. The other—logical, human, and appealing—draws the eye, grips, sways, convinces me. One is the outcome of careless routine. The other is the outcome of conscious creativity."

The purpose of this section has been to show you how you, too, can learn to develop messages *that are the product of creative word choice.*

• *APPLYING EFFECTIVE ENGLISH*

Oral Applications

• 1. In the description of the engineering triumph in the Mosul Province of Iraq (page 407), pick out each verb and noun that evokes a picture or impression. Cite examples of descriptive adjectives and adverbs that enrich the description.

• 2. In the quotation from Lafcadio Hearn (page 408), pick out each description of different kinds of words. What makes the description forceful? What role does the imagination play in phrasing ideas excitingly? Use Hearn's description of words to illustrate your ideas.

• 3. List all the specific, picture-evoking verbs you can think of for each of the following general verbs:

1 — to eat	6 — to clean
2 — to say	7 — to work
3 — to build	8 — to hold
4 — to go	9 — to buy
5 — to move (something)	10 — to see (something)

• 4. Bring to class three full-page advertisements for different products or services. For example, select advertisements for such things as automobiles, airplane transportation, soap, television sets, clothing, furnaces, tools, sewing machines, and business machines. Select advertisements from such magazines as *Life, Look, U.S. News and World Report, Newsweek,* and *Time.* Discuss the ways in which words and pictures are used in each of the advertisements to make the product or service seem desirable to the reader.

Written Applications

• 1. The following message is abstract, colorless, and vague. Rewrite the message in vivid language. Provide appropriate details and examples to increase the appeal of the message.

> The coffee pot we sell is called the Perk-O-Perfect. It is electric. It is a good product, and many people use it. Why don't you buy one?

• 2. Consult the list of specific, image-forming verbs on page 409. Use each verb in a separate sentence such as might occur in a sales message.

• 3. Write a 50-word sales message for any three of the following items of merchandise. Phrase your message as vividly as you can. Provide details. Use lively, picture-forming language whenever possible.

1 — an electric typewriter
2 — a tape recorder
3 — a vacuum cleaner
4 — a power lawn mower
5 — a tooth brush

• 4. Rephrase the following general statements in vivid, specific, and pictorial language. For examples, see page 422.

1 — Thermopane windows are good.
2 — The radio was a nice thing.
3 — Dacron clothing is durable.
4 — Dictionaries are valuable.
5 — The desk is big.
6 — Volkswagens are economical.
7 — Proofreading is important.
8 — This truck can carry a lot.
9 — Air-conditioning is fine.
10 — That chair is cute.

SECTION 3

Be Natural: Use the Words <u>You</u> Would Naturally Use

Let the experts guide you. They talk their messages naturally on to the paper. They avoid the pompous and the artificial.

"Please tell me in one-syllable words what you mean." What a revealing comment is lodged in those telling words! "A few days ago," writes a well-known executive, "one of our dictating staff showed me a reply that had just come in. It read, 'Please tell me in one-syllable words what you mean.' I directed that the reply be circulated to our entire dictation staff. *For every one it packed a powerful lesson!"*

Cultivate the use of "talk-words." Think in conversational terms. Go through each written line and underscore each word that seems fancy or formal. Then bring those formal words down to an easy level of talking. Translate each one into its conversational equivalent.

Simplify. Shun big words when simpler words are just as effective. The English language has forceful one-syllable words for many-syllable words. Often the one-syllable word "packs the heavier punch."

Try this experiment: The following word-pairs, although not in all cases strict equivalents, are close enough to be often interchangeable. They illustrate the art of conversing through writing.

WHY SAY THIS . . .	When you can say this?	WHY SAY THIS . . .	When you can say this?
Formal	*Talk-Language*	*Formal*	*Talk-Language*
approximately	about	inquire	ask
ascertain	find out	obtain	get
assist	help	participate	share
conclusion	end	permit	let
construct	build	procure	get
contribute	give	provided	if
demonstrate	show	purchase	buy
difficult	hard	render	give
initial	first	sufficient	enough

Investigate can become *probe;* instead of *difficulty* we run into a *snag;* instead of *frustrate* or *circumvent* we can *foil* the opposition; a *division* or *disagreement* can become a *split.* Words like *go, slay, flay, pact, foe, wed, hop, bid, tilt, bloc, scan, dig, snag, foil,* and *split* are simple, direct, and often more forceful than their fancy equivalents.

Consider this example of a public sign written in a typical "Polysyllabic Municipalese." Because there had been so many accidents at a dangerous triple street intersection, the street department put up signs that warned: "Pedestrians Please Cross at Signalized Intersections." It would probably have saved more lives to say "Cross at the Lights."

WHY SAY IT THIS WAY . . .	WHEN YOU CAN SAY IT THIS WAY?
When reporting a conflagration, caller will please specify with precision the site of the conflagration.	When you report a fire, tell exactly where it is.

Lincoln's writing, many believe, reached its climax in the Gettysburg Address. In this masterpiece *one hundred and ninety-five words have only one syllable.* Forty-three have two syllables. Most of the rest have three.

Simplify your phrases. Just as it is wise to use simple "talk-words" when they are as clear and as accurate as formal "write-words," so it is wise to simplify phrases. The following contrasts (close enough to be reasonably interchangeable) will illustrate:

WHY SAY THIS . . . *Formal*	When you can say this? *Natural Talk-Words*	WHY SAY THIS . . . *Formal*	When you can say this? *Natural Talk-Words*
at all times	always	in the event that ...	if
at the present time .	now	in the near future ..	soon
costs the sum of	costs	in view of the fact	
due to the fact that .	because	that	since
enclosed herewith for		owing to the fact that	because
your information .	enclosed	report to the effect	
first of all	first	that	report that
for the period of a		under date of	on
year	for a year	until such time as ..	until
for the month of		we would ask that	
June	for June	you	please
in the amount of ...	for		

When you are wound up in your words and are struggling to untangle yourself, check these questions: "What am I really trying to tell him? In talking, how would I say it?" Then choose the little words—*when they are denotatively and connotatively* exact.

Also avoid involved sentences. In an analysis of 100,000 words chosen from forty different kinds of writing, Godfrey Dewey found that the average sentence length was a fraction over nineteen words.

SIMPLIFICATION: TALK THROUGH WRITING

Remember: 1. The fewer syllables in your word, the easier it is to read.

2. The fewer words in your sentence, the easier it is to read.

3. The more personal "human-relations" references in your message, the more natural it will seem.

Choose your words for natural power. For greatest naturalness, power, clearness, and swiftness, choose your words with care. When a clear, modern, incisive statement of an idea swings into action, it becomes the shortest distance between two minds.

In the following pages, you will learn how well-written statements made up of simple, natural, modern words can do these things:

1 — Present facts
2 — Negotiate agreements
3 — Close contracts
4 — Make requests
5 — Ask and answer questions
6 — Extend and accept invitations

7 — Give advice
8 — Settle difficulties and make adjustments
9 — Extend credit and collect money
10 — Sell goods and services
11 — Get jobs

Say to yourself, "I'm going along with my message. I'm going to *be myself* when I write. Then when my message arrives, my words will make me climb out of the envelope and talk!"

The shortest distance between two minds. Finding the shortest possible distance between your mind (the sender) and your reader's mind (the receiver) is vastly important in this new missile age. For you live in an age in which electronic data computers can make ten million computations in a fraction of the flicker of an eyelash. Through the rest of your life you will operate in this kind of environment. Every business hour you must seek for *word economy*.

Twenty winning messages used these words. Under the supervision of a consulting organization, a contest to discover some of the best current communication was held recently. Commenting on the twenty winners, the judges highlighted the spirit of optimism that ran through them. "The writers," they observed, "drew up words so gracious, so genuine, so sincere that the readers would say, 'These are men we would like to do business with.' Such words cannot be ignored. They are like friendly handshakes . . . signs of goodwill."

Here are several of the words that the judges ranked at the top:

appreciation	effective	good folks	loyal	splendid
approval	enjoy	grateful	satisfying	thank you
best wishes	excellence	helpful	serve you	willingness
clean slate	genuine	honestly	smile	your confidence

HOW DO THE EXPERTS POWER THEIR WRITING?

"How I *wish I* could write like that!"

If that exclamation has been uttered once, it has probably been uttered a hundred million times or more. Naturally, everyone would like to know how to write and speak well. But not everyone is willing to summon up the effort it takes to learn how.

A champion always makes things look easy. If he is a world's champion high jumper, he makes it look easy to jump seven feet. If he is a world's champion long jumper, he makes it look easy to jump twenty-nine feet. If he is a champion writer, he makes it look easy to write with natural, incisive clarity. But how much day-in-and-day-out disciplined training do you think it may have taken for those champions to win their championships?

How, then, do the experts power their writing? How do they reach out and get your attention? What kind of magic do they put into their words to stop you in your tracks and cause you to focus upon them? *How do they generate such high word power?*

1 — They review their knowledge of people. They classify their intended reader.
2 — They fit their writing and vocabulary level to the reading level of the reader.
3 — They follow the slogan: *"Be Natural—Be Yourself."*

The experts visualize the reader. Effective writers make a continuing study of human nature. They find out what makes people act as they do. They discover what makes people "tick." They learn what appeals can be used to get people to take certain actions. They find out the basic interests of people and bring their appeals to bear on those basic interests.

A knowledge of human behavior at its various levels enables a writer to visualize the person to or for whom he is writing so that his messages have a "right-now-across-the-desk" tone.

The experts fit the writing level to the reader's reading level. Topflight communicators, from their studies of people, know that not all readers can be reached with the same level of vocabulary or with the same level of sentence length. To the average individual, they put their thoughts into fairly short, simple words that slide into the mind so that he reads on. But when they are aiming their words at those of higher education and broader experience, they may justly choose less familiar words. They may use some longer sentences of more complex patterns. In short they select the appropriate word channel that accurately suits their readers.

At whatever level they pitch their communication, they choose the words that turn the reader's "interest-key." They know, by experience, the truth of the slogan, "Be natural. Be yourself. Make what you say conversational. Then everyone understands."

HOW NOT TO WRITE

In a long bygone century business exchanges were made up largely of a combination of dusty lingo and ceremonial formality. If you look far enough into old business files, you may still find evidence of the ancient "horse-and-buggy" lingo. But you will be wise to shun all the old "rubber stamp" language of a now forgotten day. Anyone who uses dusty phrases should write his messages with a quill pen (ever hear of one?) and blot the signature with powdered sand (yes, that's the way they used to do it). Those were the days of the "ho-hum" expressions that are now merely ridiculous. Those were the days when "pomposity" was thought to be impressive.

Imagine, if you can, that you are living a hundred years ago. This is what dictation may have sounded like: "Gentlemen: Replying . . . er . . . uh . . . to yours of the tenth, comma, in which . . . hummmmm . . . you give facts to support your claim for credit with us, comma, we regret to advise you that same is inadequate from the point of view of our company, period, paragraph.

"Although . . . ah . . . hum . . . we are sorry that the information given us . . . er . . . makes it impossible to grant credit as requested, comma, we will . . . uh . . . fill your order provided check is sent in advance as . . . er . . . specified per our quotation of . . . uh . . . recent date, period, paragraph.

"Trust this arrangement will be satisfactory. Regret that we are unable to extend credit on an open account at this time."

The preceding recital may seem only a ridiculous comedy, an effort at "spoofing" and at "poking fun." But the defects in word choice are not the most serious violation. The tone is so offensive that it would not be surprising if the reader were never to place another order with the concern. This writer was killing off his business in his own century.

"Ho-Hum" language. The archaic language of a bygone era is as old fashioned as a buggy whip. Great-grandfather read by the flicker of a tallow candle. We read by scientifically designed lighting units. Great-grandfather's communications may have been formal. Ours must be freshly worded. After a study of old carbon copies, one executive calculated that cancelling "Ho-Hum" phrases would have cut by one-third last century's average message length.

Power your first sentence. Your golden opportunity to serve your reader and tell him what he wants to know will be found in your first sentence. For example, the writer of the following message highlights his coming with fresh, natural language. He skillfully heightens the desire of the reader to see his designs and illustrations.

> Thank you for your note of July 26, inviting me to come over to show you some of our interesting fixtures. I expect to reach Santa Barbara on August 8 or 9. Just as soon as I arrive, I'll arrange to call on you at a time convenient to you.
> You will admire some of our distinctive work in wrought iron and copper, in which you have expressed interest. I shall also bring along some hand-drawn designs and my illustrated brochures.
> Thank you for your inquiry and your invitation.

Choose these expert strong openings presented below and at the top of the next page:

1 — Show action that has been taken:

> "Our vice president, Mr. Thompson, has just reported to me the figures on the excellent showing you made in your recent regional contest." "We have decided to accept your recommendation of April 10, after conferring with our departmental executives."

2 — Express pleasure or regret:

"We are pleased indeed to have you take us into your confidence in the matter of the AAA action." "Thank you for your August 3 remittance of $121.50."

3 — Make a specific statement:

"The latest figure for airmail ton-miles for June, about which you inquire in your note of July 27, is 997,000,000."

These three procedures, or a reasonable combination of them, **add** power, originality, and variety.

| *How Not to Say It:* | *How to Say It:* |
| *"Ho-Hum," Wordy* | *Clear, Modern, Direct* |

Your inquiry of November 21 re *Encyclopaedia Britannica,* 13th Edition Prospectus, at hand, and in reply wish to state that we are this day forwarding to you, under separate cover, copy of prospectus asked for, which we think will serve to give you a fair idea of the latest edition.

We are glad to send you at once, in response to your request of November 21, a copy of the *Britannica* Prospectus. From it you can get an excellent idea of the contents of the latest *Britannica.*

• • •

We have received your inquiry of April 14, in which you ask about the current Xerox program. In reply we wish to say that we shall be glad to give you the information requested.

Here is the information asked for in your inquiry of April 14, about the current Xerox program. We are glad to serve you.

• • •

This is in reply to your inquiry of April 19, which was received today and in which you ask about a bond of the New York Central issue, No. 82, for $1,000. In answer we wish to state that this bond was cashed on the date of maturity, June 26, 19—, by the University Avenue National Bank, and we wish to say further that the bank credited the account in question with principal and interest in full.

The New York Central bond No. 82 of $1,000, about which you inquire in your note of April 19, was cashed on June 26, 19—, the date of maturity, by the University Avenue National Bank, which credited the account in full.

In a parade the most prominent place is the head of the column. At a public gathering it is the platform. At a banquet it is the speakers' table. At a circus it is the center ring where the most spectacular acts are presented. At a theater it is the stage. *In the written message it is the first sentence.* Upon these places attention is centered. Make the first impression good.

Each closing sentence a climax. The closing sentence gives the final impression. It brings everything to its peak. A short-story writer works for a strong climax. A good salesman knows that he must make the most of his last minute. An experienced trial lawyer, in making his closing argument, may lower his voice to a whisper or may end on a crashing shout. These experts want their parting words to clinch their efforts. They know that the closing position is second in importance only to the opening paragraph in terms of emphasis. Let your closing sentences do likewise.

A GUIDE TO EFFECTIVE TONE

1 — **Make the message attractive.** Human nature is attracted by the beautiful. See that the message is handsomely typed.

2 — **Be unselfish.** Consider the reader's viewpoint. To put yourself in his place is to exert one of the strongest forces at your command. Say the things that you would want said if you and your reader exchanged places.

3 — **Be sincere.** Remember that half-truths defeat themselves.

4 — **Be courteous.** Courtesy means straightforward consideration of the other man's point of view. Courtesy costs nothing and has been known to pay rich dividends.

5 — **Be clear and think straight.** Tell the story in simple language.

6 — **Write as if the reader were sitting on the other side of the desk and you were talking to him** *carefully.*

7 — **Make the message interesting.** See through the eyes of the reader. Write not to please yourself but to interest him.

8 — **Make every line count,** whether you write five lines or six pages. Strip off the excess. Carve away the surplus.

9 — **The first sentence is the headline.** Find out what the reader wants to know and tell it to him—first.

10 — **Keep paragraphs and sentences moderate in length.**

11 — **Use the simple little word** when it is as accurate in its meaning as the big polysyllabic word.

12 — **Use the positive tone.**

You will find the twelve points of the foregoing guide of great value when you begin to draft your solutions to the interesting problems that follow.

A test of the ridiculous. Imagine having one of your friends walk up to you and in a singsong voice start in: "Replying to your statement of yesterday when I met you on this same corner, would state that you were in error re the matter of our previous conversation. Hope my conclusion meets with your approval, and trust that we shall have the pleasure of meeting again on this corner tomorrow." Your friend *might* escape before you led him off to the psychiatrist's office.

The golden secret. The golden secret of writing is to *be natural.* "It's always a pleasure to meet new friends," runs the opening sentence of a message welcoming new customers. "You feel it in business just as you do in everyday life." Natural talk like this is the sure cure for "Ho-Hum" habits. Address your reader as if you were speaking to him naturally as he sits on the other side of the desk. Visualize him. Say to yourself, "I am talking to my reader as if he were now with me, but I am putting my words in writing only because distance makes it necessary." One businessman makes a practice of saying to his secretary, "Now, if you please, I want to *talk* to Mr. Windsor about our Spectra 70-701 computers"; and he proceeds to *talk* in a conversational manner that suggests a living-and-breathing discussion with Mr. Windsor at that very moment in time.

Conversations in writing. All effective messages are simply *careful, natural* conversations put down in written form. Notice the emphasis on *careful* and *natural.* A message must be more concise, more logical, than average conversation. But it uses the same principles of personal force and conversational directness that guide a discussion between living-and-breathing people face to face. In short, you *talk.* But, maintaining natural ease, you talk *carefully.*

Wise word choice is simply verbal intelligence. When, a couple of centuries ago, a famous man named Lord Chesterfield was giving some advice to his son, he was actually discussing what we now call *verbal intelligence.* This was the way he put it: "To write well, we must write easily and naturally. For instance, if you want to write to me, you should consider what you would say if you were with me. Then write it in plain terms just as if you were conversing." This is precisely the kind of verbal intelligence that is basic to the development of all lasting and favorable human relations. Master this instrument of verbal intelligence, and you will enjoy an assured future success.

• APPLYING EFFECTIVE ENGLISH

Oral Applications

• **1.** How does the intended audience influence the writing of messages? Take into consideration such factors as age-groups; for example, elementary school, college, young adult, middle-aged, elderly. Give examples of the products directed at each of these age-groups (or combinations of them) as a principal sales audience. What illustrations might be expected to catch the attention of each group? What features of language might be especially appropriate for each? For example, do you think that extremely technical language or slang would ever be effective in a sales message? Give examples.

Give examples of other audience-groupings besides age-groups that thoughtful writers should keep in mind. Discuss the influence audience-groupings may have in regard to the language and illustrative materials used in messages addressed to these groups.

• **2.** What is your judgment concerning the effectiveness of the following message? Cite evidence to support your conclusions.

> With reference to yours of the tenth, in which you give facts to support your claim for credit with us, we regret to advise you that same is inadequate from the point of view of our company.
>
> Although we are sorry that the information given us makes it impossible to grant credit as requested, we will send your order, provided check is sent in advance as specified per our quotation of recent date.
>
> Trust this arrangement will be entirely satisfactory. Regret that we cannot extend credit to you on an open account at this time.

• **3.** The following illustration of an ineffective business message was included in an article in the *Nation's Business*. Pick out each instance of "ho-hum," stereotyped phrasing.

> Your esteemed favor of the 28th instant to hand and the contents duly noted. In reply, beg to leave to state same will receive careful consideration at earliest possible moment.
>
> In re the matter of current prices please find enclosed herewith latest quotations up to this writing, as per your kind request. Please be advised that new list will be forwarded in near future as soon as same comes off the press.
>
> Thanking you in advance for valued favor referring to above subject and waiting further favors writer begs to remain.

Rewrite the replies given in Oral Applications 2 and 3. Incorporate the six C-qualities of effective writing. Eliminate unnecessary words.

• *REVIEW*

Correct all errors in the following sentences.

1 — The purpose of the newsletters are to inform employees of developments in the corporation and to encourage there interest in its policys.

2 — Evelyn Jurgens has entered southeastern university and expects to major in it.

3 — Because the shipment will be made on February 23th, so that it will reach you by February 28th.

4 — The order having been filled on September 13, and the inquires having been answered very promptly on September 15.

5 — The catalog arrived in yesterdays mail, hence Mr. Hill will be able to order the latest model fire extinguisher.

6 — The man with the briefcase that was reading *Newsweek* magazine is Mr. Westmann our supervisor.

7 — Every applicant, who mispells words on his application, is automatically rejected.

8 — Every memo and every report typed by personnel department secretarys are checked personelly by Miss Bronten.

9 — Quickly leaving Mrs. Anders merely glanced back before walking across the bisy street.

10 — Looking over the annual report, numerous awkward and misleading statements were found by the assistant manager.

Class "Corporation" Project

Corporation project 11. As "office manager," prepare an article of 250-300 words to be sent to all company employees. Using the title Effective Writing Tone, develop the article as a summary of the most important principles presented in Unit 11 of this textbook.

Procedure: (1) Review the three sections of Unit 11; (2) develop a topic outline as a guide; (3) prepare a rough draft of the article; (4) proofread and revise the rough draft; (5) type the final copy; correct all typographical errors.

UNIT 12

EFFECTIVE MESSAGES: SIMPLER TYPES

Effective messages in their simpler forms fall into seven groups. Each group is discussed in one of the following seven sections.

In Section 1 you are given some helpful guides for the preparation of effective personal messages.

Specific message types (presented in Section 2 and the following five sections) call for "human interaction" through the written word. Human interaction, in turn, involves the successful drawing of "feedback." Feedback consists of <u>informative reaction</u> to your message from your message receiver. The key to the skillful preparation of inquiries and replies is, as set forth in Section 2, to make your questions brief and your replies prompt and helpful.

Sections 3 and 4 show you how to issue announcements, extend invitations, make appointments, and handle orders and payments.

You will see in Section 5 that making, granting, and declining requests are activities that call for careful judgment and a special use of the positive approach.

Section 6 takes up three basic forms of special courtesy: the expression of appreciation, the issuing of congratulations, and the awarding of praise.

Finally, Section 7 presents ways and means for introducing and recommending people who are entering new communities, or who wish to be identified as they enter new situations.

UNIT 12

Section 1

Personal Messages: "Personal-Use" Communication: Skill in personal-use writing will help you every day in the year.

Section 2

Inquiries and Replies: Intelligent "human interaction" through the written word is called forth by inquiries and replies (as well as by the other functional message types presented in following sections). Make your inquiries brief and your replies prompt and helpful.

Section 3

Announcements, Invitations, and Appointments: Normal business operation calls for issuing announcements, extending invitations, and making appointments.

Section 4

Orders, Remittances, Simple Acknowledgments, and Order Acknowledgments: The heart of business success rests upon orders of and payments for goods and services.

Section 5

Simple Requests and Special Requests: Making, Granting, and Declining Them: Whether you make, grant, or decline a request, use the positive approach.

Section 6

Appreciation, Congratulation, and Praise: To express appreciation, congratulation, and praise is a form of courtesy.

Section 7

Introductions and Recommendations: Notes of introduction and recommendation identify people helpfully in new communities.

SECTION 1

Personal Messages: "Personal-Use" Communication

Skill in personal-use writing will help you every day in the year.

You will probably write many personal-use messages during your lifetime. Personal-use writing includes all forms of communication written for the purpose of carrying on personal affairs.

A wide area of choice is yours in personal-use writing. You may freely choose variety in details of form, margin width, character of heading, size, tint, and quality of stationery, and other matters of personal preference.

You do have one overriding obligation, however, that controls your individual choice of detail. That is to make your first impression favorable. To this end, center the layout of your message. Make the general form visually attractive. See that the physical appearance is handsome. If you prepare each message according to the following suggestions—all of which reflect acceptable and preferred practice— your personal messages will always be in good taste.

Personal stationery. A popular size for personal stationery measures 7⅛ inches wide by 10½ inches long. Both single sheets and four-page fold notepaper enjoy wide use. White stationery is always in good taste. Light tints are also acceptable.

Should you use pen or typewriter? Both pen and typewriter are acceptable in this age of speed. It is quite true that much personal-use communication is still done with a pen (never use a pencil except in emergency). As you know, however, there is now widespread school instruction in the use of the typewriter. Hence tyepwritten personal messages have gained full approval and are now entirely acceptable. Whether you use pen or typewriter, you will find the following guides helpful.

Use the "picture" plan. Center your message on the page. Give it a frame of handsome margins, not less than three quarters of an inch on each side. If your stationery carries a printed or engraved address, place the date two or three line spaces below the last line of the address. If the sheet is plain, with no printed or engraved address, begin the return address about an inch and a half from the top and allow a bottom margin of not less than three quarters of an inch. Use more bottom margin if your centered layout permits you to do so. Leave an inch at the top of the second and following pages.

THE SIX PARTS OF A PERSONAL MESSAGE

A personal message contains the following six parts:

1 — Heading
2 — Message address
3 — Salutation
4 — Body
5 — Complimentary close
6 — Signature

How these parts are arranged in a handwritten message is shown in the illustration on page 431.

1—Heading. The heading must give the complete address of the writer. This is for the convenience of the reader, who may wish to reply. Do not, in personal writing, abbreviate the words "avenue," "boulevard," and "street." Shown below are headings in both block and indented style.

231 Krall Street Boise, Idaho 83702 April 8, 19--	*231 Krall Street* *Boise, Idaho 83702* *April 8, 19--*

Numbers are usually handled in personal writing just as they are in business. See pages 204 to 208 for detailed directions on handling numbers. Spell out the name of the month and write the date in figures: August 1, 19—.

2—Message address. Place the message address in the same position as in a business message. Spell out in full the words "avenue," "boulevard," and "street," as well as the state name. Write "Mr.," "Mrs.," "Miss," or other appropriate title (Dr., Professor, etc.) before the name in the address. Both block and indented styles, as illustrated below, are permissible.

Mrs. Roy Bell
634 Thrush Street
Dallas, Texas   75209

Mrs. Roy Bell
634 Thrush Street
Dallas, Texas 75209

It is also permissible to place the address at the end of the message as shown on page 431.

3—Salutation. Choose your salutation to fit the degree of your acquaintance with your reader. Make it also match the tone and spirit of what you write. If, for instance, you know your reader as a close friend, you will naturally use his or her first name. Examples of various personal salutations:

Dear Mrs. Turner	Dear Mother	Dear Aunt Anne
Dear Fred	Dear Mom	Dear Cousin
Dear Robert	Dear Uncle	Dear Cousin Jennifer
Dear Bob	Dear Uncle Arnett	Dear Rebecca

Begin the salutation at the left margin and place a comma after it. A colon is also permissible. The comma (or colon) may, if preferred, be omitted after the salutation. Spell out titles like "President," "General," and "Professor." Usage permits the abbreviation *Dr.* Examples: Dear President Martin, Dear General Hancock, Dear Doctor (or Dr.) Bruce.

4—Body. Indent the first line of each paragraph in a handwritten message. Make the indention the same as that of the second line of an indented address. This will be the penwritten equivalent of about five spaces of indention on the typewriter. The indented-paragraph style is used in penwritten material because we do not think in terms of single or double spacing when we write by hand. Hence, avoid the block style. In order to identify the paragraphs, the eye needs indentions in the body of a handwritten message.

5—Complimentary close. Choose the complimentary close to match the salutation. Let it also match the tone and spirit of the personal message. Keep them in step. If the salutation is familiar because of a long-standing acquaintance, or because of a close personal or family relationship, the complimentary close may be familiar. In personal communication the following closes are appropriate:

Yours cordially	Yours affectionately	
Cordially yours	Affectionately yours	
Cordially	Affectionately	
Yours sincerely	Yours faithfully	
Sincerely yours	Faithfully yours	
Sincerely	Faithfully	

Place the complimentary close on a line by itself. Capitalize only the first word. Use a comma after the last word, unless no punctuation follows the salutation.

6—Signature. Let the form of your signature match the tone, spirit, and measure of personal relationship shown by your salutation and close. Tie them all together so that they match. In writing to close personal friends and to members of your own family, you will probably use only your first name or some familiar variation of it. In other cases you will probably sign your full name. After the signature use no punctuation.

Women's signatures indicate whether they are married. In ordinary personal messages outside the family, they identify their status by one of the following methods:

1 — An unmarried woman writes the word *Miss* in parentheses before her name.

(Miss) Kathryn J. Ames

2 — A married woman writes her own first and last names and immediately beneath, in parentheses, the abbreviation *Mrs.* followed by her husband's name.

Madeline T. Forester
(Mrs. Harry C. Forester)

3 — Optionally a married woman may write the abbreviation *Mrs.* in parentheses just before her signature.

(Mrs.) Madeline T. Forester

563 Country Lane
Pasadena, California 91107

January 4, 19--

Dear Grace,

You wrote in your Christmas letter that
you wished you could see some of my recent
paintings. Now you can, at the Sandpiper
Gallery on Wilshire Boulevard in Los
Angeles during February. I'll be having a
one-man show of my watercolors and oils.

I hope to get there sometime during
February. Perhaps we can go together. I'll let
you know further when my plans become definite.

Cordially,
Kathryn

Mrs. Roy Burns
2301 Ocean View Avenue
Los Angeles, California 90057

Mrs. Donald Powell
563 Country Lane
Pasadena, California 91107

Mrs. Roy Burns
2301 Ocean View Avenue
Los Angeles, California 90057

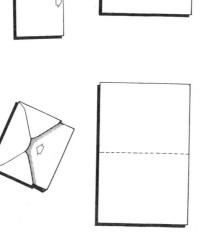

Robert R. Winston
1524 Camden Avenue
Los Angeles, California 90025

January 10, 19--

Dear Carl,

It is welcome news that you may be coming to the Pacific Coast within the next few weeks. I will be happy to tell you the optional southern routes.

As you know, during the past three years I have covered the Kansas City to Los Angeles stretch on three different routes. The most direct and, at this time, the shortest by a hundred miles, is as follows:

1. Kansas City Turnpike, Kansas City to Wichita.
2. U.S. 54, Wichita to Tucumcari, N.M., via Liberal, Kansas, and Dalhart, Texas
3. Tucumcari, N.M. to Flagstaff, Arizona, via Interstate 40 through Albuquerque
4. Flagstaff to Prescott, Arizona, via Interstate 40 and U.S. 89
5. Prescott to Los Angeles, via U.S. 89, U.S. 60, and Interstate 10

This route gives you the pleasant option of running up to the Grand Canyon for an overnight stop at the El Tovar. For this really delightful excursion, I recommend that you use U.S. 180 out of Flagstaff direct to the Southern Rim. The next morning you'll find it convenient to make a direct return to Interstate 40, via State Highway 64 southbound to Williams, Arizona, at which point you will resume your direct route to Los Angeles.

These highways are, of course, all-weather and excellently engineered. I'm sure you'll find the trip both comfortable and swift.

Further details? Just write me and I'll be happy to cover with all the information I have.

Happy traveling!

Bob

Mr. Carl J. Goldkamp
131 Everett Avenue
Kansas City, Kansas 66101

PERSONAL MESSAGE ON EXECUTIVE-SIZE STATIONERY

Robert R. Winston
1524 Camden Avenue
Los Angeles, California 90025

Mr. Carl J. Goldkamp
131 Everett Avenue
Kansas City, Kansas 66101

TYPEWRITTEN ENVELOPE ADDRESS

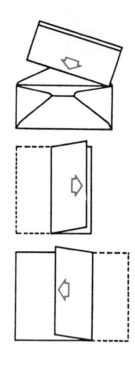

FOLDING AND INSERTING THE SHEET

Folding the sheet. Since stationery and envelopes for personal correspondence vary in size and dimensions, the best guide is to fold the sheet in accordance with the shape and size of the envelope. Many stationery sheets, including four-page sheets, fold across the center, with the top and bottom edges kept even, as illustrated on page 431. Insert the sheet so that the fold comes at the bottom of the envelope.

Addressing envelopes. The envelope address for the personal message should be essentially the same as the address on the message itself. Use the same style (block or indented) on the envelope that you have used on the heading and address of the message. Write the address on the lower half of the envelope. The top lines should not rise above the middle of the envelope and should be centered from left to right. Very long state names may, if necessary, be abbreviated. The addressed envelope illustrated on page 431 will guide you with its details.

On the back flap or in the upper left corner of the envelope, write your own name and full address so that if your message proves undeliverable, it can be returned to you. For your return address use block style only.

PREPARING THE MESSAGE ITSELF

Personal messages are written most of the time in a friendly mood with the utmost naturalness and in a manner of easy informality. Think of them as "handwritten conversation." To get conversational naturalness into your writing, you may freely use conversational features such as these contractions: *you'll, we'll, I'll, he'll, she'll, they'll, I'm, you're, he's, she's, wouldn't, couldn't, can't, won't,* and *don't.*

Let your message be interesting. You should, as a courtesy to your reader, choose your subject matter with his or her interests foremost. Remember that he or she will be most inclined to welcome information concerning matters of primary *self*-interest.

For example, if you are a girl, and your friend, Barbara, is a member of the senior swimming team, you may choose to tell her about the Aquatic Club Program of your school and how it compares with the program she wrote you about.

Or, if you are a boy, and your friend, Steve, is his school's champion half-miler, you may choose to check with him on whether he thinks the record will stand in the coming interscholastic meet.

You may also find it helpful to ask yourself guide questions like some of these: (1) What will my reader want to know? (2) What plans? (3) What events? (4) What decisions? (5) What developments? (6) What news?

Nothing could be more natural in personal writing than to use the pronoun *I*. But at the same time remember your reader. Include him frequently with the use of the *you* pronoun.

Follow such simple guides as these and your friends, acquaintances, and all your social and personal contacts will really enjoy your personal messages. With special pleasure, all your social and personal contacts will come to anticipate your messages and welcome their arrival.

Let them HEAR you TALKING! Probably the most useful single rule in personal-use writing is this: As your family and your friends read your words, let them hear you talking. Ask yourself, as you write: "How would I say this if I had the opportunity right now to sit down and talk everything over with Steve, in a personal conversation in our living room? Would I use the words I have just written down? Or would I say it more simply in talk-words?" If your answer is "yes" to the last question, cancel what you have written and say it over again as you would "talk it."

Add spring and bounce to your lines by:

1 — such informalities as the several contractions listed in an earlier paragraph (*you'll, we're, she'll, they're* and the like);
2 — use of your reader's name once or twice in your message;
3 — one or more direct questions;
4 — underlining;
5 — exclamation points; and
6 — other similar devices.

Your four-point reference key. The pages of this section have explained and illustrated how to prepare a good personal message. Let us now bring all the material together in the form of a Four-Point Reference Key:

1 — Know the purpose of your message.
2 — Concentrate on how your reader will react to what you are saying.
3 — "Write-talk" to your reader as if you were holding a living-and-breathing conversation.
4 — Be correct in fundamentals. Watch the rules of courtesy.

Now let us illustrate how you may apply the reference key.

A concrete example: Pete writes to Jeff. Pete Archer, deeply appreciative of the welcome he received in a recent visit to the city, writes his close personal friend, Jeff Farnol, and tells him what happened:

```
Dear Jeff,

Really I had no idea I'd get such a warm welcome from your
friend, Grant Andrews, when I went to Chicago the other day.
To be honest about it, he and the other fellows in the office
made me feel so much at home that I almost wondered where I
was!  I had a wonderful time.  In fact it was really the red-
carpet treatment they gave me.

I have a million thanks to send you, Jeff.  You see, just
before I left, they told me that you'd written them about me,
and that what you'd said was mighty fine and generous.

Some of these days I may be lucky enough to be able to repay
you for your thoughtfulness, and to do so several times over.
Meanwhile, believe me, I'm fully aware of how much I'm in-
debted to you for your help.


                    Cordially,

                    Pete
```

With a style as natural, as informal, as forthright, and as friendly as if the two were chatting on the front steps, Pete "write-talks" to Jeff.

When you get right down to it, of course, personal writing is never generated solely by rules. It is really created from the heart and is pervaded by a spirit that makes friendliness shine through.

To wrap it up in a capsule-summary, personal messages are threads of thoughtfulness stretching across both time and space. You may also call them personal messengers sent to tell the news you are eager to share with your friends and your family, as you write yourself into the lines and as you let your personality light up what you say.

• APPLYING EFFECTIVE ENGLISH

Oral Applications

• 1. What features of business messages and personal messages are similar? What features are different? Give examples to clarify your points.

• **2.** Name and explain the six parts of a friendly message.

• **3.** Why are accuracy, neatness, and attractiveness important in personal messages? What justification is there for regarding carelessness in correspondence as a form of rudeness?

• **4.** What features of a personal message help establish a friendly, informal tone? Cite examples from the illustration given on page 431 to support your observations.

• **5.** Discuss the message of appreciation (page 435). Cite the words, expressions, and feelings which establish a friendly, appreciative tone and help make the message effective.

• **6.** Explain the importance of each of the four points in the reference key for effective personal or social messages (page 434).

Written Applications

• **1.** Write a personal message to a close friend, using his home address. Enclose the message in an envelope. Adopt the style used for handwritten messages, and tell of some coming event that you are looking forward to eagerly.

• **2.** Assume that you have just spent a pleasant weekend visiting a cousin who lives in a town not far away. Write a personal message expressing your appreciation and telling of matters of family interest. Supply the names and address. Use the current date. Adopt the style used for handwritten messages. Prepare an envelope, using your own return address.

• **3.** Write a personal message to a friend, drawing his attention to some important magazine or newspaper article that you have read recently. Indicate where he can find the article and why you believe he may be interested in reading it.

SECTION 2

Inquiries and Replies

Intelligent "human interaction" through the written word is called forth by inquiries and replies (as well as by the other functional message types presented in following sections). Make your inquiries brief and your replies prompt and helpful.

Interpersonal communication. In the previous sections of this book we have talked about the role of interpersonal communication. We have seen how important such interpersonal communication can become in our daily lives. In person-to-person situations of *non*-business character, we have reviewed preferred methods of developing individual contact through the written word.

Human interaction. The section you are now entering takes up the business area of human interaction. The types of messages with which we shall first deal are inquiries and replies. These are the first of a series of different types of messages used by business in human interaction through the written word.

The giant scope of human interaction. The Postmaster General of the United States Post Office Department is charged with the seven-billion dollar responsibility of transferring more than 80,000,000,000 —eighty billion—pieces of mail annually through more than 44,000 local offices to every personal and business address in the world. The work force for this enormous endeavor in human interaction is more than 740,000.[1]

The *cost* of human interaction through the written word is also great. Let us take just one quick example. The IBM Corporation, through its office productions division, in a full-page message in *Newsweek*,[2] comments on the fact that it costs more than two dollars and a half to get a simple business message written and out the door. That's

---

[1] *Investor's Reader*, Vol. 53, No. 2 (July 23, 1969), p. 21.

[2] *Newsweek* (September 16, 1968), p. 16. In the relatively short period since this statement, the average cost of the individual business message, produced in the usual fashion, has continued its sharp rise. It is now past the three dollar mark.

for one letter. If you have fifty people in your office, each writing just five messages a day (which isn't a lot), it's vastly greater than two dollars and a half or three dollars or even more. In fact, says IBM, it's more than $152,000 a year—just for that one office.

Management in motion. What causes the need for the billions of inquiries, replies, announcements, invitations, appointments, orders, remittances, acknowledgments, general and special requests, congratulations, introductions, and recommendations?

The answer is not far to seek. Effective management is in continuous motion solving situations through the written word. Let's review quickly some of the actions management must take:

1 — Planning	8 — Improving	15 — Recommending
2 — Deciding	9 — Confirming	16 — Evaluating
3 — Choosing	10 — Proposing	17 — Judging
4 — Approving	11 — Building	18 — Selecting
5 — Adding	12 — Buying	19 — Specifying
6 — Expanding	13 — Selling	20 — Authorizing
7 — Changing	14 — Counseling	21 — Modernizing

Key decisions are the responsibility of the key executives who may face, each day, some of the twenty-one responsibilities listed above. Consider, for example, some of the questions that may arise: Build new? Modernize? Make do? Move? Stay put? Expand? Merge? Consolidate? Acquire? Rent? Lease? Buy? Urban or suburban? Centralize or decentralize? Ask for bids or negotiate? All the different types of messages, reflecting human interaction through the written word, help them to decide.

Feedback: the "reaction" principle. Inquiries from their very nature call for replies. These replies are the anticipated "answer-reactions." The exchange of the inquiry-and-reply pair involves the effort to transmit an idea or emotion from the mind of one person to the mind of one or more other persons, with the maximum of impact and the minimum of friction. Only when the appropriate response appears (feedback) is the transaction completed.

In an oral situation you can ask questions. From the answers, you'll be able to get a "reading" as to whether or not your listeners are properly comprehending the material you are presenting. Hence you encourage participation. You get your listeners to "play back" what the material you have presented means to them.

In the written situation you depend upon specific human interaction through the written word. The success of your effort is reflected in the feedback reaction you get. The following diagram will illustrate:

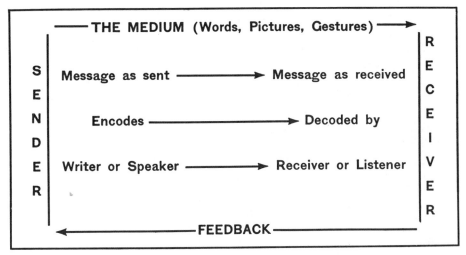

Source: *Christopher News Notes, No. 172. Adapted and Modified.*

Basic aims of business messages. Business messages usually have one or more of the following general purposes:

1 — To draw information from, or to present information to others
2 — To induce others to take a desired action
3 — To indicate to others what action is being (or has been) taken
4 — To develop good public and human relations

Although most business messages will fit into one of these general categories according to purpose, it will be more effective and efficient for us to study them by *type* according to *function*. Each of these types has a specific purpose, a plan of development, and a variation in vocabulary that is geared to its function of solving a specific business problem.

INQUIRIES

Asking for information. Inquiries are messages that ask for information. The information may be price quotations, terms of payment, folders, catalogs, articles, services, particular knowledge, or special data. Your inquiry should indicate exactly what you want.

Word your questions clearly. If your inquiry covers several points, paragraph each one or list them in numerical order. Your plan:

---

1 — Give the subject of your inquiry.
2 — Add whatever explanatory material will be helpful, such as specific details, definitions, and questions.
3 — Briefly give the reason for your inquiry, making it clear why the inquiry is addressed to the reader.
4 — End courteously.

When the answer to an inquiry will be a favor to you, enclose a stamped, self-addressed envelope. Or you may paper clip a stamp to the sheet on which the message is written. (The latter plan is recommended when an inquiry goes to a business. The business may prefer to use its own stationery.) If an inquiry is about a matter of mutual interest, or if it is sent to someone with whom you have regular exchanges, it is not necessary to enclose a stamp or a stamped, self-addressed envelope.

The inquiry may be very brief when you are (1) asking for a catalog or a booklet, (2) requesting a sample, (3) inquiring for information on timetables and the like.

AN INQUIRY

Subject
> May I ask what kind of typewriter you use in your office and why you prefer that machine?

Explanatory material
> As you may have heard, our firm expects shortly to move its business offices into new quarters with entirely new equipment. In the stenographic department thirty new typewriters are to be installed. It becomes my duty to make the choice of machine.
>
> These specific questions occur to me:
> 1. How well does the typewriter you use stand wear and tear?
> 2. Does it produce good stencils?
> 3. Does the typewriter company give good repair and replacement service?

Reason for inquiry
> I know that you have had considerable experience with the leading typewriters because your company has tried out various machines since you were employed by the firm. Your advice would be particularly valuable in helping me make a selection.

Courtesy ending
> I shall greatly appreciate your reply.

Numbering your questions and answers, as shown in the foregoing example, helps you to keep the inquiry and the answer clear and brief. But numbered lists are not always necessary. To accomplish the same purpose effective paragraphing is also a good device.

Additional examples of typical inquiries. At one time or another everyone has to make an inquiry. At a main traffic aisle on the first floor of the R. H. Macy Department Store in Kansas City, Missouri, is a wall telephone colored a "firewagon red." Beneath the telephone is the following invitation:

WHERE IS IT? ASK THE RED PHONE. JUST PICK UP THE RECEIVER AND MACY'S "RED PHONE" INFORMATION SERVICE IS READY TO ANSWER.

Here are two additional examples of typical inquiries, each representing a different type of need for information.

WHEN TO MAKE A ROOM RESERVATION?

My reminder file calls my attention to the fact that the Central States Convention is coming up in June.

I have two questions:

1. How soon will it be wise to set up reservations at the convention hotel?
2. Who is the individual reservations manager who should be addressed concerning the presidential suite?

Since I'll be leaving my office a month earlier than usual on a special conference trip, I need the requested information well in advance of departure.

Your prompt reply will be much appreciated.

A BANKING EXECUTIVE TURNS TO A COLLEAGUE FOR IMPORTANT INFORMATION

In our new branch building, now being completed, we will have four drive-in banking windows. Two of the primary problems that have confronted us so far are the lunch-hour reliefs and the handling of customers who walk up to the windows.

It will be most helpful if you will outline for us how your relief tellers keep their cash and checks separate from those of the regular tellers. What have you found is the best way to direct pedestrian customers tactfully inside the bank to a regular window?

Knowing of your long and successful operation with this phase of banking, we have come to you for advice on these matters.

We will also appreciate any further suggestions you can give us. If we may extend a similar courtesy to you, please let us know what we may do.

REPLIES

Supplying information. Whether the desired information is supplied or not, always handle an inquiry courteously and promptly. The exact information, if available, should be given in the briefest possible form.

---

1 — Give the subject of your reply.
2 — Supply the specific answer to the inquiry, if you have it.
3 — Add explanatory material that you feel may be helpful, such as specific details, technical data, background facts.
4 — End courteously.

The following reply answers the inquiry shown as an illustrative example on page 440. Note the enumeration of specific items.

ANSWER TO AN INQUIRY—ITEMS NUMBERED

Subject

In answer to your inquiry of August 23 about typewriters, we are glad to give you the benefit of our experience.

Specific answer

For the past two years we have made almost exclusive use of the SuperSpeed typewriter.

Explanatory material supporting answer

Perhaps a summary of what we consider to be the particularly good features of the SuperSpeed may help you to understand our preference.

1. It is easily handled and cleaned.
2. The touch is light; the key response is quick.
3. The parts are simple, and their uses can be learned easily.
4. Repairmen are efficient, dependable, and prompt.
5. The company allows a good rate on old machines turned in.
6. Tabulators are conveniently located and quick acting.
7. Clear-cut stencils may be produced.
8. The SuperSpeed is rugged in its resistance to office wear and tear. On this point we have interesting proof.

Courtesy ending

If you have inquiries on other office equipment, let us have them. We are glad to assist.

In the reply on page 443, note how the first paragraph shows courtesy; the second discusses the Excel; the third, the Duplex; the fourth, the Multiplex; and the last extends a courteous invitation.

ANSWER TO AN INQUIRY—ITEMS PARAGRAPHED

We are glad to tell you of our experience with duplicating machines, about which you ask in your inquiry of
January 7.

For several years we used the Excel machine for interoffice notices, but even for that purpose we did not find
it satisfactory. Clean, clear-cut copies are hard to make,
we have found. The A-B wax stencils are far better than the
blue stencils, but the stenographer must be accurate to use
the wax stencils to advantage.

For our shop orders we use a Duplex machine, which we
find satisfactory. We can make about twenty clear copies
from a Duplex carbon. By using a Duplex ribbon on the typewriter, we are able to make about fifty good copies from the
original; but because we need only seven to twelve copies
for shop orders, we do not set aside a typewriter for Duplex
work.

In our direct-mail work we make good use of the Multiplex machine that we have installed. As we use a ribbon
on the machine in preference to the ink roller, we are able
to fill in the address and the salutation either with the
typewriter or with the addresser. We have no difficulty in
obtaining matching ribbons for both the typewriter and the
addresser.

If you will call at our office before making your
selection, we shall be glad to show you the equipment in
operation.

Favorable action? "Action First" is an effective rule in many
situations, and particularly so in answers to inquiries. Every reader is
interested in action. If preparatory material must be first assembled,
make *it* the action reference. When appropriate, make the first sentence an action headline.

(a)

Immediately after your long distance call this morning,
telling us of the shortage in your Fansteel order, we sent the
seven items by fast express.

(b)

The minute your telegram reached us concerning Forms
1077A and 1077B, we secured the full confirmation you asked
for.

(c)

Thank you for your request of March 28. We are sending
you our catalog 171, which fully describes our TV line.

(d)

At our request Western Union began this morning to investigate what caused the delay in the message you sent us,
directing the sale of Consignment #4. Just as soon as we
get a report, we will write you in full.

(e)

It is a pleasure to tell you that your application has
been accepted.

(f)

You may be sure we'll get your order No. 2777 on the
way within twenty-four hours. It will have Priority One.

The high cost of delays. A startling quantity of mail is always late. Inquiries calling for an immediate answer fail to be singled out. Yet no matter how fine a reply may be in courtesy, action, or conciseness, it is not worth a nickel *if it comes too late.* To test the matter, one investigator wrote 155 businesses, asking for information on the products offered. The results:

How NOT to Do Business

10 answers came back within five days.
65 came in on the eleventh day.
12 answers arrived twenty days late.
3 were a month late.
1 came two months and five days late.
64 of the remaining businesses never answered.

Be prompt. When a concern succeeds in getting inquiries from prospective buyers, these inquiries should be handled in a way to win the largest possible amount of business and goodwill. Inquiries that may lead to valuable orders should be *answered at once.* Inquiries that involve the consulting of files, the gathering of figures, or the preparation of estimates, consuming several days' time, should be *acknowledged* at once with a confirmation reply. Give your reader a statement of progress and the probable date on which you can send the information.

A CONFIRMATION REPLY

Your inquiry regarding a package design was referred immediately to our design department. Preliminary sketches are now being made, and we shall send you our recommendations by the end of the week.

If the prospective buyer requests a catalog, a booklet, or sales information, do not merely send the impersonal catalog or booklet. To fan the flame of interest, leading firms include a carefully prepared sales presentation.

When you answer promptly, you show courtesy to the inquirer. You say in effect, "By this prompt answer I want to show you that I appreciate your inquiry, value your patronage, desire to please you, and intend to conduct my business in a manner to win your approval. This promptness is evidence of my determination."

How to win friends and please customers. Let us suppose that you maintain a savings account in the Security Bank of your former hometown two thousand miles away from your present residence. From time to time you hope to make deposits to add to your account. You ask the bank if they have "Airmail Bank Self-Mailers."

Would you be pleased if the bank president replied to you thus? "Unfortunately we do not have any Airmail Bank Self-Mailers, so we cannot forward a supply to you."

Or would you prefer this? "Yes, indeed, we do have Bank Self-Mailers. Enclosed are a half-dozen for your immediate use. Each time you send in a savings deposit, we'll send you a new self-mailing envelope. Although not Airmail, our self-mailers will bring your deposit to us safely and promptly."

The difference between these two examples of reply is a basic difference in *thinking and approach*. In the first example you run into a fusillade of negatives: "Unfortunately," "we do not have any," "so we cannot."

In the second example note the brisk current of positives:

Yes, indeed,	Each time you send
we do have	we'll send you a new
Enclosed are	our self-mailers will bring
for your immediate use	safely and promptly

In the first example everything is NO; in the second example everything is YES.

Express your thanks for especially helpful answers. Just as you say "Thank you" to acknowledge a courtesy someone has shown you, so you may choose, from time to time, to express your thanks for especially helpful replies. Of course when the interchange of questions and answers stays about even and the obligations balance off, an expression of thanks may be less needed. Express your appreciation if you are in the slightest doubt.

CASE ONE

Thank you for your helpful answer to our recent inquiry. We are surely glad to know that the divided page, the definitions, and the treatment of references have pleased you.

Your suggestion for supplying purchasers of the dictionary with later information in supplementary pages has been done with the loose-leaf encyclopedia. We have already gone so far as to supply to former customers the present department of new words (thirty-two pages) when this was not included in their volumes. We shall be glad to give some study to developing the idea further.

Feel free to write us later about any other suggestions.

We are most grateful to you for sending us the copy of the report that won the Sweepstakes at the Pacific Convention of Executives, and for granting us permission to publish the report in the <u>Quarterly Journal</u> of the Association.

CASE THREE

Thank you for your reply of May 2, telling us that the property next to you is to be sold and that, as you will not know the wishes of the new owners with reference to treatment of the tree on the property line, it is advisable to postpone this work indefinitely.

Of course we shall be glad to abide by your decision, and we are notifying our local representative immediately in order that he may govern himself accordingly. If and when the time comes that you wish to go ahead with this important work, we hope we may have the pleasure of serving you.

By making your inquiries, your replies, and your acknowledgments concise, pointed, and courteous, in the manner of the several illustrative examples in the pages of this section, you will help to reduce mail volume and costs.

• APPLYING EFFECTIVE ENGLISH

Oral Applications

• 1. Discuss various ways in which business replies can be used to win friends and please possible customers.

• 2. Identify and discuss the parts of the inquiries given on pages 440 and 441. Use the four-step plan for inquiries outlined on page 440 as a guide in your discussion.

• 3. What are the four basic purposes of business messages?

• 4. Identify the parts of the reply given on page 443. Use the four-part plan for replies outlined on page 442 as a guide.

• 5. Evaluate the following inquiry in terms of the six C-qualities.

Having scene your exhibit at the recent Minneapolis Trade Fair, the Easy-Off electric can opener, model 28, was of grate interest. As general manager of the Jurley Restaurant Chain, you can see why Im looking for ways to simplify and improve our kitchen operations at evry oppertunity.

The following questions concerning the Easy-Off model 28 concerns me. What is the unit price if bought in lots of twenty-four. What size cans are it possible to open with the Easy-Off opener. What garantee is offered by you.

Please send me any literature on this opener that is available.

● **6.** The following message is the reply sent by a furniture dealer to a woman who had not received a table and rocking chair she had ordered. Having heard nothing from the dealer for many days, she wrote the dealer, inquiring about the delay. Here is his answer:

> Dear Madam:
>
> I Found Your Letter About The Table And Traced It And Found My Two Men Were Out There To Get A Table And Rocker The Partys Gave Them The Table And Would Not Give Them The Rocer The Table Was Crated And Shiped And The Rocer Is Out Whare They Went To Get It, Did You Get The Table Yet.
>
> Yours Truly

Discuss the impression produced by this reply. Cite specific details to support your judgments.

● **7.** Evaluate the following reply:

> Unfortunately it is out of the question for Wesley's Service Station to provide indoor storage for your automobile, although we would consider renting you outdoor parking space on our property. We would be willing to accomodate you to that extent.

Written Applications

● **1.** Rewrite the reply given in Oral Application 7. Correct all errors and adopt a friendly tone.

● **2.** Rewrite the reply quoted in Oral Application 6. Incorporate in your version the six C-qualities of effective writing. Supply the heading and address.

● **3.** Rewrite the inquiry given in Oral Application 5. Incorporate the six C-qualities of effective writing.

● **4.** You are moving to Tulsa, Oklahoma. Write the secretary of Tulsa Chamber of Commerce and inquire about business colleges or other institutions offering business training in Tulsa.

● **5.** As the secretary of the Tulsa Chamber of Commerce, answer the inquiry written in connection with Written Application 4.

● **6.** (a) Write an inquiry asking about the subscription terms to *Business World,* 1760 River Road, Cleveland, Ohio 44113.

(b) Write the answer of the subscription department of *Business World.* Indicate that a sample copy is being sent and that a special introductory offer of nine issues for three dollars is available.

SECTION 3

Announcements, Invitations, and Appointments

Normal business operation calls for issuing announcements, extending invitations, and making appointments.

In the normal round of daily affairs you may find, now and then, that you want to tell some of your friends about something that happened to you last week, or that is happening to you now, or that you think may happen in the future.

You can tell your friends personally about these developments if they happen to go to the same school you do. If they go to a different school across town, perhaps you call them on the telephone. If, however, they live in a distant city, you will probably write them. In each instance you have given them information in the form of an announcement.

ANNOUNCEMENTS

Committee conferences, expansions into new quarters, management appointments, operational changes, consolidations of departments, stockholders' meetings, and myriads of similar business situations require timely and well-developed business messages. All three functions of announcements, notifications, or statements of information may sometimes be combined in one message. For example, a standing committee is going to meet to discuss and approve its annual report to the members of a club. A new business opens. A store expands into a new building. One firm absorbs another through merger. An office is moved to a new location. A board of directors elects a new president.

Under certain circumstances the announcements may be simply brief single sentences like these: "The accompanying enclosures, received by us in connection with property we are holding for your account, are forwarded to you for your information." "The Annual Report Committee of the Civic Association will meet at Association Headquarters at 8:00 p.m. Monday, November 11, to approve the financial draft report."

Under other circumstances the announcements may be of greater length. In preparing them, use the following plan:

---

1 — Make your announcement tell *who, what, when,* and *where.*
2 — Give any desirable explanatory material.
3 — Close with (a) an expression of appreciation or (b) a request for action or (c) other appropriate statement.

ILLUSTRATIVE ANNOUNCEMENTS

I

Announcement

A slight change has become necessary in the plans for our weekly luncheon at which, this week, we shall have the pleasure of hearing Dr. S. K. Dreier, nuclear scientist of the Institute of Technical Research.

Explanatory material

The luncheon will be held on Monday, April 20, at 12:30 p.m. instead of Tuesday, April 21, as originally planned. Dr. Dreier has to leave for Washington on Tuesday, and to accommodate him the luncheon is being moved up one day.

Courteous action request

Please make this announcement to all members of your section.

II

American Airlines is pleased to announce that, effective August 30, over twenty-eight million young people of this country will be offered a first-hand opportunity to see America on American Airlines luxury 707's.

Anyone--from 12 through 21 years of age--will be able to fly anywhere American Airlines operates in the U.S.A. at 50 percent of the regular first-class fare.

The only provision is that reservations for such transportation can not be made earlier than three hours prior to departure time. The reason for this, of course, is that until that time the space must be reserved for passengers paying full fares.

The new youth plan is an effort by American to create an entirely new air travel market. It is designed to encourage more young people to fly, assist in the promotion of the "Visit U.S.A." program, educate young Americans to the great advantages of air travel, broaden the base of future business and, naturally, fill airline seats that might otherwise go empty.

American, a pioneer in such passenger-promotional proposals as the Air Travel Plan and the Family Fare Plan, feels the Half Fare Plan for Young Americans opens up vast possibilities for travel by youth throughout the country. We consider it the greatest stimulant to the U.S. travel industry in recent years.

We'll be delighted to welcome you aboard!

Dictaphone Corporation
730 THIRD AVENUE
New York, N.Y. 10017

Mr. Lowell Raymond

Dear Mr. Raymond: ANNOUNCING THE DICTAPHONE SHOW

Fresh from sparkling performances in Cleveland, Memphis, and San Francisco, The
Dictaphone National Traveling Product Show will be presented in Cincinnati, Ohio.

ANNOUNCEMENT....

5.39%

It's a pleasure to send you
your Coast Federal
Savings check

TWO-MONTH BILLING for gas and electric
services during the vacation months of
July and August.

SIMPLE ANNOUNCEMENTS

III

A new "package combination" is now available that offers
you, under one unit-universal guarantee, more than four hundred home services, covering all types of repair, maintenance,
and remodeling.

Enclosed is a Peninsula Home Owners brochure that we
feel sure you will find interesting in its detailed explanation of this new enterprise. Also enclosed for your convenience is an application, should you wish to become a member.

We shall welcome the opportunity to answer your further
questions.

Illustration I, on page 450, announces a meeting date change.
Illustration II announces the offering to certain limited age groups of
a new type of air fare, with an explanation of its purpose. Illustration
III announces the news of the establishment of a new type of business
service for homeowners. As we shall see in later pages, some highly

important business announcements also carry sales promotional aspects in varying degrees. Such is the case in Illustrations II and III. But the announcement itself, in each case, is the backbone of the message.

In Illustration IV, below, a newly elected president of a nationally known mail-order firm sends the following announcement-greetings to his far-flung staff of employees. The *plan* is the same as that for announcements, with greetings being added in the opening.

IV

ANNOUNCEMENT AND GREETINGS

For the first time I greet you as president of National Products Corporation.

Before very long I hope I can shake the hand of every member of our organization from Florida to Washington, from Maine to Southern California.

You and I have a great deal in common. We have a rich heritage to live up to and a great future to strive toward. Let's do it together.

I am proud to be your president--humble in the honor, grateful for the trust, appreciative of the challenge, and confident that with your help National Products, as you and I, will continue to progress.

As your president, I pledge to you 100 percent of my time at all times. Your ideas, your suggestions, and your cooperation are needed and will be most deeply appreciated. We can go just as far as we will. Let's go forward, together!

Illustration V, below, combines the news-announcement (of the sale of a business to a new owner) with an expression of appreciation to all the loyal customers who have made the enterprise a success.

V

ANNOUNCEMENT AND APPRECIATION

As announced in the press, we have sold our business and goodwill to The Fairmont Corporation, of Kansas City, who will in the near future conduct their increased business from our State Street building, where you may expect to find many of your old Mayfair Company friends.

To most of you, some of whom have been customers for more than fifty years, we believe that "goodwill" means more than can be expressed in a general message of this kind. Of the thousands of our patrons, we find that 1,266 firms have been doing business with us for more than twenty-five years.

Of course we close these years of pleasant relations with much regret. You have our earnest thanks for all you have done for us, as well as for the cordial expression of interest that you have shown in our company, its officers, directors, department heads, salesmen, and other employees.

Announcements of a more formal character may be printed or embossed in handsome type on special paper. For examples, see the illustrations on page 450.

INVITATIONS IN BUSINESS

Formal invitations. Business invitations, like announcements, may be formal or informal. Examples of formal invitations are reproduced on page 453.

Informal invitations. Informal invitations vary in length in accordance with the amount of explanatory material that may be included. Often they contain only a sentence or two. Use this plan:

1 — Issue your invitation. (The invitation is normally placed in the opening sentence or paragraph; but sometimes, as in Illustration II below, it is optionally placed in the closing paragraph.)
2 — Give any desirable explanatory material.
3 — Close with (a) a request for favorable action and acceptance and (b) any other appropriate statement, such as a courtesy closing.

Accepting the invitation. If you accept the invitation, do so with prompt courtesy. Use this plan:

1 — State your acceptance at the opening.
2 — Repeat your understanding of the invitation you are accepting and the exact time and place of your appointment. Add any other appropriate statement.
3 — Close with (a) an expression of appreciation and (b) any other appropriate statement.

Items 1 and 2 are frequently combined in an opening sentence that confirms acceptance along with a restatement of time and place.

AN ACCEPTANCE

Acceptance	I accept with much pleasure your invitation to join you for dinner next Thursday evening, September 9, seven o'clock, at the Gibson Lodge.
Appropriate comments	It will be most interesting to discuss with you the development of Westerners, Incorporated, and to learn of the future plans you have in mind.
Appreciation	Your invitation is appreciated, and I look forward to our discussion.

YOU ARE CORDIALLY INVITED TO
A PREVIEW SHOWING OF
A FINE NEW HOUSE IN
CORRAL DE TIERRA ESTATES
ADJOINING THE CORRAL DE TIERRA
COUNTRY CLUB

ROY K. HUBBARD, BUILDER
CHARLES W. MOORE, ARCHITECT

DEC. 10 and 11
2 to 5 P.M.

You are cordially invited to an
OPEN HOUSE
at
South-Western Publishing Company's
New Office and Warehouse
Thursday, January 26, 19 —
from 3 to 5 p. m.
11 Guittard Road
Burlingame, California

The Monterey Peninsula
Visiting Nurse Association
requests the pleasure of your company
at the Annual Meeting for
members and friends
at the Casa Serrano
412 Pacific Street, Monterey
on Wednesday, January twenty-ninth
at three o'clock

Tea

CROWN ZELLERBACH CORPORATION
ONE BUSH STREET
SAN FRANCISCO, CALIFORNIA 94119

OFFICE OF THE PRESIDENT

March 17, 19 —

To Our Share Owners:

Again, it is my pleasure to invite you to attend the Annual Meeting
of Share Owners of Crown Zellerbach Corporation which will be held in
the Peacock Court of the Mark Hopkins Hotel, California and Mason
Streets, San Francisco, on Thursday, April 27, at 2 p.m.

SOME PRINTED INVITATIONS

Declining an invitation. If you decline an invitation, again do so with prompt courtesy. Use the following plan:

---

1 — State your regrets at the opening.
2 — Explain briefly why you are unable to accept.
3 — Close with a courteous expression of appreciation for having been extended the invitation.

DECLINING AN INVITATION

Declining
with regrets
{
Much as I wish I could be with you for the Annual Club Dinner at seven o'clock, August 11, to act as your master of ceremonies, I find, with regret, that I must decline.

Explanatory
material
{
A special board meeting has been called, and my presence there is required. The date and time of this special meeting is in direct conflict with the Club dinner.

Appreciation
{
Please thank the committee for the honor extended in issuing the invitation to me.

APPOINTMENTS

An appointment differs from an announcement chiefly in one particular: it usually goes to one person only. The plan you follow is extremely simple:

---

1 — State the appointment.
2 — Indicate briefly the nature of the responsibilities involved.
3 — Express your hope that the appointee will accept.

Acknowledging the appointment. Simply as a matter of courtesy, the appointee, using the following plan, should (1) acknowledge the notification of his appointment and (2) promptly accept or decline. This may be a brief but courteous one-sentence statement.

I am happy to acknowledge your note appointing me a member of the Finance Committee of the Executive Council, to take office June 1, and I am glad to accept.

Summary. A knowledge of how to prepare and handle announcements, invitations, and appointments is part of the basic equipment of a business student. In discharging these responsibilities you will find the discussion and examples in this section an effective guide.

• *APPLYING EFFECTIVE ENGLISH*

Oral Applications

• 1. Discuss the announcements on pages 449-451 in terms of the six C-qualities.

• 2. What is the difference between an announcement and an invitation?

• 3. Point out how announcements, invitations, and appointments illustrate the importance of the C-qualities in writing: (1) courtesy, (2) completeness, (3) correctness, (4) clearness, (5) concreteness, and (6) conciseness.

Written Applications

• 1. As secretary of the Kishwaukee Home Owners Association write a message announcing the meeting in February of the Executive Committee. The purpose of the meeting is to plan the annual spring meeting of the association.

• 2. As secretary of the Kishwaukee Home Owners Association write a message inviting Dr. Ellis R. Cooke, Professor of Environmental Studies, Southern State University, to be the speaker at the annual spring meeting of the Kishwaukee Home Owners Association. Explain that the theme of the meeting is "Beautifying Kishwaukee Manor this Summer" and that the committee would like Professor Cooke to speak on the topic "Beautifying City Neighborhoods."

• 3. As secretary of the Kishwaukee Home Owners Association write a message appointing Mr. Ted Hilton to a three-member panel to discuss the topic "Beautifying Kishwaukee Manor This Summer."

• 4. Mr. Hilton will not be able to participate on the panel because he will be on a business trip in New Mexico at the time of the spring meeting. Write a courteous note for Mr. Hilton declining the appointment and explaining the circumstances.

• 5. As the secretary of the Kishwaukee Home Owners Association, write a letter inviting members to the annual spring meeting. The theme of the meeting is "Beautifying Kishwaukee Manor This Summer." "Beautifying City Neighborhoods" is the title of the talk to be given by the speaker of the evening, Dr. Ellis R. Cooke, Professor of Environmental Studies at Southern State University. Request members to come with suggestions of their own for making Kishwaukee Manor more beautiful. Supply details concerning the date, time, and place of the meeting.

SECTION 4

Orders, Remittances, Simple Acknowledgments, and Order Acknowledgments

The heart of business success rests upon orders of and payments for goods and services.

You can define an order in simple terms. When you make an order, you ask for something. In return you agree to pay a certain amount. An order may take one of several forms. For example, it may be oral. You go into a record shop. You ask the clerk for the stereo record-of-the-week. You lay a five dollar bill on the counter. She gives you the change. Or, to take another example, you may make an order over the telephone. Perhaps you are ordering several items through the telephone order office of one of America's big mail-order houses. Or possibly you are placing your telephone order at the store of your choice.

Under most other circumstances you put your orders in writing. In the pages of this month's magazine you find just the special bargain offer you have been waiting for. You order it in writing. And of course the vast majority of retail, wholesale, and mercantile establishments depend heavily on written orders.

ORDERS

A written order may request the shipment of goods or the supplying of service, either (a) in exchange for an agreed payment on agreed terms or (b) under some special arrangement.

Note that an order may request the delivery of tangible things like ten VHF-UHF theatre-console color television sets with advanced remote control; or eight silver mink stoles; or twelve power mowers with electric self-starters; or fifty copies of a textbook; or five-dozen ball point pens with new silver-iridium tip. On the other hand, an order may request the supplying of an intangible service like a suite at the Beverly Plaza, or two seats first-class red carpet on Flight 747 out of San Francisco International Airport. Let's study an example or two of the latter service calling for reservations.

Reservations. A reservation is simply an order for space or for some similar service that must be arranged far in advance. Time and place are important factors. Here is a suggested plan:

---

1 — Make the specific reservation you desire indicating the exact nature of the service you want: time (hour and day and date); place; type of space or class of service; other pertinent details.
2 — Include any other appropriate instructions you think desirable.
3 — Ask for a written confirmation, if you wish one.

AIRLINES RESERVATION

Reservation made in exact terms

> Please reserve one seat, first-class, on Red Carpet AstroJet Flight 747, San Francisco to New York, leaving International Airport at 8:07 a.m., Pacific Standard Time, Thursday, May 18.

Supplementary instructions

> Charge the ticket to Air Travel Card No. 4-771-947, please.

Request for confirmation

> Your written confirmation of the reservation will be appreciated.

HOTEL RESERVATION

Please reserve a single room with bath at the Beverly Plaza for Sunday night, May 1.

A lake view is not necessary, but a quiet location is, and preferably in the new section of the Beverly Plaza just completed.

Please let me have a written confirmation at your convenience.

The customer who made this reservation was obviously acquainted with the hotel and knew what he wanted.

Orders for tangible goods. Orders for tangible goods should specify the following:

1 — *Quantity:* Give the number of feet, yards, dozens, ounces, pounds, tons, gross, reams, units, or the like. For example: "4 copies Fifth Edition, Volumes I and II, 'Color Television Spectaculars.'"
2 — *Catalog Number:* The catalog number is the short cut to the exact identification of the article. When no number is available, every possible item of identification, such as size, color, material, weight, finish, quality, or style, should be supplied.

3 — *Price of Each Article:* Give the price of each article.

4 — *Method of Shipment:* Unless there is a fixed agreement between the buyer and the seller on shipping methods and routes, specify whether the shipment is to go by freight, express, or parcel post, and if necessary indicate the route.

5 — *Destination of Shipment:* Necessary if the goods are to be sent to an address other than that of the one placing the order.

6 — *Desired Date of Shipment:* This information indicates whether the goods are to be held for later delivery or must be delivered by a certain date. Need for haste should be given special note.

7 — *Order Number:* Concerns doing a large volume of business number all orders as a means of records management and control.

8 — *Method of Payment:* This information is necessary if the method is not understood and agreed upon, or if the buyer is not a regular customer with credit terms.

The chief requirements of an order are clear arrangement and accuracy of specifications and details. Place each item on a separate line or, if necessary, in a separate paragraph of description. Tabulate all items to show the total value. Remember that a misinterpreted order based on some mistake in figures or details may result in serious delay, financial loss, or perhaps even legal troubles. Accordingly, before an order is sent, carefully verify every detail of the contents.

CENTURY SCHOOL SUPPLIES

3672 ERIE AVE.• CINCINNATI, OHIO 45208 • TELEPHONE 321-9732   Purchase Order

Order No. 5698

To
New Hope High School
271 Morrill Avenue
Lincoln, NE 68507

Date April 4, 19--

Terms 2/10, n/30

Shipped Via Mayflower Lines, Inc.

Quantity	Cat. No.	Description	Price	Total
4 M	L39082	Paper clips #1	.75 M	3.00
2 M	J36903	Paper clips #3	.75 M	1.50
3 M	X55647	Jumbo paper clips	3.50 M	10.50
2 doz.	409921	Best Test rubber cement 4 oz.	4.25 doz.	8.50
6 doz.	669208	A. W. Faber touch-up sticks	1.40 doz.	8.40
3 gro.	138890	Ticonderoga pencils #2 5/10	8.80 gro.	26.40
				58.30

BY *I. L. Peniston*
PURCHASING AGENT

PURCHASE ORDER FORM

Order blanks. Use order blanks if available. Printed forms save time and typewriting. The blank spaces of the printed form are automatic guides that indicate the required information. On page 458 a purchase order form is illustrated. Order forms may of course vary in typographic layout, depending in part on the nature of the business.

Changing or cancelling orders. Occasionally you may find it necessary to change or to cancel an order. In such instance, here is a suggested plan:

---

1 — Enter the cancellation, or state the exact change.
2 — Give any additional instructions that may be desirable or appropriate.

CANCEL AND CHANGE

Statement of cancellation and change of order

> Yesterday, through your sales representative, George Harrison, I ordered 24 Number 1267-10 bandsaws. Please cancel this order and substitute the following specifications: 12 Series 10, Number 42 Electric multi-use drills. These are quoted in your Catalog 121 at $188.95 each, F.O.B. Chicago, Illinois.

Additional instruction

> This shipment is to be sent via American Airlines Air Freight in "expedited" classification, as in the case of prior shipments to us.

REMITTANCES

A *remittance* is a money payment. When you write about a remittance, indicate the exact amount of the money payment and the form in which it is sent.

The one who owes money may, when he sends it in, specify exactly how the money is to be applied. Such instructions may be of great importance if he happens to have more than one account with the company, owes a note, or is delinquent on an overdue payment. Unless he specifies to what precise item the money is to be applied, the creditor may apply it as he sees fit. Remittances, except checks, should be acknowledged (cancelled checks are their own receipts).

When you write about remittances, therefore, include instructions such as those mentioned in the previous paragraph. Also indicate

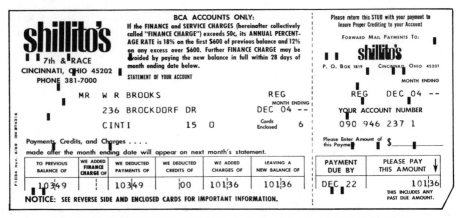

A TYPICAL BILLING FROM A RETAIL ESTABLISHMENT

This type of printed monthly bill takes care of most remittance transactions, leaving only special situations to be handled otherwise.

enclosures by a reference line (*Enclosure* or *Enclosures*) at the proper point. Use the following general plan:

---

1 — State the exact amount enclosed and indicate its form.
2 — Give exact instructions as to what account the money is to be applied.
3 — If the payment is delinquent, include an explanation.
4 — Close with whatever statement is appropriate to the particular situation.

The following illustration shows the development of this plan.

Statement of exact amount enclosed

> Enclosed is my check for $92.25.

Instructions on how to apply

> Please note that I wish to apply this remittance as payment in full on my open account to date.

Explanation of delinquency

> This payment is one month late, and I am fully aware of it. I regret this delinquency because I take pride, as I think you are aware, in keeping my credit A-1. There is just one simple explanation: an unexpected family emergency that, much to our personal regret, took all the spare cash we had in reserve.

Statement appropriate to the situation

> I'll have the next remittance in your hands promptly on the due date.

Asking for additional remittance. A customer through oversight may sometimes send in insufficient money to pay up his indebtedness. Doubtless he intends to send enough, but through some slip-up he fails to do so. He is of course not delinquent, and you have no desire to use the kind of collection pressure you might apply if he *were*. Accordingly, you turn to a different method:

---

1 — Thank the customer for his remittance.

2 — Specify the exact amount by which the payment is insufficient and ask for the additional remittance.

3 — Close with courtesy, giving any additional information or statement that may be appropriate.

ASKING FOR ADDITIONAL REMITTANCE

Expressing appreciation for payment	Thank you for telling us how pleased you are with your new typewriter, and for so promptly sending your check in payment. We're sure your new Selectric will delight you more and more with each passing day.
Request for additional payment	Incidentally, your check was "Short" of covering the full payment by $3.75, just the amount of the express charges. This, we know, was merely an oversight, and you can let us have your supplementary check for this amount whenever convenient.
Courtesy closing	The extra instruction book you requested will be on its way to you within the next few days, just as soon as we can get a new supply. We're delighted to send it to you.

This writer skillfully expresses at the outset his *double* appreciation to the customer, and with tactful informality calls attention to the payment insufficiency. Note also the equally effective final paragraph in which the writer uses a double-technique: (a) prompt action in favor of the customer, and (b) a pleasant courtesy closing.

ACKNOWLEDGMENTS

Simple acknowledgments. Certain general situations in the average business office call for simple acknowledgment. For example, an executive may be out of his office on a business trip. He knows from experience that on each business day certain items of mail will

ENCLOSED is the Metropolitan health literature you requested. For many years the Metropolitan Life Insurance Company has been active in spreading information on disease and accident prevention. The distribution of this material is a part of that activity.

We hope this literature will prove valuable to you.

Sincerely yours,

JWEcher

President

We hope you are pleased with this gift. The enclosed receipt bears important reference information regarding the gift purchase. *Please bring it with you* should you have any reason to consult us regarding it.

Marshall Field & Company

We are glad to send
this material to you.
We hope it will be
interesting and helpful.
If we can be of
further assistance
please let us know.

Public Relations
General Motors
Detroit, Michigan

SIMPLE ACKNOWLEDGMENTS IN PRINTED FORM

come in that only he can answer. He does not, however, want this material to lie unattended on his desk during his absence. Accordingly, his secretary is instructed to handle the incoming mail and to send out simple acknowledgments. Use this effective plan:

1 — Thank the writer for his note (your courteous acknowledgment).
2 — Explain the particular situation existing (for example, the executive is out of the office on a business trip, or he is in Washington for a government conference, or he is speaking at a convention in San Francisco).
3 — Assure prompt action "as soon as," and use a courtesy closing.

SIMPLE ACKNOWLEDGMENT

Thank you for your note of September 17 addressed to Mr. R. L. Culbertson. Mr. Culbertson will return to his office on September 29 from a short business trip.

Upon his return I shall be happy to bring your request to his attention. I know he will be pleased to hear from you.

Sincerely,

Arlene Huber

Secretary to Mr. Culbertson

Order acknowledgments. It is a truism that customers always like *prompt* acknowledgment of their orders. An order should, therefore, be acknowledged, if possible, on the day you receive it.

Orders that can be filled in full and without delay are often acknowledged on a printed form with blanks for inserting the necessary information. But in handling (1) orders from new customers, (2) large orders from regular customers, and (3) defective orders, personally prepared replies are usually necessary and always desirable.

Welcoming a new customer. At the time an order from a new customer is received, a personal acknowledgment is sent on the same day, carrying two important features: (1) sincere appreciation; (2) crisp definiteness. Use this effective plan:

---

1 — Thank your customer and welcome him.
2 — If it seems wise and necessary to do so, restate the order.
3 — Make clear exactly how the order is being handled.
4 — Express your cordial interest in serving him.

THE READER'S DIGEST

PLEASANTVILLE · N.Y. 10570

Dear Reader:

I thought you'd like to know right away that your gift subscription order arrived safely, and your instructions are being followed most carefully.

Enclosed is a memorandum bill which shows the amount due. You may want to pay now; many of our readers do. But if it is more convenient for you to send your check later, that will be quite all right, of course.

In either case, thank you very much! And accept our sincere wishes for a happy holiday.

Faithfully yours,

Carolyn Davis

CD:X   For the Association.

AN ORDER ACKNOWLEDGMENT IN PRINTED MESSAGE FORM

WELCOMING A NEW CUSTOMER

I

Customer welcome
> Thank you for the order given to our representative, Mr. Brock, on October 24. It is a pleasure to have you on our list of customers.

Restatement of the agreement
> Your agreement provides that the service is to be supplied for a period of one year, but you are to have the privilege of cancellation after two months if you are then convinced that the service will not prove satisfactory.

How the order is being handled
> The November release of the service is being shipped to you today by express.

Interest in serving
> We want to make our service prove of the greatest value to you in building up the reader-interest of your paper and in increasing its circulation.

II

Welcome to the First National Bank of Dover!

For most people a checking account is an essential gear in the machinery of modern living. We are pleased indeed that you have chosen us to provide this service. Our goal will be to help make your account a smoothly operating phase of your financial planning.

To acquaint you not only with our checking account department but also with our many other services, we are happy to send you the several enclosed pamphlets. These include discussions of home mortgages, installment loans, savings accounts, safe deposit boxes, and trust facilities.

If you have particular questions, feel free to call or visit any of our offices. They will be happy to serve your needs.

III

We are pleased indeed that we can count you as a new Peninsula Homeowners Service member. Welcome to our growing family!

You will find this membership of great value, both to yourself and to your home. It will give you peace of mind and savings in time, in money, and in convenience.

Enclosed is your membership card, a list of our eight personalized services, a list of your discount privileges, an appliance check-off list, a copy of our latest monthly News Letter, and a house sheet.

It will be most helpful if you will fill in the house sheet and return it to this office at your earliest convenience. The information you thus give us will enable us to handle your routine and emergency problems with maximum savings and efficiency.

Please call on us at any time of the day or night. We are here for just one purpose--to serve you twenty-four hours a day.

Acknowledging a large order from a regular customer. In acknowledging large orders from regular customers, follow the same outline as shown on page 463. Expand Section 4 of the plan to include vigorous material to center the customer's attention on the attractive features of the goods. The fact that the cusomer has sent a large order indicates that you are in a favorable position. You can stimulate enthusiasm and show a lively interest in his side of the transaction— the business efficiency that he will enjoy. Use this effective plan:

1 — Thank the customer for the continuation of his patronage and for his large order.
2 — Restate the contract-agreement.
3 — Indicate how the orders will be handled.
4 — Center the customer's attention on the favorable features of the excellent product and its potential for satisfactory profit-making service. Use a courtesy closing.

ACKNOWLEDGING A LARGE ORDER FROM A REGULAR CUSTOMER

Courteous acknowledgment

Our representative, Mr. Philip Hayden, telephoned the pleasant news to us yesterday that you are placing an exclusive contract with us for the next calendar year, covering your entire requirements of Inco-Nickel Transport Containers.

Restatement of the contract

Mr. Hayden has asked us to forward to you for your signature two copies of the contract, one to be kept for your files and the other to be returned for ours. Also enclosed with these copies is a brief summary of the major contract provisions for quick reference.

Restatement of order handling

You can rely upon us to give your orders, as they come in from time to time, our most prompt and careful attention. We shall observe your usual stipulations as to methods of shipment and routes until you give further notice.

Emphasis on excellent product features, and courtesy closing

Perhaps the fact that you have awarded us the contract for your entire year's requirements is evidence enough that you have had ample proof of the ruggedness and durability of our products. Under the most bruising conditions of service during long periods, Inco-Nickel Transport Containers with the corrugated triple-lock bindings stand the gaff of heavy-duty service.

We are glad indeed to be taking care of you again for this year as we have for so many years past. Our hope is that our business relationship will grow ever more prosperous.

Handling a defective order. Defective orders, lacking in necessary data, present a special situation. In acknowledging defective orders, never make the customer feel at fault. Ask tactfully for the additional information needed. Point out that the added information will assure accuracy in filling the order. Here is your suggested plan:

1 — Thank the customer.
2 — Ask tactfully for additional information. Never suggest that the customer is at fault.
3 — Show that your request is made in order to serve the customer well.

HOW *NOT* TO HANDLE A DEFECTIVE ORDER: NEGATIVE

We acknowledge your order for six Neverslip wrenches but can do nothing until we get more information.

You failed to state what size or sizes you want us to send these wrenches in. Naturally we can't guess at this, and we will have to hold your order up until you give us the necessary sizes. We trust you will correct this error promptly.

Note the fusillade of negatives:

Can do nothing   We will have to hold your order up
You failed to state   We trust you will correct this error
            Naturally we can't guess at this

CORRECTING THE SITUATION: POSITIVE AND HELPFUL

Thank you for your order of September 29.

The sizes in which you want these six Neverslip wrenches were not mentioned. As you know, we stock 8-inch, 10-inch, 12-inch, and 14-inch in the regular heads.

If you will indicate the exact sizes you want, we will see that your order goes out at once.

"Part-shipment," "out-of-stock," and "deferred-shipment" acknowledgments. Sometimes for some reason only a part of an order can be shipped at once. Sometimes deferred shipment is necessary when new stock is in production but has not yet been finished for shipping. Such situations call for suitable acknowledgments. Too often statements concerning exhausted stock mention only delay, inconvenience, disappointment—exactly the matters that should *not* be emphasized. Use, instead, the effective plan outlined at the top of the next page.

1 — Appreciation for the order.
2 — Speed in filling it at the earliest possible moment.
3 — A cordial request to the customer for cooperation in overcoming the present difficulty.

A "DEFERRED-SHIPMENT" ACKNOWLEDGMENT: EFFECTIVE, POSITIVE TONE

You may be sure that we are pleased to receive your instructions to forward the two black styles No. 851 and No. 805 listed on your spring order No. 1084, which was given to our representative, Mr. Sodler, for June 15 delivery.

Because of a truly unexpected call on these styles--and we believe their popularity will continue to grow throughout the season--we have had to make a new run, which is now in process and which will make it possible for us to get your order to you not later than June 25.

We are confident that you will be well pleased when you receive these two outstanding Famous Five styles. You will, we think, enjoy a fine volume of business on them. You have our best wishes for a prosperous season.

Declining orders. Under special circumstances businessmen sometimes have to decline orders. For example, exclusive agencies, restricted territories, and other established merchandising policies may make it necessary to decline orders that come to the wrong office. National manufacturers selling exclusively through local dealers, for example, usually decline orders that come to the factory itself (as some orders do). The challenge in this type of acknowledgment is a stiff one: It is to maintain a positive, willing-to-serve, assuring attitude that tactfully induces the customer to complete the transaction through the proper channel. Use the following effective plan:

1 — Express your appreciation for the order.
2 — Offer explanatory background information.
3 — Give instructions as to what the customer should do.
4 — In a courteous closing, suggest final action.

In the situations on the next page study the remarkable contrast in the sharply differing approaches of two different personalities. The first is negative. The second is positive. The first shows how to decline an order the *wrong* way. The second shows how to *save* the order and the customer by tactfully rerouting both through the local dealer.

HIGHLY DISCOURTEOUS: EMPHASIZES CUSTOMER'S IGNORANCE
AN UNPLEASANT (NEGATIVE) REFUSAL

It is impossible for us to take care of your recent request.

Apparently you are unfamiliar with the fact that all merchandise featured by us in Des Moines newspapers is presented for the attention of residents of Polk County only. Outside of the Polk County area we distribute our products only through dealers in home furnishings.

You can probably find a copy of our most recent catalog at Harrison Brothers, who are our dealers in your city. They can show you what we have to offer, and possibly you may be able to select a suitable piece if you talk with them.

In this way we can accept your order in the proper manner.

Negatives? Yes, indeed, by the dozen. Suppose we list a few:

It is impossible	If you talk with them
Apparently you are unfamiliar	(May be you won't?)
You can probably	We can accept your order
(Not certain?)	(if we feel like it)
Possibly you may be able	In the proper manner
(again, not certain?)	(implies that you ought to know better)

COURTEOUS: EMPHASIZES SERVICE TO THE CUSTOMER
THE TACTFUL AND POSITIVE APPROACH

Appreciation for the order

    Thank you very much for your recent inquiry. We shall be glad indeed to help you in completing your order.

Explanatory background information

    One of our finest representatives is Harrison Brothers, 222 Central Avenue S. W., your city. They carry a balanced selection of our home furnishings which you may see on their display floor. They also have our beautifully illustrated spring catalog from which you may make even wider selections. We are writing Harrison Brothers today with the suggestion that they call on you with our catalog so that you can examine the full line in the comfort of your own home.

    For the convenience of our customers outside Polk County we sell through home-furnishing dealers. Residents of Polk County are themselves informed of our offerings through our announcements in Des Moines newspapers. Since many customers outside the boundaries of Polk do not read Des Moines papers, we select outstanding home-furnishing dealers for service to them.

> From the wide selection on the floor at
> Harrison Brothers, and from our supplementary
> catalog, you will, we are sure, find just what
> you want. From the information in your inquiry
> we feel you will enjoy the beautifully designed
> Colonial line featured in full color on pages
> 9, 10, and 11.

> We hope you will give us the privilege of
> filling your order through Harrison Brothers.

Summary. "The heart of business success rests upon orders of and payments for goods and services." That is the statement with which this section opens. Every person, almost without exception, has to order something in writing at some time. Sooner or later, too, he needs some knowledge of handling remittances. Finally, tactful acknowledgments obviously play an important part in building good-will. All three forms of communication—orders, remittances, and acknowledgments—are part of the lifeblood of business. It is, therefore, not only desirable but *necessary* to learn how to handle these basic forms of communication.

• *APPLYING EFFECTIVE ENGLISH*

Oral Applications

• **1.** What parts should be included in a message accompanying a remittance? In a request for additional remittance? Discuss the importance of each of these parts.

• **2.** What is the distinction between orders for services and orders for goods and supplies? Give five examples of each. Explain what kinds of details must be included in each.

• **3.** What means were used to achieve a positive tone in the example, given on page 461, asking for an additional remittance.

• **4.** Assess the tone of each of the three examples welcoming a new customer (page 464). Cite evidence to support your views.

• **5.** Evaluate the following acknowledgment:

Your request of feb 13 on hand we have reviewed our agree-ment with you and will of coarse comply with it. Dependable service being our motto!

You will find inclosed literature concerning our oil burner, the Tilton boiler and enrg co deliberately set out to build the best oil burner, as to design, reliability, & eficiensy.

Hoping this will meet with your approval, and will close all prospects forwarded by you if possible, of course.

Send in you're perspective names at once so as we can close them, will expect a letter by return male.

Written Applications

• **1.** From Peter Emrod, Inc., 4478 Sherwood Road, Philadelphia, Pennsylvania 19131, order a set of the *Collected Works of Abraham Lincoln,* in eight volumes plus an index volume, published by Rutgers University Press at $115.

• **2.** Assume that you are a member of the staff of Peter Emrod, Inc., and that you have received the order (prepared in connection with Written Application 1) for one set of *The Collected Works of Abraham Lincoln.* Acknowledge the order you have received. In your acknowledgment suggest that the person who ordered the set may have friends who would appreciate owning the set. Try to sell one or more additional sets through this acknowledgment.

• **3.** Assume that the Shelby Manufacturing Co. sells its Keen-Edge electric saws only through the Sterling Hardware Company, the exclusive sales agency for this product. As a representative of the Shelby Manufacturing Co., write the proper acknowledgment of an order sent directly to the company for a 1/6 horsepower Keen-Edge eight-inch portable electric saw.

• **4.** You are employed by Houghton Tools, Inc., 1317 Miller Street, Buffalo, New York 14224. A customer has ordered a Speedway Victor 3/8 inch drill, with a 1/5 horsepower, 3.5 amp motor, Model No. 11703. The factory has been swamped with orders for this particular tool and is three weeks behind on replacement stock. Write an appropriate acknowledgment.

• **5.** (a) Write a message subscribing for one year to the *Journal of Business Analysis,* published by the Wentworth Publishing Company, 190 North Center Street, Jacksonville, Florida 32234.

(b) Write a renewal request dated one year after the message you prepared in connection with 5a, to renew your subscription to the *Journal of Business Analysis.* (Your renewal card has been mislaid.)

• **6.** The Speedway Victor drill, Model No. 13603, has been discontinued. A new two-speed 1/4 horsepower drill (Speedway Victor, Model No. 13714) has replaced the old model. Write an effective acknowledgment of an order for the obsolete model.

SECTION 5

Simple Requests and Special Requests: Making, Granting, and Declining Them.

Whether you make, grant, or decline a request, use the positive approach.

SIMPLE REQUESTS

As their name indicates, simple requests may require only a sentence or two. The basic plan for preparing a simple request consists of these two steps: (1) State your request. (2) Close with a courteous word.

Here is an example of a simple request printed on an enclosure slip:

We will appreciate your returning the premium notice with your payment.

Unless you request it, no receipt for payment will be sent you. Your check is adequate for that purpose.

Please be assured of our regard of your patronage.

Thank you

PROVIDENT LIFE & ACCIDENT INSURANCE COMPANY
Chattanooga - Since 1887

LIFE   ACCIDENT   SICKNESS   HOSPITAL   SURGICAL   MEDICAL

PRINTED IN U. S. A.   FORM 1640-U

SIMPLE REQUEST IN PRINTED FORM

Consider also the effective examples found at the top of the next page.

I

Statement of request	Will you please carefully examine the enclosed insurance policy, written in accordance with your recent instructions, and let us know if there are to be any changes, or if you would like to have further information or explanation?
Courtesy closing	We are grateful for this opportunity to serve you.

II

Statement of request	Miss Janice Raleigh, 27 Jefferson Avenue, Newport, Rhode Island, has sent in the attached request for a copy of The Communication Guide, reserves of which you keep on hand for our good customers. Can you arrange to supply her with the desired copy?
Courtesy closing	I am sure she will appreciate this brochure and find it helpful.

SPECIAL REQUESTS

Unlike simple requests, special requests are not always easy to handle. Under certain circumstances they may involve somewhat sensitive feelings. For example, did you ever make a request and get a reply that delighted you? Or a reply that, in merely a routine way, satisfied you? Or a reply that irritated you? Or a reply that depressed you? Or a reply that simply puzzled you?

Certain kinds of requests, by their very nature (together with their matching replies) involve personal feelings, sometimes very sensitive ones. These are almost always special requests.

For example, let us assume that you now have a good job. In the form of a special written request, you ask your chief for a certain privilege that, although definitely outside the regular routine, has been granted at previous times to others.

Now, if your request is given sympathetic consideration, and if it brings from your chief not only full approval but also a pat on the back for doing good work, you'll justly enjoy a sense of personal elation. Of course we all know that not all requests can be granted. But when it is not feasible to grant them, they can ordinarily be handled in such manner as to assure that they have been given full consideration and careful attention.

Illustrated at the top of the next page is a message carrying another kind of special request.

TIME
INCORPORATED
NEW YORK · CHICAGO

TIME & LIFE BUILDING
540 N. MICHIGAN AVE.
CHICAGO, ILLINOIS 60611

January 30, 19--

Dear TIME Reader:

For some time we have mailed you copies of our semiannual index. We are glad to continue doing this, if you find the indexes useful, but it may be that you no longer have need for them.

We would appreciate your letting us know if you still wish to receive TIME indexes by initialing the enclosed card and mailing it back to us. If we do not hear from you by April 1, we will remove your name from our index list.

This in no way affects your subscription to TIME Magazine.

Sincerely,

T. I. Williamson

T. I. Williamson
TIME Magazine

SPECIAL REQUEST

Occasionally you may find it necessary to ask others for some special kind of cooperation. Whether your special request is great or small, prepare it in as persuasive a manner as you can in order that it may enjoy as favorable a reception as possible. Use the following plan:

> 1 — Make your specific request (with a tactful reference, if appropriate, to one or more reasons why it is addressed to your reader).
> 2 — Include explanatory material supporting your request.
> 3 — If it is a meeting, restate the exact time and place; and, in any event, restate the request.

Consider the following illustration: The manager of Del Monte Shopping Center, Incorporated, notices that his organization is suffering increasing loss through the unjustified late return of goods taken out on approval. The loss is directly due to the fact that selections taken out on approval by customers are kept for too great a number of days before being returned.

It is felt that the loss can be sharply reduced through agreement of all the stores in the city to restrict the privilege of returning goods to a set time-limit. Such an agreement calls for city-wide retail cooperation. How would you solve this problem? Here is the actual special request that went out:

REQUESTING SPECIAL COOPERATION

Tactful opening and Specific invitation

> This request is addressed to you because of your long experience in department-store management and because of your keen interest in all questions pertaining to the management of department stores in general. Will you attend a vitally important meeting to be held at the Continental Club at noon on May 3, for the purpose of discussing the question of limiting to forty-eight hours the privilege of returning department-store goods?

Supporting material urging cooperation

> It is hoped that this meeting will be attended by the managers of all the department stores of our city and by others interested in this question, which is of paramount importance not only to the merchants but also to our patrons--a question deserving our most careful consideration.
>
> All who have discussed the matter with me believe that only at such a meeting as that which has been arranged can the question be weighed frankly and a possible solution be reached.

Restatement of exact time and place; request repeated

> Your presence and your wise counsel will do much to make this meeting a great success. The place is the Continental Club, and the time is twelve o'clock Thursday, May 3. Will you let me have a line indicating that you can be present?

Negative suggestion is dangerous. If negative suggestion creeps in, it is likely to defeat you before you start. Suggesting that the action your reader may take is likely to be unfavorable, or that your suggestion is unlikely to be a success, or that someone will try to block the scheme, or that you know the reader is busy, is thoroughly negative and may defeat the proposal before it is well under way. Revealing how easy it is to slip into sheer negativism, here is a typically "defeatist" appeal.

NEGATIVE, UNSUCCESSFUL

I know that you are extremely busy, and I further realize that you are bothered a great deal by people who are trying to sell you something. I know also that you have some purchasing connections which have undoubtedly proved satisfactory to you. But I want to explain that the only reason I am trying to sell you my product is that I am satisfied you can buy my brand to your advantage.

Energize your request with a positive approach. Choose an approach that courteously states your request in a reasonable and positive manner. Consider the following example:

POSITIVE, SUCCESSFUL

The specific request
> In preparing a semester report for one of my courses in the Warfield School of Business, I am asked to analyze the quality of business communication in the state of Minnesota.
>
> Do you have file examples of the following nature, for which you have no further use?
>
> An inquiry or an answer to an inquiry.
> A request and the granting or refusing of one.
> An acknowledgment.
> An application; a report.

Explanatory material
> The examples may be good, bad, or indifferent. If it is your wish not to reveal the name of either the sender or the recipient, I shall be glad to make copies without this information.

Courteous closing
> Your help will be greatly appreciated.

GRANTING REQUESTS

You would certainly expect it to be easy to find cordial language when it is possible to *grant* favors. But oddly enough, many efforts of this kind are ruined by a *grudging* consent. *A request should be granted cheerfully or not at all.* To give grudging consent is to destroy the spirit of willingness and the value of the act. In granting requests, you will find the following plan useful:

> 1 — Express your favorable action at once.
> 2 — Add such comment as may be appropriate.
> 3 — Close with a courteous word.

An excellent example of granting a request will be found on page 476. This reply, with cheerful cordiality, begets the full measure of goodwill it so highly deserves. Paragraph 1 carries out the first two steps of the plan set forth above. Paragraph 2 exemplifies Step 3.

Let us look at still another example. Note the courteous tone and the desire to assist, evident in the reply at the top of page 477 from a large manufacturer.

UNION CARBIDE CORPORATION
270 PARK AVENUE
NEW YORK 10017

To Our Stockholders:

It is a pleasure to send you "The Exciting Universe of Union Carbide," which appeared as a supplement to THE NEW YORK TIMES on Sunday, October 30.

This booklet is also being presented to those visiting the scientific exhibit featuring atomic energy, which we have just opened in the lobby of our new headquarters building in New York. Be sure to stop in to see this exhibit if you are in the vicinity. I believe that you will find your visit worthwhile.

If you would like additional copies of the booklet, let us know and we shall be pleased to send them to you.

Sincerely,

Birny Mason, Jr.
Chairman of the Board

A PRINTED ACKNOWLEDGMENT

We appreciate your interest and are glad to send you the enclosed material which you requested.

Please call on us whenever we may be of further assistance.

Cordially yours,

Paul E. Traum
Public Relations Director

ACKNOWLEDGMENT OF A REQUEST ON A SMALL MEMORANDUM CARD

NATIONAL BROADCASTING COMPANY, INC.
A RADIO CORPORATION OF AMERICA SERVICE
RCA BUILDING
30 ROCKEFELLER PLAZA
NEW YORK

This is the material you recently requested.

We hope that you will find it interesting and useful.

Very truly yours,

E. P. H. James
Promotion Manager

EPHJ:NC

ACKNOWLEDGMENT OF A REQUEST ON A LETTER-HEAD SLIP

AMERICAN AIRLINES

November 18, 19--

Dr. Melvin H. Hass, President
Hass, Incorporated
321 Joselin Avenue
Cincinnati, OH 45220

Dear Dr. Hass

As promised in my note of November 13, I am enclosing the two speeches by Mr. C. R. Smith that you requested: "The Turbine Engine and Air Transportation" issued in 19-- and "The Outlook for Jets" issued in 19--.

Thank you for your interest in American Airlines. Please let me know if I can help you further.

Sincerely yours

AMERICAN AIRLINES

Paul W. Wilmore
Zone Sales Manager

ag
Enclosures

A TYPED ACKNOWLEDGMENT OF A REQUEST ON AN 8½ BY 11 INCH LETTERHEAD

COURTEOUSLY GRANTING A FAVOR

Pleasing action first

> On its way to you, with our compliments, is a complete portfolio of our fall campaign including our salesmen's helps, store material, and other services.

Expression of interest

> It gives us a great deal of pleasure to assist students in their work. The merchandising field is in great need of trained men. The improvements in the methods used rest largely with young men who are now training themselves for this activity. We are much interested in what the western schools are doing for the merchants. Each month we carefully read their bulletins.
>
> The portfolio now on its way to you is entirely self-explanatory, and we therefore need not go into any discussion of the material here. Of one thing we are sure: you will find it interesting.

Courteous closing

> When we can help you further, call on us.

When the request is for a booklet, a reprint, a catalog, a pamphlet, or the like, it may be acknowledged with the enclosure of a printed slip or card (see the courteously worded examples illustrated on page 476). Or it may be acknowledged with a brief one-sentence note mailed either with the item asked for, or as a notice that the item is on its way. Such a note offers an opportunity for generating much goodwill. A typical example:

> It is a pleasure to send you, in a separate envelope, the reprint you have requested, presenting the debate, "How Soon Will Educational Television Replace Teachers?" between Frank MacDonald and John Hamilton, which appeared in the July issue of Saturday Review.

DECLINING REQUESTS

In your business and personal life you will probably find it necessary a good many times to decline a request. When this necessity faces you, seize any positive factor you can find. State what you can do, if anything. Follow this opening with a frank statement of what cannot be granted, giving the reason if you believe it should be given. Impersonal reasons for refusal (such as fixed company policies, regulations laid down by the board of directors, or the like) are effective simply because they are impersonal. They tend to disarm the reader's possible irritation. Under no circumstances should you give a curt refusal. When you must decline, courtesy in tone and tact in choice of words are of the highest importance.

Tact and courtesy. As rare as the finding of the proverbial needle in the haystack is the one who can decline a request and leave his reader in (almost) as pleased a frame of mind as if the request had been granted. In declining the request, still leaving his reader not unhappy, he will probably have applied the following tested plan:

---

1 — In pleasing tone give your explicit reason for declining.
2 — Express your interest in the situation.
3 — Close with a courteous word.

In developing a positive tone and attitude, the writer of the following example is skillful. Note, however, that he declines the request.

DECLINING WITH TACT AND COURTESY

Pleasing tone; gives reason for declining	I wish that it were possible to accept your kind invitation of July 22 to serve as a member of the Adjustment Bureau Committee. So many responsibilities rest upon me just now, however, that it would be inadvisable for me to add to them.
Expression of interest and support	The effort you are putting forth to stimulate an interest and a spirit of loyalty in our local market is most gratifying. It is a fine project and one that I know will be of decided advantage to the general welfare and best interests of this city.
Courteous close	Accept my best wishes for your continued success.

Emphasize what CAN be done. Almost every situation, however dark it may seem at first glance, has *some* feature, faint perhaps, that may carry favorable emphasis. *Look for that feature and give it prominence.* Emphasize it. Use the following tested plan:

---

1 — EMPHASIZE WHAT CAN BE DONE
2 — Give your explicit reason for declining the original request.
3 — Close with a courteous word.

A customer of a certain bank makes a request. What he asks is neither feasible nor desirable from the viewpoint of the bank. The bank can, however, suggest something that will in some degree meet the customer's request.

EMPHASIZING *WHAT CAN BE DONE*

What CAN
be done;
favorable
action first

> We are glad to be able to send you, with our compliments, a sample copy of <u>Effective Management</u>, which we hope will be of service to you in planning your campaign. We have found the book of exceptional value in all our work. The success of our recent campaign was due to this practical volume.

The refusal

> Unfortunately, in our type of business, requests for examining our management methods are so numerous and the expense involved in keeping the material open for inspection is so great, that it has been necessary to decline all such requests.

Courteous
closing

> We appreciate, however, your interest in our campaign and are glad that you like it enough to inquire.

"The clumsy refusal" a classic case. A civic-minded citizen accepted the leadership of a part of the Community Chest drive for collecting money for charity. Others in his circle of friends and associates normally cooperated in bringing the program to a successful conclusion. From one cantankerous citizen, however, the following request drew ill-tempered refusal.

COURTEOUS REQUEST

> Accompanying this note are several cards of the Community Chest. Can you arrange to take care of them or delegate someone in your department to do so?
>
> I shall be glad to call someone personally to help you if you wish. The cards are so few in number that I am taking this informal means of reaching your department with them.
>
> You may be sure I shall appreciate your help.

CLUMSY REFUSAL

> I found on my desk this morning a bunch of Community Chest literature with a request from you asking me if I would take care of the matter for the department. I have never done any soliciting, and I do not intend to begin now. Consequently, I shall refuse to help you in this matter. I do not want to start a thing of this kind, for it would result in a volume of such work being shifted to me. Ask somebody else.

The curt expressions—"a bunch," "I do not intend to begin now," "I shall refuse to help you," "I do not want to start a thing of this kind"—are highly ill-mannered in their irritability and ruinous, of course, to goodwill. Imagine the "fix" in which this man will find himself when, sometime in the future, the situation is reversed and *he* wants some help from the one he so clumsily rebuffed.

How to win (or lose) business friends. By their very nature, inquiries, requests, and the replies that follow are often related to what may become important purchases and sales. No matter whether such requests are granted or declined, they often lead to pleasant outcomes if they are handled with tact. If, on the other hand, the handling is clumsy, the outcome may be grim indeed. Suppose we study an actual case or two.

Case I. Would you like to see how an order for fifty books is hopelessly lost? Study this instructive contrast.

A CLUMSY REPLY IN A SCOLDING TONE

Your request for a copy of *The Story of Outer Space* has just reached us. You state that this is wanted as a desk copy. If we were to furnish copies free of charge for all requests, we would be pretty busy, as every day such requests pour in.

If an order is received for the book, we supply desk copy. That is, if a quantity of books are ordered, we furnish the teacher with desk copy. But we don't think we should be called upon to furnish such a copy unless an order comes along with the request.

Remember, we have to pay a royalty on every copy sent out, whether for desk use or sale. We will send desk copy only when you submit an order.

The person who made the original request actually received the scolding reply. "That discourteous reply," he said, "has lost that company the sale of fifty books. I had just about made up my mind to use their edition anyhow, without seeing a desk copy, but now? Now I wouldn't use their book, even if it turned out to be the best and last one in the world!"

The basic causes of the failure? Suppose we list them:

Irascible indulgence in a "scolding" tone
Blundering ignorance of human nature
Failure to recognize all the positive possibilities
Failure to see through the eyes of the reader

According to the testimony of the one who made the original request the purchase was almost decided. *One tactful sentence of reply would have cinched it.* But the fifty-book sale was irretrievably lost because the one tactful sentence never came.

Now let us see how the business might have been won.

THE CORDIAL REPLY: IT MIGHT HAVE SAVED
THE BUSINESS

Positive and courteous: promises instant action

> We shall be glad indeed to send you a complimentary desk copy of <u>The Story of Outer Space</u> if you will accompany your request with a minimum ten-copy order. Of course, we'll be glad to have you order more!

Explanatory material

> <u>The Story of Outer Space</u> is an extraordinary text. As a result of the great attention it is attracting, we have scores of requests each month for desk copies. For this reason we have found it necessary to limit our free copies to instructors using the book as a text in the classroom. With every order for ten or more copies, we are happy to furnish the desk copy on a complimentary basis.

Courtesy close with favorable action offered

> As soon as your order arrives, your desk copy will be promptly on its way.

Case II. Your house construction enterprise features its service in *Time* magazine. From one of your *Time* announcements you receive the following request:

> Please send me a copy of the booklet you mention in your full-page announcement in <u>Time</u> last week. We are expecting to build fairly soon, and your booklet may be helpful.

This request you can handle in two sharply different ways: the failure way or the success way.

The failure way. The loser lets the request gather dust on the desk for a week or two. When he finally answers it, he writes thus:

KILLING INTEREST AND GOODWILL (NEGATIVE)

In reference to your recent request in which you ask for a copy of our booklet "Ideal Comfort 365 Days In The Year," we regret to inform you that the last edition has been completely exhausted. We are unable to tell you when other copies will be available, if at all, inasmuch as no new edition is planned. We regret, therefore, that we cannot comply with your request.

Note that the irritating negatives are all there. In fact they appear to be holding a "Negative Convention." Suppose we list a few:

we regret to inform you
completely exhausted
We are unable
if at all

no new edition is planned
We regret, therefore
we cannot comply

The success way. You reply to the request on the same day you receive it. Promptness is never more crucial than when an interested customer has requested information. If your reply is to be sent at all, *send it at once!* It will reach the peak of its power if it arrives while the impulse that prompted your reader's original request is alive and fresh, while the fever of interest is upon him. With his interest at peak, he will give warm and favorable attention to all the facts you persuasively offer.

GENERATING INTEREST AND GOODWILL (POSITIVE)

Favorable, positive action first

> Thank you very much for your recent request. We're glad to send you at once our four-page multigraphed brief summarizing the extraordinary performance of our new "MagiControl Warm-Cool Thermostat."

Explanatory material

> This brief presents the essential facts regarding installation and costs of our new thermostatic control system that has revolutionized one segment of the building industry. Our supply of the original "MagiControl" booklet, <u>Ideal Comfort 365 Days in the Year</u>, has run out because of an unusual volume of requests, but the enclosed brief supplies much the same information. If the original booklet is reprinted, we'll see that you have your copy right away.

Specific reference to enclosure

> Study the performance figures on page 3 of the enclosure, and you will see that the new "MagiControl" saves a substantial part of its installation cost in its first year of operation.

Courtesy close inviting further inquiry

> Please write us again when you are further along in your building plans.

A communication like this generates interest and shows courtesy through promptness. You also generate large measures of goodwill through your obvious willingness to serve. Finally, you capitalize on every aspect of the request that has positive impact, in order to develop your excellent business opportunity.

Summary. You will probably find it an almost daily duty to prepare a request, to grant a request, or to decline a request. When you are faced directly with these kinds of responsibilities, the material in this section will stand you in good stead as a vital reference source. Use it systematically to enhance the effectiveness of your efforts.

• APPLYING EFFECTIVE ENGLISH

Oral Applications

• **1.** Explain why the message granting a favor (page 477) can be expected to increase the goodwill of the recipient. Cite specific words and phrases to support your explanation.

• **2.** In your opinion what words and phrases make the request for special cooperation on page 474 effective?

• **3.** State the two parts of a simple request. What is the purpose of each part?

• **4.** Pick out the words and phrases which, in your judgment, spoil the appeal given on page 474.

• **5.** What special problems confront a person when he writes a special request?

Written Applications

• **1.** Rewrite the discourteous refusal to the request for assistance in the Community Chest drive (page 479). Make your refusal tactful and courteous so that it will preserve the goodwill of the person who made the request.

• **2.** You are one of two druggists in the town of Elm Grove, Wyoming. You wish to invite Mr. Elmer Cox, the other druggist, to discuss a plan by which each drugstore would remain open on alternate Sundays. This arrangement will mean that the volume of business conducted over the year by each drugstore will not be affected. The purpose of the plan is to enable each druggist to have alternate Sundays as holidays without losing business to the competitor.

　　1 — Make an outline of the message to be sent to Mr. Cox.
　　2 — Write the message, organizing it in accordance with your outline.

• **3.** Your close friend Dr. Bernard T. Elston is the director of the Heart Fund Drive in Hamilton County. He has written requesting that you serve as chairman of the Heart Fund Drive in your town, Franklin Park. The assignment would entail arranging for twelve captains, who in turn would secure volunteer collectors to work in various parts of Franklin Park. Arrangements for the Drive should be completed by January 23. Since you will be away during January you cannot accept the appointment as chairman. Write a courteous refusal. Emphasize your willingness to serve as a captain or as a volunteer collector since you will be available during February.

SECTION 6

Appreciation, Congratulation, and Praise

To express appreciation, congratulation, and praise is a basic form of courtesy.

To whom should you send a thank you note? To whom should you send a note of congratulation? To whom should you send a birthday card? To whom should you send a clipping of interest? To whom should you send a few sentences of praise? Almost every person knows a number of people he ought to visit, in person or through the written word, to make sure they get the word of thanks, congratulations, or praise before the appropriate time has gone.

Like recognition of a noteworthy achievement, appreciation for service well done is something that should be given basic priority. To do so is simply a part of good manners. Every person in the world likes to know when he has done well. This is true no matter how illustrious or humble he may be. To say "Thank you" doesn't take many words. In fact it takes just two. To convey praise or congratulations doesn't take many words. A sentence or two may do it, or perhaps only a dozen words or so. But what important words!

There is an odd contradiction in some strains of human nature. The unhappy truth is that many individuals find their chief pleasure in discovering weaknesses in others, weaknesses that they can gloat over. Aware of the many faults of which they themselves may be guilty, they unconsciously defend themselves by searching hopefully for even more numerous faults in their associates. Lively attention is devoted to something that can be criticized in others. Only jealous silence greets something worthy of praise. The fact is that some persons should not attempt to write any words of appreciation because they are unable to put themselves into a sufficiently generous frame of mind. You must appraise yourself to determine where *you* stand on the scale of generosity of spirit and thoughtfulness of others.

If one were to take a conservative estimate, prickly expressions of complaint probably outnumber expressions of praise about a hundred to one. For that reason large enterprises have highly trained staffs specializing in nothing but handling complaints and completing adjustments. The irony is this: The very instruments that prevent many complaints from ever getting started are often the notes of appreciation, congratulation, and praise we are discussing in this section.

What are some of the occasions that may properly call for expressions of appreciation, congratulation, or praise? Here are a selected few:

1 — Appreciative acknowledgment of special consideration
2 — Appreciation for a request granted
3 — Congratulations for success well earned
4 — Commendation for an act of public service
5 — Praise for good work

APPRECIATION

Expressions of appreciation, like those of congratulation and praise, show an interest in the welfare and progress of others as well as a generosity of thought that reflects inbred good manners. In preparing expressions of appreciation, you will find the following plan useful:

---

1 — State your appreciation in simple, direct words.
2 — Include an explanatory word or two, if appropriate.
3 — Close with a courteous word.

The nature of the appreciative expression will determine whether Step 1 alone is enough. In many instances Step 1 and Step 3 will be reflected in a single sentence. In saying "Thank you" to others, you will soon learn the wide flexibility you enjoy. Here are seven effective examples:

I

Appreciation
```
     The Board of Directors of the Gallery
Association, speaking for all the association
members, join together to thank the Camera Club
for the generous gift of last week.
```

Explanatory comment
```
     You may be assured that it will be grate-
fully used in some specific form to make our
newly remodeled central display room more
efficient for our mutual use.
```

Courtesy closing
```
     May your Camera Club enjoy continued
success in the coming year!
```

THANKS FOR LETTING US SERVE YOU AGAIN!

THANK YOU.

Thank You!
We appreciate
your patronage.

 THANK YOU!

And we hope you come again soon

THANK YOU
FOR USING TEXACO PRODUCTS

YOUR DIVIDEND...OUR THANKS

PRINTED CARDS THAT SAY "THANK YOU"

II

As chairman of hostesses for our most successful Peninsula Voluntary Services project on Wednesday, I wish to thank you for serving so graciously at the Hawaii exhibit. You played a most important part in making the whole affair such a pleasant and enjoyable event.

III

Mr. Crail gave me your letter and asked me to thank you for your complimentary remarks about our Free Enterprise Program. We are greatly encouraged to hear from good people like you.

We are most happy to forward to you some extra copies of our Self-Reliance quotation and hope you can make good use of them.

IV

Please let me take this means of thanking you, on behalf of the American Union of Arts, for your cooperation in making our Collector's Show of last month a success.

We are most grateful to you for lending us your Laurencin print, which helped so much to give the exhibit the depth and variety we believe it achieved.

V

You were most kind in complying so promptly with my request for reference books on Space Science and Design of Space Craft. The title selections are just what I need for my study. Your guidance has indeed been helpful.

VI

On behalf of the Washington High School Communications class, I am happy to express our deep appreciation for your courteous treatment during our visit to the Xerox Corporation plant. The luncheon given by your Company was most enjoyable.

Most interesting, too, was the manner in which the staffs of the various departments demonstrated the various pieces of equipment to us.

In expressing our thanks to you, may we add that we shall long remember our enjoyable and instructive visit.

VII

Let me express our whole-hearted appreciation for the speed you showed in producing and shipping the battery of equipment we ordered for the Super-Nova Space Project at Huntsville. The way in which you handled the order is worthy of admiration.

For the exceptional performance you turned in, you have our thanks.

The daily relationship between individuals may, for the most part, be in the realm of business. Yet such association may give rise to the exchange of pleasant words that build vital goodwill. Some expressions of appreciation may seem far removed from the commercial stream. But they generate the kind of mutual understanding and pleasant friendship that may profoundly affect the course of important future transactions.

CONGRATULATIONS

To indicate pleasure in the good fortune and success others have attained is the purpose of expressions of congratulations. Of course anyone who strives to create an expression of congratulation that rings true must himself feel a *genuine* pleasure in the good fortune of his reader. He must lay aside every tinge of envy and mean what he says. In expressing congratulations, the following plan is effective:

> 1 — State your congratulations in simple, direct words.
> 2 — Include an explanatory word or two, if appropriate.
> 3 — Close with a courteous word.

The nature of the congratulatory expression will determine whether Step 1 alone is enough. In many instances a sentence or two will cover all three steps. You again enjoy a wide range of flexibility in saying "Congratulations." Here are four effective examples:

I

Congratulations	{	The members of the Speech Club have asked me to speak for them in congratulating you on winning the Cup at the Interscholastic Speech Meet in Atlanta last week.
Explanatory comment	{	We have some idea of the amount of effort you expended in preparing for the Meet.
Courtesy closing	{	We're proud of you for the honor you have brought Montgomery High.

II

This brief note is to tell you how pleased I was to read, on page 196 of The Review for April, of the honor you received last January from the State Association of High School Editors. Congratulations!

Everyone knows how well you deserve the honor.

III

Let me congratulate you on the distinction you have won in being awarded the coveted national George Washington Honor prize for your current Americanism program.

This recognition from the Freedoms Foundation is well-merited. You have the warm commendations of those of us who, like you, would like to see a still-free America as the environment for our children and our children's children.

I hope that you and Coast Enterprises will keep up the powerful campaign.

Expressions of appreciation have been used in the past and will be used in the future by presidents, princes, and potentates. By their example all of us may profit. Typical are these lines to Thomas A. Edison, world-famed inventor, on his eightieth birthday. From whom did they come? From a former president of the United States.

IV

I am glad to have an opportunity to join with your friends throughout the world in extending hearty congratulations upon your eightieth birthday. To your energy, courage, industry, and strong will the world owes a debt of gratitude which it is impossible to compute. Your inventions, placing the forces of nature at the service of humanity, have added to our comfort and happiness and are a benefaction to all mankind for generations to come. I trust that there are in store for you many more years of health and usefulness.

PRAISE

Expressions of praise follow the "congratulations" plan:

---

1 — Express your praise in simple, direct words.
2 — Include an explanatory word or two, if appropriate.
3 — Close with a courteous word.

Praise
> You have my unlimited praise for your article on the subject, "Creativity," which I have just read in this morning's copy of <u>Grey Matter</u>.

Explanatory comment
> You earn this praise for your clear-cut analysis of the true nature of this none-too-simple subject.

Courteous closing
> Give your associates, Mr. Kingston and Mr. Taft, my regards and pass along my message of commendation.

SYMPATHY

Of one thing you may be sure: sorrow will, at one time or another, come to all of your friends and associates, just as it will, at one time or another, unalterably come to you. An expression of sympathy is simply the effort of a friend or an associate to lighten in some small way the burden of the sorrow when it strikes. The true meaning of an expression of sympathy comes only from the reality of the event that brings it forth. Every person will inevitably suffer sorrow. But it may be softened through expressions of sympathy from those who understand. The following plan is useful:

---

1 — Express your sympathy in simple, direct words.
2 — Close courteously with word of quiet understanding.

Anything as individual and personal as a note of sympathy can never of course be reduced to set definition. But it can, in its almost unlimited range of flexibility, be described and exemplified.

I

Expression of sympathy
> The folks here at the office have just learned that you have been under the weather with an illness. This distresses all of us very much.

Courtesy closing
> We hope that you are much better and that you're making a fast recovery. Everyone sends "Get Well" greetings.

Although it is difficult indeed to make words serve in a
situation of great sorrow, at least we can try to tell you
how much we all wish to express our deepest personal sympathy
for what is not only your great loss but ours as well.

You have only to ask if there is anything that we can do
to help assuage that loss, even a little. Your friends are
all about you and near you, and we hope you will remember
that truth, each day, and continuously.

Summary. Appreciation, congratulation, praise, commendation, sympathy—all these forms of expression involve highly personal approaches and attitudes that call for a wide range of flexibility. Much of the time these forms will be purely personal. From time to time they will also involve business relationships. To each, the same creative principles apply.

• *APPLYING EFFECTIVE ENGLISH*

Oral Applications

• **1.** In the sample messages of appreciation given on pages 485 to 487, identify (a) the statement of appreciation, (b) the explanatory remarks (if any), and (c) the courteous close.

• **2.** Discuss the advantages, in terms of friendly personal relations, of messages of appreciation, congratulation, and praise. Examine the advantages of such messages with reference to desirable business relations.

• **3.** List some of the situations in business in which a note of appreciation would be appropriate, a note of praise, and a note of congratulation. Cite at least three situations with reference to each of these types of messages.

Written Applications

• **1.** Write a note of appreciation:

1 — to a friend who has recommended you for a desirable position; assume that you have obtained the position.
2 — to the students in the senior art class at Aurora East High School; thank them for making posters which were used in the current Aurora civic clean-up campaign. You have been chairman of this campaign.

3 — to Dr. Howard Larr, Professor of Biology at North Central University, who has addressed a meeting of the nature study group of which you are secretary.

- **2.** Write a note of congratulation:
  1 — to your cousin Susan, who has just been graduated with high honors from Merton College.
  2 — to a business associate, Mr. Kenneth Salisbury, who has just been made general manager of the Apex Electronics Corporation.

- **3.** Write a note of appreciation in connection with one of the situations you suggested in Oral Application 3.

- **4.** The Franklin Oil Company, 4008 East Parker Avenue, Louisville, Kentucky 40212, operates a chain of eighteen independently owned service stations in Louisville. As public relations manager of the Franklin Oil Company, write to all regular customers expressing the company's appreciation for their continued patronage during a change-over to a different brand of gasoline and oil. The change-over occurred three weeks ago. Assure each customer that Franklin stations will continue to provide efficient, courteous service, the best available petroleum products, and reliable towing and repair facilities.

- **5.** The druggist, Mr. Elmer Cox, to whom you wrote earlier suggesting that the drugstores in Elm Grove, Wyoming, be kept open on alternate Sundays (see Written Application 2, page 483) has agreed to cooperate. Write a message expressing your appreciation.

- **6.** You are secretary of the Monroe Park Chamber of Commerce. You have requested and secured the assistance of ten prominent citizens in arranging an express route for trucks through a congested part of the city. You have also had the close cooperation and expert advice of the chief of police in making the necessary arrangements. Your plan has now been adopted by the City Council.

  1 — Write a message of appreciation to Chief of Police Lester J. Farmer for the studies, reports, and advice he provided.
  2 — Write a message of appreciation to be sent to each of the ten citizens who supported your plan and encouraged the Monroe Park City Council to adopt it.
  3 — Write a message of appreciation to members of the City Council for their understanding and cooperation.

SECTION 7

Introductions and Recommendations

Notes of introduction and recommendation identify people helpfully in new communities.

You are about to start on a new job in San Francisco, California. You have never been to San Francisco, although you have heard many pleasant reports about the city on the Golden Gate.

You have no acquaintances in San Francisco. But your present employer has business connections there. Through these connections he can introduce you. He gives you an unsealed message of introduction to one of his good friends. Now you have an anchor to the new community through his courteous action.

Arriving at your new location, you hand the introduction to the person addressed. He helps you to make the acquaintance of others. In a much shorter time than would otherwise have been possible, you find that you have developed a number of new friends.

INTRODUCTIONS

You will find it relatively simple to prepare an introduction. What you are about to do is to make a statement about another person. You are simply going to tell who he is and why he is being introduced. The following plan is useful:

> 1 — Make the introduction.
> 2 — Give your reason for writing.
> 3 — Offer brief information about the one introduced.
> 4 — Express appreciation for any courtesies.

As an alternative for written introduction, a business card bearing the words "Introducing Mr. Fairmont" is sometimes used.

In the usual manner, address the envelope carrying the written introduction. Then place this notation in the lower left corner:

```
Introducing
Mr. Charles Fairmont
```

AN INTRODUCTION

The intro-duction	It is a pleasure to introduce Mr. Charles Fairmont, who has up to the first of this month been on the staff of Metropolitan Construction Company of Cincinnati as assistant manager in charge of contracts.
Reason for writing	Mr. Fairmont has been commissioned to open and take charge of the new San Francisco office.
Background information	It has been my good fortune to be associated with Mr. Fairmont for the past ten years. He possesses the kind of energy, enthusiasm, and leadership that should make him the type of community citizen San Francisco will like.
Courtesy closing	Any help you can give him in making desirable contacts in his new post will indeed be appreciated.

ANOTHER EFFECTIVE INTRODUCTION

I am pleased to introduce Mr. Jonathan Stanley, who has been our assistant personnel manager here at the Omaha plant of Topco Metals, Inc., for the last five years. Mr. Stanley will be the new personnel manager of our Dallas plant. He and his family will be moving to Dallas about May 3.

I'll appreciate any assistance you may be able to give Mr. Stanley in establishing associations in Dallas.

RECOMMENDATIONS

Recommendations may be *specific* (addressed to a particular individual) or *general* (intended for anyone interested). A specific recommendation carries more weight because it contains more detail. The following plan is useful:

---

1 — Give the exact prior employment status of the one recommended.
2 — Supply a brief summary of experience and background.
3 — In a courteous close, state why the individual left your employ.

The specific type is often written to cover an inquiry from an employer who is following up a reference given in an application. An example of an employment inquiry:

THE EMPLOYMENT INQUIRY

Mr. Charles Fairmont has applied for a position in our Engineering Department. He has given your name as a reference. We shall appreciate it if you will give us your impression of Mr. Fairmont's character and ability.

An example of the answering (specific) recommendation:

THE ANSWERING SPECIFIC RECOMMENDATION

Exact prior employment status

> Mr. Charles Fairmont, the subject of your March 1 inquiry, was employed in our Engineering Department from 19-- to 19--. Before coming to us, he spent several years in marine and stationary engineering work.

Experience and background

> His experience in stationary and marine engineering is, from the operating standpoint, of great value in boiler and power-plant engineering. Moreover, during the time he was with us, he developed into a skilled draftsman. Mr. Fairmont is industrious, of distinctly superior ability, and of high character.

Reason for leaving employ

> Temporarily laid off during a slump, he found other employment. Frankly, we were sorry to lose him. He is a man who made a definite place for himself in our enterprise.

Intended to be read by anyone interested, the general recommendation, usually carries the opening address "To Whom It May Concern." Use the following plan:

1 — Give the exact prior employment status of the one recommended.
2 — In a sentence or two, supply information about the person's experience and background.

A GENERAL RECOMMENDATION

Exact prior employment status

> Mr. Arthur Nevins, bearer, has been in the employ of Chancellor Industries, Inc., since 19--. During the last six years he has been in the Accounting Department.

Experience and background

> Mr. Nevins has applied himself well to his duties and has demonstrated thorough reliability in his work. He is an excellent detail man and has given us entire satisfaction.

A general recommendation is essentially little more than a "certificate of good standing." It is included in this discussion simply to let you know of its nature and occasional use.

In contrast, the specific recommendation, giving definite information, is "tailored to fit" a concrete employment situation. It is therefore of measurable value because it sets forth concrete facts directly related to the opportunity.

● APPLYING EFFECTIVE ENGLISH

Oral Applications

● 1. State the four parts of an effective note of introduction. Identify each of these four parts in the following introduction. Then discuss the tone and effectiveness of the message. Cite specific words and phrases to justify your views.

> It is a pleasure for me to introduce Mr. Oliver N. Smalley, who has been our assistant personnel manager here at the Knoxville office of Newcomb Insurance Agency for the last five years.
>
> Mr. Smalley will be the new personnel manager of our Seattle office. He and his family will be moving to Seattle about October 17.
>
> During the years of my association with Mr. Smalley I have been impressed by his conscientious interest in civic and school affairs, as well as by his valuable contributions to the Newcomb Agency. He has served on the Knoxville Board of Education for many years and was chairman of our Community Chest campaign last year. I know that he will be a real asset to Seattle and his new community.
>
> I shall greatly appreciate any assistance you can give Mr. Smalley in establishing worthwhile associations in Seattle.

● 2. What are the parts of a specific recommendation? Identify these parts in the following recommendation. Discuss the tone of this recommendation and cite specific words and phrases to illustrate your points.

> Miss Myrna Utley, about whom you inquired in your letter of October 3, was employed as my secretary from February, 1963, to April of this year. Before she joined our firm, she had had four years of experience as secretary with the Eberhardt Took & Die Company.
>
> Miss Utley is an outstanding private secretary. She is highly intelligent and conscientious. She is careful in her work and completely reliable. She is the most dependable, imaginative, and accurate secretary I have encountered in twenty years of business experience.
>
> Since her family now live on the West Coast, Miss Utley has decided to join them there. I recommend her without qualification. I believe that you will find that she is a delightful person, as well as a loyal and efficient secretary.

• **3.** What is the main difference between a specific and a general recommendation? Why is a specific recommendation so much more valuable? Point out in detail the difference between the specific recommendation given in Oral Application 2 and the following general recommendation. Why is the former more desirable?

> Mr. Derwood Harper has been employed from 1960 to 197- in the personnel department of Trunbul Foundries. Before 1960 he worked for three years in our shipping department.
>
> Mr. Harper has always been reliable and trustworthy. He is a willing worker and cooperative employee. He is leaving our firm because he wishes to seek employment in a warmer climate.

Written Applications

• **1.** Write a recommendation for a classmate, Jerome Clauson, who wishes to secure a position as a file clerk with the Emmet C. Wilson Company, a mail-order firm in Phoenix, Arizona. Jerome knows no one in the concern. Emmet C. Wilson is a personal friend of your father and has known you for years.

• **2.** A close friend, Miss Elsie Hartnet, is moving to Cleveland, Ohio, where you lived for a number of years before moving to your present home. Write an introduction for Miss Hartnet to Mrs. Sylvia Martin, a good friend of yours who lives in Cleveland.

• **3.** Mr. Omar S. Manser has been a watchman at your firm for three years. He has been adequate in his work but has never been outstanding. His doctor has recommended that he move to the Southwest for reasons of health. Write a general recommendation for Mr. Manser.

• **4.** Invent a situation in which a specific written introduction would be appropriate. Supply the appropriate information, and write the introduction.

• *REVIEW*

Check the following sentences and correct all errors.

1 — The arrangements for the interviews which Miss Conford was responsible for was completely satisfactory.
2 — Miss Marksens suggestion having the effect of encouraging every one to work harder then ever.
3 — The college scheduled asemblys for the incoming students, and they were all excellent.

4 — Clara is one of those girls who is always ready to help.

5 — We sold two hundred sixteen articles at $3.75 each, thirty-seven articles at $.85 cents each, and one hundred thirty-four articles at 1.50 dollars each.

6 — The salesman consulted their copys of the wall street journal.

7 — Miss Hazelwood Mr. Gardners secretery use to assist in keeping the companie's financial records.

8 — The staff is bringing there individual recommendations to the january conferance, through discussion the best ideas will be choosen and utilized in next springs sails campaign.

9 — Miss Harts note was the kine that gives reel encouragement.

10 — The merchandize can be transported by railway accross the county in less than a weak.

11 — To many students have difficulty in writting messages simply because affective study and proofreading habits have not been thoroghly masterred by them.

12 — For there march activity, the girls scouts visited the field museum of natural history in chicago they all agreed that it was an exiting and interesting trip.

13 — Responsibal and considerate, a very good impression was produced on the Rotary Club member by that group of student's.

14 — Mrs. Rodgers planed speakers for the Fall and Winter programs and to arrange for a consert at the Spring meeting.

15 — The firm plans to take a pole of public opinion the purpose of the pole will be to determine the publics reception of compact cars'.

16 — The arrangements having been made for the enlargement of the office and for accomodating additional personnal.

17 — While watching a television program, the emergency announcement of the whether warning was heard by millions of people.

18 — The employees' of the manufacturing firm located North of town is prejudice against the plan, more information is suppose to be maid available to them.

19 — Three proposals had been under consideration for some month's at the April meeting the board announced publically that Miss Schrams plan would be adapted exactly as submitted.

20 — Prepared carefully, Alan Bookwright's delight at the news of Mr. Farmer's promotion was expressed in a handwriten personal message.

Class "Corporation" Project

Corporation project 12-A. Contemporary School Supplies, Inc., will move into its new quarters at 1480 West Lamont Boulevard a week from today. Dennis R. Washer, President, has asked you to prepare for his signature a message announcing the move to customers and giving the new address and telephone number. Suggest that henceforth all mail and telephone orders should be placed at the new address. State that a new catalog of equipment and supplies is being sent in a separate envelope.

Since this is to be a duplicated form message, omit the inside address and use the salutation *Dear Customer:*

Corporation project 12-B. On *(use yesterday's date)* a shipment of office equipment arrived from the Courtway Manufacturing Company, 4622 Sherbourne Avenue, Duluth, Minnesota 55807. The shipment lacks six fluorescent desk lamps, bronze finish, Catalog No. 87802. These items, however, were listed on Invoice No. 631017.

As "order department manager," write to Harvey T. Keller of the Courtway Manufacturing Company to secure prompt shipment of the missing equipment. Organize your request as follows:

1 — Acknowledge receipt of the partial shipment of your order.
2 — Specify exactly what items were not included in the shipment.
3 — Indicate your willingness to accept the lamps in black or white finish if they are not available in bronze.
4 — Courteously request prompt shipment.

Corporation project 12-C. Contemporary School Supplies, Inc., has received an order from the Warren School District, Warren, Vermont 05674, for sixty gallons of special gymnasium floor varnish. Your company no longer handles paint or varnish. As "assistant public relations director," write Mr. Russell K. Topps, superintendent of the Warren School District, explaining that Contemporary School Supplies, Inc., has discontinued handling paints and varnishes. Suggest that Mr. Topps order the varnish from the Mohawk Paint and Varnish Company, 4817 North Lincoln Avenue, Chicago, Illinois 60625. Explain that this company specializes in varnishes for gymnasium and dance floors and that you feel confident the proper varnish will be available there.

Mr. Topps is a potential customer of Contemporary School Supplies, Inc. Take the opportunity afforded by this situation to invite Mr. Topps' attention to your extensive line of school supplies. Indicate that you are sending him Contemporary's latest catalog and that Contemporary School Supplies, Inc. will always be ready to serve in any way possible.

UNIT 13

EFFECTIVE APPLICATIONS

Among the most personally rewarding demonstrations of your communication power is your use of words to get the job you want. Nowhere is this ability more important than in the application for a job. Here your skill in personal expression meets its toughest test: Can you get the job you need through your words alone?

To this test question no one can answer yes except you. You alone can properly tell the facts about yourself. No one else can do it successfully.

Outlined for you in Section 1 are the effective application methods that have won the most consistent successes over the years. Here you learn what a tested application system can actually do for you as an individual.

In the construction of an effective data sheet, Section 2 guides you with systematic accuracy, step-by-step.

The data sheet is the all-important reference device presented for the instant convenience of your prospective employer. It keys your outstanding points in such a way that your prospective employer can most effectively evaluate you in relation to the job you hope to get. In effect, your data sheet powerfully reinforces and amplifies everything you present in your message of application.

UNIT 13

Section 1

How to Create an Effective and Successful Application: Your personal skill in telling what you can do is your best insurance for Job security.

Section 2

The Successful Application Team: Data Sheet, Application Message, and Interview: Give convincing facts and impressions about yourself in the data sheet, the application message itself, and the interview.

SECTION 1

How to Create an Effective and Successful Application

Your personal skill in telling what you can do is your best insurance for job security.

RESEARCH AND CREATIVITY: SECRETS OF APPLICATION SUCCESS

Among the most personally rewarding demonstrations of your communication power is your use of words to get the job you want. The power is there. Everyone can recognize it. It can be accurately measured in the form of the job you have won. So no one any longer doubts the crucial importance of self-expression. This power of self-expression is, in essence, simply the ability to shape into meaningful language your own creative "job-getting" thoughts.

One of the central purposes of this section is to review for you the exact process of effectively applying for employment. To apply successfully for employment requires research on the one hand; and creativity on the other. Research is the process of discovering information and transforming it into knowledge. Creativity is producing what is new or refreshing what is less new.

You engage in research when you (1) formulate a purpose; (2) plan methods of fulfilling that purpose; (3) collect, analyze, synthesize, and interpret information; (4) record, report, and use your findings.

You engage in creativity when you bring into being that which has not existed, or when you alter that which has. The terms *research* and *creativity* are not mutually exclusive. Rather, creativity is involved in effective research. And research is often the basis of creativity. Thus, the research phase and the creativity phase of applications "dovetail" into each other, as you will presently see in your study of this section.

Related to employment applications, research involves your discovering or rediscovering information about (1) yourself as a prospective worker, (2) other people as prospective employers or co-workers, and (3) circumstances that are likely to associate you with those other people. Creativity, related to employment applications, involves your producing words and actions that represent your research findings so that you will effectively fulfill your purpose and get your job.

At this point it would be natural for you to ask this question: How should I combine research and creativity when I apply for a job? In this and the following section you will cover such research stages as (1) the preliminary planning, (2) the digging for facts about yourself, your career field, and specific positions, (3) the sifting, resifting, and organizing of those facts to fit a basic plan of action. You will also cover such creative stages as (1) the systematic fitting of your attributes to job requirements, as you understand them, through (2) application messages and (3) data sheets that are logically as well as psychologically effective.

What's your competition? A simple fact of life is this: You are now at this moment in the midst of stiff competition. It is all around you in the form of your classmates. And for all the rest of your life you will probably be in the midst of stiff competition. Its pressure will, in fact, quite probably accelerate as jobs and the various new technologies increase in complexity. Hence, the very wisest and smartest thing you can do is to take every possible creative step to make yourself competent to meet this competition and to take every possible step to prepare for it.

Again, in the Help Wanted section of a city newspaper, the following insertion appears: "*Wanted*: A man to work eight hours a day to replace one who didn't. Call 624-6789 between 2 and 4 p.m. for an appointment. Or write Box A 777, Peninsula-Herald."

Concise? Yes. Clear? Yes. Reflecting the current competitive conditions? Yes.

As a third example, turn now to still another job-search:

> *Communicator Junior-Executive:* Must have effective command of language. Able to meet people well. Course' in Communication for Business highly desirable. State in detail your education and experience. Address L G 449, Times-Express.

Supremely clear in this job-search message are the requirements. The company states with maximum brevity exactly what their requirements are. "Effective language command." "Able to meet people well." "Course in Communication for Business highly desirable." If you apply, you are left in no doubt as to what capacities you must have to fill the stated requirements.

Have you the word-command to get the job? The type of job-search reflected in the foregoing examples is becoming more and more usual. "Every business student," writes expert Paul Nystrom, "needs to study not only what to do and how to do it, but also how to tell it. No matter what the course in business may be, no matter what the practical experience, the development of the ability to speak and to write well comes very near to being at least half of the problem of education."

Dr. Nystrom's statement is overwhelmingly supported by the experience of millions. Knowledge, skill, business ability—these attributes will be of use *only* if the person has the ability to convert them into ideas and words that may be easily understood by others. In the following pages you will find the precise guidance to convert into intelligible words (1) what you can do for a prospective employer, and (2) why you are sure you can do it.

TOP RATING FOR PERSONAL USE VALUE

On the practical scale no kind of communication ranks higher for personal use than the job application message. Most people readily agree with this assertion, but few summon up enough willpower to master the skill. Yet this powerful tool for economic protection is always ready at your hand. It is in truth your insurance protection each time you may need it in the future. It offers you two priceless levers: (1) It helps you to multiply your own strength. (2) It helps you to project your personal power lines. What we are really talking about is your personal future, how to insure your employment and livelihood, how to promote your future success.

You and the placement director. One whose professional task is to find jobs for those who want them is called a placement director. These officers testify that an astonishing number of job seekers do not have the remotest idea of how to prepare an application. Although many applicants have acceptable or even good educations, they have for some reason *learned nothing whatever about how to apply for a job*.

"Yet the application a candidate prepares probably has most weight," concludes a recent survey, "in securing him an interview and a job. Most men complain that applicants for a job have no conception of what a good application looks like."

Some time ago a New York financial publication carried an item significant to every business student and every person who will ever need a job. It offered an unusual opportunity for a sales executive.

The man, said the notice, must have a personality that will enable him to win the full cooperation of his associates and to inspire confidence in his subordinates. "This man must be old enough," the notice continued, "to have had the experience which will qualify him for this position and still be young enough to work with an organization planning aggressive expansion.

"The man securing this position must be of a caliber and ability to command a salary of at least $35,000 a year to start.

"WRITE, giving in detail your qualifications. Your application will be treated in strictest confidence. Address Box CC87."

This invitation was directed to men who believed they were competent to handle the executive burdens of a $35,000-a-year position. Yet you will notice that it asked them to *write*. Before they grant personal interviews, prospective employers looking for men of this caliber still want to examine written qualifications.

YOU are your application. Your application will be one of the most intensely personal documents you will ever write. It represents you as it reaches your prospective employer's desk; in one sense *it will be you*. It will be as if you said: "This, Mr. Employer, is my accredited representative, my chief ambassador. This application shows you what I think I am.

As we have emphasized in earlier pages, your skill and ability will be sold in competition. So prepare yourself to compete with other applicants who, just as earnestly as you, may want the same job. They too will send their accredited representatives to plead their cases. Like you, they will put their dependence on an application in which they picture themselves as well as they know how. Your task is to make yourself more skillful so that you may outperform the others.

"Personal use for everyone." Young people seek their first job. They turn to the application. Maturer people with energy and ambition are readying themselves for better positions than those they have. They turn, likewise, to the application.

Prospective employers want to "size up" applicants ahead of the interview. They want to determine in advance whether the applicants are worth further contact. The impression their applications make literally determine whether they are worth taking the time to see.

How "what you can do" fits "what must be done." Let us take two men, equal in training and ability. Each one wants the same job. The one who knows better the procedure of an application will get the position. He wins it for two reasons: (1) He knows how to state to advantage what he can do, and (2) he has the all-essential knack of showing how *what he can do* measures up with *what the employer wants done.* He fits together the teeth of two gears—"what he can do" gears into "what must be done"—and shows to his prospective employer how these two gears mesh.

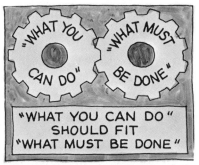

"WHAT YOU CAN DO"
SHOULD FIT
"WHAT MUST BE DONE"

The art of a good application is to fit these two gears together.

Yourself and the "market." To introduce a product, you study it to find its superior qualities and uses. You next study your market to find who are your prospective buyers, where they live, what their buying habits are, what features and qualities they are looking for, and what appeals will be strongest.

You follow the same process in winning a job. You study yourself to discover your personal qualities. You get ready to put into persuasive words a description of your training, your skill, your knowledge, and your ability. You study the services you can offer in order to be able to present them effectively.

Next you search out prospective employers who might have a need for the kind of ability you can offer. You find out where these employers work, when they do their interviewing, what opportunities are open, what qualifications are needed for handling these jobs. You then put yourself on the "examining stand" and decide whether the qualifications you have are those the employer wants. You proceed to the third and final step, the application itself, only if your completed study of yourself and the job shows that your qualifications fit.

Thus you complete the preparatory study that gives your application the advantage over aggressive competition. For competition you will have! To meet it, you must make every preparatory step count. Here is a summary:

THE PRODUCT: yourself, your skills, your abilities.
THE MARKET: prospective employers whose locations, job opportunities, and needs have been studied.
THE CONTACT: your application itself.

Major classes of applications: (1) *solicited,* written in response to advertisements (usually "want ads"), and (2) *unsolicited.*

An unsolicited application is one written by an applicant who hopes that there may be an employment opening or who happens to hear of a vacancy. But more commonly it is written at the suggestion of a third person who may know the prospective employer or who may have knowledge of a definite job that is open. The "third person" may be a friend, an employment agency, or a representative of an appointment bureau.

On the other hand, advertisements draw the greater number of applications. Because of the scores of applications that result, your message, if it is to obtain more than casual notice, must stimulate attention and interest through its expression, tone, and appearance.

Blind employment advertisements. A blind advertisement is one in which the employer's name is not revealed. The requirements of the job are mentioned only in general terms. In this case it is hardly worthwhile to attempt a market study or to write more than the essentials of age, extent of education, and experience. Your application will be one of scores. Hence some mechanical feature like a long or tinted envelope may prove helpful in distinguishing your reply.

From twenty-five to two hundred applications, a prospective employer may select not more than ten or twenty of the best-looking for examination. A fine-looking one has far more chance of attention than those less attractive. Employers know by experience that a poor entry usually means a poor applicant. They put their attention on the "fine-looker." They know that it usually means a superior applicant. Handsome appearance is always essential of course. But it is doubly essential when the effectiveness of your message depends upon it.

Complete employment advertisements. A complete advertisement is one that gives enough information so that the applicant can make a study of the job and can fit his abilities to it. Complete advertisements generally offer opportunities far more desirable and better-paying positions than do blind advertisements. Therefore you are justified in putting more effort into showing how you fill the employer's needs— in demonstrating how "what you can do" fits "what needs to be done."

PLANNING YOUR APPLICATION

For anything as individual and personal as an application a plan should be flexible. Then it will easily adapt itself to many circumstances. Sometimes a man of rich personality and engaging expression can win a position with an application that seems to have no plan at all. In his case he wins the job, not because of lack of plan, but in spite of it. For applicants less gifted, it is wise to follow a tested procedure that is known to work.

The "A I D A" plan. A handy memory device to guide you through the main steps of application procedure is the name "Aida." Here is a simple outline of these four steps:

1	A	ttention	Attracting favorable attention
2	I	nterest	Arousing interest
3	D	esire	Stimulating desire and convincing the mind
4	A	ction	Getting action

These four "AIDA" functions are not necessarily "boxed off" in separate compartments. Although you may study them separately as a convenience in identifying them, you will recognize that they flow together. The several "AIDA" functions shade into one another like the colors of a rainbow. The illustrations below show, in contrast, how the thought stream flows smoothly ahead from one part to the next.

The four main "AIDA" functions outlined below translate themselves into the six steps of an effective application shown on page 509.

Attract favorable attention. The *best-looking* application will always seize top attention. Accordingly, as your first step, buy a few sheets of fine-quality bond paper with envelopes to match. Select a white bond in the standard business sheet size of 8½ by 11 inches. At this point we come to several "Don'ts." Don't use social, club, fancy, or hotel stationery. To do so will almost always seriously prejudice your case. If you are currently employed, don't use the letterhead of your firm. You are not justified in doing so. For the same reason, don't use the letterhead of your father's business. Simply use plain, unadorned, fine white bond.

I ATTENTION	II INTEREST
III DESIRE	IV ACTION

NOT LIKE THIS . . .   *. . . BUT LIKE THIS*

1 — **Establish a point of contact** (attract favorable attention).
   a. Physical appearance and arrangement
   b. Statement of nature and purpose

2 — **Outline your understanding of the requirements of the position** (arouse interest with a study of the needs of this specific job opening).

3 — **Show how your experience and education fit these requirements** (sustain interest and stimulate desire for a personal interview, as your qualifications begin to appear valuable).

4 — **Mention personal qualifications** (reinforce desire for a personal interview that will check your application against your actual personality).
   a. Your interest in the employer's type of business
   b. Reasons for leaving your present connection
   c. Personal desires and chief aim or interest
   d. Why you feel you can fill the requirements

5 — **Give references** (reinforce the employer's desire to look further into your qualifications).

6 — **Make a request for an interview** (get action—the result you desire).

THE SIX STEPS OF AN EFFECTIVE APPLICATION

Typewrite your application (or have it typewritten). To give the application a competitive advantage, typewrite your application or have it typewritten. Its typed form will distinguish it from the large number of others that may come in handwriting. By contrast your effort will stand out. Typewriting may mean the difference between losing and winning.

You may have been asked to submit the application in your own handwriting. In this case do so, but send along an excellent type-written copy. Your prospective employer will then read the type-writing, may do no more than glance at the handwriting. Thus, you follow the employer's instructions without losing your competitive advantage.

A favorable first impression lays the groundwork for your success. "If this fine-looking presentation truly represents the caliber of the one who wrote it," thinks the prospective employer as he admires the neatness of the layout, "then I want to interview that person. Set up the appointment, please."

Visualize. When you prepare for a personal interview, you are careful as to dress. The application by which you hope to gain the interview should be equally attractive. Its appearance must command respect. Its strength will be tested by how it looks. Balance the material. Set it up in symmetrical form and proper arrangement. "Make it a picture." Frame it in the same careful proportions as those of the sheet upon which it is placed.

Step One: The point of contact. The opening sentence, your point of contact, shows your purpose and tells where you, the applicant, learned of the position (through an advertisement or otherwise), or mentions the name of the individual with whom the prospective employer is acquainted and who has suggested that you write. Your opening sentence should be followed by a specific statement that you are applying. The fact that you *are* applying should not be left to suggestion or imagination. It should be said outright. Apply in clearcut terms: "May I be considered an applicant?" "Please consider me an applicant." "I should like to apply for this position."

"HERE IS ONE OF THE BEST APPLICATIONS I HAVE SEEN. I THINK YOU SHOULD HAVE A LOOK AT IT."

Point of contact

    In Thursday's <u>Daily Herald</u> I noticed your advertisement for a private secretary and correspondent. May I be considered an applicant for this position?

Step Two: Your understanding of the requirements. If you are making your first application, your statement here will be fairly brief. Your understanding of the employer's needs must come from general knowledge. But if you were a person of experience and maturity, this part would offer you a chance to show your understanding, your capacity, and your grasp of the requirements. Develop this section as far as your experience permits.

It is my understanding that you want a young man
with a working knowledge of office methods. He must
also be able to take dictation rapidly and accurately,
and he must have a background of general business
training.

Step Three: How your education and experience fit the requirements. This part will give facts taken from your career. All facts should be chosen and sifted several times until you have found the ones that bear on the employer's needs. Take the you-attitude. Assume the point of view of the employer. Try to see how what you can do fits into what he wants done. From your experience and training, sift until you find the facts that focus on the employer's needs.[2]

How experience and education fit these requirements

I am a graduate of Western Technical High School,
where I took the four-year commercial course. During
the past four years since my graduation, I have been
private secretary to Mr. Arthur F. Graham, executive
director of the Higbee Company, Cleveland, Ohio. My
work with Mr. Graham has been widely varied. I can
take dictation at 145 words a minute, transcribe my
notes at 45 words a minute, and type straight copy at
80 words a minute. On my own responsibility I have
handled much of the routine correspondence and have
found this experience highly valuable in broadening
my general business and secretarial ability. I have
become thoroughly familiar with commercial and legal
forms, including leases, deeds, mortgages, releases,
affidavits, and vouchers.

Step Four: Personal qualifications. State why you feel confident you can make a success in the position for which you are applying. Here you may include touches of human interest—items revealing your human side.

"Sometimes I have had to scramble hard for money with which to continue my education," runs a sentence that held the interest of one employer. "During the summer months between school terms, I have had jobs as a hodcarrier, a mason's assistant, a salesman for two hardware stores, and a bill collector."

"Your 'hard scramble' for money to continue your education got you your job," the employer said later. "I like the kind of ambition that carried you through four jobs to your graduation."

Explain why you are interested in the employer's kind of business, your reasons for leaving your present position if you have one, your

---

[2] This part may also be enlarged by use of a data sheet. The data sheet, discussed and illustrated in later pages, carries a summary of further details of your training and experience. See page 518 for an illustration of an effective data sheet. While the application scores the first impression, it is often the data sheet that the prospective employer keeps in front of him for further consideration.

chief aim, and why you feel confident that you can take care of the work involved in the new job.

Personal
qualifica-
tions
> I believe I have developed, through my training and experience, the ability to handle the duties you require. I enjoy this kind of work. My reason for making a change is to improve my position. Mr. Graham tells me that I have now reached the maximum salary permitted by the Board, and he fully understands and approves my wishes for further advancement.

Step Five: References. References, like guarantees, increase the employer's confidence in your ability. Give at least three references with correct and exact addresses, and make clear that you give these references with the permission of the persons named. The following expressions are suitable and courteous: "I have permission to refer. . . ." "I refer by permission. . . ." and "(place names here) have permitted me to refer. . . ." Choose references that represent both business and personal areas.

References
and men-
tion of data
sheet
> Mr. Arthur F. Graham has kindly permitted me to use his name as a reference. On the enclosed data sheet you will find additional references and also data with regard to my general qualifications.

Step Six: Request for an interview—getting action. Let your closing sentence (1) suggest an interview and (2) make that action easy. Make a direct request for an interview. Tell how and when the prospective employer may reach you. "May I have a personal interview at your convenience? I can be reached by telephone at 351-6866 or by mail at 8508 Concord Hills Circle" is typical of many possible requests for action. Practice variety through use of different kinds of closings.

Request for
interview
> May I have a personal interview? If you wish to telephone me, my number is 791-6926.

An effective effort. Now let us see how the whole application looks and sounds when it is put together in one piece. It will be well worth your while to review carefully, sentence by sentence, the complete draft as reproduced on page 513. For obvious reasons, this draft was successful in winning a new position for the person who wrote it. Logical and well developed, the material emphasized facts that the employer wanted to know and was pleased to get. You will note, however, that it did not waste the executive's time with unnecessary facts, wording, or any other kind of unnecessary material.

Appearance	*Content*
1. Stationery. Does it impress favorably or otherwise?	1. Plan. Is it logical in corethought, sequence?
2. Letterhead. Is it suitable?	2. Paragraphs. Do they indicate thought units?
3. Neatness. Is the paper clean?	
4. Folding. Is it exact, straight?	3. Sentences. Are they grammatical, varied, clear?
5. Ink (ribbon). Is it clear?	
6. Typing. Is it accurate, even?	4. Punctuation. Is it correct?
7. Layout. Is it pleasing, balanced, centered?	5. Spelling. Is it correct?
	6. Tone. Is it positive?

HOW NOT TO WRITE AN APPLICATION

Let us now turn for a moment to two true stories to find out why some applicants fail.

True story number one concerns a thumb-marked postal card in careless handwriting. See the illustration on page 513. Needless to say, this applicant did not get the job. His careless card was the first to be tossed into the wastebasket.

True story number two concerns a page of poor-grade scratch-paper carelessly torn from a notebook and bearing several lines of hastily scrawled words, obviously dashed off in a great rush. Addressed to a famous manufacturing company, this "application" is illustrated on page 513. This effort was instantly consigned to the wastebasket.

But the effective effort on page 513 carries out the rules for an effective business message as well as an effective application. It is placed attractively on the sheet, well typed, and neat. To incorporate the C-qualities of effective writing, the applicant has carefully worked out each step.

What went wrong? The two defective examples you have just read reveal similar faults. Regarding ability, they depend on unsupported statements. They make unjustified requests that put the burden of continued contact on the prospective employer. When an applicant tries to shift the load of further negotiation over to the prospective employer, he almost guarantees his own failure. In ninety-nine cases out of a hundred the employer will carry the matter no further.

Avoid these dangers. Graduating seniors in astonishing numbers write "applications" in which the plan and the material violate all basic principles. (1) The points of contact are weak. (2) The plan and the organization are illogical. (3) The facts are thin and poorly

AN INSTANT FAILURE

April 2

Dear Sir—

Noticed your add of wanting reliable man for responsible position in local fort. Think I can meet your requirements so please mail me particulars by return mail and when I can may have interview.

Very truly yours,
Joe Doakes

A SECOND FAILURE

Aug. 7

Dear Sir:

Mr. A. B. Bliss of the Bliss School advises me that you have a vacancy in your research bureau. I am well qualified for such a position and would enjoy employment with your company. Please consider me. Awaiting your early reply,

I am
Yours truly,
John Doe

AN EFFECTIVE MESSAGE

271 Chester Court
Billings, Montana 59102
June 3, 19--

Mr. John Lux
Sales Presentations, Inc.
208 North Broadway Street
Billings, Montana. 59101

Dear Mr. Lux

In Thursday's Daily Herald I noticed your advertisement for a private secretary and correspondent. May I be considered an applicant for this position?

I understand that you want a young man with a working knowledge of office methods, a background of general business training, and the ability to take dictation rapidly and accurately.

I am a graduate of Western Technical High School, where I took the four-year commercial course. Since my graduation four years ago, I have been private secretary to Mr. Roy J. Bell, executive director of the Higbee Company. My work with Mr. Bell has been widely varied. I can take dictation at 145 words a minute, transcribe my notes at 45 words a minute and type straight copy at 80 words a minute. On my own responsibility I have handled much of the routine correspondence and have found this experience highly valuable in broadening my general business and secretarial ability. I have become thoroughly familiar with commercial and legal forms, including leases, deeds, mortgages, releases, affidavits, and vouchers.

My training and experience have helped me develop the ability to handle the duties you require. I enjoy this kind of work. My reason for making a change is to improve my position. Mr. Bell tells me that I have now reached the maximum salary permitted by the Board, and he understands and approves my wishes for further advancement.

Mr. Bell has given me permission to use his name as a reference, and the enclosed data sheet shows additional references and general qualifications.

May I have a personal interview? If you wish to telephone me, my number is 791-6926.

Sincerely yours

Vernon F. Baker
Vernon F. Baker

Enclosure

marshaled. (4) Personal claims appear without supporting details. (5) The requests in the action paragraph are often unjustified. This is the factual record of the majority of most graduating classes in the country. Poor though the record may seem, it can be improved by study and effort, the material for which is given in these pages. And it may confidently be added that you will be rewarded with hours of later happiness for every minute you spend upon these pages.

Summary. This section has offered you guides for preparing application materials that will satisfy the needs of personnel executives. Remember that these men are the selectors. They are the experts through whom the company chooses its employees. The guides given in this section have gone through the fire of experience. They are suggested, not to cramp your creativity but only to free it. Properly used, they will work for you as they have worked for many others.

• APPLYING EFFECTIVE ENGLISH

Oral Application

As a prospective employer, discuss the sentences below which have been taken from applications. Explain all errors. Discuss the impression you think each sentence in its original form might make upon a prospective employer. Give reasons for your conclusions.

1 — Your companie's vacation policy and it's bonus plan is described in the current issue of business week.
2 — The principle at the school that had an exellent repetation wear I went has promised to reccommend me highly.
3 — My former employers having written me there redy to right me a reccomendation if I left.
4 — While studing public speaking, my instructor said my poise would an aset as a salesman.
5 — I was a clerk-typist with the Lyle Harris Plumbing Company last year I became secretary to the general manager Mr. Oscar L. Nieman.

Written Applications

• **1.** Write a paragraph establishing your point of contact for each of the following advertisements.

1 — Bookkeeper, knowledge of typing, and some business experience essential; state age, experience, and expected salary. M217 *Daily Telegraph.*
2 — Secretary-stenographer, for mail-order firm; two-years' experience; high school graduate; age 19-25; beginning salary $110; give education, experience, references, age. R1907 *Daily Telegraph.*

• **2.** Write an application in response to a help-wanted advertisement in your local newspaper. Clip the advertisement from the newspaper and attach it to your finished draft.

• **3.** Write closing paragraphs requesting interviews for each of the jobs involved in Written Application 1.

• **4.** From your friend Miss Jennifer Klass, an assistant supervisor in the design department of the Alton Manufacturing Company, you have learned that Mr. J. C. Barnes, general manager of the firm, is looking for a competent secretary. As a college graduate with four years of secretarial experience, write an application requesting an interview. Provide details and references as appropriate.

SECTION 2

The Successful Application Team: Data Sheet, Application Message, and Interview

Give convincing facts and impressions about yourself in the data sheet, the application message itself, and the interview.

You are fortunate to live in an age when well-trained, well-educated, and capable people enjoy many opportunities for success. Even before you set forth on a formal career, you will often find useful part-time and summer jobs that will acquaint you with business and the men who make business run.

Remember that the world does not *owe* you a living. You need to discover and develop your abilities so that, by serving other people well, you can fulfill yourself. Your task is to bring employment opportunities and yourself together in the most effective way you can. Your means of carrying out that task are winning and well-selected words that produce rewarding results.

The curious fact is that relatively few applicants ever think *creatively* about employment. "I am constantly staggered," says Walter Hoving, a famous merchandising executive, "by this passive waiting for someone else to do the thinking that they should do for themselves." And Alex F. Osborn, discussing the topic of self-selling, presents forceful suggestions for fact-gathering preparation. Mr. Osborn suggests that you:

1 — Scan the classified section of the telephone directory.
2 — Then go to the library and survey the career books.
3 — Then talk to an experienced friend and seek his seasoned guidance.
4 — *But* do your creative self-sales thinking for yourself.[1]

Good fact-gathering preparation finds its ultimate reward in the form of a convincing and effective data sheet.

---

[1] Alex F. Osborn, *Applied Imagination, Principles and Procedures of Creative Problem-Solving* (2d ed.; New York: Charles Scribner's Sons, 1961), p. 335.

THE PERSONAL DATA SHEET

The personal data sheet tells who you are and what knowledges and skills you have to offer. The application message itself ties directly to the data sheet, shows how what you can do fits what must be done, and requests the interview.

Classified information in quick-reference form. The data sheet is a carefully organized presentation of classified personal details and general information. The use of the data sheet relieves the application message of much routine detail and lifts from it the weight of many cataloged facts. Classified lists and tabulations present details.

You will note the clear distinction between the application message on the one hand and the data sheet on the other. The personal message reflects individuality and personality and aims to present a well-rounded impression of the applicant's background and ability.

On the other hand, the data sheet is the proper place to classify details in tabular form, summarized for quick reference. Employers may file the personal message but keep the data sheet on their desks.

PERSONAL DATA SHEET
OF
[NAME HERE]

1. *General details—personal*

Name	Physical condition
Age	Height and weight
Address and telephone	Single or married

2. *Education*

High school	Major field of study
Business college	Courses taken in major field
Junior college	Courses allied to major field
Institute	Books read on major field and
University	allied subjects
	Special skills

Theoretical training, laboratory training, field training

3. *Experience and practical training*
    Positions held, with dates of tenure and names of employers
    Any special training gained from practice

4. *Special interests, hobbies, sports*

5. *Affiliations, lodges, clubs*

6. *References* (by permission): names, correct addresses

DATA SHEET GUIDE

```
                    PERSONAL DATA SHEET
                           OF
                     JEAN L. BELL
```

Personal Information

```
    Age:          18 (as of April 3, 19--)
    Address:      128 Brown Avenue, Baltimore, Maryland   21224
    Telephone:    662-4721
    Health:       Excellent
    Height:       5'4"
    Weight:       110
```

Education

```
    High School:       Baltimore Technical High School
    Degree Received:   Diploma, upon graduation in June
    Major:             Academic-Business
    Grade Average:     B (upper third of graduating class)
    Business Subjects: Typewriting I, II (speed, 65 words a minute
                          with appropriate production skills)
                       Shorthand I, II (dictation speed, 110 words
                          a minute; transcription speed, 30 words
                          a minute)
                       Business Writing        Office Practice
                       Consumer Economics      Business Machines
                       Bookkeeping I           Retailing
```

Practical Work Experience

```
    Stenographer              Duties:  Handling customer corre-
    Claims Department         spondence, filing and finding
    Prudential Insurance Co.  customer records, keeping records
    Baltimore, Maryland       of claims paid and denied, answering
                              telephone (part-time employment)

    Sales Clerk               Duties:  Selling girls' dresses and
    Junior-Miss Department    accessories, handling merchandise
    Bycks Brothers, Inc.      exchanges, keeping sales records
    Baltimore, Maryland       (summer employment)
```

References (by permission)

```
    Miss Janet G. Meyer                Mr. James K. Fawley
    Business Department                Claims Department
    Baltimore Technical High School    Prudential Insurance Company
    231 West 23rd Street               321 North Wind Road
    Baltimore, Maryland   21211        Baltimore, Maryland   21204
```

AN EFFECTIVE DATA SHEET (A SECOND SHEET)

The data sheet guide. The data sheet guide presented on page 518 reflects the tabular form that makes quick reference easy. You should, of course, adapt these headings to suit your requirements, shaping the data to fit your particular needs, and making omissions or adding new headings where appropriate.

The data sheet shown on page 518 was attached to an application for a position in a stenographic pool of a customer-relations department in a large department store. Note how its tabular plan approximates that shown on page 517.

Company data sheets. Companies hiring employees by the score develop their own data sheets. To each applicant is given a printed information blank to be filled out in detail. When an information blank is supplied, the data sheet becomes unnecessary (see page 520).

EXAMPLES OF CONCRETE, CONVINCING APPLICATIONS

Concreteness is one of the most important of all the requirements that enter into an effective application. Concreteness is based upon facts that make it possible for the prospective employer to see:

1 — What activities you have been engaged in
2 — What your major interests are
3 — What types of work you have a natural aptitude for
4 — Where you have gathered your experience
5 — Some of the individual happenings and accomplishments that give background to your personality

What are some of the convincing *concrete* details that make applications effective? Examine the paragraph in the middle of page 510. Note its concreteness. Now read the following passage:

> For one year I was employed half time as a stenographer by Prudential Insurance Company. During this time, I performed a wide variety of office duties--

Let us interrupt the paragraph for a moment. Note how weak and unconvincing the statement would have been had the applicant stopped at the dash at the end of the last typewritten line above. But she did not stop there. She continued with this sharp detail:

> --These duties included: taking dictation and transcribing for the manager of the claims department, filing and finding customer records, checking specific insurance coverages of claimants, keeping records of claims approved and denied, and taking claim information over the telephone.

HAYMOND AND ASSOCIATES
623 Lexington Road   Baltimore, Maryland 21207

■■■

PLEASE TYPE

Date __May 20, 19--__

Name _____ LaMaster _____ Mary _____ Arnett _____
        Last   *First*   *Middle*

Address __12 Glendale Road   Portland Maine 04106__   Telephone Number __207-351-1737__
          Street and Number   *City*   *State*   *ZIP Code*

Position Desired __Secretary__   Social Security No. __301-43-4569__

How Long Have You Lived at the Above Address? __2 years__   Do You Live with Your Parents? __No__
                                                                                          Yes/No

Date and Place of Birth __June__   __13__ __19--__   __Louisville Kentucky__ Citizen of United States? __Yes__
                         Month   *Day*   *Year*   *City*   *State*   *Yes/No*

Weight __115__   Height __5__ __2__   Right or Left Handed __Right__
        Pounds   *Feet* *Inches*
                                                       No. of Dependents
Single (X)   Married ( )   Widowed ( )   Separated ( )   Divorced ( )   Other than Self _____

EDUCATION

	School Name	Address	Major	From Year	To Year	Grad. Degree
Grammar	Lakeside Elementary	Louisville, Kentucky		19--	19--	Diploma
High School	Blake High School	Louisville, Kentucky	College prep.	19--	19--	Diploma
Business						
Evening						
University or College	Scott Junior College	Portland, Maine	Bus.	19--	19--	Diploma
Other						

PREVIOUS EMPLOYMENT

From Mo. Yr.	To Mo. Yr.	Name and Address of Employer	Position	Salary	Reason for Leaving
June 19--	Aug. 19--	Kerr Sales Co., Waco, Texas	Clerk	$350	Summer
June 19--	Aug. 19--	Allen Mfg. Co., Akron, Ohio	Typist	$425	Summer

PERSONAL REFERENCES *

Name	Address	Occupation
Mr. Robert Keen	Blake High School Louisville, Kentucky	Principal
Mr. J. K. Adams	Scott Junior College Portland, Maine	Business Professor
Mrs. Emily J. Burks	Filing Dept., Kerr Sales Co. Waco, Texas	Secretary

* If you have never been employed, give names of two responsible persons (not relatives) to whom we can refer.

Signature *Mary Arnett LaMaster*

THE FIRST PAGE OF A FOUR-PAGE PRINTED INFORMATION BLANK

This is the first page of a four-page information blank used by a large concern in obtaining information from applicants. The remaining pages ask for (1) details of education and experience, (2) information about physical qualifications, (3) data on past employment.

Unit 13 • Effective Applications

Applications that give only a weak impression almost always lack *concrete facts*. Nothing but generality appears. Concreteness is the success secret. Here are additional examples.

1 — A graduating student answers a magazine advertisement:

> I wish to apply for the position of assistant laboratory technician noted in your advertisement in the February issue of the <u>Electrical World.</u>

A later part of his statement reads:

> Our work consisted of pole setting, stringing of drop wire, poling conduit, pulling in cable, and office survey work. In the last-named project we laid out and designed a cable line and made a drop-wire survey of the city of Phoenix.

2 — A young woman applies for a position in a public library. These details give a definite picture of her background.

> As a library worker, I have been a Jack-of-all-trades. Some of my tasks were mending books, keeping registration records, taking charge of the contingent fund, and acting as reference librarian in the periodical room of the library.

Flashes of human interest. Just as concreteness focuses attention on specific details, rays of human interest light up an application. These may fall in the paragraph on personal qualifications. On page 523 may be found an example of the use of human interest. Sometimes the flash of *one phrase* or *one detail* that takes your prospective employer into some odd little corner of your personality or background is enough to make him remember you and your application out of the large number he has examined.

"My work," writes one applicant, "was interrupted by the war, during which I served as an ensign in the navy." This is a flash of human interest. Others, taken from actual applications, center about items like these:

1 — Exceptional proficiency in a special field—mathematics, copywriting, secretarial skills, etc.
2 — Leadership in any particular activity—social, athletic, musical. [Handle this item with care in order to avoid any appearance of boasting]
3 — Any special apprenticeship
4 — Domestic or foreign travel, in war service or as a civilian
5 — Skill in design, layout, and related techniques
6 — Knowledge of draftsmanship
7 — Musical training or skill with certain instruments
8 — Ability at handling foreign languages

A student who applies for a position with a market-research organization lights up his effort in the following way:

> During my spare time in the last few semesters I have been conducting market investigations for agencies and research concerns. I have made studies of the consumer's breakfast habits, radios, and conditions in the building supply and material trades in Chicago. My thesis led me into a study of eleven hundred different commodities in groceries, pharmaceuticals and confectioneries. I analyzed such areas as package weights and shapes.

On the back of the application containing this paragraph, the employer penciled this note: "Frank, I'd like to meet this young man. *He sounds interesting.*"

Students in large schools often have some unusual occupational experience, the very mention of which compels attention and interest. Most of these young men and women will doubtless apply for work when they have finished their schooling. They will have plenty of material with which to supply flashes of human interest.

PITFALLS TO WATCH

Tone. Tone must strike a balance between two dangers. On the one side is the danger of arrogance, vanity, and self-conceit. On the other is the danger of timidity, diffidence, and self-abasement. Between these dangers you, the applicant, must make your way. You must avoid a cheap display of egotism, self-praise, and ostentation. Yet likewise you must avoid timorousness, overconstraint, and humility. The desirable tone is that of rational and modest confidence in your ability. Study the illustrative cases in this unit for examples of satisfactory tone balance.

The Pronoun *I*. The pronoun I is a good pronoun and more popular among people than any other. You are talking about yourself.

HANDLE WITH CARE!

You are giving information about your training and experience. You are conveying some idea of your personality and your individuality. If your general tone is modest, there is nothing objectionable in using I *when you need to*. To avoid *I* by devious means may make your message seem insincere and artificial.

On the other hand, the unpleasant repetition of *any* word should be avoided. A little attention to the phrasing will disclose ways of keeping the *I's* down to a reasonable number without straining to hide them. As a general rule, try to begin paragraphs with some word other than *I*. The beginnings of paragraphs are conspicuous. The same pronoun may gather unpleasant attention through over-emphasis, if it opens very many paragraphs.

Negatives. Negative suggestions sometimes creep into applications. Guard against them. (1) Do not let your attempt sound like a wholesale broadcast. It should be tailored to fit the specific situation. (2) If you have had no experience, do not mention experience at all. To say, "Although I lack experience in your type of business," or "I regret that I have no business experience," is to put yourself on the defensive. Use the space to tell what your positive qualifications are and leave the rest of the matter for discussion in the interview. (3) Defer a discussion of salary, if possible, until the interview. You will be unwise to write, "Salary is unimportant," "I care nothing about salary," or "I am willing to start at almost any wage." Such a statement may paint an unfair picture of you. It may cause the prospective employer to dismiss you from consideration as unambitious.

Never copy. The greatest mistake you can make is to attempt to express your individuality in the phrases of someone else. To use the phrases, the sentences, the paragraphs, or even the entire work of another is only to masquerade in their costume and to parade in borrowed plumage. You misrepresent yourself and risk your chances.

Let us see how this risk may actually take place. Two applications came to an executive in a firm located in Chicago. The two *were identical from beginning to end*. The first paragraph of each was:

> You probably have been swamped with applications, both personal and written, for positions with your company. Probably each and every one of those applicants thinks he is essential to your success. And probably you are tired of reading applications, but here is mine.

Each application *killed* the other. Moreover, to make matters worse, a tone of negative suggestion ran through the "master model" from which these were copied. The executive, disgusted, dropped both applicants from consideration. "There," he said, "are two applicants who will 'probably' never get positions with this firm!"

The applications just read are illustrations of how certain individuals presented their cases. They are *not* models. *So personal is an application that it must be the individual effort of each writer.*

Employers applaud good applications. A young woman applied for a position in a large public school system. She received this acknowledgment:

> To our regret, your application for a position in the Business Department of our school reached us after the contract for the position had been signed.
>
> We are sorry for the simple reason that yours is one of the best-constructed applications we have received this year. We would have been pleased indeed to study your credentials. Next year, perhaps, you can try us again earlier in the season.

In another instance a student wrote to his teacher: "I found out, after I had secured an excellent position, that the leading reason for my success was the application I wrote. Believe me, I most earnestly value and appreciate all the things you taught me in the courses I had with you."

A PERSONAL NOTE

You live in a world of opportunities. The information in this and in the preceding section can help you make not merely the most but the best of these opportunities.

We enjoy the privilege of advising you. What you do with our advice, however, is up to you. You have our counsel and our good wishes for your success. Use them to create and develop the career of which you are capable. The guides reviewed for you in these two sections have been tested and proved. Put them to good use.

• APPLYING EFFECTIVE ENGLISH

Oral Applications

• **1.** Explain the significance to applications of the term *concreteness*. Discuss the areas in which concrete details can be offered. Why are vague, general statements unsatisfactory in an application? Give examples.

• **2.** What are the principal differences between a letter of application and a data sheet? How do they differ in form? in content? in tone?

• **3.** Evaluate the following unsolicited application. Be prepared to cite specific evidence from the application to support each point you make.

> I suspect that you probably have been swamped with applications, both personal and written, for positions with your company.

I wouldn't be surprised if each and every one of those applicants thinks he is essential to your success. I know you must be tired of reading applications, but I think you will find my qualifications somewhat different from those run-of-the-mill job hunters.

To begin with, I need a position. I am a recent graduate of Bellwood Business College, and I know that I am capable of handling a stenographic position. All I need is the chance to prove it. Surely in view of the predicted increase of business, you are going to need an additional stenographer.

May I hope for your consideration within the next two or three days. I am enclosing a self-addressed, stamped envelope for your reply.

Written Applications

- 1. From your own experience, list some personal human-interest incidents to have available to light up the applications you will write for Written Applications 3 and 5.

- 2. Rewrite the application quoted in Oral Application 3, making it more effective. Assume that you have the preparation necessary and give concrete details.

- 3. You need a part-time position while you attend college. Assume that you have been graduated from high school. Select the kind of work for which you are best qualified and write an unsolicited application to the H. C. Carter Business Supply Company.

- 4. Prepare a data sheet to accompany the unsolicited application you wrote for Written Application 3.

- 5. From your local newspaper, clip three advertisements for positions that interest you. Write an application in answer to one of the advertisements. Prepare a data sheet to accompany it. Paste the three advertisements on a separate sheet, circling the one you have answered, and attach the sheet to your written material.

In composing your reply, direct your attention to these questions:

1 — *What* special knowledge, skill, and experience do I have to offer?
2 — *Who* might be interested in profiting from my abilities?
3 — *Where* are such prospective employers to be found?
4 — *Why* do I want to work for such an employer and *why* should he be interested in my abilities?
5 — *When* is the appropriate time to address the employer?
6 — *How* can I show that *what I can do fits what must be done?*

• REVIEW

Correct all errors in the following sentences.

1 — That companies' vacation policy for executives are excellant.
2 — The paints' shipment was short four ounces of blue pigment painting cannot be started until this pigment arrives.
3 — Their was a conference last night.
4 — The conclusion's of the report agreed on earlier will be reconsidered at this afternoons session.
5 — There is in the proposal three main points.
6 — Except for Loretta and I, everyone went.
7 — The office staff has their own directaries.
8 — 17 students signed vaucher's for food.
9 — Laying on the desk was his schedule and checkbook.
10 — Among the contestants was a secretary and a typist.
11 — Yesterdays storm may effect business adversely.
12 — Each clerk in those departments keep their own record of expences.
13 — Agitated because of his mistake, the financial report was revised by Mr. Cockran.
14 — Mr. Buchanon was lead to a similar conclusion.
15 — They were prejudice against the expansion.
16 — Well designed and elegant, the helpful movers arranged the new lounge furniture for us.
17 — Heather is a girl whom Miss Moore believes will succeed.
18 — The salesmen, as well as the general manager, are here.
19 — Either the director or the assistant managers is attending.
20 — The firm reported its' plans.

Class "Corporation" Project

Corporation project 13-A. You are W. H. Mobberly, the personnel director of Contemporary School Supplies, Inc. Evaluate the application you prepared as Written Application 2 of Section 1. Then invite the applicant for an interview with Mr. Mobberly. Set a date and time for the interview and state that you are enclosing the standard application blank of Contemporary School Supplies, Inc., to be completed and brought to the interview.

Corporation project 13-B. As Mr. Mobberly, assume that the interview was successful. Write to the applicant offering the position at a monthly salary of $500. State that the applicant's duties will begin at 8 a.m. Monday, July 7. Add a cordial note of welcome to the company.

UNIT 14

SALES MESSAGES: MAKE THEM EFFECTIVE THROUGH CREATIVE PLANNING

Are you interested in sports car convertibles, Hawaiian vacations, three-dimensional color TV, or stereo hi-fi FM? The very existence of these and hundreds of other pleasant potential possessions depends on selling.

These goods and services would simply not exist without the function of selling. Unless you have buyers or can be sure that you can find buyers, you cannot afford (1) to make the product or (2) develop and offer the service. Without an assured market of active buyers, the risk is too great.

To manufacture things (a color TV) or to provide planes or ships (for a Hawaiian vacation), capital (money) is required. People who have this money to invest will not risk it in a venture to provide goods and services until they are sure a market exists, a market created through constructive sales skills.

The importance of plan in preparing sales material is the subject of Section 1. Once the plan is clear, the material controlled by your plan fits neatly into place.

Section 2 explains why it is important to focus attention on an outstanding feature. In doing so, you will serve the needs of both unity and emphasis. Sections 3 and 4 show you how to fan your reader's interest into desire to buy. They also show you how to transform that desire into action—the decision to purchase.

Concluding the unit is Section 5 with a presentation of certain appeals—psychological channels through which you trigger the effective buying action you seek.

UNIT 14

Section 1

Plan the Sales Message: A sound basic plan guides you in creating a clear and persuasive presentation.

Section 2

Center Attention on Your Main "Product Feature": Highlight the central feature of your product. This central feature is probably the one of greatest interest to your buyer.

Section 3

Arouse Your Reader's Interest and Desire for the Product: To cause your reader to want to buy, fan his interest and desire through helpful information.

Section 4

Get Favorable Action: Make It Easy to Act: You will heighten your persuasive power if you present your offer in an "easy-action" form.

Section 5

Satisfy the Reader's Wants: Use Powerful Appeals: Trigger favorable action through powerful appeals, carefully selected to fit your precise market.

SECTION 1

Plan the Sales Message

A sound basic plan guides you in creating a clear and persuasive presentation.

With its vast geographical area and its population of more than two hundred million, the United States creates huge demands for manufactured goods and personal services. Rail, truck, and airfreight tonnage mounts daily. This steady industrial expansion depends heavily upon *the power of the written word*. Through this power, marketing management extends major effort to win the favorable buying response of more and more people. The scope of that response is reflected in the size of our GNP (gross national product).

The engine that powers the massive American marketing machine is called selling. The sales process distributes goods and services throughout the fifty states and around the world. An order for a specific product or service sets in motion a series of management activities. Some of these activities are the extension of credit, making adjustments, managing time-payment contracts, and collecting overdue accounts. The engine that sets these management activities in motion is the total sales program, a dynamic process that brings products, services, and the customer finally together.

In its simplest and most basic form, selling is the function of turning people into customers and keeping them as friends. Almost every message that you write for business purposes is in one important sense a selling message. Whether it answers requests and inquiries, whether it adjusts problems and troubles, whether it collects money and extends credit, it strives to turn people into customers and keep them as friends over many future years.

The force that keeps the wheels turning. No matter where you choose to exert it, sales effort is the thrust that pulls behind it a long and productive train of orders for goods and services, remittances of money and payments, profitable inquiries and persuasive replies, and interested requests with swift acknowledgments.

Generated through the selling process, sales volume keeps the industrial and commercial wheels turning. Whether you are selling maps or microscopes, Christmas cards or hundred-ton cranes, door locks or diesel locomotives, the selling function—the process by which *you* help the customer to select—is what creates billions of dollars in the marketing network. This is equally true whether you are selling at retail, at wholesale, or at the manufacturing level.

Let us for a moment trace the process: (1) Purchases make sales. (2) Sales make jobs. (3) Jobs make business. (4) Good business brings good times. (5) Good times assure prosperity. (6) Prosperity makes purchases possible.

You are back at the beginning again. Through this endless chain of cause and effect, you have come full circle.

Master this vital difference. Before we get into the techniques and procedures of sales, let us establish once and for all one vital distinction: There is a *chasm* of difference between (1) attempting to sell someone something on the one hand and (2) causing someone to *want* to buy on the other. The besetting fault of thousands of inferior sales messages is that they try to "force" something upon the reader. In contrast, note that effectively created sales messages cause the reader *to want to buy,* through interest fanned into keen desire.

"Transferring convictions." "Selling, you know, is just transferring convictions from your mind to somebody else's." So states internationally known Paul Hoffman, one of the greatest salesmen ever developed in America. One effective way for transferring sincere convictions from your mind to somebody else's is through a personal message in written form—a sales message. If you managed a small store, you could probably enjoy pleasant, conversational, personal contacts with all your customers. Suppose, however, that your store begins to prosper under your good management, attracts many more customers, becomes far larger and more successful, until you have ten or twenty times as many people coming into your establishment as in the beginning. Much as you might like to do so, you would probably no longer be able to talk to each customer. There would simply be too many.

As the nearest approach to a personal visit, you can turn to the written sales message. If you develop the right skills, you can give your message the winning qualities of naturalness, enthusiasm, logical plan, and courtesy. In such a way you can multiply your personality and your personal contacts, talking not to one customer alone but to a hundred or a thousand. Thus you make use of a "self-multiplier."

Major advantages. A written message has these advantages:

Flexible	—you may make it reach as many people as you wish, and with a message as long or as short as you wish.
Adaptable	—you may use it as a medium for marketing products that cost as little as $5 or as much as $5,000 or more.
Economical	—if properly used, a written message costs only a fraction of the services of a personal salesman. Except for postage it has no traveling expenses and no hotel or motel bills.
Exact Results	—you can check a written message for exact results. Your mailing list shows where each message has gone.
Personal	—you can make your message personal and direct because you are sending it to an individual.

Unifying the qualities. In fusing flexibility, adaptability, economy, precise results, and your own personality into an integrated message that will "pull" effective results, you must depend upon your skill in translating into words your carefully arranged ideas.

When a written message pulls on your reason and emotions and builds up a desire to buy, you may be sure that the words have been chosen and put together expertly into smooth-flowing sentences. You may be sure that the sentences, in turn, have been linked together into smooth-flowing paragraphs. Finally, you may be sure that the paragraphed ideas have been welded together into a full statement of clearness and selling force. Such a statement is what you will be aiming for in solving the situations to be laid before you in these pages.

"MORE SMOKE IN THE STACK"   "MORE HUM IN THE ASSEMBLY LINE"   "MORE MONEY IN THE PAY ENVELOPE"

Is the market there? Let us suppose that you are a member of a Junior Achievement Corporation. A Junior Achievement Corporation is a going business, staffed by high-school students who are interested in business and who, through their corporation, actually make and sell a product (like footstools, small cabinets, ashtrays, and wallets). These students usually have the guidance of mature and experienced business executives who act as counsellors. But these men leave the actual decisions to the boys and girls who manage the business. These boys and girls strive to locate an existing market for what they plan to make. If they make the right products for this market they may gain valuable business experience in addition to making a profit.

As sales manager of your Junior Achievement Corporation, you would learn, along with your fellow-executives, that it takes money (called "capital" in investor-language) to make things like ashtrays, footstools, and TV sets for people who want them, and that it takes money to operate steamships and airlines so that people can take a Caribbean vacation or an around-the-world trip. You would also learn that people who have some money (capital) to invest will not want to risk it in an enterprise to make products or offer services unless they are convinced that there is an existing market for such goods or services. If, in fact, you yourself had a hundred dollars that you might invest in your corporation, you would certainly not want to risk that money to make your chosen products unless you were sure there was a market. You would also want to be sure that you had a reasonable chance not only to get your money back but also to make a profit.

STUDY YOUR PRODUCT AND YOUR MARKET

Before you make your first attempt to draft a sales message, you will find it necessary to get the answers to these eight major questions:

1 — What is your product (or service)?
2 — What is the market for your product?
3 — What is the aim of your message?
4 — How interested is your reader?
5 — Will the results justify writing to him or her?
6 — What is your central selling (buying) point?
7 — What facts will have the strongest appeal?
8 — What message plan will have the most force?

Now let us take this list, step by step, and see how the answer to each question will help us.

1—*Study the product.* Learn what it is made of, how it is made, what its uses are, what its advantages are. (Analyze services similarly).

Dig for facts about your product. How can you find these facts? Suppose we select a miniature camera and a student zipper briefcase as illustrations. What facts can we gather about these articles? We may discover facts about (a) materials, (b) manufacturing methods, (c) construction, (d) method of operation, (e) design and appearance of the finished product, and (f) uses.

MINOX—THE CAMERA THAT NEVER STAYS HOME

Minox, the ultra-miniature camera . . . world's most remarkable ultra-miniature photography system, the MINOX B is the world's smallest, lightest, easiest-to-use precision camera.

People in the know . . . people on the go . . . have more fun using the $3\frac{1}{4}$ oz. Minox. So easy to use. Just drop in film cartridge. Look through the crystal-clear finder. Then SNAP! Thrilling pictures or brilliant color slides of family, friends, or business associates every time. Just $3\frac{7}{8}$ inches short, the Minox tucks away in your pocket or nestles in your belt. Truly a precision masterpiece with built-in exposure meter, f. 3.5 lens, speeds to 1/1000 second, and many, many other big camera features.

When a picture is worth 10,000 words, Minox is the one camera you'll always have with you in pocket or purse ready for instant action . . . the priceless shot! It's a smart way to take notes!

STUDENT ZIPPER BRIEFCASE

3 pockets—split cowhide, $19.95.

Carry a briefcase or envelope. A good-looking, full-sized case. No straps to fuss with. The heavy slide fastener zips smoothly across the top, protects the contents. Special design takes all strain off the slide fastener . . . the new D-type drop style leather handle is attached so that the pull is evenly divided over entire case. Ideal for carrying books, papers, music. Made of full 4-ounce stock, split cowhide leather in baby shark grain. Leather handle. 3 spacious pockets with partitions. Strong leather gussets. Sewing: extra heavy. Size: 16 x 11 inches. Black or dark brown. Initials free.

2—*Study the market for the product (or service).* Who is the person to whom you are about to write? Where does he or she live?

Is he or she an old customer or a new one? Are you answering an inquiry from an already interested prospective buyer?

If the prospective buyer is a man, is he young or old? wealthy, middle class, or poor? married or single? a laborer, mechanic, farmer, professional man, or businessman? of broad, average, or slight education?

If the prospective buyer is a woman, what is her age? ability to buy? station in life—housewife, servant, office or factory worker, club woman, or society leader? We aim the message at the central interests of the man or the woman to whom we are about to write.

3—*Define the exact aim of your message.* Get it in sharp focus. Do you want to persuade your reader to visit your store? To order your article by mail? To try your article for a few days? To take some other definite action?

4—*Determine how interested the reader is.* How much interest has your reader in your product? How much does he know about it? If he has never heard of an ultra-modern "heat-pump" for heating *and* cooling his home the year 'round, you will have to describe it for him in order to develop his interest. If he knows all about a heat-pump and its usefulness in his home, you can assume that he is already interested. You can then go on to list superior features of your particular brand.

5—*Determine whether the results will justify writing to him.*[1] This point must be decided by past records and experience. If a similar statement to a similar prospect under similar conditions has been successful, this one is likely to be also.

6—*Choose the central selling point (buying feature).* The central selling point of the article is the same as the central buying feature. The central buying feature is the one best designed (a) to make the strongest impression and (b) to make the product most wanted by your reader.

7—*Assemble the supporting facts and choose those of strongest appeal to your particular reader.*

8—*Organize your selected facts according to an effective plan.* When you have completed a careful study of the product (or service) and the market, chosen the central selling point, and assembled

---

[1] All of these steps except the fifth may be followed in class work. For the fifth step you may assume a favorable answer.

the supporting facts, you should observe a step-by-step plan in writing the sales message. These are the steps:

THE SALES PROCESS
1 — Center favorable attention on your main "product-feature."
2 — Arouse your reader's interest and desire for the product.
3 — Get favorable action; make it easy for your reader to act.

• APPLYING EFFECTIVE ENGLISH

Oral Applications

• **1.** In a competitive economy, what are the implications and importance of *selling?*

• **2.** Explain the sense in which *every* business message is a sales message.

• **3.** State and discuss the six steps in the cause-and-effect chain of the marketing cycle.

• **4.** What is the vital psychological difference between (1) a message that leads the customer to *want* to buy something and (2) one that merely sells a product.

• **5.** Bring three full-page magazine advertisements to class. Be prepared to explain how the sales message in each is designed to arouse the reader's desire for the product or service.

• **6.** State the eight major questions that must be answered before an effective sales message can be drafted. Explore the significance of each question.

Written Applications

• **1.** List relevant facts that you feel could be used effectively in selling the following products: (1) a high school class ring, (2) an air-conditioner, (3) a portable television set, (4) a dictionary, (5) a ball-point pen, (6) a flashlight, (7) a portable typewriter.

• **2.** List relevant facts that you feel could be used effectively in selling the following services: (1) a special accelerated course in Spanish, (2) a three-minute car wash, (3) a guided tour of Washington, D.C., (4) a bath soap, (5) a correspondence course in speed reading.

SECTION 2

Center Attention on Your Main "Product Feature"

Highlight the central feature of your product. This central feature is probably the one of greatest interest to your buyer.

Human wants are what make people buy. To satisfy their various wants, they buy many different kinds of goods and services. Among the many methods for stimulating human wants are three that deserve more than ordinary attention: (1) the article or the service in actual use; (2) the article or the service presented through personal salesmanship; (3) the article or the service presented through written sales messages. All three methods may be used in various combinations to achieve the outcome you want.

For example, a personally prepared written sales message sent to a single person may so stimulate the interest of that person in the article that he or she will send in an inquiry for further information. Then a personal sales representative may call upon the interested inquirer, present by word of mouth still more facts, and leave the article for two weeks' trial. During that time it is put to actual use. Note that in this example the whole buying process has been triggered by a written sales message.

Structure of the written message. A written sales message is a statement presenting persuasive business information that stimulates a desire to buy. Such a message normally aims to do four things: (1) attract attention (favorable attention); (2) arouse interest; (3) stimulate desire and convince the mind; (4) get action.

Rarely, do you express these four aims with precisely the same emphasis on each one. One aim may dominate. If this is the case, the other aims will be suggested in the background. For example, if you are answering an inquiry about your product or your service, you may properly assume that you have successfully secured attention and aroused interest, and you may launch at once into the process of completing the remaining three steps.

You never "box off" the four structural parts into separate compartments. You do study them separately for your convenience in discussing and illustrating them and in practicing their different approaches. But you will quickly recognize that they flow together, shading into one another sometimes imperceptibly, like rainbow colors. From one part to the next the thought stream flows smoothly ahead until it reaches the fourth and final stage—favorable action.

The case of the airmail stamp. Let us now study a sales message that, in simple straightforward fashion, carries out all four functions in a complete sales appeal. The Superintendent of Postal Service for United Air Lines, an American air carrier, wishes to expand the service of his organization to sales executives. Let us now analyze his message. It appears on page 539.

"Are you looking for a real 'super-salesman'?" (The sales executive reading this line probably answers a resounding "YES," his answering thought perhaps continuing with a comment like "YES—where is he? I've been looking for him and about a dozen like him ever since I became executive vice president in charge of sales!")

"There's one available to you, and he's tops without exception." (Replies the executive, mentally, "Good! If you've got him hidden somewhere, trot him out right now! I can certainly use him and several more like him!") Thus in two opening sentences your attention has been ensnared.

"There are a few things he can't do, but he's willing to try anything," runs the opening sentence of the Interest-Desire sections. "He makes it a point always to get inside offices that often are closed to salesmen. He doesn't put up a fight when you take him to a 'cold beat.' He never grows old and has to be pensioned. He never seems to have those personal problems that make salesmen fall down on the job. You never have to worry about his demanding a large bonus when he completes a big job. He can deliver any sales talk—no matter how complicated—in the least possible time. And he'll bring back those signed contracts without fuss or fanfare." ("This," says the executive to himself, "is the phenomenon I've been looking for. Who is he, and where can I find him?")

"Wages?" concludes the interest-desire section, "He costs only ten pennies the call." ("Ten pennies?" mentally replies the sales executive incredulously, "How can that be?") The answer then comes:

"You guessed it. He's an Airmail stamp. Yet he screams for attention. Always dress him well in a red-, white-, and blue-bordered envelope." ("Hmmm . . ." muses the sales executive, "Come to think of it, that's right . . . I *could* use direct Airmail for those selective campaigns in which I want to sharpshoot for my markets. Perhaps I'd better try that." You have aroused his interest, stimulated his desire to try the Airmail experiment, brought him into a mood to take a concrete action-decision.)

"For your direct-mail campaign, use Airmail. Get in touch with us for further information." (Replies the sales vice president mentally, "That's just what I'm going to do. Miss Farrington," he says, turning to his secretary, "Let's get in touch with United Air Lines, Attention John J. Hart, Superintendent of Postal Service.") Thus does the United Air Lines sales message complete its successful mission: Attention, Interest, Desire, and Action: the four stages flow into one another, but they are still clearly definable in their effect on the mind of the airlines executive.

The case of the auto-typist. Suppose we now look at a second example. The vice president of Auto-Typist Sales & Service Agency, representing a manufacturer of automatic typewriting equipment, sets out to capture the interest of a publishing company executive. On page 539 appears the complete message.

He plunges directly into his subject with a challenging statement: "An Auto-typist produces error-free, individually typewritten messages in volume, economically." (Note the sharply factual points: "error-free," "individually typewritten," "in volume, economically.") Your attention has been captured.

"You can produce, on your premises, with your own help and supervision, messages such as this, Mr. Robinette, all day long, . . ." (Perhaps Mr. Robinette now asks himself, "Yes, but what kind? Sales messages only? Is this a sharply limited service? If so, wouldn't it be too expensive for us?" Almost before he has time to raise the questions, the answer is forthcoming.) ". . . messages such as this, Mr. Robinette, soliciting inquiries, welcoming new customers, reviving inactive accounts, collecting from delinquents, etc. All manner of company communication can be handled efficiently as part of your daily program." ("Well," thinks Mr. Robinette, "this gets to be interesting. I think there may be something here we had better look into. I'd like to have this kind of equipment in the shop.")

". . . you can produce 100, 200, 300, or 400 units, each day, at a labor cost of only five to ten cents each unit, depending on the length and volume required." ("Indeed," thinks Mr. Robinette, desiring to

AUTO-TYPIST

AMERICAN AUTOMATIC TYPEWRITER COMPANY

2323 N. PULASKI ROAD · CHICAGO, ILLINOIS 60639 · (AREA CODE 312) 384-5151

February 20, 19--

Mr. Jerry W. Robinette
E. W. Carr Company
781 Main Avenue
St. Louis, MO 63136

Dear Mr. Robinette

ATTENTION
{ An Auto-Typist automatic message-writer produces error-free, individually typewritten messages in volume, economi-cally.

INTEREST
DESIRE
CONVICTION
{ You can produce, on your premises, with your own help and supervision, messages such as this, Mr. Robinette. All day long, Auto-Typist can solicit inquiries, welcome new customers, revive inactive accounts, collect from delin-quents, and the like. All manner of repetitive company correspondence can be handled efficiently as part of your daily routine.

What is most interesting, however, is that you can produce 100, 200, 300, or 400 messages each day at a labor cost of only five to ten cents each, depending on the length and volume required. You can purchase Auto-Typist equip-ment outright; you can purchase on a time-payment basis over twelve or eighteen months, paying out of savings; or you can lease over a thirty-six months period, on a tax economy leasing program.

ACTION
{ Initial the enclosed carbon copy and return it to me in tonight's mail, Mr. Robinette; I shall send you complete details.

Sincerely yours

John C. Clark

John C. Clark
Vice President, Sales Manager

bd

Enclosure

UNITED AIR LINES

Mailing address: P.O. Box 66141, Chicago, Illinois 60666 Phone: (312) 437-2300

October 28, 19--

Mr. Kenneth Keller
Sales Manager
Baker Heating Company
611 Eridsen Drive
Chicago, IL 60615

Dear Mr. Keller

ATTENTION
{ Are you looking for a real "super-salesman"? There's one available to you, and he's tops without exception.

INTEREST
DESIRE
CONVICTION
{ There are a few things he can't do, but he's willing to try anything--makes it a point always to get inside offices that often are closed to salesmen, doesn't put up a fight when you take him to a "cold beat," never grows old and has to be pensioned, never seems to have those personal problems that make salesmen fall down on the job. You never have to worry about his demanding a large bonus when he completes a big job. He can deliver any sales talk--no matter how complicated--in the least possible time. And he'll bring back those signed con-tracts without fuss or fanfare. Wages? He costs only ten pennies the call.

You guessed it--he's an airmail stamp. He screams for attention. Always dress him well in a red-white-and-blue-bordered envelope.

ACTION
{ For your direct-mail campaign, use airmail.

Get in touch with us for further information.

Sincerely yours

J. J. Hart

J. J. Hart
Superintendent of Postal Service

JJHart:ea

learn more about the equipment and now convinced that it may be well worth installing, "let's find out more.")

"If you would initial the attached carbon copy and return it to me in tonight's mail, Mr. Robinette, I shall send you complete details." (Acting favorably without delay—and note that the action was made extremely easy—Mr. Robinette initials the carbon copy, hands it to his secretary, and another successful sale is generated.

The case of the twenty thousand dollar sale. Suppose we take the final case of a sales message that, singlehandedly, sold twenty thousand dollars worth of books. Note carefully how the four structural steps flow smoothly together in the example on page 541.

Seizing your attention in the first line is a startling concrete fact. The first three short paragraphs place you in the midst of a little drama and whip up your curiosity. Then come two paragraphs of factual material to develop and sustain your interest. These paragraphs then swing around to *you,* showing how you, too, may master the same methods that brought such unexpected success to the general manager. These two paragraphs, and the two that follow, develop desire for the book and convince the mind that it is worthy. Finally come three paragraphs to stimulate and make easy the desired action. Throughout, note how the thought stream flows forward in a steady unbroken current.

The central feature (product or service). Use as your central point of emphasis that feature of the product or service most likely to make the strongest impression upon the prospective buyer (the central "buying point"). That feature is also called the central "selling point." From the buyer's view it is the feature that makes him most want what your company has to offer.

To find the central feature (product or service) you will need to know (1) what the reader wants and (2) what the product or service can give. Then you bring these two points forcefully together. Among the many qualities discovered in studying the product or service, there will be one—possibly a striking feature that sets it off from all others of its type—that makes it particularly desirable to the class of readers you are addressing. This is your central feature. You determine this central point by studying the features of the product or service in relation to the needs and the desires of the reader. You sift the qualities of the product or service (through your market study). Then you draw forth the one central point that most powerfully matches the product or service to the chief need of your buyer.

"TWENTY THOUSAND DOLLARS FROM A SINGLE SHOT? IMPOSSIBLE!" HE EXCLAIMED TO HIMSELF.

Attention

The General Manager was astonished. He hadn't the remotest idea that _he_ could bring in more than $20,000 worth of business through the written word. But there were returns to prove it--order after order from his campaign to win back 1,305 old customers.

Was this result pure luck?

Not exactly! For when the General Manager heard of our unusual publication containing the actual working methods of Dr. Harold Ames, the well-known communications specialist, he was among the first to send for a copy. A few weeks later he wrote us:

"I must say that I never knew there were so many fine points in writing as I found in Mr. Ames' work. Below are the detailed results of my campaign to win back 1,305 old customers.

```
Business received from first unit............$22,267.64
Business received from second unit...........  3,879.67
Total.........................................$26,147.31
Average invoice.....................................$82.74
Average business for each name......................$20.03
Percentage of returns from first unit............17.90%
Percentage from second unit.....................10.70%"
```

Interest

This is the frank statement of the treasurer and general manager (the name is on file in our office). Seldom has there been such a wholehearted endorsement of a publication. Nonetheless interesting, however, is the experience of George Anderson of Cincinnati, Ohio, who, after reading the part dealing with the power of good writing made a $1,200 sale through his own writing! As soon as Empire Builders, Inc., heard of the publication, they bought a copy and later reordered five. Hundreds of concerns are using this book to increase sales, collect slow accounts, and soothe disgruntled customers.

Desire and conviction

Now, the same methods that these concerns have found so valuable are offered to you in Effective Communication in Business, the new 650-page book by Dr. Harold Ames. Here are explained, illustrated, and applied the basic principles of powerful writing, including those that win orders, bring delinquents up to date, build up goodwill and prestige.

This remarkable book shows how to express feelings or ideas in words, how to overcome indifference or opposition, how to make your meaning clear; how to get attention and action, how to organize communications work, how to test writing, how to find and use ideas-- 650 pages on creative business writing. (See the circular enclosed.)

Action

Send no money now. The book is yours on approval for five days' free examination. So send the convenient examination card today--now!

Find the central feature. An electrical equipment maker brings out a new electric fan. It has all the qualities of competing fans: handsome in appearance, attractive in finish, efficient in operation, equipped with several speeds, capable of delivering large quantities of air, silent motor. But it needs no safety guard because its blades are made of harmless rubber. Near this fan small children can play in safety. Buyers are seeking a safe fan. Hence this feature is the central selling point.

Match the reader's wants. You have now brought your electric fan into line with the desire of your reader for a safe fan. You have matched your product to your reader's need. The one point about which everything else turns is the rubber blade.

The class of buyer determines the central selling point. The central selling point shifts as the class of buyer shifts. For example, to the careful mother the central point is the harmless rubber blades of the fan. To the electric-appliance dealer the central point is that the fan sells faster than other competing fans in the same price class. Therefore it will give him more profit through faster sales. To a purchasing agent buying fifty fans for a company with a large office, the central point may be that the fan costs no more than competing fans and needs little adjustment or repair.

Reinforce the central feature. Emphasize one central feature. Then add *concrete facts* that support the central point. See that they are sharp, definite, and detailed. For example, you will probably want to tell the reader, in addition to the central safety feature of the rubber-bladed electric fan, that the new model is streamlined and crinkle-finished in soft shades of brown, green, or ivory; operates for two hours at a cost of one cent; has three speeds from zephyr to whirlwind; delivers by test a quarter more air volume than any earlier model; and has an improved whisper-quiet motor with bearings permanently oiled and sealed.

WINNING FAVORABLE ATTENTION

The skillful writer "swings aboard" the reader's train of thought in opening his sales message. He seizes the reader's attention and centers it upon what he has to say. He does so through the statement of an arresting fact, or through a question, or through an agreeable assertion. Perhaps he makes a statement that puts the reader into an attitude of assent. Perhaps he makes him say, "Yes, I've often thought of that myself," or "No question about that; it's true." Such openings incline the reader to say, several paragraphs later, "Yes, I am certain that I want this article."

SEIZE ATTENTION:
INVOLVE YOUR READER

1 — *Paint an Action Picture:*

A flash . . . a flame . . . a puff of smoke . . . and precious papers gone! [For a unit on safe deposit boxes.]

A snap of the wrist . . . the line sails out over the stream, the reel hums merrily . . . a strike! [For a unit on fishing rods and reels.]

2 — *Flash a "Short-Short" Story:*

Why the Troy Company signed—the other contract!

She gets more attention than a movie star!

How twenty men won a fortune. . . .

3 — *Offer a Miniature Testimonial:*

Remarked one of our owners recently, "Torsion-Aire Ride has given my car and me the most velvety travel I have ever enjoyed. How did you invent it?" May we tell you the story?

4 — *Ask a Question:*

Are you a genius size?

How long does it take you to read a movie title?

Have you a hungry wastebasket?

Could you obtain a blank piece of U.S. bank-note paper? No, because each sheet is guarded.

5 — *Flash a Piece of News:*

This year, over a million quarter-inch drills will be sold—not because people want quarter-inch drills, *but because they want quarter-inch holes.*

A milk so rich it whips like cream. . . .

6 — *Strike a Parallel:*

Everything afloat rises and falls fifty feet every 24 hours in the Bay of Fundy. But the up-and-down cycle of business in Canada and the United States is much slower.

7 — *Supply a Startling Fact:*

The message that lighted two million lamps!

$22,267.64 from a single effort!

8 — *Use an "If" Opening:*

If we should place in your office an electric typewriter and show that it would save you 40% of your daily typing cost. . . .

Dear Friend:

Believe it or not...it took us several years to write this letter.

LOOK BUILDING • 111 TENTH STREET • DES MOINES, IOWA 50304

If I sent you a 'round-the-world ticket for only $3.00 . . .

. . . you would probably think I was crazy!

your name is news . . .

What's wrong with your present car? Why are you thinking of trading it in? Is it because the tires are getting worn out, rattles and squeaks driving you to distraction?

how
10 minutes
changed
the course
of our lives

WHY SETTLE FOR LESS...?

SOME ATTENTION-GETTING DEVICES

9 — *Make a Pleasant and Agreeable Assertion:*
> For a newspaper you readily pay a few pennies. But for this booklet, much more interesting than a newspaper, I believe you will willingly pay several pennies more.
> The life of a bubble is fleeting seconds.

10 — *Use a Quotation:*
> Carried to the seventh degree by the famous old Scottish warrior was the famous quotation, "If at first you don't succeed, . . ."

11 — *Refer to Current Events:*
The President, the members of his Cabinet, the members of the Supreme Court, and the members of the Senate and the House of Representatives are this morning receiving their copies of. . . .

12 — *Use a "Power"-Phrase That Compresses the Point:*
To present you with a $20 bill is the desire of the Scottish woolen weavers (to stress a price reduction.)

13 — *Use a Touch of Human Interest:*
Andrew Carnegie's recipe for a poor man to get rich: Save $1,000 and then begin prudent investing.

14 — *Make Your Reader Hungry:*
Would you like to make mouth-melting pies: lemon chiffon, old-fashioned pumpkin, brandied mincemeat with hard sauce, Southern pecan, deep-dish apple, strawberry angel, chocolate. . . ?

15 — *"Thumb-Nail" a Situation:*
While I was waiting at the Cypress Point Golf Club's famous Sixteenth Hole, where the ball sails 200 yards over the Pacific Ocean, I watched a foursome trying to make this shot.

Things to avoid. Take caution in advance: avoid falling into five common errors. In opening "attention" paragraphs, avoid:

Negative suggestions: "We know that you are beset on all sides by those wanting to sell you things, but we would also like a moment with you."

Irrelevant beginnings: "Armstrong's 25,000 mile-an-hour space flight may be fast but so is our speed in rushing this special offer to you!"

Trite questions: "Have you ever stopped to think . . . ?

Scare openings: "Danger! Act at once!" "Beware!"

Empty generalities: "We want to give you some facts about our service that we think you will want to know."

Pictures and color. Often used in sales work are illustrations and stationery in various tints and colors, such as blue, buff, or pink. In a revealing test two mailings, one on white and the other on tinted paper, were released. Returns from the white were 10.5 percent; those from the tinted, 19.2 percent. To each mailing there was then added an illustration, and another test was run. The illustrated white drew returns of 20 percent; the illustrated tint, 34 percent.

Attention through action. A store display window with something moving in it attracts scores of passersby. The same window without the moving feature may pass unnoticed. One display expert gives this example: "One of our windows had a moving toy train in it. A crowd four deep instantly gathered along the entire twenty-foot window length. Then, as a test, we stopped the train. The crowd almost immediately melted away. We started up the train again—and within moments the crowd was back." Action always arrests attention. If your product (or service) lends itself to the appeal of action, use it.

• APPLYING EFFECTIVE ENGLISH

Oral Applications

• **1.** What methods can be used to stimulate a desire for any product? Explain how such methods can be used in combination.

• **2.** What are the four objectives of a written sales message?

• **3.** Explain the central "buying point" in each of the sample sales messages on pages 539 and 541.

• **4.** What do you anticipate might be the reaction of a potential customer to each of the sales-message openings given on pages 543-545?

• **5.** Explore the possible advantages of pictures, color, and action in sales presentations.

• **6.** Bring to class three full-page magazine advertisements. Be prepared to point out and discuss in each (1) the central "buying point" and (2) effective use of scenes, action pictures, or color.

Written Application

Write an attention-getting opening sentence for sales messages concerning the following products. Use the technique specified.

1 — Elco Carbon Paper (supply a startling fact)
2 — Rainbow Crayons (strike a comparison between black-and-white and colored movies)
3 — Colonial Wheat Flakes Cereal (use a quotation from a professional football player)
4 — An Ernie Banks First Baseman's Mitt (flash a "short-short" story)
5 — Appleman's Pure Honey (ask a question)
6 — A Bentley Carpet Sweeper (paint an action picture)
7 — *Newstate Magazine* (refer to current events)

SECTION 3

Arouse Your Reader's Interest and Desire for the Product

To cause your reader to want to buy, fan his interest and desire through helpful information.

"Originally designed for undercover intelligence work, the amazing Minox camera is a gem of precision engineering by West German craftsmen. It has 302 parts, requires 2,000 painstaking procedures to manufacture and assemble. Some 388 inspection controls are necessary to comply with 1,973 dimensions having mechanical tolerances of 4/10,000 of an inch."

Sentences like these demonstrate how the experts get attention and how they direct that attention to the product (or service) in a dramatic manner.

"Because it is spectacularly small—a mere 37⁄8 inches long—and because it is featherlight—a mere 31⁄4 ounces—the Minox B is always with you in pocket or purse for instant photo action."

Making a forceful impression, the experts have aroused your interest. They have caused you to want to know more. You are now willing to read on. You now believe that the product (or service) has usefulness, specifically for you yourself.

Note how, in the brief quotations you have just read, the vivid detail sharpens your interest. Through the colorful concreteness, the details catch your desire. You visualize in full measure the usefulness of the Minox B. You reach the point where you want it because you recognize your need.

AROUSE INTEREST, STIMULATE DESIRE

On page 549 are illustrations, packed with helpful and informative facts, carefully replying to people who have already shown their attention-interest in your product or service (1) by asking for it, (2) by accepting an invitation to use it on a trial basis, or (3) by visiting your commercial exhibit. In each case these people have demonstrated their interest in hearing more. They have inquired, accepted a trial offer, or have inspected an exhibit. Note how each message carefully presents concrete, explanatory sales *facts*.

Learn to describe. The two important types of description are (1) physical and (2) emotional. Each of these you will have occasion to use often.

Physical description. What is the magical source of the rich musical tone of the Stereo-FM? What is the velvety texture of the decorator drapes? What is the tensile strength of your steel girder, the brute power-output of your compound, double-shaft, heavy-duty tractor, or the cutting rate of your diamond drill? What is the secret of the artistry of the fragile lace, the petal delicacy of the subtle perfume?

What is the length, breadth, height, texture, scent, sound, taste, color, shape, size—all the literal details of the exterior, interior, construction, dimensions, and nature of your article or your service? Physical description presents facts to answer these questions.

Emotional description. Vivid pictures of satisfaction in use call for emotional description, stimulating desire for the product (or service) and action to get it. It powerfully translates the velvety cloth, the rich musical tone, the fragile lace, the subtle perfume, the girder strength, the tractor power, and the diamond-drilling rate into vividly described uses that fill the buyer's wants. Less tangible but no less important are these joys, these satisfactions, these pleasures the buyer may experience.

Let us take a color-television console and picture it first by *physical* methods. There it stands in the corner of your recreation room, a handsome combination color-TV-Stereo-Hi-Fi-AM-FM-Multiplex-Tape Recorder; four-speed; diamond-stylus; sleek mahogany matched cabinet; sliding-door concealed 30-inch super-color screen; dimensions 72 inches by 36 inches by 27 inches in cabinet-console size, with ample interior stereo-record storage space.

But now, by the magic of *use*-interpretation, you translate the very same color-television instrument into a miraculous source of mystery. Suddenly you find you can vault the hemispheres and "see around the earth," view from your own armchair the tossing waves of the Atlantic and Pacific at the same instant on a split screen, see the London World's Fair, Shakespeare's *Twelfth Night* and *The Merry Wives of Windsor* at Stratford-on-Avon, the Prime Minister

BABSON'S REPORTS Inc.   WELLESLEY HILLS, MASS. 02181 • TELEPHONE: 235 • 0900

THE ORIGINAL BABSON SYSTEM • FOUNDED BY ROGER W. BABSON IN 1904

Thank you--

     for accepting our invitation to consider Babson's
Washington Service.

     The Weekly Forecasts promised you will be mailed
each week by first-class mail.

PERCEPTUAL DEVELOPMENT
LABORATORY

6767 SOUTHWEST AVENUE
ST. LOUIS, MISSOURI 63143

Mr. Lawrence Gabriel
Premium Oil Company
5432 Chef Menteur Highway
New Orleans, Louisiana 70126

Dear Mr. Gabriel:

Thank you for visiting our exhibit at the convention and
for your interest in our unique, multi-function projector,
the PerceptoScope, and our accompanying program services.

I am sure you will gain some further ideas regarding the
advantages of the PerceptoScope as a training aid and the
content and quality of our programs from the enclosed
brochure.

EVELYN WOOD READING DYNAMICS INSTITUTE
READING DYNAMICS OF D.C., INC.

1000 Vermont Avenue, N.W., Washington, D.C. 20005 (202) 737-4234

Dear Friend:

Thank you for your letter expressing interest in our rapid
reading process. Perhaps you have already read, seen or
heard one or more challenging accounts in national publications or major radio and TV network programs.

BUILDING EXPRESSED INTEREST INTO FUTURE SALES

addressing the House of Commons, or the President of the United
States addressing the Australian Parliament.

Sec. 3 • Arouse Your Reader's Interest and Desire for the Product

Running together like mercury, materials generating interest and desire, based upon both fact and emotional appeal, reinforce each other. Rarely are they separated into segments. Beginning with useful and informative facts, interest moves on to personal, emotional appeals linked directly to the reader's needs.

Effective use of evidence. The types of evidence most useful to arouse interest, to stimulate desire, to lay the basis for confidence and belief, and to give proof of value that will convince the mind are:

1 — *Facts* and *Figures*
2 — *Explanation of construction:* how the product is built
3 — *Tests* by the maker, laboratory, dealer, consumer
4 — *Samples,* sometimes enclosed
5 — *Trial use:* the customer makes his *own* test
6 — *References,* such as a list of satisfied owners
7 — *Testimonials:* (a) user's testimony as to satisfaction; (b) expert testimony of scientists or authorities. A testimonial, like a guaranty, is a powerful action device because it removes doubt.
8 — *The product in use:* lively and pleasant pictures of the product in use—not merely the air-conditioning unit, but "a living room of cool comfort through summer heat"
9 — *Savings and economies made by purchase:* thrift
10 — *Guaranties*

Give force to your writing through the use of these ten types.

Proof of value. The buyer will be interested in any article—a dictating machine, a calculating machine, a duplicator, a tabulator, a typewriter—if you can supply facts, figures, evidence, and definite proof to show that he can make more money, cut his costs, stop losses, increase his output, simplify his routine, or increase his sales. These centers of interest call for sharp facts. If you present such facts with proof of value, you tap these interest centers and convince his mind.

PROOF OF VALUE:
CARTRIDGE LOADING TAPE RECORDER

Now . . . this revolutionary new 3-in-1 cartridge loading tape recorder. . . . To record, just snap in a blank tape cartridge, switch on the sensitive remote control microphone, and talk . . . or record any other sound you want—speeches, music, phone conversations. All sounds are picked up with amazing precision . . . plays with rich, full fidelity. In seconds you hear your own voice, or any other sound you record, played back so clear and true it's hard to believe it's coming from such a lightweight and such a compact three-pound recorder.

When you record something that you don't want to keep permanently, such as school notes or office dictation, you can use the same tapes over again any time you wish. With just a touch of a button you erase what you recorded before, and you've got a fresh tape to use again and again.

Fast rewind lets you go back to any spot on your tape quickly. If you wish to go back to an earlier part, you just push a button. Your recorder immediately reverses itself and speeds back to the point you want to hear again. Hear what you've just recorded. Make corrections in dictation. Hear a favorite song played again and again, if you wish.

Get a full hour of recording and listening pleasure. Whether you're using your recorder for pleasure listening or making your own tapes, no worry about running out of tape. Each tiny cartridge plays for a full hour for your recording pleasure.

And the accessories at no extra cost! You get the tape cartridge free to play the minute your recorder arrives. Second, you get an earphone for private listening or transcribing notes or dictation. Third, you get a special phonograph, radio, or TV input jack so you can record directly from your phonograph, radio, or TV. Fourth, even the batteries are included! You don't have to buy a thing to start using your recorder. The recorder comes complete with five long-life batteries all ready to pop in to start recording.

JUST A FEW OF THE WAYS YOUR FAMILY WILL USE THIS VERSATILE, LIGHTWEIGHT RECORDER:

Business

Dictation in home, office
Record interviews
Practice speeches
Record verbal agreements
Record meetings

School

Record notes
Record lectures
Dictate term paper
Practice languages
Record debates

Family

Make an album
Fun at parties
Record favorite records
Improve speaking habits
Send voice greetings to
   loved ones

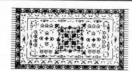

eugene f lacey
oriental rugs and carpets

529 MAIN STREET
ALEXANDRIA, VA 22309
703-251-1673

Dear Mr. Smith:

Just two little pieces of yarn--but what an important
story they tell you.

Pull the ends of the red yarn and notice how the strands
separate and fray easily. Now pull the blue yarn and
notice the difference--it will <u>not</u> fray.

The red yarn was spun by machine. The blue yarn was spun
by hand in far-off Persia.

Genuine oriental rugs are made only with hand-spun yarn.
The wool for this yarn comes from the backs of sheep
that graze most of the year in the warm, sunny pastures
of lands across the sea. It is the extra strength of
this wool and the skill of the hand weaver which enables
the genuine oriental rug to hold its beauty for centuries.

I would like you to see the exceptional oriental rug in
my shop which was hand-woven so firmly that there are
as many as 400 knots to the square inch, compared to 200
knots in the average oriental rug.

I would like to show you some of the genuine orientals
which have journeyed thousands of miles across oceans and
continents to reach my shop from far-off lands. I can
promise you one of the most pleasant half hours you have
ever enjoyed, just "talking rugs" . . . telling you some
of the truly romantic legends behind these rugs and showing you the magnificient pieces which will add charm,
distinction, and character to your home.

Of course, you will not be under the slightest obligation.
Either stop at the store the next time you are downtown
or telephone 251-1673 for an evening appointment.

Sincerely yours,

Eugene F. Lacey

efl:a   Eugene F. Lacey

THIS DRAMATIC "TEST-IT-YOURSELF" MESSAGE DOUBLED SALES

*On the original, the two pieces of yarn—red and blue—were stapled into position
near the top.*

The crisp explanation of usefulness, detail by detail, convinces
the reader that the product is excellent. Proof of value is abundant.

A sales effort is like a short story or a hundred-yard dash. To
win, it must get a fast start and keep up the pace to the final spurt.
"Write a first sentence," says a short-story critic, "that will drop the
reader into the opening of the action and make him read on to find
out what spurs his curiosity."

Unit 14 • Sales Messages: Make Them Effective Through Creative Planning

The following paragraphs choose details of construction, carefully selected to highlight desirable features and to convince the reader with proof of value:

WIDE ANGLE CENTER FOCUS BINOCULARS, 7 x 35

These precision glasses put you right in the middle of the action! Get 3-dimension effects with micro-sharp clarity through precision-ground optics. These extra-wide angle binoculars *stretch* the scene to give you a huge panorama of all the action in your favorite sports. Engineered trim, compact, and light-weight for people on the go . . . yet rugged enough for hard use even by youngsters in the family!

High 7-power magnification puts you right up front so you can see all the finest details. Individual eye adjustment. Clearly calibrated eyepiece collar, so once you set your own individual sights, you can remember what calibration is best for you for the future.

Convenient center-focus adjustment. 35mm objective lenses let in greatest light for brilliance even at night or under dim lighting conditions. Lenses especially coated to end glare and reduce reflection. Center focus extends field of view of normal vision from 525 feet to 1300 yards. With these fine coated lenses featuring *stereo vision,* see a bigger area and twice the action. Included free: four lens caps. Neck strap. Carrying case.

Use vivid facts and dramatic material to add power. Note in the unusual examples illustrated on pages 539 and 552 the extraordinary character of the structural features: attention, interest, desire, action, drama, change of pace, emphasis.

Observe that interest flows imperceptibly into desire. Although the reader may have remained interested in only a mild degree through facts alone, he finds his attitude quite different the moment he discovers that the facts have a special and particular application to himself.

When you fit the product or service to the reader's needs by picturing it in use and by showing the many advantages of its use, you begin to stimulate desire. Without pressure your reader puts himself into the picture once you have (1) aroused his interest, (2) sharpened his desire, (3) convinced his mind, and (4) established his buying mood.

Generate force with sharp detail. Search for vivid, pictorial, concrete words. With a little practice you will find them all about you. Sample some of them: sparkles, glitters, starfire, crystal-flash, petal-fragile, luminous, crash, glow, sledge-hammer blow, menacing, burly, razor-sharp, siren-scream, thug, foundry-tough, soft as down— the number is limitless.

Paint word pictures. You hear often enough: "A picture is worth ten thousand words." Whether this ancient dictum is true depends on the particular circumstances. Pictures of any kind, we know, whether painted by cameras, by watercolor, by brushes and oils, or by words, can be enormously powerful as witness our great magazines that use both pictures and words. Editors of these great magazines know that vivid nouns, colorful verbs, and picture-making adjectives add power to their pages. With a sledge-hammer blow here, a frightful crash there, burly adjectives can transform their printed pages into sheer terror. Or with nimble hint here and a deft touch there, neat words can turn their printed pages into a luminous glow.

Colorful verbs, concrete nouns, and pictorial adjectives surrounding carefully chosen illustrations are the plastic materials out of which professional writers develop powerful sales brochures, booklets, catalogs, and other sales pieces. In the following contrasts, check the paragraphs at the right for their professional approach:

Empty Generality	*Dynamic Vividness*
For high-quality glassware look over these varieties of glass in table sets of your choice.	Crystal of rare design and excellence sparkles here. Formal patterns glitter starlike in rock crystal, decorative Bohemian glass, fragile Venetian ware. Choose from crystal salad sets, cocktail sets, and grapefruit sets—gallant gifts, all of them.
Our carefully made glassware is attractive because it has a combination of light, color, and design.	In the beautiful nothingness of crystal is hidden magic; its secret art is reflection of dancing lights and mysterious colors. There's a deep-etched ware encrusted with coin fold; iridescent crystal of conspicuous loveliness; hand-blown glass with fairylike etching.

Professional writers created the paragraphs at the right. In the first example, Ovington's, a famous gift shop with headquarters in New York and Chicago, captures the delicate tracery, the crystalline sparkle, and the fragile glitter of its wares. In the second example, the Fostoria Company, famous glass manufacturer, generates a sense of beautiful delicacy through chosen words of vividness, power, and point. Consider, also, these contrasts:

Empty Generality	*Dynamic Vividness*
Our new car is a good buy because it has features you want.	New! . . . Under the hood is a revolution in powerplants! A Space-Arrow powered with a Thunder-Streak 490 double overhead cam engine can leave America's costliest luxury car in its dust! . . . combines penny-saving economy with horsepower punch.
Fishing can be a lot of fun.	Suddenly the line runs taut . . . The reel sings merrily . . . the rod bends double . . . A strike! Fifty feet away a flash of silver slices the placid waters, shakes itself vigorously, and darts swiftly for the weedy depths . . . Man! What a whopper!

Note that the "Pro's" put YOU right in the center of the situation, paint pictures all around you, make you the hero. In the second paragraph at the right above, you can *feel* the snap of the rod.

The case of the Wells Fargo Bank: Power through vividness. You have just been appointed manager of the safe-deposit department of the Wells Fargo Bank American Trust Company. One of your first objectives is to increase the number of rentals of safe-deposit boxes in your vault. For this purpose you are planning a direct-mail sales message. Your first step will be to make a simple market study:

The service: Rental of a safe-deposit box for one year for the positive safeguarding of valuable papers
The market: Persons of sufficient means to have papers or valuables important enough to need safeguarding
The medium: A sales message with a descriptive enclosure

The central feature? Perhaps it will be safety, protection against thievery, and freedom from the worry of possible destructive loss. Assemble supporting facts. Decide on a narrative appeal to the emotion of fear and the desire to protect personal property. One of the examples on page 556 may be similar to your work.

SUSPENSE-GRIPPING ATTENTION

And then--

"There was a crash, and the room was plunged into darkness. I turned and fired at a masked figure silhouetted against the open window--"

Now go on with the story in "Security," the folder enclosed. This has probably never happened to you, and we hope it never will. But it did happen to . . . [and so on].

STRIKING APPEAL TO PROTECTION

Passing his fingers over one of the twenty-seven expanding bolts on the seventeen-ton steel door of our new vault, the manager of our safe-deposit department said to me: "You know, this department is really offering the patrons of this bank fire insurance without any premium."

That remark set me thinking. It flashed into my mind that we are doing something even more tnan insurance could ever hope to do--we guarantee to our patrons the return of an article when it is called for, and not merely payment of its assessed value after the article is smoldering in ruins.

Your bonds, your contracts, your insurance policies, your wife's bracelet heirloom, or perhaps the ring great grandmother bequeathed to her great granddaughter, all will be safe in our massive new vault. Safe! No matter if all Atlanta should be swept by a holocaust! For a penny a day you can place your valuables behind heavy concrete reinforcements with thick walls of bent railroad iron and battleship steel.

Before red tongues of flame sear into ashes the precious documents you would not lose, think and--ACT!

Vivid safety (or positive) appeals are usually preferred to vivid fear (or negative) appeals. But when the product or the service is one of protection to human life or property—as in the case of safe-deposit boxes, life and fire insurance, automobile chains, firearms, inspection services, alarm equipment, and the like—appeals to the motives of fear and self-protection are strong and suitable.

"Test-it-yourself!"—a famous technique. Suggest that your reader himself *do something to test your product, to try out your article, to put it through its paces.* Whether you do this in a postscript on your message, or on an enclosed slip or leaflet or folder, you are inviting your reader to "test-it-yourself."

Here are some examples of this effective technique:

1 — "A sample of Sisalkraft is enclosed. Tear this little piece lengthwise. Then tear it crosswise. Note how tough it is. Note how sturdily it resists your pulling and tugging. More than anything we can say, this test demonstrates Sisalkraft's quality and great strength."

2 — A rubber company attaches a small sample of sponge rubber about the size of a nickel to the upper left corner of the message. The opening sentence: "A little piece of ordinary sponge rubber like the sample attached gave our tire engineers their first clue to a revolutionary discovery for adding months to the life of a tire tread." At the bottom is a second sample, a tiny strip of the new tread rubber, which you are invited to detach: "Notice how smooth it feels. Bite it. See how live and springy it is. Take it in both hands and stretch it. Pull hard! Try to break it! It's the toughest!"

3 — The manufacturer of an automobile, noted for its aerodynamic streamlining, urges the reader to carry out this quick test:

> Hold a lighted match behind a flat surface such as a safety match packet. Then blow at it. The flame is sucked toward you. Then use a tumbler, instead of the match packet. Blow again. The air flows around the tumbler without any disturbance and the flame is blown away from you, if not completely extinguished.
>
> This simple test explains the basic aerodynamics behind the new Air-Missile. This car has no flat surfaces and therefore no wind resistance. The air flows around and over it exactly in the manner illustrated in the tumbler test.

4 — Duplan Corporation stockholders received a sample of glass cloth woven by the company, with the following invitation: "Touch a lighted match to this fabric. It will not burn!" The glass-cloth sample was enclosed with a folder telling where and how the cloth is used. Results of the mailing surpassed all expectations. Not only did stockholders try the match test, but they also started telephoning the company before ten o'clock the day the sample was received, asking where the fabric could be bought.

5 — To demonstrate the fire-proof safety of its rock-wood fiber insulation, the maker enclosed a small sample with the same test-it-yourself suggestion: "Strike a match, hold the rock wool in the flame, and try to burn it!"

6 — The NCR Company (originally the National Cash Register Company) does not say what one of its machines will do. They suggest that the prospect press a button and *see* what it will do: "Press this button, Mr. Forbes. See what happens."

Valuable outcomes from "Test-it-yourself." Not less than four valuable results flow from your reader's trial actions and self-tests.

1 – The prospect *does* something that dramatizes the central point.
2 – A mental association is built up on this strong point.
3 – Active interest is stimulated.
4 – The prospect is put into a receptive mood for further action.

Look again at the illustration on page 552. On the original mailing piece, two pieces of yarn—red and blue—were stapled into position at the top.

"Just two little pieces of yarn," runs the opening, "but what an important story they tell you. Pull the ends of the red yarn and notice how the strands separate and fray easily. Now pull the blue yarn and notice the difference—it will *not* fray."

The test-it-yourself action demonstrates first hand the superiority of the hand-spun yarn made in Persia, the yarn out of which are made genuine oriental rugs.

Enclosures motivate the buying decision. Supplementary material such as leaflets, folders, pamphlets, testimonials, samples, an order blank, and a business reply card or envelope may be enclosed with the sales message itself, in various groupings. Such additional material should be clearly identified for action. Examples:

Test the enclosed sample in every way you can think of! Wet it. Fold it. Try to tear it. See how tough and rugged it really is! Turn to page 3 of the enclosed folder and check Diagram A and Table B. Then for further valuable information just slip the enclosed coupon, validated for you alone, into the postpaid envelope now while you are thinking of it.

Investigate this remarkable program at no risk or cost: to get your sample kit, send the enclosed Preview Certificate today! Also enclosed to make it easy is your postpaid Airmail envelope. Use it now!

Testimonials as "reinforcers." Copies of testimonials are sometimes enclosed to reinforce the value of the product (or service). Two types in common use are (1) user's (ordinary) testimony; (2) expert (authoritative) testimony.

The second is preferred because the expert knowledge of the person giving the testimony enables him to be more accurate and more influential.

The procedure of a famous hotel chain demonstrates the force of a testimonial. Each day the hotel management places a fresh transparent envelope around its hotel stationery packet provided for each room desk. On the face of the envelope appears the following suggestion:

When you're writing, please note

Just a few words of praise about us—any kind of praise—can do us more good than hundreds of advertising words of our own. The reason, of course, is simple. You're sincere. You're a good judge of hotels. When you approve of your room, your service, your meals, it has "sock-force!"

Well do we understand your influence on others. Any pleasant or complimentary comments about us that you may pass on to your friends we will appreciate!

Slant your appeal to your prospect. Make every effort to plant your reader squarely in the center of the action. "What is there in this for me?" is the typical reader response. Hence the you-attitude becomes triply important. No buyer willingly spends his money unless he sees a clear advantage accruing to *him*.

Visualize one buyer—a single individual—and focus your message upon him. Select one person out of the group you are addressing and write to him. Forget the others. Convince him. You will then convince the others. Picture one person. Think of him as a living being with human weaknesses, prejudices, likes, motives, and instincts. Then in a perfectly natural manner you will talk to him—in writing. Maintaining the sense of close understanding and of direct person-to-person communication, you can forget the other thousand who may be on your mailing list. In persuading *your* reader to take favorable action, you are influencing all the rest.

The subscriber to a mass magazine is almost never consciously aware that his magazine has millions of other readers. Almost never does he say to himself, consciously, "Imagine this: At the very instant I pick up this magazine, there are probably a million other people doing the same thing." No . . . so far as each individual is concerned, that magazine has a circulation of *one,* and he is the one. In the same way a customer about to purchase an article (or a service) sees only himself. He is interested only in information that penetrates his own *personal* centers of interest. It matters to him not at all that there may be other thousands of buyers acting as he acts. His own act is to him the only act of importance.

When you have a choice **choose simple words.** Time and again, the experts prove how powerful are SIMPLE words! With years of experience behind him as a sales writer, expert Joseph A. Ecclesine, writing in *Printers' Ink,* hammers home the point in an article entitled "Big Words Are for the Birds." The *Reader's Digest,* in a later issue, gave enormous circulation to Mr. Ecclesine's article under the heading, "Words of One Syllable." And that is exactly Mr. Ecclesine's triumph: *In words of one syllable he proves how powerful simple words can be.*

> When you come right down to it, there is no law that says you *have* to use big words when you write or talk.
> There are lots of small words, and good ones, that can be made to say all the things you want to say, quite as well as the big ones. It may take a bit more time to find them at first. But it can be well worth it, for all of us know what they mean. Some small words, more than you might think, are rich with just the right feel, the right taste, as if made to help you say a thing the way it should be said.
> Small words can be crisp, brief, terse—go to the point, like a knife. They have a charm all their own. They dance, twist, turn, sing. Like sparks in the night they light the way for the eyes of those who read. They are the grace notes of prose. You know what they say the way you know a day is bright and fair —at first sight. And you find, as you read, that you like the way they say it. Small words are gay. And they can catch large thoughts and hold them up for all to see, like rare stones in rings of gold, or joy in the eyes of a child. Some make you feel, as well as see: the cold deep dark of night, the hot salt sting of tears.
> Small words move with ease where big words stand still—or, worse, bog down and get in the way of what you want to say. There is not much, in all truth, that small words will not say— and say quite well.[1]

Fit your words to your reader. Adapt your language, your general references, and your words themselves to your reader. *Choose the particular vocabulary that your reader understands.*

Examples: (1) If you were talking to a person who had never been inside the walls of a factory, or who had never been anywhere near an assembly line, of what use would it be to talk of "driving fit,"

---

[1] Reproduced here by permission of Joseph A. Ecclesine, the author; *Printers' Ink* (issue of February 17, 1961); and *Reader's Digest* (Vol. 79, No. 471).

"sliding fit," or "running fit"? (2) If you were talking to a woman who had never in her life gone to a football game and had never bothered to watch one on television, of what use would it be to talk of a smash off left tackle, a double wing-back formation, or an end-around play? (3) If you were talking to a man who had never played a game of golf in his life, who never watched championship golf on television, and who didn't "give a hoot" about golf, of what use would it be to talk of rimming the lip of the cup and sliding past, or of using a wedge to blast out of a sandtrap, or of studying the green in order to read the break?

On the other hand, if in each of these instances you were talking instead to (1) a production engineer, (2) former champion football coach Forrest Evashevski, or (3) professional golfer Bill Casper, you would have an audience who would understand precisely every word you have used.

Coach yourself to watch your word choice. Choose your words to fit the scene. For example, special sports terms will be intelligible only to people who are familiar with those sports. Special trade terms will be intelligible only to members of the trade. Accordingly, scientific terms are suitable in messages to scientists; electronic terms to electronics engineers; chemical terms to chemists; legal terms to lawyers; medical terms to doctors; skiing terms to ski enthusiasts, and so on. Study your reader. Then choose the words that fit. This is the essence of effective communication.

• APPLYING EFFECTIVE ENGLISH

Oral Applications

• 1. Examine the sales message given on pages 550 and 551. What are the physical and emotional factors which help make the message effective?

• 2. What are the possible advantages of each of the ten kinds of evidence frequently used in sales messages? Bring to class two full-page magazine advertisements which illustrate the use of different kinds of evidence. Discuss the advantage that results from the inclusion of such evidence.

• 3. In the magazine advertisements you brought to class for Oral Application 2, indicate any of the following techniques for adding power to a sales message: (1) attention-arousing questions, (2) dramatic statements, (3) sharp details. If other techniques are used, try to identify them.

• 4. In your opinion, what are the main advantages of the "test-it-yourself" approach? Cite examples from your own or your family's experience.

• 5. What kinds of enclosures can be used to increase sales interest? Bring to class any enclosures that have come through the mail to your home in the last few days. How have such enclosures contributed to the effectiveness of the mailing?

Written Applications

• 1. Write a description that combines physical and emotional factors for any three of the following products: (1) typing paper made for easy erasures, (2) a stereo-tape cartridge of the Beatles, (3) a self-winding, calendar wrist watch, (4) an electric coffee pot, (5) a book containing color photographs of Yellowstone National Park.

• 2. Write an attention-getting, concrete, and detailed statement as a substitute for each of the following ineffective generalities. Try to place the reader in the center of the situation.

1 — A Sweep-King Vacuum Cleaner cleans well.
2 — Reach-Master extension ladders are good.
3 — My visit to the White House was nice.
4 — The sound on this stereo recording is pleasant.
5 — This encyclopedia contains lots of information.

SECTION 4

Get Favorable Action: Make it Easy to Act

You will heighten your persuasive power if you present your offer in an "easy-action" form.

FAVORABLE ACTION IS YOUR TARGET

To bring your reader to a favorable decision and to call forth favorable action, you have available three successful methods: (1) Offer your reader certain inducements. (2) Make it easy for him to act. (3) Suggest that he act at once.

Through thousands of trials, each method has been exhaustively tested. Each has been found highly effective in surmounting the two major obstacles to favorable action. These two obstacles, as you probably well know, are:

> 1 — *Procrastination:* "There's no hurry; let's think it over for a while." "I'll wait a little while and give it some thought." "I'm not sure; I think I'll talk it over with Mary." "Maybe I'll order it tomorrow." "I'll put this aside for now and order next week."
>
> 2 — *Reluctance to part with money:* "Wonder if it's worth the price?" "Gee, I think this costs too much!" "Doubt if I can afford it." "Should I dip into my reserve fund for this?" "Maybe I'm being extravagant if I should decide to get this." "Why don't I hang on to my money and wait—they may make a better offer."

As you see, everyone has a tendency to put things off, to defer decisions, to wait a little longer. It takes *energy* to decide things. It takes *willpower* to show initiative. As you can also see, everyone instinctively dislikes to part with money.

The following pages suggest ways to get around these roadblocks.

Offer inducements. Offer your reader certain inducements. These inducements you may offer singly or in various combinations, as shown on page 564.

1 — Your money refunded if not completely satisfied.
2 — You have our unqualified guarantee.
3 — Free trial for ten days on approval: no money down; no obligation.
4 — You need send no money in advance.
5 — Order now. Pay in thirty days.
6 — Pay in ten easy installments.
7 — This offer expires on November 30.
8 — The price goes up 5 percent after January 15: Act now.
9 — Send your order within ten days and earn the special 20 percent discount.

Make it easy to act. To make it as easy as possible for your reader to act is simply common sense. Here are tested methods to make action easy:

1 — Enclose an order blank.
2 — Keep the blank simple.
3 — Plan the blank, if possible, so that the customer can use check marks in spaces. Some companies omit the blank and suggest to the customer, "Don't bother to make out an order blank or to write a note. Just check off the items you want right on this sheet, sign your name, and mail to us." These sentences are placed at the bottom of the sheet. Listed at some convenient point are the items, with a checking space before each one.
4 — Enclose a business reply card or envelope when feasible. (Such units usually carry the printed caption, "Business Reply Mail.") When mailings are sent to home addresses, a certain percentage of the readers will have neither stamps nor envelopes. The business reply card and the business reply envelope, widely used for mailings in which action is important, leave nothing for the reader to do except check, sign, and drop in the mail. Under postal regulations the business concern pays postage on business reply cards and envelopes only if they are returned. Hence cards and envelopes not used cost the concern nothing for postage.
5 — When money is to be sent, state to the exact detail in what form you want it sent [stamps, cash, check, draft, money order]. Examples: "Use the enclosed coin card," or "Fold a dollar bill in this special container; slip the container into the envelope, which needs no postage; and drop it in the mail."

Suggest that your reader act at once. Shown on page 565 are three successful methods of suggesting immediate action. Each of these methods has repeatedly proved its effectiveness.

The American College Dictionary, with the scope of dictionaries selling for as much as $15.00, is yours for only $6.00 — after you've examined it, compared it, USED it Free in your home for 10 days. If after that time you are not convinced that this is the greatest dictionary value you've ever seen, return it and owe nothing. Otherwise, send us just $6.00 plus postage and handling costs at the end of 10 days — that's all.

So mail the enclosed postage-free card back to us now. It will insure a copy for you -- but it must be returned promptly to entitle you to the special price. Won't you sign this special numbered Reservation Certificate today -- and put it with your outgoing mail at once?

SEND PAYMENT, AND... GET THIS HELPFUL BONUS **FREE!**

EFFECTIVE ACTION DEVICES

1 — The definite command: "Mail the card now." "Fill out the order and send it today." "Sign the card and drop it in the mail at once."

2 — The persuasive suggestion: "Why not fill out the order blank now, slip it into the mail, and let us send you a set of these attractive samples?" "Signing the enclosed card is all you need to do to obtain your copy of this valuable reference source."

3 — The brisk action request: This takes a middle position. Examples: "If you'll print your name and address on the enclosed blank, place the blank in the business reply envelope, and drop the envelope in the mail at once, we'll see that your name is stamped in gold on the cover of each one of the twenty-four volumes." "Check the word *yes* on the handy card now and get your pair of Britannica bookends free."

Sec. 4 • Get Favorable Action: Make it Easy to Act

ENCYCLOPÆDIA BRITANNICA

17.68

425 NORTH MICHIGAN AVENUE • CHICAGO, ILLINOIS 60611

January 19, 19--

NOW AS NEVER BEFORE
YOU NEED IT!

We made you the unusual offer, two weeks ago, of a set
of the Encyclopaedia Britannica at a sharp reduction in
price.

> Now--as a final surprise, we enclose a special
> order form which will enable you to buy the
> Britannica, in dark blue cloth binding, <u>on a
> payment basis of only $5 a month</u>, if you wish.

May we now remind you that orders for this greatest knowledge book in the world, under the special sales-price
reduction, <u>must be sent in promptly</u>.

This offer--with its attractive saving to you--is of such
exceptional nature that it is, and must be, only a short-
time privilege. To gain the substantial advantage of this
Short-Time Sale, <u>you must act quickly</u>.

More than 60,000 families own sets of this, the most
brilliantly illustrated harvest of practical information
ever published. Thousands of unsolicited letters tell us
that all users of the new Britannica, whether their ages
be 8 or 80, find it to be an unfailing source of help.

<u>Now as never before you need it</u>! And now, for a brief
period, you may buy it at an extraordinarily low cost.
But you must be quick.

We, therefore, cordially urge you to take advantage of
this inviting offer to send in your order <u>now</u>.

Additional information is enclosed--with an order blank
for your <u>immediate use</u>.

Don't miss this splendid opportunity.

Sincerely yours,

L. E. Seaber

LESeaber/bja   Vice President

Enclosure

---

*A FORCEFUL MAILING ILLUSTRATING THE USE OF
EMPHASIS DEVICES*

Business reply envelopes, cards, and other action devices. Action devices are illustrated on page 565. Note how the details of each reply unit picture the desired action.

Also illustrated on page 566 is an example of a sales message devoted to action. The targets of the enclosures are to offer powerful inducements, to make action extraordinarily easy, and to enhance the probability of a successful sale.

EMPHASIS GETS ACTION

In the order of importance three chief methods of getting emphasis are: (1) logical arrangement, (2) short paragraphs and sentences, (3) mechanical aids.

Logical arrangement. Emphasis by logical arrangement is the most forceful method. Emphasis in (1) sentences, (2) paragraphs, and (3) the whole message has been discussed in preceding sections. To review these pages at this point would not only be wise but would also reinforce your grasp of methods for applying emphasis in every phase of sales writing.

Use relatively short paragraphs and sentences. When professional typographers "let daylight into a job," they mean that a type set-up should not be jammed into a black mass. They want enough white space to be left around the edges of the type and between the lines so that the eye can more easily locate openings at which to begin to read. The experts call such open areas "daylight," or "breathing space."

Break your message into frequent paragraphs for emphasis. The space between paragraphs supplies contrast. Sales writing, for this reason, has frequent paragraphs.

A solid mass of typing forces your reader to hunt for the points. Frequent paragraphing, on the other hand, helps him to see the points because they stand out. Make reading easy with well-judged paragraphs.

Practice using a relatively short sentence. A long sentence strains the reader's attention, is often obscure, and may fail to make its point. Short sentences carry the reader along instead of requiring him to carry them. They move with the kind of life and zest that one expects in material designed to trigger interest.

In the illustrations on pages 552 and 566 note the qualities of (1) sentence vigor, (2) paragraphing, (3) clearness, (4) attractiveness to the eye.

Visual aids. To guide the eye to the point you want to stress visual aids add great emphasis. Available to you are some of these aids:

1 — Capitalization.
2 — Exclamation points.
3 — Dashes and asterisks.
4 — Unexpected blank spaces.
5 — Underlining.
6 — Illustrations in varying positions; or a boldface heading—like the headline of a newspaper or the title of a chapter; sometimes used as an opening or greeting.
7 — A postscript: Emphatic because, like the heading above the first line, it is set off by white space. In sales messages specific points are often featured in postscripts.
8 — Short paragraphs: emphatic by contrast with medium-length paragraphs and long paragraphs. In single-spaced messages with double spacing between paragraphs, the extra white area sets off the short paragraphs.
9 — Short sentences: emphatic because the eye leaps to them and absorbs their content in a flash.
10 — Ample margins.
11 — Extra wide margins for one or more paragraphs or for important material: emphatic because of the contrast with the narrower margins.
12 — A short double-spaced paragraph in the body of a single-spaced message: emphatic by contrast.
13 — Indention, special indention, or extension of first words of a paragraph beyond the regular margin.
14 — The direct parallel: two short columns of contrasted facts, placed side by side. This arrangement offers powerful contrast because each column sets off the other.
15 — Special paragraphing: Breaking a sentence in the middle and showing the break by a dash at the end of the first paragraph and one at the beginning of the second. Double spacing is used between the separated parts of the sentence.
16 — A few words or a check mark in the margin.
17 — Several words or sentences typed in red.

Emphasize—with restraint. A good speaker gets attention by talking in a conversational tone and only now and then raising his voice. He holds attention by emphasizing only those points that deserve emphasis. If he megaphoned everything he had to say in loud and harsh language, he would lose his audience in a hurry because, disgusted, they would leave. Why do we discount nine tenths of what the circus barker shouts at us through *his* megaphone? The answer to this question is not difficult. We discount his megaphoning because, failing to change his pace, he attempts to emphasize everything.

True emphasis comes only from contrast. For example, if the great pyramids of Egypt were dropped among the peaks of the High Sierras or the Colorado Rockies, you would never know they were there. But standing as they do in the vast reaches of the Sahara Desert, they form one of the world's "spectaculars." Similarly, if in a piece of writing you sprinkle a hatful of dashes and exclamation points indiscriminately among your words, and if you pepper your page with capital letters with little rhyme or reason, it might be surmised that you were trying for emphasis. But weak writing can not thus be propped up. Like the pyramids on the Sahara, you would win more emphasis if you call on these devices only at chosen intervals. If saved properly for your climax points, block letters, the underscoring line, and other visual devices retain their maximum power because they supply strong visual contrast.

Direct maximum attention to climax points. Remember that you are the one who will have to do the directing. Why is this so? Because there is only a very low measure of "self-propulsion" in the general public. Hence if you expect to get action, you must ask for it, must make it easy to take, and must urge it.

Summarizing the four-part structure. You have now completed a study of the basic structure of a well-planned sales message:

1 — Attention: directs the reader's thought to the message.

2 — Interest: crisp facts and informative details arouse interest in the offer and show that it is worthy.

3 — Desire: persuasive material and effective appeals show how the offer fills a particular need.

4 — Action: suitable inducements and convenient aids (checklist order blanks, business reply cards and envelopes) invite a favorable decision.

• APPLYING EFFECTIVE ENGLISH

Oral Applications

• **1.** What methods do you feel are most helpful in bringing the reader of a sales message to a favorable decision about the product?

• **2.** Discuss the techniques a company can use to make it easy for a potential customer to make a purchase. What sales strategy lies behind such techniques?

• **3.** What can be done in a sales message to encourage a potential customer to act promptly? Why is prompt action so desirable?

• **4.** Examine various ways of determining the effectiveness of a mailing.

• **5.** What is the relationship between contrast and emphasis? Explore the possible dangers of excessive emphasis.

• **6.** Bring to class two full-page magazine advertisements which illustrate the following sales-message techniques: (1) visual aids (identify these aids and point out their functions), (2) suggestions that the reader act promptly, (3) devices to simplify action for the potential customer, and (4) offers used as inducements.

Written Applications

• **1.** Try to improve the effectiveness of the following sales message. Emphasize each point by expressing it in a separate sentence, and group related sentences into short paragraphs.

> Imagine the shrieks of delight as your youngsters coast down hill or push one another gaily in their roller-bearing Glideway Wagons (wagons built to stand up for years under tough use; built to resist bumps, spills, and the collisions that inevitably occur when kids are giving their wagons really hard use; painstakingly undercoated to provide life-long protection against rust; and painted with the same durable enamels used on modern automobiles), and remember that Glideway Wagons, which come in small, medium, and large sizes (and have removable sides for use in hauling heavy loads of groceries or in carrying very small children) cost only pennies more than ordinary kinds.

• **2.** Write a 150-word explanation of the sales techniques (such as offers, order blanks, action suggestions, effective emphasis, visual aids, and careful structure) used in one of the advertisements you selected in connection with Oral Application 6.

SECTION 5

Satisfy the Reader's Wants: Use Powerful Appeals

Trigger favorable action through powerful appeals, carefully selected to fit your precise market.

People always want things. This is one of the basic facts of human nature. The things that people want are products (or services) that fill certain definite needs. *Buying drives* and *sales appeals* are two special terms with which you will now need to become familiar.

Buying drives are a set of feelings or inclinations within the buyer's mind that press him toward the purchase of what you are offering.

Sales appeals are the triggers that set off the buying drive. The appeals themselves are not the direct cause of the action. They are the *activators* that, when brought into play, trigger the buying drives.

You will review in the following pages some of the basic psychological appeals (triggers, activators) available to you for sales efforts directed to markets that you have carefully defined.

HELP PEOPLE TO GET WHAT THEY WANT

A market is not a geographical area of ten square miles, a hundred square miles, or a thousand square miles. It is instead a community of active human beings with certain needs and a certain amount of money with which to satisfy them. The more you learn about the drives that cause your personal friends to act as they do, the more ably you will write and the better you will help them to fulfill their wants.

Find out how buyers act today when they buy, if you want to learn something about how buyers are going to act tomorrow. People are driven by certain motives, called psychological drives, that cause them (by habit or instinct) to do the things they do and to want the things they want. Therefore first identify the wants with which you are dealing. Then you can select the appeals that will most powerfully energize the wants.

HOW DO YOU SLAY A DRAGON????

Why, hire an expert dragon slayer . . . of course.
Whenever there's an important job to be done, there's
no point in paying good money for anything less than
expert service.

Dear Friend:

When one of the outstanding publishing organizations in the world, in collaboration
with the University of Chicago, develops a single literary effort . . . at a cost of
two million dollars . . .

. . . it becomes a venture which should be brought to the attention of every man and
woman who enjoys creative thinking and fine writing.

HEADED FOR A WARMER CLIMATE ???

That's not necessary if what you're looking for
is more warmth to your printed message.

FITTING POWERFUL APPEALS TO HUMAN WANTS

Choose your appeals accurately by studying your market. To
choose the appeal that will energize the want into an outright purchase,
study (1) the offer you make and (2) the reader to whom you make it.
Study the offer in order to determine what it can do for your reader,
how it will benefit him, and what want it will satisfy. Study the reader
in order to determine how he can use what you offer, why he needs
it, and what desires are present that it will satisfy. By this process you
bring the offer and the need together. Then you fit one into the other.
If the circumstances are favorable, what you have written may energize
the want into a purchase.

Consider some illustrations:

(1) If we are to sell Foremost Dairy ice cream, we know by experience and past buying behavior that it will satisfy a certain craving
for a cold delicacy. As for the buyer we know that his normal hunger
want will impel him to act.

(2) If we are to sell the Sears Steel-Belted Radial automobile tire,
we know by field tests on thousands of roads that it will save a car
from serious blowouts. As for the reader, we know that he earnestly
wants safety of life and limb whether he goes out for a short pleasure
drive or a long cross-country motor trip.

(3) If we are to sell the Flex-Air, rubber-blade fan, we know it will circulate fresh air with the minimum risk of harming the fingers of an inquisitive child. As for the reader we know that, aside from his desire to keep cool, he also wants a fan that is safe to have around.

The right appeal. The choice of the appeal varies with what you have found in your study of the product and the buyer. The choice is also guided by (1) how much the buyer already knows about the

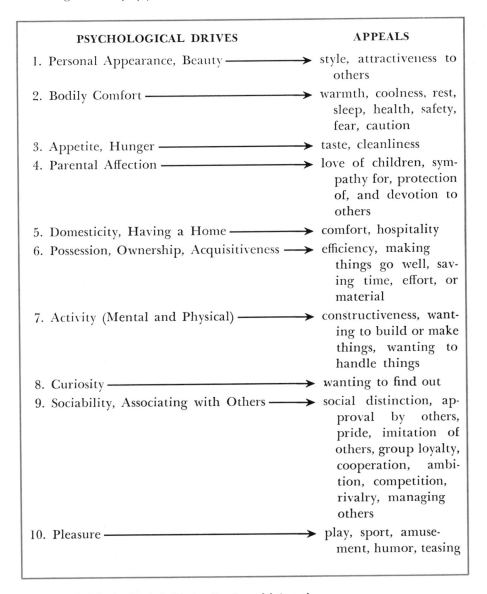

PSYCHOLOGICAL DRIVES	APPEALS
1. Personal Appearance, Beauty	style, attractiveness to others
2. Bodily Comfort	warmth, coolness, rest, sleep, health, safety, fear, caution
3. Appetite, Hunger	taste, cleanliness
4. Parental Affection	love of children, sympathy for, protection of, and devotion to others
5. Domesticity, Having a Home	comfort, hospitality
6. Possession, Ownership, Acquisitiveness	efficiency, making things go well, saving time, effort, or material
7. Activity (Mental and Physical)	constructiveness, wanting to build or make things, wanting to handle things
8. Curiosity	wanting to find out
9. Sociability, Associating with Others	social distinction, approval by others, pride, imitation of others, group loyalty, cooperation, ambition, competition, rivalry, managing others
10. Pleasure	play, sport, amusement, humor, teasing

product; (2) what season of the year it is, what holiday or special event may be near; (3) what class of buyers may be involved—whether housewives, high school students, or stamp collectors, for example; and (4) what appeals are in use by your competitors.

Powerful appeals. Powerful appeals stimulate desire, increase the force of the message, and get action. Considering the human mind as a whole unit in the way it reacts to a given appeal, one may correctly say that the sales writer learns how to touch off the "psychological trigger" that impels a customer to buy.

On page 573 are listed some of the powerful motives for human action. The motives have been brought together into related groups to make them easier to study. Each motive is an energizer that, when used under the proper circumstances, impels the prospective customer to buy. To these drives powerful appeals may be directed.

Test the appeals. Let us test this list of appeals. Suppose we develop them by applying them to *yourself* and to *your* own daily routine. Read the paragraphs on page 575, line by line. How many apply to you? How many apply to your fellow students?

How many appeals can you identify? Consider a typical mailing sent by a local dealer to a prime list of customers. Let us see how the mailing is built around some of the action triggers listed on page 576.

NAME THE ACTION TRIGGERS

Attention

> Incredible? Perhaps the things we say below may seem so. But we have hundreds of testimonials from satisfied users to prove that the Stream-Kleen Automatic Dishwasher makes handling dishes practically a pleasure!

Interest and desire

> Three times a day, if you wish it, the Stream-Kleen spotlessly cleans your dishes, glasses, silverware, even the pots and pans. It's all simple, effortless--you simply fill the basket and press the button! The Automatic Stream-Kleen does the rest, completes all cycles, stops itself.
>
> Enameled in soft, charming shades of blue, green, gray, ivory, lavender, or brown, as well as in the popular white, and with an added special choice, if you wish, of stainless steel door, your Stream-Kleen Automatic keeps its lifetime beauty.

Action

> See this remarkable new Automatic. We'll demonstrate, with pleasure, its handling ease, its fully automatic operation, its amazing economy. And you'll win a factory discount of ten percent from the regular price if you select one of the models within the next fourteen days.

About three times a day you are hungry. You enjoy the taste of delicious things, but you must have confidence that they are clean. You instinctively prefer living in cleanliness to living in dirt.

You are cautious in traffic and in avoiding disease and infection, for the sake of safety and health and because of fear. You complain with everyone else about the heat and the humidity, or about zero weather and slush. You dislike frostbite as much as you do severe sunburn. And about the same time each night you yawn with sleepiness.

You like to have people think you good looking, and you would rather be in style than out of it.

Among the precious things in life to you are your mother, father, brother, and sister; and if the last-named are little, you take part of the responsibility in shielding them from harm. If you are normal, you feel sorry for others when they are in trouble, and you try to help them.

You like to have your home a place where friends may come and have a good time.

You like to have things of your own—each one of us has his pet likes and possessions—and yet you like to save up a surplus for the future.

You want people to invite you to social events in which you would be glad to stand out as a center of attraction, approved by all. If such distinction seems not immediately possible, you tend to imitate someone who holds the focus of attention, whether you consciously do so or not. You are without doubt loyal to your school; well mannered in public and, it is hoped, in private; ambitious to hold a class office or a managership or a chairmanship. If you have the instinct of leadership, you unquestionably have the trait of ambition. You back your athletic team against all comers, triumph with it in victory, and support it in defeat.

You want to do things and to be in things. From class activity, political, social, forensic, or athletic, you get pleasure, sport, or amusement, as the case may be.

For the "fun of it" you do many things not in the school calendar. You may have a special skill in editing a school publication, in designing or building scenery for a class play, or in making models of objects. Doubtless you enjoy driving a car, a motor boat, or possibly an airplane.

Finally, there will never come a time when you will not instinctively want to follow the flashing fire trucks, sirens screaming, as they rocket by in a thundering roar.

In the order in which they appear, some of the major action triggers (appeals) are pleasure, curiosity, manipulation, cleanliness, health, bodily comfort, relaxation and rest, enjoyable activity, efficiency and convenience, home comfort, saving of time and effort, domesticity, beauty and attractiveness, social distinction, hospitality, durability (economy), ownership and acquisitiveness, efficiency, and thrift.

Requests present sales avenues. A potential customer requests a Sears' catalog. The general manager, Mr. J. C. Grable, expertly uses the opportunity to trigger interest through selective appeals, as shown in the illustration at the left on page 577.

Again, in the order in which they appear, some of the major action triggers (appeals) are possession, ownership, efficiency, saving time, saving effort, convenience, and guaranteed satisfaction.

People enjoy curiosity. R. E. Smallwood, vice president of *Sales Management,* the marketing magazine, opens his message, illustrated at the right on page 577, with an appeal to curiosity—wanting to find out—followed by appeals to efficiency, intellectual progress, making things go smoothly, and constructiveness.

Adjust tone to the situation. Adjust your words to suit your reading audience. Upon the way you select your words depends the *tone* of your writing. Scientific terms to scientists take a tone of dignified seriousness. Messages to scholars and professional men strike an informative tone. Messages to women may be characterized by a tone of femininity or sprightliness. Sporting terms to sportsmen may appropriately take a tone of jauntiness or buoyancy. Let your words arouse acceptable images, suggest desirable situations, and spur constructive motives.

Consider the difference in the following examples. The first, from the Detroit Diesel Engine Division of General Motors Corporation, is *"economic and performance efficiency"* through and through. Note how the message below and on page 576 hammers on saving time, effort, and material for greater management efficiency:

> The first time you try a Detroit Diesel engine, it may take a bit of "getting used to." So our new customers tell us.
>
> You'll discover smoother operation. Anything else? Yes: Faster response. Improved performance. Better fuel economy. And you'll discover a lot of other advantages that are also worth getting used to. Like rugged, lightweight construction.

Sears

SEARS, ROEBUCK AND CO.

February 8, 19--

Mr. William Guffy
623 Banff Lane
Los Angeles, CA 90049

Dear Mr. Guffy:

Thank you so much for requesting a copy of Sears new Spring and
Summer General Catalog. We are happy to send it and hope that
it reaches you promptly.

This new book--the most complete storehouse of values to be found
in America--features over 100,000 items, representing the best in
product development. Over half the merchandise offered was either
developed or significantly improved during the past decade.

When you order from your new Sears Catalog, please remember: The
easiest way to shop is by phone. It will save you time, and will
speed the delivery of your order. Simply refer to the Index Section for the telephone number to call.

In many locations you can shop by phone any hour of the day or
night . . any day of the week! Telephone salesgirls are always
on duty, waiting to take your Sears Catalog order.

Whether you shop by phone, by mail, or in person . . . it's an
added convenience to be able to say "Charge it!" The enclosed
folder and application explain how simple it is to have a Charge
Account at Sears. You may also open an account over the phone.

Please be sure to check your new Sears Spring and Summer Catalog
first before you buy anything . . anywhere. Your complete
satisfaction is guaranteed. The Sears folks will look forward
to serving you soon.

Sincerely yours,

J. C. Grable

J. C. Grable
General Manager
Los Angeles Catalog Order

Jm

Enclosure

thank you, for shopping at Sears

Sales Management
THE MARKETING MAGAZINE

630 THIRD AVENUE • NEW YORK, N.Y. 10017

YUkon 6-4800

August 7, 19--

Mr. David C. Parker, Editor
Comstock Publishing Company
981 Madison Avenue
Baltimore, MD 21201

Dear Mr. Parker:

I once saw a letter that sold a yacht. It was four paragraphs long!

I saw another letter which sold 3,500 $1 subscriptions.
It was three pages long!

And there you have communication--one authority will tell
you never to write a two-page effort. Another will counsel you to tell the whole story, regardless of length.

But they both agree on one thing: It's ideas that make
sales messages click. An idea that sold a mailing house
service was used by Du Pont to sell Cellophane! And this
idea first appeared in the "Sales Letter Round Table."

We don't tell you what you already know . . : how to write
your sales program. But we do keep you continually supplied with ideas.

That is why I present the enclosed invoice with confidence.
I am sure you will want another twelve months' helping of
"Round Table" ideas.

Sincerely,

P. C. Smallwood

P. C. Smallwood
Vice President

RESmallwood:rc

Enclosure

Detroit Diesels are built to last longer. They have fewer parts. So there's less to go wrong, less to maintain. And when worn parts do need replacing, Detroit Diesels are faster and easier to repair. They spend less time in the shop. You spend less for parts, maintenance, and overhauls.

Why not take the trouble to find out about our engine? It's worth getting used to. Just write Detroit Diesel Engine Division, General Motors, Detroit, Michigan 48228. "We'll "fill you in!"

In contrast, consider a second example of far different appeal:

Commander Riley Services Limited

17 BLENHEIM ROAD, LONDON, N.W.8

Telephone: MAIda Vale 8726

DIRECTORS: P. W. C. RILEY, O.B.E., V.R.D.,   M. M. F RILEY (U.S.A.)

9 January, 19--

Mrs. Robert R. Aurner
Post Office Box 3434
Carmel, California 93921
U.S.A.

Dear Mrs. Aurner

    Once again we are writing from midwinter London to remind you of the pleasures of touring in Britain in the Spring.

    It is some time since we have heard from you, and we want to assure you that the Riley Services are still here, ready to plan a delightful and personal holiday in the British Isles for you and your friends.

    We are sending you one of our brochures in the hope that it will tempt you to return. In the meantime, all good wishes from us for 19--.

        Yours sincerely

        Peter Riley

        Commander Riley Services Limited

USE OF PERSONAL APPEAL TO TRIGGER ACTION

No Diesel Engine efficiency this time! Commander Riley makes his low-pressure appeal to pleasure in the form of a delightful and personal holiday of play or perhaps sport and amusement in the British Isles.

Small shifts may have powerful outcomes. Changes and shifts so small as to be beyond the detection of the inexperienced sometimes change a mailing from an average performance into a major success. We can draw a parallel: An original painting by the master painter Whistler differs from an inferior copy only in the minutest shifts in color, only in the minutest differences in brush strokes. But Whistler's painting continues the priceless masterpiece. So it is that experts recognize what moves machines and men. They have learned how to make the adjustments needed to assure fresh power and multiplied persuasiveness in every program of writing.

Completing sales communication through feedback. Feedback is the evidence of your having informed or persuaded, proof that your message has been received. You need to know whether your recipient has associated your message with his own interests, expectations, requirements, and concerns.

In a sense all communications are much like radar. "They work on the echo principle. When no echo comes back from the communications effect, then perhaps the echo is not really impinging on anyone . . . effort must be made to encourage, record, and evaluate echoes." [1]

"When you . . . write . . . is anybody listening?" [2] is the intriguing question appearing on a cover of *Fortune*. When you send a carefully prepared piece of mail to a selected individual, you hope that he will not only listen to you but that he will do so in a receptive mood. You hope he will understand and interpret correctly what is being said. Finally you hope he will remember, apply, and act on what he has heard.

Five major advantages of mail as a sales channel. Among major advantages of the United States mail as a sales instrument are these: (1) Selectivity. You pick the people you want your message to reach. (2) Timing. You can choose when your message will be received.

---

[1] Bela Gold, "Office Radar," *Advanced Management—Office Executive*, Vol. 1, No. 12 (December, 1962), p. 14.

[2] "Is Anybody Listening?" *Fortune*, Vol. XLII (September, 1950), pp. 77-79. See also Wesley Wiksell, *Do They Understand You?* (New York: The Macmillan Company, 1960), p. 86.

(3) Flexibility. You can control the size, the shape, and the format of the mailing. (4) Cost effectiveness. If you can think in terms of influence upon the person the message reaches, mail is the least expensive medium. (5) Action. Mail is the only medium in which the selling message may be shaped to contain the elements making it easy for the prospect to take action.

Summary. Will your reader comprehend the exact nature of your message? Will he be inclined to act favorably now? If not, will he retain the kind of information that may lead him to act favorably in the future? To bring about a favorable decision now, or to supply information that will eventually lead to such a decision, is your basic aim.

As long as a growing number of products and services compete for shares of the market, and as long as we are a part of a free, competitive system, the people responsible for guiding and creating sales efforts will be able to earn rich rewards. The purpose of this unit has been to help you to learn how to share in those rewards.

• *APPLYING EFFECTIVE ENGLISH*

Oral Applications

• **1.** Identify the appeals shown in the sales messages reproduced on page 572.

• **2.** What appeals would you recommend to trigger favorable action for the following products or services?

    1 — A stereo 8-track tape player for use in an automobile
    2 — A life-insurance policy
    3 — A gourmet steak sauce
    4 — A catering service
    5 — Automobile seat belts
    6 — An electric blanket
    7 — A set of golf clubs
    8 — An automobile tire
    9 — A savings account
    10 — A charity drive for the local Children's Hospital
    11 — A correspondence course in effective communication

• **3.** Discuss the appeals that you feel would be most likely to trigger favorable action on the part of teenagers, college students, young married couples, your parents, and your grandparents.

Written Applications

● 1. Guided by the examples given on pages 572-573, make a list of the basic needs and appealing offers that are suggested by the following products:

    1 — The Speedwrite Portable Typewriter
    2 — The Groom Master Electric Shaver
    3 — The Gentel-Air Clothes Dryer
    4 — The Order-Guide Appointment Calendar
    5 — The Executive Attache Case

● 2. Select an effective advertisement that makes an offer of some kind. Write a 150-word statement explaining how the advertiser's offer is carefully fitted to the consumer's need and is designed to convert the underlying want (or desire) into a purchase. Submit a copy of the advertisement along with your statement.

● 3. The tone of the following sales message is negative, and the message is monotonous and dull. Revise the message, injecting a pleasing, enthusiastic tone by the use of words that arouse pleasant images or suggest desirable situations. Try to prepare a truly effective sales message.

> Shine-O Cleanser will remove dirt from utensils. Shine-O Cleanser does a good job. Shine-O Cleanser works fast. If you are dissatisfied with your present cleanser, why not drop us a line. If you take the little bit of trouble to do this and thus show us that you want to give Shine-O Cleanser a fair trial, we'll send you a small sample free of charge, and we'll pay the postage!

● 4. Work out a preliminary statement of the basic need in connection with each of the following products. Then make a list of some effective appeals that could be used to sell each product. Finally, write a 100-word sales message for two of the products.

    1 — The Arctic Explorer Sleeping Bag
    2 — Williamson's Sky-King Sun Glasses
    3 — The Memson Kitchen Clock
    4 — *Merriam-Webster's New Collegiate Dictionary*, Seventh Edition
    5 — The Splash-Pal Plastic Beach Ball

• *REVIEW*

Correct all the errors in the following sentences taken from sales messages.

1 — High in capacity and low in weight, you will be delighted and astonished by Fiber-Tough Luggage.

2 — Swiming is more fun with Water-Boy Fins you will be amazed at how fast you can swim when you are wearing Water-Boy Fins.

3 — The Beckwith Travel Service provides guides in every city of the United States that is thoroughly familiar with thier areas.

4 — Similiar in construction to a kyack, you will be delighted with are stable new sixteen-foot Wave-Breaker boat.

5 — Scientific experiments with Sunray Toothpowder at Eastern University has prooved that Sunray helps privent tooth decay.

6 — Sure-Coat Wax providing a durable, long-lasting protective coat which will increase the beaty of any car finish and making it easy to keep your cars' clean.

7 — Tough-tred linoleum will stand up for years under constant hard use its' finish will remain bright and never require hard scrubing.

8 — When using the Paulford Rangemaster Golf Ball, extra distances are noticed by golfers on coarses all over the United States.

9 — Max-Hold Trucks will carry there load effortlessly up the steepest hill over the roughest roads through sand mud or snow.

Class "Corporation" Project

Corporation project 14-A. As Mr. Jerome Nason, sales promotion manager of Contemporary School Supplies, Inc., plan a sales message for Contemporary's Wide-View Fluorescent Lighting Fixtures, which are designed for use in modern classrooms. This message will be sent to superintendents and principals in all parts of the country.

1 — Write out (a) the underlying need schools have for modern lighting and (b) the sales points most likely to convert that need into a purchase of Wide-View Fluorescent Fixtures.

2 — List two or three possible inducements that might enhance the appeal of your merchandise.

3 — Review the four-point structure of a well-planned sales message (page 569) and outline your sales message.

Corporation project 14-B. Write the sales message for Contemporary's Wide-View Fluorescent Light Fixtures—the message you planned in Corporation Project 14-A.

UNIT 15

EFFECTIVE ADJUSTMENTS: HOW TO SMOOTH OUT TROUBLE

No business wants trouble. Management makes arrangements that avoid trouble if possible; but, if trouble occurs in spite of all precautions, management tries to deal with it promptly and effectively.

To do so, management sets up systems designed to prevent trouble from arising in the first place and to take care of it systematically when it does.

Unit 15 discusses systems and procedures that fall under the general heading of adjustment.

A certain amount of trouble is inevitable, as Section 1 points out. To smooth trouble, you must emphasize the positive factors in the problem.

Reviewing the four chief types of adjustment, Section 2 guides you in using the proper methods for finding out precisely where the fault lies, and in getting the right answer to the central question: "Who made the error?" It then points out how to take prompt steps to correct the trouble.

UNIT 15

Section 1

Effective Adjustments: The Positive Tone: To smooth out trouble, search for the positive factors in your problem. Use the customer approach. See through his eyes.

Section 2

Effective Adjustments: The Four Chief Types: Find out precisely where the fault lies. Take prompt steps to correct it or to help others to do so.

SECTION 1

Effective Adjustments: The Positive Tone

To smooth out trouble, search for the positive factors in your problem. Use the customer approach. See through his eyes.

"How to get along with people at a distance." If you have developed skill in handling the English language, you really have also developed skill in getting along with other people. Let us see why this is true: In adjusting to other people, either nearby or at a distance, you make most of your adjustments through the oral or written word.

This and the following section discuss how to get along with people at a distance. You will presently be examining adjustment examples directed both to the business student and also to the student who is preparing for a career not necessarily in business itself, but perhaps in a life associated with or affected by our industrial environment. These adjustment examples will illustrate the powerful principles of the written word and its usefulness in getting along with and adapting to others.

Are you perfect? If you are perfect, you are certainly the exception. A certain quota of trouble is simply a part of the process of living. No person can be certain of always being right. Organizations are never precision machines. They are collections of human beings subject to human weaknesses. Recognizing these typical human frailties, Alexander Pope more than two centuries ago created the immortal line, "To err is human, to forgive, divine."

Blunders are unpredictable. No matter how superbly managed a firm may be, sooner or later it will make some errors. What kinds of errors? It may incorrectly compute some invoices. It may, through misunderstanding, cancel some orders. Some imperfect products may slip through the assembly line at the factory. An assistant misplacing some papers may cause serious and disruptive shipping delays. Some addresses may be radically wrong.

At one time or another all these blunders have actually happened in almost every business. But the company itself is by no means the only source of mistakes! Sometimes the customer himself is to blame. Let's take the simplest kind of illustration. The customer sends you an order for an article that you offer in twelve sizes and six colors. He fails to specify either size or color. (Customers constantly commit just this fault.) You write, politely requesting the additional information. He reads your note too hurriedly and answers only half your request. Now you have to write your second request asking for the other half. When you finally get all necessary information, the whole procedure adds up to four wasteful exchanges. Customer carelessness was the villain.

Oversight, carelessness, and neglect. Size, color, and catalog number are not the only items that customers forget. As long as we have people around, as long as human nature is as human nature is, we shall have human oversight. Probably no one knows this fact better than executives of mail-order houses, men who can predict, almost to the decimal, how many incoming orders out of every hundred will be missing some essential fact or item, such as the typical message that opens with the words, "Enclosed are several samples. . . ." But the enclosures aren't there.

The burden of blunders is rather well distributed over companies, customers, transportation agents (airlines, railways, buses, trucks), and others. Blunders are simply a common problem. It is the responsibility of everyone to hold them down, to reduce them, if possible to eliminate them and, when necessary, to correct them.

Trouble's best antidote: prompt courtesy. Yet experienced adjusters, highly skilled in the art of smoothing out trouble, know that if complaints are handled fairly, promptly, and cheerfully, they can become rich sources of goodwill. "When there's trouble around," wrote famed John T. McCutcheon, "politeness is the word's greatest trouble-smoother. Try courtesy. You'll find it is positively 'catching'." In a similar vein another keen observer writes, "A smile is a *curve* that can set lots of things *straight!*"

REQUESTING AN ADJUSTMENT

An effective request for adjustment calls for three qualities: clearness, careful details, and courtesy. When trouble happens to you, it may loom larger than it really is. You may be tempted to fall into worry, even annoyance over the matter. Yet if you wish to make fully effective your request for the correction, you must hold rigidly in check your worry and annoyance.

Let us now suppose that you are the customer doing the asking. McAlpin's, a local store, has sent you a bill that doesn't belong to you. It's the store's mistake and you want it corrected. How should you set up your request? Here is one version:

Subject and request for adjustment	The enclosed monthly statement, sent to me by mistake, is returned to you with the request that this charge be removed from my credit account.
Explanatory detail	If you will carefully note the name on the invoice, you will see that the purchaser was Mrs. J. E. Robinson--not Jerry W. Robinson. While Mrs. J. E. Robinson's street address and mine are the same, she lives in Apartment 32. I, on the other hand, live in Apartment 4.
Courteous suggestion for prompt action	I'm glad to be able to help you correct this error promptly.

The plan here is simple, clear, direct, and comprehensive:

1 — Subject first, with a request for the adjustment in the same sentence
2 — Explanatory detail giving the reason for making the request
3 — Courteous suggestion for prompt action

When you ask someone to make an adjustment, you will, as a general rule, find it most effective to search for the main subject ("What is it I want them to do?") and put it first. Here is an example:

The enclosed monthly statement, sent to me by mistake, is returned to you with the request that this charge be removed from my credit account.

Everybody now knows what you want: "Remove this charge from my credit account." The subject is up front where your reader will see it instantly. Now that you have asked for what you want, you can give the reason why, in the form of the explanation that comes later. To place the subject first and the explanation later is called the *analytical order*.

Occasionally, however, if the situation is out of the ordinary, or if the trouble is somewhat serious, you may wish to turn to the *chronological order*. In the chronological order you "set the stage" by giving your explanation first.

SPECIAL SITUATION: CHRONOLOGICAL ORDER

Pleasant, positive opening

> Our new Norman Rockwell Album, Regular Edition, has just arrived. It is from every point of view a beautiful piece of editing and printing, on which we congratulate you all.

Explanatory detail

> But we've got trouble. By some unfortunate mischance, perhaps during the binding process, a splattering of tiny black ink dots appears irregularly sprinkled on portions of the front cloth hard-cover, marring its appearance. Several light smudges appear likewise on the back cover. We realize that this kind of thing can happen and can sometimes escape the eye of inspectors, no matter how carefully they perform their duties. As your records will show, the Album is already paid for in full by Check 3994, dated December 22, 19--, for $14.50.

Direct request for adjustment

> Please send a replacement copy in perfect condition, and let us know to what address you wish the damaged copy returned. We are sure you would want us to have a perfect copy to place on our library table for others to admire.

In this instance the plan is also simple, clear, direct, and comprehensive:

> 1 — Positive opening with some type of pleasant reference to the main subject
> 2 — Explanatory detail giving the reason for making the request
> 3 — Direct request for the adjustment with a courteous suggestion for prompt action

Expect the best. Be confident. Be positive. Be courteous. Your approach goes like this: You've got trouble on your hands. You know it. But you are confident and positive that it is going to be corrected with the help of your reader, once he hears about it. The positive tone suggests that your reader is fair and honest. It emphasizes the remedy for the trouble and specifies, in courteous words, the correction that is about to set things straight. You work constructively toward a confident solution.

Setting things right. To take care of things that have gone askew and to set them right is the sole purpose of an adjustment department. An adjustment correspondent may at times meet outright dishonesty, sometimes stupidity, often carelessness and ignorance. Indeed his patience may be drawn to the breaking point. But, as a professional in his specialty, he forces himself to remember that his company is in business to keep its customers, not to antagonize them, and that he is paid to take these troubles and handle them in the proper manner. He has one great slogan, one tested guide ever before him. It takes the form of one sentence seven words long: *Settle the trouble and keep the customer.*

Note how this seven-word guide has been constructively applied in the following paragraph closing a skillful adjustment:

```
        I am sorry that our handling of your trial subscription
has given you a wrong impression of the NATIONAL SPACE
RESEARCH COMPANY.  Of course I deeply appreciate your frank-
ness in writing us and giving us this opportunity to explain
the situation to you.  We certainly want to create goodwill
rather than lose it, and we earnestly hope that we may be
able to count you as one of our friends.
```

The friendship approach. The psychology of adjustments is, in fact, the use of the friendship approach. Adjustments can run a full scale of approaches from the positive, cordial, and constructive at the top, to the curt, blunt, and blundering at the bottom. "In building up a business," writes the chief executive of a famous company, "we have much less to fear from outside competition than from inside inefficiency, blunders, and clumsy communication. These are the dangerous dragons to watch out for!" Especially is this fact true of mailings granting or refusing adjustments. A *good* adjuster is an individual acquainted with human motives. He possesses an even temper. He knows the power of constructive psychological appeals and is able to use them in such a way as to bring about a satisfactory cooperative result. A customer cannot be kept unless he feels that he has been well treated. A part of the successful adjustment approach is to make the customer feel so. The adjustment department deals with men and women who may be disappointed, disgruntled, and irritated over real or fancied wrongs. Accusation, discontent, suspicion—these are the attitudes that the adjuster must often face. He meets negative attitudes with powerful positive offsets. This procedure is, indeed, his professional obligation.

"We're the *adjustment* department—*NOT* the complaint department!" The right approach to adjustment should also be used in naming the department that handles the trouble. Years ago it was the custom to call it the "complaint department." But *complaint* is an ugly, negative, snarling word, bristling with irritation and resentment. When this fact was discovered, companies looked around for a word that more truly represented the function of the department. Today we deal more frequently with "adjustment departments." The change is worthwhile. The term *complaint* suggests only the trouble (negative). The term *adjustment* suggests the settling of the trouble (positive). Correcting the problem is the objective.

Granting an adjustment. When you grant an adjustment, arrange your material in the following manner:

1 — Be prompt, courteous.
2 — Grant the request at once.
3 — Give any necessary explanation showing why you grant the request.
4 — Close with a cordial invitation for future business.

Refusing an adjustment. When you refuse an adjustment, arrange your material in the following manner:

1 — Be prompt; if possible, affirm the customer's mood.
2 — Explain the circumstances surrounding the claim.
3 — Give your decision.
4 — Close with a cordial invitation for future business.

Whether you grant the adjustment or decline to make it, note that each plan closes with a cordial invitation for future business. This is an important action to take. It may mean the difference between losing the customer or keeping him in your company circle.

What happens sometimes is this: you make the adjustment— apparently to the satisfaction of your customer. You forget the episode . . . and your customer vanishes into thin air, never to return. Because of faulty tone, or an insufficient explanation of how the trouble occurred, your adjustment (at first apparently successful) has failed. Your former customer now belongs to someone else.

Let's go back to Mr. Jerry W. Robinson and his trouble with McAlpin's, the store that sent him the wrong bill. How did the store reply?

Prompt courtesy	Thank you, Mr. Robinson . . . for so promptly returning the monthly statement that, through the mix-up in initials, went to you in error.
Immediate granting of request	The charge has been removed from your credit account, and we now have everything straightened out.
Cordial invitation for future business	We like all the Robinsons on our list, and we hope you'll soon come in again.

Then, in turn, suppose we go back to the situation involving the smudged copy of the new Norman Rockwell Album. The customer, you will recall, has already laid fifteen dollars on the line for what has turned out to be a damaged book. He is doubtless confident that he will get his replacement, but you, as the company adjuster, will want to be particularly careful to see that he does. How do you reply? You capitalize on every indication your customer has given you that he is happy with the Norman Rockwell Album. And you act with swift promptness. This version proves highly successful:

Courteous opening	Thank you very much for your note of January 24 in which you explained how much you enjoyed receiving the Norman Rockwell Album.
Request granted at once	We are delighted to send you at once a replacement copy, and we're going to take special pains to see that your new copy is in perfect condition.
Explanatory material	We're sorry the first one, with its smudges, escaped the eagle eyes of our inspectors, but they'll see that your new one is A-OK! Enclosed is a return address label for your convenience in returning the damaged copy.
Invitation for future business	By all means show your new copy to your friends-- maybe several of them will want their own!

Positives versus negatives. When you are feeling rather negative yourself, you may be tempted to think, "What's all this about positive and negative? If you make an adjustment, it's made, isn't it? The customer ought to take it and like it. Isn't that about all there is to it?" The answer is simply "No." In order to illustrate just how much more there is to it, let the next few pages demonstrate several instructive contrasts.

Small shift: big differences. Suppose we start with a simple situation and see what a small shift can do.

I

We are disappointed to learn that some of your stereo records in our Sing-Along Album are defective. The replacements are on the way but in the meantime will you please destroy the imperfect records?

Thank you for your comments. Your payment has been credited.

II

Courteous opening action	Thank you for your favorable comments on our Sing-Along Album, Stereo Edition. Your payment has been promptly credited--with our appreciation.
Adjustment granted at once	Two perfect stereo replacements are on the way to you right now to take the place of the two records you found defective.
Explanatory material	Meanwhile we'll really be grateful if you'll destroy the imperfect records to get them out of the way.
Cordial close	It is a privilege to serve you. Enjoy happy stereophonic music!

Which is the better version? It will not take you long to decide. If you were the "Director of Presentations"—or the communications supervisor—of this company, and you were to analyze these two examples, you would rate the power index of Number II much higher. Even Number I, however, does possess a basic courtesy that makes it superior in effectiveness to perhaps nine out of ten mill-run adjustments at this moment traveling the mails.

If you are going to grant the request, do it WILLINGLY; don't be a grudge! One of the great unsolved mysteries is why an otherwise efficient management will allow an occasional adjustment to slip through, literally bristling with a chip-on-the-shoulder "you-ought-to-know-better-than-to-impose-on-us-like-this" grudge. Even if the adjustment were generous, even if it were to refund double the money, if it is made with a grudge it is worse in its effect than an outright refusal.

If you make an adjustment, make it cheerfully. This is the inviolable rule. When management goes to the expense of granting an adjustment, it is an inexcusable waste of opportunity not to gain from the adjustment every atom of goodwill. If, therefore, the business is going to concede, it should take pains to make a cheerful concession. As has been well said, "You cannot sweeten a cup of coffee into which you have first poured vinegar." Here, then is the prize way *not* to adjust: " (1) We are right; (2) you are wrong; (3) we will, however, grant your claim." If you were to follow this plan (and some firms still do), you would utterly destroy your effort.

I

CHIP-ON-THE-SHOULDER

Frankly, we don't believe your claim of August 3 is justified at all. We are very much surprised at this claim, regarding our very best line of waders. We have sold thousands to hunters all over the country and have hardly ever had any trouble like this reported.

Your customer ought to know that any wader of this type has a thin top and should be strapped.

Since your customer seems much disturbed, we have in this instance, however, decided to grant your claim, although we still think it is unfair to us to ask us to do so.

Don't you think customers ought to be able to read plain directions? We are enclosing another folder. Please see that the customer reads this through. Get the facts into his head somehow.

II

CHEERFUL

As a mark of our appreciation for your care in handling the trouble you wrote us about on August 3 and as an aid to you in giving satisfaction to your customer, we are happy to honor your claim in full.

A new pair of waders is being sent you at once. Please help to ensure the customer's future satisfaction by telling him that this pair will give the finest service if it is strapped snugly according to the directions enclosed.

You can assure your customer that he can be proud of this boot . . . . (continue here with descriptive material.)

Look for the points of agreement. When you have to decline a request for adjustment—and there will always be times when this is necessary—your first move should be to search out all the possible points of agreement. You get in step with your customer. To get in step with him means to bring to the fore those points on which you

```
┌─────────────────────────────────────────────────────────────┐
│                                                               │
│    Dear Subscriber:                                           │
│                                                               │
│    Your inquiry and request regarding your subscription to    │
│    The Executive will have our prompt attention.              │
│                                                               │
│    It will take a few days to complete the investigation and  │
│    make the proper adjustment, which you may be sure will be  │
│    promptly followed up as you have requested.                │
│                                                               │
│    Thank you for writing.                                     │
│                                                               │
│                               Sincerely yours,                │
│                                                               │
│                               THE EXECUTIVE                   │
│                               Subscription Department         │
│                                                               │
│                                                               │
└─────────────────────────────────────────────────────────────┘
```

GRANTING AN ADJUSTMENT REQUEST WITH A
COURTEOUS POSTCARD ACKNOWLEDGMENT

Note the cordial tone, and the effective suggestion of prompt action.

and he are agreed. Emphasize agreement at the beginning and you go far toward removing resentment at the same time that you put the reader into a receptive mood.

Get in step. To get in step with another person calls for a thorough knowledge of the problem he has put before you and some familiarity with human nature. You will find helpful one or more of the following specific approaches:

> 1 — Thank your customer for calling attention to the need for adjustment.
> 2 — If the trouble is serious, express emphatic regret.
> 3 — Take a sympathetic attitude.
> 4 — If you can grant *part* of the request, do so at once.

Whether the request must be declined wholly or may be granted in part will determine your choice of one or more of these approaches. Affirming your customer's mood at the beginning is wise because it is simply good diplomacy, no matter what you must do with the claim. You establish friendly relations before you give your explanation and your decision: "We certainly agree with you that your Airfreight order, Number 1019, should have arrived long before this. We're vigorously tracing it now and as soon as we have the facts, we'll call you."

Note carefully, however, that to affirm your customer's mood, to get in step with him, does not necessarily mean to grant the request. It merely helps to swing into stride with him and to win his cooperation. You demonstrate that his interests will be guarded; that the decision will be fair; that you are with him, not against him.

SWING INTO STEP WITH HIM

"Gunpowder" words and phrases can blow you up! Anytime a controversial discussion gets under way—and begins to heat up—there are certain taunts that are almost certain to make matters worse. If it is a domestic squabble, you are likely to hear some such expression as "It's not my fault if she takes after your side of the family!" If it is a business situation, you are likely to hear such irritating expressions as "you claim," "you state," "we cannot understand," and similar dangerous word combinations. If you plan to become an adjuster, you must rigidly avoid all the harsh words and phrases that carry unhappy, even vicious, associations. Here are a few of them:

1 — Your complaint. An irritable, cantankerous, and generally disagreeable atmosphere surrounds this word.

2 — You state, you say, you claim, you assert. Such expressions are dangerous because they suggest disbelief. Use, instead, *you report, which were reported.* When criticism hovers in the air, it is well to avoid the pronoun *you* because it tends to fasten an accusation upon the reader.

Accusing, Dangerous	*Impersonal, Safe*
You failed to enclose the sample.	The sample, which was not enclosed, . . .
You are wrong in saying that.	There is a misunderstanding.
You never heard us make such a statement.	We were in error not to have made the matter clearer.
You neglected to give the size.	As size was not mentioned.

3 — We cannot understand. We are utterly at a loss. These discourteous expressions imply ignorant carelessness on the part of the customer. They are often mistakenly used in situations involving customer errors. The expressions also suggest incompetence on the part of the business itself. Contrast:

Helpless, Tactless	*Alert, Courteous*
We are at a loss to know what has become of your order.	We are sending a duplicate shipment of your order.
We cannot understand why you failed to include the sizes.	Just as soon as you let us know what sizes you wish, . . .

4 — Never happen again. Too broad a promise. The error is bound to happen again sometime. But it must not happen too frequently. A successful business is one that holds the goodwill of customers and, through careful supervision of its activities, permits only the fewest possible mistakes. "We shall be careful to guard against this mistake," is a safer assurance.

5 — If this is not satisfactory; or *we hope* (or *trust*) *this will be satisfactory.* Such expressions suggest that the management itself is uncertain whether its adjustment has been correct. If the management is uncertain, the reader most certainly will be. The closing sentence should clinch the action taken. "Because we prize our business associations with you, we are glad to make this adjustment" is a positive and clinching close.

Summary. To win the favorable response and to hold the favorable regard of more customers, adjustment executives are alert to deal with every kind of trouble with the utmost speed, tact, and courtesy. They know how delicate and perishable customer goodwill can be. Such goodwill, staunch when it flourishes on satisfactory products, services, and company policies, can be destroyed in an instant if adjustment procedure is faulty.

Whatever the causes of an adjustment request, the remedies are usually found in customer-centered courtesy, the lubricant that cools the world's friction points. Recognizing how delicate and perishable goodwill can be, the skillful adjuster employs empathy while acknowledging his role as company spokesman. He realizes that adjustment requests are a form of feedback that his company should recognize and profitably use.

• *APPLYING EFFECTIVE ENGLISH*

Oral Applications

• **1.** What advantages does the name "adjustment department" have over the name "complaint department"? How can these advantages be carried over into adjustment (rather than *complaint*) procedures?

• **2.** Discuss the tone of each sentence in the following refusal to grant an adjustment:

> The check you say you sent us on June 7, 19--, has never reached us, although three weeks have elapsed since that date. Your complaint about not receiving a second Tone-Master Transistor Radio is hard for us to understand, inasmuch as we still have never received payment for the first one. We cannot understand what could have happened to your check. After all, we have only your word that you sent it. When your payment arrives (and *if* it arrives!) it will be a pleasure for us to send the merchandise and wash our hands of this unpleasant and time-consuming correspondence.
>
> We trust that you will agree that we are being completely fair about this problem. After all, we can't very well be expected to send out our merchandise as gifts.

• **3.** Discuss the tone of each sentence in the following **example** granting an adjustment.

> We have received a complaint from you in which you claim that the switch on your Sure-Spot Flashlight was defective. We note that three weeks elapsed between the time you bought the flashlight and the time you wrote us about the "defective switch." As soon as you return the so-called "defective" flashlight, however, we shall mail you a replacement.

Written Applications

• **1.** Rewrite the adjustment example given in connection with Oral Application 3. Eliminate the "chip-on-the-shoulder" tone. Incorporate, instead, a positive, smiling tone.

• **2.** Rewrite the discourteous example of the refusal message given in Oral Application 2. Decline to send a second Tone-Master Transistor Radio until payment has been received for the first, but do so in a courteous, friendly way that will lead the customer to want to do business with your firm in the future.

SECTION 2

Effective Adjustments: The Four Chief Types

*Find out precisely where the fault lies. Take prompt
steps to correct it or to help others to do so.*

Utopia isn't here yet. You've heard of Utopia. That is the glass-
perfect world in which everyone does everything in precisely the right
way at the right time and in the right place.

What would it be like if we all lived in Utopia? First of all,
companies would so perfect their management procedures that they
would never make mistakes. Customers, too, would never make mistakes. Airlines, railways, truck lines, steamship companies, and all
other baggage and freight carriers would make no mistakes. Professional adjusters would have to look for other jobs. Adjustment
departments, like a puff of smoke, would vanish into an historical
yesterday. We would all be living in a glass-perfect world. The
millennium, indeed, would be here.

Someday Utopia may arrive. But it isn't here yet. And it won't
be in your lifetime, or in many lifetimes thereafter. No glass-perfect
world is in sight. And it would be painfully unrealistic to expect it.
The stream of human error will continue to flow. The struggle
against human mistakes will go on and on. To smooth out trouble,
to recapture endangered goodwill, and to maintain cordial business
relationships will continue to be the prime responsibility of trained
professional adjusters.

"WHERE DOES THE FAULT LIE?"—THE FOUR ADJUSTMENT APPROACHES

The first question you will face in handling an adjustment will
probably be this: "Whose fault is it?" "Who's responsible?" When
you get the right answer to that question, you will know what you
must do. Clearly you must find out where the trouble comes from
before you can apply the right solution.

"Where does the trouble come from?" Adjustments fall into four classic patterns based upon who is at fault. To handle these four patterns, you call upon the tested plans outlined in the following pages. Let us examine more fully each of the classic patterns listed below:

1 — When the company is at fault
2 — When a third party is at fault
3 — When the fault is divided between the company and the customer
4 — When the customer is at fault

When the company is at fault. In this situation, grant the adjustment instantly and completely. Use this plan:

---

1 — Grant the request promptly.
2 — Give any needed explanation.
3 — Close by cordially inviting future business.
4 — Recheck the adjustment for (a) completeness, (b) positive tone, (c) retention of goodwill.

Example I: On pages 589, 591, and 592 review the series of adjustments exchanges falling in Class I, the company at fault. These exchanges present excellent illustrations of effective Class I adjustments.

Example II: Following an audit of its accounts, a firm finds an error in one of the invoices sent it by another company from which it has made a series of purchases. Here is their adjustment request:

> Please send us a credit memorandum for $45 to adjust a discrepancy in your invoices covering our purchase orders No. A-1287 and No. A-1391.
>
> On order No. A-1391 you charge us $74.75 for each item, less 20 percent. On order No. A-1287 you charge us $75 for each item, with no discount.
>
> It appears that this slip-up is due to an oversight of both your billing department and our invoice department. We'll appreciate the correction.

This request tells clearly (a) what the customer wants and (b) what the trouble is that gives rise to the request. The precise detail aids in getting the correction.

Dear Subscriber:

Have you ever felt happy and sorry at the same time?

That's the feeling we have right now. We are happy to have your order (it is being processed now), but we are sorry we cannot start your subscription immediately.

Response to our "New Subscriber" offer has been so much greater than ever before that the stock of current issues has been exhausted. But, rest assured your copies will start at the earliest possible date and you will receive the full term of the subscription.

Thanks again for your order, and especially for your patience.

J. L. Marshall
for ESQUIRE

INTERNATIONAL MOVEMENT FOR ATLANTIC UNION

North American Headquarters:

1736 COLUMBIA RD., N.W., WASHINGTON, D. C. 20009

By clerical error, a number of bad copies of our leaflet, "A Rising Tide," were included with invitations to join our Advisory Council which we mailed a few days ago. Fearing that you may have received one of them, we enclose a readable copy of it, with our apologies.

Mrs. Chase Osborn
Vice President

July 19, 19--

WHEN THE COMPANY IS AT FAULT

Shortly after this request comes the following reply:

THE PROMPT CORRECTION

Prompt action first

Here's our credit memorandum for $44.40 to cover the discount asked for in your April 3 request.

Explanation

The correct price on these items is $75 each, with a discount of 20 percent. Through on oversight, we did not allow the discount on your order No. A-1287; we are happy to do so now. The adjusted discount at the correct price on your order No. A-1391, however, brings the amount due you to $44.40. We have credited your account accordingly.

Cordial close

Thank you for discovering the error. We are glad to rectify it at once and to assure you that we are ready for your next order.

Example III: Mr. J. W. Roberts sends a request to the American Mutual Benefit Insurance Company, asking them to correct their records. The company has incorrectly referred to Mr. Roberts' son as a daughter. Explanation for the curious mistake: the son's first name. The company takes quick steps to adjust the matter.

THE COMPANY PROMPTLY CORRECTS A MISTAKE IN A NAME

Prompt action first

> We're sorry! It is one hundred percent our fault that we referred to your son as a daughter in our note of October 11. There was no excuse for this error because we had your son's complete record in our files. Shelley's address has been changed to 941 Shoreham Avenue, Duluth, in accordance with your correction.

Explanation

> As in all insurance companies, we assume that the address on our records is correct until we receive a change of address notice from either our policyholder or from the Post Office Department. Until your request reached us yesterday, we had not received such a notice and were unaware that your address had changed.

Cordial close

> The American Mutual is most eager to be of every possible help to its policyholders. We thank you for writing us with the request for correction. Shelley's records are now all straight. Please call on us further whenever you have questions.

When a third agency (usually the carrier) is at fault. Your transporting agent (plane, train, truck, etc.) may be at fault because of delay or damage in transit. If the carrier is found to be responsible for either or both, the company's adjustment reply explains the action the customer should take to protect the company in case of damage, or to speed the delivery.

The person or firm who receives the shipment must make sure that there is no shortage or apparent damage before he signs the receipt acknowledging that the shipment was received in good condition. Concealed damage—which sometimes occurs in goods crated or wrapped in such a manner as to keep the damage from being apparent —may be made the subject of a claim later. When goods have been damaged in transit, the person or firm who received the shipment (called the "consignee") has the freight agent make a notation of the damage on the freight receipt before it is signed. Afterwards the consignee may take the goods and make a claim against the carrier. No claim can be made against the shipper. He is not at fault.

Even though they may not be legally responsible for the safe delivery of a shipment by the carrier, many companies gain much goodwill by making a prompt adjustment themselves and putting in their own claim against the carrier. When necessary, they obtain the aid of the customer. But they win his valuable goodwill by taking the weight of the responsibility upon themselves. The plan followed is substantially the same as that which would be used had the company itself been at fault. The difference is that the customer, knowing that the company is not obligated to act, doubly appreciates the help.

---

1 — Promptly grant the adjustment.
2 — Give any needed explanation. Request such information as you may need to complete your claim against the carrier.
3 — Close with assurance to your customer that you have been happy to act in his behalf.

Example I: Progressive companies win goodwill by assuming some of the customer's troubles caused by damage or loss in shipment. The customer is often unfamiliar with the steps to be taken; he may even be much distressed about the damaged or lost shipment. He finds it a welcome relief to have the company's specialists take over the responsibility and save him the worry.

ON BEHALF OF THE CUSTOMER
A COMPANY ADJUSTS A CARRIER'S FAULT

Prompt action first
```
        We are pleased to be able to send you today
another matched pair of television console lamps like
those you ordered previously.
```

Explana-tion
```
        It appears that the first shipment was damaged in
transit, for we have a receipt from the Southern Pacific
indicating that the stand was received in a perfect
carton.  This fact throws the responsibility for the
adjustment on the Southern Pacific Company.  But
railroad adjustments are usually slow; and knowing how
much you wish to present this gift to your husband on
his birthday, we have taken this means to see that the
beautiful set gets to you in perfect condition at the
time you want it most.

        Please leave the damaged shipment in the hands of
the rail agent.  We shall enter an immediate claim, and
you will not be troubled further.
```

Cordial close
```
        You may be sure it's a pleasure for us, too, to
get the gift to you in time.  May the birthday be a
most pleasant occasion, and a memorable one for you both!
```

Example II: Again illustrating how companies sometimes take extraordinary action to protect customer goodwill, consider the following case. On a television program a manufacturer offered, for one dime, a small hi-fi phonograph record bearing a popular theme song.

The company bought the miniature records in good faith from one of the largest record manufacturers in the country and promptly sent them by thousands to program viewers who asked for them. Soon, however, complaints began to drift in that on many 4-speed changers the miniature records could not be played.

Then arose the major question: what should the company do? Some would have handled this adjustment merely by refunding the money to those who actually complained. But this particular organization was worried about the possibility (and a likely one) that many others might be dissatisfied without taking the trouble to complain. Hence, instead of simply returning the money to those who wrote, it sent—to everyone who had received the record—a note beginning, "May we extend to you an apology and an explanation?" The mailing refunded the dime plus postage. In this manner through aggressive adjustment action a large measure of goodwill, so painstakingly built up over the years, was protected.

When the fault is divided between the company and the customer. This type of situation is a common one. When the error is divided, *search first for the positive elements and emphasize them.* Follow this plan:

---

1 — Be prompt and courteous.
2 — Adjust at once your part of the fault.
3 — Mention the customer's share tactfully and impersonally.
4 — Give any necessary further explanation.
5 — Close on the note of future satisfaction.

Example I: A customer may write urgently asking for an instant correction of what he thinks is the company's error, but he may mention that in the past he has had pleasant dealings with the firm. Here you have the positive element you are looking for. Open with it.

```
        We are always pleased to have our customers tell us of
their many satisfactory dealings with us.  We are then even
more determined to keep up the good record.  Thank you for
mentioning your past satisfaction.  To us this is the most
gratifying news we could have, and we shall certainly strive
to merit your confidence in the coming years.

        Here is what we plan to do in the present matter:
(the adjustment then continues.)
```

Example II: In the following case there are at least two distinct possibilities: (a) That the company's product in this particular instance was actually defective for some exceptional reason; or (b) that the customer was simply not a good gardener. There is a reasonable chance that both *a* and *b* play a part in this adjustment.

One thing is certain: The company has a brilliant opportunity to win goodwill at small cost through willingly duplicating the order. With the possibility that the fault is half the company's, half the customer's, or that it is at least divided in some proportion, the company here will be wise to take prompt and positive initiative.

Suppose we try an experiment in this case and show first "How NOT to Make an Adjustment." Or, for the following example, you may prefer to use the title, "How to Lose a Customer."

How to Lose a Customer

"We are all right!"	We certainly cannot understand why those plantings about which you complain didn't do any better. We almost never get any complaints at all about these.
"You are all wrong!"	Moreover, it is not usually our policy to duplicate orders of this type, because if we tried to guarantee them, we would always be getting all kinds of false claims.
"We will, however, . . ."	In this instance, however, we have decided to replace the order, but this time we must ask you to be more careful.

Now suppose we turn the situation around and put some words together in a way that may help to please the customer and hold his hard-earned goodwill:

HOW TO HOLD A CUSTOMER

Prompt adjustment first	By air parcel post we are rushing a replacement order to you covering the pyrocanthus about which you have just written us. We have made a careful selection, and with it we send our best wishes for good luck.
Explanatory material	Last season was not a good one and was a rather trying period in practically all regions. We hope that this spring will more than offset the disappointing results of last year.
Cordial invitation for future business	Be sure to study our new catalog when it reaches you toward the end of next month, and plan to make your selections early. You'll find a beautiful variety waiting for you.

Unit 15 • Effective Adjustments: How to Smooth Out Trouble

When the customer is at fault. Customers are just as liable to commit errors as the companies from which they buy. Everyone makes his quota of mistakes. He puts the wrong figure down. He forgets something. He omits the samples, seals the envelope, and sends it on, not noticing his error. He neglects to give the size, the color, the quality, or the serial number. He misunderstands the directions on the order blank. He may commit scores of other human errors. And the curious fact is that he rarely blames himself, because it is human nature to gloss over one's own mistakes. The disappointments arising from the customer's own shortcomings do not make his grievances any the less real. Nor does he feel any obligation to keep his disappointments to himself. In such a situation, use the following plan:

1 — Say something pleasant first: "Thank you for your order. . . ."
2 — Courteously state the facts and make the statement *impersonal*. Don't say: "You neglected to mention the color." "You failed to give the size." Better: "As color was not mentioned," or "As the size was not given, . . ."
3 — Indicate prompt and favorable action as soon as the customer error is corrected.

Example I: Mr. William Guffy, Secretary, Bennington Corporation, 1528 Walton Way, Augusta, Georgia, complains to his bank that he has not received his checking account statements for the months ending January 31 and February 28. It turns out that Mr. Guffy is himself to blame for the trouble.

IT WAS THE CUSTOMER'S FAULT:
THE BANK IS DIPLOMATIC

Pleasant & courteous opening

> Thank you very much for your note of March 18, telling us that you have not received statements for the months ending January 31 and February 28.

Impersonal statement of the facts

> A careful check of our control file indicates that the latest address we have for mailing your statements is 242 David Street, Augusta, Georgia, given to us June 21, 19--. If this address should be changed to the one now shown on your letterhead, please complete the enclosed mail authority card and return it to us in order to authorize the change.

Prompt and helpful action

> To assist you temporarily until your original statements are either returned to us or forwarded on to the proper address, we are happy to enclose duplicate copies of the ledger sheets showing the activity on this account for the months of January and February.

Example II: Almost three years after the job had been completed, James Frazier of Lewisville, Idaho, asks for an adjustment on his slate roofing. He sends his complaint to the president of the mail-order house from which he had made the purchase. Mr. Frazier is completely at fault, as an impartial examination of the facts clearly proves.

The task here is to place the blame where it belongs and yet, if possible, to keep Mr. Frazier as a customer. This will obviously be no easy job. So serious is this case that the facts, as you will note in the following version, are fully reviewed and carefully summarized. The positive decision is given. The skillful adjustment then closes on a cordial note.

THE SERIOUS CASE OF MR. FRAZIER

Courteous
neutral
opening

Your request of July 19 addressed to the president of this company, applying for an adjustment on your slate roof, has been referred to me for an answer. I am glad to reply.

Careful
review of
all facts

To be able to write understandingly and clearly on this subject and also to review the facts for you, I have gathered the following information from those who have handled the previous correspondence:
We received your order for this roofing on October 18, 19—, and shipment was made ten days later.
Two years later after this purchase was made, your request dated September 20, 19—, was received. It asked for an adjustment on this job, which apparently was not giving satisfaction.
Investigation was made to find the reason. It was discovered that the shingles, which should have been nailed at the apex of each triangular point according to directions, were also nailed at the sides. The necessary expansion and contraction of the roofing consequently tore holes in the shingles.
In order to help you out of this difficulty, we offered, on November 7, 19—, to pay half the price of a new job. This is the last correspondence up to the present time.

Decision

We now renew our offer to you, subject to acceptance within ten days. After August 3, 19—, it will be withdrawn.

Cordial
close

You will agree that this concession is liberal, considering the lapse of time since our original offer. We shall be glad to receive your order for the job in accordance with our offer, and for any additional material that you may need.

The general manager emphasizes the liberal steps that the house has taken to retain the customer's goodwill. The customer's long delay justifies the firmness of the tone of the final offer.

Each time a customer asks for an adjustment, you are dealing with a person who is disappointed: a person dissatisfied with the purchase he has made. Of course if an article is actually faulty, the solution is simple. It is returned for credit. If a service is in some respect not satisfactory, the solution is equally simple. It is suspended and the payment refunded.

There are, however, many adjustment situations in which the error may be corrected without having the article returned or the service suspended. These situations are in what might be defined as the "twilight zone." The actual trouble has been ironed out. As far as the product or the service itself is concerned, things are back to normal. But not so with the customer in many cases. The customer's confidence has been shaken. Some psychological damage has been done.

Entering at this point is *"re-sale,"* meaning, literally, *selling again.* Resale material literally resells the buyer what he originally bought, shows him that he has done the right thing after all, and repaints for him the genuine value of the article or the service ordered.

Resale paragraphs in adjustments are designed (1) to refresh the desire to keep the article or continue to use the service, (2) to keep the customer's confidence from being undermined, (3) to prevent his estimate of the value of the article or service from unjustifiably shrinking. In reclaiming the wavering loyalty of a customer about to be lost, adjusters find that resale material is especially effective.

Recapturing goodwill by rebuilding confidence. Suppose we look in on two separate department store episodes, each involving a troublesome and potentially dangerous problem in customer relations. Let us consider first the case of Hoffman Corporation. Mr. F. C. Pilgram has just notified the store that he is withdrawing his trade, amounting to several hundred dollars a year, as of July 1 because of careless treatment given to an adjustment request made by Mrs. Pilgram. Mrs. Pilgram had asked that a metal fitting on a recently purchased dressing table be replaced because of a defect that caused it to break a few days after it was put into use. Hoffman Corporation blundered in handling the matter. There was a long delay. Mr. Pilgram then wrote as indicated above.

At this point the situation was placed in the hands of Adjustment Manager Robert Jackson. Mr. Jackson, a skilled executive, wrote as shown on page 608.

THE COMPANY WINS BACK A CUSTOMER WITH
EXPERT "RESALE"

You are entirely justified in your expression of lack of confidence in our store service.

It appears that when Mrs. Pilgram gave the metal piece to the salesman, Mr. Chupka failed to record properly the name and address. When the manager of our furniture department returned without being successful in replacing the broken part, we could do nothing but wait until we should receive a letter from the unknown patron. Mrs. Pilgram told us on April 7, much more courteously and patiently than was justified, that we had not taken care of the difficulty.

In the beginning, the buyer of the furniture department took with him this piece of hardware to the Chicago Merchandise Mart and made a sincere effort to replace the broken piece but was unsuccessful; nor could he find anything sufficiently similar to it to be of use to you. When he returned, he made an effort to have a local metal worker repair it by welding but was told that, while it could be done, it would not be a permanent job because of the nature of the metal.

We have given you this lengthy explanation because we want you to know that we tried to give you the kind of service you have experienced with us in the past.

Our representative, Mr. Chupka, will call at your office tomorrow and will bring back with him, if you will permit it, the original fitting, which will now be reproduced through hand-fashioning without cost to you.

More than anything else we regret deeply that you should have been so annoyed by the faulty service of our employees. We shall be grateful to you if you will make to Mrs. Pilgram such explanation on our behalf as will erase the disagreeable impression she has received.

So pleased was Mr. Pilgram with Mr. Jackson's reply that he wrote thus:

MR. PILGRAM IS PLEASED

Your note reached me this morning--and at the same time your representative, Mr. Chupka, called upon me with reference to the difficulty we have had in getting the dressing table hardware piece fixed up. Mr. Chupka's apologies were so wholehearted that I was some what ashamed of myself for having written such a stiff protest as I did. I promised him I would ask Mrs. Pilgram to call upon him when she is next in Chicago. The situation has been ironed out. We're happy.

Mr. Jackson proved himself an expert adjustment officer. The action he proposed was the correct one in this situation. The store should take the initiative in sending its representative to correct the error. Throughout the paragraphs appear expressions that aim to reestablish in the customer's mind an esteem for the store and a loyalty to it as a place to trade. This is the process of *resale*.

Especially well-chosen are the following expressions:

"You are entirely justified. . . ."

"Mrs. Pilgram told us . . . much more courteously and patiently than was justified. . . ."

". . . we want you to know that we tried to give you the kind of service you have experienced with us in the past."

"Our representative, Mr. Chupka, will call at your office tomorrow and will bring back with him, if you will permit it. . . ."

More than anything else we regret deeply. . . ."

"We shall be grateful to you if you will make to Mrs. Pilgram such explanation on our behalf as will erase the disagreeable impression she has received."

Another classic case is that of Trammell's, Inc., the proud name of which has just been seriously damaged by an unfortunate episode involving two store employees who have blundered: They have been ill-mannered to a valued customer, Mrs. J. L. Thornberry. As accredited representatives of the store, they have not only brought serious harm to the store's reputation but may also have caused the loss of a valuable patron. Yet to take the easy way out and simply dismiss the two may cripple the personnel of the department and may not bring the customer back. How would you solve this puzzle? Here is how one executive approached the problem:

AN ADJUSTMENT OFFICER SOLVES A "PUZZLER"

Courteous
apology
and action
first

> We can't tell you how sorry we are to learn of the discourtesy shown you recently by two of our employees. The matter has been carefully investigated. Let us assure you there will be no further annoyance.
>
> With your fairmindedness we hope you will forgive the two individuals for their conduct. The two have apologized most sincerely. Please do not hold any ill feeling toward them or this organization.

Explana-
tory
material,
store
policy

> You have helped us greatly by bringing this matter to our attention because it has made it possible for us to guard against this kind of incident. Our hope is always to give service with courtesy. To perfect this system is our aim.
>
> You have placed great confidence in us in the past, if we are to judge by the amount of patronage that you have given us. Will you not overlook this episode and give us an opportunity to make good our policy?

Cordial
selling
close

> Recently a new feature has been added to our shopping helps. Miss Peggy Doerger, our professional shopper, will give you personal suggestions and assist you in selections. Ask for Miss Doerger--she awaits your request to serve.

How an angry patron became a friend. Steve Bing was angry. He ordered a book from a leading and highly respectable publishing company. In some incredible fashion the shipping department sent him a "second," a damaged copy with scratched cover and torn pages, obviously a "reject" destined for the scrap pile.

Mr. Bing, in irritable mood, fires off a note stating that he "is going to put the book on his desk with a sign on it telling the public about the kind of merchandise this company attempts to foist onto its customers."

If you were the publisher's adjuster, how would you approach this situation? Would you assume an air of superior dignity and "tut-tut" the customer for losing his temper? Would you humble yourself in a tearful apology, assenting to every slur he has made? Or would you take a sporting attitude, as did the adjuster in the following reply? Note how the executive gets in step with the complainant in the first sentence, vigorously affirms his mood, and, with constructive sporting appeals, makes every effort to recapture goodwill.

GETTING IN STEP WITH HIM!
CONVERSATIONAL SPORTING ANSWER

You certainly have every right to rise up in wrath if that book is only half as bad as you report it to be. In putting it up on your desk with a big sign telling the story about your experience, you are doing the right thing. You are doing it because at the present time you are convinced that people cannot deal with us without getting "stung."

But as your only wish is to be fair--and we are sure of that--you must also tell on that sign what we did when you called to our attention our failure to give you 100 percent service.

This is what we are doing: First of all, we are asking the shipping clerk to send a brand-new book, and heaven help him if he doesn't! Then we are going to say this: You can have your money back in addition to the new book, or we will do any other thing you want us to do that will convince you that we are a fairly decent and respectable lot of folks in this office.

This reply recaptured the customer's goodwill. The informal tone, just touched with whimsical humor, gives the impression that the adjuster is talking to Mr. Bing face to face. There shines through the lines the personality of a man who wants to work with others in the spirit of fairness. A few months later Bing called upon the company and met the man who had written. The two became personal friends, and a once-angry patron was "back in the fold."

If you wish to follow the experts, whose professional job is to smooth out trouble, your guides to success are shown below.

---

1 — *Analyze each situation for the right solution.* An **adjustment** is a delicate instrument.

    a. Determine what is best to do in the given situation.

    b. Make a plan.

    c. Choose tactful expressions. The man who complains is sensitive. Choose words to fit the delicate adjustment instrument.

2 — *Be genuinely helpful in smoothing out the trouble.* Work for the next order. Many companies adjust generously because of what such policy may mean in future patronage.

3 — *Be sure to satisfy as far as satisfaction can be carried*—with justice to both the company and the customer.

4 — *Take each request seriously.* To the customer the smallest claim is important. What may seem to the company the tiniest trifle is to the customer perhaps mountainous in importance. Never underestimate.

To get a customer is expensive! Settle the trouble and keep him! "To get a new customer costs our company several hundred dollars," writes the chief executive of a big retail enterprise catering particularly to women. "Each one of our customers has a circle of friends who are or may in the future become our customers. We know of actual cases where other companies, our competitors, have, by mishandling one customer, lost the patronage of from ten to twenty of her friends. Seldom is it realized how like wildfire ripples of discontent can spread! Happily, however, a skilled adjustment officer can turn most of the outgoing ripples into those of positive contentment and satisfaction and can thus *multiply our friends!*"

Instead of saying "NO," say "YES" to something else. Many successful adjustment managers have been salesmen. Men with a selling background can quickly sense what customers really want. And what customers really want—not merely what they ask for—should, if feasible, be given to them.

Often an offer to render an alternative service is more valuable to the claimant than the remedy for which he originally asked. The adjuster who senses this situation, and who offers what the customer *really wants,* generates abundant goodwill. Therefore you should gain selling experience, if you can, before entering the adjustment division. To a professional adjuster nothing may be more valuable than calm patience, psychological insight, sales ability, and communication proficiency.

The adjustment officer welds together business insight and a practical knowledge of human nature. Using this equipment, he confidently approaches and solves problems. The experienced adjuster knows, from the cases he has handled, how the shift of a word can completely alter the tone of his message and how to communicate a calm and conciliatory attitude through his choice of words. His experience proves that adjustment management, and the handling of adjustment language, can be an exact undertaking, requiring word precision and word control.

Summary. A good adjuster knows human motives. He has an even temper. He knows the power and use of constructive appeals. A customer bestows his loyalty and his patronage only when he feels that he has been well treated. Adjustment psychology aims to make the customer feel so. Necessarily the adjustment department deals with men and women who are disappointed, disgruntled, and irritated over real or fancied wrongs. Discontent, suspicion, sometimes even accusation—these are the attitudes that the adjustment department must handle. It must meet these negative mental attitudes with well-planned and constructive solutions put in the form of powerful, positive communications.

• *APPLYING EFFECTIVE ENGLISH*

Oral Applications

• **1.** State the basis on which the four chief classes of adjustments are set up. What are the main differences in the way the four classes of adjustments are handled?

• **2.** Explain the steps in the basic adjustment procedure when the company itself is at fault.

• **3.** Why do many companies accept the extra burden of handling customer complaints that actually involve the carrier rather than the shipper? How is this same attitude reflected in correspondence regarding adjustments?

• 4. Discuss the reason why companies play down—minimize—errors which a customer may make in submitting his order, his payment, or a request for adjustment. How can such errors be minimized? Be prepared to give examples.

Written Application

As adjustment officer of the Masterson Department Store, you have received the following complaint from Mrs. Harold Dresser:

> Last Monday, April 16, I bought a bronze floor lamp for $43.97 and requested that it be shipped at once, since I needed it for a party I was to give that Friday, April 20. It is now Tuesday, April 24, and the lamp still has not arrived. Cancel my order and close my charge account at your store. I am not accustomed to doing business with a careless and irresponsible firm.

Write the adjustment acknowledging the error on the part of Masterson's Shipping Department. Try to win back Mrs. Dresser's goodwill. She has been an excellent customer of the Masterson Department Store for years, and you want to do everything possible to keep her business and win back her approval.

• *REVIEW*

Correct all errors in the following sentences from sales messages.

1 — Benton Pioneer Bicycles, manufactured by the Benton Arms Company, provides handbreaks and three-speed gear shift on all models the most expensive model costs less than $87 dollars.

2 — Wearing any of the current models of Sure-Press Wear, people will be impressed by your good taste and appresiation of elegent style.

3 — Oriental Airways, Inc., have daily flights to Tokyo and Singapore from Hololulu these flights leave at 830 AM and 415 PM, respectively.

4 — The Desert-Zone Dehumidifier being able to control the humidity in a basement measuring 20 feet by forty feet by 8 feet.

5 — The Clip-King Power Mower can be easily adjust to cut grass to any hieght from one-half inch to two and one-half inches it is also completely self-sharpenning.

6 — The four models of this AM-shortwave radio, the Diplomat, is capable of bringing in broadcasts from as far away as Copenhagen Madrid and Athens.

7 — Everlock Adhesive Company now offering a waterproof, extremely strong, quick-setting, and versatile sement.

Corporation project 15-A. As manager of the Adjustment Department of Contemporary School Supplies, Inc., you have received the following request for adjustment from Dr. Ernest Evans, principal of the Booker T. Washington School, Seattle, Washington:

> On August 7, I ordered seventy-two kindergarten-size aluminum folding chairs from Contemporary School Supplies, Inc. The shipment arrived on August 23, but it contained only seventy chairs. School is scheduled to open in just six days, and two additional chairs will be needed badly. Please send these chairs as soon as possible. I feel strongly that the added shipping charge should not be billed to us.

Write the adjustment, indicating that the two chairs are being sent by special shipment, that the mistake was made by your Shipping Department, that the additional shipping charge will be borne by Contemporary, and that you look forward to doing business with Dr. Evans in the future.

Corporation project 15-B. As assistant manager of the Adjustment Department of Contemporary School Supplies, Inc., you have received the following request for adjustment from Mr. Charles Reed, Superintendent of the Woodlawn School District, Milwaukee, Wisconsin:

> The shipment of twenty-five Hixon Fluorescent Light Fixtures arrived yesterday. Unfortunately, five of the fluorescent light bulbs which accompanied the order were broken in shipment. Please send us five replacement bulbs, and ten spare bulbs, for which you may bill us at your standard price, less our usual discount. Since night school classes are scheduled to begin in two weeks, we shall appreciate your expediting the order.

Though the carrier is at fault, Contemporary School Supplies, Inc., wishes to cooperate with Mr. Reed fully and thus increase his goodwill. Write an adjustment indicating that the replacement bulbs will be shipped today, that the extra bulbs will accompany the shipment, and that the claim for the broken bulbs will be submitted to the Mercury Shipping Company, which is responsible for the damage, on behalf of Mr. Reed. Take special care to make the tone of the adjustment positive, so that it increases Mr. Reed's satisfaction in doing business with Contemporary School Supplies, Inc.

UNIT 16

CREDITS AND COLLECTIONS: HOW TO EXTEND CREDIT AND COLLECT MONEY

Credit is founded firmly on the assumption that people are basically honest. The word credit comes from the Latin word <u>Credo</u>, meaning "I believe."

A businessman who extends credit says in effect: I have faith that my customer will carry out his obligation to me. I believe that, when he makes this purchase agreement, he will keep his word. I believe he will pay his bill when it is due. Hence I am willing to extend him the privilege of taking the goods now because I am confident he will pay me at the proper time.

Only when something happens to interfere with the payment at the time it is due do collections become necessary. What things can happen? The buyer may fall ill. He may suffer unexpected financial reverses. These reverses may impair his power to pay. Such things happen. When they do, the collection officer must deal with them as contingencies. And on those few debtors who default, he must apply continuous and increasing pressure.

Discussed in Section 1 is the nature of credit and why it must be granted with great care.

Reviewed in Section 2 are the basic principles and psychological appeals through which it becomes possible to get the money and save the customer.

UNIT 16

Section 1

Credit Is a Privilege: How to Grant It, and How to Refuse It—Tactfully: Credit—the power to buy without paying cash—is a privilege that must be granted with care or, if necessary, declined with tact.

Section 2

Collection Messages: Following Up the One Who Owes: A good collection officer gets the money and saves the customer, through the use of carefully selected appeals.

SECTION 1

Credit is a Privilege: How to Grant It, and How to Refuse It—Tactfully

Credit—the power to buy without paying cash—is a privilege that must be granted with care or, if necessary, declined with tact.

You will have a credit record. Seventeen hundred members of the Associated Credit Bureaus of America maintain a total of over 100,000,000 credit records. If yours is not already one of these, it soon will be. That, at least, is the strong probability. These one thousand seven hundred credit bureaus constantly flash exchanges of information throughout the country. So your credit rating will follow you wherever you go. One large metropolitan credit bureau answers more than forty thousand credit inquiries each month and maintains records on more than three million individuals and businesses.

Basic credit information sources. Credit ratings by EDP—electronic data processing—reporting a profile of each customer are now standard procedure. Local credit bureaus feed data to a local processing center. The data flow in from banks, credit card operations, central charge headquarters, department stores, municipal license bureaus, utilities, and other sources. These sources help to determine instantaneously the customer's bill-paying habits.

When you apply for credit, you are normally asked to fill out a credit application form. From this form, credit bureaus draw additional information about your age, parents, the schools you have attended, the jobs you have held, and the length of time you have spent in each job. Other information comes from former employers, from high school and college records, from vital-statistic bureaus, from the corner druggist, from news items about you that may bear in any way upon your credit, your character, or your integrity. In summary, the purpose of credit information is to supply answers to blunt questions like these: "Are you a dependable person?" "Do you pay your bills?" "Do you pay them promptly?" "Do you honor *all* your obligations?"

Guard your credit as if it were gold. If you can go to your bank, ask for credit, and get it, what your bank is really saying is, "You're OK—we believe in you." Again, if you were a store owner and could go to your distributor-supplier, ask for a "line of credit," and get it, what your supplier would really be saying is, "You're OK—I believe in you." Whenever an individual or an organization extends credit, that action itself is saying, "I'm putting a wager on this customer. I think he's dependable. My wager says that he'll be willing and able to pay his bill on the dot when the time comes."

CREDO

"I Believe!"

When you are given credit, you have received a privilege, a privilege that can never be given to everybody because not everybody can earn it. What you have been granted is the privilege of getting what you want *now* and paying for it *later*. The "now" and the "later" are the factors that form the essence of credit. Of course this kind of privilege is valuable because it means that you can, *for the time being,* get something for nothing.

But now note carefully the next step: When you are given credit, somebody expresses faith, belief, and confidence in your *ability to pay* for your purchase within the specified time. This specified time may be thirty, sixty, ninety days, or even longer, depending upon the character of the business that has given you the credit.

Taking the discount is smart management. Businessmen try to "take their discounts" as a matter of business efficiency. Under terms of 2/10, for example, they pay a bill within ten days from the date of purchase. They are then privileged to deduct 2 percent from the amount of the bill and to remit the balance. They are credited with payment in full. Thus the businessmen make 2 percent (by saving it) besides the normal profit they will receive on the resale of the goods. A merchant who discounts his bills is never subject to collection pressure because he is never delinquent. He belongs to the gilt-edge group.

Character, capital, capacity, and business condition. The credit man appraises every application for four factors:

1 — Has the applicant *character?* Is his record that of a man who is steady and dependable? Does it indicate integrity in the man behind it? In dealings with others, does the applicant show a sense of obligation? Is he honest, straightforward, aboveboard?

2 — Has the applicant *capital?* Does he have enough money in his business? Is he, in other words, adequately capitalized? What is the ratio of his assets to his liabilities? What is the ratio of his assets quickly convertible into cash (liquid assets) to his current liabilities? What is his general financial status?

3 — Has the applicant *capacity?* Does his record show that he can manage a successful business, that he has a business head? Is he making progress or losing ground? Has he chosen his location well? Has he chosen a business in which there are expanding opportunities? In general, does he show good management judgment?

4 — What is the general *condition* of business? What is the general business trend? In other words, is business good, average, or poor? Is the condition of business likely to improve? Or simply to continue average? Or is it likely to decline?

Among these four factors the most important is character. A famous banker once lent a large sum to a young man who had neither ready cash ("liquid capital"), no material security ("collateral"). Asked why he was willing to assume such a risk, the famous financier replied, "First and foremost, character. Second, capacity. That young man has both. I'm supplying the capital. Business conditions are satisfactory and may even improve a little. If they don't, it still makes no difference to me. I've seen to it that he has adequate life insurance. The rest is a foregone conclusion. *I'll get my money back.*"

INVESTIGATING CREDIT

How a credit account is opened. A credit account may be opened in one of several ways: (1) The customer may request credit orally or in writing; (2) he may request it with his first order; (3) he may send in the first order and leave the credit decision to the company; or (4) a businessman buying for cash may build an excellent credit rating, and the seller may offer him credit.

Reviewing the sources of credit information. As we have seen, the credit officer has a number of sources of information channels available to him. Among the more important are these:

1 — *The customer himself:* Most persons are reasonably well informed about credit procedures and expect to give information regarding credit responsibility. For example, the customer applying for

credit at a retail store supplies information about salary, banking connection, annual income, ownership of real estate or an automobile, and credit accounts with other firms. Business firms seeking credit supply copies of commercial references and financial statements.

2 — *Other business firms:* Other firms with which the applicant has had credit accounts are prepared to supply details of their experience when asked. Banks likewise serve as references.

3 — *Local and national credit bureaus:* Credit bureaus such as the National Retail Credit Men's Association and the National Association of Credit Men maintain files on concerns and individuals with whom their members have done credit business. Credit information from the local and national credit bureaus is available to members. There is usually a nominal annual membership fee for joining such organizations.

4 — *Special credit-rating agencies:* A credit-rating agency such as Dun & Bradstreet publishes volumes containing credit information on business firms. If you are a subscriber to the service and you find that a firm about which you need credit information is not listed, Dun & Bradstreet will furnish you with a special report upon request.

Whether the information needed refers to the credit of a consumer or the credit of a businessman, the basic credit considerations are the same. In writing, you follow the same plan and use the same principles. And you keep well informed about important sources like those just listed in order to be able to make wise decisions quickly.

Asking for credit information. Whatever method is used, credit is granted only after careful investigation. When you ask for information from the customer, emphasize that the facts requested are simply a part of the usual requirements for credit extension. This statement avoids the suggestion that you are in any way questioning the customer's financial standing. Use the following plan:

---

1 — Open with a suitable courteous and pleasant reference.

2 — Request the necessary credit information.

3 — Close with (a) sales material or (b) some equally suitable reference.

The request at the top of the next page goes to a retail customer who has asked for the privilege of opening a charge account.

ASKING FOR CREDIT INFORMATION

Courtesy opening
> Thank you for your interest in becoming a credit customer. It is a pleasure to consider the matter of opening a charge account in your name.

The request for credit information
> In order to open this account, we shall need certain references and information as a matter of customary routine. Please let us have the name of the bank with which you have an account, and the names and addresses of two persons in the city to whom we may refer. From the period of time during which we have enjoyed your patronage, we judge that you have been for several years a resident of the city. Is this correct? At what other stores do you have accounts?

"Sales material" close
> Received this week in our music department are some additional models of the Royal Stereo Portables you were considering on Tuesday when you asked about credit. Come and see them soon.

USEFUL CREDIT-INFORMATION GUIDE

Credit information needed varies somewhat according to the type of business, but in general it should include the following:

1 — How long have you known the customer?
2 — Does he attend to business?
3 — How good is his location?
4 — What kind of progress is he making?
5 — What is his competition?
6 — How does his management compare with his competitor's?
7 — Does he own real estate? What is his equity (ownership)?
8 — Has he ever been in financial trouble?
9 — How do the local bankers rate him?
10 — What does his whole record show?

GRANTING AND REFUSING CREDIT

A message granting credit follows the same principles of structure as does that granting a favor. See the illustration on page 475. Use the following plan:

1 — Extend credit with courtesy.
2 — Express your wish for cordial relations.
3 — Refer to the credit privilege (a) as a commercial advantage to the businessman, or (b) as a convenience to the customer.

A card acknowledgment of credit is shown on page 623.

A message refusing credit follows the same principles of structure as does that refusing a favor (see pages 477-482). A man who can refuse credit and make a friend proves himself an expert. Use this plan:

---

1 — Thank the customer for his order, for his information and references, and for his cooperation.
2 — Be frank in explaining the situation, mentioning first the favorable factors, then the less favorable ones.
3 — Suggest as a temporary solution that dealings be undertaken on a cash basis. Offer full cooperation toward reaching a satisfactory future credit basis.

In the example below, the writer refuses credit; but in doing so, he makes every effort to maintain the goodwill of the customer.

REFUSING CREDIT TO A BUSINESSMAN

Thank you for your order of February 23 and for your courtesy in enclosing credit information and references.

We have gathered some complimentary opinions about your personal character and business ability, showing that you have developed an enviable reputation among those with whom you have done business. Our study of your balance sheet reveals, however, certain aspects that might easily endanger your entire financial position. The ratio of assets to liabilities shows that at the moment you need additional capital. This should not be difficult to obtain in view of the favorable opportunities promised by your location. A capital addition of $5,000 would be satisfactory.

You may be sure we want to cooperate with you to the fullest extent in any way that may lead to a satisfactory future credit basis. Meanwhile we shall be glad to take care of your current needs with our most favorable cash terms. You will find this arrangement an excellent basis, we believe, for us to become better acquainted.

If we may have your favorable answer, our first shipment will go to you at once.

Courtesy is a part of credit. Whether you grant or decline a credit request, you can surround your decisions with the basic tone of courtesy. When you grant credit, what you have done, in effect, is to compliment your customer on his good credit rating. When you decline credit, you courteously hold out the prospect that, with improving conditions in the customer's personal situation, credit extension may later prove possible.

Summary. As you study this section, you note that the proper handling of credit requires knowledge of people and *proficiency in communication—a shrewd adroitness in the choice of words.* For

Marshall Field & Company

CREDIT AND
COLLECTION DEPARTMENT

February 17, 19--

Mrs. Richard L. Wendt
243 North Kolmar Avenue
Chicago, Illinois 60624

Dear Mrs. Wendt:

Thank you for your recent inquiry.

At the moment we are unable to locate an account in the name shown above. Perhaps it has been removed from our files because of inactivity.

If you are interested in an account with us, please fill in the enclosed application and return it in the envelope provided. As soon as it is received, the information will have our prompt attention.

We look forward to hearing from you.

Cordially yours

M. L. Socha

M. L. Socha

mbs

Enclosures

①

APPLICATION FOR CREDIT

Marshall Field & Company

PERSONAL DATA ◇ IF MARRIED USE HUSBAND'S NAME & OCCUPATION

| MR. MRS. MISS | FIRST NAME | INITIAL | LAST NAME |

STREET ADDRESS

| CITY | STATE | ZIP CODE | HOME TELEPHONE NO. |

IF LESS THAN 2 YEARS AT PRESENT ADDRESS PLEASE GIVE FORMER ADDRESS:

WIFE'S NAME: SINGLE / MARRIED / WIDOWED / DIVORCED / SEPARATED / AGE IF UNDER 21

HAVE YOU HAD AN ACCOUNT WITH US BEFORE? YES NO / HOW LONG THERE / I RENT / I OWN / HOW LONG

NAME & ADDRESS OF NEAREST RELATIVE OR PERSONAL REFERENCE IF SO, PLEASE GIVE DETAILS ON REVERSE SIDE

BANK AND TRADE REFERENCES: ◇

NAME OF BANK & CITY WHERE LOCATED

NAME OF BANK & CITY WHERE LOCATED

BUYERS AUTHORIZED TO CHARGE TO THIS ACCOUNT—NAME & RELATIONSHIP

☐ I HAVE THESE BUDGET ACCOUNTS. (PLEASE LIST APPROXIMATE BALANCES OUTSTANDING)

☐ I HAVE MONTHLY CHARGE ACCOUNT WITH

☐ I HAVE CHARGE ACCOUNT WITH

INCOME ◇

| | FOR | USE | D O ▷ E | C O ◁ U B R |

ACCOUNT NO.

SHOPPING CARD NO.

BUSINESS CONNECTION OR SOURCE OF INCOME

ADDRESS / POSITION / HOW LONG YRS. / TELEPHONE NO. / INCOME $

IF LESS THAN 2 YEARS AT PRESENT OCCUPATION PLEASE GIVE PREVIOUS EMPLOYER.

WIFE'S EMPLOYER / ADDRESS / POSITION / HOW LONG YRS. / TELEPHONE NO. / INCOME $

LETTER NO.

POSITION / ADDRESS / HOW LONG YRS. / TELEPHONE NO. / INCOME $

| TYPE OF ACCOUNT | APPROVED | DATE |
| INTERVIEWER | FOLIO NO. | ISSUE CARDS | CODE |

OUR TERMS: PLEASE READ AND SIGN

STATEMENT CLOSING DATE:
CARDS ISSUED TO ME.

I AGREE TO PAY ALL CHARGES WITHIN FIFTEEN DAYS OF STATEMENT CLOSING DATE.

I AGREE, ALSO, TO RETURN UPON REQUEST ANY CHARGE CARDS ISSUED TO ME.

MARSHALL FIELD & COMPANY WELCOMES NEW CHARGE CUSTOMERS. ACCOUNTS ARE OPENED WITH THE UNDERSTANDING THAT THE RELATIONSHIP WILL BE A CONTINUING ONE, AND THE ACCOUNT WILL BE OF SERVICE THROUGHOUT THE YEAR.

SIGNATURE

---

②

Tucked
inside
is your
Pogue's
Charge
Card

Miss Rosanne Sabatelli
6342 Montgomery Road
Cincinnati, Ohio 45213

Pogue's

Take your Pogue's Charge Card out. Take a look. Then hurry to Pogue's. Downtown, Kenwood or Tri-County. For quick reference, keep your Pogue's Charge Card always at your fingertips. One never knows when the urge for something grand might strike!

---

③

GUMP'S

It is indeed a pleasure to welcome you as a charge customer.

Your account has been opened and we hope that there will be many occasions for you to enjoy its conveniences.

You may be assured that everything will be done to make your shopping with us both pleasant and advantageous.

S. & G. GUMP COMPANY

example, subscribers to the *Harvard Business Review* recently rated "the ability to communicate" as the prime requisite of a promotable executive.[1]

The promotable credit executive is the one who has developed a flexible and sensitive control of words related to people's actions and intentions. It is "our sensitivity to the needs, the wishes . . . of others that . . . make us truly effective communicators. . . . In the long run, what we are will shine through what we say and how we say it." [2]

Particularly is this statement true in the world of financial management where credit is built on the belief that others will live up to their promises. In carrying out his duties, the credit officer, like the collection officer, must be a specialist in energizing the impulse of personal responsibility.

Only when obligations become overdue, and personal responsibility is defaulted, does collection pressure become necessary. The collection process is the subject of the next section.

• *APPLYING EFFECTIVE ENGLISH*

Oral Applications

• **1.** Explain the meaning of the expression "taking the discount."

• **2.** What are some of the ways in which a credit account may be opened?

• **3.** Analyze the example refusing credit to a businessman (page 622). In this example, cite specific words, phrases, and ideas which are calculated to maintain the goodwill of the addressee.

• **4.** What is the assumption on which all credit is based?

• **5.** When credit information is requested from a customer, what advantages may result from emphasizing that the facts requested are simply part of the usual requirements for extending credit?

• **6.** State the four factors that form the basis for approving any application for credit.

• **7.** Why isn't all business done on a cash basis?

• **8.** Indicate the main sources of information available to a credit officer.

---

[1] John Fielden, "What Do You Mean I Can't Write?" *Harvard Business Review* (May-June, 1964), p. 144. See also, C. Wilson Randle, "How to Identify Promotable Executives," *Harvard Business Review* (May-June, 1956), p. 122.

[2] John Fielden, "For Better Business Writing," *Harvard Business Review* (January-February, 1965), p. 172.

• **9.** What is the importance of each of the ten questions contained in the "Useful Credit-Information Guide" given on page 621.

Written Applications

• **1.** As Mrs. Leslie Morris, write to the credit manager of the Carleton Department Store, 4398 Madison Avenue, Sacramento, California 95842, requesting that a charge account be opened in your name. State that you have lived at your present address, 3709 Canterbury Road, Sacramento, California 95815, for the last eleven years and that you have been a regular cash customer at the Carleton store during all those years.

• **2.** Mrs. Leslie Morris has made application to become a credit customer of the Carleton Department Store in Sacramento, California. (See Written Application 1.) As Mr. Marvin Carman, credit manager of the Carleton Department Store, write to Mrs. Morris requesting credit information. Close with an invitation to Mrs. Morris to attend Carleton's Carnival of Summer Values, July 23-28, during which all merchandise will be discounted from five to forty percent.

• **3.** As Mrs. Leslie Morris, answer Mr. Carman's request for credit information. (See Written Application 2.) Make clear that you have had a checking account at the Westwood National Bank of Sacramento for two years. Give as references the names of Dr. Donald C. Vast, 927 Claremont Way, Sacramento, California 95822, and Professor Ronald Oldberg, 1400 Cody Way, Sacramento, California 95825. Explain that you currently have a charge account at the Richard Mark Department Store and at Thomas R. Lenox, Inc.

• **4.** As Mr. Carman, credit manager of the Carleton Department Store, 4398 Madison Avenue, Sacramento, California 95842, write Mrs. Leslie Morris. Inform her that a charge account has been opened in her name. Extend a warm welcome to Mrs. Carman as a new credit customer at Carleton.

• **5.** As Mr. Carman, credit manager of the Carleton Department Store, 4398 Madison Avenue, Sacramento, California 95842, refuse credit to Mr. Jeffrey Sill, 124 Berg Avenue, Sacramento, California 95822. Explain that credit accounts at Carleton's are extended only to persons having established accounts at a Sacramento bank, and that Mr. Sill had indicated in his latest message to you that he did not have such an account. Make your refusal as courteous as possible, so as to encourage and retain Mr. Sill's valuable cash patronage at your store.

SECTION 2

Collection Messages: Following Up the One Who Owes

A good collection officer gets the money and keeps the customer through the use of carefully selected appeals.

Holding a sensitive post. In finance management the modern credit-collection officer knows that he holds a highly sensitive post. His responsibilities require insight, understanding, and tact. Sensitively guiding the extension of credit, carefully applying collection pressure, he is aware that his obligations are not less than three in number.

First, he must strive to protect his company's financial interests. Second, he must help to hold customer loyalty. Third, he must help the company to make profitable sales. Yet he is always aware that sales are futile unless the customer *pays in full* for his purchases. Hence, using careful selection standards, he extends the credit privilege only to those he rates good risks. Through credit education he trains his customers to appreciate the credit privilege. Together, selective credit extension and wise credit education combine to minimize bad-debt loss. The wiser the credit extension, the lighter the collection load.

But no matter how keen the credit officer, he will now and then make a mistake in detecting a poor risk. Working as he does with human factors, he cannot be expected to make a perfect record. To handle delinquent situations, the collection system is put into operation, but *only after* the customer is in default.

Classes of credit customers. Credit customers are classified as those who are: (1) good pay; (2) good pay but slow; (3) uncertain.

1 — **Those who are good pay** are reliable. They pay when notified. They are anxious to keep their credit unimpaired. They cooperate with the credit department when they delay a payment. This class is gilt-edged.

2 — **Those who are good pay but slow** are usually reliable in the long run. But they cause the collection department most of its correspondence. These customers may be careless but rarely dishonest. They intend to pay—eventually.

3 — **Those who are uncertain** will creep into the credit list in spite of the shrewdest judgment of the credit officer. They are unreliable. Their unreliability may at first fail to come to light, even under careful investigation. Some of them are dishonest. They pay under pressure. When discovered, they are reduced to cash basis. This class is a bad risk.

STAGES OF COLLECTION FOLLOW-UP

Collections are written in a series with the pressure increasing from the first phase to the last. Collection procedure falls into four stages: (1) Reminder; (2) Stronger Reminder; (3) Discussion; (4) Urgency.

How to use collection appeals. Important appeals to your customer may be mild or increasingly vigorous, depending on the stage at which they are used. Choose your appeals to match the stage you have reached. Appeals are mild in Stages 1 and 2, the Reminders. Appeals become far more forceful in Stages 3 and 4.

IMPORTANT COLLECTION APPEALS

In most messages: fairness, cooperation, self-respect

Helpful in every stage: pride, self-interest, honor

Useful in any stage: success, fair play, wish to avoid unpleasant things, force of habit

To be used when appropriate: self-esteem, community prestige, desire for comfort, acquisitiveness, family affection, imitation (of other good businessmen), loyalty (to a friendly house), competition, curiosity, shame (to be used sparingly)

Important in later stages: fear, annoyance of legal force, ultimatum

Never to be used: pity, anger, contempt.

Let us now apply these appeals to the three main classes:

1 — *To those who are good pay:*
   Have you overlooked this account? Is our record of the account correct? May we have your check so that we can close accounts by [date]? Is there some reason for delay? Perhaps this statement has escaped your attention. We suggest that with your check you also make a trial order. [Sales material inserted.]

2 — *To those who are good pay but slow:*

Self-interest (reselling the customer the value of the goods originally ordered: Reinstating in his mind how the goods looked when they arrived; suggesting concrete ways in which he has been benefited). Pride. Goodwill. Cooperation. Fair dealing. Honesty. Good nature. Wish to avoid annoyance. Good reputation. Success. Family affection. Imitation. Competition. Value of keeping credit undamaged. Are you short of capital? Are your own collections slow? Is business lagging? Won't you tell us why your account has gone unpaid? If you will only give us the details of your present problem, perhaps we can arrange a partial-payment plan. Fear, phrased gently. Alternative steps, growing stronger.

3 — *To those who are uncertain, perhaps bad, pay:*

Appeal to discouraged delinquents through pride, imitation of other successful merchants, shame, fear, and possibility of a lawsuit. Appeal to dishonest delinquents simply through fear, possibility of a lawsuit, and direct legal steps.

ILLUSTRATING COLLECTION PROCEDURE

Examples of the four stages. Most customers pay when they receive a statement. If they did not, business could not be done on credit because the confidence that supports the credit structure would collapse. A customer is not delinquent until his bill runs unpaid past the due date. Not until after the first reminder does collection pressure begin.

1 — *Reminder.* Collection reminders are memory helps. They keep the accounts before the eyes of the delinquents. They may include sales material suggesting reorders; they may carry an enclosure introducing new goods. You assume that the customer has overlooked the invoice and will pay as soon as he reads the reminder.

STAGE I: REMINDER (INCLUDING SALES MATERIAL)

Timely contact	Vacation days like these are just the kind to invite the enjoyment of a fine 15-transistor radio like the new one you recently bought from us.
Reminder	May we count on receiving promptly a check for $57.50, the balance due on your account?
Sales-material "softener"	You'll like the new stereophonic rhythm records just arrived in our music department. Check the list enclosed. Then come in and hear some of them soon.

2 — *Stronger reminder.* The stronger reminder is a second memory jog put in stronger terms. The news item or the sales material (which

A PRINTED COLLECTION REMINDER

insulated the request in the first notice) is now withdrawn. Attention must be concentrated on getting the check. The wording becomes more definite. Added pressure appears. The request for the check is direct and forthright.

Courtesy is maintained. The assumption is again oversight. You assume that the customer has once more overlooked the invoice and will pay as soon as he receives the second notice. Questions may be included to make sure that the amount is correct and that the purchase is satisfactory.

STAGE II: STRONGER REMINDER (REQUEST MORE DEFINITE)

Direct strong reminder

You will note from the attached statement that our April bill has apparently been overlooked. This amount is small. We rely on you to make payment now in order to avoid the annoyance of further correspondence.

Making action easy

A stamped, self-addressed envelope is enclosed for your convenience.

3 — Discussion. The discussion stage aims to get the check or to draw a reply. The customer has now ignored a simple reminder and a stronger reminder of his obligation. His account has run perhaps several weeks past the due date. He must be made to send a check or to break his silence and tell what the difficulty is.

The appeal to friendly cooperation is now brought into play: "Won't you tell us frankly what the trouble is?" The assumption is financial difficulty. You assume the customer is in the midst of money troubles and has hesitated to tell about them. Your request for a check or an explanation is now insistent. The customer must pay. Although you apply sharply increasing pressure, your tone is courteous.

Contact:
restates
facts

> Won't you tell us frankly just what the difficulty is? Six weeks have now gone by since your account, itemized on the enclosed statement, became due. To our notices of May 15 and June 1, calling attention to the evident oversight, we have had no answer.

Appeal to
cooperation

> As we have had no word to the contrary, we feel confident that the purchase has proved satisfactory, that our records are correct, and that you are indebted for the amount indicated. We want to enjoy the most cordial relations with our customers. We want them to buy freely and to use their credit privileges to the fullest extent. But to make it possible for us to offer such services, we must have equal cooperation from our customers. We must have prompt payment of accounts when they become due.

Rehearses
credit
material

> Your credit privilege is valuable. Your credit record has been sound. We want you to keep it so because of the advantages it opens to you. For example, we are just now beginning to receive our new fall stock, fresh, beautiful, and promising splendid selections. We want you to be among the customers who will enjoy a chance to make advance selections. We are therefore anxious that you do not allow this small amount to prevent your taking advantage of the opportunity.

Appeal to
fair play

> You have already enjoyed a liberal extension of time. As a matter of fair play and in justice to other customers, we cannot longer permit a delay. Please let us know at once the difficulty that has caused the delay. We strongly urge you to retain your past credit standing in our establishment.

Direct
demand

> To do so, your check to cover the full amount of the statement must be in our hands by noon of June 21.

The discussion rehearses credit material and stresses the appeals of fair play and cooperation. Attention is called to the exact amount of the statement, the dates of previous notices, and the amount of time during which the debt has been overdue. The message closes with a direct, imperative demand for explanation and payment.

4 — *Urgency.* The urgency stage calls for force, delivering the ultimatum to the customer who has chosen to ignore two reminders and a third message inviting discussion. *The urgency ultimatum should be promptly followed by the action it threatens to take.*

The language of urgency is sharp and imperative. The keynote is finality: an insistence on immediate payment. But the insistence must be in a matter of fact manner to avoid show of anger. The threat of action to be taken may be (a) to place the account in the hands of a collection agency or (b) to institute a suit at law.

STAGE IV: URGENCY (THREAT OF OTHER ACTION)

Final
restatement
of facts

> It is a matter of deep regret that our efforts calling attention to your indebtedness and urging payment of your account have received no consideration. The attached statement indicates the exact amount of your account and the full period of your delinquency.

Appeal to
fair play

> You have already enjoyed an extension of time far in excess of that permitting good credit standing. Justice to other customers makes a further delay of payment out of the question.

Appeals
to fear,
self-esteem,
community
standing

> It now becomes necessary to inform you that, unless your check for your account in full is in our hands by July 10, we shall assume that you have no desire whatever to cooperate with us. Your account will then be transferred to a collection agency. You are aware, of course, that such action damages your credit rating in the community. We feel certain that you will prevent such an unfavorable situation by attending to this matter at once.

Final
action;
urgent
demand

> Let us urge you to act immediately so that it will not be necessary for us to resort to this drastic method of protecting our interests. To avoid this unpleasant action, you must have your check in our hands not later than July 10.

Note how this ultimatum uses one insistent phrase after another to emphasize the necessity for final fast action on the part of the debtor if unpleasant measures are to be avoided. Appeal is made to self-esteem, community prestige, fair play, and fear.

TIME INTERVALS

The time interval between collection efforts depends on several factors: (1) The credit standing of the customer on the basis of the original credit investigation and his past record, (2) the fact that the customer has or has not been delinquent before, (3) the nature of the business, (4) whether usual credit practice allows long or short collection periods, (5) business conditions. Businessmen are in general agreement that the more serious the case, the shorter should be the time between efforts and the sooner the matter should go to a collection agency or to legal action.

Save the customer. The collection effort must not only get the money but it must also strive to save the customer. Modern collection methods rely heavily on the constructive appeals of pride, self-esteem, reputation, fair play, and the Golden-Rule cooperative spirit. So vivid do they make the obligation that the debtor's conscience spurs him into paying. He is almost literally "sold" into paying his account. The old-style, run-of-the-mill, hammer-and-tongs, fear-and-threat, customer-killer approach gives way to the modern collection persuasiveness of today. All tests show that the sales point of view wins the best collection results. The persuasive appeal of "you can still save your credit rating if . . ." plays a potent part even in closing stages when legal action looms and last-chance urgency takes the center of attention.

Thank the prompt-pay customer. Customers who pay, and do so promptly, are likely to remain your most valuable patrons. They are the ones who most deserve your warm recognition. The Installment Loan department of a banking institution expresses its thanks:

APPRECIATION TO A PROMPT-PAY CUSTOMER

Opening of warm thanks	Thank you for the excellent manner in which you have so promptly taken care of your Instaloan. It has been a pleasure to serve you.
Explanatory material	Your final remittance has been credited to your account and your Instaloan has been marked "Paid in Full." Your note will be mailed to you within ten days of the date you made your final payment.
Closing suggestion for new business	Now that you have paid your loan, may we suggest that you continue your monthly payment habit, this time with regular monthly deposits into a National Bank savings account or checking account. You will thus establish a reserve for cash payments to take advantage of sudden opportunities or to meet emergencies.

Customers who pay, and do so promptly, are likely to remain your most valuable patrons. Recognize them. Treat them well.

Summary. The credit-collection officer performs a pivotal function in business management. Using creative ingenuity, he strives to get the money and keep the customer. Both are necessary outcomes. The degree to which he brings them both about is one measure of his performance efficiency. He relies heavily upon the written word because the written word stays on the record. He uses the written message because he considers the subject *too crucial or too significant to be entrusted to casual, short-lived verbal form.* Even with all the ultra-modern help now available to him through electronic data processing, he finds that in his particular sector of business management, *he is absolutely dependent upon the carefully controlled written word.* How such written words function in his field of financial specialization has been the subject of this section.

• *REVIEW*

Correct all errors in the following statements from sales messages.

1 — With Varnish Spot Cleaner youll save dollars in cleaning bills and still keep you're cloths more imaculate than ever.

2 — Youll love playing tennis with Marnworth Tennis Balls on cement courts there new synthetic covers resist ware much longer than any ball on the market.

3 — Sending Scene-View Postcards give pleasure to friends at home.

4 — The 2½ house power engine on the Yard-King Powermower, available cost to cost at Koleby Stores, has a oversize muffler that reduces engine noise to a pur.

5 — Looking over your correspondense tomorrow, the letters typed on a Kimberly Crown Electric typewriter are the one's likely to catch your eye and win you're approval for a even right-hand margin gives a letter a real proffessional and artistic touch and enbales them to win special attention from busy executive's every time.

6 — So much fun, such good exercise, and so wonderfully relaxing, your guests will delight in playing table tennis on Robertson Companies sturdy regulation table.

7 — Fine-textured, delicious, and easy to bake, you will love the latest Miracle Taste cake mix—Triple Fudge Delight.

8 — Have you come in with aching arms and wrenched back from clipping bushes with the new electric Hedge-Master Trimmer you can trim seventy-five feet of hedge in a matter of minutes and get proffesional results.

9 — The price for dry cleaning two or more dresses are 25 per cent less if they are brought in at the same time then if they are brought in separately.

10 — The Frigid Zone Refrigerator freezes ice cubes in minutes in its' huge freezer compartment one hundred pounds of frozen foods can be conveniently stored.

11 — So reliable and elegant that many leading airline pilot's insist on owning it, the Flight Guide Calendar Wrist Watch is the watch of men who's responsibilities demand the utmost in accuracy.

12 — Rugged and durable, you will find that the Husky-Boy Card Table has strength as well as outstanding style in addition it is available in a number of finishes.

Corporation project 16-A. As credit manager of Contemporary School Supplies, Inc., write to Dean Wesley L. Matsler, Hoover School of Business, 4958 Beulah Avenue, Chattanooga, Tennessee 37409, asking for references in connection with credit information. Dean Matsler has just submitted a large order for fifty electric typewriters, fifty standard typewriters, one hundred typewriter desks, five teachers' desk-and-chair sets, and twenty-five three-shelf, 36-inch bookcases. At the same time the school submitted this large order, it asked for credit.

Corporation project 16-B. Assume that you have received, from five reliable references, uniformly favorable information concerning the credit reputation of the Hoover School of Business. Write to Dean Matsler granting credit to the school. State that their recent order is being shipped at once and that you are sending him the latest catalog of Contemporary School Supplies, Inc. Close with an invitation for future business.

Corporation project 16-C. As collection manager of Contemporary School Supplies, Inc., write a message of appreciation to Mr. Clark R. Denton, Superintendent of the Hillcrest School District, Maple City, Michigan 49664. This school district has just completed its final payment on a 90-day credit arrangement covering a large purchase of school fittings and equipment for a new school. Thank Mr. Denton for the large order from the Hillcrest School District and for their prompt payment of each credit installment. Close by reminding Mr. Denton that Contemporary carries a full line of school equipment and supplies. Invite him to do business with Contemporary School Supplies, Inc., in the future.

Corporation project 16-D. As assistant collection manager of Contemporary School Supplies, Inc., prepare a four-stage collection message series for use by Contemporary collection correspondents. Assume that the "reminder" and the "stronger reminder" messages are to be sent as printed postal card messages requesting payment. Assume that the "discussion" and "urgency" units are to be developed as messages, individually typed.

Make your language fit the collection stage for which you are writing. In each stage be understanding and courteous, yet firm. Remember that the purpose of a collection message is "to collect the money and keep the customer."

SECTION 1

Sentence X-Ray (Diagram)

R
E
F
E
R
E
N
C
E

G
U
I
D
E

 **Introduction**

This section is a guide to the "x-raying" of sentences. It provides what many teachers and students have found to be a valuable supplementary approach for mastering the grammatical and rhetorical resources of English. X-raying sentences is a technique for analyzing constructions and representing them graphically, so that the interrelationships among their elements are displayed in outline form and thus clarified and emphasized.

Medical doctors and teachers rely upon x-rays to explain and diagnose certain kinds of health problems. Similarly, many writers find that a sentence chart—a kind of x-ray of the constructions appearing in any sentence—provides practical assistance in perceiving (1) whether the parts of a sentence fit together unambiguously and (2) whether the word forms are appropriate to their functions. Thus, the sentence x-ray offers a visual aid for diagnosing various kinds of possible errors, weaknesses, and ambiguities in writing.

To demonstrate the diagnostic value of visually displaying the various elements in a sentence, let us consider three examples. Take first this sentence: "Larry is one of those students who cooperates/cooperate enthusiastically." Students who have trouble deciding whether *cooperates* (the singular form of the verb) or *cooperate* (the plural form of the verb) is appropriate in such a sentence can perceive instantly from a sentence x-ray that the antecedent of *who* is plural and that the plural form of the verb is appropriate.

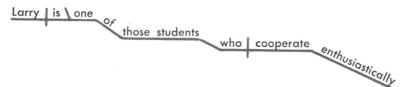

Note that the effect of the x-ray is to reveal visually the way in which the parts of the sentence fit together and are interrelated. The x-ray "loosens" the parts that make up the sentence and arranges them in a pattern that focuses attention upon their differing functions and interdependence.

A second example will further clarify the usefulness of this technique. Suppose we consider this sentence: "Each of the members is/are enthusiastic." The noun *members* standing immediately before the verb sometimes influences a writer or speaker to choose the plural form of the verb. An x-ray shows at once that *members* is part of a modifying element and should not influence the form of the verb:

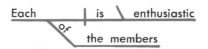

Before we learn the tricks of sentence x-raying, it may be helpful to look at one more example illustrating the usefulness of the technique. Let's examine this sentence: "Roger is someone *who/whom* I think will succeed." Here the problem involves the function of the relative pronoun *who/whom*. If the pronoun itself is functioning as the object of the verb *think*, it should be in the objective (accusative) case *whom*. On the other hand, if it is functioning as the subject of the verb phrase *will succeed*, it should be in the subjective (nominative) case *who*. Once the sentence is x-rayed we see at once the nature of the relationship between the pronoun and the other elements in the sentence.

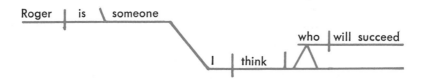

Thus, the x-ray reveals that *who* serves as the subject of the dependent clause. Furthermore, the x-ray shows that the clause *who will succeed* functions as the direct object of the transitive verb *think*. In addition we can see that the whole clause *who I think will succeed* serves to modify *someone*.

While the fundamental x-raying technique is the same for all types of sentences, there are two or three simple tricks than can be very useful for emphasizing the various kinds of constructions related to the four basic patterns of sentences. Let's start with Pattern 1 sentences to get the idea of the basic technique.

Guide 1: SENTENCE X-RAYS FOR UNDERSTANDING THE FOUR BASIC SENTENCE PATTERNS

A. X-Raying Pattern 1 Sentences

Transitive verb with direct object. *(See page 33)* As we noted in the Introduction to this guide, many students understand the grammatical relationships among the parts of a sentence better if they see those relationships represented pictorially, graphically. When one is confused by the syntax of a sentence, a diagram will display the parts of the sentence so that their interrelationships are clarified.

In this first section we shall learn how to chart modifying words and phrases, as well as how to chart the essential parts of Pattern 1 sentences—subject, transitive verb, and object. Let's take an easy example for a start and consider this sentence: "The students completed their assignment." Here is the sentence in x-ray form:

Subject	Transitive Verb	Direct Object
The students	completed	their assignment

It's useful to let the vertical line between subject and verb project beneath the horizontal line. This vertical line divides the subject from the predicate, the two basic parts of a sentence.

The words *the* and *their* might be placed on slanted lines beneath *students* and *assignment*. *The* and *their* are, however, essential elements in communicating the grammatical meaning of the sentence. By keeping limiting modifiers of this kind on the same level as the words they modify, we symbolize that they are essential. Other examples of limiting modifiers (determiners) are *a, an, that, those, this, these, his, her, your, Jean's, some, any, all, seven.*

In contrast, descriptive modifiers like *happy, mature, smiling, pleasant, fortunate, eager,* and *powerful*—optional modifiers that contribute to the meaning of the sentence but are not essential for stipulating how a noun is related to its context—are placed on slanted lines beneath their head. Adverbial modifiers of verbs, adjectives, or adverbs are also placed on slanted lines beneath their head. Whenever possible, connect such slanted lines at a point that suggests the word order of the original sentence.

To see how this practice helps us to visualize the parts of a sentence, let's expand our original example by adding various optional
modifiers: "The serious and diligent students quickly and efficiently
completed their very challenging assignment." Here is the expanded
sentence in x-ray form:

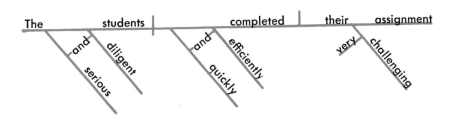

Prepositional phrases are charted in a similar way, except that the
preposition is placed on a line that connects the object of the preposition to its head. Let's alter our original sentence to illustrate this
possibility: "The students from Denver completed their assignment
in mathematics without delay."

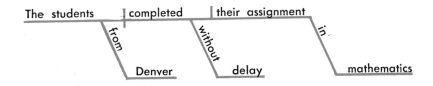

Note how neatly the x-ray reveals the linking function of the prepositions, the noun-modifying function of two of the prepositional phrases
(indicating *which* students and *which* assignment), and the verb-
modifying function of the third (indicating the manner in which they
completed their assignment).

Single-word and phrasal modifiers are displayed in this same way
in x-rays of all sentence types.

Transitive verb in passive form. *(See pages 123-125)* Sentences
containing transitive verbs always can have an alternative form with
the verb expressed in passive voice. Take as an example the sentence
we discussed in this section: "The students completed their assignment." With its verb in passive voice, the sentence would read as
follows: "Their assignment was completed by the students."

Sec. 1 • Sentence X-Ray (Diagram)

Sentences with verbs in passive voice may be x-rayed essentially in the same way as sentences with verbs in active voice. Note how neatly the x-ray indicates that the performer of the action is expressed by a prepositional phrase:

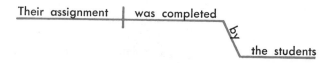

Sending-type transitive verb with indirect object and direct object. *(See page 34)* The main feature of such sentences is the inclusion of an indirect object, in addition to the structures we have already learned to display graphically. Let's use the following sentence for purposes of illustration: "The secretary gave her supervisor the memorandum."

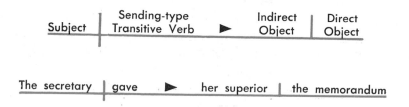

In some forms of diagramming, the indirect object is placed beneath the verb, as a kind of adverb. Thus, in the sentence above, *her superior* might have been placed on a slanted line under *gave*. While either method of x-raying the indirect object is helpful, the form suggested here has the advantage of (1) preserving the original word order of the sentence and (2) graphically symbolizing that a special type of verb is always involved in such a construction.

When modifiers occur, represent them in the x-ray as explained on pages 638 and 639.

With a prepositional phrase substituted for the original indirect object. *(See page 34)* Since the distinguishing feature of such Pattern 1 sentences is the occurrence of a sending-type transitive verb and an indirect object, a writer always has available the resource of expressing the indirect object by means of a prepositional phrase introduced by *to* (sometimes by *for*). One of the effects of this alternative phrasing is to make possible greater emphasis on the recipient, by allowing the recipient to stand last in the sentence.

Let's experiment with the sentence we used in our earlier discussion: "The secretary gave her superior the memorandum." If we use the preposition *to* as a link to connect *superior* to the rest of the sentence, we get this result: "The secretary gave the memorandum *to her superior*." Here is our x-ray of this sentence:

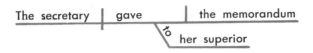

Sending-type transitive verb in passive form. *(See pages 68-69)* Only such Pattern 1 sentences can have two kinds of transformation with verbs in passive voice. Either the direct object or the indirect object may be made the subject of the passive verb. If the direct object becomes the subject, the indirect object (after a passive verb called a "retained indirect object") is retained and is x-rayed exactly like an ordinary indirect object. Let's experiment with the sentence we used in our discussion: "The secretary gave her superior the memorandum." Making the direct object the subject of the verb in passive voice, we get this: "The memorandum was given her superior by the secretary." In x-ray form, we discover these relationships:

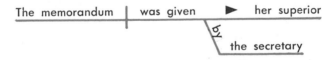

In the second kind of transformation, the indirect object becomes the subject, and the direct object (after a passive verb called a "retained direct object") is retained and is x-rayed exactly like an ordinary direct object. Here is our sentence transformed in this way: "Her superior was given the memorandum by the secretary." In x-ray form the sentence looks like this:

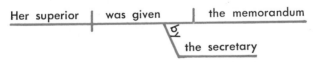

Altering-type transitive verb with objective complement. *(See pages 34-35)* The main feature of such sentences is the inclusion of an objective complement (a noun or adjective indicating the effect of the verb with reference to the direct object). The following sentences illustrate this pattern: "The directors consider Lester their representative" and "The promotion made Laura happy." Here is the x-ray form appropriate for such sentences:

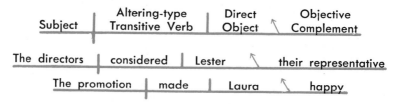

The noun or adjective which serves as an objective complement stands on the main line after the direct object and separated from it by an arrow-headed line slanted toward the direct object. The slant and arrow-head of this line symbolize that the objective complement indicates the result (or effect) upon the direct object of whatever action the verb names. Sometimes the objective complement is introduced by the expletive *as*: "Wilkins regarded him as a friend." Here is a convenient form for x-raying this pattern:

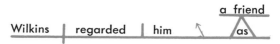

Altering-type transitive verb in passive form. *(See page 68)* Since transitive verbs occur in such Pattern 1 sentences, we can transform the verbs into passive voice and thus alter the emphasis placed upon different parts of the sentence. For example, the sentences we examined above ("The directors considered Lester their representative" and "The promotion made Laura happy") can be transformed and then x-rayed as follows:

Lester was considered by the directors as their representative.

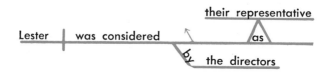

Laura was made happy by the promotion.

Objective complements retained after verbs in the passive voice can be called "retained objective complements." One could also regard them as predicate nouns or predicate adjectives, names which have the advantage of simplicity.

B. X-Raying Pattern 2 Sentences *(See pages 36-37)*

Though Pattern 2 sentences may have both single-word and phrasal modifiers, they lack the objects characteristic of Pattern 1 sentences and the predicate nouns and predicate adjectives characteristic of Pattern 3 sentences. Here is an example: "The members worked hard." The x-ray clarifies the distinctive pattern of this type of sentence:

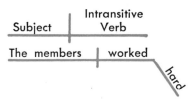

A noun-adverb often follows an intransitive verb, indicating where or when the action took place. Again, the x-ray draws attention to the fact that a Pattern 2 sentence is involved. Take these examples: "The members worked Monday" and "Jim walked home."

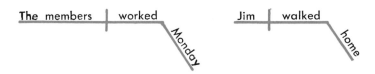

C. X-Raying Pattern 3 Sentences *(See pages 40-42)*

Like sentences of all other patterns, Pattern 3 sentences may have modifiers of all kinds. What distinguishes Pattern 3 sentences is the occurrence of a linking verb that joins a subject modifier to the subject. Since such a modifier is essential for completing the information being given about the subject, the modifier is called a *subjective complement*. Here are sample sentences, with their x-rays: "Eleanor became a supervisor" and "Stenographers must be efficient."

Eleanor | became \ a supervisor

Stenographers | must be \ efficient

The line separating the linking verb from the subjective complement (whether predicate noun or predicate adjective) is slanted toward the subject. The slant of this line reminds us (1) that the predicate noun renames the subject (refers to the same person or thing as the subject) or (2) that the predicate adjective describes the subject.

Review: Pattern 1, 2, and 3 Sentences for Practice X-Raying

1 — The employees submitted their recommendations.
2 — Each representative of the classes has offered his explanation.
3 — The teacher taught her students the principles of writing.
4 — Many companies send their regular customers catalogs.
5 — Sharon wrote her teacher a long letter.
6 — Sharon wrote a long letter to her teacher.
7 — Many companies send catalogs to their regular customers.
8 — The teacher taught the principles of writing to her students.
9 — The corporation made Mr. Franklin their local agent.
10 — Our coach considers Dick the best swimmer on the team.
11 — That simple idea made the man rich.
12 — The volunteers painted the walls of the basement blue.
13 — Many delegates left yesterday.
14 — A similar event will occur each week.
15 — The couples strolled home from the library.
16 — Many girls become expert stenographers.
17 — Each student will eventually become a competent typist.
18 — The secretary was unusually intelligent.
19 — Any brochure must be neat.
20 — The recommendations of our committee are ready.
21 — The audit seemed entirely accurate.
22 — The sophomores appear happy about the results.
23 — Ellen rearranged her office.
24 — The audience applauded thunderously.
25 — The senior accountant surely will receive the promotion.

D. X-Raying Pattern 4 Sentences

With *there* as an expletive. *(See pages 42-43)* X-rays of the first three sentence patterns essentially preserve the normal work order of the original sentences. It is desirable to preserve the actual word order of the sentence whenever possible, because word order is the basic signal in English grammar. The study of grammar is really the study of the signalling system by which meaning is communicated.

A serious problem in x-raying Pattern 4 sentences is that the logical subject occurs *after* its verb. A second problem is caused by the fact that the expletive *it* determines the form of the following verb, while the expletive *there* does not. The x-rays suggested below draw attention to these special features of Pattern 4 sentences and retain the original word order so far as possible.

Let us consider first those Pattern 4 sentences using the expletive *there*. The following sentence provides a typical example: "There are many advantages in systematic study." Here is the recommended technique for x-raying such sentences:

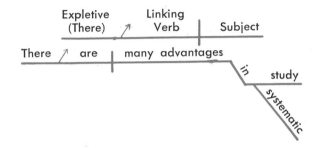

The arrow slanted toward the subject reminds us graphically that the expletive *there* has caused a postponement of the subject. The vertical line separating the linking verb from the subject reminds us that the subject (rather than a predicate noun) follows the verb.

With *it* as an expletive. *(See pages 43-44)* Pattern 4 sentences using *it* as an expletive entail somewhat different considerations: (1) the logical subject of the verb is an infinitive construction or a dependent clause, (2) the *it* substitutes for the logical subject and occupies the "subject position" to the left of the verb, and (3) a subjective complement follows the linking verb. Take these examples: "It is necessary to complete the report," "It seems fortunate that we sent the letter," and "It was an advantage to review the lesson." Here is a helpful method for x-raying such sentences:

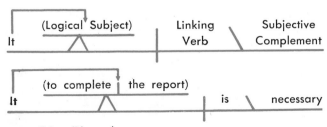

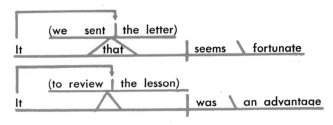

In these x-rays the logical subject is placed in parentheses after the expletive *it*. The arrow and parentheses remind us graphically that *it* has caused the logical subject to be postponed. The vertical line separating the subject and verb and penetrating the base line reminds us that *it* (unlike *there* in the other type of Pattern 4 sentence) is the grammatical subject of the verb and determines the form of the verb.

Review: Pattern 1, 2, 3, and 4 Sentences for Practice X-Raying

1 — There are three available copies of the book.
2 — His promotion will probably occur next year.
3 — The coach gave his team careful advice.
4 — It seems certain that Lester will succeed.
5 — The principal considered Nancy the outstanding graduate.
6 — Our team has seemed extremely energetic.
7 — There have been many suggestions for improvement.
8 — The contest will undoubtedly continue in the future.
9 — Esther gave the counselor copies of her essays.
10 — The corporation has scheduled a meeting of stockholders.

Guide 2: SENTENCE X-RAYS FOR UNDERSTANDING THE FUNCTIONS OF NOUNS

In this section we shall learn effective methods of x-raying all of the structures in which nouns frequently appear. The most frequent of these structures (subject, direct object, indirect object, objective complement, predicate noun, and adverbial noun) have already appeared in connection with the x-raying of the four basic sentence patterns. To make this survey comprehensive and convenient, we shall repeat these structures here and proceed to treat the many other structures characteristic of nouns. The presentation will be an illustrative sentence (with the noun in question italicized) and the recommended x-ray.

1 — Noun as subject (See page 65): *Writers* check their work.

| Writers | check | their work |

2 — Nouns as direct object (See page 65): The secretary prepared a *memorandum*.

```
The secretary | prepared | a memorandum
```

3 — Noun as indirect object (See page 65): The principal sent each *student* the form.

```
The principal | sent ▶ each student | the form
```

4 — Noun as objective complement (See page 65): The teacher considered his students *friends*.

```
The teacher | considered | his students \ friends
```

5 — Noun as object of a preposition (See page 65): The agent of the *company* brought copies to the *meeting*.

6 — Noun as appositive (use the same method for x-raying restrictive and nonrestrictive appositives) (See page 65): Miss Cousins, our *advisor,* is fascinated by Shaw's play *Saint Joan*.

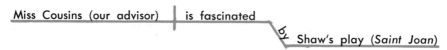

7 — Noun as noun-adjunct (See page 66): The *house* builder consulted the landowner about the *tax* rate.

8 — Noun used in direct address (See page 66): *Lowell,* we need your assistance.

```
(Lowell)
we | need | your assistance
```

9 — Noun as possessive modifier (See page 66): The *company's* van delivered the *customer's* package.

```
The company's van | delivered | the customer's package
```

10 — The possessive form of a noun used in ways other than as an attributive modifier (See page 67):

"That letter of *Father's* is too long."

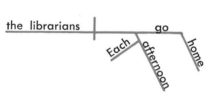

"This dictionary is Cora's."

This dictionary | is \ Cora's [dictionary]

11 — Noun as subjective complement (predicate noun) (See page 67): Donald has become the *leader.*

Donald | has become \ the leader

12 — Noun as adverb (See page 68): Each *afternoon* the librarians go *home.*

the librarians | go

13 — Noun as retained direct object (after passive voice verbs of transformed sentences in which the former indirect object is serving as subject): The consultant was given that *explanation* by Kent. (This sentence is a passive transformation of this one: Kent gave the consultant that explanation.) (See pages 68-69)

14 — Noun as retained indirect object (after passive voice verbs of transformed sentences in which the former direct object is serving as subject): That explanation was given the *consultant* by Kent. (This sentence is a passive transformation of this one: Kent gave the consultant that explanation.) (See page 69)

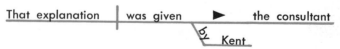

15 — Noun as retained objective complement (after passive voice verbs of transformed sentences in which the former direct object is

serving as subject): Jerome was appointed the company's *representative* by the president. (This sentence is a passive transformation of this: The president appointed Jerome the company's representative.) This structure can be regarded simply as a predicate noun. (See page 68.)

$$\underline{\text{Jerome} \quad | \quad \text{was appointed} \qquad \diagdown \quad \text{the company's representative}}$$
$$\underset{\diagdown}{\overset{}{b_{\!\!y}}} \quad \underline{\text{the president}}$$

Guide 3: SENTENCE X-RAYS FOR UNDERSTANDING INFINITIVE PHRASES AND GERUND PHRASES
(See pages 88-89)

Infinitives and gerunds are sometimes accompanied by "subjects" —by a noun or pronoun indicating the performer of the action expressed by the infinitive or gerund. In this situation, objective case forms are used with an infinitive. For example: The assistant asked him to complete the application.

$$\underline{\text{him} \; | \; \text{to complete} \; | \; \text{the application}}$$
$$\underline{\text{The assistant} \quad | \quad \text{asked} \quad | \qquad \bigwedge \qquad \qquad \qquad \qquad}$$

Accompanying a gerund, a noun or pronoun occurs in the possessive case. For example: Winifred complimented his singing.

$$\underline{\text{Winifred} \quad | \quad \text{complimented} \quad | \quad \text{his singing}}$$

Note that as a verbal noun, the gerund is x-rayed like other nouns. Its function determines its place in the x-ray.

Guide 4: SENTENCE X-RAYS FOR UNDERSTANDING FLEXIBILITY IN ADJECTIVE PLACEMENT
(See page 98)

There are four principal positions which descriptive adjectives can occupy in a sentence:

1 — Attributive position (immediately before the term modified): The *clever* advertisement attracted many *enthusiastic* customers.

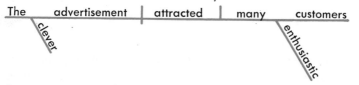

Descriptive adjectives in the attributive position are optional stylistic features. A writer may omit or multiply them at will.

2 — Appositive position (immediately following the term modified): The secretary, *eager* and *competent,* began the assignment.

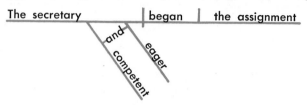

Descriptive adjectives in the appositive position are optional stylistic features. A writer may omit or multiply them at will.

3 — Predicate position (as a predicate adjective required after a linking verb): The report will be comprehensive.

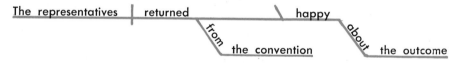

After a linking verb, a subjective complement regularly occurs. The subjective complement (i.e., completer of the subject) may be a predicate adjective or a predicate noun. Note that in the x-ray a predicate adjective (or noun) is placed on the main line.

Predicate position (as a predicate adjective optional after an intransitive verb): The representatives returned from the convention happy about the outcome.

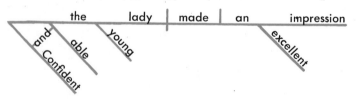

4 — Introductory position (set off by a comma—by a pause in speaking—from the subject of the sentence, the term modified): *Confident* and *able,* the young lady made an excellent impression.

Misplaced modifiers result if descriptive adjectives in the introductory position cannot logically modify the subject of the sentence.

SENTENCE X-RAYS FOR UNDERSTANDING COMPOUND STRUCTURES
(See pages 139-140)

The x-ray is a useful tool for demonstrating grammatical parallelism—the identical use of two or more structures within a single sentence. Often the parallel structures are joined by means of a coordinating conjunction (*and, or, but*) or by means of correlative conjunctions (*either/or, neither/nor, not only/but also, not/but,* etc.). Here are examples of sentences with various kinds of compound structures. Note how clearly the x-ray is able to picture the parallel use of the compound elements.

1 — Compound subject: The manager and his assistant examined the document.

2 — Compound verb: The official drafted and carefully revised his speech.

3 — Compound direct object: Wendy closed both the door and the window.

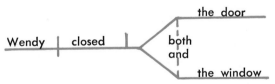

4 — Compound indirect object: The editor gave Mel and Carl additional suggestions.

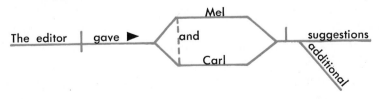

5 — Compound predicate noun: Henry has become an impressive speaker and effective writer.

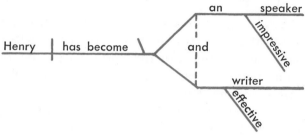

6 — Compound predicate: Nan brought her typewriter and prepared all the notices.

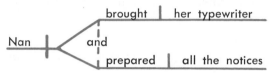

7 — Compound sentence—two main clauses: These students finished the assignment, but the others completed only one sentence.

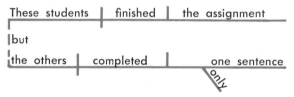

Compound sentence—two main clauses: Either the plan must be approved, or no change will be possible.

the plan | must be approved
|Either
|or
|no change | will be \ possible

Guide 6: SENTENCE X-RAYS FOR UNDERSTANDING COMPLEX SENTENCES
(See pages 141-144)

A complex sentence contains one main clause and one or more dependent clauses. The central value of the x-ray for such sentences is that it pictures the function of the dependent clause. One can see at a glance, for example, whether a dependent clause is serving as subject, direct object, appositive, predicate noun, object of a preposition, some kind of modifier, or some other structure.

Dependent clauses introduced by a subordinating conjunction.
(See pages 141-143):

1 — As subject: That an improvement had occurred was undeniable.

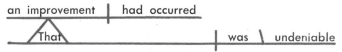

2 — As direct object: The manager believes that the advertisement improved sales. Note that the subordinating conjunction *that* may be omitted in such sentences.

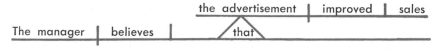

3 — As appositive: The idea that services win customers seems basic to success.

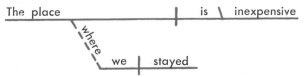

4 — As noun modifier: The place where we stayed is inexpensive.

5 — As verb modifier: Prices have risen because copper has become scarce.

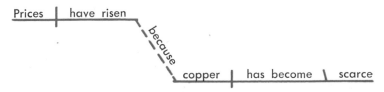

6 — As adjective modifier: The lecture was so excellent that Jim forgot to take notes.

Dependent clauses introduced by a relative pronoun. *(See pages 143-144):*

1 — As noun modifier (the relative pronoun serving as subject in the dependent clause): The brackets which arrived this morning will be installed without delay.

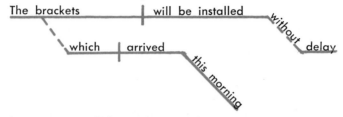

2 — As noun modifier (the relative pronoun serving as direct object in the dependent clause): The suggestion that Miss Janiss offered at the conference has not been tried.

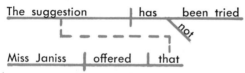

[In the dependent clause the relative pronoun *that* replaces the noun *suggestion*]

3 — As subject (the indefinite relative pronoun serving as subject in the dependent clause): Whoever remembered to check the oil deserves our thanks.

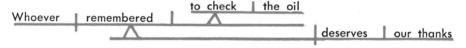

4 — As subject (the relative pronoun serving as direct object in the dependent clause): Whomever Hollis selects will be assigned those responsibilities.

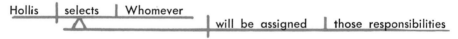

5 — As object in a prepositional phrase used to modify a noun: The investigation into who made the decision has begun already.

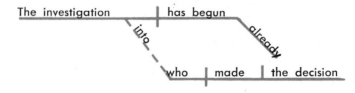

6 — As object in a prepositional phrase used to modify a verb:
The registrar sends the forms to whoever requests them.

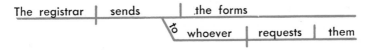

Guide 7: **SENTENCE X-RAYS FOR UNDERSTANDING QUESTIONS**
(See pages 150-152)

Questions are x-rayed in the same way as statements, with one important difference: If the question entails a reversal in the sequence of the subject and verb, the x-ray must draw attention to this essential signal. The following sentences illustrate the technique: "Tim does study frequently" and "Does Tim study frequently?"

Statement: Question:

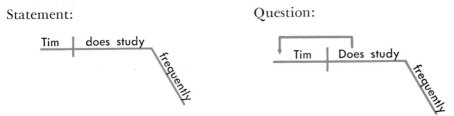

One advantage of the question x-ray is that it emphasizes that the same bond exists between subject and finite verb in questions as in statements. Another is that the arrow reminds us that the reversal in the sequence of the subject and verb is an essential grammatical signal.

Questions signalled only by a reversal in the order of subject and verb. *(See pages 150-151):*

"Have the students submitted their assignment yet?"

"Are the foremen coming to the meeting?"

"Will the shipment arrive today?"

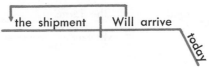

"Must all students send the college a copy of their transcripts?"

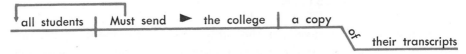

Questions signalled by both an interrogatory function word and a reversal in the order of subject and verb. *(See pages 151-152):*

"To whom were the instructions given?"

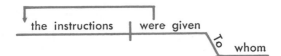

"When will the new edition be ready?"

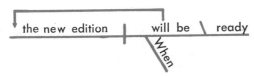

"Why have the rooms not been painted?"

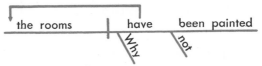

"Where will the consultant have his office?"

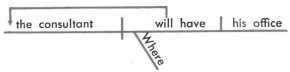

"How soon must the sponsor receive an answer?"

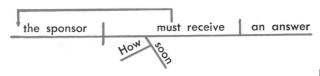

Questions signalled only by an interrogatory function word. *(See page 151):*

"Who sent the principal this obsolete outline?"

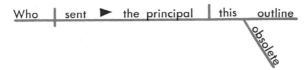

"Which entrance will be refinished?"

"What caused Jill to leave so suddenly?"

Guide 8: SENTENCE X-RAYS FOR UNDERSTANDING REQUESTS AND COMMANDS
(See page 152)

The most distinctive feature of requests and commands is that a subject does not occur. A proper name or the pronoun *you* may be used in direct address to secure the attention of the person concerned, but the term in direct address is always set off by a pause in speech and by commas in writing. For example: Lester, bring in the files.

```
(Lester)

    x  |  bring   |  the files
                  \
                   in
```

Note how an x-ray emphasizes the difference between a command/request and the corresponding statement: Lester brings in the files.

```
Lester  |  brings  |  the files
                   \
                    in
```

Using parentheses around the term in direct address, placing it higher than the regular subject position, and inserting an *x* in the regular subject position are techniques designed to emphasize the difference in grammatical signals between a command/request and a statement.

Please is an especially important function word for signifying politeness and consideration in commands and requests. In business communications, both oral and written, there is no substitute for the tone of courtesy conveyed by *please*. *Please* is best x-rayed as a special kind of auxiliary verb:

"Pauline, please retype these summaries."

(Pauline)

$$\underline{\quad x \quad | \quad \text{please retype} \quad | \quad \text{these summaries} \quad}$$

"Please be careful, ladies and gentlemen."

(ladies and gentlemen)

$$\underline{\quad x \quad | \quad \text{Please be} \quad \backslash \quad \text{careful} \quad}$$

"Jack, please consult a current dictionary to find the correct spelling of this word."

(Jack)

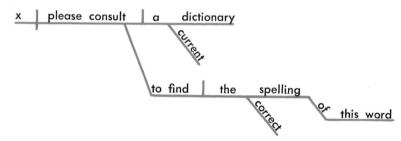

Reference Guide

SECTION 2

Guide to Correct Typewritten Form

Footnotes, quotations, and reference lists occur from time to time in general papers and in business reports. You will find it useful and necessary to know how to handle the manuscript details set forth in the following pages.

FOOTNOTES

Footnotes are used in three important ways:

1 — To make it easier for subsequent students to take up an investigation
2 — To explain and amplify matters referred to in the main text
3 — To protect the writer against any possible charge of improper use of his materials (plagiarism)

Footnotes should be attached to important statements of fact and to any interpretations or inferences taken from other writers. Footnotes may be numbered consecutively throughout a short report, or they may be numbered anew for each chapter of a long report. In theses and books the numbering usually begins anew at the opening of each chapter.

Placement of footnote references. The footnote reference figures (superscripts) can be placed in one of two places:

1 — At the end of the quoted material
2 — At the end of the statement that introduces the quoted material

With numerical charts, graphs, and tables, where superscripts might be confusing, symbols may be used in this order:

1 — Asterisk (*)
2 — Dagger (†)
3 — Double dagger (‡)
4 — Section mark (§)
5 — Parallel (‖)

Spacing. Footnotes are separated from the text by a single space, a 1½-inch line from the left margin, and a double space. There should be a margin of approximately one inch below the footnotes on all pages. Footnotes are single-spaced with a double space between them. The first line is indented to paragraph point.

Footnotes illustrated. The first reference to a work should be given in full. The following forms are acceptable; and once a form or style is adopted, it should be used consistently.

For books, the order of presenting the various elements is:

1 — Author's name, comma (John J. Jones,)
2 — Title of book, underlined, no comma
3 — Facts of publication in parentheses, comma (edition number, location and name of publisher, year of publication)
4 — Page reference, period

For an article or other portion of a magazine or periodical, the order is:

1 — Author's name, comma
2 — Title of article (or chapter, etc.) in quotation marks, with a comma
3 — Title of publication, underlined, comma
4 — Volume number, comma, "No." reference, no comma, date of issue in parentheses, comma
5 — Page reference, period

For an article in a bound volume, the order is:

1 — Author's name, comma
2 — Title of article in quotation marks, comma
3 — Title of publication, underlined, no comma
4 — Facts of publication as for books

5 — Volume number, issue number and date, page reference, period

Subsequent footnotes. When two footnotes referring to the same work occur without intervening footnotes, use *ibid.* (for *ibidem,* in the same place). Add the page number of the second reference if it differs from the first.

For reference to a different page of a work already cited but with intervening footnotes, use the author's surname and the notation *op. cit.* (for *opere citato,* in the work cited), and the page number. For a reference precisely like a reference not immediately preceding, use the author's name and *loc. cit.* (for *loco citato,* in the same place) with no page number.

Additional use of footnotes. It is customary also to use textual footnotes to discuss or amplify points in the text.

One-Author Book→
Two-Author Book→
Three-Author Book→
Unpublished Material→
Magazine Article→
Newspaper Article→

[1]Lois Irene Hutchinson, "Postal Information," Standard Handbook for Secretaries (8th ed.; New York: McGraw-Hill, Inc., 1969), p. 345.

[2]Robert R. Aurner and Paul S. Burtness, Effective English for Business Communication (6th ed.; Cincinnati: South-Western Publishing Co., 1970), pp. 429-457.

[3]J Marshall Hanna, Estelle L. Popham, and Esther Kihn Beamer, Secretarial Procedures and Administration (5th ed.; Cincinnati: South-Western Publishing Co., 1968), pp. 234-237.

[4]James E. Silverthorn, The Basic Vocabulary of Written Business Communications (Doctoral dissertation, Indiana University, 1955), p. 32.

[5]Dorothy Betts, "Let's Communicate," The Balance Sheet, Vol. LI, No. 6 (February, 1970), pp. 254-256.

[6]Cincinnati Enquirer (April 25, 1970), p. 14.

MODEL FOOTNOTES

QUOTATIONS

Quotations should be brief and pertinent. They should be accurate and should be verified by direct comparison with their sources. An omission is permissible if the sense of the whole passage is not distorted by it. It is customary to use omission marks (. . .) to show that part of a quotation has been dropped.

Omission marks, also called ellipses, are printed devices signifying the omission of letters or of words in quoted material. Three marks or dots (. . .) are used to signify an omission at the beginning of the quoted discourse, or at any other point if the omitted portion or section does not end on a period. Four marks or dots (. . . .) are used when the omitted portion or section does end on a period.

An editorial explanation within a quotation is enclosed in square brackets, [ ].

> "President [Arthur W.] White pioneered in the use of the plan."

If parentheses are used, the reader understands that the material enclosed, as well as the parentheses, was taken verbatim from the original source:

> "President White (always a bold executive) pioneered in the use of the plan."

REFERENCE LIST

A reference list (or bibliography) is a list of the sources of information used in the preparation of the report or paper. It should, if possible, accompany every piece of written work in which a considerable amount of source material is used.

Arrange the list of books, articles, periodicals, or documents in alphabetical order by authors; by editors; or by titles (if the authors are unknown, as for some articles in periodicals and encyclopedias). The items may be accompanied by a few words of description.

Give exact information as to author, title, place, publisher, and year of publication in order to identify each reference. In special cases (government documents, periodicals, etc.) even more information may be required in order to complete positive identification.

The titles of books, booklets, and periodicals are ordinarily underlined in typewritten material and *printed in italics;* the titles of magazine and encyclopedia articles are enclosed in quotation marks.

A correct form for listing books, magazine articles, and periodicals, with all necessary punctuation, is given in the following examples. Note that (1) the first author's name is written with the last name first and (2) the punctuation differs from that in footnotes.

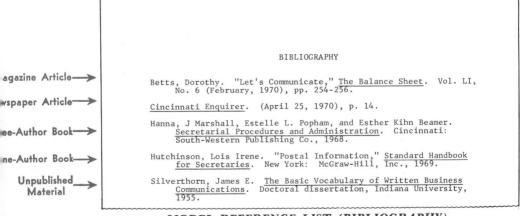

BIBLIOGRAPHY

agazine Article→ Betts, Dorothy. "Let's Communicate," The Balance Sheet. Vol. LI, No. 6 (February, 1970), pp. 254-256.

wspaper Article→ Cincinnati Enquirer. (April 25, 1970), p. 14.

ee-Author Book→ Hanna, J Marshall, Estelle L. Popham, and Esther Kihn Beamer. Secretarial Procedures and Administration. Cincinnati: South-Western Publishing Co., 1968.

ne-Author Book→ Hutchinson, Lois Irene. "Postal Information," Standard Handbook for Secretaries. New York: McGraw-Hill, Inc., 1969.

Unpublished Material → Silverthorn, James E. The Basic Vocabulary of Written Business Communications. Doctoral dissertation, Indiana University, 1955.

MODEL REFERENCE LIST (BIBLIOGRAPHY)

SECTION 3

Transcription Guide

The common aim of both the executive and his secretary is to produce truly effective messages. You will instantly recognize two outstanding qualities in a message produced by an expert secretary-executive team:

1 — Handsome external form
2 — Effective message content

Select a layout that is attractive, symmetrical, and accurate in detail. Learn to "visualize." Visualizing is seeing in your mind's eye how a message ought to look when you lay it on paper. Develop an eye for symmetry, proportion, and balance.

The guides to good usage and accurate detail provided in this section are definite. Follow them consistently. These guides, based on the authoritative practice of business leaders, give you quick, clear-cut answers to the fifty-one questions most frequently asked about transcription.

The numbered paragraphs below refer to the matching numbers in the ILLUSTRATED GUIDE on page 663.

1 — Type the message in a form symmetrical and attractive to the eye.
2 — A ZIP Code number is now used on the line with the city and state, two spaces after the state without punctuation. An approved 2-letter state-name abbreviation may be used with the ZIP Code number.
3 — Position the dateline to conform to the letter style or to the letterhead itself. Datelines may be blocked at the left margin, typed to end at the right margin, begun at the horizontal center of the sheet, or aligned with an element of the letterhead.
4 — Spell names of months in full, both in the dateline and in the body.
5 — Omit *st, d,* and *th* after the number of the day unless the month is not mentioned.
6 — Place a comma between the day of the month and the year.
7 — Omit punctuation after the year in a dateline. Within a sentence, insert a comma.
8 — Type the address in block form at the left margin three blank spaces below the date.
9 — To make the lines of the address as nearly equal in length as possible, place the addressee's title (a) on the same line as his name, (b) on the next line, preceding the name of the firm, or (c) on a separate line, below the name.
10 — Use a comma between the addressee's title and his name or the firm name.

The AURNER Corporation

Management Consultant Division

Post Office Box 3434
Carmel, California 93921

September 11, 19--

Mr. G. W. Knight, President
Burke & Webb Company, Inc.
12 North Third Street, N.W.
Philadelphia, PA 19106

My dear Mr. Knight:

Your active interest in improving communications efficiency--and in cutting communications costs--is noteworthy. Special studies in the practical research laboratory of the small, medium, and large business office can give you some startling cost figures.

Some otherwise ultramodern executives are only self-trained in the difficult art of maintaining consistent quality in their communications output. What is commonplace knowledge to the expert is to some of them startling news and shocking fact: A letter is often much more expensive than a comparable telegram!

R. R. Roe, President of Roe and Associates, has written a book entitled Effective Communication in Business. In Chapter I, "Can You Slash the High Cost of Business Communication?" Mr. Roe states, "Business messages are expensive production tools that may be costing you more than $2.50 each--at least three times *more* than the old estimate of 75 cents each."

Mr. Roe concludes that the effective message wins because:

1. It becomes the executive's right arm and extends his personal power. Says one president, "It enlarges my business field, gives me greater personal 'weight'!"

2. It can be made to win business friendship in summer and winter, spring and fall.

If 40 letters cost you $100, a 10 percent increase in dictating-executive efficiency returns $10 in clear capital to your treasury.

Sincerely yours,

THE AURNER CORPORATION

RRAurner/kd

President and Director

Copy to Communications, Inc.

ILLUSTRATED GUIDE

11 — Capitalize the principal words of titles and the names of departments (Credit Department).

12 — Use end-of-line punctuation only after permissible abbreviations.

13 — Write the firm name as it appears on the firm's own letterhead.

14 — Use the ampersand "&" [and] only when the firm itself uses it.

15 — It is permissible to abbreviate *Incorporated (Inc.)* and *Limited (Ltd.)*. A comma may or may not occur before *Incorporated* or *Inc.* and *Limited or Ltd.* When *Incorporated* or *Inc.* and *Limited* or *Ltd.* occurs within a sentence, use a comma immediately after them. Write in full the words *Company* and *Corporation.*

16 — Write in full the words North, South, East, and West in street directions.

17 — Spell out the number naming a street if it is ten or below; for eleven or above, use figures. For example: 555 North 79th Street.

18 — For postal sections of a city (N.E., S.E., N.W., S.W.; e.g., 711 - 14th Street, N.W.), use initials followed by periods, but do not abbreviate Avenue, Boulevard, or Street.

19 — Type the name of the city and the state on the same line, **sep**arated with a comma.

20 — The state name may be spelled in full, abbreviated in the standard manner, or abbreviated according to the 2-letter ZIP abbreviation. The inside address and the envelope address should agree.

21 — If an "attention" line is necessary, place it a double space below the inside address and a double space above the salutation. Since the attention line is part of the address, the preferred placement is at the left margin. The attention line may, however, be centered. Capitalize only the principal words. When the letter is addressed to a company, use the salutation *Gentlemen.*

22 — The first word of a salutation is always capitalized. Note that the word *dear* is not capitalized unless it is the first word.

23 — Type the salutation even with the left margin, a double space below the last line of the inside address, followed by a colon in mixed punctuation. *Do not* use a hyphen.

24 — Begin the body a double space below the salutation. Indent the paragraphs five to (not more than) ten spaces. The block form (no indention) is optional.

25 — To maintain a reasonably even right margin requires occasional hyphenation. Divide a word only when necessary and never at the end of more than two successive lines.

26 — Leave two spaces after a colon, exclamation point, question mark, or period (one space after a period following an initial or abbreviation used within the sentence). Leave one space after a comma or semicolon. Leave two spaces between sentences.

27 — Type the hyphen or dash at the end of a line rather than at the beginning of the next.

28 — Use a comma to point off words or word groups used in a series of at least three units. Place a comma before *and, or,* or *nor* in a series of three or more items.

29 — The dash (--) is made by typing the hyphen twice, without spacing before or after.

30 — Double-space between paragraphs.

31 — The hyphen (-) is used to link together compound words.

32 — Capitalize the first word of a fully stated direct quotation.

33 — Use figures and spell out the word *cents*.

34 — A comma or a period should precede the closing quotation mark. A semicolon or a colon should follow the quotation mark. A question mark or an exclamation point is placed inside the quotation mark when a part of the quoted matter; outside when not a part.

35 — Set off with commas a word or words in apposition.

36 — When referring to articles and books, place in quotation marks the titles of articles, short monographs, and chapters. Underline or type entirely in capitals the titles of books, magazines, and other full-length works. Such titles are preceded and followed by commas only when they are in apposition.

37 — Use a colon after the words that introduce an enumeration or a long quotation. Use a comma before a short quotation.

38 — Indent enumerations and long quotations equally from both margins. Double-space between paragraphs.

39 — Place a period after a point number of an enumeration, and space twice after the period.

40 — Begin the second and following lines of centered material directly under the first letter of the first word of the first line.

41 — A quotation within a quotation is enclosed in single quotation marks (' '). Double quotation marks are placed with relation to other punctuation marks according to Guide No. 34.

42 — Seasons of the year are capitalized only when they are personified. (Example: "Harsh Winter and his minions fade . . . and gentle SPRING takes o'er her reign."

43 — Express even sums of money without the decimal and ciphers.

44 — Express percentages in figures; spell out *percent*.

45 — Use a hyphen to connect two/or more words compounded to express a single idea.

46 — Type the complimentary close a double space below the last line of the body. It is begun at the left margin in block style, begun at the horizontal center of the sheet, or placed so that the longest line ends at the right margin.

47 — When the company name is used, type it in solid capital letters on the second line below and even with the complimentary close.

48 — Type the official title (if used) on the fourth line below the complimentary close or the company name.

49 — Type the signature identification and stenographic reference flush with the left margin and on a line with the dictator's official title, or a double space below.

50 — Type the word *Enclosure,* or the abbreviation *Enc.* (if necessary) flush with the left margin a double space below the signature identification. More than one enclosure is indicated by adding the correct figure: *Enclosures 2* or *Enc. 2.*

51 — The phrase *Copy to* or *Copies to* is typed a double space below the last item of the letter followed by the name or names of those to whom carbon copies are being sent.

 **SECTION 4**

Word-Division Guide

You will find it desirable to keep relatively even the right margin of typewritten messages, general papers, reports, and other types of manuscripts. To achieve this aim, you must often divide words. When a word is divided at the end of a line, you indicate the division by a hyphen (-) following the syllable or syllables at the end of the line.

Syllabication is of three kinds:

1 — Dictionaries show *all* the syllables into which a word may be divided. For readability, however, it may not be desirable to divide at a point permitted by the dictionary.

2 — In printed material the left margin and the right margin must be exactly even. To keep these margins even, it is now and then necessary to divide a word at a point that does interfere somewhat with the readability of the material.

3 — In *typewritten* material, unlike books, the right margin does not have to be exactly even. Hence it becomes possible for the typist to make a choice with regard to how words are divided. To aid the typist, a set of principles has been developed for the syllabication of typewritten material. Their use will make the right margin as attractive as possible

without interfering with the readability of the copy.

There are certain word-division rules that must always be followed. There are certain other rules that it is desirable to follow but that may be suspended if following them would make the right margin too uneven. Generally, however, the typist can follow the "desirable" rules as well as the "must" rules.

"MUST" RULES

1. Divide words only between syllables. One-syllable words, therefore, should never be divided. (E.g., filed, missed, typed, through)

2. There must be more than one letter with the first part of the word and more than two letters with the last part of the word.

alone *not* a-lone	truly *not* tru-ly
above *not* a-bove	into *not* in-to
steady *not* stead-y	teacher *not* teach-er

It follows, then, that four- and five-letter words cannot be divided. Furthermore, it is *preferred* that six-letter words not be divided.

letter	*is preferred to*	let-ter
enlist	*is preferred to*	en-list

3. A syllable that is separated from the remainder of the word must contain a vowel.

con-trol	*but not*	could-n't
doc-trine	*but not*	does-n't

4. When a final consonant, preceded by a single vowel, is doubled before adding a suffix, divide between the two consonants.

run-ning	*not*	runn-ing
step-ping	*not*	stepp-ing

BUT when a root word ends in a double consonant before a suffix is added, divide between the root word and the suffix.

tell-ing	*not*	tel-ling
spell-ing	*not*	spel-ling
assess-ing	*not*	asses-sing

"DESIRABLE" RULES

5. A single-letter syllable within a word should generally be written with the first part of the word.

busi-ness	*not*	bus-iness
sepa-rate	*not*	sep-arate

Exceptions

(a) When two one-letter syllables occur together within a word, divide between the one letter syllables.

gradu-ation	*not*	gradua-tion
perpetu-ation	*not*	perpetua-tion

(b) When the single-letter syllable *a, i,* or *u* is followed by the ending syllable *ble, bly, cle,* or *cal,* the two ending syllables should be joined when carried over to the next line.

mir•a•cle	*divided*	mir-acle
di•vis•i•ble	*divided*	divis-ible
de•pend•a•ble	*divided*	depend-able
cler•i•cal	*divided*	cler-ical
a•gree•a•bly	*divided*	agree-ably

Note that this rule applies only when the vowel is correctly written as a syllable by itself. In the following examples the vowels *a* and *i* are *not* single-letter syllables.

du•ra•ble	*divided*	dura-ble
mu•si•cal	*divided*	musi-cal

6. Divide hyphened words and compounds—such as *two-thirds, three-fourths, self-discipline, self-explanatory,*

record-breaking, and *brother-in-law*—only at the hyphen that connects the words.

7. Put on the first line enough of the divided material to suggest what the complete word will be.

stenog-rapher	*not*	ste-nographer
recom-mend	*not*	rec-ommend
clearing-house	*not*	clear-inghouse
diffi-cult	*not*	dif-ficult
gentle-man	*not*	gen-tleman

8. Avoid dividing a surname. When it is necessary to divide parts of a proper name, divide at the logical point for readability.

Cheltenham	*not*	Chelten-ham
Mr. Robert R./ White	*not*	Mr. Robert/ R. White
Mr. James/ Smith	*not*	Mr./ James Smith

9. Avoid dividing the last word of more than two consecutive lines, the final word on a page, or the word at the end of the last complete line of a paragraph.

10. Avoid the division of figures and abbreviations.

$11,700	*not*	$11,/700
A.T.&S.F.	*not*	A.T./&S.F.

11. If it is impossible to place an entire address on a single line, separate the parts of the address as shown below.

1234 Monterey/ Street	*not*	1234/ Monterey Street
7890 South/ Bridgeport	*not*	7890 South Bridge-port
2345 - 77th/ Street	*not*	2345 - 77th Street
Akron,/ Ohio 44305	*not*	Akron, Ohio/ 44305

12. If separating the parts of a date proves unavoidable, separate the day of the month from the year, not the month from the day.

September 23,/ 19 - -	*not*	September/ 23, 19 - -

SECTION 5

Guide-Forms for Addresses and Salutations [1]—Special Groups

THE PRESIDENT AND VICE PRESIDENT

Address	*Salutation*
The President The White House Washington, D.C. 20500	Sir: To the President: Mr. President: Dear Mr. President:
The Honorable Richard M. Nixon The White House Washington, D.C. 20500	My dear President Nixon:
The Vice President United States Senate Washington, D.C. 20510	Sir: My dear Sir: Dear Sir:
The Honorable the Vice President of the United States Washington, D.C. 20510	Mr. Vice President: My dear Mr. Vice President: Dear Mr. Vice President:
The Honorable Spiro T. Agnew The Vice President of the United States Washington, D.C. 20501	

SPEAKER OF THE HOUSE

The Honorable the Speaker of the House of Representatives Washington, D.C. 20515	Sir: My dear Sir: Dear Sir:
The Speaker of the House of Representatives Washington, D.C. 20515	Mr. Speaker: My dear Mr. Speaker: Dear Mr. Speaker:
The Honorable John McCormack Speaker of the House of Representatives Washington, D.C. 20515	My dear Mr. McCormack Dear Mr. McCormack (informal)

THE SUPREME COURT

The Chief Justice of the United States Washington, D.C. 20543	Sir: Mr. Chief Justice:
The Honorable Warren E. Burger Chief Justice of the Supreme Court of the United States Washington, D.C. 20543	
The Honorable Thurgood Marshall Associate Justice of the Supreme Court Washington, D.C. 20543	Sir: Mr. Justice: Your Honor:
The Honorable Thurgood Marshall Justice, Supreme Court of the United States Washington, D.C. 20543	My dear Mr. Justice: My dear Justice Marshall: Dear Justice Marshall:

THE CABINET

The Honorable the Secretary of State Washington, D.C. 20520	Sir: My dear Sir: Dear Sir:
The Honorable William P. Rogers Secretary of State Washington, D.C. 20520	My dear Mr. Secretary: Dear Mr. Secretary:

[1] All salutations are listed in the order of decreasing formality.

Address	Salutation

The Under Secretary of the Navy Department
Washington, D.C.   20350

Sir:
My dear Sir:
Dear Sir:

The Honorable John W. Warner
Under Secretary of the Navy Department
Washington, D.C.   20350

My dear Mr. Warner:
Dear Mr. Warner: (but never Mr. Secretary):

OTHER WASHINGTON OFFICIALS

The Honorable Clinton P. Anderson
The United States Senate
Washington, D.C.   20510

Sir:
My dear Sir:
Dear Sir:
My dear Mr. Senator:

Senator Clinton P. Anderson
The United States Senate
Washington, D.C.   20510

My dear Senator:
My dear Senator Anderson:
Dear Senator Anderson:

The Honorable Clinton P. Anderson
United States Senator
Santa Fe, New Mexico   87501
(When at headquarters away from Washington)

The Honorable William O. Cowger
The House of Representatives
Washington, D.C.   20515

Sir:
My dear Sir:
Dear Sir:
My dear Representative Cowger:
Dear Representative Cowger:

Representative William O. Cowger
The House of Representatives
Washington, D.C.   20515

My dear Mr. Cowger:
My dear Congressman:
Dear Mr. Cowger: (informal)

The Honorable William O. Cowger
Representative in Congress
Frankfort, Kentucky   40601
(When at headquarters away from Washington)

The Honorable James E. Allen, Jr.
Commissioner of Education
Department of Health, Education, and Welfare
Washington, D.C.   20201

Sir:
My dear Sir:
Dear Sir:
My dear Mr. Commissioner:
My dear Mr. Allen:
Dear Mr. Allen: (informal)

STATE OFFICIALS

His Excellency
The Governor of Alaska
Juneau, Alaska   99801

Sir:
My dear Sir:
Dear Sir:
My dear Governor Miller:

The Honorable Keith H. Miller
Governor of Alaska
Juneau, Alaska   99801

Dear Governor Miller:
Dear Governor: (informal)

The Honorable the Governor of Alaska
Juneau, Alaska   99801

The Honorable Joseph T. Edger
Lieutenant Governor of Maine
Augusta, Maine   04330

Sir:
My dear Sir:
Dear Sir:

The Lieutenant Governor of the State of Maine
Augusta, Maine   04330

The Honorable J. Edward Lumbard
Chief Judge of the Court of Appeals
New York, N.Y.   10007

Sir:
My dear Sir:
Dear Sir:
My dear Judge Lumbard:
Dear Judge Lumbard:

The Honorable Allen J. Busby
The State Senate
Madison, Wisconsin   53702

Sir:
My dear Sir:
Dear Sir:

Senator Allen J. Busby
Senate Chamber
The State Capitol
Madison, Wisconsin   53702

My dear Mr. Senator:
Dear Senator:
My dear Senator Busby:
Dear Senator Busby

Address	*Salutation*
The Honorable George W. Alexander Member of the Assembly Harrisburg, Pennsylvania 17102	Sir: My dear Sir: Dear Sir: My dear Representative Alexander: My dear Mr. Alexander:
Representative George W. Alexander **or** Assemblyman George W. Alexander Assembly Chamber The State Capitol Harrisburg, Pennsylvania 17102	Dear Mr. Alexander: (informal)

CITY OFFICIALS

The Honorable B. T. Schleicher Mayor of the City of Rockford City Hall Rockford, Illinois 61104	Sir: My dear Sir: Dear Sir: My dear Mr. Mayor: Dear Mr. Mayor:
The Mayor of the City of Rockford City Hall Rockford, Illinois 61104	My dear Mayor Schleicher: Dear Mayor Schleicher: (informal)

EDUCATORS

President or Chancellor (of a College or University)

Dr. Kingman Brewster, Jr. President of Yale University New Haven, Connecticut 06520	My dear Sir: Dear Sir: My dear President Brewster: Dear President Brewster:
Roger W. Heyns, LL.D. (**or** if not an LL.D., use the initials of his highest degree) Chancellor, University of California Berkeley, California 94720	

Doctor of Philosophy (or Laws, or Medicine)

Edwin E. Green, Ph.D. (**or** LL.D., **or** M.D.) **or** Dr. Edwin E. Green **or** (to man and wife) Dr. and Mrs. Edwin E. Green 6810 Dickerson Street Detroit, Michigan 48213	My dear Sir: Dear Sir: My dear Dr. Green: Dear Dr. Green: **and** Dear Dr. and Mrs. Green:

Doctor of Divinity

W. S. Stevens, D.D. **or** Dr. W. S. Stevens **or** The Reverend Dr. W. S. Stevens (Specific address here)	My dear Sir: Dear Sir: My dear Dr. Stevens: Dear Dr. Stevens:

Professor (in a College or University)

Professor Neville Hughes Department of Electrical Engineering University of Wisconsin Madison, Wisconsin 53706	My dear Sir: Dear Sir: My dear Professor Hughes: Dear Professor Hughes:
N. W. Hughes, Ph.D. (**or** LL.D., M.D., etc., using only the initials of his highest degree) Professor of Electrical Engineering University of Wisconsin Madison, Wisconsin 53706	

CHURCHMEN

Bishop (Protestant Episcopal)

To the Right Reverend Anson Phelps Stokes, Jr. Bishop of Massachusetts	Right Reverend and dear Sir: My dear Bishop Stokes: Dear Bishop Stokes: (informal)

Bishop (Methodist Episcopal)

Reverend Bishop T. Otto Nall Bishop of the Northern Area Methodist Episcopal Church St. Paul, Minnesota 55102	Dear Sir: My dear Bishop Nall: Dear Bishop Nall:

Bishop (Anglican)

The Right Reverend the Lord Bishop of (name of bishopric here) (Specific postal address here)	My Lord Bishop: My Lord:

Address	*Salutation*
Clergyman (Protestant)	Reverend Sir: (formal)
The Reverend M. S. Tibbetts	My dear Sir:
341 Virginia Avenue	Dear Sir:
Pittsburgh, Pennsylvania 15221	My dear Mr. (or Dr.) Tibbetts:
or (if a doctor of divinity)	Dear Mr. (or Dr.) Tibbetts:
The Reverend Dr. M. S. Tibbetts, etc.	Right Reverend Sir:

(**Note:** Most authorities disapprove the use of Reverend with the last name alone. There is also a well-defined preference for spelling the word Reverend in full.)

Rabbi	
Rabbi Dudley Weinberg	Reverend Sir: (formal)
The Reverend Dudley Weinberg	My dear Sir:
(Place specific address here)	Dear Sir:
	My dear Rabbi Weinberg:
(**Note:** If a doctor's degree is held, **Dr.** may be	Dear Rabbi Weinberg:
substituted for **Rabbi.**)	

ROMAN CATHOLIC HIERARCHY [2]

Pope	
To His Holiness Pope	Most Holy Father:
	Your Holiness:

Cardinal	
His Eminence, James Cardinal McIntyre	Your Eminence:
Archbishop of Los Angeles	My Lord Cardinal: (to cardinals of foreign
100 Fremont Place	countries)
Los Angeles, California 90010	

(**Note:** Such salutations as My Lord, Your Lordship, My Lord Cardinal, etc., are not ordinarily used in the United States of America, but should be used by an American writing to dignitaries of foreign countries entitled to such a title.)

Archbishop	
The Most Reverend Albert G. Meyers	Your Excellency:
Archbishop of Chicago	
Holy Name Cathedral	
Chicago, Illinois 60608	

Bishop	
The Most Reverend John Muldoon	Your Excellency:
Bishop of Oklahoma	Dear Bishop Muldoon:
Oklahoma City, Oklahoma 73102	

Monsignor	
The Right Reverend Monsignor Joseph Ryan	Right Reverend and dear Monsignor:
St. Brendan's Church	Dear Monsignor Ryan:
Chicago, Illinois 60606	

Priest	
Very Reverend William R. Rand **or**	Dear Reverend Father:
Reverend William R. Rand	Reverend and dear Sir:
164 Lansing Place	Dear Father Rand:
Mobile, Alabama 36627	

Brother of a Catholic order	
Brother Brendon, O.F.M.	Dear Brother:
St. Francis Seminary	Dear Brother Brendon:
Quincy, Illinois 62301	

Mother Superior	
Reverend Mother Mary Louise, O.C.A.	Reverend Mother:
Sacred Heart Convent	Dear Reverend Mother:
New Orleans, Louisiana 70108	

Sister	
Sister Mary Margaret	Dear Sister:
St. Catherine's School	Dear Sister Mary Margaret
Rochester, Minnesota 55901	

[2] The list of proper titles and salutations for churchmen of the Roman Catholic Hierarchy has been checked for acceptability by competent and eminent authorities. It has, according to the confirmation of the **Catholic School Journal**, the consent of the Hierarchy and the Clergy.

INDEX

A

A, 49, 114

Abbreviations, in a letter, 369; ZIP Code, 380

Abstract nouns, 63

Accuracy, proofreading for, 20

Acknowledgments, 461; examples of, 462; of declining orders, 467; of defective orders, 466; of deferred shipment, 466; of large orders, 465; of orders, 463; out-of-stock, 466; part-shipment, 466; welcoming new customer, 463

Action, 563, 567; easy, 564; favorable, offer inducements for, 563

Action devices, 565

Active voice, 126; for punch, 235

Address, envelope, 377, 381; numbers in, 206, 358; of a letter, 344, 357, 358; placement of, in a letter, 357; postal card, 380, 385; return, on envelopes and postal cards, 378

Addressee notation on the envelope, 380

Addresses, special groups, guide-forms for, 668

Addressing, for Optical Character Reader, envelopes and postal cards, 378; general guides for, 378

Adjectival noun, 66

Adjective clauses introduced by subordinating conjunctions, 142

Adjective-forming suffixes, 97

Adjectives, 94; comparative degree, 95; comparison of, 95; definition of, 94; descriptive, 63, 94; formal characteristics of, 94; generating idea power with, 407; in appositive position, 98, x-ray of, 650; in attributive position, 98, x-ray of, 649; in introductory position, 98, x-ray of, 650; positions of occurrence, 98; positive degree, 95; predicate, 40, 98, x-ray of, 650; superlative degree, 95; test-frames for identifying, 94

Adjustments, effective, 585; four chief types of, 598; granting, 590; guide for, 611; positive tone in, 585; refusing, 590; requesting, 586

Adverb clauses introduced by subordinating conjunctions, 141

Adverbial modifier, 36

Adverbial noun, 36

Adverbs, 100; comparative degree, 102; comparison of, 102; constructions occurring in, 102; definition, 100; distinguished from prepositions, 104; formal characteristics of, 101; linking, 140; nouns as, 68; superlative degree, 102; test-frames for identifying, 100

Advertisements, blind employment, 506; complete employment, 506

Age, numbers for expressing, 207

Agreement, 53; in number, 86; in person, 86; of subject and verb, 85

AIDA plan, 507

Aim in studying English, 5

Ain't, 12

Altered word order, 41

Altering-type transitive verb, 34; x-ray of, 641

Amounts of money, rules for expressing numbers in, 206

AMS Simplified letter style, 350

An, 49, 114

Announcements, 448; examples of, 449, 450, 451

Antecedents, 77

Apostrophe, 178; placement of, 180; plural possessive, 179; singular possessive, 179; to show possession, 178; use in a contraction, 182

Appeals, how to test for, 574; market, 572; powerful, 574; right, 573

Application, 501; attract favorable attention by your, 507; examples of, 519; how not to write, 512; pitfalls to watch in, 522; planning your, 506; six steps of an effective, 508; solicited, 505; typewritten, 508; unsolicited, 505

Appointments, 454; acknowledging, 454

Appositive, nonrestrictive, 66; noun as, 65; restrictive, 65

Appreciation, 485

Approaches to language study, 24

Articles, indefinite, 47

Attention, involve your reader, 543; things to avoid in winning favorable, 545; through action, 546; through color, 545; through pictures, 545; winning favorable, 542

Attention line, 361; used with subject line, 363

Attributive position, adjective in, 98

Auxiliaries, 118; in future tense, 119; in perfect tenses, 120; indicating obligation, 128; related to passive voice, 123; related to progressive aspect, 125; related to tense, 119; single-form, 126

Auxiliary verbs, 49

Awareness of your reader, 337

B

Bibliography, 661

Blind employment advertisements, 506

Block letter style, 347

Body, of a letter, 344, 368, paragraphing in, 368

Book, divisions of a, rules for expressing numbers in, 208

Brackets, 187

Business condition, 618

Business letters, basic aims of, 439

Buying drives, 571

C

"C's," 285-334

Capacity, 618

Capital, 618

Capitalization, 198; proper nouns, 198

Carbon copy notation, 374

Carbon copy of a letter, 374

Careful speech, importance of, 11

Character, 618

Clarity, generate power through, 313

Classification, paragraph development by, 249

Clause, dependent, 146; descriptive, comma with, 164; elliptical, 225; identifying, comma with, 165; main, 146; nonrestrictive, comma with, 164; restrictive, comma with, 165

Clearness, 308; focus-phrases for, 312; pointer-words for, 312; test for, 310

Climactic arrangement, 237; for emphasis, 237

Closing sentences, climax, 421; forceful, 281

Coherence, characteristic of an effective message, 270; repetition of key words and phrases for, 259; sentence, 222; tying ideas together for, 258; use of limiting adjectives for, 259; use of pronouns for, 259

Collection, reminders, 628; stages of follow-up, 627; stronger reminders, 628

Collection appeals, how to use, 627

Collection messages, 626; time intervals for, 631

Collective nouns, 61

Colon, 174; capitalization with, 201

Comma, 164

Comma fault, 218

Commands, 152; x-ray of, 657

Common nouns, 61

Company data sheet, 519

Company name in closing lines of a letter, 371

Comparative degree, 102

Comparison, paragraph development by, 250

Complete employment advertisements, 506

Completeness, 299; build an effective plan for, 299; chief guides for, 305; greatest single threat to, 304

Complex sentence, 147

Complimentary close, match with salutation, 370; in a letter, 344, 370; placement in a letter, 371

Compound-complex sentence, 148

Compound numbers, hyphen with, 189

Compound sentence, 147; joined by phrases and transitional words, semicolon with, 172; no conjunction, semicolon with, 172; x-ray of, 652

Compound words, hyphen with, 188

Conciseness, 324; word saving for, 325

Concrete nouns, 63

Concreteness, 324; flashes word pictures, 329

Condense, learn to, 326

Congratulations, 487

Conjunctions, coordinating, 139

Conjunctions, correlative, 139

Conjunctions, subordinating, 141; introducing adjective clauses, 142; introducing adverb clauses, 141; introducing noun clauses used as appositives, 142; introducing noun clauses used as direct objects, 142; introducing noun clauses used as predicate nouns, 143; introducing noun clauses used as subject, 142

Conjunctive adverbs, 49

Connectors, 139; coordinating conjunctions as, 139; linking adverbs as, 140; relative pronouns as, 143; subordinating conjunctions as, 141

Contraction, apostrophe in, 182

Coordinate clauses, comma with, 166

Coordinating conjunctions, 49, 139

Correctness, 316; checklist for, 320; to show good manners, 320

Correlative conjunctions, 139

Courtesy, 287; test for, 287; you attitude for, 290

Credit, granting, 621; guard it, 618; information, asking for, 620; investigating, 619; refusing, 622

Credit account, opening a, 619

Credit customers, classes of, 626

Credit information guide, 621

Credit information sources, 617, 619

Credit record, 617

Credo, 618

address on, 380; small, folding the letter for, 382; window, 383, folding the letter for, 384

Errors block thought flow, 317; cost money, 317; tiny ones may grow into towering trouble, 318

Exclamation point, 176

Expletive, 42, 43

Expression, effective oral, 7; effective written, 16

F

Fact writing, 392

Fault, carrier at, 601; company at, 599; customer at, 605

Figures, hours and minutes, colon with, 175

Finite verb, 85

First impression, 337

First sentence, duties of, 278; powerful, 419

Focus-phrases, clearness through, 312

Folding the letter for the envelope, 382, 383, 384

Footnotes, 659; illustrated, 659, 660; placement of references for, 659; spacing for, 659

Force generated with detail, 660

Formal invitations, 452

Fractions, rules for expressing numbers in, 207

Fragment, sentence, 216

Friendship approach to adjustments, 589

Function words, grammatical meaning through, 26; types of, 49

Future perfect tense, 121

Future tense, 119

G

General case, 57

Geographical differences in language, 7

Gerunds, 89, 225; x-ray of, 649

Getting along with others, 305

Golden secret of writing, 433

Good manners, 320

Goodwill, 287; recapturing, 607

Grammar, 25; signalling system of, 25

Grammatical agreement, 27

Grammatical meaning, through function words, 26; through punctuation, 28; through word form, 27; through word order, 26

"Gunpowder" words and phrases, 595

Granting requests, 475

H

Heading in a letter, 344, 356

Historical differences in language, 7

"Ho-Hum" language, 419

Honorable, 359

Hyphen, 188

I

I, 522

Identifying clauses, comma with, 165

Illustrated Guide, 663

Importance of parts of speech, 47

Impression, first, make an excellent, 337

Impression, favorable, through writing, 17; how to make a good, 13

Incompleteness, risks of, 302

Independent clauses, no connecting word, colon with, 174

Indirect object, 34; noun as, 65; personal pronoun as, 77

Indirect object, retained, noun as, 69; personal pronoun as, 78

Inductive reasoning, paragraph development by, 250

Infinitives, 88, 225; x-ray of, 649

Informal invitations, 452

Inquiries, 439

Interest, arousing, by generating force, 553; by word pictures, 554; through effective use of evidence, 550; through emotional description, 548; through physical description, 548; through proof of value, 550; through the "test-it-yourself" technique, 556; through use of dramatic material, 553; through use of vivid facts, 553

Interesting tone in writing, 397

Interrogatory function words, question signal, 49, 151

Intransitive verb, 36

Introductions, 492

Introductory phrase containing verb form, comma with, 167

Introductory position, descriptive adjective in, 98

Invitations, 452; accepting, 452; declining, 454; formal, 452, examples of, 453; informal, 452

Irregular verbs, 83

PUNCTUATION MADE EASY

On the next two pages is a highly condensed quick-reference punctuation table for the use of those who wish a source of punctuation information in easily accessible space. This table is of special value to executives, secretaries, and other office workers who use this book continuously as a reference.

How to Use

For a continuous reference 1—open the book at the back cover, 2—put a rubber band around the front cover and the body of the book, 3—stand the book upright, 4—place it at the right or left of the working space on the desk, and open at a convenient angle.

PUNCTUATION

(Page references are to pages in this book.)

PERIOD: Pages 161-162

1. At the end of a declarative sentence.
2. At the end of an imperative sentence.
3. After all initials and after most abbreviations (C.O.D., Inc., f.o.b. But: TWA, FDIC).
4. Between dollars and cents expressed in figures.

COMMA: Pages 164-169

1. To point off a subordinate clause preceding its principal clause (clauses often introduced by words like *if, unless, since, because,* etc.).
2. To set off a nonrestrictive clause.
3. To set off a nonrestrictive appositive but not a restrictive appositive.
4. To separate coordinate clauses joined by one of the pure conjunctions (*and, but, for, or, neither, nor*).
5. To point off an introductory phrase containing a verb.
6. To point off a dependent word or word group that breaks the direct continuity of the sentence.
7. To point off parenthetic words, phrases, and clauses.
8. To point off words or word groups used in a series when there are at least three units.
9. To point off words used in direct address or in explaining other words.
10. To point off sentence elements that might be wrongly joined in reading if there were no commas.
11. To indicate the omission of words that are understood by the reader.
12. Before a short quotation.

SEMICOLON: Pages 172-173

1. Between the members of a compound sentence when no conjunction is used.
2. Between the clauses of a compound sentence that are joined by such words as *also, consequently, for, hence, however,* etc.
3. Before the expressions *as, that is, namely, i. e., e. g., to wit, viz.,* when they introduce an illustration that is a complete clause or an enumeration that consists of several items.
4. To separate the members of a compound sentence when one or both members are punctuated with commas.
5. Between serial phrases or clauses having a common dependence on something that precedes or follows.
6. Between the members of a series of clearly defined units, upon each of which special emphasis is to be laid.

COLON: Pages 174-175

1. Between two independent groups having no connecting word between them, the first group pointing forward to the second.
2. After forward-looking expressions.
3. Before a series of expressions.
4. Before a long quotation.
5. To separate hours and minutes when expressed in figures.

QUESTION MARK: Page 175

1. After a direct question.
2. After the individual members of a series, each one of which might be expanded into a complete sentence.